WITHDRAWN
Columbia College
1001 Rogers Street
Columbia, MO 65216

Principles of Computer-aided Design

Principles of
Computer-aided Design

Editor
Joy Crelin

SALEM PRESS
A Division of EBSCO Information Services, Inc.
Ipswich, Massachusetts
GREY HOUSE PUBLISHING

Cover photo: New generation ergonomics footwear design. Photo by Devrimb, iStock.

Copyright © 2022, by Salem Press, A Division of EBSCO Information Services, Inc., and Grey House Publishing, Inc.

Principles of Computer-aided Design, published by Grey House Publishing, Inc., Amenia, NY, under exclusive license from EBSCO Information Services, Inc.

All rights reserved. No part of this work may be used or reproduced in any manner whatsoever or transmitted in any form or by any means, electronic or mechanical, including photocopy, recording, or any information storage and retrieval system, without written permission from the copyright owner. For permissions requests, contact proprietarypublishing@ebsco.com.

For information contact Grey House Publishing/Salem Press, 4919 Route 22, PO Box 56, Amenia, NY 12501.

∞ The paper used in these volumes conforms to the American National Standard for Permanence of Paper for Printed Library Materials, Z39.48 1992 (R2009).

Publisher's Cataloging-In-Publication Data
(Prepared by The Donohue Group, Inc.)

Names: Crelin, Joy, editor.
Title: Principles of computer-aided design / editor, Joy Crelin.
Description: Ipswich, Massachusetts : Salem Press, a division of EBSCO Information Services, Inc. ; Amenia, NY : Grey House Publishing, [2022] | Series: [Principles of science] | Includes bibliographical references and index.
Identifiers: ISBN 9781637000977
Subjects: LCSH: Computer-aided design. | Computer-aided engineering.
Classification: LCC TA174 .P75 2022 | DDC 620.00420285—dc23

FIRST PRINTING
PRINTED IN THE UNITED STATES OF AMERICA

Contents

Publisher's Note vii
Editor's Introduction ix
Contributors xv

Aeronautics and Aviation 1
Aerospace Design 8
Algorithm 13
Applied Mathematics 15
Applied Physics 22
Archaeology 27
Architecture and Architectural Engineering 34
Architecture Software 41
Artificial Organs 43
Audiology and Hearing Aids 49
AutoCAD 54
Automated Processes and Servomechanisms 56
Avionics and Aircraft Instrumentation 61
Biomechanical Engineering 69
Bridge Design and Barodynamics 73
Building Information Modeling (BIM) 77
CATIA 81
Cell and Tissue Engineering 83
Civil Engineering 88
Communications Satellite Technology 94
Computer-aided Design (CAD) in Education 99
CAD Research and Theory 101
Computer-aided Engineering (CAE) 103
Computer-aided Mechanical Design (CAM) 106
CAD/CAM, Popularization of 110
CAD/CAM Software, Overview of 112
Computer Animation 114
Computer Languages, Compilers, and Tools 117
Computer Memory and Storage 121
Computer Modeling 123
Computer Numerical Control (CNC) Milling 125
Computer Simulation 127
Contract Manufacturing 130
Control of Manufacturing Systems 133
DAC-1 139
Deep Submergence Vehicle Design 140
Dentistry 143
Design 149

Design for Manufacturability 151
Design Thinking 155
Ecodesign 159
Electric Automobile Technology 161
Electrical Engineering 168
Electronic Design Automation (EDA) 175
Electronics and Electronic Engineering 178
Engineering Design 183
Engineering Tolerances 186
Environmental Engineering 188
Epoxies and Resin Technologies 193
Ergonomics 199
Fossil Fuel Power Plants 205
Fuel Cell Technologies 211
Functional Design 215
Game Programming 219
Gas Turbine Technology 221
Generative Design 226
Geometry 230
Graphical User Interface (GUI) 236
Graphics Formats 238
Graphics Technologies 240
Heat-Exchanger Technologies 245
Hybrid Vehicle Technologies 250
Hydraulic Engineering 254
Hydroponics 259
Integrated-Circuit Design 267
International System of Units 272
Isometric Drawing 278
Jet Engine Technology 281
Just-In-Time Manufacturing 286
Kinematics 293
Lean Manufacturing 295
Manufacturing, Energy Use in 299
Manufacturing Processes 302
Manufacturing Strategies 308
Manufacturing Systems Design 311
Measurement and Units 316
Microscale 3D Printing 323
Naval Architecture and Marine Engineering 327
NX 332
Open-Source CAD Software 335

Optics 337	Solar Panel Design 414
Plastics Engineering 343	SolidWorks 416
Polymer Science 350	Spacecraft Engineering. 418
Process Management for Manufacturing 356	Sports Engineering. 424
Product Design 361	Submarine Engineering 429
Product Lifecycle Management (PLM) 362	Technical Drawing 435
Propulsion Technologies. 364	3D Printing 438
Prosthetics 369	UNISURF 441
Prototyping 374	Urban Planning and Engineering 443
Quality Control 377	Vectors. 449
Random-Access Memory (RAM) 383	Web Graphic Design 453
Reconfigurable Agile Manufacturing 385	Wireframes 455
Reconfigurable Manufacturing Systems 390	
Robotics. 395	Timeline 457
Roller-Coaster Design. 403	Glossary. 463
Douglas T. Ross. 405	Organizations 471
Scandinavian Design. 409	Bibliography 473
Sketchpad 412	Subject Index 499

Publisher's Note

Computer-aided Design is the next volume in Salem's *Principles of Science* series, which includes *Microbiology, Energy, Marine Science, Geology, Information Technology,* and *Mathematics.*

This new resource explores the use of computers in the design process of many products and applications. CAD is used in such wide-ranging industries as shipbuilding, aerospace, and automotive design as well as in the medical field and architecture. In addition, CAD is used in the film industry to produce special effects and computer animation. CAD is a part of the design and manufacturing of almost anything imaginable. The introduction of this groundbreaking technology in the 1950s changed how many businesses approached design, engineering, and manufacturing. Initially used by only a small number of industries, CAD in the twenty-first century has become a part of nearly every facet of modern life. It is a valuable tool not only for engineers but also for artists, doctors, and entertainers.

This volume begins with a comprehensive Editor's Introduction to the topic of computer-aided design written by Joy Crelin.

Following the Introduction, *Computer-aided Design* includes 110 entries that discuss such topics as computer modeling, 3D printing, CAD and manufacturing, product lifecycle managing, technical drawing, aviation and aeronautics, and CAD software, to name a few.

Entries begin with an Abstract defining the key elements of a topic and end with a helpful Further Reading section.

This work also includes helpful appendices, including:
- Timeline;
- Glossary;
- Organizations;
- Bibliography;
- Subject Index

Salem Press extends appreciation to all involved in the development and production of this work. Names and affiliations of contributors to this work follow the Editor's Introduction.

Principles of Computer-aided Design, as well as all Salem Press reference books, is available in print and as an e-book. Please visit www.salempress.com for more information.

Editor's Introduction

Consider, for a moment, a recently constructed house. That house was based on architectural drawings created on a computer rather than on paper and visualized for the benefit of its developer or future owner through the creation of a three-dimensional (3D) computer model rather than a physical one. Following the design phase of the project, the house was built in part by workers operating heavy equipment, which was in turn made up of smaller components produced through the use of computer-aided manufacturing (CAM) systems. Following its completion, the house's owners filled their new home with consumer goods designed using CAD technology, from furniture to decorative items to shoes. Electronics in the home featured circuit boards and other components with complex layouts that were planned out through the use of specialized electronic CAD software. The electrical wiring system of the house itself was laid out using a similar program, as were the home's heating and plumbing systems. The car parked in the driveway was designed by digital means, as was the airplane flying overhead, and CAM systems were used to fabricate components for both vehicles to exacting specifications.

All of the objects and structures present in this example, from the house to the furniture to the plane overhead, could exist in a world without CAD technology. Indeed, traditional forms of creating architectural, engineering, and conceptual-design drawings predate the invention of CAD by centuries, and traditional design processes remain the preferred methods in some contexts. What this example demonstrates, however, is how ordinary and ubiquitous computer-aided design, manufacturing, and engineering technologies have become. Just as those technologies operate together in a multitude of ways, the products and structures they help to create fit together to form the environment in which people carry out their everyday lives in the twenty-first century developed world.

WHAT IS COMPUTER-AIDED DESIGN?

Introduced in the late 1950s, the definition of computer-aided design as a concept fluctuated in scope over the decades, particularly as CAD came to serve as an umbrella term encompassing a host of related technologies often used in conjunction with one another. To understand the technology's origins, however, it can be helpful to think about the understanding of CAD articulated by the researchers affiliated with the Massachusetts Institute of Technology's Computer-Aided Design Project, an initiative that officially began operations in 1959. In the 1960 technical memorandum *Computer-Aided Design: A Statement of Objectives*, Douglas J. Ross, the MIT researcher typically credited with coining the term CAD, explained that the project's goal was "to evolve a man-machine system"—a CAD system—"which will permit the human designer and the computer to work together on creative design problems." In proposing that system, Ross and his colleagues sought to strike an ideal balance between human and computer contributions to the design process in which neither human nor computer would take on an inordinate role in solving the design problem with which they were presented. As such, the 1960 memorandum specifically excluded "automatic design" procedures from the researchers' definition of a CAD system, as they considered such procedures to be too heavily reliant on computers. They likewise excluded "automatic programming" systems such as the computer numerical control (CNC) tool systems previously developed at MIT and by researchers such as Patrick J. Hanratty of General Electric (later of General Motors), which they deemed overly dependent on human intervention.

While the researchers planned to investigate traditional design practices as part of the process of designing their CAD system, Ross noted that CAD technology would not simply replicate preexisting design techniques and processes in a computing environment. Rather, the researchers sought to replace inefficient existing design practices with "more efficient, more natural, more expressive techniques" that would be "made possible only through the combining of man and machine into a design system." Further, Ross and his colleagues hoped to combine the results of their research and development with existing numerical control manufacturing technologies and develop a means of "going almost directly from the requirement for a machined part to the finished product." While CAD as an umbrella concept would come to diverge significantly from the MIT researchers' understanding of it over the subsequent decades, the researchers' emphasis on a smooth path from design to manufactured product would remain highly relevant, signaling the close ties between CAD and CAM throughout the history of those technologies.

THE EVOLUTION OF CAD
Though far from the only institution exploring the potential of CAD during that period, MIT remained a hotbed of CAD research throughout the 1960s, a period that resulted in the creation of groundbreaking technologies such as Sketchpad. Introduced by doctoral student Ivan Sutherland in 1963, Sketchpad was computer software that enabled users to draw and manipulate graphics on a screen and featured an interface that computer historians would later come to consider the first graphical user interface (GUI). Early CAD technologies such as Sketchpad typically fell within the category of two-dimensional (2D) CAD, in that they could be used to produce an array of 2D drawings similar to the blueprints and technical drawings already in use in many industries. The next decades saw the rise of 3D CAD, which moved beyond the bounds of 2D drawings to allow for the creation of 3D shapes that could be manipulated and viewed on screen in a manner similar to manipulating and viewing an object in the real world.

As Ross and his colleagues at MIT had hoped when writing *Computer-Aided Design: A Statement of Objectives*, CAD and CAM technologies became increasingly linked over the decades, resulting in the widespread use of the combined term CAD/CAM, and both saw improvements in functionality as they became increasingly capable of interfacing with one another. Indeed, the need for different computer systems and job functions to interface and work in conjunction with one another would become a crucial factor in the development of advanced CAD software and related technologies over the late twentieth and early twenty-first centuries. When designing a product or structure intended to be produced in the real world, one must focus not only on the visual aspects of design but also on the engineering and manufacturing considerations at hand to ensure that the product or structure is both visually appealing and capable of functioning as intended. For instance, an individual with a strong understanding of visual design could use CAD software to create a drawing or model of a visually appealing bridge. To bring that bridge into existence in the real world, however, that individual—or potentially a team of skilled professionals—would also need to ensure that the design is engineered to stand up to the stresses the bridge would need to endure, such as the weight of the cars crossing it and potential motion caused by earthquakes. Similarly, the individual or team would need to ensure that the appropriate materials would be used in the bridge's construction and that the bridge could, in fact, be constructed as designed. In light of such requirements, CAD software came to be often used in conjunction with technologies such as computer-aided engineering (CAE) software to ensure the viability of the products or structures being designed.

A substantial advance in the realm of CAD software—and in the software market as a whole—in the twenty-first century was the advent of cloud-based software solutions and the software-as-a-service (SaaS) model, both of which arose amid improvements to internet infrastructure that allowed for faster speeds and more reliable connections. Whereas software of the late twentieth and early twenty-first centuries was traditionally distributed in physical form, such as on CD-ROMs, cloud-based services can be accessed remotely through the internet. The move to the cloud was, for some software companies, likewise accompanied by a move to a subscription model in which users would pay a monthly or yearly subscription fee to use the software rather than a one-time licensing fee. While some software companies previously offered multiple distinct versions of their software solutions, each targeted toward a particular industry or function, companies moving to the cloud- and subscription-based model often experimented with offering industry-specific solutions as add-ons to a base-level subscription rather than unique software options in their own right. A major focus of software developers during that period was also ensuring that a company's products—for instance, the company's separate CAD and CAE offerings—were capable of working in tandem with one another and could easily output files suitable for use in manufacturing contexts, including the burgeoning field of 3D printing.

CAD IN INDUSTRY AND THE WORKPLACE

While some early CAD systems were developed in research laboratories at institutions such as MIT, other early systems and a selection of later ones arose out of industry and were initially developed to meet individual corporations' unique manufacturing and design needs, which were not yet being addressed by commercially available technology. The automotive industry was particularly active in that space, with car manufacturers developing innovative computer technologies for use in their factories and design facilities. Such technologies included the Design Augmented by Computer (DAC-1) system developed at General Motors in the early 1960s and the UNISURF system introduced by the French car manufacturer Renault later that decade. The aerospace industry was also a field notable for its extensive experiments with CAD, CAM, CAE, and related technologies, carried out within government-funded organizations as well as both private and public corporations. The National Aeronautics and Space Administration (NASA), for instance, made use of CAD technology at least as early as the 1980s, and the publicly traded aerospace corporation Boeing became the first company to produce a digitally designed commercial airliner with the introduction of the Boeing 777 in the mid-1990s.

By the third decade of the twenty-first century, CAD software and its related technologies were used in a multitude of industries and for a seemingly endless array of purposes, contributing to the design and production of the smallest components as well as to the planning of entire urban areas.

An analysis of reviews of general-purpose CAD software—CAD software designed for a wide range of industries rather than for a specific industry or purpose—posted to the website G2 between 2013 and 2020 found that businesses using such software belonged to more than one hundred individual industries, including industries commonly associated with the use of CAD, such as design, construction, and civil engineering, as well as the utilities, transportation, and food production industries, among many others. In addition, companies in a number of industries make use of specialized CAD software solutions that meet specific, rather than general, needs and are thus more appropriate for use by workers in those industries than their general-purpose counterparts.

Alongside facilitating numerous design and engineering tasks in the workplace, CAD software itself constitutes a notable sector of the software industry. A report on the global CAD software market published by the market-research firm Prescient & Strategic Intelligence in 2020 estimated that the value of that market in 2019 was $9.3 billion. The firm went on to project that the CAD software market would experience substantial gains over the next decade and would attain an estimated global value of $18.7 billion by 2030. Prescient & Strategic Intelligence projected that significant gains would be made in industries such as healthcare during that period and likewise highlighted the Asia-Pacific region as a geographic market that would likely experience notable growth over the course of the decade.

While CAD is a profitable sector unto itself and has been widely credited with improving the efficiency of design and manufacturing processes in a wide range of industries, the use of CAD software and related technologies in the workplace can have far-reaching ramifications for the workers themselves. A key factor to consider is that the creation of technical drawings and similar content was once the responsibility of dedicated drafters, who worked to provide visual representations of designs often ideated by other professionals. Following the introduction of CAD software into many industries, however, professionals who were not dedicated drafters increasingly became capable of creating such drawings themselves. As of 2020, the US Bureau of Labor Statistics' Occupational Outlook Handbook projected that employment of drafters would decline over the next decade and specifically attributed that decline to the adoption of CAD and related technologies and the resulting elimination of that specialized role. Such phenomena have sparked concerns that widespread implementation of CAD technology could result in the loss of jobs, although those concerned about the employment ramifications of such technology tend to focus more substantially on the relationship between job losses and automation in manufacturing.

CAD BEYOND THE WORKPLACE
Though CAD is perhaps best known for its benefits to industry, its uses in the twenty-first century are hardly constrained to workplace functions. Indeed, the introduction of free or low-cost options to the software market has opened CAD and related technologies up to widespread use by hobbyists and has arguably eliminated or reduced the technological or artistic barriers that in the past prevented some individuals from creating visual depictions of their design concepts. An individual with little freehand drawing ability, for example, might struggle to create scale plans for a design the individual hopes to build or outsource to a manufacturer. The drawing tools offered by many CAD software packages, however, can assist such an individual in completing a design, help the individual visualize what the completed object or structure would look like, and potentially detect problems in the design that would prevent successful construction. The advent of consumer-oriented CAD software, along with the rise of 3D printers, has arguably democratized the processes of design and small-scale manufacturing, enabling hobbyists to design and manufacture physical products that meet their specific needs without having to engage the services of a professional designer or manufacturing company. An avid costumer might design and 3D print masks or other accessories based on original designs or inspired by favorite characters from media, a board game enthusiast might design custom box inserts for organizing game components, or an avid gardener might design plant holders or small components for a home hydroponics system, among other possibilities. The use of CAD and related technologies for such projects emphasizes the versatility of those technologies and likewise demonstrates that design, in such cases, need not necessarily be motivated by profit.

The influence of CAD beyond the workplace likewise extends to education. Increasingly incorporated into curricula at all levels during the first decades of the twenty-first century, CAD education can encompass one-off projects that teach students to use basic CAD tools as well as career-focused courses that prepare students to pursue work in fields such as engineering, architecture, or product design. CAD education can also serve as a valuable component of a broader STEM (science, technology, engineering, and mathematics) or STEAM (science, technology, engineering, arts, and mathematics) curriculum, due to the strong connections between CAD and fields such as engineering, geometry, physics, and the visual arts. In addition, research suggests that making use of CAD software can have measurable effects on students' skills that could extend beyond CAD projects and benefit them throughout their studies. A study of freshman engineering students at Turkey's Afyon Kocatepe University carried out in 2013 and 2014, for instance, sought to assess whether the students' participation in an engineering drawing course that focused on the use of CAD tools would have an effect on those students' spatial visualization skills, as measured through the Purdue Spatial Visualization Test: Visualization of Rotation (PSVT:R) assessment. The resulting paper, published in the *European Journal of Engineering Education* in 2017, revealed that the students who participated in the class demonstrated greater improvements in their spatial visualization skills over the study period than a control group of students who were not enrolled in the class. While further research is likely needed to establish as clear relationship between the study of CAD and improvements in spatial visualization skills, that study indicates that using CAD tools in educational contexts may offer lasting benefits that are not limited to practical and career skills.

MOVING FORWARD

As CAD, CAM, CAE, and related technologies become increasingly prevalent in the twenty-first century, a key question to be asked is where such technologies will go next. One likely development is a shift among software companies toward cloud-based CAD solutions and the SaaS model, a process that was already underway by late 2021. That shift appeared poised to continue; in its 2020 report, for instance, Prescient & Strategic Intelligence predicted that a substantial increase in the use of cloud-based CAD solutions would take place between 2020 and 2030. In many industries, the widespread move to remote work following the emergence of the COVID-19 pandemic in 2020 stressed the importance of a worker's ability to access files and essential software from home, a process heavily reliant on the use of cloud- and web-based services. While the long-term ramifications of that move within the design, manufacturing, and engineering fields remain to be seen, the pandemic era raised important questions about the most appropriate means of accessing CAD tools in the twenty-first century.

Alongside newfangled methods for the delivery of CAD services, an area of increasing interest is the integration of artificial intelligence and machine learning into the field of computer-aided design. The development of machine-learning algorithms trained with appropriate datasets could result in the creation of tools that could automate elements of product design or other tasks typically carried out via CAD or CAE software. The use of CAD software in the design of nanotechnology also shows significant promise, and the development of smaller and smaller computer components can in turn result in the creation of smaller and more efficient computers capable of performing resource-intensive CAD tasks with ease. Other areas of interest include the use of CAD and CAM technologies to improve the health of humankind, including though the design and manufacturing of customized medical implants and through developing technologies such as bioprinting, which researchers hope will one day be used to 3D print living human tissue or organs. These and other areas at the frontier of CAD research and development are well worth monitoring as scientists and software developers continue to expand the boundaries of CAD technology over the next decades.

—Joy Crelin

Further Reading

Beck, Adam. "60 Years of CAD Infographic: The History of CAD since 1957." *CADENAS PARTsolutions*, 2019, partsolutions.com/60-years-of-cad-infographic-the-history-of-cad-since-1957. Accessed 23 Dec. 2021.

"CAD Software Market Research Report." *Prescient & Strategic Intelligence*, Sept. 2020, www.psmarketresearch.com/market-analysis/cad-software-market. Accessed 23 Dec. 2021.

"Drafters." US Bureau of Labor Statistics, 8 Sept. 2021, www.bls.gov/ooh/architecture-and-engineering/drafters.htm#tab-1. Accessed 23 Dec. 2021.

Gigante, Michael. "Computer-Aided Design (CAD): State of Category." *G2*, 15 July 2020, www.g2.com/articles/computer-aided-design-cad-state-of-category. Accessed 23 Dec. 2021.

Krahe, Carmen, Maximilian Iberl, Alexander Jacob, and Gisela Lanza. "AI-Based Computer Aided Engineering for Automated Product Design—A First Approach with a Multi-View Based Classification." *Procedia CIRP*, vol. 86, 2019, www.sciencedirect.com/science/article/pii/S2212827120300524. Accessed 23 Dec. 2021.

Kösa, Temel, and Fatih Karakus. "The Effects of Computer-Aided Design Software on Engineering Students' Spatial Visualisation Skills." *European Journal of Engineering Education*, vol 43, no. 2, 3 Sept. 2017, www.researchgate.net/publication/319467497_The_effects_of_computer-aided_design_software_on_engineering_students%27_spatial_visualisation_skills. Accessed 23 Dec. 2021.

Ross, Douglas T. *Computer-Aided Design: A Statement of Objectives*. MIT, 1960.

Torpey, Elka. "CAD Designer." *US Bureau of Labor Statistics*, May 2019, www.bls.gov/careeroutlook/2019/youre-a-what/cad-designer.htm. Accessed 23 Dec. 2021.

Williams, Joe. "Autodesk Is Dragging the Industrial World into the Cloud — And Showing It the Future." *Protocol*, 9 July 2021, www.protocol.com/enterprise/autodesk-cloud-cad-profile#toggle-gdpr. Accessed 23 Dec. 2021.

Contributors

Jeongmin Ahn, MS, PhD
Syracuse University

Michael P. Auerbach, MA
Marblehead, MA

Harlan H. Bengtson, BS, MS, PhD
Illinois University, Edwardsville

Kimberly Edginton Bigelow
University of Dayton

Tyler Biscontini
Independent Scholar

Victoria M. Breting-García, MA
Independent Scholar

Brian Burns
Massachusetts General Hospital

Josephine Campbell
Independent Scholar

Byron D. Cannon, MA, PhD
University of Utah

Roger V. Carlson
Jet Propulsion Laboratory

Anne Collins
Independent Scholar

Sue Ann Connaughton, MLS
North Adams, MA

Joy Crelin
Independent Scholar

Joseph Dewey
University of Pittsburgh

Mark Dziak
Northeast Editing

Marlanda English, PhD
Capella University

Michael Erbschloe
Kent State University

Jennifer L. Gibson, BS, DP
Excalibur Scientific

Jim Greene, MFA
University of Tennessee

Joyce Gubata, MBA
Mavenlink

Jan Hall
Miami University

Mary Woodbury Hooper
Dynamed

April D. Ingram, BSc
Kelowna, British Columbia

Micah L. Issitt
Independent Scholar

Vincent Jorgensen, BS
Sunnyvale, CA

Bassam Kassab, BEng, MEng, MSc
Santa Clara Valley Water District

Marylane Wade Koch, MSN, RN
University of Memphis

Narayanan M. Komerath, PhD
Georgia Institute of Technology

Bill Kte'pi
Independent Scholar

Jeanne L. Kuhler, BS, MS, PhD
Benedictine University

Jeffrey Larson, PT, ATC
Northern Medical Informatics

M. Lee, BA, MA
Independent Scholar

R. C. Lutz, BA, MA, PhD
University of California

Marianne M. Madsen, MS
University of Utah

Michael Mazzei
Independent Scholar

Ashwin Mudigonda
Universal Robotics Inc.

Robert J. Paradowski, MS, PhD
Rochester Institute of Technology

Ellen E. Anderson Penno, BS, MS, MD, FRCSC, Dip ABO
Western Laser Eye Associates

Elena Popan, PhD
Texas Tech University

Steven J. Ramold, PhD
Eastern Michigan University

Richard M. J. Renneboog, MSc
Independent Scholar

Elizabeth Rholetter Purdy, PhD
Independent Scholar

Lars Rose, MSc, PhD
The Nature of Matter

Julia A. Rosenthal, BA, MS
Independent Scholar

Elizabeth D. Schafer, Ph
Loachapoka, AL

Abhijit Sen
Suri Vidyasagar College

Billy R. Smith Jr., PhD
Anne Arundel Community College

Polly D. Steenhagen, BS, MS
Delaware State University

John Teehan
Independent Scholar

Bethany Thivierge, BS, MPH
Technicality Resources

Janine Ungvarsky
Kings College

Maura Valentino, MSLIS
Central Washington University

Ruth A. Wienclaw, PhD
University of Memphis

Edwin G. Wiggins, BS, MS, PhD
Webb Institute

Scott Zimmer, MLS, MS, JD
Alliant International University

Aeronautics and Aviation

ABSTRACT
Aeronautics is the science of atmospheric flight. Aviation is the design, development, production, and operation of flight vehicles. Transonic airliners, airships, helicopters, fighter planes, and unmanned aerial vehicles (UAVs) are all applications of aeronautics.

DEFINITION AND BASIC PRINCIPLES
Aeronautics is the science of atmospheric flight. The terms "aero" (referring to flight) and "nautics" (referring to ships or sailing) originated from the activities of pioneers who aspired to navigate the sky. These early engineers designed, tested, and flew their own creations, many of which were lighter-than-air balloons. Twenty-first-century aeronautics encompasses the science and engineering of designing and analyzing all areas associated with flying machines.

Aviation (based on the Latin word for "bird") originated with the idea of flying like the birds using heavier-than-air vehicles. "Aviation" refers to the field of operating aircraft, while the term "aeronautics" has been largely superseded by "aerospace engineering," which specifically includes the science and engineering of spacecraft in the design, development, production, and operation of flight vehicles.

A fundamental tenet of aerospace engineering is to deal with uncertainty by tying analyses closely to what is definitely known, for example, the laws of physics and mathematical proofs. Lighter-than-air airships are based on the principle of buoyancy, which derives from the law of gravitation. An object that weighs less than the equivalent volume of air experiences a net upward force as the air sinks around it.

Two basic principles that enable the design of heavier-than-air flight vehicles are those of aerodynamic lift and propulsion. Both arise from Sir Isaac Newton's second and third laws of motion. Aerodynamic lift is a force perpendicular to the direction of motion, generated from the turning of flowing air around an object. In propulsion, the reaction to the acceleration of a fluid generates a force that propels an object, whether in air or in the vacuum of space. Understanding these principles allowed aeronauts to design vehicles that could fly steadily despite being much heavier than the air they displaced and allowed rocket scientists to develop vehicles that could accelerate in space. Spaceflight occurs at speeds so high that the vehicle's kinetic energy is comparable to the potential energy due to gravitation. Here the principles of orbital mechanics derive from the laws of dynamics and gravitation and extend to the regime of relativistic phenomena. The engineering sciences of building vehicles that can fly, keeping them stable, controlling their flight, navigating, communicating, and ensuring the survival, health, and comfort of occupants, draw on every field of science.

BACKGROUND AND HISTORY
The intrepid balloonists of the nineteenth century were followed by aeronauts who used the principles of aerodynamics to fly unpowered gliders. The Wright brothers demonstrated sustained, controlled, powered aerodynamic flight of a heavier-than-air

aircraft in 1903. The increasing altitude, payload, and speed capabilities of airplanes made them powerful weapons in World War I. Such advances improved flying skills, designs, and performance, though at a terrible cost in lives.

The monoplane design superseded the fabric-and-wire biplane and triplane designs of World War I. The helicopter was developed during World War II and quickly became an indispensable tool for medical evacuation and search and rescue. The jet engine, developed in the 1940s and used on the Messerschmitt 262 and Junkers aircraft by the Luftwaffe and the Gloster Meteor by the British, quickly enabled flight in the stratosphere at speeds sufficient to generate enough lift to climb in the thin air. Such innovations led to smooth, long-range flights in pressurized cabins and shirtsleeve comfort. Fatal crashes of the de Havilland Comet airliner in 1953 and 1954 focused attention on the science of metal fatigue.

The Boeing 707 opened up intercontinental air travel, followed by the Boeing 747, the supersonic Concorde, and the EADS Airbus A380. A series of crewed research aircraft designated X-planes since

Space Shuttle Atlantis on a Shuttle Carrier Aircraft. Photo via NASA/Wikimedia Commons. [Public domain.]

the 1930s investigated various flight regimes and also drove the development of better wind tunnels and high-altitude simulation chambers. Combat-aircraft development enabled advances that resulted in safer and more efficient airliners.

The rise of computer-aided design (CAD) programs in the latter half of the twentieth century proved beneficial to the aeronautics and aviation industry, enabling aircraft designers to design and modify plans for flying machines and their components using computers rather than paper blueprints. A relatively early adopter of CAD technology, the aerospace company Boeing began using CAD programs for aircraft design by the early 1980s and in 1995 introduced the commercial Boeing 777 airliner, the first known airliner to have been designed entirely through digital means. Over the subsequent decades, CAD software became an indispensable tool within the industry, facilitating the digital creation and testing of three-dimensional (3D) models of aircraft in development.

HOW IT WORKS

Force balance in flight. Five basic forces acting on a flight vehicle are: aerodynamic lift, gravity, thrust, drag, and centrifugal force. For a vehicle in steady level flight in the atmosphere, lift and thrust balance gravity (weight) and aerodynamic drag. Centrifugal force due to moving steadily around the earth is too weak at most airplane flight speeds but is strong for a maneuvering aircraft. Aircraft turn by rolling the lift vector toward the center of curvature of the desired flight path, balancing the centrifugal reaction due to inertia. In the case of a vehicle in space beyond the atmosphere, centrifugal force and thrust countergravitational force.

Aerodynamic lift. Aerodynamics deals with the forces due to the motion of air and other gaseous fluids relative to bodies. Aerodynamic lift is generated perpendicular to the direction of the free stream as the reaction to the rate of change of mo-

Illustration of Montgolfier brothers flight, 1784. Image via Wikimedia Commons. [Public domain.]

mentum of air turning around an object, and, at high speeds, to compression of air by the object. Flow turning is accomplished by changing the angle of attack of the surface, by using the camber of the surface in subsonic flight, or by generating vortices along the leading edges of swept wings.

Propulsion. Propulsive force is generated as a reaction to the rate of change of momentum of a fluid moving through and out of the vehicle. Rockets carry all of the propellant onboard and accelerate it out through a nozzle using chemical heat release, other heat sources, or electromagnetic fields. Jet engines "breathe" air and accelerate it after reaction with fuel. Rotors, propellers, and fans exert lift force on the air and generate thrust from the reaction to this force. Solar sails use the pressure of solar radiation to push large, ultralight surfaces.

Static stability. An aircraft is statically stable if a small perturbation in its attitude causes a restoring aerodynamic moment that erases the perturbation. Typically, the aircraft center of gravity must be ahead of the center of pressure for longitudinal stability. The tails or canards help provide stability about the different axes. Rocket engines are said to be stable if the rate of generation of gases in the combustion chamber does not depend on pressure stronger than by a direct proportionality, such as a pressure exponent of 1.

Flight dynamics and controls. Static stability is not the whole story, as every pilot discovers when the airplane drifts periodically up and down instead of holding a steady altitude and speed. Flight dynamics studies the phenomena associated with aerodynamic loads and the response of the vehicle to control surface deflections and engine-thrust changes. The study begins with writing the equations of motion of the aircraft resolved along the six degrees of freedom: linear movement along the longitudinal, vertical and sideways axes, and roll, yaw, and pitch rotations about them. Maneuvering aircraft must deal with coupling between the different degrees of freedom, so that roll accompanies yaw, and so on.

The autopilot system was an early flight-control achievement. Terrain-following systems combine information about the terrain with rapid updates, enabling military aircraft to fly close to the ground, much faster than a human pilot could do safely. Modern flight-control systems achieve such feats as reconfiguring control surfaces and fuel to compensate for damage and engine failures; or enabling autonomous helicopters to detect, hover over, and pick up small objects and return; or sending a space probe at thousands of kilometers per hour close to a planetary moon or landing it on an asteroid and returning it to Earth. This field makes heavy use of ordinary differential equations and transform techniques, along with simulation software.

Orbital missions. The rocket equation attributed to Russian scientist Konstantin Tsiolkovsky related the speed that a rocket-powered vehicle gains to the amount and speed of the mass that it ejects. A vehicle launched from Earth's surface goes into a trajectory where its kinetic energy is exchanged for gravitational potential energy. At low speeds, the resulting trajectory intersects the earth, so that the vehicle falls to the surface. At high enough

Designs for flying machines by Leonardo da Vinci, circa 1490. Image via Wikimedia Commons. [Public domain.]

speeds, the vehicle goes so far so fast that its trajectory remains in space and takes the shape of a continuous ellipse around Earth. At even higher kinetic energy levels, the vehicle goes into a hyperbolic trajectory, escaping Earth's orbit into the solar system. The key is thus to achieve enough tangential speed relative to Earth. Most rockets rise rapidly through the atmosphere so that the acceleration to high tangential speed occurs well above the atmosphere, thus minimizing air-drag losses.

Hohmann transfer. Theoretically, the most efficient way to impart kinetic energy to a vehicle is impulsive launch, expending all the propellant instantly so that no energy is wasted lifting or accelerating propellant with the vehicle. Of course, this would destroy any vehicle other than a cannonball, so large rockets use gentle accelerations of no more than 1.4 to 3 times the acceleration due to gravity. The advantage of impulsive thrust is used in the Hohmann transfer maneuver between different orbits in space. A rocket is launched into a highly eccentric elliptical trajectory. At its highest point, more thrust is added quickly. This sends the vehicle into a circular orbit at the desired height or into a new orbit that takes it close to another heavenly body. Reaching the same final orbit using continuous, gradual thrust would require roughly twice as much expenditure of energy. However, continuous thrust is still an attractive option for long missions in space, because a small amount of thrust can be generated using electric propulsion engines that accelerate propellant to extremely high speeds compared with the chemical engines used for the initial ascent from Earth.

APPLICATIONS AND PRODUCTS

Aerospace structures. Aerospace engineers always seek to minimize the mass required to build the vehicle but still ensure its safety and durability. Unlike buildings, bridges, or even (to some degree) automobiles, aircraft cannot be made safer merely by making them more massive, because they must also be able to overcome Earth's gravity. This exigency has driven development of new materials and detailed, accurate methods of analysis, measurement, and construction. The first aircraft were built mostly from wood frames and fabric skins. These were superseded by all-metal craft, constructed using the monocoque concept (in which the outer skin bears most of the stresses). The Mosquito high-speed bomber in World War II reverted to wood construction for better performance. Woodworkers learned to align the grain (fiber direction) along the principal stress axes. Metal offers the same strength in all directions for the same thickness. Composite structures allow fibers with high tensile strength to be placed along the directions where strength is needed, bonding different layers together.

Aeroelasticity. Aeroelasticity is the study of the response of structurally elastic bodies to aerodynamic loads. Early in the history of aviation, several mysterious and fatal accidents occurred wherein pieces of wings or tails failed in flight, under conditions where the steady loads should have been well below the strength limits of the structure. The intense research to address these disasters showed that beyond some flight speed, small perturbations in lift, such as those due to a gust or a maneuver, would cause the structure to respond in a resonant bending-twisting oscillation, the perturbation amplitude rapidly rising in a "flutter" mode until structural failure occurred. Predicting such aeroelastic instabilities demanded a highly mathematical approach to understand and apply the theories of unsteady aerodynamics and structural dynamics. Modern aircraft are designed so that the flutter speed is well above any possible speed achieved. In the case of helicopter rotor blades and gas turbine engine blades, the problems of ensuring aeroelastic stability are still the focus of leading-edge research. Related advances in structural dynamics have enabled development of composite structures and of highly efficient turbo machines that use counterrotating stages, such as those in the F135 engines used in the F-35 Joint Strike Fighter. Such advances also made it possible for earthquake-surviving high-rise buildings to be built in cities such as San Francisco, Tokyo, and Los Angeles, where a number of sensors, structural-dynamics-analysis software, and actuators allow the correct response to dampen the effects of earth movements even on the upper floors.

Smart materials. Various composite materials such as carbon fiber and metal matrix composites have come to find application even in primary aircraft structures. The Boeing 787 is the first to use a composite main spar in its wings. Research on nano materials promises the development of materials with hundreds of times as much strength per unit mass as steel. Another leading edge of research in materials is in developing high-temperature or very low-temperature (cryogenic) materials for use inside jet and rocket engines, the spinning blades of turbines, and the impeller blades of liquid hydrogen pumps in rocket engines. Single crystal turbine blades enabled the development of jet engines with very high turbine inlet temperatures and, thus, high thermodynamic efficiency. Ceramic designs that are not brittle are pushing turbine inlet temperatures even higher. Other materials are "smart," meaning they respond actively in some way to inputs. Examples include piezoelectric materials.

Wind tunnels and other physical test facilities. Wind tunnels, used by the Wright brothers to develop airfoil shapes with desirable characteristics, are still used heavily in developing concepts and proving the performance of new designs, investigating causes of problems, and developing solutions and data to validate computational prediction techniques. Generally, a wind tunnel has a fan or a high-pressure reservoir to add work to the air and raise its stagnation pressure. The air then flows through means of reducing turbulence and is accelerated to the maximum speed in the test section, where models and measurement systems operate.

The power required to operate a wind tunnel is proportional to the mass flow rate through the tunnel and to the cube of the flow speed achieved. Low-speed wind tunnels have relatively large test sections and can operate continuously for several minutes at a time. Supersonic tunnels generally operate with air blown from a high-pressure reservoir for short durations. Transonic tunnels are designed with ventilating slots to operate in the difficult regime where there may be both supersonic waves and subsonic flow over the test configuration. Hypersonic tunnels require heaters to avoid liquefying the air and to simulate the high stagnation temperatures of hypersonic flight and operate for millisecond durations. Shock tubes generate a shock from the rupture of a diaphragm, allowing high-energy air to expand into stationary air in the tube. They are used to simulate the extreme conditions across shocks in hypersonic flight. Many other specialized test facilities are used in structural and materials testing, developing jet and rocket engines, and designing control systems. While the development of computer-based testing programs has enabled aircraft designers to perform some testing virtually, such as by subjecting a 3D model of an airplane to a simulated wind tunnel, such technologies have yet to replace physical test facilities as the primary testing venue for the aerospace industry..

Avionics and navigation. Condensed from the term "aviation electronics," the term "avionics" has come to include the generation of intelligent software systems and sensors to control unmanned aerial vehicles (UAVs), which may operate autonomously. Avionics also deals with various subsystems such as radar and communications, as well as navigation equipment, and is closely linked to the disciplines of flight dynamics, controls, and navigation.

During World War II, pilots on long-range night missions would navigate celestially. The gyroscopes in their aircrafts would spin at high speed so that their inertia allowed them to maintain a reference position as the aircraft changed altitude or accelerated. Most modern aircraft use the global positioning system (GPS), Galileo, or GLONASS satellite constellations to obtain accurate updates of position, altitude, and velocity. The ordinary GPS signal determines position and speed with fair accuracy. Much greater precision and higher rates of updates are available to authorized vehicle systems through the differential GPS signal and military frequencies.

CAREERS AND COURSEWORK
Aerospace engineers work on problems that push the frontiers of technology. Typical employers in this industry are manufacturers of aircraft or their parts and subsystems, airlines, government agencies and laboratories, and the defense services. Many aerospace engineers are also sought by financial services and other industries seeking those with excellent quantitative (mathematical and scientific) skills and talents.

University curriculum generally starts with a year of mathematics, physics, chemistry, computer graphics, computer science, language courses, and an introduction to aerospace engineering, followed by sophomore-year courses in basic statics, dynamics, materials, and electrical engineering. Core courses include low-speed and high-speed aerodynamics, linear systems analysis, thermodynamics, propulsion, structural analysis, composite materials, vehicle performance, stability, control theory, avionics, orbital mechanics, aeroelasticity and structural dynamics, and a two-semester sequence on capstone design of flight vehicles. High school students aiming for such careers should take courses in mathematics, physics, chemistry and natural sciences, and computer graphics. Aerospace engineers are frequently required to write clear reports and present complex issues to skeptical audiences, which demands excellent communication skills. Taking flying lessons or getting a private pilot license is less important to aerospace engineering, as exhilarating as it is, and should be considered only if one desires a career as a pilot or astronaut.

The defense industry is moving toward using aircraft that do not need a human crew and can perform beyond the limits of what a human can survive, so the glamorous occupation of combat jet pilot may be heading for extinction. Airline pilot salaries are also decreasing significantly. Aircraft approach, landing, traffic management, emergency response, and collision avoidance systems may soon become fully automated and will require maneuvering responses that are beyond what a human pilot can provide in time and accuracy. Opportunities for spaceflight may also be minimal, although the emergence of multiple competing private spaceflight companies in the twenty-first century could potentially lead to an increase in related jobs. This is not a unique situation in aviation history. Early pilots, even much later than the intrepid "aeronauts," also worked much more for love of the unparalleled experience of flying, rather than for looming prospects of high-profile careers or the salaries paid by struggling startup airline companies. The only reliable prediction that can be made about aerospace careers is that they hold many surprises.

SOCIAL CONTEXT AND FUTURE PROSPECTS
Airline travel is under severe stress in the first part of the twenty-first century. This is variously attributed to airport congestion, security issues, rising fuel prices, predatory competition, reduction of route monopolies, and leadership that appears to offer little vision beyond cost cutting. The decline in consumer travel following the emergence of the COVID-19 pandemic in 2020 likewise proved detrimental to the industry. Nevertheless, the global demand for commercial aircraft remained significant: a 2021 report by the market research firm Global Industry Analysts projected that the global commer-

cial aircraft market would increase from $197.4 billion in 2020 to $218.8 billion in 2026.

Detailed design and manufacturing of individual aircraft are distributed between suppliers worldwide, with the wings, tails, and engines of a given aircraft often designed and built in different parts of the world. Japan and China are expected to increase their aircraft manufacturing, while major US companies appear to be moving more toward becoming system integrators and away from manufacturing.

Just over one century into powered flight, the human venture into the air and beyond is just beginning. Aircraft still depend on long runways and can fly only in a very limited range of conditions. Weather delays are still common because of uncertainty about how to deal with fluctuating winds or icing conditions. Most airplanes still consist of long tubes attached to thin wings, because designing blended wing bodies is difficult with the uncertainties in modeling composite structures. The aerospace and aviation industry is a major generator of atmospheric carbon releases. This will change only when the industry switches to renewable hydrogen fuel, which may occur faster than most people anticipate.

—*Narayanan M. Komerath, PhD*

Further Reading

Anderson, John D., Jr., and Mary L. Bowden. *Introduction to Flight*. 9th ed., McGraw-Hill, 2021.

"Commercial Aircraft: Global Market Trajectory & Analytics." *StrategyR*, 2021, www.strategyr.com/market-report-commercial-aircraft-forecasts-global-industry-analysts-inc.asp. Accessed 28 Nov. 2021.

Design Engineering Technical Committee. *AIAA Aerospace Design Engineers Guide*. 6th ed., American Institute of Aeronautics and Astronautics, 2012.

Fielding, John P. *Introduction to Aircraft Design*. 2nd ed., Cambridge UP, 2017.

Gudmundsson, Snorri. *General Aviation Aircraft Design: Applied Methods and Procedures*. 2nd ed., Butterworth-Heinemann, 2021.

Hill, Philip, and Carl Peterson. *Mechanics and Thermodynamics of Propulsion*. 2nd ed., Prentice Hall, 1991.

Liepmann, H. W., and A. Roshko. *Elements of Gas Dynamics*. Dover, 2001.

Peebles, Curtis. *Road to Mach 10: Lessons Learned from the X-43A Flight Research Program*. American Institute of Aeronautics and Astronautics, 2008.

"777 Commercial Transport." *Boeing*, www.boeing.com/history/products/777.page. Accessed 28 Nov. 2021.

Wong, Kenneth. "Fly into a Wind Tunnel with Autodesk Project Falcon." *Digital Engineering 247*, 14 Dec. 2011, www.digitalengineering247.com/article/fly-into-a-wind-tunnel-with-autodesk-project-falcon/. Accessed 28 Nov. 2021.

Aerospace Design

ABSTRACT

Aerospace design is crucial to the development and manufacturing of aircraft and spacecraft. Since the introduction of aircraft in the nineteenth century, aerospace design has led to the production of countless flight vehicles, including spacecraft used for space exploration. Aerospace design involves a design process, which may take several years to complete. The phases of this process typically are system/mission requirements, conceptual design, preliminary design, and critical design. With spacecraft, the design generally includes major components such as the mission payload and the platform.

LEARNING TO FLY

The term "aerospace" refers to Earth's atmosphere and the space beyond. Aerospace design or aerospace engineering is the branch of science and technology that focuses on creating and manufacturing effective aircraft and spacecraft. Aerospace design is divided into two subfields: aeronautic design and astronautical design. Aeronautic design refers to the creation of machines that fly in Earth's atmosphere. Astronautical design deals with designing and developing spacecraft and their launch vehicles, generally powered by highly powerful rockets. The aerospace industry caters to military, industrial, and commercial consumers.

The history of aerospace design begins with the history of aviation. The first powered lighter-than-air craft existed as early as the 1850s. Jules Henri Giffard (1825-82) invented a steam-powered airship in 1852. Ferdinand von Zeppelin (1838-1917) introduced rigid airships in 1900; they came to be known as "zeppelins" and later as "blimps." Brothers Orville (1871-1948) and Wilbur Wright (1867-1912) designed a heavier-than-air, piloted airplane that is generally credited as the first of its kind to execute a successful powered flight, in 1903. Air flight designs continued to progress throughout the twentieth century, paving the way for the development of rotary winged aircraft such as helicopters, which use revolving wings or blades to lift into the air. Powerful air flight engines that fuel modern aircrafts did not emerge until the mid-twentieth century.

At the same time that engine design was advancing, aerospace engineers also began developing machinery that would take humans to the upper atmosphere and into space. Konstantin Tsiolkovsky (1857-1935), known as the "Russian father of rocketry," was a pioneer of astronautics with his insightful studies in space travel and rocket science. American engineer Robert Goddard launched the first liquid-fueled rocket in 1926. Goddard continually improved his rocket design over the years. His calculations contributed to the development of other rocket-powered devices such as ballistic missiles. Tsiolkovsky and German scientist Hermann Oberth (1894-1989) independently made similar breakthroughs in the same time period.

During World War I and World War II, aerospace design saw rampant progress as military engineers pursued higher performance aircraft design. In particular, advances in rocket research during World War II laid the foundation for astronautics. Continued advances in aerospace design were spurred by the Cold War and the space race between the United States and the Soviet Union. The competition to reach outer space led to the launch of the first artificial satellite, *Sputnik 1*, by the Soviet Union in 1957. Artificial satellites would later prove critical to twenty-first-century communications systems and become widespread, with a variety of designs and functions.

The United States established the National Aeronautics and Space Association (NASA) in 1958. Aerospace engineers designed a wide range of spacecraft to explore space, incorporating new technologies and capabilities as they became available. For example, in 1969, an American-made spacecraft successfully sent astronauts to the moon, which marked the first time humans landed on the moon. Many other spacecraft went on to be used to carry out missions elsewhere in the solar system. The design and manufacturing of spacecraft was increasingly carried out by private aerospace companies in the first decades of the twenty-first century, particularly after the conclusion of NASA's Space Shuttle program in 2011. In addition to producing their own spacecrafts and launch systems, private companies such as SpaceX positioned themselves as key suppliers of aerospace technology for NASA missions.

DESIGN PROCESS

The design process of a spacecraft generally occurs in the following phases: system/mission requirements, conceptual design, preliminary design, and critical design. Some of these phases can take years to complete. In the system/mission requirements phase, the requirements of the spacecraft are addressed. The type of mission the spacecraft will be used for helps determine these requirements, as specific tasks may dictate certain design elements. For example, a deep space probe would require a significantly different design than a weather monitoring satellite.

The US Space Shuttle flew 135 times from 1981 to 2011, supporting Spacelab, Mir, the Hubble Space Telescope, and the ISS. (Columbia's maiden launch, which had a white external tank, shown) Photo via NASA/Wikimedia Commons. [Public domain.]

The conceptual design phase deals with several possible system concepts that could fulfill the requirements of the mission. These concepts are first conceived and then analyzed. After the most suitable concept is chosen, costs and risks are examined and schedules are made.

The preliminary design phase involves several tasks. Variations of the selected concept are identified, examined, and improved. Specifications for each subsystem and component level are identified. The projected performance of the systems and subsystems is analyzed. Documents are composed, and an initial parts list is put together. This phase may run for several years depending on the novelty and complexity of the mission.

Lastly, the critical design phase, or detailed design phase, takes place. During this phase, the detailed characteristics of the structural design of the spacecraft are established. Equipment, payload, the crew, and provisions are all taken into account. Plumbing, wiring, and other secondary structures are reviewed. Various tests involving design verification are performed, including tests of electronic circuit models and software models. Design and performance margin estimates are improved. Test and evaluation plans are settled. Like the preliminary design phase, the critical design phase may take several years to complete. Once the design process has been completed, the spacecraft can finally be built. It is then tested before being delivered for use.

By the early twenty-first century, computer-aided design (CAD) technology played an essential role in the aerospace design process, enabling employees of NASA, international space agencies, and private aerospace corporations to design spacecraft, launch systems, robotic rovers, and a host of related components by digital means. CAD was likewise crucial to the processes of testing new crafts or components as well as developing new components to be used in conjunction with existing technology.

TYPICAL COMPONENTS

Most spacecraft share two key components: the mission payload and the platform, or the bus. The mission payload includes all of the equipment that is specific to the mission, such as scientific instruments and probes, rather than general operation. The platform comprises all other parts of the spacecraft, used to deliver the payload. It consists of several subsystems, including the structures subsystem, thermal control subsystem, electrical power subsystem, attitude control subsystem, and telemetry, tracking, and commanding (TT&C) subsystem.

The structures subsystem serves various functions such as enclosing, supporting, and protecting the other subsystems, as well as sustaining stresses and loads. It also provides a connection to the launch vehicle. Two main types of structure subsystems exist: open truss and body mounted. The open-truss type typically has the shape of a box or cylinder, while the body-mounted type does not have a definite shape. The choice of structural materials is an important consideration in aerospace design. Light, durable, and heat-resistant materials, such as aluminum, titanium, and some plastics, are typically used.

The thermal control subsystem regulates the temperature of the spacecraft's components. This helps guarantee that the components function properly throughout the mission. Different components require different temperatures. Thermal control systems may be active or passive. Active thermal control involves the use of electrical heaters, cooling systems, and louvers. Passive thermal control includes the use of heat sinks, thermal coatings and insulations, and phase-change materials (PCM). With passive thermal control, electrical power is not needed and there are no moving parts or fluids.

The electrical power subsystem provides the power the spacecraft needs for the duration of the mission, which can last for years. In most cases, the subsystem includes the following components: a source of energy; a device that converts the energy into electricity; a device that stores the electrical energy; and a system that conditions, charges, discharges, distributes, and regulates the electrical energy. The source of energy is generally solar radiation, nuclear power, or chemical reactions.

The attitude control subsystem deals with the process and hardware necessary for obtaining and sustaining the proper orientation in space, or attitude. It has several functions, including maintaining an orbit (station keeping), adjusting an orbit, and stabilization. That subsystem typically includes navigation sensors, a guidance section, and a control section. As with thermal control, the attitude control may be either active or passive. Active attitude control uses continuous decision-making and hardware that are closed loop. This includes the use of thrusters, electromagnets, and reaction wheels. Passive attitude control uses open-loop environmental torques to sustain attitude, such as gravity gradient and solar sails.

The TT&C subsystem involves communication with operators on the ground. Telemetry uses a radio link to transmit measurement data to those operators. It is typically used for improving spacecraft performance and for monitoring the health of the spacecraft, including the payload.

Tracking and commanding deals with the spacecraft's position. Tracking is used to report the spacecraft's position to the ground station, while commanding is used to change the spacecraft's position. Some common tracking methods are the use of a beacon or a transponder, Doppler tracking, optical tracking, interferometer tracking, and radar tracking and ranging. Commanding is achieved through coded instructions that the ground station sends to the aircraft.

PRACTICAL EXAMPLE

A good example of aerospace design is that of the Space Shuttle, officially called the "Space Transportation System" (STS). In 1969, US president Richard Nixon established the Space Task Group to study the United States' future in space exploration. Among other things, the group envisioned a reusable spaceflight vehicle. It was not long before NASA, along with industry contractors, began the design process of such a vehicle. The process involved numerous studies, including design, engineering, cost, and risk studies. Some of the studies focused on the concepts of an orbiter, dual solid-propellant rocket motors, a reusable piloted booster, and a disposable liquid-propellant tank.

In 1972, the design of the Space Shuttle was moved forward. It would feature an orbiter, three main engines, two solid rocket boosters (SRBs), and an external tank (ET). The orbiter would house the crew, the SRBs would provide the shuttle's lift at the beginning of its flight, and the ET would hold fuel for the main engines. All of the components would be reusable, except for the ET, which would be jettisoned after launch. Refinements continued to be made as the project continued and systems were tested.

The first orbiter spacecraft, named Enterprise, was completed in 1976 and underwent several flight tests. However, Enterprise was merely a test vehicle and was not used for any actual space missions. In 1981, the first Space Shuttle mission took place. *Columbia* lifted off from the Kennedy Space Center and became the first orbiter in space. Over the next several decades, several shuttles successfully performed many space missions. The Space Shuttle program concluded in 2011 following the final flight of the shuttle *Atlantis*.

—*Michael Mazzei*

Further Reading

Anderson, John D., Jr., and Mary L. Bowden. *Introduction to Flight*. 9th ed., McGraw-Hill, 2021.

Garino, Brian W., and Jeffrey D. Lanphear. "Spacecraft Design, Structure, and Operations." *AU-18 Space Primer*. Air U, 2009, www.airuniversity.af.edu/Portals/10/AUPress/Books/AU-18.PDF. Accessed 28 Nov. 2021.

Goldstein, Phil. "How Computer-Aided Design Is Used in Government." *FedTech*, 24 June 2020, fedtechmagazine.com/article/2020/06/how-computer-aided-design-used-government-perfcon. Accessed 28 Nov. 2021.

"History of the Space Shuttle." *NASA*, history.nasa.gov/shuttlehistory.html. Accessed 28 Nov. 2021.

"Part I. Historical Context." *Space Transportation System*. Historic American Engineering Record, Nov. 2012.

Wall, Mike. "The Private Spaceflight Decade: How Commercial Space Truly Soared in the 2010s." *Space.com*, 20 Dec. 2019, www.space.com/private-spaceflight-decade-2010s-retrospective.html. Accessed 28 Nov. 2021.

Algorithm

ABSTRACT

An algorithm is a set of steps to be followed in order to solve a particular type of problem. Having originated within the field of mathematics, algorithms make it easier for mathematicians to think of better ways to solve certain types of problems, because looking at the steps needed to reach a solution sometimes helps them to see where an algorithm can be made more efficient by eliminating redundant steps or using different methods of calculation. Algorithms are also key to computer science and enable the automation of various processes, including the generation and manipulation of curves in computer-aided design (CAD) programs.

HISTORY AND BACKGROUND

The word algorithm originally came from the name of a Persian mathematician, Al-Khwarizmi, who lived in the ninth century CE and wrote a book about the ideas of an earlier mathematician from India, Brahmagupta. At first the word simply referred to the author's description of how to solve equations using Brahmagupta's number system, but as time passed it took on a more general meaning. First it was used to refer to the steps required to solve any mathematical problem, and later it broadened still further to include almost any kind of method for handling a particular situation. The concept has been analogized to a recipe for baking a cake; just as the recipe describes a method for accomplishing a

Ada Lovelace's diagram from "note G," the first published computer algorithm. Photo via Wikimedia Commons. [Public domain.]

goal (baking the cake) by listing each step that must be taken throughout the process, an algorithm is an explanation of how to solve a problem that describes each step necessary.

ALGORITHMS IN MATHEMATICS
Algorithms are often used in mathematical instruction because they provide students with concrete steps to follow, even before the underlying operations are fully comprehended. There are algorithms for most mathematical operations, including subtraction, addition, multiplication, and division.

For example, a well-known algorithm for performing subtraction is known as the left to right algorithm. As its name suggests, this algorithm requires one to first line up the two numbers one wishes to find the difference between so that the units digits are in one column, the tens digits in another column, and so forth. Next, one begins in the leftmost column and subtracts the lower number from the upper, writing the result below. This step is then repeated for the next column to the right, until the values in the units column have been subtracted from one another. At this point the results from the subtraction of each column, when read left to right, constitute the answer to the problem.

By following these steps, it is possible for a subtraction problem to be solved even by someone still in the process of learning the basics of subtraction. This demonstrates the power of algorithms both for performing calculations and for use as a source of instructional support.

ALGORITHMS IN COMPUTER-AIDED DESIGN
Algorithms are also important within the field of computer science. For example, without algorithms, a computer would have to be programmed with the exact answer to every set of numbers that an equation could accept in order to solve an equation—an impossible task. By programming the computer with the appropriate algorithm, the computer can follow the instructions needed to solve the problem, regardless of which values are used as inputs. Algorithms are crucial to a wide range of computer technologies, facilitating the sorting and analysis of data, the use of automated decision-making processes, and other key functions. In computer-aided design (CAD) programs, algorithms are particularly useful in automating the drawing of shapes that would otherwise require time-consuming calculations. For example, CAD programs use algorithms to generate curves and to enable designers to manipulate those curves in accordance with their needs.

—*Scott Zimmer, MLS, MS, JD*

Further Reading
Cormen, Thomas H. *Algorithms Unlocked*. MIT Press, 2013.
Ferguson, R. Stuart. *Practical Algorithms for 3D Computer Graphics*. 2nd ed., AK Peters/CRC Press, 2013.
Fitter, Hetal N., Akash B. Pandey, Divyang D. Patel, and Jitendra M. Mistry. "A Review on Approaches for Handling Bezier Curves in CAD for Manufacturing." *Procedia Engineering*, vol. 97, 2014, pp. 1155-66.
MacCormick, John. *Nine Algorithms That Changed the Future: The Ingenious Ideas That Drive Today's Computers*. Princeton UP, 2012.
O'Leary, Timothy, Linda O'Leary, and Daniel O'Leary. *Computing Essentials 2021*. McGraw-Hill, 2020.
Parker, Matt. *Things to Make and Do in the Fourth Dimension: A Mathematician's Journey through Narcissistic Numbers, Optimal Dating Algorithms, at Least Two Kinds of Infinity, and More*. Farrar, 2014.
Sarkar, Jayanta. *Computer Aided Design: A Conceptual Approach*. CRC Press, 2017.
Schapire, Robert E., and Yoav Freund. *Boosting: Foundations and Algorithms*. MIT Press, 2012.
Steiner, Christopher. *Automate This: How Algorithms Came to Rule Our World*. Penguin, 2012.
Valiant, Leslie. *Probably Approximately Correct: Nature's Algorithms for Learning and Prospering in a Complex World*. Basic, 2013.

Applied Mathematics

ABSTRACT

Applied mathematics is the application of mathematical principles and theory in the real world. The practice of applied mathematics has two principal objectives: One is to find solutions to challenging problems by identifying the mathematical rules that describe the observed behavior or characteristic involved, and the other is to reduce real-world behaviors to a level of precise and accurate predictability. Mathematical rules and operations are devised to describe a behavior or property that may not yet have been observed, with the goal of being able to predict with certainty what the outcome of the behavior would be.

DEFINITION AND BASIC PRINCIPLES

Applied mathematics focuses on the development and study of mathematical and computational tools. These tools are used to solve challenging problems primarily in science and engineering applications and in other fields that are amenable to mathematical procedures. The principal mathematical tool is calculus, often referred to as the mathematics of change. Calculus provides a means of quantitatively understanding how variables that cannot be controlled directly behave in response to changes in variables that can be controlled directly. Thus, applied mathematics makes it possible to make predictions about the behavior of an environment and thus gain some mastery over that environment.

For example, suppose a specific characteristic of the behavior of individuals within a society is determined by the combination of a large number of influencing forces, many of which are unknown and perhaps unknowable, and therefore not directly controllable. Study of the occurrence of that characteristic in a population, however, allows it to be described in mathematical terms. This, in turn, provides a valid means of predicting the future occurrence and behavior of that characteristic in other situations. Applied mathematics, therefore, uses mathematical techniques and the results of those techniques in the investigation or solving of problems that originate outside of the realm of mathematics.

The applications of mathematics to real-world phenomena rely on four essential structures: data structures, algorithms, theories and models, and computers and software. Data structures are ways of organizing information or data. Algorithms are specific methods of dealing with the data. Theories and models are used in the analysis of both data and ideas and represent the rules that describe either the way the data were formed or the behavior of the data. Computers and software are the physical devices that are used to manipulate the data for analysis and application. Algorithms are central to the development of software, which is computer specific, for the manipulation and analysis of data.

BACKGROUND AND HISTORY

Applied mathematics, as a field of study, is newer than the practices of engineering and building. The mathematical principles that are the central focus of applied mathematics were developed and devised from observation of physical constructs and behaviors and are therefore subsequent to the development of those activities. The foundations of applied mathematics can be found in the works of early Egyptian and Greek philosophers and engineers. Plane geometry is thought to have developed during the reign of the pharaoh Sesostris, as a result of agricultural land measurements necessitated by the annual inundation of the Nile River. The Greek engineer Thales of Miletus is credited with some of the earliest and most profound applications of mathematical and physical principles in the construction of some of his devices, although there is no evidence that he left a written record of those principles. The primary historical figures in the development of applied mathematics are Euclid and Archimedes. It is perhaps unfortunate that the Greek method of phi-

Applied Mathematics

PRINCIPLES OF COMPUTER-AIDED DESIGN

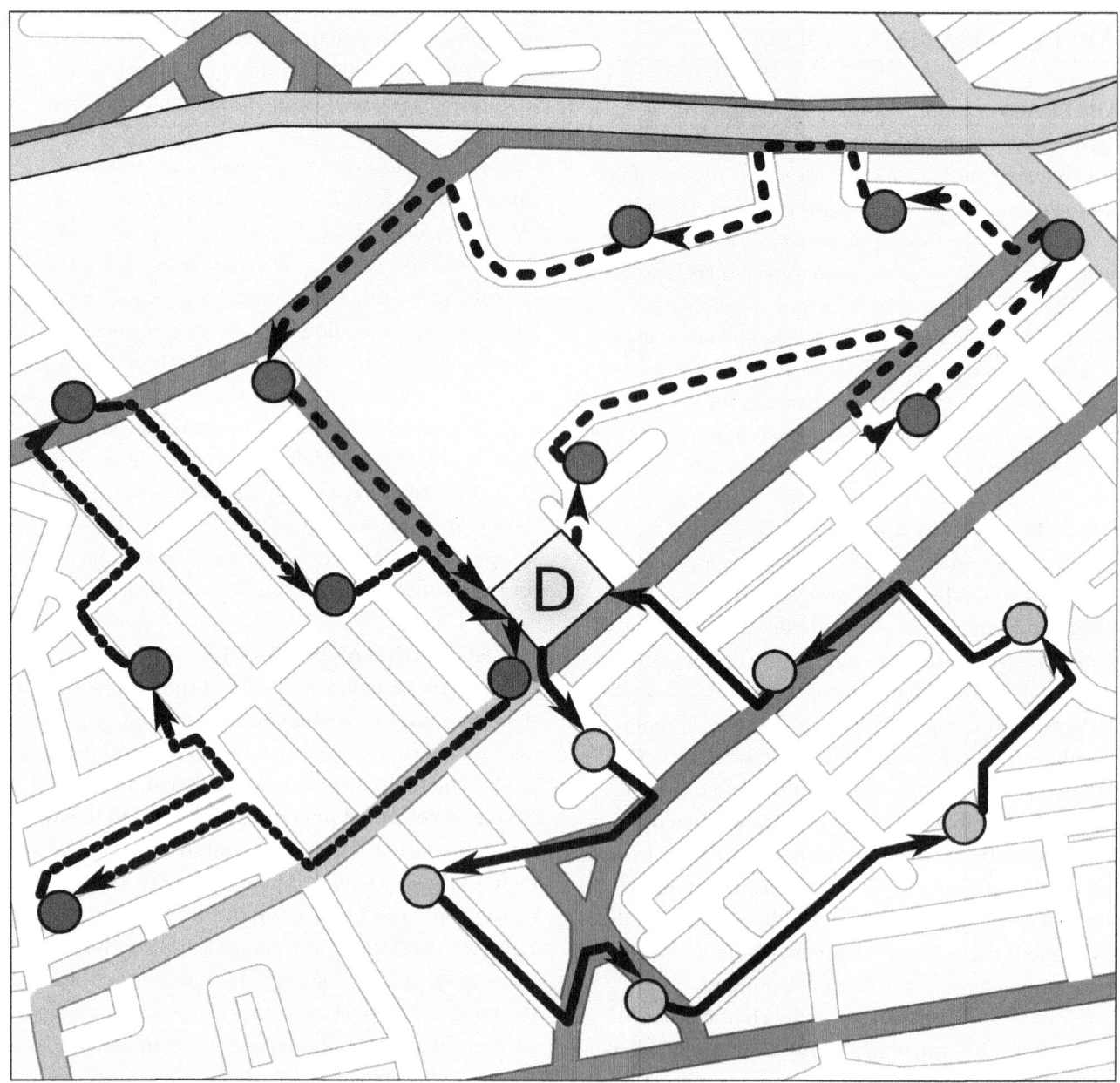

Efficient solutions to the vehicle routing problem require tools from combinatorial optimization and integer programming. Paddington Station location map. Image by Maly LOLek, via Wikimedia Commons.

losophy lacked physical experimentation and the testing of hypotheses but was instead a pure thought process. For this reason, there is a distinction between the fields of pure mathematics and applied mathematics, although the latter depends strictly on the former.

During the Middle Ages, significant mathematical development took place in Islamic nations, where *al geber*, which has come to be known as "algebra," was developed, but the field of mathematics showed little progress in Europe. Even during the Renaissance period, mathematics was the realm almost exclusively of astronomers and astrologers. It is not certain that even Leonardo da Vinci, foremost of the Renaissance engineers and artists, was adept at mathematics despite the mathematical brilliance of his designs. The major historical development of applied mathematics began with the development of calculus by Sir Isaac Newton and Gottfried Wilhelm Leibniz in the seventeenth century. The applicability of mathematical principles in the development of scientific pursuits during the Industrial Revolution brought applied mathematics to the point where it has become essential for understanding the physical universe.

HOW IT WORKS
Applied mathematics is the creation and study of mathematical and computational tools that can be broadly applied in science and engineering. Those tools are used to solve challenging problems in these and related fields of practice. In its simplest form, applied mathematics refers to the use of measurement and simple calculations to describe a physical condition or behavior.

A simple example might be the layout or design of a field or other area of land. Consider a need to lay out a rectangular field having an area of 2,000 square meters (m2) with the shortest possible perimeter. The area (A) of any rectangular area is determined as the product of the length (l) and the width (w) of the area in question. The perimeter (P) of any rectangular area is determined as the sum of the lengths of all four sides, and in a rectangular area, the opposite sides are of equal length. Thus, $P = 2l + 2w$, and $A = l \times w = 2000$ m2. By trial and error, pairs of lengths and widths whose product is 2,000 may be tried out, and their corresponding perimeters determined. A field that is 2,000 meters long and 1 meter wide has an area of 2,000 square meters and a perimeter of 4,002 meters. Similarly, a field that is 200 meters long and 10 meters wide has the required area, and a perimeter of only 420 meters. It becomes apparent that the perimeter is minimized when the area is represented as a square, having four equal sides. Thus, the length of each side must be equal to the square root of 2,000 in magnitude. Having determined this, the same principles may be applied to the design of any rectangular area of any size.

The same essential procedures as those demonstrated in this simple example apply with equal validity to other physical situations and are, in fact, the very essence of scientific experimentation and research. The progression of the development of mathematical models and procedures in many different areas of application is remarkably similar. Development of a mathematical model begins with a simple expression to which refinements are made, and the results of the calculation are compared with the actual behavior of the system under investigation. The changes in the difference between the real and calculated behaviors are the key to further refinements that, ideally, work to bring the two into ever closer agreement. When mathematical expressions have been developed that adequately describe the behavior of a system, those expressions can be used to describe the behaviors of other systems.

A key component to the successful application of mathematical descriptions or models is an understanding of the different variables that affect the behavior of the system being studied. In fluid dynamics, for example, obvious variables that affect a fluid are the temperature and density of the fluid. Less obvious perhaps are such variables as the viscosity of the fluid, the dipolar interactions of the fluid atoms or molecules, the adhesion between the fluid and the surface of the container through which it is flowing, whether the fluid is flowing smoothly (laminar flow) or turbulently (nonlaminar flow), and a number of other more obscure variables. A precise mathematical description of the behavior of such a system would include corrective terms for each and every variable affecting the system. However, a number of these corrective terms may be considered together in an approximation term and still produce an accurate mathematical description of the behavior.

An example of such an approximation may be found in the applied mathematical field of quantum mechanics, by which the behavior of electrons in molecules is modeled. The classic quantum mechanical model of the behavior of an electron bound to an atomic nucleus is the so-called "particle-in-a-box model." In this model, the particle (the electron) can exist only within the confines of the box (the atomic orbital), and because the electron has the properties of an electromagnetic wave as well as those of a physical particle, there are certain restrictions placed on the behavior of the particle. For example, the value of the wave function describing the motion of the electron must be zero at the boundaries of the box. This requires that the motion of the particle can be described only by certain wave functions that, in turn, depend on the dimensions of the box. The problem can be solved mathematically with precision only for the case involving a single electron and a single nuclear proton that defines the box in which the electron is found. The calculated results agree extremely well with observed measurements of electron energy.

For systems involving more particles (more electrons and more nuclear protons and neutrons), the number of variables and other factors immediately exceeds any ability to be calculated precisely. A solution is found, however, in a method that uses an approximation of the orbital description, known as a "Slater-type orbital approximation," rather than a precise mathematical description. A third-level Gaussian treatment of the Slater-type orbitals, or STO-3G analysis, yields calculated results for complex molecular structures that are in excellent agreement with the observed values measured in physical experiments. Although the level of mathematical technique is vastly more complex than in the simple area example, the basic method of finding an applicable method is almost exactly identical.

APPLICATIONS AND PRODUCTS

Applied mathematics is essentially the application of mathematical principles and theories toward the resolution of physical problems and the description of behaviors. The range of disciplines in which applied mathematics is relevant is therefore very broad. The intangible nature of mathematics and mathematical theory tends to restrict active research and development to the academic environment and applied research departments of industry. In these environs, applied mathematics research tends to be focused rather than general in nature. Applied mathematics is generally divided into the major areas of computational mathematics: combinatorics and optimization, computer science, pure mathematics, and statistical and actuarial science. The breadth of the research field has grown dramatically, and the diversity of subject area applications is indicated by the applied mathematics research being conducted in atmospheric and biological systems applications, climate and weather, complexity theory, computational finance, control systems, cryptography, pattern recognition and data mining, multivariate data analysis and visualization, differential equation modeling, fluid dynamics, linear programming, medical imaging, computer-aided design, and a host of other areas.

Computational mathematics. Simply stated, computational mathematics is the process of modeling systems quantitatively on computers. This is often referred to in the literature as *in silico*, indicating that the operation or procedure being examined is carried out as a series of calculations within the silicon-based electronic circuitry of a computer chip and not in any tangible, physical manner. Research in computational mathematics is carried out in a wide range of subject areas.

The essence of computational mathematics is the development of algorithms and computer programs that produce accurate and reliable models or depictions of specific behaviors. In atmospheric systems, for example, one goal would be to produce mathematical programs that precisely depict the behavior of the ozone layer surrounding the planet. The objective of such a program would be to predict how the ozone layer would change as a result of alterations in atmospheric composition. It is not feasible to observe the effects directly and would ultimately be counterproductive if manifesting an atmospheric change resulted in the destruction of the ozone layer. Modeling the system *in silico* allows researchers to institute virtual changes and determine what the effect of each change would be. The reliability of the calculated effect depends directly on how accurately the model describes the existing behavior of the system.

Medical imaging. An area in which applied mathematics has become fundamentally important is the field of medical imaging, especially as it applies to magnetic resonance imaging (MRI). The MRI technique developed from nuclear magnetic resonance (NMR) analysis commonly used in analytical chemistry to determine molecular structures. In NMR, measurements are obtained of the absorption of specific radio frequencies by molecules held within a magnetic field. The strength of each absorption and specific patterns of absorptions are characteristic of the structure of the particular molecule and so can be used to determine unequivocally the exact molecular structure of a material.

One aspect of NMR that has been greatly improved by applied mathematics is the elimination of background noise. A typical NMR spectrum consists of an essentially infinite series of small random signals that often hide the detailed patterns of actual absorption peaks and sometimes even the peaks themselves. The Fourier analysis methodology, in which such random signals can be treated as a combination of sine and cosine waves, also known as "wavelet theory," eliminates a significant number of such signals from electromagnetic spectra. The result is a much more clear and precise record of the actual absorptions. Such basic NMR spectra are only one dimensional, however. The second-generation modification of NMR systems was developed to produce a two-dimensional (2D) representation of the NMR absorption spectrum, and from this was developed the three-dimensional (3D) NMR imaging system that is known as MRI. Improvements that make the Fourier analysis technique ever more effective in accord with advances in the computational abilities of computer hardware are the focus of one area of ongoing applied mathematics research.

Population dynamics and epidemiology. Population dynamics and epidemiology are closely related fields of study. The former studies the growth and movements of populations, and the latter studies the growth and movements of diseases and medical conditions within populations. Both rely heavily for their mathematical descriptions on many areas of applied mathematics, including statistics, fluid dynamics, complexity theory, pattern recognition, data visualization, differential equation modeling, chaos theory, risk management, numerical algorithms and techniques, and statistical learning.

In a practical model, the movements of groups of individuals within a population are described by many of the same mathematical models of fluid dynamics that apply to moving streams of particles. The flow of traffic on a multilane highway or the movement of people along a busy sidewalk, for example, can be seen to exhibit the same gross behavior as that of a fluid flowing through a system of pipes. In fact, any population that can be described in terms of a flow of discrete particles, whether molecules of water or vehicles, can be described by the same mathematical principles, at least to the extent that the variables affecting their motion are known. Thus, the forces of friction and adhesion that affect the flow of a fluid within a tube are closely mimicked by the natural tendencies of drivers to drive at varying speeds in different lanes of a multilane highway. Window-shoppers and other slow-moving individuals tend to stay to the part of the sidewalk closest to the buildings, while those who walk faster or more purposefully tend to use the part of the sidewalk farthest away from the buildings, and this also follows the behavior of fluid flow.

The spread or movement of diseases through a population can also be described by many of the same mathematical principles that describe the movements of individuals within a population. This is especially true for diseases that are transmitted directly from person to person. For other disease vectors, such as animals, birds, and insects, a mathematical description must describe the movements of those particular populations, while at the same time reflecting the relationship between those populations and the human population of interest.

Statistical analysis and actuarial science. Perhaps the simplest or most obvious use of applied mathematics can be found in statistical analysis. In this application, the common properties of a collection of data points, themselves measurements of some physical property, are enumerated and compared for consistency. The effectiveness of statistical methods depends on the appropriately random collection of representative data points and on the appropriate definition of a property to be analyzed.

Statistical analysis is used to assess the consistency of a common property and to identify patterns of occurrence of characteristics. This forms the basis of the practice of statistical process control (SPC) that has become the primary method of quality control in industry and other fields of practice. In statistical process control, random samples of an output stream are selected and compared to their design standard. Variations from the desired value are determined, and the data accumulated over time are analyzed to determine patterns of variation. In an injection-molding process, for example, a variation that occurs consistently in one location of the object being molded may indicate that a modification to the overall process must be made, such as adjusting the temperature of the liquid material being injected or an alteration to the die itself to improve the plastic flow pattern.

In another context, one that is tied to epidemiology, the insurance and investment industries make very detailed use of statistical analysis in the assessment of risk. Massive amounts of data describing various aspects of human existence in modern society are meticulously analyzed to identify patterns of effects that may indicate a causal relationship. An obvious example is the statistical relationship pattern between healthy lifestyle and mortality rates, in which obese people of all age groups have a higher mortality rate than their counterparts who maintain a leaner body mass. Similarly, automobile insurance rates are set much higher for male drivers between the ages of sixteen and twenty-five than for female drivers in that age group and older drivers because statistical analysis of data from accidents demonstrates that this particular group has the highest risk of involvement in a traffic accident. This type of data mining is a continual process as relationships are sought to describe every factor that plays a role in human society.

CAREERS AND COURSEWORK

The study of applied mathematics builds on a solid and in-depth comprehension of pure mathematics. The student begins by taking courses in mathematics throughout secondary school to acquire a solid foundational knowledge of basic mathematical principles before entering college or university studies. A specialization in mathematics at the college and university level is essential to practically all areas of study. As so many fields have been affected by applied mathematics, the methodologies being taught in undergraduate courses are a reflection of the accepted concepts of applied mathematics on which they are constructed. As the depth of the field of applied mathematics indicates, career options are, for all intents and purposes, unlimited. Every field of endeavor, from anthropology to zoology, has a component of applied mathematics, and the undergraduate must learn the mathematical methods corresponding to the chosen field.

Students who specialize in the study of applied mathematics as a career choice and proceed to postgraduate studies take courses in advanced mathematics and carry out research aimed at developing mathematics theory and advancing the application of those developments in other fields. Particular programs of study in applied mathematics are included as part of the curriculum of other disciplines. The focus of such courses is on specific mathematical operations and techniques that are relevant to that particular field of study.

SOCIAL CONTEXT AND FUTURE PROSPECTS
Human behavior is well suited and highly amenable to description and analysis through mathematical principles. Modeling of population dynamics has become increasingly important in the contexts of service and regulation. As new diseases appear, accurate models to predict the manner in which they will spread play an ever more important role in determining the response to possible outbreaks. Similarly, accurate modeling of geological activities is increasingly valuable in determining the best ways to respond to such natural disasters as a tsunami or earthquake. Earth itself is a dynamic system that is only marginally predictable. Applied mathematics is essential to developing models and theories that will lead to accurate prediction of the occurrence and ramifications of seismic events. It will also be absolutely necessary for understanding the effects that human activity may be having on the atmosphere and oceans, particularly in regard to the issues of global warming and the emission of greenhouse gases. Climate models that can accurately and precisely predict the effects of such activities will continue to be the object of a great deal of research in applied mathematics.

The development of new materials and the engineering of new applications with those materials is an ongoing human endeavor. The design of extremely small nanostructures that employ those materials is based on mathematical principles that are unique to the realm of the very small. Of particular interest is research toward the development of the quantum computer, a device that operates on the subatomic scale rather than on the existing scale of computer construction. Research into such technology remains ongoing, with some researchers investigating the potential applications of computer-aided design (CAD) and computer-aided manufacturing (CAM) technologies in designing and manufacturing the necessary nanostructures.

—*Richard M. J. Renneboog, MSc*

Further Reading
Anton, Howard. *Calculus: A New Horizon*. 6th ed., Wiley, 1999.
De Haan, Lex, and Toon Koppelaars. *Applied Mathematics for Database Professionals*. Springer, 2007.
Higham, Nicholas J., editor. *The Princeton Companion to Applied Mathematics*. Princeton UP, 2015.
Howison, Sam. *Practical Applied Mathematics: Modelling, Analysis, Approximation*. Cambridge UP, 2005.
"IonQ Chooses Onshape's Cloud CAD Platform for Quantum Computer Design." *Duke*, 23 Jan. 2019, otc.duke.edu/news/ionq-chooses-onshapes-cloud-cad-platform-for-quantum-computer-design/. Accessed 28 Nov. 2021.
Moore, David S., William I. Notz, and Michael Fligner. *The Basic Practice of Statistics*. 9th ed., Macmillan, 2021.
Rubin, Jean E. *Mathematical Logic: Applications and Theory*. Saunders College Publishing, 1990.
Sedivy, Josef, and Stepan Hubalovsky. "Mathematical Foundations and Principles in Practice of Computer Aided Design Simulation." *International Journal of Mathematics and Computers in Simulation*, vol. 6, no. 1, 2012, pp. 230-37.
Washington, Allyn J. *Basic Technical Mathematics with Calculus*. 10th ed., Pearson, 2014.

APPLIED PHYSICS

ABSTRACT

Applied physics is the study and application of the behavior of condensed matter, such as solids, liquids, and gases, in bulk quantities. Applied physics is the basis of all engineering and design that requires the interaction of individual components and materials. The study of applied physics now extends into numerous other fields, including physics, chemistry, biology, engineering, medicine, geology, meteorology, and oceanography.

DEFINITION AND BASIC PRINCIPLES

Applied physics is the study of the behavior and interaction of condensed matter. Condensed matter is commonly recognized as matter in the phase forms of solids, liquids, and gases. Each phase has its own unique physical characteristics, and each material has its own unique physical suite of properties that derive from its chemical identity. The combination of these traits determines how something consisting of condensed matter interacts with something else that consists of condensed matter.

The interactions of constructs of condensed matter are governed by the interaction of forces and other vector properties that are applied through each construct. A lever, for example, functions as the medium to transmit a force applied in one direction so that it operates in the opposite direction at another location. Material properties and strengths are also an intimate part of the interaction of condensed matter. A lever that cannot withstand the force applied to it laterally will bend or break rather than function as a lever. Similarly, two equally hard objects, such as a train car's wheels and the steel tracks upon which they roll, rebound elastically with little or no generation of friction. If, however, one of the materials is less hard than the other, as in the case of a steel rotor and a composition brake pad, a great deal of friction characterizes their interaction.

BACKGROUND AND HISTORY

Applied physics is of necessity the oldest of all practical sciences, dating back to the first artificial use of an object by an early hominid. The basic practices have been in use by builders and designers for many thousands of years. With the development of mathematics and measurement, the practice of applied physics has grown apace, relying as it still does upon the application of basic concepts of vector properties (force, momentum, velocity, weight, moment of inertia) and the principles of simple machines (lever, ramp, pulley).

The modern concept of applied physics can be traced back to the Greek philosopher Aristotle (ca. 350 BCE), who identified several separate fields for systematic study. The basic mathematics of physics was formulated by Pythagoras about two hundred years before, but was certainly known to the Babylonians as early as 1600 BCE. Perhaps the greatest single impetus for the advance of applied physics was the development of calculus by Sir Isaac Newton and the fundamental principles of Newtonian mechanics in the seventeenth century. Those principles describe well the behaviors of objects composed of condensed matter, only failing as the scale involved becomes very small (as below the scale of nanotechnology). Since the Industrial Revolution and into the twenty-first century, the advancing capabilities of technology and materials combine to enable even more advances and applications, yet all continue to follow the same basic rules of physics as the crudest of constructs.

HOW IT WORKS

As the name implies, applied physics means nothing more or less than the application of the principles of physics to material objects. The most basic principles of applied physics are those that describe and quantify matter in motion (speed, velocity, acceleration, momentum, inertia, mass, force). These principles lead to the design and implementation of devices and structures, all with the purpose of performing a physical function or action, either individually or in concert.

A second, and equally important, aspect of applied physics is the knowledge of the physical properties and characteristics of the materials being used. This includes such physical properties as melting and boiling points, malleability, thermal conductivity, electrical resistivity, magnetic susceptibility, density, hardness, sheer strength, tensile strength, compressibility, granularity, absorptivity, and a great many other physical factors that determine the suitability of materials for given tasks. Understanding these factors also enables the identification of new applications for those materials.

DESIGN

Applied physics is the essential basis for the design of each and every artificial object and construct, from the tiniest of nanoprobes and the simplest of levers to the largest and most complex of machines and devices. Given the idea of a task to be performed and a device to perform that task, the design process begins with an assessment of the physical environment in which the device must function, the forces that will be exerted against it, and the forces that it will be required to exert in order to accomplish the set task. The appropriate materials may then be selected, based on their physical properties and characteristics. Dimensional analyses determine the necessary size of the device, and also play a significant role in determining the materials that will be utilized.

All of these factors affect the cost of any device, an important aspect of design. Cost is an especially important consideration, as is the feasibility of replacing a component of the designed structure. For example, a device operating in a local environment in which replacement of a component, such as an actuating lever, is easily carried out may be constructed using a simple steel rod. If, however, the device is something like the Mars Rover, for which replacement of worn parts is not an option, it is far more reasonable and effective to use a less corrosive, stronger, but more costly material, such as titanium, to make movable parts. The old design tenet that "form follows function" is an appropriate rule of thumb in the field of applied physics.

APPLICATIONS AND PRODUCTS

In many ways, applied physics leads to the idea of creating devices that build other devices. At some point in time, an individual first used a handy rock to break up another rock or to pound a stick into the ground. This is a simple example of applied physics, when that individual then began to use a specific kind of rock for a specific purpose; this action advanced again when someone realized that attaching the rock to a stick provided a more effective tool. Applied physics has advanced far beyond the crude rock-on-a-stick hammer, yet the exact same physical principles apply now with the most elegant of impact devices. It would not be possible to itemize even a small percentage of the applications and products that have resulted from applied physics, and new physical devices are developed each day.

Civil engineering. Applied physics underpins all physical aspects of human society. It is the basis for the design and construction of the human environment and its supporting infrastructure, the most obvious of which are roads and buildings, designed and engineered with consideration of the forces that they must withstand, both human-made and natural. In this, the highest consideration is given to the science and engineering of materials in regard to the desired end result, rather than to the machines and devices that are employed in the actual construction process. The principles of physics involved in the design and construction of supporting structures, such as bridges and high-rise towers, are of primary importance. No less important, however, are the physical systems that support the function of the structure, including such things as electrical systems, internal movement systems, environmental control systems, monitoring systems, and emergency response systems, to name a few. All are relevant to a specific aspect of the overall physical construct, and all must function in coordination with the other systems. Nevertheless, they all also are based on specific applications of the same applied physics principles.

Transportation. Transportation is perhaps the single greatest expenditure of human effort, and it has produced the modern automotive, air, and railway transportation industries. Applied physics in these areas focuses on the development of more effective and efficient means of controlling the movement of the machine while enhancing the safety of human and nonhuman occupants. While the physical principles by which the various forms of the internal combustion engine function are the same now as when the devices were first invented, the physical processes used in their operation have undergone a great deal of mechanical refinement.

A particular area of refinement is the manner in which fuel is delivered for combustion. In earlier gasoline-fueled piston engines, fuel was delivered via a mechanical fuel pump and carburetor system that functions on the Venturi principle. This has long since been replaced by constant-pressure fuel pumps and injector systems, and this continues to be enhanced as developers make more refinements based on the physical aspects of delivering a liquid fuel to a specific point at a specific time. Similarly, commercial jet engines, first developed for aircraft during World War II, now utilize the same basic

Experiment using a laser. Photo via US Air Force/Wikimedia Commons. [Public domain.]

physical principles as did their earliest counterparts. Alterations and developments that have been achieved in the interim have focused on improvement of the operational efficiency of the engines and on enhancement of the physical and combustion properties of the fuels themselves.

In rail transport, the basic structure of a railway train has not changed; it is still a heavy, massive tractor engine that tows a number of containers on very low friction wheel-systems. The engines have changed from steam-powered behemoths made up of as many as one-quarter-million parts to the modern diesel-electric traction engines of much simpler design.

Driven by the ever-increasing demand for limited resources, this process of refinement for physical efficiency progresses in every aspect of transportation on land, sea, and air. Paradoxically, it is in the area of railway transport that applied physics offers the greatest possibility of advancement with the development of nearly frictionless, magnetic levitation systems upon which modern high-speed bullet trains travel. Physicists continue to work toward the development of materials and systems that will be superconducting at ambient temperatures. It is believed that such materials will completely revolutionize not only the transportation sector but also the entire field of applied physics.

Medical. No other area of human endeavor demonstrates the effects of applied physics better than the medical field. The medical applications of applied physics are numerous, touching every aspect of medical diagnostics and treatment and crossing over into many other fields of physical science. The most obvious of these is medical imaging, in which X-ray diagnostics, magnetic resonance imaging (MRI), and other forms of spectroscopic analysis have become primary tools of medical diagnostics. Essentially, all of the devices that have become invaluable as medical tools began as devices designed to probe the physical nature of materials.

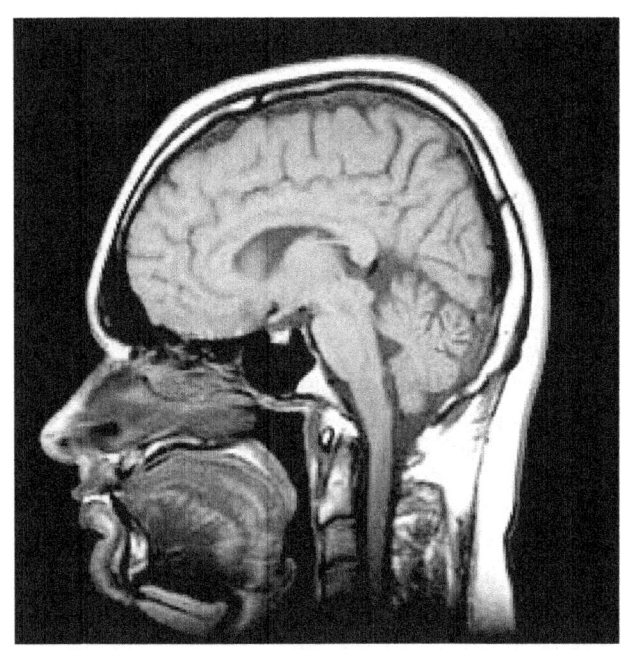

A magnetic resonance image. Photo by Ranveig, via Wikimedia commons.

Spectrographs and spectrometers that are now routinely used to analyze the specific content of various human sera were developed initially to examine the specific wavelengths of light being absorbed or emitted by various materials. MRI developed from the standard technique of physical analytical chemistry called "nuclear magnetic resonance spectrometry," or NMR. In this methodology, magnetic signals are recorded as they pass through a material sample, their patterns revealing intimate details about the three-dimensional (3D) molecular structure of a given compound. The process of MRI that has developed from this simpler application now permits diagnosticians to view the internal structures and functioning of living systems in real time. The diagnostic X-ray that has become the single most common method of examining internal biological structures was first used as a way to physically probe the structure of crystals, even though the first practical demonstration of the existence of X-rays by German physicist Wilhelm Röntgen in 1895 was as an image of the bones in his wife's hand.

Military. It is not possible to separate the field of applied physics from military applications and martial practice, and no other area of human endeavor so clearly illustrates the double-edged sword that is the nature of applied physics. The field of applied physics at once facilitates the most humanitarian of endeavors and the most violent of human aggressions. Ballistics is the area of physics that applies to the motion of bodies moving through a gravitational field. The mathematical equations that describe the motion of a baseball being thrown from center field equally describe the motion of an arrow or a bullet in flight, of the motion of the International Space Station in its orbit, and of the trajectory of a warhead-equipped rocket. The physical principles that have permitted the use of nuclear fission as a source of reliable energy are the same principles that define the functioning of a nuclear warhead.

In the modern age it is desired that warfare be carried out as quickly and efficiently as possible as the means to restore order and peace to an embattled area, with as little loss of life and destruction of property as possible. To that end, military research relies heavily on the application of physics in the development of weapons, communications, and surveillance systems.

Digital electronics. Applied physics has also led to the development of the transistor, commonly attributed to William Shockley, in 1951. Since that time, the development of ever-smaller and more efficient systems based on the semiconductor junction transistor has been rapid and continuous. This has inexorably produced the modern technology of digital electronics and the digital computer. These technologies combine remarkably well to permit the real-time capture and storage of data from the many and various devices employed in medical research and diagnostics, improve the fine control of transportation systems and infrastructure, and advance a veritable host of products that are more efficient in their use of energy than are their nondigital counterparts.

SOCIAL CONTEXT AND FUTURE PROSPECTS

Applied physics has become such a fundamental underpinning of modern society that most people are unaware of its relevance. A case in point is the spin-off of technologies from the National Aeronautics and Space Administration (NASA) space program into the realm of everyday life. Such common household devices as microwave ovens and cell phones, medical devices such as pacemakers and heart monitors, and the digital technology that permeates modern society were developed through the efforts of applied physics in exploring space. For most laypersons, the term "applied physics" conjures images of high-energy particle accelerators or interplanetary telescopes and probes, without the realization that the physical aspect of society is based entirely on principles of applied physics. As these cutting-edge fields of physical research continue, they will continue to spawn new applications that are adapted continually into the overall fabric of modern society.

The areas of society in which applied physics has historically played a role, particularly those involving electronics, will continue to develop. Personal computers and embedded microcontrollers, for example, will continue to grow in power and application while decreasing in size, as research reveals new ways of constructing digital logic circuits through new materials and methods. The incorporation of the technology into consumer products, transportation, and other areas of the infrastructure of society is becoming more commonplace. As a result, the control of many human skills can be relegated to the autonomous functioning of the corresponding device. Consider, for example, the now-built-in ability of some automobiles to parallel park without human intervention.

The technologies that have been developed through applied physics permit the automation of many human actions, which, in turn, drives social change. Similarly, the ability for nearly instantaneous communication between persons in any part of the world, which has been provided through applied physics, has the potential to facilitate the peaceful and productive cooperation of large numbers of people toward resolving significant problems.

—*Richard M. Renneboog, MSc*

Further Reading
Askeland, Donald R., and Wendelin J. Wright. *The Science and Engineering of Materials*. 7th ed., Cengage Learning, 2015.
The Britannica Guide to the One Hundred Most Influential Scientists. Constable & Robinson, 2008.
Ewen, Dale, Neill Schurter, and P. Erik Gundersen. *Applied Physics*. 11th ed., Pearson, 2017.
Giancoli, Douglas C. *Physics for Scientists and Engineers with Modern Physics*. 4th ed., Pearson, 2008.
Helliwell, T. M., and V. V. Sahakian. *Modern Classical Mechanics*. Cambridge UP, 2021.
Robbins, Charles. *Applied Mechanical Physics Using Computer Aided Design*. World Class CAD, 2007.
Sen, P. C. *Principles of Electric Machines and Power Electronics*. 3rd ed., Wiley, 2014.
Valencia, Raymond P., editor. *Applied Physics in the Twenty-First Century*. Nova Science, 2010.

Archaeology

ABSTRACT
Archaeology is the field of applied science concerned with the techniques and practice of collecting, preserving, and analyzing the artifacts and physical remains left behind by human civilizations. The central purpose of archaeology is to study the lives and cultural practices of past societies, both ancient and modern. Archaeology has a deep intangible impact on human experience, as a means of understanding and maintaining the multifaceted cultural heritage produced by the human species. It also has many practical applications; for example, archaeological studies of rural agriculture can help farmers increase the yield of their crops, and urban archaeologists can advise municipal administrators on issues such as transit patterns and garbage disposal.

DEFINITION AND BASIC PRINCIPLES
Archaeology is the study of past human cultures, both historic and prehistoric, through the systematic excavation, inspection, and interpretation of material remains such as tools, toys, clothing, bones, buildings, and other artifacts. In the United States, archaeology is considered a subfield of anthropology, which is the science concerned with the origin, evolution, behavior, beliefs, culture, and physical features of humankind.

The traditional image of archaeology held by many people (and reinforced by television programs and motion pictures featuring adventurous archaeologists such as Indiana Jones) is that it is a field largely concerned with examining ancient artifacts drawn from the extremely distant past. This is certainly true of many subfields of archaeology, such as Egyptology, Assyriology (study of ancient Assyria), classical archaeology, and prehistoric archaeology. However, archaeological tools and techniques can be and frequently are applied to the analysis of human cultures across all segments of time, from the very beginning of the species to much later epochs. For example, industrial archaeologists study the development and use of industrial methods, most of which did not truly come into being on a large scale until the eighteenth century, while urban archaeologists study the patterns of life revealed by the material past of metropolises—such as New York or Paris—that still exist and that have a long history of human habitation.

Archaeology as practiced in the modern world is characterized by several key principles. First, the field is not simply descriptive but rather explana-

CAD programs are used to create 3D models of archaeological sites and artifacts. Photo via iStock/gorodenkoff. [Used under license.]

tory. Archaeologists are concerned not just with the question of what happened in the past but also how and why it happened. To that end, they attempt to interpret the artifacts and features they uncover for clues about the belief systems, behaviors, traditions, and social, political, and economic lives of the cultures at hand. For example, archaeological excavations of the artifacts buried in the tombs of ancient Egyptian pharaohs have revealed a great deal of specific knowledge about what Egyptians believed to be true about the afterlife. Second, it is multiscalar, meaning that the examination of a particular culture takes place simultaneously on many scales, each of which is intertwined with the others. For instance, an archaeologist may combine the small-scale analysis of individual pots, vases, and other clay artifacts—which give insight into the specific production processes used by the artisans who created them—with large-scale evidence about how those objects were handled on trade routes and marketplace procedures—which give insight into the overall historical trajectory of an entire civilization. By the same token, no matter which geographic region an archaeologist is studying, he or she is likely to examine collected data in the light of wider global trends.

BACKGROUND AND HISTORY

People have always been fascinated by the cultures that came before them. Even in ancient Babylon, for example, relics such as ruined temples were objects of interest. During the European Renaissance, an early form of archaeology arose that was mainly focused on classical antiquities and the investigation of large prehistoric sites and monuments, such as Stonehenge. The eighteenth century witnessed the first formal archaeological excavations, one of which was conducted by future president Thomas Jefferson on an Indigenous burial mound located on his Virginia estate. In the nineteenth century, the site of the ancient city Pompeii, destroyed by a sudden volcanic eruption, became the focus of intensive archaeological investigations. Innovative techniques, such as the use of plaster of Paris to create molds of bones and other artifacts, were developed by early practitioners such as Italian scholar Giuseppe Fiorelli.

During the nineteenth century, archaeology began to develop the formality of a scientific discipline. The simultaneous maturation of the field of geology, with its theory of the stratification of rocks, helped establish similar ideas in archaeology. In addition, archaeologists began to work with the principle of uniformitarianism for the first time; this was the idea that past and present societies had more commonalities with each other than differences. Finally, the nineteenth century was the age in which naturalist Charles Darwin's theory of evolution, combined with the accumulating weight of physical evidence, led archaeologists to search for material evidence of human activity in the very distant past, far beyond the age of the earth as defined by biblical scholars.

Archaeology underwent a transformation during the twentieth century, when many useful field techniques were developed that helped transform the field into a true science. Detailed records were kept at every excavation, including the location and description of each artifact. Sites were also divided into grids and searched systematically, and drawings and models were made of every dig. Advances were also made in absolute dating; particularly significant was the invention of radiocarbon dating by chemist Willard Libby in the United States. Partly as a result of these techniques, archaeology became far more quantitative, or driven by data and statistical analysis, than it had previously been. Hypotheses and theories were carefully tested before being accepted.

Computer technology became increasingly important within the field of archaeology throughout the late twentieth and early twenty-first centuries, offering archaeologists new means of storing, organizing, and analyzing the data collected. Computer-aided design (CAD) and graphics programs were used to digitize existing materials, such as maps, as well as to create three-dimensional (3D) models of archaeological sites or artifacts. At times, archaeologists used CAD programs to create digital reconstructions of artifacts that existed in partial or fragmented form. Virtual models of artifacts likewise proved useful for preservation purposes; researchers and the public could view and interact with the models, while the fragile original artifacts could be protected from further wear or damage.

HOW IT WORKS

Archaelogical surveys. The first step in conducting any archaeological investigation is to identify and take stock of the location in which the study will be held. This is known as a "survey." The choice of location can be determined in several ways. Documentary sources, such as old maps or other written materials, can sometimes be used to accurately discover the location of an archaeological site. For example, clues in the writings of the ancient Greek poet Homer helped scientists find the ruined city of Troy (in northwest Turkey). In other cases, archaeologists attempt to survey sites on which new developments such as roads or buildings are planned to unearth important remains before they are destroyed. This is known as "salvage archaeology." On occasion, developers have integrated remains found by salvage archaeologists into their construction plans, as in the case of an Aztec temple dug up in Mexico City and used as part of the subway station that was built on that site. Other archaeological sites of interest are discovered through ground reconnaissance, in which either a judgmental or probabilistic sampling method is used to search for physical evidence, or aerial reconnaissance, which can sometimes turn up traces of human activity that cannot be seen from the ground.

Once a site has been identified as being of archaeological interest and an excavation begins, a deeper survey is conducted of the selected area. The same kinds of sampling methods used in ground reconnaissance are available to archaeologists at this point. Judgmental sampling is based solely on an archaeologist's judgment about which locations within the site should be searched for evidence. For example, since humans tend to settle near sources of water, judgmental sampling might concentrate the excavation along a river bed that runs through the site. Probabilistic sampling, in contrast, is subject to chance and variation, and may help archaeologists turn up unexpected discoveries or make more accurate predictions about areas not sampled. Probabilistic sampling can take the form of simple random, stratified random, or systematic sampling. Simple random sampling is where any given location within a site has an equal chance of being sampled. Stratified random sampling is where the site is divided into naturally occurring regions, such as forest versus cultivated land, and the number of searches conducted in each region is based on its size in relation to the entire site. Systematic sampling is where a site is divided into equal parts and then sampled at consistent intervals (e.g., a search is made every 100 meters).

Types of archaeological evidence. The evidence used by archaeologists to form a picture of an ancient or past society can be classified into four major categories: material, environmental, documentary, and oral evidence. Of the four, material evidence is perhaps the most fundamental. It can consist of either organic or inorganic remains that have been used by or constructed by people. Material evidence includes buildings, tools, pottery, toys, textiles, baskets, and food remains. Environmental evidence can take many forms, including soil samples, minerals, pollen, spores, animal bones, shells, and fossils.

Because Earth has undergone many significant geological and climate-related changes over the course of its history, environmental evidence can help reveal what the world looked like during the time of a particular group's existence in an area. Environmental evidence can also offer clues about people's relationships with the landscape around them. For example, if the materials in a lower layer of a dig consisted mostly of wood, charcoal, and pollen, while those in a higher layer of a dig consisted mostly of cattle bones, one hypothesis might be that a region that had once been wooded had at some point been cleared by the inhabitants of the area and used for the rearing of animals.

Documentary evidence, or written records, can be extremely useful to archaeologists whenever it is available. Depending on the epoch, or span of history, from which these documents arise, they may consist of text inscribed on stone slabs, clay tablets, papyrus, or other types of materials. They may record laws, serve as proof of legal contracts (such as marriages or business agreements), list births and deaths in a city, or inventory commodities such as grain or shells. Finally, oral and ethnographic evidence—interviews and oral histories with modern-day inhabitants of a particular area—can help supplement the physical remains collected in an excavation. Certain practices such as the techniques of rural architecture or traditions of marriage, for instance, may have been preserved without much variation over time. In such cases, living members of a culture that has been around for many generations may be able to provide key information about the habits of their ancestors.

Dating archaeological evidence. Archaeologists have a plethora of techniques for placing objects in time. Relative dating methods identify artifacts as being older or younger than others, thus placing them into a rough inferred sequence. One of the most straightforward techniques of relative dating is to note the depth at which a particular object was found at a site; that is, in which strata, or deposit layer, it was contained. This method, known as "stratigraphy," is an effective way to gauge the relative age of objects because layers build up on top of other layers over time. Other means of relative dating include pollen analysis, ice-core sampling, and seriation. Seriation uses the association of artifacts with known dates of use, along with knowledge about how the frequency of use of those artifacts changed over time, as markers for other items found in close proximity.

Absolute dating methods are far more accurate than relative dating techniques (which can be confused by the effects of natural disasters or animal activity on the organization of strata). They also produce more specific results. The absolute dating technique that is used more than any other by archaeologists is radiocarbon dating, which is capable of assigning an accurate age to artifacts of biological origin (including bone, charcoal, leather, shell, hair, textiles, paper, and glues) that are 50,000 years old or younger. Radiocarbon dating relies on the fact that the element carbon has a particular isotope—carbon 14—which is radioactive. Radiocarbon dating is also known as "carbon-14 dating." This radioactive carbon combines with oxygen in the atmosphere to form carbon dioxide, which is absorbed by plants as they photosynthesize. Because plants form the base of every food chain, all living things on Earth contain some amount of radiocarbon within their bodies. Because scientists know the half-life of radiocarbon (the time it takes for half the amount in a given sample to decay), they are able to measure the radiocarbon in any organic material and calculate how long it has been around. Besides radiocarbon dating, other absolute dating techniques include dendrochronology, which relies on the annual growth rings present in the trunks of long-lived trees, and thermoluminescent dating, in which trace amounts of radioactive atoms in rock, soil, and clay can be heated to produce light, the intensity of which varies depending on the age of the object. This method is primarily used to date pottery and other human-created artifacts.

Interpreting evidence. Three basic concepts dominate the approach an archaeologist takes when he or she approaches an artifact, a feature, or a site: context, classification, and chronology. Context, or where an object is found and what other items surround it, can reveal more of a complete story than any single artifact. For example, a decorated container found within a tomb could serve one purpose; the same container found in the kitchen of a dwelling could have been intended for an entirely different one. Classification (also known as "typology") also helps place unearthed artifacts within a particular frame of reference. For example, determining that all the items found at a particular location belong to the same type—such as cooking utensils, hunting supplies, or bathing vessels—could indicate how a location was used or who used it. Finally, chronology is essential to understanding the relationship between the elements of any archaeological investigation. For example, unless they have been disturbed, objects located at lower levels, or strata, of a particular excavation site will be older than those located at higher levels. This can help archaeologists trace the development of a particular tool over time or to see and identify important changes in the cultural practices of a given society.

APPLICATIONS AND PRODUCTS

Cultural resource management. The major practical application of archaeological tools and techniques can be found in the area of cultural resource management (CRM). In a sense, CRM is a form of institutionally legislated salvage archaeology. It involves the use of archaeological skills to identify, preserve, and maintain important features of historic and prehistoric culture to benefit the public interest. In most countries, including the United States and Canada, any planned development of any significance, including the building of new gas or oil pipelines, residences, highways, golf courses, or any other construction, requires the developer—whether private or public—to conduct a CRM survey to comply with legal requirements. The goal of CRM is to ensure that important pieces of a nation's past are conserved. CRM studies are generally performed by trained archaeologists serving as consultants and involve reconnaissance and sampling intended to scan the area for the presence of significant archaeological sites, features, or artifacts. If any are found, the developers are responsible for safely excavating and preserving them. If this is impossible or the site is identified as especially historically significant, the project may be terminated.

Waste management. The field of garbage archaeology, or garbology, was pioneered by American urban archaeologist William Rathje in the 1970s. By applying the tools of archaeology to the waste dumped in landfills, Rathje and other scientists have been able to provide many practical insights that are useful to waste management specialists and city, state, and federal administrators concerned with reducing waste and conserving energy. For instance, they showed that even supposedly biodegradable artifacts, such as paper, wood, and even food, are preserved for far longer when packed tightly together in a landfill than they otherwise would be. This is because the dense conditions reduce the amount of oxygen available for decomposition to take place. One of the implications of this discovery is that simply switching from nonbiodegradable to biodegradable materials in the production process—banning plastic disposable cups in favor of paper ones, for example—will not be enough to reduce the amount of effectively permanent waste that is generated by consumers and filling landfills to the point of overflowing.

Agriculture. In some parts of the world, environmental archaeologists have discovered evidence that areas of land that are marked by barren soil in fact used to be rich and fertile. For example, the Negev Desert in Israel, with its high temperatures and meager rainfall, used to be the site of an ancient urban society that cultivated crops such as wheat and grapes. Archaeologists also established that the climate in the area had not changed over the 2,000-year period in between. Using aerial reconnaissance techniques, scientists were able to show that the ancient farmers had employed a water-delivery system composed of terraces and cisterns to collect and redirect rainwater from the infrequent flash floods that occur in the area. This insight has proved to be of immense importance to modern-day agricultural scientists and farmers in Israel and has played a role in the country's successful efforts to "green" the Negev. Similarly, local farmers in rural Peru have begun using prehistoric field technologies unearthed by environmental archaeologists—primarily elevated fields that improve drainage and help protect plants from chilly nights—to dramatically increase their crop yields.

Crime investigation. Forensic archaeologists apply the methodologies of archaeology to the investigation of crimes, working closely with coroners and police officers to collect and analyze physical evidence from the scene. They investigate fragments of bone, teeth, soil, fabric, jewelry, or other artifacts, while more subtle clues such as disturbed soil or markings from tools or weapons may also provide important leads. Just as in other forms of archaeology, the forensic archaeologist first establishes the boundaries of the site to be surveyed, divides it into grids, and performs a thorough excavation of the material and environmental evidence found in the area. Stratigraphy is an important element of forensic archaeology, particularly so when a body has been buried before being found; the deeper into the soil digging proceeds, the older the remains, personal artifacts, or other evidence that is found will be.

CAREERS AND COURSEWORK
The typical archaeology career path begins with an undergraduate degree in anthropology, with an em-

phasis on coursework covering the fields of biological, linguistic, and cultural anthropology. In addition, the aspiring archaeologist should be sure to take a set of courses in related sciences—such as geology, chemistry, ecology, environmental studies, evolutionary science, geophysics, anatomy, and paleontology. Mathematics and statistics are equally important subjects, since much archaeological analysis requires a keen understanding of these areas. In the humanities, history courses—preferably focused on a particular geographic area or epoch in time—are essential, as is an advanced knowledge of at least one foreign language. In addition, business management and technical writing skills will assist any archaeologist who chooses to go into the field of CRM. Finally, if at all possible, students should attempt to pursue archaeological internships, fieldwork placements, or other forms of practical work experience during their undergraduate careers. Such experiences not only are a means of gaining hands-on knowledge of the field techniques used in archaeology but also provide students with professional contacts.

A bachelor's degree will serve as sufficient minimum qualification for many professional archaeological positions in the private sector, particularly in consulting firms hired by developers to perform CRM surveys—in such settings, practical work experience is more important. However, additional graduate study at the master's or doctoral level is necessary to obtain a role as a crew supervisor and enter higher pay brackets. For archaeologists who wish to become faculty in academic institutions, a doctoral degree in archaeology and evidence of original research is required. Other organizations for which archaeologists work include museums, city and state governments, and the federal government. Typical roles for archaeologists include conducting field investigations, performing analyses of found artifacts, curating museum archaeology collections, teaching courses, and publishing research papers.

SOCIAL CONTEXT AND FUTURE PROSPECTS

Archaeology is one of the most important and influential lenses through which scientists, historians, and other scholars view pieces of the past that otherwise would be lost. Its findings often reveal stunning insights into the nature of human civilization and the growth of human culture. For example, archaeologists piecing together skeletons found in Africa have been able to uncover the point at which the protohuman species Neanderthal died out and *Homo sapiens* (anatomically identical to modern humans) replaced it, while the ancient cave paintings discovered in Lascaux, an area in the southwest of France, demonstrate that human beings were creating art as long ago as 15,000 BCE. In other words, archaeology is a science dedicated to telling the story of humanity itself.

Although archaeology is at its core a science concerned with the investigation of material objects, the future of archaeology may be surprisingly metaphysical: a small but growing movement exists that is determined to treat the World Wide Web as a treasure trove of archaeological artifacts. "Internet archaeology," as this nascent subfield of archaeology is called, seeks to archive and interpret websites, pages, and graphics that were created during the early years of the internet and are no longer being updated by their owners.

—M. Lee, BA, MA

Further Reading

Eiteljorg, Harrison II, Kate Fernie, Jeremy Huggett, Damian Robinson, Bernard Thomason, et al. "CAD: A Guide to Good Practice." *Archaeology Data Service/Digital Antiquity Guides to Good Practice*, 2011, guides.archaeologydataservice.ac.uk/g2gp/Cad_Toc. Accessed 28 Nov. 2021.

Gamble, Clive. *Archaeology: The Basics*. 3rd ed., Routledge, 2015.

Garstki, Kevin. *Digital Innovations in European Archaeology*. Cambridge UP, 2020.

Haindl, Michal, and Matìj Sedláèek. "Virtual Reconstruction of Cultural Heritage Artifacts." *2016 International Workshop on Computational Intelligence for Multimedia Understanding (IWCIM)*, 2016, pp. 1-5.

Kelly, Robert L., and David Hurst Thomas. *Archaeology*. 7th ed., Cengage Learning, 2017.

Liarokapis, Fotis, Athanasios Voulodimos, Nikolaos Doulamis, and Anastasios Doulamis, editors. *Visual Computing for Cultural Heritage*. Springer Nature Switzerland, 2020.

Murray, Tim. *Milestones in Archaeology: A Chronological Encyclopedia*. ABC-CLIO, 2007.

Renfrew, Colin, and Paul G. Bahn, editors. *Archaeology: The Key Concepts*. Routledge, 2005.

Architecture and Architectural Engineering

ABSTRACT

Architecture and architectural engineering are fields involved in the design and construction of buildings. Working in close association with architects, architectural engineers translate people's needs and desires into physical space by applying a wide range of engineering and other technologies to provide building systems that are functional, safe, economical, environmentally healthy, and in harmony with the architect's aesthetic intent.

DEFINITION AND BASIC PRINCIPLES

Architecture and architectural engineering are complex and highly skilled fields. Architects develop the graphic design of buildings or dwellings and are often directly involved in their construction. Architectural engineers are certified professionals specializing in the application of engineering principles and systems technology to the design and function of a building. The term "architecture" sometimes includes the engineering technologies of building design. Architecture applies aesthetics, measurement, and design to the cooperative organization of human life. An essential dynamic of this process is the creation of technology. The engineering profession designs a magnitude of objects, structures, and environments to meet human needs and purposes. Building engineers specialize in the technologies that benefit human health and well-being within a built environment. These technologies are the direct result of exponential advances in the manipulation of chemical, hydraulic, thermal, electrical, acoustical, computational, and mechanical systems. Solar, wind, and nuclear power play an important role in the creation of sustainable buildings and environments, and the innovative use of new and recycled construction materials is an essential part of efficient planning and design.

BACKGROUND AND HISTORY

As early as about 10,000 BCE, small human settlements began to form along the fertile banks of the Nile River in Egypt, the Tigris and the Euphrates rivers in the Middle East, the Indus River in India, and the Yellow and Yangtze Rivers in China. These settlements grew, becoming prosperous city-states that supported the erection of large buildings. Temples, pyramids, and public forums served as religious and political symbols of increasing private and public wealth and power. Elaborate structures of a grand scale required specialized instruments such as levers, rollers, inclined planes, saws, chisels, drills, cranes, and right-angle tools for surveying land surfaces and for masonry construction.

In ancient Egypt, individuals noted for their ability to provide shelter, public works, water supplies, and transportation infrastructure for their communities were known as "master builders." The ancient Greeks called these individuals *architektons*. In Roman armies, military engineers termed "architects" designed siege engines and artillery and built roads, bridges, baths, aqueducts, and military fortifications.

Developing technologies. During the Middle Ages, craftsmen and artisans contributed considerable expertise and know-how to building construction and helped refine the tools of the trade. With the advent of the printing press, classical Greek, Roman, and Arabic treatises covering topics in architecture, mathematics, and the sciences were disseminated, and their content found its way into practical uses. Advances in graphic representation (such as the use of perspective) and the geometric manipulation of the Cartesian coordinate system enhanced the conceptual art of two (2D)- and three-dimensional (3D) spatial translations. Technologies flourished, creating the impetus that came to a head during the Industrial Revolution.

The modern era. Population pressures on urban centers during the eighteenth and nineteenth centuries accelerated the forward momentum of numerous technologies. The transition to fossil fuels, the development of steam power, and the distribution of electric power, as well as improvements in the production of iron and steel, transformed societies. These technologies had a profound impact on the principles of architectural design and building systems.

During the nineteenth century, the availability of energy and the technologies of mass production accelerated the standardization and distribution of construction materials worldwide. Heating flues, air ducts, elevator shafts, internal plumbing, and water and sewage conduits were developed in Great Britain and installed in hospitals, mills, factories, and public buildings. These innovative technologies were

Virtual models of architectural structures are an essential tool in creating physical spaces. Photo via iStock/Paul Bradbury. [Used under license.]

quickly adopted for private and commercial use in the United States, the British Commonwealth, and the continental nations.

New technologies for lighting, internal heating, and ventilation were first greeted with misgiving, but over time, building environments took on a life of their own in the minds of city health experts, architects, and engineers. A robust educational system developed to enable architects to master the increasing complexity and diversity of building design and construction technologies. Professional trade associations were formed to administer programs of certification and to determine public standards of health and safety that were codified and set within applicable statutory frameworks.

In the second half of the twentieth century, computers began to enable architects and architectural engineers to function with a greater degree of precision. Computers could be used to create detailed presentation graphics, tables, charts, and models in a relatively short period of time. Computer-aided design (CAD) software likewise became an essential tool for architects over the course of the late twentieth and early twenty-first centuries, enabling them to create virtual models of the structures they designed.

HOW IT WORKS

Architects and architectural engineers play prominent roles in the planning, design, construction, maintenance, and renovation of buildings. All processes of a project are initiated and directed to reflect the needs and desires of the project owner. These directives are modified by detailed sets of construction documents and best practices. Building codes are enforced to safeguard the health and safety of the owner, users, and residents; environmental standards are followed to protect property and to ensure the efficient use of natural resources; and attractive design features are chosen to enhance the community. The choice of construction materials, the visual and spatial relationship of the building to the environment and community, traffic safety, fire prevention, landscaping, and mechanical, electrical, plumbing, ventilation, lighting, acoustical, communication, and security systems are all essential features that determine the quality, functionality, and character of a building.

Articulating the owner's intent. The contract process begins with the owner's interest in a residential, public, or commercial building. The selection of an architect for the project will be based on the type of construction (light or heavy) and the particular purpose the building is intended to serve. The plans for simple one- and two-family dwellings frequently follow well-established homebuilder association guidelines and designs that can be modified to meet the future owner's budget and lifestyle. Larger, more complex designs (such as a church or a school) will be managed by a team of architects and engineers carefully chosen for their expertise in key aspects of the project. The selections of the architectural engineering team and the project manager are considered the most important steps in the design process.

The careful and deliberate coordination of effort and timely verbal and written communication are essential at all stages of the project. At the outset, the owner and those directly involved in the corporate administration of the project must work closely together to establish the values and priorities that will guide the design. Detailed feedback loops of self-assessment are conducted throughout the different phases of the project to ensure multiple levels of engagement and evaluation. In the introductory phase, questions are raised to clarify the owner's intentions and to begin addressing key issues such as the scope of the project, the projected use and life cycle of the building, the level of commitment to environmental quality issues, and health and energy requirements. Once these issues have been formulated, a site evaluation is conducted. This process further refines the relationship of the project to the natural surroundings and includes a thorough review of the environmental integrity of the land; local codes governing transportation, water supply, sewage, and electrical infrastructure; health and safety issues; and the relationship of the surroundings to the projected indoor environment.

Project design. The architect, working with other professionals, uses the information obtained in the introductory phase to create a design that fits the owner's needs and desires, complies with all building codes, and suits the site.

In situations where project turnaround is rapid, a design charrette may be scheduled. This is an intense, rapid-fire meeting of key professionals to quickly develop a schematic design that meets the primary objectives of the project. Participants include administrative representatives from all the internal offices involved in the project. In addition, utilities managers, key community and industrial partners, technology experts, financial institutions, and other stakeholders in the project are invited to set goals, to discuss problems, and to resolve differences. The process is a demanding one, challenging participants to think beyond the boundaries of their professional biases to understand and bring to focus a building design that reflects the highest standards of their respective trades.

Project documentation. Project documentation is a highly technical orchestration of graphics, symbols, written correspondence, schematic sequencing and scheduling, and audiovisual representation. Construction drawings are a precise, nonverbal map that translates physical spatial relationships into intelligible two- and three-dimensional projections and drawings. The sequence of presentation and the lexicographical notations used to represent and to communicate the dimensions, systems, materials, and objects within a constructed space are highly refined, requiring years of careful study and practice. Project documentation also includes all the legal and civic certifications, permits, and reviews required before a certificate of occupancy is finally issued.

The documents of the project must be recorded in a narrative that can be understood by the owner and the different teams of workers involved. Documentation is particularly important for those project teams working toward LEED (Leadership in Energy and Environmental Design) certification. The LEED Green Building Rating System is an internationally recognized, voluntary certification program that assists commercial and private property owners to build and maintain buildings according to the best practices of green building design. It is administered by the US Green Building Council, a nonprofit organization whose members adhere to industry standards set to maximize cost savings, energy efficiencies, and the health of the indoor environment.

Systems analyses and energy efficiencies. Whole-building performance is an essential concept for achieving energy efficiencies and sustainable engineering of mechanical systems. Critical decisions regarding the choice of materials, the orientation of the building and its effect on lighting, the dimensions of the space in question, and the requirements for heating, cooling, mechanical, electrical, and plumbing systems demand a high level of technical analysis and integration among a number of building professionals to create a viable base design amenable for human use and habitation. Other factors incorporated into quality building designs include accessibility for the disabled, the mitigation of environmental impacts, and legal compliance with building codes and requirements.

As a result of the tremendous advantages of computational technologies, systems engineers have an expanding pool of resources available to assist in the optimization of energy efficiencies. Simulation software packages such as EnergyPlus, DOE-2, and ENERGY-10 make it possible to evaluate the potential for using renewable energy sources, the effects of daylight, thermal comfort, ventilation rates, water conservation, potential emissions and contaminant containment strategies, and scenarios for recycling building materials. Landscape factors that affect a building's energy use include irrigation systems, the use of chemical insecticides and fertilizers, erosion control factors, the conservation of native vegetation, and adequate shade and wind protection. Engineers use simulations to evaluate a series of alternatives to provide mechanical, solar, electrical, hydraulic, and heating, ventilation, and air-conditioning systems that optimize critical energy features of the design.

Statement of work and contract bid. The final construction documents include all the drawings, specifications, bidding information, contract forms, and cost features of the project. Certifications of compliance with all regulatory standards and applicable codes are included in the documentation and are verified and signed by the project architects and engineers. Once a bid is secured and a final contract is signed, the design team maintains a close relationship with the contractors and subcontractors to monitor the details of construction and systems installation. The final commissioning process serves to verify the realization of the owner's intent and to thoroughly test the systems installed in the building. The integrity of the building envelope, the function of all mechanical systems, and the stability of energy efficiency targets are validated by a third party.

APPLICATIONS AND PRODUCTS

The primary applications of architecture and architectural engineering are residential, commercial, and public structures. The Bauhaus school, founded in 1919 in Weimar, Germany, expanded the traditional view of architecture by envisioning the construction of a building as a synthesis of art, technology, and craft. Walter Gropius, the founder of the school, wanted to create a new architectural style that reflected the fast-paced, technologically advanced modern world and was more functional and less ornate. Another architect associated with the school, Ludwig Mies van der Rohe developed an architectural style that is noted for its clarity and simplicity. The S. R. Crown Hall, which houses the College of Architecture at the Illinois Institute of Technology in Chicago, is considered to be among the finest examples of his work.

Modern architecture, characterized by simplicity of form and ornamentation that arises from the building's structure and theme, became the dominant style in the mid-1900s and has continued into the twenty-first century, despite the rise of postmodern architecture in the 1970s. Postmodernism incorporated elements such as columns strictly for aesthetic reasons. American architect Robert Venturi argued that ornamentation provided interest and variation. Venturi's architectural style is represented by the Guild House, housing for the elderly in Philadelphia, which originally featured a television antenna as a decorative element.

New paths. Architect Christopher Alexander has combined technology with architecture, incorporating inventions in concrete and shell design into aesthetically pleasing works, including the San Jose Shelter for the Homeless in California and the Athens Opera House in Greece. He argues for an organic approach to architecture, with people participating in the designs of the buildings that they will use and of the environments in which they will live.

Alexander's work concerns itself with the environment in which buildings are constructed, which is a major part of architecture in the twenty-first century. Innovations in architecture and architectural engineering involve creating sustainable buildings or communities or creating buildings in unusual environments.

The Eden Project houses a series of eight large geodesic domes constructed in 2001 at St. Austell in Cornwall. These domes, or biomes, provide self-sustaining environments housing thousands of plants gathered from around the world. The tubular steel and thermoplastic structures use active and passive sources of heat, and innovative ventilation and water systems collect rainwater and groundwater for recirculation in the building envelope. The project's architects, Nicholas Grimshaw and Partners, have developed a system that helps other building professionals understand natural impacts on human environments.

In the Netherlands, innovative designers are experimenting with amphibious housing, or homes that rise and fall with water levels. Along the banks of the Meuse River in Maasbommet, the internationally recognized construction company Dura Vermeer opened a small community of amphibious and floating homes in 2006. Designed by architect Ger Kengen, the amphibious models rest on a hollow foundation filled with foam and anchored on two mooring poles located at the front and back of the structure. The poles allow the house to float on rising water to a height of 18 feet.

Similar structures were designed in New Orleans, Louisiana, following Hurricane Katrina. In 2010, the Special No. 9 House, designed by John C. Williams Architects for the Brad Pitt Make It Right Foundation, won the American Institute of Architects Committee on the Environment (AIA/COTE) Top Ten Green Projects Award. The FLOAT house, also in New Orleans, is another Make It Right Foundation project developed by Morphosis Architects under the direction of Los Angeles-based architect and professor Thom Mayne.

Habitats in space. Perhaps the most spectacular applications of the methods of architectural engineering involve the crewed space flight program. Many of the mechanical systems that make homes and public places so livable are essential for creating similar environments in space. The International Space Station is a monumental project involving the efforts of fifteen nations to develop sustainable human habitats in space. Orbiting nearly 250 miles above Earth at a speed of 22,000 miles per hour, the space station uses eight massive solar and radiator panels to control heat and provide energy for the ship's modular systems. Heating and cooling systems are essential for the maintenance of the ship, the internal environment, and the space suits worn during maneuvers outside the spaceship. Construction materials are in continuous development to find products that can withstand severe cold, radiation, and heat during reentry into Earth's atmosphere. The National Aeronautics and Space Administration (NASA) developed a lightweight ceramic ablater material able to withstand temperatures of 5,000° Fahrenheit. Other insulation materials are used for electric wires, paints, and protective cladding for the ship. Many of the thermal fabrics designed for space have been adapted by athletes and health providers worldwide.

Inside the ship, mechanical systems generate heat and other emissions. Air quality is regularly monitored for carbon dioxide and oxygen levels. Waste materials are carefully recycled or packaged for shuttle return to Earth for disposal. Transportation routes, cycles of delivery, points of entry and egress, fire safety, lighting and electrical systems, oxygen generators, efficient waste disposal systems, water distiller and filtration systems for the storage, treatment, and recycling of water—all the technologies that add so much to the quality of human life—have been engineered to meet the needs of space travel. In turn, these novel space systems have enormous applicability in the design of products for use in homes and places of work on Earth. They also continue to be developed and refined as government space agencies and private companies explore the potential for further space or planetary colonization, such as a potential base on the planet Mars.

CAREERS AND COURSEWORK

Most careers in architecture require, at a minimum, a five-year bachelor's degree in architecture or a four-year bachelor's degree plus a two-year master's degree in architecture. Those with undergraduate degrees in other areas may attend a three-year master's program in architecture. Usually, students gain experience through an internship in an architectural firm. Architects with a degree from an accredited school and some practical experience must pass the Architect Registration Examination to obtain a license to practice in the United States.

The successful completion of a general program of study in architectural engineering requires demonstrated competencies in the mechanics of heating, ventilation, air-conditioning, plumbing, fire protection, electrical, lighting, transportation, and structural systems. Students may pursue a five-year program that terminates with a bachelor's degree in architectural engineering and generally leads to certification or a four-year program, followed by a master's degree. Students may also obtain a degree in architectural engineering technology, which specializes in the technology of building design. Architectural engineering graduates must pass a series of exams administered by the National Council of Examiners for Engineering and Surveying to obtain a license to practice.

SOCIAL CONTEXT AND FUTURE PROSPECTS

From the earliest records of human history, architects and engineers have advanced human civilization. The practical and aesthetic dimensions of architecture and engineering technologies have had profound social, political, economic, and religious impacts. The practices of architecture and engineering are just as much a product of cooperative human evolution as they are catalysts of change. Indeed, no thorough study of these fields is complete without a thoughtful and rigorous understanding of the environmental and cultural forces that stimulated their advances. Topographies, geographies, climates, political economies, known technologies, the commodities of exchange, and the natural resources available for human use stimulated human imagination and invention in novel and diverse ways in particular times and places. These innovations are reflected in the range of human responses to the need for food, shelter, safety, hygiene, and social interaction.

In twenty-first-century society, these needs are modified by larger global concerns including the efficient use of energy and natural resources, pollution containment, and the need for sustainable life systems. Green architecture is likely to become an increasingly prominent part of the field. Architects will increasingly explore sustainable architecture that looks at not only the building but also the environment and community, and they will continue to pursue construction in unusual environments, such as housing on the water or in space. They will also look at ways to reuse existing buildings and structures, particularly those worthy of preservation. In choosing materials and systems, they will be investigating ways to recycle building materials and to incorporate systems that reduce pollution and minimize energy usage.

Modern architectural theory also considers the implications of architecture as a field that in many cases has divided into two camps: mass produced, functional structures and custom, aesthetically minded works by individual architects or notable firms. This division may be seen as highlighting economic inequality, as the wealthy are able to commission construction that incorporates health-minded and sustainable design and is built on the most desirable sites, while buildings used by the poor may be neglected or shoddily constructed and pay little attention to factors such as ecology and health. Some architects and firms have taken a socially conscious position to combat such inequality. Another development is the growth of open-source architecture, collaborative design, mass customization, and other architectural processes and techniques inspired by the open access movement. Resources such as the internet, architectural CAD software, and

3D printing increasingly offer challenges to the traditional model of architecture.

—*Victoria M. Breting-García, MA*

Further Reading

Allison, Eric, and Lauren Peters. *Historic Preservation and the Livable City*. Wiley, 2011.

Bacus, John. *Digital Sketching: Computer-Aided Conceptual Design*. Wiley, 2020.

DeKay, Mark, and G. Z. Brown. *Sun, Wind, and Light: Architectural Design Strategies*. 3rd ed., Wiley, 2014.

Farin, Gerald, Joseph Josef Hoschek, and Myung-Soo Kim. *Handbook of Computer-Aided Geometric Design*. Elsevier, 2002.

Fisanick, Christina, editor. *Eco-Architecture*. Greenhaven, 2008.

Garrison, Ervan G. *A History of Engineering and Technology: Artful Methods*. 2nd ed., CRC Press, 1999.

Goldberger, Paul. *Why Architecture Matters*. Yale UP, 2009.

Huth, Mark W. *Understanding Construction Drawings*. 7th ed. Cengage Learning, 2019.

La Roche, Pablo. *Carbon-Neutral Architectural Design*. 2nd ed., CRC Press, 2017.

McMorrough, Julia. *The Architecture Reference & Specification Book*. Rev. ed., Rockport, 2018.

Pohl, Jens G. *Building Science: Concepts and Applications*. Wiley, 2011.

Ratti, Carlo, and Matthew Claudel. *Open Source Architecture*. Thames & Hudson, 2015.

Thomas, Katie Lloyd, Timo Amhoff, and Nick Beech. *Industries of Architecture*. Routledge, 2016.

Architecture Software

ABSTRACT

Architecture software is a category of specialized computer software intended for use by architects. Through the use of such software, architects may design, model, and modify plans for homes or other buildings digitally rather than on paper. As the type and scale of the structures being designed vary greatly, many types of architecture software are available to address the differing requirements of individual projects.

THE INTRODUCTION OF SOFTWARE TO ARCHITECTURE

During the late twentieth and early twenty-first centuries, architecture became one of many fields to be dramatically transformed through the use of computer technology. For centuries, architects designed single structures such as homes as well as larger, multibuilding facilities by hand. They drafted plans on paper and created three-dimensional (3D) scale models out of materials such as cardboard, wood, and foam. These processes relied heavily on physical components. Therefore, it was relatively difficult to collaborate with fellow architects or other professionals who were not located nearby. Making changes to one's work, particularly to models that were already assembled, could be time-consuming and difficult. The advent of architecture software brought advances in areas such as drafting, modeling, and modifying models and floorplans as well as collaborating with other professionals.

Architecture software is designed to assist in one or more of the many tasks required for building information modeling (BIM). Depending on one's role and how one relates to the building process, certain tasks may be more important. Determining the proper architecture software first requires one to know what BIM tasks one hopes to take on.

Although typically designed for and marketed to architects, architecture software is similar in many ways to other types of software used in the broader field of art and design. Some architecture programs are essentially specialized versions of computer-aided design (CAD) software. For example, one particularly popular producer of CAD programs, Autodesk, offers an industry-specific architecture toolset for use with its flagship CAD software, AutoCAD. Architects began to adopt the use of CAD programs in the 1980s. By the following decade, such software was widely used in the field.

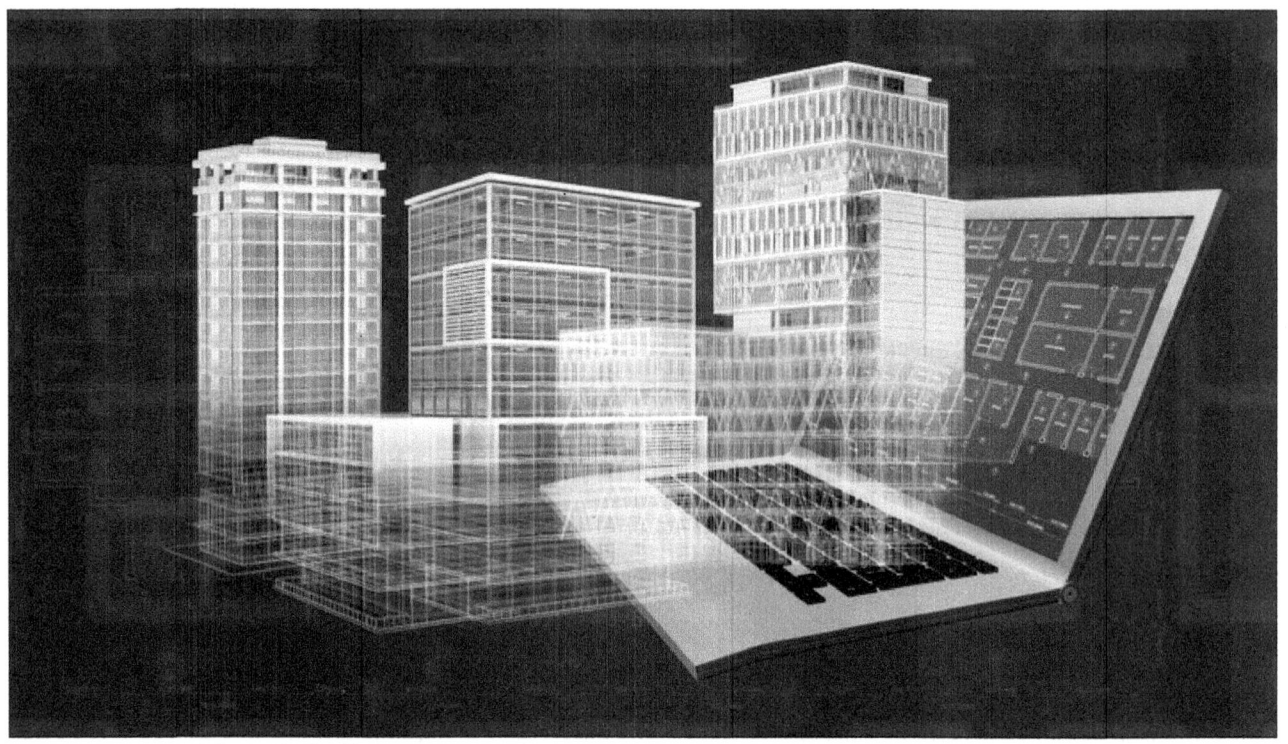

Photo via iStock/Maxiphoto. [Used under license.]

FEATURES

Architecture software is created and sold by a number of different technology companies. Therefore, the available programs vary in terms of features, although there are certain common ones. The first and perhaps most essential feature is the ability to draft floor plans, a process that was historically done with paper and pencil. Architecture software also typically allows users to create 3D models of structures and easily insert elements such as doors and windows. Unlike physical models of proposed structures, digital models can be modified with just a few clicks of a mouse. Architecture software also sometimes includes features that support collaboration among architects and other professionals. These can include the ability to check files in and out, add notes to floor plans, and record measurements.

Specialized software devoted to BIM has much in common with standard architecture software. However, BIM software also allows the user to incorporate information such as expected time frames, costs, and the functions of a particular building or facility into the design. BIM software allows the various professionals involved in the design process to evaluate and modify the design prior to moving forward with the project.

RENDERING AND POSTPRODUCTION

In addition to creating floor plans and 3D models, architects are frequently tasked with creating images of their designs for clients. Transforming a 3D model into a two-dimensional (2D) image is known as "rendering." In postproduction, an architect may use graphic design software to add visual effects to the rendered image. For instance, if the architect has designed a waterfront apartment complex, he or she may use a graphic design program such as Adobe Photoshop to add photorealistic water textures to the image and increase its aesthetic appeal.

When creating floor plans and models, architects typically use vector images. Vector images are based on defined points and lines. This allows the images to remain true to scale no matter how much their overall size is modified. Graphic design software such as Photoshop, on the other hand, is a raster-based program. In a raster-based program, the images are based on individual pixels. As such, architects also sometimes use software capable of converting from vector to raster.

ADVANTAGES AND DISADVANTAGES

The use of specialized software in the field of architecture has a number of advantages and disadvantages. Chief among the advantages is a potential increase in productivity and time savings. Digital tools to draft floor plans and create models have largely replaced more time-consuming physical methods. The abilities to modify designs, test designs through digital modeling, and easily collaborate with fellow professionals on a project are cited as key benefits of architecture software.

However, the use of architecture software is not a substitute for architectural training. Some architects argue that the availability of such software can enable some users to produce substandard work. In addition, ongoing changes in the field require architects to maintain up-to-date knowledge of current technology. This can put architects accustomed to working with older systems at a disadvantage.

—*Joy Crelin*

Further Reading

Ambrose, Gavin, Paul Harris, and Sally Stone. *The Visual Dictionary of Architecture*. AVA, 2008.

Bacus, John. *Digital Sketching: Computer-Aided Conceptual Design*. Wiley, 2020.

Bergin, Michael S. "A Brief History of BIM." *ArchDaily*, 7 Dec. 2012, www.archdaily.com/302490/a-brief-history-of-bim. Accessed 28 Nov. 2021.

Ching, Francis D. K. *Architectural Graphics*. 6th ed., Wiley, 2015.

Kilkelly, Michael. "Which Architectural Software Should You Be Using?" *ArchDaily*, 4 May 2015, www.archdaily.com/626972/which-architectural-software-should-you-be-using. Accessed 28 Nov. 2021.

McMorrough, Julia. *The Architecture Reference & Specification Book*. Rev. ed., Rockport, 2018.

Artificial Organs

ABSTRACT

Artificial organs are complex systems of natural or manufactured materials used to supplement failing organs while they recover, sustain failing organs until transplantation, or replace failing organs that cannot recover. Some whole organs have artificial counterparts: heart, kidneys, liver, lungs, and pancreas. Smaller body parts also have artificial counterparts: blood, bones, heart valves, joints, skin, and teeth. In addition, there are mechanical support systems for circulation, hearing, and breathing. Artificial organs are composed of biomaterials, biological or synthetic materials that are adapted for use in medical applications.

DEFINITION AND BASIC PRINCIPLES

Artificial organs are complex systems that assist or replace failing organs. The human body is composed of ten major organ systems: nervous, circulatory, respiratory, digestive, excretory, reproductive, endocrine, integumentary (skin), muscular, and skeletal. The nervous system transmits signals between the brain and the body via the spinal cord and nerves. The circulatory system transports blood to deliver oxygen and nutrients to the body and to remove waste products. Its organs are the heart, blood, and blood vessels. It works closely with the respiratory system, in which the lungs and trachea perform oxygen exchange between the body and the environment. The digestive system breaks down food and absorbs its nutrients. Its organs include the esophagus, stomach, intestinal tract, and liver. The excretory system rids the body of metabolic waste in the forms of urine and feces. The reproductive system provides sex cells and in females the organs to develop and carry an embryo to term. The endocrine system consists of the pituitary, parathyroid, and thyroid glands, which secrete regulatory hormones. The integumentary system is the body's external protection system. Its organs include skin, hair, and nails. The muscular system recruits muscles, ligaments, and tendons to move the parts of the skeletal system, which consists of bones and cartilage.

BACKGROUND AND HISTORY
While he was still a medical student in 1932, renowned cardiac surgeon Michael DeBakey introduced a dual-roller pump for blood transfusion. It has since become the most widely used type of clinical pump for cardiopulmonary bypass and hemodialysis. Physician John H. Gibbon, Jr., of Philadelphia, developed the first clinically successful heart-lung pump. He initially demonstrated it in 1953, when he closed a hole between the atria of an eighteen-year-old girl.

In 1954, American physician Joseph Murray performed the first successful human kidney transplant from one identical twin to the other in Boston. In 1962, he performed the first kidney transplant in unrelated persons. In 1967, surgeon Christiaan Barnard performed the first successful human heart transplant in Cape Town, South Africa. The patient, a fifty-four-year-old man, lived another eighteen days.

Physician Willem J. Kolff is considered to be "the father of the artificial organ." After emigrating from the Netherlands in 1967, he spent a good deal of his career at the University of Utah, where he became a distinguished professor emeritus of internal medicine, surgery, and bioengineering. He led the designing of numerous inventions, including the modern kidney dialysis machine, the intra-aortic balloon pump, an artificial eye, an artificial ear, and an implantable mechanical heart.

American physician Robert K. Jarvik refined Kolff's design into the Jarvik-7 artificial heart, intended for permanent use. In 1982, at the University of Utah, American surgeon William C. DeVries implanted it into retired dentist Barney Clark, who survived 112 days. Research into artificial organs continued over the next decades, resulting in the development of medical devices designed to mimic essential functions of organs such as the kidneys, liver, lungs, and pancreas. In the first decades of the twenty-first century, one area of particular interest was the computer-aided design (CAD) and computer-aided manufacturing (CAM) of biomaterials such as human tissues. Some researchers suggested that advances in CAD and three-dimensional (3D) printing could one day grant scientists the ability to print replacement organs that could be transplanted into the individuals in need of them. 3D-printed organs could also potentially be used to test new medications or surgical techniques.

HOW IT WORKS
The existence and performance of artificial organs depend on the collaboration of scientists, engineers, physicians, manufacturers, and regulatory agencies. Each of these groups provides a different perspective of pumps, filters, size, packaging, and regulation.

Hemodynamics. The human heart acts as a muscular pump that beats an average of seventy-two times a minute. Each of the two ventricles pumps 70 milliliters of blood per beat or 5 liters per minute. Blood pressure is measured and reported as two numbers: the systolic pressure exerted by the heart during contraction and the diastolic pressure, when the heart is between contractions. Hemodynamics is the study of forces related to the circulation of the blood. The hemodynamic performance of artificial organs must match that of the natural body to operate efficiently without resulting in damage. Calculations may be made using computational fluid dynamics (CFD); relevant parameters include solute concentration, density, temperature, and water concentration. In addition to artificial hearts, which are intended to perform all cardiac functions, there is a mechanical circulatory implement called a "ventricular assist device" (VAD) that supports the function of the natural heart while it is recovering from a heart attack or surgery. Its pumping action may be pulsatile, in rhythmic waves matching those of the beating heart, or continuous.

Mass transfer efficiency. The human kidney acts as a filter to remove metabolic waste products from the blood. A person's kidneys process about 200 quarts of blood daily to remove 2 quarts of waste and extra water, which are converted into urine and excreted. Without filtration, the waste would build to a toxic level and cause death. Patients with kidney failure may undergo dialysis, in which blood is withdrawn, cleaned, and returned to the body in a periodic, continuous, and time-consuming process that requires the patient to remain relatively stationary. Portable artificial kidneys, which the patient wears, filter the blood while the patient enjoys the freedom of mobility. Filtration systems may involve membranes with a strict pore size to separate molecules based on size or columns of particle-based

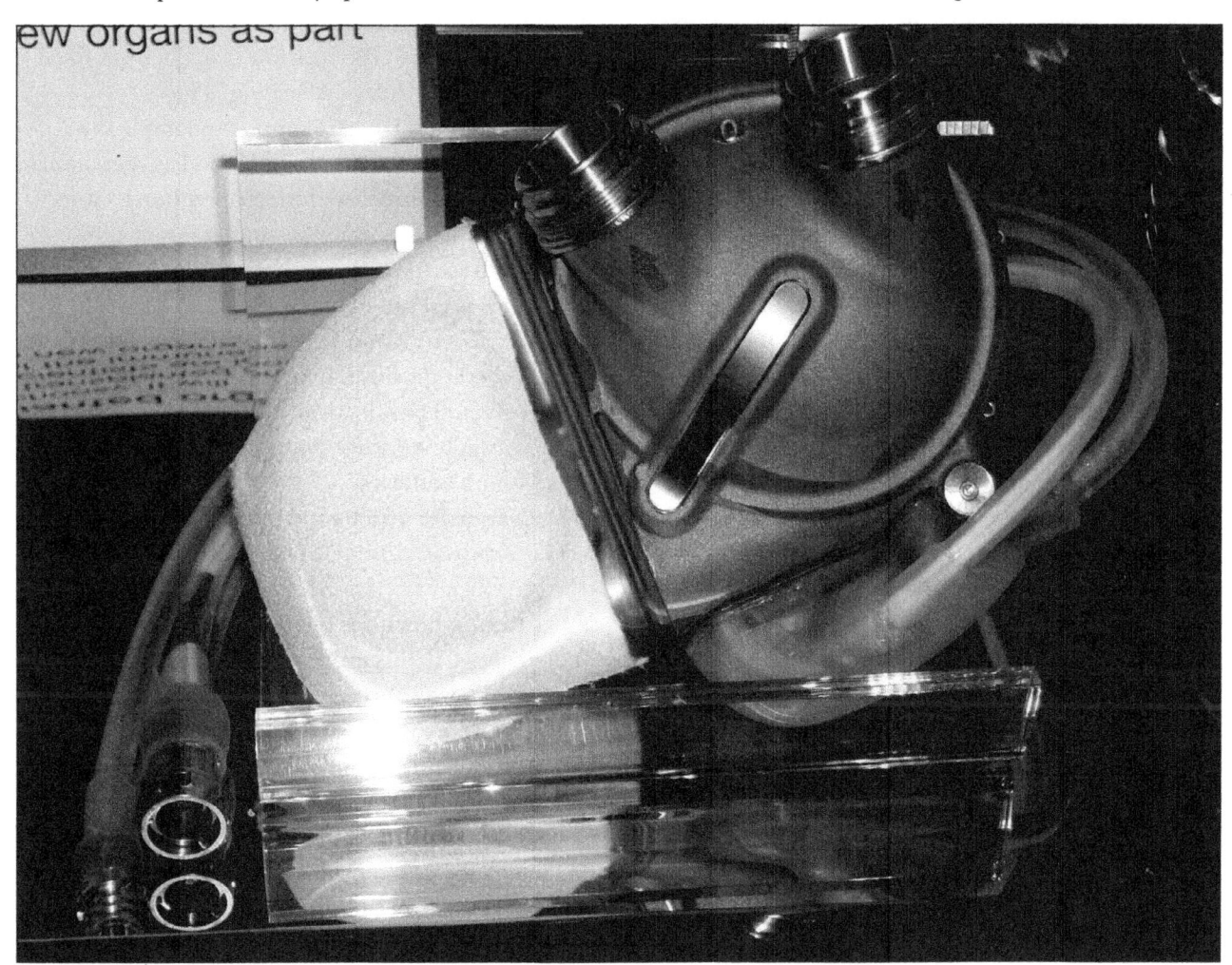

An artificial heart on display at the London Science Museum. Photo by Rick Proser, via Wikimedia Commons.

adsorbents to separate molecules by chemical characteristics. Mass transfer efficiency refers to the quality and quantity of molecular transport.

Scale. The development of artificial organs requires that biological processes that can be duplicated in the laboratory be scaled up to work within the human body without also magnifying the weaknesses. Biological functions occur at the organ, tissue, cellular, and molecular levels, which are on micro- and nanoscales. In addition, machines that work in the engineering laboratory must be scaled down to work within the human body without crowding the other organs. Novel power sources and electronic components have facilitated miniaturization. Size must also be balanced with efficiency and cost. CAD software is being used to create virtual 3D models before fabrication, while CAM technologies such as 3D printing allow for quick and cost-effective prototyping of medical devices.

Biomaterials. Artificial organs are made of natural and/or manufactured materials that have been adapted for medical use. The properties of these materials must be controlled down to the nanometer scale. The biological components may serve in gene therapy, tissue engineering, and the modification of physiological responses. The synthetic materials must be biocompatible, which means that they do not trigger an adverse physiological reaction such as blood clotting, inflammatory response, scar-tissue formation, or antibody production. The biomechanics of the artificial organ, such as friction and wear, must be known and parts must be sterile before use. Biomaterials have been developed for subspecialties such as orthopedics and ophthalmics.

Regulation. The body has natural feedback systems that allow the exchange of information with the brain for optimal regulation. Artificial organs that communicate directly with the brain are still in development. The present models require sensors and data systems that may be monitored by physicians. Implanted devices must be able to be inspected without direct observation. Another aspect of regulation is the uniform manufacturing of artificial organs in compliance with performance and patient safety specifications.

APPLICATIONS AND PRODUCTS

The collective knowledge of scientists, engineers, physicians, manufacturers, and regulatory agencies has produced the applications and products in the interdisciplinary realm of artificial organs.

Hemodynamics. Knowledge of hemodynamics, the study of blood-flow physics, has led to the development of artificial circulatory assistance. The VAD supplements the contraction of the two lower chambers of the heart so the heart muscle does not have to work as hard while it is healing. The cardiopulmonary bypass pump, also known as a "heart-lung machine," provides blood oxygenation and circulating pressure during open-heart surgery when the heart is stopped. A similar application called "extracorporeal membrane oxygenation" (ECMO) is used to assist neonates and infants in the intensive care unit and to maintain the viability of organs pending transplantation. The natural pressure generated by a healthy heart is used to send blood through versions of artificial lungs and kidneys without batteries.

Mass transfer efficiency. Information about molecular transport and delivery, known as "mass transfer efficiency," has been applied to separation and secretion functions of artificial organs. In hemodialysis, toxins are removed from circulating blood that passes through a filter called a "dialyzer." This process also removes excess salts and water to maintain a healthy blood pressure. The dialyzer is composed of a semipermeable membrane or cylinder of hollow synthetic fibers that separates out the metabolic-waste solutes in the incoming blood by diffusion into dialysate solution, leaving cleaner outgoing blood. Hemofiltration is a similar process; however, the filtration occurs without dialysate solution because instead of diffusion, the solutes are removed more quickly by hydrostatic pressure. Another separation technique in medical applications is apheresis, in which the constituents of blood are isolated. This may be achieved by gradient density centrifugation or absorption onto specifically coated beads. The therapeutic application is the absorptive removal of a specific blood component that is causing an adverse reaction in a patient, with the remaining components returned to the patient's circulatory system. The pathogenic blood component might be malignant white blood cells, excess platelets, low-density lipoprotein, autoantibodies, or plasma. The second application of apheresis is the separation of components following blood donation. Concentrated red blood cells are administered in the treatment of sickle-cell crisis or malaria. Plasmapheresis is used to collect fresh frozen plasma as well as rare antibodies and immunoglobulins.

Scale. Miniaturization of artificial organs has been facilitated by the application of smaller, more efficient batteries, transistors, and computer chips. For example, hearing aids once had to be worn with cumbersome amplifiers and batteries disguised in a purse or camera case with a carrying strap. Existing models fit completely in the ear canal, and a computer chip facilitates digital rather than analog processing for crisper sound. The artificial kidney has evolved into a wearable model, introduced in 2012, that weighs 10 pounds and is seventeen times smaller than a conventional dialysis machine. Its hollow-fiber filter must be replaced once a week and its dialysate solution must be replenished daily. However, this maintenance is a trade-off that many patients are willing to make for freedom of movement. On the horizon is an artificial retina that depends on a miniature camera to transmit images. Conversely, research is under way to produce large-scale cultures of tissues on biohybrid matrices and scaffolding for transplantation.

Biomaterials. Synthetic materials are used in artificial organs. Dacron (polyethylene terephthalate) is a polyester fiber with high tensile strength and resistance to stretching whether wet or dry, chemical degradation, and abrasion. Patches of it are sewn to arteries to repair aneurysms. When tubing of it is used as an aortic valve bypass, the patient will not require subsequent blood-thinning medications. Gore-Tex (expanded polytetrafluoroethylene) is an especially strong microporous material that is waterproof. Vascular grafts made from it are supple and resist kinks and compression. It is also used for replacing torn anterior and posterior cruciate ligaments in the knee.

Perfluorocarbon fluids are synthetic liquids that carry dissolved oxygen and carbon dioxide with negligible toxicity, no biological activity, and a short retention time in the body. These features make them ideal for medical applications. One of these fluids, perfluorodecalin, is typically used as a blood substitute (also called a "blood extender") because it mixes easily with blood without changing the hemodynamics. It increases the oxygen-carrying capacity of the blood and penetrates ischemic (oxygen-deprived) tissues especially easily because of its small particle size. This makes it particularly useful in the healing of ulcers and burns. It is also used in conjunction with ECMO in the life support of preterm infants to increase oxygenation and to keep the lungs inflated, reducing exertion. Furthermore, it is used in the preservation of harvested organs and cultured tissue for transplantation, extending their viable storage time.

Regulation. The application of regulatory systems has allowed artificial organs to be adjusted while they are in use. Artificial cardiac pacemakers, which supplement the natural electrical pacemaking capabilities of the heart to normalize a slow or irregular heartbeat, are externally programmable so that cardiologists are able to establish the optimal pacing parameters for each patient. Adjustments are made with radio frequency programming, so no further surgery is required. Contemporary hearing aids have volume controls that the wearer can adjust to suit changing surroundings. The inability to detect high- or low-pitch sounds is not a function of volume, yet pitch range can be adjusted in a hearing aid by an audiologist. Other parameters are also adjustable, and the audiologist can reprogram the hearing aid as a person's hearing loss changes.

CAREERS AND COURSEWORK

Universities offer various undergraduate and graduate programs related to artificial organs. The University of Pittsburgh's Swanson School of Engineering, for instance, offers undergraduate degrees in bioengineering, while Brown University offers graduate degrees in biomedical engineering that focus on areas such as tissue engineering and biomaterials. Medical schools likewise support researchers in the field of biotechnology development. The Michael E. DeBakey Department of Surgery at Baylor College of Medicine in Texas encompasses multiple divisions related to organ transplantation and implant-based support. The University of Maryland School of Medicine's Department of Surgery has an Artificial Organs Laboratory as one of its surgical research laboratories.

This is a collaborative field, and scientists, biomedical engineers, physicians, and businesspeople work together in commercial ventures to design and fabricate functional artificial organs. Because artificial organs fall under the regulatory domain of the Food and Drug Administration (FDA) as medical devices, manufacturers must undergo rigorous product development, clinical trials, and patent protection prior to FDA approval. Components are then made to custom specifications. Some companies produce a multitude of medical devices, while some specialize in specific technologies such as biotransport, dialysis, perfusion, and cell culture matrices.

SOCIAL CONTEXT AND FUTURE PROSPECTS

The number of Americans older than sixty-five years of age is expected to double between 2018 and 2060. The fastest growing age group is people older than eighty-five years of age. Increasing life span of the general population is a direct result of improved health care. The shortage of donor organs is also an issue of concern. In 2020, more than 91,000 people in the United States were waiting for kidney transplants, but only about 23,000 kidneys were received that year. About 107,000 individuals in the United States were on the national transplant waiting list in 2021, and about seventeen Americans died each day while waiting for a transplant. The need for artificial organs as a bridge to transplantation or even as a permanent substitute for failed organs, then, is becoming increasingly urgent.

Once only made of synthetic components, artificial organs are becoming biohybrid organs: a combination of biological and synthetic components. Examples include functionally competent cells enveloped within immunoprotective artificial membranes and tissues cultured on chemically constructed matrices. Experiments are underway to develop an antibacterial agent that can be incorporated into biomaterials to reduce the risk of infection from these organ surfaces. Emerging technologies also involve sensors and intelligent control systems, biological batteries and alternate power sources, and innovative delivery systems.

Other areas of research include the miniaturization of artificial organs for pediatric use and the development of smaller and more efficient batteries and sensors that will be capable of more accurate communication between the artificial organ and the brain. Another goal is to incorporate wireless capabilities so the artificial organ may be programmed, monitored, and recharged remotely so the patient has increased freedom of mobility.

—*Bethany Thivierge, BS, MPH*

Further Reading

Hasan, Anwarul, editor. *Tissue Engineering for Artificial Organs*. 2 vols. Wiley, 2017.

Hench, Larry L., and Julian R. Jones, editors. *Biomaterials, Artificial Organs, and Tissue Engineering*. CRC Press, 2005.

McClellan, Marilyn. *Organ and Tissue Transplants: Medical Miracles and Challenges*. Enslow, 2003.

Mironov, Vladimir, Thomas Boland, Thomas Trusk, Gabor Forgacs, and Roger R. Markwald. "Organ Printing: Computer-Aided Jet-Based 3D Tissue Engineering." *Trends in Biotechnology*, vol. 21, no. 4, 2003, pp. 157-61.

"Organ Donation Statistics." *Health Resources & Services Administration*, Oct. 2021, www.organdonor.gov/learn/organ-donation-statistics. Accessed 28 Nov. 2021.

Sharp, Lesley A. *Bodies, Commodities, and Biotechnologies: Death, Mourning, and Scientific Desire in the Realm of Human Organ Transfer*. Columbia UP, 2008.

Tripathi, Anuj, and Jose Savio Melo, editors. *Advances in Biomaterials for Biomedical Applications*. Springer Nature Singapore, 2017.

Yasinski, Emma. "On the Road to 3-D Printed Organs." *Scientist*, 26 Feb. 2020, www.the-scientist.com/news-opinion/on-the-road-to-3-d-printed-organs-67187. Accessed 28 Nov. 2021.

Audiology and Hearing Aids

ABSTRACT

Audiology is the study of hearing, balance, and related ear disorders. Hearing disorders may be the result of congenital abnormalities, trauma, infections, exposure to loud noise, some medications, and aging. Some of these disorders may be corrected by hearing aids and cochlear implants. Hearing aids amplify sounds so that the damaged ears can discern them. Some fit over the ear with the receiver behind the ear, and some fit partially or completely within the ear canal. Cochlear implants directly stimulate the auditory nerve, and the brain interprets the stimulation as sound.

DEFINITION AND BASIC PRINCIPLES

Audiology is the study of hearing, balance, and related ear disorders. Audiologists are licensed professionals who assess hearing loss and related sensory input and neural conduction problems and oversee treatment of patients.

Hearing is the ability to receive, sense, and decipher sounds. To hear, the ear must direct the sound waves inside, sense the sound vibrations, and translate the sensations into neurological impulses that the brain can recognize.

The outer ear funnels sound into the ear canal. It also helps the brain determine the direction from which the sound is coming. When the sound waves reach the ear canal, they vibrate the eardrum. These vibrations are amplified by the eardrum's movement against three tiny bones behind the eardrum. The third bone rests against the cochlea; when it transmits the sound, it creates waves in the fluid of the cochlea.

The cochlea is a coiled, fluid-filled organ that contains thirty thousand hairs of different lengths that resonate at different frequencies. Vibrations of these hairs trigger complex electrical patterns that are transmitted along the auditory nerve to the brain, where they are interpreted.

BACKGROUND AND HISTORY

The first hearing aids, popularized in the sixteenth century, were large ear trumpets. In the nineteenth century, small trumpets or ear cups were placed in acoustic headbands that could be concealed in hats and hairstyles. Small ear trumpets were also built into parasols, fans, and walking sticks.

Electrical hearing devices emerged at the beginning of the twentieth century. These devices, which had external power sources, could provide greater amplification than mechanical devices. The batteries were large and difficult to carry; the carrying cases were often disguised as purses or camera cases. Zenith introduced smaller hearing aids with vacuum tubes and batteries in the 1940s.

In 1954, the first hearing aid with a transistor was introduced. This led to hearing aids that were made

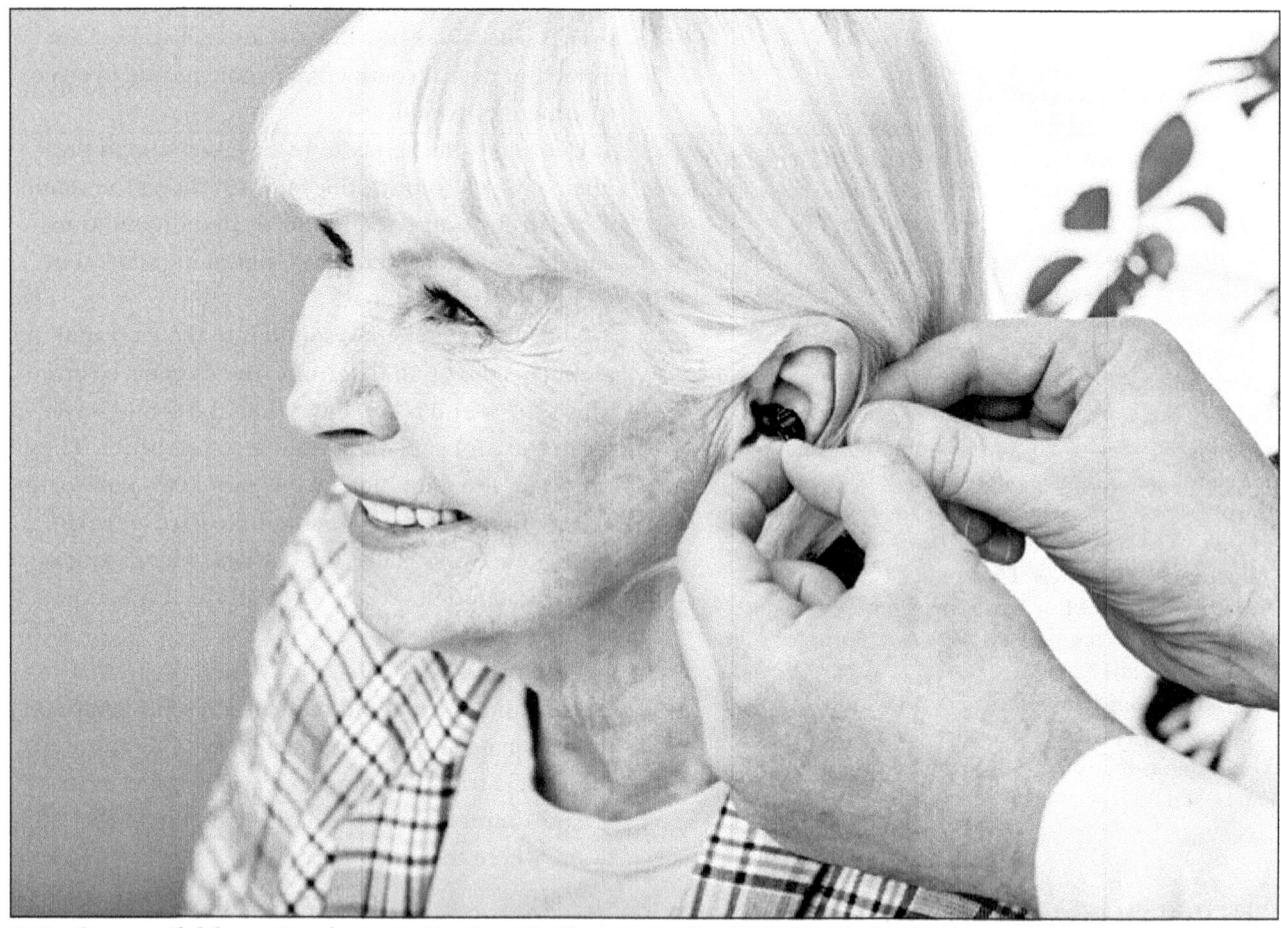

CAD software enabled the creation of customized hearing aids. Photo via iStock/peakSTOCK. [Used under license.]

to fit behind the ear. Components became smaller and more complex, leading to the marketing of devices that could fit partially into the ear canal in the mid-1960s and ones that could fit completely into the ear canal in the 1980s.

HOW IT WORKS

Audiologists are concerned with three kinds of hearing loss: conductive hearing loss, in which sound waves are not properly transmitted to the inner ear; sensorineural hearing loss, in which the cochlea or the auditory nerve is damaged; and mixed hearing loss, which is a combination of these.

Conductive hearing loss. Otosclerosis, inefficient movement of the three bones in the middle ear, results in hearing loss from poor conduction. This disease is treatable with surgery to replace the malformed, misaligned bones with prosthetic pieces to restore conductance of sound waves to the cochlea.

Meniere's disease is thought to result from an abnormal accumulation of fluid in the inner ear in response to allergies, blocked drainage, trauma, or infection. Its symptoms include vertigo with nausea and vomiting and hearing loss. The first line of treatment is motion sickness and antinausea medications. If the vertigo persists, treatment with a Meniett pulse generator may result in improvement. This device safely applies pulses of low pressure to the middle ear to improve fluid exchange.

Hearing loss may result from physical trauma, such as a fracture of the temporal bone that lies just behind the ear or a puncture of the eardrum. These injuries typically heal on their own, and in most cases, the hearing loss is temporary.

A gradual buildup of earwax may block sound from entering the ear. Earwax should not be removed with a cotton swab or other object inserted in the ear canal; that may result in infection or further impaction. Earwax should be softened with a few drops of baby oil or mineral oil placed in the ear canal twice a day for a week and then removed with warm water squirted gently from a small bulb syringe. Once the wax is removed, the ear should be dried with rubbing alcohol. In stubborn cases, a physician or audiologist may have to perform the removal.

Foreign bodies in the ear canal, most commonly toys or insects, may block sound. If they can be seen clearly, they may be carefully removed with tweezers. If they cannot be seen clearly or moved, they may be floated out. For toys, the ear canal is flooded with warm water squirted gently from a small bulb syringe. For insects, the ear canal should first be filled with mineral oil to kill the bug. If the bug still cannot be seen clearly, the ear canal may then be flooded with warm water squirted gently from a small bulb syringe. Once the object is removed, the ear canal should be dried with rubbing alcohol.

Sensorineural hearing loss. Some medications have adverse effects on the auditory system and may cause hearing loss. These medications include large doses of aspirin, certain antibiotics, and some chemotherapy agents. Doses of antioxidants such as vitamin C, vitamin E, and ginkgo biloba may ameliorate these ototoxic effects.

Exposure to harmful levels of noise, either over long periods or in a single acute event, may result in hearing loss. If the hair cells in the cochlea are destroyed, the hearing loss is permanent. Hearing aids or cochlear implants may be necessary to compensate.

An acoustic neuroma is a noncancerous tumor that grows on the auditory nerve. It is generally surgically removed, although patients who are unable to undergo surgery because of age or illness may undergo stereotactic radiation therapy instead.

Presbycusis is the progressive loss of hearing with age as a result of the gradual degeneration of the cochlea. It may be first noticed as an inability to hear high-pitched sounds. Hearing aids are an appropriate remedy.

Mixed hearing loss. Infections of the inner ear by the viruses that cause mumps, measles, and chickenpox and infections of the auditory nerve by the viruses that cause mumps and rubella may cause permanent hearing loss. Because fluid builds up and viruses do not respond to antibiotics, viral ear infections may require surgical treatment. In a surgical procedure called "myringotomy," a small hole is created in the eardrum to allow the drainage of fluid. A small tube may be inserted to keep the hole open long enough for drainage to finish.

Some children are born with hearing loss as the result of congenital abnormalities. Screening to determine the nature and severity of the hearing loss is difficult. Children are not eligible for cochlear implants before the age of twelve months. Young children often do well with behind-the-ear hearing aids, which are durable and can grow with them.

APPLICATIONS AND PRODUCTS

Audiological products consist mainly of hearing aids and cochlear implants.

Hearing aids. Although hearing aids take many forms, basically, all of them consist of a microphone that collects sound, an amplifier that magnifies the sound, and a speaker that sends it into the ear canal. They require daily placement and removal, and must be removed for showering, swimming, and battery replacement. Most people do not wear them when sleeping.

Hearing aids that sit behind the ear consist of a plastic case, a tube, and an earmold. The case contains components that collect and amplify the sound, which is then sent to the earmold through the tube. The earmold is custom-made to fit comfortably. This type of hearing aid is durable and well suited for children, although their earmolds must be replaced as they grow.

Hearing aids that sit partially within the ear canal are self-contained and custom-molded to the ear canal, so they are not recommended for growing children. Because of the short acoustic tube that channels the amplified sound, they are prone to feedback, which makes them less than ideal for people with profound hearing loss. Newer models offer feedback cancellation features.

Hearing aids that sit completely within the ear canal are self-contained and custom-molded. However, thin electrical wires replace the acoustic tube, so this type of hearing aid is free of feedback and sound distortion. They are not well suited for elderly people because their minimal size limits their volume capabilities.

Traditionally, in-ear hearing aids were customized for the individual user through a physical molding process that involved making a cast of the individual's ear canal. That cast was used to make a mold, which was in turn used to shape the exterior of the hearing aid, also known as the "hearing aid shell." By the early twenty-first century, hearing aid manufacturers had begun to experiment with digital processes for creating customized hearing aids. The digital design process, much like the earlier method, typically began with making a physical cast of the individual's ear canal. Afterward, however, the cast itself would be scanned and digitized, and any modifications to the resulting three-dimensional (3D) model would be made via specialized computer-aided design (CAD) software. Following the completion of the design process, the customized hearing aid shell would be manufactured using 3D printing technology, a form of additive manufacturing in which the shell would gradually be formed out of layers of resin.

The first hearing aids were analog, a process that amplified sound without changing its properties. Although amplification was adjustable, the sound was not sorted, so background noise was also amplified. New hearing aids are digital, a process in which sound waves are converted into binary data that can be cleaned up to deliver clearer, sharper sounds.

The choice of hearing aid depends on the type and severity of hearing loss. Hearing aids will not restore natural hearing. However, they increase a person's awareness of sounds and the direction from which they are coming and heighten discernment of words.

Cochlear imprints. The US Food and Drug Administration (FDA) approved cochlear implants in the mid-1980s. A cochlear implant differs from a hearing aid in its structure and its function. It consists of a microphone that collects sound, a speech processor that sorts the incoming sound, a transmitter that relays the digital data, a receiver/stimulator that converts the sound into electrical impulses, and an electrode array that sends the impulses from the stimulator to the auditory nerve. Hearing aids compensate for damage within the ear; cochlear implants avoid the damage within the ear altogether and directly stimulate the auditory nerve.

Whereas hearing aids are completely removable, cochlear implants are not. The internal receiver/stimulator and electrode array are surgically implanted. Three to six weeks after implantation, when the surgical incision has healed, the external portions are fitted. The transmitter and receiver are held together through the skin by magnets. Thus, the external portions may be removed for sleep, showering, and swimming.

CAREERS AND COURSEWORK

Audiologists are licensed professionals but not medical doctors. Physicians who specialize in ears, nose, and throat disorders are called "otorhinolaryngologists." Audiologists must have a minimum of a master's degree in audiology; a doctoral (AuD) degree is becoming increasingly desirable in the workplace and is required for licensure in some states. State licensure is required to practice in all fifty states. To obtain a license, an applicant must graduate from an accredited audiology program, accumulate supervised clinical experience, and pass a national licensing exam. To get into a graduate program in audiology, applicants must have had undergraduate courses in biology, chemistry, physics, anatomy, physiology, math, psychology, and communication. Most states have continuing education requirements to renew a license. An audiologist must pass a separate exam to mold and place hearing aids. The American Board of Audiology and the American Speech-Language-Hearing Association (AHSA) offer professional certification programs for licensed audiologists.

Audiologists can go into private practice as sole proprietors or as associates or partners in larger practices. They may also work in hospitals, outpatient clinics, and rehabilitation centers. Some are employed in state and local health departments and school districts. Some teach at universities and conduct academic research, and others work for medical device manufacturers. Audiologists may specialize in working with specific age groups, conducting hearing protection programs, or developing therapy programs for patients who are newly deaf or newly hearing.

SOCIAL CONTEXT AND FUTURE PROSPECTS

As the population of older people continues to grow, so will the incidence of hearing loss from aging. In addition, the market demand for hearing aids is expected to increase as devices become less noticeable and existing wearers switch from analog to digital models. At the same time, advances in medical treatment are increasing the survival rates of premature infants, trauma patients, and stroke patients, populations who may experience hearing loss.

Hearing aid manufacturers have continued to innovate over the decades, and digital devices are becoming smaller and providing increasingly better sound processing. Neurosurgical techniques also are improving. Public health programs are promoting hearing protection. Excessive noise is the most common cause of hearing loss, and one-third of noise-related hearing loss is preventable with proper protective equipment and practices. Researchers are continuing to study the genes and proteins related to specialized structures of the inner ear. They hope to discover the biological mechanisms behind hearing loss in order to interrupt them or compensate for them on the molecular level.

—*Bethany Thivierge, BS, MPH*

Further Reading

Dalebout, Susan. *The Praeger Guide to Hearing and Hearing Loss: Assessment, Treatment, and Prevention*. Praeger, 2009.

DeBonis, David A., and Constance L. Donohue. *Survey of Audiology: Fundamentals for Audiologists and Health Professionals*. 3rd ed., Slack Incorporated, 2020.

Gelfand, Stanley A. *Essentials of Audiology*. 4th ed., Thieme Medical, 2016.

"How 3D Printed Hearing Aids Silently Took Over the World." *3D Sourced*, www.3dsourced.com/editors-picks/custom-hearing-aids-3d-printed/. Accessed 28 Nov. 2021.

Kramer, Steven, and David K. Brown. *Audiology: Science to Practice*. 3rd ed., Plural, 2018.

Lass, Norman J., and Charles M. Woodford. *Hearing Science Fundamentals*. Mosby, 2007.

Moore, Brian C. J. *Cochlear Hearing Loss: Physiological, Psychological and Technical Issues*. 2nd ed., Wiley, 2007.

Noorani, Rafiq. *3D Printing: Technology, Applications, and Selection*. CRC Press, 2017.

"3D Printing Technology for Improved Hearing." *Sonova*, www.sonova.com/en/story/innovation/3d-printing-technology-improved-hearing. Accessed 28 Nov. 2021.

AutoCAD

ABSTRACT
Computer-aided design (CAD) enables engineers, scientists, architects, manufacturers, and other individuals to use specialized software to carry out and document the design process. Of the many CAD software packages available in the third decade of the twenty-first century, AutoCAD by Autodesk is one of the most popular and is often seen as an industry standard. It offers a wide range of tools suitable for an equally wide range of purposes, from manufacturing to animation.

INTRODUCTION
Computer-aided design (CAD) allows engineers, scientists, architects, manufacturers, and others to use computer software and technology to carry out and document the design process. Using points, lines, planes, curves, and set shapes, a user can create a detailed description of an item, create schematics and blueprints, render three-dimensional (3D) models, or even create 3D-printed prototypes. By the third decade of the twenty-first century, the Autodesk-produced CAD software AutoCAD had become one of the most popular software packages for CAD. To appreciate everything AutoCAD offers fully, one must have an understanding of the history of CAD and the early technologies out of which AutoCAD arose.

HISTORY OF COMPUTER-AIDED DESIGN
Engineering drawings have been around for a long time. They have helped build such diverse items and structures as churches, war machines, scientific instruments, and nearly all modern electronic devices, from radios to medical scanning machines. For a long time, schematics and plans were drawn out by hand on paper. By the 1940s, however, general-purpose computers were beginning to come into use. The potential for computers to handle complex equations and design was immediately noted.

First coined in the 1950s, the term "computer-aided design" and the abbreviation "CAD" are typically attributed to Douglas T. Ross, a pioneering computer scientist who led the Computer-Aided Design project at the Massachusetts Institute of Technology (MIT). Early innovations in the development of CAD systems included Sketchpad, described by MIT doctoral student Ivan Sutherland in his 1963 dissertation, and Design Augmented by Computer (DAC-1), a product of a collaboration between General Motors (GM) and International Business Machines (IBM). Sketchpad enabled users to draw and manipulate shapes on a screen. DAC-1, among other functions, facilitated the digitization and sharing of drawings that already existed on paper. Over the subsequent decades, advances in computing technology and software development led to the creation of increasingly complex CAD software packages that offered an array of advanced features, AutoCAD among them.

TYPES OF CAD
Since emerging in the 1960s, CAD software has been subject to constant development and improvement. Broadly, CAD encompasses several distinct forms of design.

2D CAD. Two-dimensional (2D) CAD images are essentially digital versions of hand-drawn technical drawings, blueprints, or sketches. Images are printed or plotted on a flat surface and depict only two dimensions.

3D CAD. 3D CAD models are drawn in three dimensions. All sides of the object exist in the model, even if they are not visible at a given time due to the model's orientation. 3D CAD models can typically be rotated or otherwise moved to allow the designer to view any side, angle, or component of the model.

3D Wireframe and surface modeling. Wireframe models represent 3D objects by outlining all edges of an object. However, the surfaces of the object are not modeled, and the model itself is not solid. As they do not rely on surface textures and shadowing, wireframe models can be displayed quickly and can be rotated, sized, and adjusted without waiting for surfaces or solid sections to be rendered. In surface modeling, the external surfaces of the object are modeled and can be viewed from any external angle. However, the model is not solid, and the interior of the model is typically hollow.

Solid modeling. In contrast to wireframe and surface modeling, solid modeling entails the modeling of a solid object, not merely the object's outlines or surfaces. Designers can test the viability of their designs through the use of simulation tools that analyze how the modeled object fares when subjected to pressure, motion, or other forces.

INTRODUCING AUTOCAD

Due to the intense processing power required, early CAD packages required large time-sharing computers to operate. While that worked for a while in some industries and government settings, there was a great need for CAD technology for smaller engineering and mechanical design firms.

In 1982, the California-based computer software company Autodesk released a full-featured program called "AutoCAD." Initially developed for CP/M (a precursor to DOS [disk operating system]) machines, it was later utilized on many microcomputer workstations, including those running Microsoft Windows, Unix, and Macintosh operating systems. AutoCAD soon became a popular choice for CAD projects due to its numerous add-ons and enhanced functionality. Its DXF file format became importable and exportable to a wide range of graphics programs.

USES AND ADVANTAGES OF AUTOCAD

AutoCAD is primarily used to develop preliminary design concepts and layouts; work with different design options; make calculations; and create drawings, schematics, and 3D models. Like other CAD programs, AutoCAD can output to formats required for machine manufacturing and interact with analysis and marketing tools.

One of the many advantages of using AutoCAD is that editing and reviewing technical details becomes

A man using AutoCAD 2.6 to digitize a drawing of a school building, 1987. Photo by Suspiciouscelery, via Wikimedia Commons.

more efficient than attempting the same acts by hand. AutoCAD streamlines the manufacturing process by converting detailed information about items into a format that can be universally accessed. Using AutoCAD, users can view an object from any angle. CAD software such as AutoCAD can also reduce design time by allowing designers to run precise simulations before taking the time and expense involved in constructing physical prototypes or models.

With AutoCAD's advanced rendering and animation capabilities, engineers and designers can further visualize product designs with various textures and shading. These options are utilized heavily in computer-generated animated features. Artists can use select object descriptors to draw, render, and shade anything from a nail to a skyscraper and allow animators to move, scale, and rotate images with ease.

IMPACT OF AUTOCAD

In the twenty-first century, CAD software is used in a broader variety of industries than it was when first introduced in the 1960s. In addition to the aerospace, electronics, and manufacturing industries, CAD is used in the film and game-design industries, in urban planning, and elsewhere. Overall, AutoCAD software encourages efficiency and design quality, increases productivity, and helps improve documentation and record keeping throughout the design and testing process.

Because AutoCAD software can increase productivity and nurture creativity, it has become a vital tool for visualizing products and mechanical interactions before introducing a manufacturing process. Autodesk provides extensive support for AutoCAD, including image and texture libraries, subscription licenses, and more. As technology improves, AutoCAD software will likely continue to have relevance and usefulness in even more fields and industries.

—*John Teehan*

Further Reading

Alton, Larry. "How CAD Software and 3D Printing Are Allowing Customized Products at Scale." *Inc.*, 1 Feb. 2020, www.inc.com/larry-alton/how-cad-software-3d-printing-are-allowing-customized-products-at-scale.html. Accessed 16 Dec. 2021.

Bernstein, Larry. "What Is Computer-Aided Design (CAD) and Why It's Important." *Jobsite*, 11 Oct. 2021, www.procore.com/jobsite/what-is-computer-aided-design-cad-and-why-its-important. Accessed 16 Dec. 2021.

"Computer-Aided Design (CAD) and Computer-Aided Manufacturing (CAM)." *Inc.*, 6 Feb. 2020, www.inc.com/encyclopedia/computer-aided-design-cad-and-computer-aided-cam.html. Accessed 16 Dec. 2021.

Goldstein, Phil. "How Computer-Aided Design Is Used in Government." *FedTech*, 24 June 2020, fedtechmagazine.com/article/2020/06/how-computer-aided-design-used-government-perfcon. Accessed 16 Dec. 2021.

"The History of Design, Model Making and CAD." *Creative Mechanisms*, 14 Dec. 2015, www.creativemechanisms.com/blog/the-history-of-design-model-making-and-cad. Accessed 16 Dec. 2021.

Ziden, Azidah Abu, Fatariah Zakaria, and Ahmad Nizam Othman. "Effectiveness of AutoCAD 3D Software as a Learning Support Tool." *International Journal of Emerging Technologies in Learning (JET)*, vol. 7, no. 2, 2012, pp. 57-60.

Automated Processes and Servomechanisms

ABSTRACT

An automated process is a series of sequential steps to be carried out automatically. Servomechanisms are systems, devices, and subassemblies that control the mechanical actions of robots by the use of feedback information from the overall system in operation.

DEFINITION AND BASIC PRINCIPLES

An automated process is any set of tasks that has been combined to be carried out in a sequential order automatically and on command. The tasks are not necessarily physical in nature, although this is the most common circumstance. The execution of the instructions in a computer program represents an automated process, as does the repeated execution of a series of specific welds in a robotic weld cell. The two are often inextricably linked, as the control of the physical process has been given to such digital devices as programmable logic controllers (PLCs) and computers in modern facilities.

Physical regulation and monitoring of mechanical devices such as industrial robots is normally achieved through the incorporation of servomechanisms. A servomechanism is a device that accepts information from the system itself and then uses that information to adjust the system to maintain specific operating conditions. A servomechanism that controls the opening and closing of a valve in a process stream, for example, may use the pressure of the process stream to regulate the degree to which the valve is opened.

Another essential component in the functioning of automated processes and servomechanisms is the feedback control systems that provide self-regulation and auto-adjustment of the overall system. Feedback control systems may be pneumatic, hydraulic, mechanical, or electrical in nature. Electrical feedback may be analog in form, although digital electronic feedback methods provide the most versatile method of output sensing for input feedback to digital electronic control systems.

BACKGROUND AND HISTORY

Automation begins with the first artificial construct made to carry out a repetitive task in the place of a person. One early clock mechanism, the water clock, used the automatic and repetitive dropping of a specific amount of water to measure the passage of time accurately. Water-, animal-, and wind-driven mills and threshing floors automated the repetitive action of processes that had been accomplished by humans. In many developing areas of the world, this repetitive human work remains a common practice.

With the mechanization that accompanied the Industrial Revolution, other means of automatically controlling machinery were developed, including self-regulating pressure valves on steam engines. Modern automation processes began in North America with the establishment of the assembly line as a standard industrial method by Henry Ford. In this method, each worker in his or her position along the assembly line performs a limited set of functions, using only the parts and tools appropriate to that task.

Servomechanism theory was further developed during World War II. The development of the transistor in 1951 enabled the development of electronic control and feedback devices, and hence digital electronics. The field grew rapidly, especially following the development of the microcomputer in 1969. By the twenty-first century, digital logic and machine control could be interfaced in an effective manner, enabling automated systems to function with an unprecedented degree of precision and dependability.

HOW IT WORKS

An automated process is a series of repeated, identical operations under the control of a master operation or program. While simple in concept, it is complex in practice and difficult in implementation and execution. The process control operation must be designed in a logical, step-by-step manner that will provide the desired outcome each time the process is cycled. The sequential order of operations must be set so that the outcome of any one step does not prevent or interfere with the successful outcome of any other step in the process. In addition, the physical parameters of the desired outcome must be established and made subject to a monitoring protocol that can then act to correct any variation in the outcome of the process.

A plain analogy is found in the writing and structuring of a simple computer programming function. The definition of the steps involved in the function must be exact and logical because the computer, like any other machine, can do only exactly what it is instructed to do. Once the order of instructions and the statement of variables and parameters have been finalized, they will be carried out in exactly the same manner each time the function is called in a program. The function is thus an automated process.

The same holds true for any physical process that has been automated. In a typical weld cell, for example, a set of individual parts are placed in a fixture that holds them in their proper relative orientations. Robotic welding machines may then act upon the setup to carry out a series of programmed welds to join the individual pieces into a single assembly. The series of welds is carried out in exactly the same manner each time the weld cell cycles. The robots that carry out the welds are guided under the control of a master program that defines the position of the welding tips, the motion that it must follow, and the duration of current flow in the welding process for each movement, along with many other variables that describe the overall action that will be followed. Any variation from this programmed pattern of movements and functions will result in an incorrect output.

The control of automated processes is carried out through various intermediate servomechanisms. A servomechanism uses input information from both the controlling program and the output of the process to carry out its function. Direct instruction from the controller defines the basic operation of the servomechanism. The output of the process generally includes monitoring functions that are compared to the desired output. They then provide an input signal to the servomechanism that informs how the operation must be adjusted to maintain the desired output. In the example of a robotic welder, the movement of the welding tip is performed through the action of an angular positioning device. The device may turn through a specific angle according to the voltage that is supplied to the mechanism. An input signal may be provided from a proximity sensor such that when the necessary part is not detected, the welding operation is interrupted and the movement of the mechanism ceases.

The variety of processes that may be automated is practically limitless given the inter-

Globe control valve with pneumatic actuator and "positioner." This is a servo which ensures the valve opens to the desired position regardless of friction. Photo by Rafa? Rygielski, via Wikimedia Commons.

face of digital electronic control units. Similarly, servomechanisms may be designed to fit any needed parameter or to carry out any desired function.

APPLICATIONS AND PRODUCTS

The applications of process automation and servomechanisms are as varied as modern industry and its products. It is perhaps more productive to think of process automation as a method that can be applied to the performance of repetitive tasks than to dwell on specific applications and products. The commonality of the automation process can be illustrated by examining a number of individual applications, and the products that support them.

"Repetitive tasks" are those tasks that are to be carried out in the same way, in the same circumstances, and for the same purpose a great number of times. The ideal goal of automating such a process is to ensure that the results are consistent each time the process cycle is carried out. In the case of the robotic weld cell, the central tasks to be repeated are the formation of welded joints of specified dimensions at the same specific locations over many hundreds or thousands of times. This is a typical operation in the manufacturing of subassemblies in the automobile industry and in other industries in which large numbers of identical fabricated units are produced.

Automation of the process requires the identification of a set series of actions to be carried out by industrial robots. In turn, this requires the appropriate industrial robots be designed and constructed in such a way that the actual physical movements necessary for the task can be carried out. Each robot will incorporate a number of servomechanisms that drive the specific movements of parts of the robot according to the control instruction set. They will also incorporate any number of sensors and transducers that will provide input signal information for the self-regulation of the automated process. This input data may be delivered to the control program and compared to specified standards before it is fed back into the process, or it may be delivered directly into the process for immediate use.

Programmable logic controllers (PLCs), first specified by the General Motors Corporation in 1968, have become the standard devices for controlling automated machinery. The PLC is essentially a dedicated computer system that employs a limited-instruction-set programming language. The program of instructions for the automated process is stored in the PLC memory. Execution of the program sends the specified operating parameters to the corresponding machine in such a way that it carries out a set of operations that must otherwise be carried out under the control of a human operator.

A typical use of such methodology is in the various forms of computer numeric control (CNC) machining. CNC refers to the use of reduced-instruction-set computers to control the mechanical operation of machines. CNC lathes and mills are two common applications of the technology. In the traditional use of a lathe, a human operator adjusts all of the working parameters such as spindle rotation speed, feed rate, and depth of cut, through an order of operations that is designed to produce a finished piece to blueprint dimensions. The consistency of pieces produced over time in this manner tends to vary as operator fatigue and distractions affect human performance. In a CNC lathe, however, the order of operations and all of the operating parameters are specified in the control program and are thus carried out in exactly the same manner for each piece that is produced. Operator error and fatigue do not affect production, and the machinery produces the desired pieces at the same rate throughout the entire working period. Human intervention is required only to maintain the machinery and is not involved in the actual machining process.

Servomechanisms used in automated systems check and monitor system parameters and adjust operating conditions to maintain the desired system output. The principles upon which they operate can range from crude mechanical levers to sophisticated and highly accurate digital electronic-measurement devices. All employ the principle of feedback to control or regulate the corresponding process that is in operation.

In a simple example of a rudimentary application, units of a specific component moving along a production line may in turn move a lever as they pass by. The movement of the lever activates a switch that prevents a warning light from turning on. If the switch is not triggered, the warning light tells an operator that the component has been missed. The lever, switch, and warning light system constitute a crude servomechanism that carries out a specific function in maintaining the proper operation of the system.

In more advanced applications, the dimensions of the product from a machining operation may be tested by accurately calibrated measuring devices before releasing the object from the lathe, mill, or other device. The measurements taken are then compared to the desired measurements, as stored in the PLC memory. Oversize measurements may trigger an action of the machinery to refine the dimensions of the piece to bring it into specified tolerances, while undersize measurements may trigger the rejection of the piece and a warning to maintenance personnel to adjust the working parameters of the device before continued production.

Two of the most important applications of servomechanisms in industrial operations are control of position and control of rotational speed. Both commonly employ digital measurement. Positional control is generally achieved through the use of servomotors, also known as stepper motors. In these devices, the rotor turns to a specific angular position according to the voltage that is supplied to the motor. Modern electronics, using digital devices constructed with integrated circuits, allows extremely fine and precise control of electrical and electronic factors, such as voltage, amperage, and resistance. This, in turn, facilitates extremely precise positional control. Sequential positional control of different servomotors in a machine, such as an industrial robot, permits precise positioning of operating features. In other robotic applications, the same operating principle allows for extremely delicate microsurgery that would not be possible otherwise.

The control of rotational speed is achieved through the same basic principle as the stroboscope. A strobe light flashing on and off at a fixed rate can be used to measure the rate of rotation of an object. When the strobe rate and the rate of rotation are equal, a specific point on the rotating object will always appear at the same location. If the speeds are not matched, that point will appear to move in one direction or the other according to which rate is the faster rate. By attaching a rotating component to a representation of a digital scale, such as the Gray code, sensors can detect both the rate of rotation of the component and its position when it is functioning as part of a servomechanism. Comparison with a digital statement of the desired parameter can then be used by the controlling device to adjust the speed or position, or both, of the component accordingly.

SOCIAL CONTEXT AND FUTURE PROSPECTS
While the vision of a utopian society in which all menial labor is automated, leaving humans free to create new ideas in relative leisure, is still far from reality, the vision becomes more real each time another process is automated. Paradoxically, since the mid-twentieth century, knowledge and technology have changed so rapidly that what is new becomes obsolete almost as quickly as it is developed, seeming to increase rather than decrease the need for human labor.

New products and methods are continually being developed because of automated control. Similarly, existing automated processes can be reautomated using newer technology, newer materials, and modernized capabilities. Particular areas of growth in automated processes and servomechanisms are found in the biomedical fields. Automated processes greatly increase the number of tests and analyses that can be performed for genetic research and new drug development. Robotic devices become more essential to the success of delicate surgical procedures each day, partly because of the ability of integrated circuits to amplify or reduce electrical signals by factors of hundreds of thousands. Someday, surgeons may be able to perform the most delicate of operations remotely, as normal actions by the surgeon are translated into the miniscule movements of microscopic surgical equipment manipulated through robotics.

Concerns that automated processes will eliminate the role of human workers are unfounded. The nature of work has repeatedly changed to reflect the capabilities of the technology of the time. The introduction of electric streetlights, for example, did eliminate the job of lighting gas-fueled streetlamps, but it also created the need for workers to produce the electric lights and to ensure that they were functioning properly. The same sort of reasoning applies to the automation of processes today. Some traditional jobs will disappear, but new types of jobs will be created in their place through automation.

—*Richard M. Renneboog, MSc*

Further Reading

"History of CNC Machining." *Bantam Tools*, 12 Apr. 2019, medium.com/cnc-life/history-of-cnc-machining-part-1-2a4b290d994d. Accessed 28 Nov. 2021.

James, Hubert M. *Theory of Servomechanisms*. McGraw, 1947.

Krar, Steve, Arthur Gill, and Peter Smid. *Technology of Machine Tools*. 8th ed., McGraw-Hill, 2020.

Mehta, B. R., and Y. Jaganmohan Reddy. *Industrial Process Automation Systems: Design and Implementation*. Butterworth-Heinemann, 2014.

Seal, Anthony M. *Practical Process Control*. Butterworth, 1998.

Seames, Warren S. *Computer Numerical Control Concepts and Programming*. 4th ed., Delmar, 2002.

Smith, Carlos A. *Automated Continuous Process Control*. Wiley, 2002.

Avionics and Aircraft Instrumentation

ABSTRACT
Flight instrumentation refers to the indicators and instruments that inform a pilot of the position of the aircraft and give navigational information. Avionics comprises all the devices that allow a pilot to give and receive communications, such as air traffic control directions and navigational radio and satellite signals. Early in the history of flight, instrumentation and avionics were separate systems, but these systems have been vastly improved and integrated. These systems allow commercial airliners to fly efficiently and safely all around the world. Additionally, the integrated systems are being used in practically all types of vehicles—ships, trains, spacecraft, guided missiles, and unmanned aircraft—both civilian and military.

DEFINITION AND BASIC PRINCIPLES
Flight instrumentation refers to the instruments that provide information to a pilot about the position of the aircraft in relation to the earth's horizon. The term "avionics" is a contraction of "aviation" and "electronics" and has come to refer to the combination of communication and navigational devices in an aircraft. This term was coined in the 1970s after the systems were becoming one integral system.

The components of basic flight instrumentation are the magnetic compass, the instruments that rely on air-pressure differentials, and those that are driven by gyroscopes and instruments. Air pressure decreases with an increase in altitude. The altimeter and vertical-speed indicator use this change in pressure to provide information about the height of the aircraft above sea level and the rate that the aircraft is climbing or descending. The airspeed indicator uses ram air pressure to give the speed that the aircraft is traveling through the air.

Other instruments use gyroscopes to detect changes in the position of the aircraft relative to the earth's surface and horizon. An airplane can move around the three axes of flight. The first is pitch, or the upward and downward position of the nose of the airplane. The second is roll, the position of the wings. They can be level to the horizon or be in a bank position, where one wing is above horizon and the other below the horizon as the aircraft turns. Yaw is the third. When an airplane yaws, the nose of the airplane moves to the right or left while the airplane is in level flight. The instruments that use gyroscopes to show movement along the axes of flight are the turn and bank indicator, which shows the angle of the airplane's wings in a turn and the rate of turn in degrees per second; the artificial horizon, which indicates the airplane's pitch and bank; and the directional gyro, which is a compass card connected to a gyroscope. Output from the flight instruments can be used to operate autopilots. Modern inertial navigation systems (INS) use gyroscopes, sometimes in conjunction with a global positioning system (GPS), as integrated flight instrumentation and avionics systems.

The radios that comprise the avionics of an aircraft include communications radios that pilots use to talk to air traffic control (ATC) and other aircraft and navigation radios. Early navigation radios relied on ground-based radio signals, but many aircraft have come to use GPS receivers that receive their information from satellites. Other components of an aircraft's avionics include a transponder, which sends a discrete code to ATC to identify the aircraft and is used in the military to discern friendly and enemy aircraft, and radar, which is used to locate rain and thunderstorms and to determine the aircraft's height above the ground.

BACKGROUND AND HISTORY

Flight instruments originally were separated from the avionics of an aircraft. The compass, perhaps the most basic of the flight instruments, was developed by the Chinese in the second century BCE. Chinese navy commander Zheng He's voyages from 1405 to 1433 CE included the first recorded use of a magnetic compass for navigation.

The gyroscope, a major component of many flight instruments, was named by French physicist Jean-Bernard-Léon Foucault in the nineteenth century. In 1909, American businessman Elmer Sperry invented the gyroscopic compass that was first used on US naval ships in 1911. In 1916, the first artificial horizon using a gyroscope was invented. Gyroscopic flight instruments along with radio navigation signals guided American pilot Jimmy Doolittle to the first successful all-instrument flight and landing of an airplane in 1929. Robert Goddard, the father of rocketry, experimented with using gyroscopes in guidance systems for rockets. During World War II, German rocket scientist Wernher von Braun further developed Goddard's work to build a basic guidance system for Germany's V-2 rockets. After the war, von Braun and 118 of his engineers immigrated to the United States, where they worked for the US Army on gyroscopic INS for rockets. Massachusetts Institute of Technology (MIT) engineers continued the development of the INS to use in Atlas rockets and eventually the space shuttle. Boeing was the first aircraft manufacturer to install INS into its 747 jumbo jets. Later, the Air Force introduced the system to their C-141 aircraft.

Radios form the basis of modern avionics. Although there is some dispute over who actually invented the radio, Italian physicist Guglielmo Marconi first applied the technology to communication. During World War I, in 1916, the Naval Research Laboratory developed the first aircraft radio. In 1920, the first ground-based system for communication with aircraft was developed by General

Electric (GE). The earliest navigational system was a series of lights on the ground, and the pilot would fly from beacon to beacon. In the 1930s, the nondirectional radio beacon (NDB) became the major radio navigation system. This was replaced by the very high frequency omnidirectional range (VOR) system in the 1960s. In 1994, the GPS became operational and was quickly adapted to aircraft navigation. The great accuracy that GPS can supply for both location and time was adapted for use in INS.

As computer-aided design (CAD) and computer-aided manufacturing (CAM) technology developed during the latter decades of the twentieth century, those technologies came into widespread use within the aviation industry and facilitated the design and manufacturing of a wide range of aircraft components, from a plane's fuselage to its engines. The first known aircraft to be designed entirely through digital means, the Boeing 777 airliner, made its first commercial flight in 1995. Flight instruments and avionics systems likewise benefited from the rise of CAD technology: CAD software could be used to design and model physical instruments, such as altimeters, and to design and refine the layout of aircrafts' instrument panels. Specialized electrical design software could likewise be used to design the electrical systems underlying the avionics technology, while the ground- and satellite-based systems on which the avionics relied could likewise incorporate digitally designed components.

HOW IT WORKS

Flight instruments. Flight instruments operate using either gyroscopes or air pressure. The instruments that use air pressure are the altimeter, the vertical speed indicator, and the airspeed indicator. Airplanes are fitted with two pressure sensors: the pitot tube, which is mounted under a wing or the front fuselage, its opening facing the oncoming air; and the static port, which is usually mounted on the side of the airplane out of the slipstream of air flowing past the plane. The pitot tube measures ram air; the faster the aircraft is moving through the air, the more air molecules enter the pitot tube. The static port measures the ambient air pressure, which decreases with increasing altitude. The airspeed indicator is driven by the force of the ram air calibrated to the ambient air pressure to give the speed that the airplane is moving through the sky. The static port's ambient pressure is translated into altitude above sea level by the altimeter. As air pressure can vary from location to location, the altimeter must be set to the local barometric setting in order to receive a correct altimeter reading. The vertical speed indicator also uses the ambient pressure from the static port. This instrument can sense changes in altitude and indicates feet per minute that the airplane is climbing or descending.

Other flight instruments operate with gyroscopes. These instruments are the gyroscopic compass, the turn and bank indicator, and the artificial horizon. The gyroscopic compass is a vertical compass card connected to a gyroscope. It is either set by the pilot or slaved to the heading indicated on the magnetic compass. The magnetic compass floats in a liquid that allows it to rotate freely but also causes it to jiggle in turbulence; the directional gyro is stabilized by its gyroscope. The magnetic compass will also show errors while turning or accelerating, which are eliminated by the gyroscope. The turn and bank indicator is connected to a gyroscope that remains stable when the plane is banking. The indicator shows the angle of bank of the airplane. The artificial horizon has a card attached to it that shows a horizon, sky, and ground and a small indicator in the center that is connected to the gyroscope. When the airplane pitches up or down or rolls, the card moves with the airplane, but the indicator is stable and shows the position of the aircraft relative to the horizon. Pilots use the artificial horizon to fly when they cannot see the natural horizon. The artificial hori-

Avionics refers to both the navigational and communication systems used by pilots. Photo via iStock/Ratstuben. [Used under license.]

zon and directional gyro can be combined into one instrument, the horizontal situation indicator (HSI). These instruments can be used to supply information to an autopilot, which can be mechanically connected to the flight surfaces of the aircraft to fly it automatically.

Ground-based avionics. Ground-based avionics provide communications, navigational information, and collision avoidance. Communication radios operate on frequencies between 118 and 136.975 megahertz (MHz). Communication uses line of sight. Navigation uses VOR systems. The VOR gives a signal to the aircraft receiver that indicates the direction to or from the VOR station. A more sensitive type of VOR, a localizer, is combined with a glide slope indicator to provide runway direction and a glide path for the aircraft to follow when it is landing in poor weather conditions and the pilot does not have visual contact with the runway. Collision avoidance is provided by ATC using signals from each aircraft's transponders and radar. ATC can identify the aircrafts' positions and advise pilots of traffic in their vicinity.

Satellite-based systems. The limitation of line of sight for ground-based avionic transmitters is a major problem for navigation over large oceans or in areas of the world that have large mountain ranges or few transmitters. The US military was very concerned about these limitations and the Department of Defense spearheaded the research and implementation of a system that addresses these problems. GPS is the United States' satellite system that provides navigational information. GPS can give location, movement, and time information. The system uses a minimum of twenty-four satellites orbiting Earth that send signals to monitoring receivers on Earth. The receiver must be able to get signals from a minimum of four satellites in order to calculate an aircraft's position correctly. Although originally designed solely for military use, GPS is widely used by civilians.

Inertial navigation systems (INS). The INS is a self-contained system that does not rely on outside radio or satellite signals. INS is driven by accelerometers and gyroscopes. The accelerometer houses a small pendulum that will swing in relation to the aircraft's acceleration or deceleration and so can measure the aircraft's speed. The gyroscope provides information about the aircraft's movement about the three axes of flight. Instead of the gimbaled gyros, more precise strap-down laser gyroscopes have come to be used. The strap-down system is attached to the frame of the aircraft. Instead of the rotating wheel in the gimbaled gyroscopes, this system uses light beams that travel in opposite directions around a small, triangular path. When the aircraft rotates, the path traveled by the beam of light moving in the direction of rotation appears shorter than the path of the other beam of light moving in the opposite direction. The length of the path causes a frequency shift that is detected and interpreted as aircraft rotation. INS must be initialized: The system has to be able to detect its initial position or it must be programmed with its initial position before it is used or it will not have a reference point from which to work.

APPLICATIONS AND PRODUCTS

Military INS and GPS uses. Flight instrumentation and avionics are used by military aircraft as well as civilian aircraft, but the military have many other applications. INS is used in guided missiles and submarines. It can also be used as a stand-alone navigational system in vehicles that do not want to communicate with outside sources for security purposes. INS and GPS are used in bombs, rockets, and, with great success, unmanned aerial vehicles (UAVs) that are used for reconnaissance as well as delivering ordnance without placing a pilot in harm's way. GPS is used in almost all military vehicles such as tanks, ships, armored vehicles, and cars, but not in submarines as the satellite signals will not penetrate deep water. GPS is also used by the United States Nuclear Detonation Detection System as the satellites carry nuclear detonation detectors.

Navigation. Besides the use of flight instrumentation and avionics for aircraft navigation, the systems can also be used for almost all forms of navigation. The aerospace industry has used INS for guidance of spacecraft that cannot use earthbound navigation systems, including satellites that orbit the planet. INS systems can be initialized by manually inputting the craft's position using GPS or using celestial fixes to direct rockets, space shuttles, and long-distance satellites and space probes through the reaches of the solar system and beyond. These systems can be synchronized with computers and sensors to control the vehicles by moving flight controls or firing rockets. GPS can be used on Earth by cars, trucks, trains, ships, and handheld units for commercial, personal, and recreational uses. One limitation of GPS is that it cannot work where the signals could be blocked, such as under water or in caves.

Cellular phones. GPS technology is critical for operating cell phones. GPS provides accurate time that is used in synchronizing signals with base stations. If the phone has GPS capability built into it, as smartphones do, it can be used to locate a mobile cell phone making an emergency call. The GPS system in cell phones can be used in cars for navigation as well as for guidance while hiking, biking, boating, or geocaching.

Tracking systems. In the same manner that GPS can be used to locate a cell phone, GPS can be used to find downed aircraft or pilots. GPS can be used by biologists to track wildlife by placing collars on the animals, a major improvement over radio tracking that was line-of-sight and worked only over short ranges. Animals that migrate over great distances can be tracked by using only GPS. Lost pets can be tracked through GPS devices in their collars. Military and law enforcement use GPS to track vehicles.

Other civilian applications. Surveyors and mapmakers use GPS to mark boundaries and identify locations. GPS units installed at specific locations can detect movements of the earth to study earthquakes, volcanoes, and plate tectonics..

Next-generation air transportation system (NextGen). While radar and ground-based navigational systems such as the VOR remained in use during the first decades of the twenty-first century, the Federal Aviation Administration (FAA) in 2007 began researching and designing NextGen, a new system for navigation and tracking aircraft that would be based on GPS in the National Airspace System (NAS). Using NextGen GPS navigation, which was expected to be in place by 2025, aircraft would be able to fly shorter and more direct routes to their destinations, saving time and fuel. ATC would change to a satellite-based system of managing air traffic.

CAREERS AND COURSEWORK

The possible careers associated with flight instruments and avionics include both civilian and military positions ranging from mechanics and technicians to designers and researchers. The education required for these occupations usually requires at least two years of college or technical training, but research and design may require a doctorate.

Maintenance and avionics technicians install and repair flight instruments and avionics. They may work on general aviation airplanes, commercial airliners, or military aircraft. With more and more modes of transportation using INS and GPS, mechanics and technicians may also be employed to install and repair these systems on other types of vehicles—ships, trains, guided missiles, tanks, or UAVs. The National Aeronautics and Space Administration (NASA) and private companies employ technicians to work with spacecraft. Most of these positions require an associate's degree with specialization as an aircraft or avionics technician, or the training may be acquired in the military.

As computers are becoming more and more important in these fields, the demand for computer technicians, designers, and programmers will increase. Jobs in these fields range from positions in government agencies such as the FAA or NASA to private-sector research and development. The education required for these occupations varies from high school or vocational computer training to doctorates in computer science or related fields.

Flight instrument and avionics systems are being designed and researched by persons who have been educated in mechanical, electrical, and aeronautical engineering, computer science, and related fields. Some of these occupations require the minimum of a bachelor's degree, but most require a master's degree or doctorate.

SOCIAL CONTEXT AND FUTURE PROSPECTS

Aviation, made possible by flight instrumentation and avionics, has revolutionized how people travel and how freight is moved throughout the world. It has also dramatically changed how wars are fought and how countries defend themselves. In the future, flight instrumentation and avionics will continue to affect society not only through aviation but also through applications of the technology in daily life.

Military use of UAVs controlled by advances in flight instrumentation and avionics will continue to change how wars are fought. However, this technology may also be used in civilian aviation. UAVs could be used to inspect pipelines and perform surveys in unpopulated areas or rough terrain, but it is unclear whether they will be used for passenger flights. Many people will certainly be fearful of traveling in airplanes with no human operators. The FAA would have to develop systems that would incorporate unmanned aircraft into the airspace. However, the use of unmanned vehicles may be an important part of future space exploration.

Perhaps the avionics system that has had the most impact on society is GPS. As GPS devices are being made more compact and more inexpensively, they are being used more and more in daily life. GPS can permit underdeveloped countries to improve their own air-navigation systems more rapidly without the expense of buying and installing ground-based navigational equipment or radar systems used by air traffic control facilities.

—Polly D. Steenhagen, BS, MS

Further Reading

Collinson, R. P. G. *Introduction to Avionics Systems*. 3rd ed., Springer Netherlands, 2011.

"Computer Graphics, Purpose and Function, Care and Use, Types of Drawings." *Aeronautics Guide*, Oct. 2019, www.aircraftsystemstech.com/2019/10/aircraft-drawings-computer-graphics.html. Accessed 28 Nov. 2021.

Dailey, Franklyn E., Jr. *The Triumph of Instrument Flight: A Retrospective in the Century of US Aviation*. Dailey International, 2004.

El-Rabbany, Ahmed. *Introduction to GPS: The Global Positioning System*. 2nd ed., Artech House, 2006.

Federal Aviation Administration. *Instrument Flying Handbook*. US Department of Transportation, 2012.

Helfrick, Albert D. *Principles of Avionics*. 9th ed., Avionics Communication, 2015.

"Next Generation Air Transportation System (NextGen)." *Federal Aviation Administration*, 7 Sept. 2021, www.faa.gov/nextgen/. Accessed 28 Nov. 2021.

"777 Commercial Transport." *Boeing*, www.boeing.com/history/products/777.page. Accessed 28 Nov. 2021.

Spitzer, Cary R., editor. *Avionics: Development and Implementation*. CRC Press, 2007.

Tooley, Mike. *Aircraft Digital Electronic and Computer Systems: Principles, Operation and Maintenance*. 2nd ed., Routledge, 2013.

Tooley, Mike, and David Wyatt. *Aircraft Communications and Navigation Systems*. 2nd ed., Routledge, 2017.

Wang, Guoqing, and Wenhao Zhao. *The Principles of Integrated Technology in Avionics Systems*. Academic Press, 2020.

Biomechanical Engineering

ABSTRACT

Biomechanical engineering is a branch of science that applies mechanical engineering principles such as physics and mathematics to biology and medicine. It can be described as the connection between structure and function in living things. Researchers in the field investigate the mechanics and mechanobiology of cells and tissues, tissue engineering, and the physiological systems they comprise. The work also examines the pathogenesis and treatment of diseases using cells and cultures, tissue mechanics, imaging, microscale biosensor fabrication, biofluidics, human motion capture, and computational methods. Real-world applications include the design and evaluation of medical implants, instrumentation, devices, products, and procedures. Biomechanical engineering is a multidisciplinary science, often fostering collaborations and interactions with medical research, surgery, radiology, physics, computer-aided design (CAD), and other areas of engineering.

DEFINITION AND BASIC PRINCIPLES

Biomechanical engineering applies mechanical engineering principles to biology and medicine. Elements from biology, physiology, chemistry, physics, anatomy, and mathematics are used to describe the impact of physical forces on living organisms. The forces studied can originate from the outside environment or generate within a body or single structure. Forces on a body or structure can influence how it grows, develops, or moves. Better understanding of how a biological organism copes with forces and stresses can lead to improved treatment, advanced diagnosis, and prevention of disease. This integration of multidisciplinary philosophies has led to significant advances in clinical medicine and device design. Improved understanding guides the creation of artificial organs, joints, implants, and tissues. Biomechanical engineering also has a tremendous influence on the retail industry, as the results of laboratory research guide product design toward more comfortable and efficient merchandise.

BACKGROUND AND HISTORY

The history of biomechanical engineering, as a distinct and defined field of study, is relatively short. However, the application of principles of physics and engineering to biological systems has been developed over centuries. Many overlaps and parallels to complementary areas of biomedical engineering and biomechanics exist, and the terms are often used interchangeably with biomechanical engineering. The mechanical analysis of living organisms was not internationally accepted and recognized until the definition provided by Austrian mathematician Herbert Hatze in 1974: "Biomechanics is the study of the structure and function of biological systems by means of the methods of mechanics."

Greek philosopher Aristotle introduced the term "mechanics" and discussed the movement of living beings around 322 BCE in the first book about biomechanics, *On the Motion of Animals*. Leonardo da Vinci proposed that the human body is subject to the law of mechanics in the 1500s. Italian physicist and mathematician Giovanni Alfonso Borelli, a student of Galileo's, is considered the "father of biomechanics" and developed mathematical models to describe anatomy and human movement mechanically. In the 1890s German zoologist Wilhelm Roux and German surgeon Julius Wolff determined the effects of loading and stress on stem cells in the development of bone architecture and healing. British physiologist Archibald V. Hill and German physiologist Otto Fritz Meyerhof shared the 1922 Nobel Prize for Physiology or Medicine. The prize was divided between them: Hill won "for his discovery relating to the production of heat in the muscle"; Meyerhof won "for his discovery of the fixed relationship between the consumption of oxygen and the metabolism of lactic acid in the muscle."

The first joint replacement was performed on a hip in 1960, and the first joint replacement in a knee took place in 1968. The development of imaging, modeling, and computer simulation in the latter half of the twentieth century provided insight into the smallest structures of the body. The relationships between these structures, functions, and the impact of internal and external forces accelerated new research opportunities into diagnostic procedures and effective solutions to disease. In the 1990s, biomechanical engineering programs began to emerge in academic and research institutions around the world, and the field continued to grow in recognition throughout the first decades of the twenty-first century.

HOW IT WORKS
Biomechanical engineering science is extremely diverse. However, the basic principle of studying the relationship between biological structures and forces, as well as the important associated reactions of biological structures to technological and environmental materials, exists throughout all disciplines. The biological structures described include all life forms and may include an entire body or organism or even the microstructures of specific tissues or systems. Characterization and quantification of the response of these structures to forces can provide insight into disease process, resulting in better treatments and diagnoses. Research in the field extends beyond the laboratory and can involve observations of mechanics in nature, such as the aerodynamics of bird flight, hydrodynamics of fish, or strength of plant root systems, and how these findings can be modified and applied to human performance and interaction with external forces.

As in biomechanics, biomechanical engineering has basic principles. Equilibrium, as defined by British physicist Sir Isaac Newton, results when the sum of all forces is zero and no change occurs and energy cannot be created or destroyed, only converted from one form to another.

The seven basic principles of biomechanics can be applied or modified to describe the reaction of forces to any living organism.

- The lower the center of mass, the larger the base of support; the closer the center of mass to the base of support, and the greater the mass, the more stability increases.
- The production of maximum force requires the use of all possible joint movements that contribute to the task's objective.
- The production of maximum velocity requires the use of joints in order—from largest to smallest.
- The greater the applied impulse, the greater increase in velocity.
- Movement usually occurs in the direction opposite that of the applied force.
- Angular motion is produced by the application of force acting at some distance from an axis, that is, by torque.
- Angular momentum is constant when a body or object is free in the air.

The forces studied can be combinations of internal, external, static, or dynamic, and all are important in the analysis of complex biochemical and biophysical processes. Even the mechanics of a single cell, including growth, cell division, active motion, and contractile mechanisms, can provide insight into mechanisms of stress, damage of structures, and disease processes at the microscopic level. Imaging and computer simulation allow precise measurements and observations to be made of the forces impacting the smallest cells.

APPLICATIONS AND PRODUCTS

Biomechanical engineering advances in modeling and simulation have tremendous potential research and application uses across many healthcare disciplines. Modeling has resulted in the development of designs for implantable devices to assist with organs or areas of the body that are malfunctioning. The biomechanical relationships between organs and supporting structures allow for improved device design and can assist with planning of surgical and treatment interventions. The materials used for medical and surgical procedures in humans and animals are being evaluated and some redesigned, as biomechanical science is showing that different materials, procedures, and techniques may be better for reducing complications and improving long-term patient health. Evaluating the physical relationship between the cells and structures of the body and foreign implements and interventions can quantify the stresses and forces on the system, which provides more accurate prediction of patient outcomes.

Biomechanical engineering professionals apply their knowledge to develop implantable medical devices that can diagnose, treat, or monitor disease and health conditions and improve the daily living of patients. Devices that are used within the human body are highly regulated by the US Food and Drug Administration (FDA) and other agencies internationally. Pacemakers and defibrillators, also called "cardiac resynchronization therapy" (CRT) devices, can constantly evaluate a patient's heart and respond to changes in heart rate with electrical stimulation. These devices greatly improve therapeutic outcomes in patients afflicted with congestive heart failure. Patients with arrhythmias experience greater advantages with implantable devices than with phar-

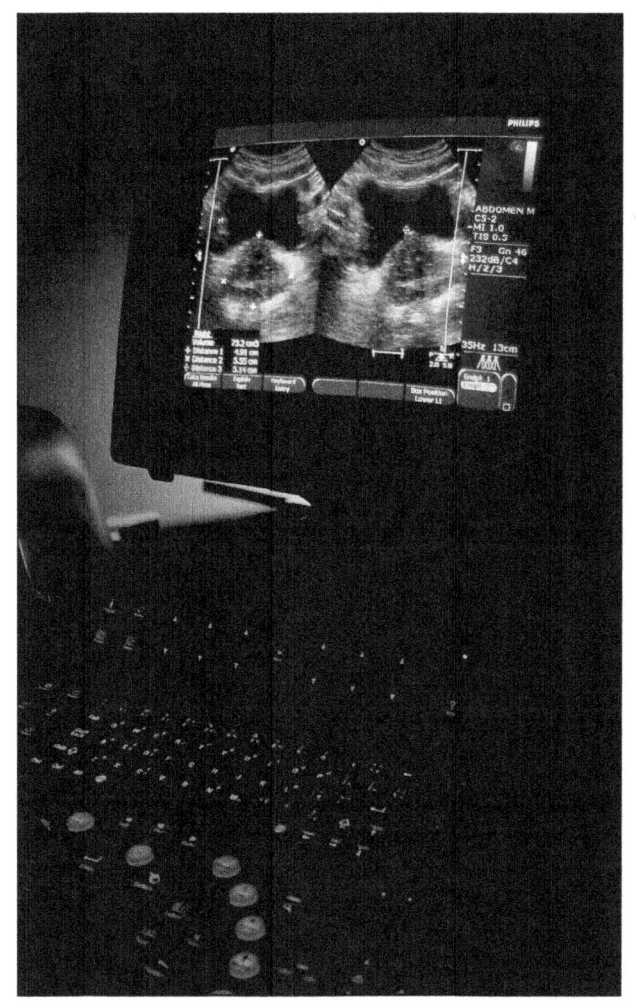

Ultrasound representation of urinary bladder (black butterfly-like shape) with a hyperplastic prostate. An example of engineering science and medical science working together. Photo by Etan J. Tal, via Wikimedia Commons.

maceutical options. Cochlear implants have been designed to be attached to a patient's auditory nerve and can detect sound waves and process them in order to be interpreted by the brain as sound for deaf or hard-of-hearing patients. Patients who have had cataract surgery used to have to wear thick corrective lenses to restore any standard of vision, but with the development of intraocular lenses that can be implanted into the eye, their vision can be restored, often to a better degree than before the cataract developed.

Artificial replacement joints comprise a large portion of medical-implant technology. Patients receive joint replacement when their existing joints no longer function properly or cause significant pain because of arthritis or degeneration. Hundreds of thousands of hip replacements are performed in the United States each year, a number that has grown significantly as the baby boomer portion of the population ages. Artificial joints are normally fastened to the existing bone by cement, but advances in biomechanical engineering have led to a new process called "bone ingrowth," in which the natural bone grows into the porous surface of the replacement joint. Biomechanical engineering contributes considerable knowledge to the design of the artificial joints, the materials from which they are made, the surgical procedure used, fixation techniques, failure mechanisms, and prediction of the lifetime of the replacement joints.

The development of computer-aided design (CAD) and computer-aided manufacturing (CAM) proved to particularly crucial to the field of medical implant design, as CAD programs facilitated the design of implants customized to fit the unique body of the recipient, at times by incorporating anatomical data gleaned through computed tomography (CT) scans or other forms of medical imaging. The resulting implants could subsequently be manufactured via three-dimensional (3D) printing technology or through traditional means. The advent of CAD has likewise allowed biomechanical engineers to create complex models of organs and systems that can provide advanced analysis and instant feedback. This information provides insight into the development of designs for artificial organs that align with or improve on the mechanical properties of biological organs. Biomechanical engineering can provide predictive values to medical professionals, which can help them develop a profile that better forecasts patient outcomes and complications. An example of this is using finite element analysis in the evaluation of aortic-wall stress, which can remove some of the unpredictability of expansion and rupture of an abdominal aortic aneurysm. Biomechanical computational methodology and advances in imaging and processing technology have provided increased predictability for life-threatening events.

Nonmedical applications of biomechanical engineering also exist in any facet of industry that impacts human life. Corporations employ individuals or teams to use engineering principles to translate the scientifically proven principles into commercially viable products or new technological platforms. Biomechanical engineers also design and build experimental testing devices to evaluate a product's performance and safety before it reaches the marketplace, or they suggest more economically efficient design options. Biomechanical engineers also use ergonomic principles to develop new ideas and create new products, such as car seats, backpacks, or even specialized equipment and clothing for elite athletes, military personnel, or astronauts.

SOCIAL CONTEXT AND FUTURE PROSPECTS

The diversity of studying the relationship between living structure and function has opened up vast opportunities in science, health care, and industry. In addition to conventional implant and replacement devices, the demand is growing for implantable tissues for cosmetic surgery, such as breast and tissue implants, as well as implantable devices to aid in weight loss, such as gastric banding.

Reports of biomechanical engineering triumphs and discoveries often appear in the mainstream media, making the general public more aware of the scientific work being done and how it impacts daily life. Sports fans learn about the equipment, training, and rehabilitation techniques designed by biomechanical engineers that allow their favorite athletes to break performance records and return to work sooner after being injured or having surgery. The public is accessing more information about their own health options than ever before, and they are becoming knowledgeable about the range of treatments available to them and the pros and cons of each.

Biomechanical engineering and biotechnology is an area that is experiencing accelerated growth, and billions of dollars are being funneled into research and development annually. This growth is expected to continue.

—*April D. Ingram, BSc*

Further Reading

"Biomechanics." *Engineering in Medicine and Biology Society*, 2018, www.embs.org/about-biomedical-engineering/our-areas-of-research/biomechanics/. Accessed 28 Nov. 2021.

Ethier, C. Ross, and Craig A. Simmons. *Introductory Biomechanics: From Cells to Organisms*. Cambridge UP, 2007.

Hall, Susan J. *Basic Biomechanics*. 9th ed., McGraw-Hill, 2021.

Hamill, Joseph, Kathleen M. Knutzen, and Timothy R. Derrick. *Biomechanical Basis of Human Movement*. 5th ed., Wolters Kluwer, 2021.

Hayenga, Heather N., and Helim Aranda-Espinoza. *Biomaterials Mechanics*. CRC Press, 2017.

Memon, Afaque Rafique, Enpeng Wang, Junlei Hu, Jan Egger, and Xiaojun Chen. "A Review on Computer-Aided Design and Manufacturing of Patient-Specific Maxillofacial Implants." *Expert Review of Medical Devices*, vol. 17, no. 4, 2020, pp. 345-56.

Özkaya, Nihat, David Goldsheyder, and Margareta Nordin. *Fundamentals of Biomechanics: Equilibrium, Motion, and Deformation*. 4th ed., Springer International Publishing, 2018.

Peterson, Donald R., and Joseph D. Bronzino, editors. *Biomechanics: Principles and Practices*. CRC Press, 2017.

Prendergast, Patrick, editor. *Biomechanical Engineering: From Biosystems to Implant Technology*. Elsevier, 2007.

Bridge Design and Barodynamics

ABSTRACT

Barodynamics is the study of the mechanics of heavy structures that may collapse under their own weight. In bridge building, barodynamics is the science of the support and mechanics of the methods and types of materials used in bridge design to ensure the stability of the structure. Concepts to consider in avoiding the collapse of a bridge are the materials available for use, what type of terrain will hold the bridge, the obstacle to be crossed (such as river or chasm), how long the bridge needs to be to cross the obstacle, what types of natural obstacles or disasters are likely to occur in the area (high winds, earthquakes), the purpose of the bridge (foot traffic, cars, railway), and what type of vehicles will need to cross the bridge.

DEFINITION AND BASIC PRINCIPLES

Barodynamics is a key component of any bridge design. Bridges are made of heavy materials, and many concepts, such as tension and compression of building materials, and other factors, such as wind shear, torsion, and water pressure, come into play in bridge building.

Bridge designers and constructors must keep in mind the efficiency (the least amount of material for the highest-level performance) and economy (lowest possible costs while still retaining efficiency) of bridge building. In addition, some aesthetic principles must be followed; public outcry can occur when a bridge is thought to be "ugly." Conversely, a beautiful bridge can become a landmark symbol for an area, such as the Golden Gate Bridge has become for San Francisco.

The four main construction materials for bridges are wood, stone, concrete (including prestressed concrete), and iron (from which steel is made). Wood is nearly always available and inexpensive but is comparatively weak in compression and tension. Stone, another often available material, is strong in compression but weak in tension. Concrete, or "artificial stone," is, like stone, strong in tension and weak in compression.

The first type of iron used in bridges, cast iron, is strong in compression but weak in tension. The use of wrought iron helped in bridge building, as it is strong in compression but still has tensile strength.

Steel, a further refinement of iron, is superior in compression and tensile strength, making it a preferred material for bridge building. Reinforced concrete or prestressed concrete (types of concrete with steel bars running through concrete beams) are also popular bridge-building materials because of their strength and lighter-weight design.

BACKGROUND AND HISTORY

From the beginning of their existence, humans have constructed bridges to cross obstacles such as rivers and chasms using the materials at hand, such as trees, stones, or vines. In China during the third century BCE, the emperor of the Qin Dynasty built canals to transport goods, but when these canals interfered with existing roads, his engineers built bridges of stone or wood over these canals.

However, the history of barodynamics in bridge building truly begins in Roman times, when Roman engineers perfected the keystone arch. In addition to the keystone and arch concepts, the Romans improved bridge-building materials such as cement and concrete and invented the cofferdam so that underwater pilings could be made for bridges. These engineers built a network of bridges throughout the Roman empire to keep communication with and transportation to and from Rome intact. The Romans made bridges of stone because of its durability, and many of these bridges remained intact into the twenty-first century.

In the Middle Ages, bridges were an important part of travel and transportation of goods, and many bridges were constructed during this period to support heavy traffic. This is also the period when peo-

CAD software offered new flexibility in the design and modifying of bridge models. Photo via iStock/ehrlif. [Used under license.]

ple began to live in houses built on bridges, in part because in walled cities, places to build homes were limited. Possibly the most famous inhabited bridge was London Bridge, the world's first stone bridge to be built over a tidal waterway where the water rose and fell considerably every twelve hours. However, in Paris in the sixteenth century, there were at least five inhabited bridges over the Seine to the Île de la Cité.

The first iron bridge was built in 1779. Using this material changed the entire bridge-building industry because of the size and strength of structure that became possible. In the 1870s, a fall in the price of steel made bridges made of this material even more popular, and in 1884, Gustave Eiffel, of Eiffel Tower fame, designed a steel arch bridge that let wind pass through it, overcoming many of the structural problems with iron and steel that had previously existed. Iron and steel are still the most common materials to use in bridge building.

Suspension bridges began to be quite popular as they are the most inexpensive way to span a longer distance. In the early 1800s, American engineer John Augustus Roebling designed a new method of placing cables on suspension bridges. Famous examples of suspension bridges include the Golden Gate Bridge (completed in 1937) and Roebling's Brooklyn Bridge (completed in 1883).

Girder bridges were often built to carry trains in the early twentieth century. Though capable of carrying heavyweight railroad cars, this type of bridge is usually only built for short distances as is typical with beam-type bridges. In the 1950s, the box girder was designed, allowing air to pass through this type of bridge and making longer girder bridges possible.

While traditional methods of designing and evaluating the safety of bridges proved successful over the centuries, advances in computer technology during the late twentieth and early twenty-first centuries brought with them a host of new tools for bridge design. Perhaps the most valuable new tool was computer-aided design (CAD) software, which offered new means of designing the physical structure and appearance of bridges, creating three-dimensional models, and modifying those designs in response to the needs of a given project. Specialized CAD software for bridge design existed as early as the mid-1980s, when the French civil engineering firm Campenon Bernard developed bridge-design software to be used in house. By the third decade of the twenty-first century, major producers of CAD software such as Autodesk offered specialized software for the design and analysis of bridges.

HOW IT WORKS

The engineering principles that must be used to construct even a simple beam bridge are staggering. Supports must be engineered to hold the weight of the entire structure correctly as well as any traffic that will cross the bridge. The bridge itself, or "span," must be strong enough to bear the weight of traffic and stable enough to keep that traffic safe. Spans must be kept as short as reasonably possible but must sometimes be built across long distances, for example, over deep water.

Arch. The Roman arch concept uses the pressure of gravity on the material forming the arch to hold the bridge together with the outward thrust contained by buttresses. It carries loads by compressing and exerting pressure on the foundation, which must be prevented from settling and sliding. This concept allowed bridges to be built that were longer than ever before. For example, a surviving bridge over the Tagus River in Spain has two central arches that are 110 feet wide and 210 feet above the water level. These arches are made of uncemented granite, and each keystone weighs 8 tons. This type of bridge is constructed by building a huge timber structure to support the bridge during the building phase, then winching blocks into place with a pulley system. After the keystone to the arch is put into place, the scaffolding is removed, leaving the bridge to stand alone.

Beam. This is the most common form of bridge and may be as simple as a log across a stream. This type of bridge carries a load by bending, which horizontally compresses the top of the beam and simultaneously causes horizontal tension on the bottom of the beam.

Truss. A truss bridge is popular because it requires a relatively small amount of construction material to carry a heavy load. It works like a beam bridge, carrying loads by bending and causing compression and tension in the vertical and diagonal supports.

Suspension. Suspension bridges are essentially steel-rope bridges: thick steel cables are entwined like ropes into a larger and stronger steel cable or rope. These thick, strong cables then suspend the bridge itself between pylons that support the weight of the bridge. A suspension bridge can be thought of as an upside-down arch, as the curved cables use tension and compression to support the load.

Cantilever. Cantilevered means something that projects outward and is supported at only one end (similar to a diving board). This type of bridge is generally made with three spans with the outside spans supported on the shore and the middle span supported by the outside spans. This is a type of beam bridge that uses tension in the lower spans and compression in the upper span to carry a load.

Pontoon. A pontoon bridge is built across water with materials that float. Each pontoon, or floating object, can support a maximum load equal to the amount of water it displaces. If the load placed on one pontoon-supported section exceeds the water displaced, the pontoon will submerge and cause the entire bridge to sink.

APPLICATIONS AND PRODUCTS

Bridges are continuously being built to cross physical obstacles, and as the nature of materials changes, the ability to cross even larger obstacles becomes reality. Nature is the defining force on a bridge; most bridges fail because of flooding or other natural disasters.

Improvements in building materials are ongoing. For example, the Jakway Park Bridge in Buchanan County, Iowa, was the first bridge in North America to be built with ultrahigh performance concrete (UHPC) with pi-girders. This moldable material combines high compressive strength and flexibility and offers a wide range of design possibilities. It is very durable and has low permeability.

Bridge-building products may even be developed that help the environment. For example, the rebuilt I-35W bridge in Minnesota, completed in 2008, uses a concrete that is said to "eat smog." The concrete contains photocatalytic titanium dioxide, which accelerates the decomposition of organic material. Similarly innovative materials, such as self-healing concrete, may change the future of bridge building.

CAREERS AND COURSEWORK

Those who engineer and design bridges may have backgrounds in a variety of fields, including architecture and design. However, those who are involved in the barodynamic aspects of bridge building are engineers, usually either civil engineers, materials, or mechanical engineers. Earning a degree in one of these fields is required to get the training needed in geology, math, and physics to learn about the physical limitations and considerations in bridge building. Many bridge engineers have advanced degrees in a specific related field. After earning a degree, a candidate for this type of job usually works for a few years as an assistant engineer in a sort of apprenticeship, learning the specifics of bridge building such as drafting, blueprint reading, surveying, and stabilization of materials. To become a professional engineer (PE), one must then take a series of written exams to get his or her license.

SOCIAL CONTEXT AND FUTURE PROSPECTS

Barodynamics is a rapidly changing field. As new materials are created and existing materials change, the possibilities for future improvements in this field increase. Development of future lightweight materials may change the way bridges are engineered and designed to make the structure stable and avoid collapse. Just as innovations in iron refinement changed the face of bridge building in the late 1800s, new materials may refine and improve bridge building even further, bringing more efficient and economical bridges.

Materials engineers are usually the people who provide the technological innovation to create these kinds of new materials. They examine materials on the molecular level to understand how materials can be improved and strengthened in order to provide better building materials for structures such as bridges. Possible future bridge-building materials include ceramics, polymers, and other composites. Two other rapidly growing materials fields that may affect bridge barodynamics are biomaterials and nanomaterials.

—*Marianne M. Madsen, MS*

Further Reading

Blockley, David. *Bridges: The Science and Art of the World's Most Inspiring Structures*. Oxford UP, 2010.

Fu, Chung C., and Shuqing Wang. *Computational Analysis and Design of Bridge Structures*. CRC Press, 2015.

Gaudin, Sharon. "WPI Researcher Develops Self-Healing Concrete That Could Multiply Structures' Lifespans, Slash Damaging CO2 Emissions." *WPI*, 8 June 2021, www.wpi.edu/news/wpi-researcher-develops-self-healing-concrete-could-multiply-structures-lifespans-slash. Accessed 28 Nov. 2021.

Pipinato, Alessio, editor. *Innovative Bridge Design Handbook: Construction, Rehabilitation, and Maintenance*. 2nd ed., Elsevier, 2021.

Tonias, Demetrios E., and Jim J. Zhao. *Bridge Engineering: Design, Rehabilitation, and Maintenance of Modern Highway Bridges*. 4th ed., McGraw-Hill, 2017.

Unsworth, John F. *Design and Construction of Modern Steel Railway Bridges*. 2nd ed., CRC Press, 2018.

Yanev, Bojidar. *Bridge Management*. Wiley, 2007.

Building Information Modeling (BIM)

ABSTRACT

Building information modeling (BIM) is a field within architecture, design, and construction that focuses on creating, altering, and managing digital representations of buildings and other structures. BIM involves the use of modeling software and is considered an evolution of computer-aided design (CAD) as well as a superior alternative to two-dimensional (2D) CAD, which uses software to produce 2D models of physical structures.

Unlike traditional CAD, BIM models are parametric, meaning that each element of the design can be linked to each other element so that any change made to the design or plan affects all parts of the overall design. BIM models typically have an informational layer that can be used to integrate data about pricing and sourcing, maintenance, deterioration, thermal conservation, and energy usage. Data associated with a BIM model can also be integrated in such a way that the information changes automatically if the model is altered.

BRIEF HISTORY

Building information modeling (BIM) is one of several computer-aided design models used by engineers, architects, and contractors working on construction and design projects. BIM is a form of computer design and is an evolution of the first digital design programs. The first computer-aided design (CAD) program was Sketchpad, developed in 1963 by Ivan Sutherland. The program used a light pen and a button interface to allow users to draw designs on a computer screen. When personal computers became a reality in the 1980s, the first practical digital design programs began to appear.

Building information model of a mechanical room developed from lidar data. Image by Oregon State University, via Wikimedia Commons.

Charles Eastman was the first to propose creating a three-dimensional architecture system with linked data files. He first wrote about the concept in a 1974 paper and later received funding to begin working on the project. The Building Description System (BDS), a database that contained a library of building elements and was searchable by factors such as building material, cost, supplier, or subcontractor, was his first step.

Eastman went on to design the Graphical Language for Interactive Design (GLIDE) program in 1977, which contained many of the elements that became standard in later BIM programs. In 1982, the company Autodesk released its first version of AutoCAD software using 2D design. The next major step in the development of BIM came from Budapest, Hungary, where physicist Gábor Bojár launched the ArchiCAD system in 1984. ArchiCAD used many of the same elements as Eastman's BDS system and was considered a major technical leap forward, though the lack of widespread personal computer use limited the adoption of the program and many architecture firms continued to use traditional CAD programs.

The personal computer explosion of the 1990s led to the development of a host of new BIM programs. Advancements in the complexity of computer processing and data storage allowed new versions of BIM software to incorporate more detailed data management systems, making BIM more practical for commercial use.

OVERVIEW

While architects and engineers differentiate between BIM and CAD, both are models for creating and modifying three-dimensional (3D) data about physical structures. BIM software available by 2021 integrated drawing and visualization tools that are part of CAD programs but tended to include additional functionality that is not present in traditional CAD software.

One of the major advantages of BIM systems is the use of a parametric method for representing the relationship between objects. Traditional CAD systems tend to use explicit or coordinate-based models that treat each object as an individual, separate structure. By contrast, BIM systems are parametric, meaning that each element is modeled according to behaviors and attributes that are linked to every other element. If a designer changes the pitch, weight, thickness, or other qualities assigned to a roof, for instance, the other elements of the design automatically change as a result.

BIM systems also typically include data files associated with each component. In a BIM model, a wall will have an associated list that can show the materials needed for the project, the time needed to complete the component, the sourcing of materials, and a variety of other parameters. If a wall is supposed to have a door, the list connected to the wall will contain what designers call a "door schedule" that plans when the door is supposed to be installed within the wall. The data lists in BIM models are similarly linked to every related component in the model so that the lists automatically update whenever changes are made to any related element in the design.

While BIM systems are often described as 3D, some architects and designers see BIM as "n-dimensional," meaning that additional dimensions can be modeled within the program. In addition to the three physical dimensions, BIM models can also integrate and model other aspects of the project that include the time needed for completion of individual components as well as the entire project, cost and maintenance of the project, and even estimates of how use will affect the structure.

By 2021, architects and engineers often used BIM for projects with specific needs or goals. When constructing a concert venue, engineers, designers, and contractors can use BIM programs to model the acoustic properties of components, materials, and rooms within a structure. Similarly, BIM modeling can help estimate factors including thermal and electrical conservation, energy use, and the environmental impact of materials. All of this information and any changes can be shared with the entire team working on the project, keeping the planning and building process smooth and updated.

Despite significant advantages, the widespread adoption of BIM systems only began in the 2010s, due partly to the complexity of earlier BIM software and conservatism in the building industry that inspired loyalty to the AutoCAD methodology. One of the trends in BIM design is for contractors and designers to use BIM models to involve the consumer in the design process. Using a BIM model, a contractor can demonstrate alterations or options to a customer.

—*Micah L. Issitt*

Further Reading
Bergin, Michael. "A Brief History of BIM." *ArchDaily*, 7 Dec. 2012, www.archdaily.com/302490/a-brief-history-of-bim. Accessed 28 Nov. 2021.
Borrmann, André, Markus König, Christian Koch, and Jakob Beetz, editors. *Building Information Modeling: Technology Foundations and Industry Practice*. Springer International Publishing, 2018.
Deutsch, Randy. *BIM and Integrated Design: Strategies for Architectural Practice*. Wiley, 2011.
Goldstein, Phil. "What Is Building Information Modeling Technology in Government?" *FedTech*, 16 June 2020, fedtechmagazine.com/article/2020/06/what-building-information-modeling-technology-government-perfcon. Accessed 28 Nov. 2021.
Hardin, Brad, and Dave McCool. *BIM and Construction Management: Proven Tools, Methods, and Workflows*. 2nd ed., Wiley, 2015.
Kensek, Karen M., and Douglas E. Noble. *Building Information Modeling: BIM in Current and Future Practice*. Wiley, 2014.
Knapp, Chris. "Forward History: Practice Beyond BIM." *ArchitectureAU*, 5 Apr. 2013, architectureau.com/articles/forward-history-practice-beyond-bim/. Accessed 28 Nov. 2021.

Sacks, Rafael, Chuck Eastman, Ghang Lee, and Paul Teicholz. *BIM Handbook: A Guide to Building Information Modeling for Owners, Designers, Engineers, Contractors, and Facility Managers*. 3rd ed., Wiley, 2018.

"3D-4D Building Information Modeling." *US General Services Administration*, 4 Sept. 2020, www.gsa.gov/real-estate/design-construction/3d4d-building-information-modeling. Accessed 28 Nov. 2021.

C

CATIA

ABSTRACT
CATIA is a proprietary software product developed and marketed by Dassault Systèmes and focused on three-dimensional computer-aided design. Through the 3DEXPERIENCE cloud platform, CATIA can integrate with a range of engineering, simulation, and manufacturing tools.

ORIGINS OF CATIA
CATIA has its roots in the aerospace industry and specifically in the French aerospace company Dassault Aviation, known during the 1960s and 1970s as Avions Marcel Dassault and later Avions Marcel Dassault—Breguet Aviation. In the late 1960s, Dassault Aviation began to investigate the possibility of using computers in the design and manufacturing process after obtaining the company's first two IBM 1800 computer systems. Within a matter of years, the company had established a dedicated team of engineers tasked with developing computer-aided design (CAD) and computer-aided manufacturing (CAM) systems to be used for the development of aircraft bodies. To that end, Dassault Aviation in 1975 licensed the Computer-graphics Augmented Design and Manufacturing (CADAM) product that had originally been developed by the US-based Lockheed Corporation. CADAM, however, did not meet all of Dassault Aviation's unique needs, and the company subsequently began to develop its own proprietary CAD software for in-house use.

In 1977, work began on a proprietary three-dimensional (3D) CAD product named Conception Assistée Tridimensionnelle Interactive (CATI). The product would later be renamed Conception Assistée Tridimensionnelle Interactive Appliquée (CATIA) and referred to as Computer-Graphics Aided Three-dimensional Interactive Application in English-speaking countries. In 1981, the team working on CATIA was split off from Dassault Aviation to form a new company, Dassault Systèmes, under the leadership of Francis Bernard, one of the engineers who had led the development of the software. Rather than continuing to work on in-house CAD systems, Dassault Systèmes was tasked with developing CATIA into a commercial software product that could be licensed for use by other companies, much as Dassault Aviation had previously purchased a license for CADAM.

CATIA SOFTWARE
Announced in 1981, the debut commercial version of CATIA, CATIA Version 1, officially entered the market by the following year. While the initial version of CATIA focused primarily on 3D CAD, two-dimensional (2D) CAD functionality was added to CATIA Version 2, which was released in 1984. Initial incarnations of CATIA ran exclusively on mainframe computers. However, CATIA Version 3, launched in 1988, could be used on both mainframe computers and on some workstations running the UNIX operating system. Later releases of that version, including Version 3 Release 2, were compatible with a wider range of workstations and offered enhanced functionality. Version 4 debuted in 1993, and Version 5, better known as V5, was launched in 1999. CATIA V5 was the first version of the product to be compatible with some Windows workstations,

and it notably offered enhanced product lifecycle management (PLM) functions.

In keeping with its origins, CATIA was popular in the aerospace industry from early on, with early clients including Dassault Systèmes' progenitor, Dassault Aviation, as well as the aerospace company Grumman. The product came into use at Boeing by the mid-1980s and was similarly adopted by a number of major companies in the automotive industry, including BMW and Honda. CATIA likewise became a commonly implemented CAD solution in a variety of other fields, including architecture and product design. While Dassault Systèmes acquired several additional CAD, CAM, and computer-aided engineering (CAE) software products over the decades, including SolidWorks in 1997, CATIA remained a core brand for the company into the early twenty-first century.

CLOUD SERVICES

A popular CAD solution throughout the first decade of the twenty-first century, CATIA took on new significance the following decade when it became one of the first major CAD products to be integrated into a cloud-computing platform. In 2012, Dassault Systèmes launched the 3DEXPERIENCE platform, a cloud-based means of accessing Dassault products such as CATIA and SolidWorks. 3DEXPERIENCE CATIA was designed to facilitate collaboration among professionals working in different physical locations as well as integration of design tools such as CATIA with Dassault Systèmes' range of computer-aided engineering, simulation, manufacturing, and marketing products. As of early 2022, the 3DEXPERIENCE cloud platform operated on a subscription-based, software-as-a-service (SaaS) model that allowed for automatic updates and the integration of new tools, features, and services as they were developed. One such feature, the 3DEXPERIENCE Marketplace, launched in 2018 for the purpose of connecting designers with manufacturing companies that could produce physical versions of the objects being designed. The 3DEXPERIENCE Marketplace also encompassed a PartSupply catalogue, from which designers could choose digital models of components to incorporate into their designs.

In the years following the debut of the 3DEXPERIENCE platform, Dassault Systèmes also continued to offer customers the non-cloud-based CATIA V5 product, new releases of which were published on a regular basis throughout that period. While the company sought to allow customers to transition easily between the V5 and 3DEXPERIENCE incarnations of CATIA, there were some technical challenges that for several years made moving between the two systems a difficult task. In 2018, however, Dassault Systèmes introduced its PLM Collaboration Services gateway, a gateway through which users of CATIA V5 could access a range of 3DEXPERIENCE tools. Both CATIA V5 and 3DEXPERIENCE CATIA remained available to designers by early 2022. Other products offered under the CATIA brand at that time included CATIA Magic, a product based on systems engineering solutions brought under the CATIA umbrella through Dassault Systèmes' 2018 acquisition of the software developer No Magic, and CATIA Composer, a tool for creating product documentation and other deliverables.

—*Joy Crelin*

Further Reading

Bernard, Francis. "How the Inventor of CATIA Became the Founder of Dassault Systèmes." *Isicad*, 3 Mar. 2021, isicad.net/articles.php?article_num=21729. Accessed 10 Jan. 2022.

———. *A Short History of CATIA & Dassault Systemes*. Bernard, 2003.

"CATIA." *Dassault Systèmes*, 2021, www.3ds.com/products-services/catia/. Accessed 10 Jan. 2022.

"CATIA CAD/CAM/CAE System Version 3 Release 2 Overview." *IBM*, 2 Oct. 1990, www.ibm.com/common/ssi/cgi-bin/ssialias?appname=skmwww&htmlfid=897%2FENUS290-643&infotype=AN&mhq=service%20

initializer&mhsrc=ibmsearch_a&subtype=CA. Accessed 10 Jan. 2022.

"History." *Dassault Systèmes*, 2021, www.3ds.com/about-3ds/what-we-are/history. Accessed 10 Jan. 2022.

"Moving from CATIA V5 to 3DEXPERIENCE CATIA." *Dassault Systèmes*, 2021, www.3ds.com/3dexperience/cloud/moving-catia-v5-3dexperience-catia. Accessed 10 Jan. 2022.

Ogewell, Verdi. "Dassault Launches Long-Awaited Migration Bridge for CATIA V5 to 3DEXPERIENCE." *Engineering.com*, 20 Nov. 2018, www.engineering.com/story/dassault-launches-long-awaited-migration-bridge-for-catia-v5-to-3dexperience. Accessed 10 Jan. 2022.

Weisberg, David E. "Chapter 13: IBM, Lockheed and Dassault Systèmes." *The Engineering Design Revolution: The People, Companies and Computer Systems That Changed Forever the Practice of Engineering*. Weisberg, 2008, www.cadhistory.net/13%20IBM,%20Lockheed%20and%20Dassault.pdf. Accessed 10 Jan. 2022.

CELL AND TISSUE ENGINEERING

ABSTRACT

Cell and tissue engineering are fields dedicated to discovering the mechanisms that underlie cellular function and organization to develop biological or hybrid biological and nonbiological substitutes to restore or improve cellular tissues. The most immediate goal of cell and tissue engineering is to allow physicians to replace damaged or failing tissues within the body. The field was first recognized as a distinct branch of bioengineering in the 1980s and has since grown to attract participation from numerous medical and biological disciplines.

Engineered cellular materials may be used to grow new tissue within a patient's heart or to replace damaged bone, cartilage, or other tissues. In addition, research into the mechanisms affecting cellular organization and development may aid in the treatment of congenital and developmental disorders. Cell and tissue engineering has developed in conjunction with stem cell research and is therefore subject to debate over the ethics of stem cell research.

DEFINITION AND BASIC PRINCIPLES

Cell and tissue engineering is a branch of bioengineering concerned with two basic goals: studying and understanding the processes that control and contribute to cell and tissue organization and developing substitutes to replace or improve existing tissues in an organism. Substitute tissues can be composed either of biological materials or of a blend of biological and nonbiological materials.

The basic goal of cell and tissue engineering is to create more effective treatments for tissue degeneration and damage resulting from congenital disorders, disease, and injury. Engineers may, for instance, introduce foreign tissues that have been modified to stimulate healing within the patient's own tissues, or they may implant synthetic structures that help control and stimulate cellular development. Another goal in cell and tissue engineering is to create tissues that are resistant to rejection from the host organism's immune system. Rejection is one of the primary difficulties in organ transplantation and limb replacement surgery.

One of the basic principles of cell and tissue engineering is to use and enhance an organism's innate regenerative capacity. Engineers therefore examine the ways that tissues grow and change during development. Using cutting-edge development in genomics and gene therapy, engineers are working to develop ways to stimulate a patient's immune system and enhance healing.

Cell and tissue engineering have a wide variety of potential applications. In addition to creating new therapies, engineering principles can be used to create new methods for delivering drugs and engineered cells to target locations within a patient. The potential applications of cell and tissue engineering depend on the capability to create cultures of cells and tissues to use for experimentation and transplantation. Research on cell growth is a major facet of the bioengineering field.

BACKGROUND AND HISTORY

Cell and tissue engineering emerged from a field of study known as "regenerative medicine," a branch concerned with developing and using methods to enhance the regenerative properties of tissues involved in the healing process. Ultimately, cell and tissue engineering became most closely associated with transplant medicine and surgery.

Medical historians have found documents from as early as 1825 recording the successful transplantation of skin. The first complete organ transplants occurred in the 1950s, and the first heart transplant was completed successfully in 1964.

The science of cell and tissue engineering arose from attempts to combat the problems that affect transplantation, including scarcity of organs and frequent issues involving rejection by the host's immune system. In the 1970s and 1980s, scientists began working on ways to build artificial or semiartificial substitutes for organ transplants. Most early work in tissue engineering involved the search for a suitable artificial substitute for skin grafts.

By the mid-1980s, physicians were using semisynthetic compounds to anchor and guide transplanted tissues. The first symposium for tissue engineering was held in 1988, by which time the field had adherents around the world. The rapid advance of research into the human genome and genetic medicine in the mid-1990s had a considerable effect on bioengineering. In the twenty-first century, cell and tissue engineers work closely with genetic engineers in an effort to create new and better tissue substitutes.

HOW IT WORKS

Broadly speaking, cell and tissue engineering involves creating cell cultures and tissues that are introduced to an organism to repair damaged or degenerated tissues. There are a wide variety of techniques and specific applications for cell and tissue engineering, ranging from cellular manipulation at the chemical or genetic level to the creation of artificial organs for transplant.

Most cell and tissue engineering methods share several common procedures. First, scientists must produce cells or tissues. Next, engineers must tell the cells what to do. This can be done in a variety of ways, from physically manipulating cellular development and tissue formation to altering the genes of cells in such a way as to direct their function. Finally, engineered tissues and cells must be integrated into the body of the host organism under controlled conditions to limit the potential for rejection. Cell and tissue engineering can be divided into two main categories, *in vitro* engineering and *in vivo* engineering.

In vitro engineering. *In vitro* engineering is the development of cell cultures and tissues outside of the body in a controlled laboratory environment. This method has several advantages. Producing tissues in a laboratory has the potential for growing large amounts of tissue and eventually entire organs. This could help solve a major issue with transplant surgery: the scarcity of viable organs for transplantation. Scientists can more precisely control the growing environment and can therefore exert greater control over developing cells and tissues. *In vitro* engineering allows engineers to modify and adjust cellular properties without the need for surgery or invasive techniques.

In vitro engineering is commonly used in the creation of skin tissues, cartilage, and some bone replacement tissues. Although *in vitro* techniques have certain advantages, they have serious drawbacks, including a higher rejection rate for cells and tissues created *in vitro*. In addition, there are physiological advantages to engineering within the host organism's body, including the presence of accessible cellular nutrients.

In addition to practicing established techniques for producing tissues *in vitro*, some researchers in the first decades of the twenty-first century focused their energies on a technique known as "bioprinting." With the assistance of computer-aided design (CAD) software and computer-aided manufacturing (CAM) technology such as specialized three-dimensional (3D) printers, researchers used the process of additive manufacturing to print thin layers of living tissue. Researchers suggested that bioprinted tissues could be used for a variety of purposes in the future, including for transplantation and the testing of pharmaceuticals. Some researchers likewise proposed that advances in bioprinting could one day facilitate the laboratory-based production of complete, functioning human organs.

In vivo engineering. *In vivo* engineering is the family of techniques that involves creating engineered cellular cultures or tissues within the host's body. It involves the use of chemicals to alter cellular function and the use of synthetic materials that interact with the host's body to stimulate or direct cellular growth.

In vivo procedures typically involve introducing only minor changes to the host's internal environment, and therefore, these tissues are more likely to be resistant to rejection. In addition, working *in vivo* allows engineers to take full advantage of the host's existing cellular networks and the physiological environment of the body. The body provides the essential nutrients, exchange of materials, and disposal of waste, helping create healthy tissues.

The primary disadvantages of the *in vivo* approach are that engineers have less direct control over the development of the cells and tissues and cannot make exact changes to the microenvironment during development. In addition, *in vivo* engineering does not allow for the production of mass quantities of cells and is therefore not an avenue toward addressing the shortage of available tissues and organs for transplant.

APPLICATIONS AND PRODUCTS

Hundreds of bioengineers are working around the world, and they have created a wide variety of applications using cell and tissue engineering research. Among the most promising applications are cell matrices and bioartificial organ assistance devices.

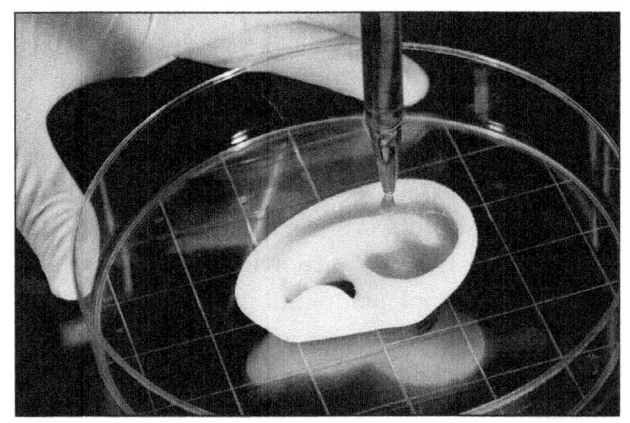

Regenerating a human ear using a scaffold. Photo by Army Medicine, via Wikimedia Commons.

Cell matrices. In an effort to improve the success of tissue transplants, bioengineers have developed a method for using artificial matrices, also called "scaffolds," to control and direct the growth of new tissues. Using cutting-edge microengineering techniques and materials, engineers create three-dimensional structures that are implanted into an organism and thereafter serve as a "guide" for developing tissues.

The scaffold acts like an extracellular matrix that anchors growing cells. New cells anchor to the artificial matrix rather than to the organism's own extracellular material, allowing engineers to exert control over the eventual size, shape, and function of the new tissue. In addition, scaffolds can aid in the diffusion of resources within the growing tissue and can help engineers direct the placement of functional cells, as the scaffold can be installed directly at the site of an injury.

Matrices may be constructed from a variety of materials, including entirely synthetic combinations of polymers and other structures that are created from derivatives of the extracellular matrix. Many researchers have been designing scaffolds that dissolve as the tissues form and are then absorbed into the organism. These biodegradable scaffolds allow engineers to avoid further surgical procedures to remove implanted material.

Cellular scaffolds represent a middle ground between *in vivo* and *in vitro* engineering. Engineers can create a scaffold in a laboratory environment and can allow tissue to anchor and grow around the matrix before implantation, or they can place a scaffold in their target area within the organism and allow the organism's own cells to populate the matrix.

Scaffolds have been used successfully in cardiac repair, especially in conjunction with stem cells. A scaffold seeded with stem cells may be implanted directly into a heart valve, roughly at the site where a cardiac infarction has occurred. The scaffold then directs the growing cells toward the injured area and facilitates regeneration of damaged tissue.

Artificial matrices have also been successful in treating disorders that affect the kidney, bone, and cartilage. Researchers are hopeful that cellular scaffolds could eventually allow the creation of entire organs by coaxing cells to develop around a scaffold designed as an organ template.

Bioartificial organs. One of the major areas of research in tissue engineering is the creation of machines that assist organs damaged by disease or injury. Made from a combination of synthetic and organic materials, these machines are sometimes called "bioartificial devices."

One of the most promising organ assistance devices is the bioartificial liver (BAL), which has been developed to help patients suffering from congenital liver disease, acute liver failure, and other metabolic disorders affecting the liver. The BAL consists of cells incorporated into a bioreactor, which is a small machine that provides an environment conducive to biological processes. Cells growing within the BAL receive optimal nutrients and are exposed to hormones and growth factors to stimulate development. The bioreactor is also designed to facilitate the delivery of any chemicals produced by the developing tissues to surrounding areas.

The BAL performs some of the functions usually performed by the liver: It processes blood, removes impurities, produces proteins, and aids in the synthesis of digestive enzymes. The BAL is not intended to permanently replace the liver but rather to supplement liver function or to allow a patient to survive until a liver transplant can be arranged. The bioartificial liver enables patients to forgo dialysis treatments, and some researchers hope to develop BAL devices that may function as a permanent replacement for patients in need of dialysis.

Researchers are working on bioartificial kidney devices that would aid patients with diabetes and other disorders leading to kidney failure. Again, the bioartificial kidney devices are bioreactors, using stem cells and kidney cells to perform some of the purification and detoxification functions of the kidney. Researchers are also developing bioartificial devices to treat disorders of the pancreas and the heart and to help patients suffering from nervous system or circulatory disorders. Taken as a whole, the development of organ assistance devices may be a step toward the development of bioartificial devices that can function to fully replace a patient's malfunctioning organ.

CAREERS AND COURSEWORK

Students interested in cell and tissue engineering might start at the undergraduate level, working toward a degree in biology or biochemistry, with a focus on cellular biology. Students might also enter the bioengineering field with a background in engineering, though students will still need a significant background in biology and medical science. Knowledge of CAD and 3D printing technology will also prove useful to students interested in the developing technique of bioprinting.

After achieving an undergraduate education, students can progress in the field by pursuing graduate studies in cell biology, bioengineering, or related fields. Many professionals working in other disciplines, such as orthopedic medicine, dermatology, and cardiac surgery may also become involved with cell and tissue engineering during their careers. Graduate institutions are increasingly trying to introduce programs that focus on cell and tissue engineering.

Professionals seeking work in the cell and tissue engineering field can seek employment with nonprofit research institutions, such as those in many universities. Positions in universities are generally funded by a combination of public and private funding. Additionally, those interested in bioengineering careers can find employment within a large number of corporations. Biotechnology companies in the United States employ chemists, mechanical engineers, physicians, and individuals trained specifically in bioengineering.

SOCIAL CONTEXT AND FUTURE PROSPECTS

Bioengineering is intended to improve daily life, both for those suffering from injury and illness and for the population at large. Cell and tissue engineers are focusing on ways to replace damaged tissues, providing, for instance, new skin where skin has been destroyed, and technology to supplement the function of essential organs. One of the ultimate goals of the industry is to create artificial organs that can fully and permanently replace damaged organs. Bioengineers are confident that in the future it will be possible to provide patients with a variety of organs, including a heart, liver, or pancreas.

Although most cell and tissue engineers focus on combating physical illness and injury, bioengineering also has the potential to produce technology that will allow humans to improve their functional abilities. At some point, combinations of synthetic computer technology and biological components could be used to improve human visual capacity or to endow humans with more precise access to memory.

Humans are not the only targets for bioengineers, as other organisms may also be altered to improve their basic physiological functions. Take, for instance, a 2008 project from the Australian Center for Plant Functional Genomics in which researchers attempted to bioengineer plants that could withstand higher levels of salt in the soil, a breakthrough that could turn into a major benefit for agriculture. Salt-resistant strains of important agricultural crops could grow where agriculture was previously impossible because of the soil's alkalinity.

As a distinct discipline, bioengineering is relatively new, and scientists have only begun to investigate the potential applications and discoveries possible with further research. As the field has begun to expand, so too have opportunities for scientists, engineers, and physicians interested in exploring the future of medicine and science. The bioengineering field has already created billions in revenue and is still in a state of rapid growth. Universities, hospitals, and biomedical corporations are likely to increase their investment in these emerging technologies and techniques, creating a strong and growing industry for many years to come.

—*Micah L. Issitt*

Further Reading

Douglas, Kenneth. *Bioprinting: To Make Ourselves Anew*. Oxford UP, 2021.

Fay, Cormac D. "Computer-Aided Design and Manufacturing (CAD/CAM) for Bioprinting." *Methods in Molecular Biology*, no. 2140, 2020, pp. 27-41.

Lanza, Robert, Robert Langer, Joseph Vacanti, and Anthony Atala, editors. *Principles of Tissue Engineering*. 5th ed., Academic Press, 2020.

Mataigne, Fen. *Medicine by Design: The Practice and Promise of Biomedical Engineering*. Johns Hopkins UP, 2006.

Mota, Carlos, Sandra Camarero-Espinosa, Matthew B. Baker, Paul Wieringa, and Lorenzo Moroni. "Bioprinting: From Tissue and Organ Development to *in Vitro* Models." *Chemical Reviews*, vol. 120, no. 19, 2020, pp. 10547-607.

"3D Bioprinting of Living Tissues." *Wyss Institute*, 2021, wyss.harvard.edu/technology/3d-bioprinting/. Accessed 28 Nov. 2021.

Yock, Paul G., Stefanos Zenios, Josh Makower, et al., editors. *Biodesign: The Process of Innovating Medical Technologies*. 2nd ed., Cambridge UP, 2015.

CIVIL ENGINEERING

ABSTRACT

Civil engineering is the branch of engineering concerned with the design, construction, and maintenance of fixed structures and systems, such as large buildings, bridges, roads, and other transportation systems, and water supply and wastewater-treatment systems. Civil engineering is the second oldest field of engineering, with the term "civil" initially used to differentiate it from the oldest field of engineering, military engineering. The major subdisciplines within civil engineering are structural, transportation, and environmental engineering. Other possible areas of specialization within civil engineering are geotechnical, hydraulic, construction, and coastal engineering.

DEFINITION AND BASIC PRINCIPLES

Civil engineering is a very broad field of engineering, encompassing subdisciplines ranging from structural engineering to environmental engineering, some of which have also become recognized as separate fields of engineering. For example, while environmental engineering is included as an area of specialization within most civil engineering programs, many colleges offer separate environmental engineering degree programs.

Civil engineering, like engineering in general, is a profession with a practical orientation, having an emphasis on building things and making things work. Civil engineers use their knowledge of the physical sciences, mathematics, engineering sciences, and empirical engineering correlations to design, construct, manage, and maintain structures, transportation infrastructure, and environmental treatment equipment and facilities.

Empirical engineering correlations are equations, graphs, or nomograms that are based on experimental measurements and give relationships among variables of interest for a particular engineering application. Such correlations are important in civil engineering because usable theoretical equations are not available for all the necessary engineering calculations. For example, the Manning formula is an experimental description of the average velocity of a liquid flowing in an open channel, based on the volumetric flow rate, the slope of the channel, the depth of the liquid, and the size, shape, and material of the bottom and sides of the channel. Rivers, irrigation ditches, and concrete channels used to transport wastewater in treatment plants are examples of open channels. Similar empirical relationships are used in transportation engineering, structural engineering, and other specialties within civil engineering.

BACKGROUND AND HISTORY

Civil engineering is the second-oldest field of engineering. The term "civil engineering" came into use in the mid-eighteenth century and initially referred to any practice of engineering by civilians for nonmilitary purposes. Before this time, most large-scale construction projects, such as roads and bridges, were done by military engineers. Early civil engineering projects were in areas such as water supply, roads, bridges, and other large structures—the same type of engineering work that exemplifies civil engineering in modern times.

Although the terminology did not yet exist, civil engineering projects were carried out in early times. Examples include the Egyptian pyramids (about 2700-2500 BCE), well-known Greek structures such as the Parthenon (447-438 BCE), the Great Wall of China (220 BCE), and the many roads, bridges, dams, and aqueducts built throughout the Roman Empire.

Most of the existing fields of engineering split off from civil engineering or one of its offshoots as new fields emerged. For example, the field of mechanical engineering emerged in the early nineteenth century due to the increased use of machines and mechanisms.

HOW IT WORKS

In addition to mathematics, chemistry, and physics, civil engineering makes extensive use of principles from several engineering science subjects: engineering mechanics (statics and strength of materials), soil mechanics, and fluid mechanics.

Engineering mechanics—statics. As implied by the term "statics," this area of engineering concerns objects that are not moving. The fundamental principle of statics is that any stationary object must be in static equilibrium. That is, any force on the object must be canceled out by another force that is equal in magnitude and acting in the opposite direction. There can be no net force in any direction on a stationary object, because if there were, it would not be stationary. The object considered to be in static equilibrium could be an entire structure, or it could be any part of a structure, down to an individual member in a truss. Calculations for an object in static equi-

A multi-level stack interchange, buildings, houses, and park in Shanghai, China. Photo via Wikimedia Commons. [Public domain.]

librium are often done through the use of a free-body diagram, which is a sketch of the object showing all of the external forces acting on it. The principle used for calculations is that the sum of all the horizontal forces acting on the object must be zero and the sum of all the vertical forces acting on the object must also be zero. Working with the forces as vectors helps to find the horizontal and vertical components of forces that are acting on the object from some direction other than horizontal or vertical.

Engineering mechanics—strength of materials. This subject is sometimes called "mechanics of materials." Whereas statics works only with forces external to the body that is in equilibrium, strength of materials uses the same principles and also considers internal forces in a structural member. This is done to determine the required material properties to ensure that the member can withstand the internal stresses that will be placed on it.

Soil mechanics. Knowledge of soil mechanics is needed to design the foundations for structures. Any structure resting on the earth will be supported in some way by the soil beneath it. A properly designed foundation will provide adequate long-term support for the structure above it; inadequate knowledge of soil mechanics or foundation design may lead to something such as the Leaning Tower of Pisa. Topics in soil mechanics include physical properties of soil, compaction, distribution of stress within soil, and flow of water through soil.

Fluid mechanics. Fundamental principles of physics are used for some fluid mechanics calculations. Examples are conservation of mass (called the "continuity equation" in fluid mechanics) and conservation of energy (called the "energy equation" or the "first law of thermodynamics"). Some fluid mechanics applications, however, make use of empirical (experimental) equations or relationships. Calculations for flow through pipes or flow in open channels, for example, use empirical constants and equations.

Knowledge from engineering fields of practice. In addition to these engineering sciences, a civil engineer uses accumulated knowledge from the civil engineering areas of specialization. Some of the important fields of practice are hydrology and hydrogeology, geotechnical engineering, structural engineering, transportation engineering, and environmental engineering. In each of these fields of practice, there are theoretical equations, empirical equations, graphs or nomograms, guidelines, and rules of thumb that civil engineers use for design and construction of projects related to structures, roads, stormwater management, or wastewater management, for example.

Civil engineering tools. Several tools available for civil engineers to use in practice are engineering graphics, computer-aided drafting and design (CAD), surveying, and geographic information systems (GIS). Engineering graphics (engineering drawing) has been a mainstay in civil engineering since its inception, used for preparation and interpretation of plans and drawings. Most of this work has come to be done using CAD software, and major producers of CAD technology such as Autodesk and Dassault Systèmes offered specialized programs for use by civil engineers during the first decades of the twenty-first century. Surveying is a tool that has also long been a part of civil engineering. From laying out a road or a building foundation to measuring the slope of a river or a sewer line, surveying is a useful tool for many of the civil engineering fields. Civil engineers often work with maps, and GIS, a much newer tool than engineering graphics or surveying, makes this type of work more efficient.

Codes and design criteria. Much of the work done by civil engineers is either directly or indirectly for the public. Therefore, in most fields of civil engineering, work is governed by codes or design criteria specified by some state, local, or federal agency. For example, federal, state, and local governments have building codes; state departments of transportation specify design criteria for roads and highways; and wastewater-treatment processes and sewers must meet federal, state, and local design criteria.

APPLICATIONS AND PRODUCTS

Structural engineering. Civil engineers design, build, and maintain many and varied structures. These include bridges, towers, large buildings (skyscrapers), tunnels, and sports arenas. Some of the civil engineering areas of knowledge needed for structural engineering are soil mechanics, geotechnical engineering, foundation engineering, engineering mechanics (statics and dynamics), and strength of materials.

When the Brooklyn Bridge was built over the East River in New York City (1870-83), its suspension span of 1,595 feet was the longest in the world. It remained the longest suspension bridge in North America until the Williamsburg Bridge was completed in New York City in 1903. The Brooklyn Bridge joined Brooklyn and Manhattan and helped establish the New York City Metropolitan Area.

The Golden Gate Bridge, which crosses the mouth of San Francisco Bay with a main span of 4,200 feet, had nearly triple the central span of the Brooklyn Bridge. It was the world's longest suspension bridge from its date of completion in 1937 until 1964, when the Verrazano-Narrows Bridge opened in New York City with a central span that was 60 feet longer than that of the Golden Gate Bridge.

Japan's Akashi Kaikyō Bridge, which crosses the Akashi Strait between Honshu and Awaji Island, became the world's longest suspension bridge upon its completion in 1998. It has a single suspended span of 6,532 feet and a total length of 12,831 feet.

One of the most well-known early towers illustrates the importance of good geotechnical engineering and foundation design. Italy's famous Tower of Pisa, commonly known as the Leaning Tower of Pisa, started to lean to one side very noticeably while still under construction, a process that lasted from 1173 until 1372. Its height of about 185 feet is not extremely tall in comparison with towers built later, but it was impressive at the time it was built. The reason for its extreme tilt—more than 5 meters off perpendicular—is that it was built on rather soft, sandy soil with a foundation that was not deep enough or spread out enough to support the structure. In spite of this, the Tower of Pisa has remained standing for more than six hundred years.

Another well-known tower, the Washington Monument, was completed in 1884. At 555 feet in height, it was the world's tallest tower until the Eiffel Tower, nearly 1,000 feet tall, was completed in 1889. The Washington Monument remains the world's tallest masonry structure. The Gateway Arch in St. Louis, Missouri, is the tallest monument in the United States, at 630 feet.

The twenty-one-story Flatiron Building, which opened in New York City in 1903, was one of the first skyscrapers. It is 285 feet tall, and its most unusual feature is its triangular shape, which was well suited to the wedge-shaped piece of land on which it was built. The 102-floor Empire State Building, completed in 1931 in New York City with a height of 1,250 feet, earned the title of the world's tallest building at that time, outdoing the Chrysler Building, which was still under construction, by 204 feet. The Sears Tower (now the Willis Tower) in Chicago is 1,450 feet tall and was the tallest building in the world when it was completed in 1974. Several taller buildings have been constructed since that time, including the Burj Khalifa in Dubai, which is a record-breaking 2,722 feet high.

Some of the more interesting examples of tunnels go through mountains and under the sea. The Hoosac Tunnel, built from 1851 to 1874, connected New York State to New England with a 4.75-mile railway tunnel through the Hoosac Mountain in northwestern Massachusetts. It was the longest railroad tunnel in the United States for more than fifty years. Mont Blanc Tunnel, built between 1957 and

1965, is a 7.25-mile-long highway tunnel under Mont Blanc in the Alps that connects Italy and France. The Channel Tunnel, one of the most publicized modern tunnel projects, spans a distance of 31 miles beneath the English Channel to connect Dover, England, and Calais, France.

Transportation engineering. Civil engineers also design, build, and maintain a wide variety of projects related to transportation, such as roads, railroads, and pipelines.

Many long, dramatic roads and highways have been built by civil engineers, ever since the Romans became the first builders of an extensive network of roads. The Appian Way is the best known of the many long, straight roads built by the Romans. Construction on the project was started in 312 BCE by the Roman censor Appius Claudius Caecus; by 244 BCE, it extended about 360 miles from Rome to the port of Brundisium in southeastern Italy. The Pan-American Highway, often billed as the world's longest road, connects North America and South America. The original Pan-American Highway ran for more than 15,500 miles, from Texas to Argentina; it has since been extended to go from Prudhoe Bay, Alaska, to the southern tip of South America, with a total length of nearly 30,000 miles.

The US interstate highway system has been the world's biggest earthmoving project. Started in 1956 by the Federal Highway Act, as of 2021 it covered a total distance of 46,876 miles. This massive highway construction project transformed the American system of highways and had major cultural impacts.

The building of the First Transcontinental Railroad, completed in 1869, was a major engineering feat. The railroad extended for nearly 2,000 miles, connecting San Francisco to the existing East Coast network in Council Bluffs, Iowa. Logistics was a major part of the project, with the need to transport steel rails and wooden ties great distances. An even more formidable task was construction of the Trans-Siberian Railway, the world's longest railway.

It was built between 1891 and 1904 and covers more than 5,700 miles across Russia, from Moscow in the west to Vladivostok in the east.

The Denver International Airport, which opened in 1993, was a very large civil engineering project. This airport covers more than double the area of all of Manhattan Island.

The first oil pipeline in the United States was a 5-mile-long, 2-inch-diameter pipe that carried 800 barrels of petroleum per day. Pipelines have become much larger and longer since then. The Trans-Alaska Pipeline System, with 800 miles of 48-inch diameter pipe, can carry 2 million barrels per day. At the peak of construction, twenty thousand people worked twelve-hour days, seven days a week.

Water resources engineering. Another area of civil engineering practice is water resources engineering, with projects such as canals, dams, dikes, and seawater barriers.

The oldest known canal that is still in operation is the Grand Canal in China, which was constructed between 485 BCE and 283 CE. The Grand Canal is more than 1,000- miles long, although its route has varied because of several instances of rerouting, remodeling, and rebuilding over the years. The 363-mile-long Erie Canal was built from 1817 to 1825 to connect Albany and Buffalo across the state of New York, thus overcoming the Appalachian Mountains as a barrier to trade between the eastern United States and the newly opened western United States. The economic impact of the Erie Canal was tremendous. It reduced the cost of shipping a ton of cargo between Buffalo and New York City from about $100 per ton (over the Appalachians) to $4 per ton (through the canal).

The Panama Canal, constructed from 1881 to 1914 to connect the Atlantic and Pacific Oceans through the Isthmus of Panama, is only about 50 miles long, but its construction presented tremendous challenges because of the soil, the terrain, and the tropical illnesses that killed many workers. Upon its completion, the Panama Canal reduced the travel distance from New York City to San Francisco by about 9,000 miles.

When the Hoover Dam was completed in 1936 on the Colorado River at the Colorado-Arizona border, it was the world's largest dam, at a height of 726 feet and crest length of 1,224 feet. The technique of passing chilled water through pipes enclosed in the concrete to cool the newly poured concrete and speed its curing was developed for the construction of the Hoover Dam and is still in use. The Grand Coulee Dam, in the state of Washington, was the largest hydroelectric project in the world when it was built in the 1930s. It has an output of 10,080 megawatts. The Itaipu Dam, on the Parana River along the border of Brazil and Paraguay, is also one of the largest hydroelectric dams in the world. It began operation in 1984 and is capable of producing 13,320 megawatts.

Dikes, dams, and similar structures have been used for centuries around the world for protection against flooding. The largest sea barrier in the world is a 2-mile-long surge barrier in the Oosterschelde estuary of the Netherlands, constructed from 1958 to 1986. Called the *Deltawerken* (Delta Works), the purpose of this project was to reduce the danger of catastrophic flooding. The impetus that brought this project to fruition was a catastrophic flood in the area in 1953. A major part of the barrier design consists of sixty-five huge concrete piers, weighing in at 18,000 tons each. These piers support tremendous 400-ton steel gates to create the sea barrier. The lifting and placement of these huge concrete piers exceeded the capabilities of any existing cranes, so a special U-shaped ship was built and equipped with gantry cranes. The project used computers to help in guidance and placement of the piers. A stabilizing foundation used for the concrete piers consists of foundation mattresses made up of layers of sand, fine gravel, and coarse gravel. Each foundation mattress is more than 1-foot thick and more than 650 feet by 140 feet, with a smaller mattress placed on top.

CAREERS AND COURSEWORK

A bachelor's degree in civil engineering is the requirement for entry into this field. Registration as a professional engineer is required for many civil engineering positions. In the United States, a graduate from a bachelor's degree program accredited by the Accreditation Board for Engineering and Technology is eligible to take the Fundamentals of Engineering exam to become an engineer in training. After four years of professional experience under the supervision of a professional engineer, one is eligible to take the Professional Engineer exam to become a registered professional engineer.

A typical program of study for a bachelor's degree in civil engineering includes chemistry, calculus and differential equations, calculus-based physics, engineering graphics/CAD, surveying, engineering mechanics, strength of materials, and perhaps engineering geology, as well as general education courses during the first two years. This is followed by fluid mechanics, hydrology or water resources, soil mechanics, engineering economics, and introductory courses for transportation engineering, structural engineering, and environmental engineering, as well as civil engineering electives to allow specialization in one of the areas of civil engineering during the last two years.

A master's degree in civil engineering that provides additional advanced courses in one of the areas of specialization, a master of business administration (MBA) degree, or an engineering management master's degree complement a bachelor's of science degree and enable their holder to advance more rapidly. A master of science degree would typically lead to more advanced technical positions, while an MBA or engineering management degree would typically lead to management positions.

Anyone aspiring to a civil engineering faculty or research position must obtain a doctoral degree. In that case, to provide proper preparation for doctoral level study, any master's-level study should be in pursuit of a research-oriented master of science degree rather than a master's degree in engineering or a practice-oriented master of science degree.

SOCIAL CONTEXT AND FUTURE PROSPECTS

Civil engineering projects typically involve basic infrastructure needs such as roads and highways, water supply, wastewater treatment, bridges, and public buildings. These projects may be new construction or repair, maintenance or upgrading of existing highways, structures, and treatment facilities. The buildup of such infrastructure since the beginning of the twentieth century has been extensive, leading to a continuing need for the repair, maintenance, and upgrading of existing structures. Also, governments tend to devote funding to infrastructure improvements to generate jobs and create economic activity during economic downturns. All of this leads to the projection for a continuing strong need for civil engineers.

—Harlan H. Bengtson, BS, MS, PhD

Further Reading

Arteaga, Robert F. *The Building of the Arch*. 10th ed., Jefferson National Parks Association, 2002.

Darwin, David, and Charles Dolan. *Design of Concrete Structures*. 16th ed., McGraw-Hill, 2021.

Davidson, Frank Paul, and Kathleen Lusk Brooke, editors. *Building the World: An Encyclopedia of the Great Engineering Projects in History*. 2 vols. Greenwood, 2006.

"Highway History." *Federal Highway Administration*, 27 Apr. 2021, www.fhwa.dot.gov/interstate/faq.cfm. Accessed 28 Nov. 2021.

Labi, Samuel. *Introduction to Civil Engineering Systems: A Systems Perspective to the Development of Civil Engineering Facilities*. Wiley, 2014.

Moaveni, Saeed. *Engineering Fundamentals: An Introduction to Engineering*. 6th ed., Cengage Learning, 2020.

Weingardt, Richard G. *Engineering Legends: Great American Civil Engineers; 32 Profiles of Inspiration and Achievement*. American Society of Civil Engineers, 2005.

Yasmin, Nighat. *Introduction to AutoCAD 2022 for Civil Engineering Applications*. SDC Publications, 2021.

COMMUNICATIONS SATELLITE TECHNOLOGY

ABSTRACT

Communications satellite technology has evolved from its first applications in the 1950s to become a part of most people's daily lives and thereby producing billions of dollars in yearly sales. Communications satellites were initially used to help relay television and radio signals to remote areas of the world and to aid navigation. Weather forecasts routinely make use of images transmitted from communications satellites. Telephone transmissions over long distances, including fax, cellular phones, pagers, and wireless technology, are all examples of the increasingly large impact that communications satellite technology continues to have on daily, routine communications.

DEFINITION AND BASIC PRINCIPLES

Sputnik 1, launched on October 4, 1957, by the Soviet Union, was the first artificial satellite. It used radio transmission to collect data regarding the distribution of radio signals within the ionosphere in order to measure density in the atmosphere. In addition to space satellites, the most common artificial satellites are the satellites used for communication, weather, navigation, and research. These artificial satellites travel around the earth because of human action, and they depend on computer systems to function. A rocket is used to launch these artificial satellites so that they will have enough speed to be accelerated into the most common types of circular orbits, which require speeds of about 27,000 kilometers per hour. Some satellites, especially those that are to be used at locations far removed from the earth's equator, require elliptical-shaped orbits instead, and their acceleration speeds are 30,000 kilometers per hour. If a launching rocket applies too much energy to an artificial satellite, the satellite may acquire enough energy to reach its escape velocity of 40,000 kilometers per hour and break free from Earth's gravity. It is important that the satellite be able to maintain a constant high speed. If the speed is too low, gravity may cause the satellite to fall back down to Earth's surface. There are also natural satellites that travel without human intervention, such as the moon.

BACKGROUND AND HISTORY

In 1945, science-fiction writer Arthur C. Clarke first described the concept of satellites being used for the mass distribution of television programs in his article "Extra-Terrestrial Relays," published in *Wireless World*. John Pierce, who worked at Bell Telephone Laboratories, further expanded on the idea of using satellites to repeat and relay television channels, radio signals, and telephone calls in his article "Orbital Radio Relays," published in the April 1955, issue of *Jet Propulsion*. The first transatlantic telephone cable was opened by AT&T in 1956. The first transatlantic call was made in 1927, but it traveled via radio waves. The cable vastly improved the signal quality. The Soviet Union launched Sputnik 1, the first satellite, in 1957, which began the Space Race between the Soviet Union and the United States.

The Communications Satellite Act of 1962 was passed by the United States Congress to regulate and assist the developing communications satellite industry. The first American television satellite transmission was made on July 10, 1962, five years into the Space Race, with the National Space and Aeronautics Administration's (NASA) launch of the world's first communications satellite, AT&T's Telstar. Many new communications satellites followed, with names such as Relay, Syncom, Early Bird, Anik, Westar, Satcom, and Marisat. Since the 1970s, communications satellites have allowed remote parts of the world to receive television and radio, primarily for entertainment purposes. As technology has continued to evolve, satellite technology has facilitated mobile phone communication and high-speed internet applications.

As satellite technology developed throughout the late twentieth century, manufacturers of satellites—both communications satellites and satellites intended for military or scientific purposes—experimented with the use of burgeoning computer-aided design (CAD) technology when designing satellites and their individual components. NASA had begun working with such technology by the mid-1980s, which saw the development of the Interactive Design and Evaluation of Advanced Spacecraft (IDEAS) system. IDEAS allowed for the computer-aided design and analysis of various satellites as well as other

A U.S. Space Force Extremely High Frequency communications satellite relays secure communications for the United States and other allied countries. Photo via Wikimedia Commons. [Public domain.]

aerospace systems. Later digital tools used for satellite design included the intelligent Computer Aided Satellite Designer (iCASD), a tool that facilitated the design of modular satellite components.

In addition to making satellite design an easier and more efficient process for designers working on behalf of space agencies, military branches, and major corporations, CAD software democratized the process of designing and manufacturing satellites, enabling smaller companies and educational institutions to participate in that process as well. Members of the Brown University student group Brown Space Engineering, for instance, successfully designed and built the "nanosatellite" EQUISat, which NASA helped place in orbit in July of 2018. The components of EQUISat were designed and modeled using the CAD software SolidWorks, and computer-aided manufacturing (CAM) equipment was subsequently used to manufacture the satellite's components. EQUISat continued to orbit Earth until December of 2020, when it reentered the atmosphere.

HOW IT WORKS

Communications satellites orbit Earth and use microwave radio relay technology to facilitate communication for television, radio, mobile phones, internet, weather forecasting, and navigation applications by receiving and relaying signals. Generally, there are two components required for a communications satellite. One is the satellite itself, sometimes called the "space segment," which consists of the satellite and its telemetry controls, the fuel system, and the transponder. The other key component is the ground station, which transmits baseband signals to the satellite via uplinking and receives signals from the satellite via downlinking.

These communications satellites are suspended around Earth in different types of orbits, depending on the communication requirements.

Geostationary orbits. Geostationary orbits are most often used for communications and weather satellites because this type of orbit has permanent latitude at zero degrees, which is above Earth's equator, and only longitudinal values vary. The result is that satellites within this type of orbital can use a fixed antenna that is pointed toward one location in the sky. Observers on the ground view these types of satellites as motionless because their orbit exactly matches Earth's rotational period. Numerically, this movement equates to an orbital velocity of 1.91 miles per second, or a period of 23.9 hours. Because this type of orbit was first publicized by the science-fiction writer Arthur C. Clarke in the 1940s, it is sometimes called a "Clarke orbit." Systems that use geostationary satellites to provide images for meteorological applications include the Indian National Satellite System (INSAT), the European Organisation for the Exploitation of Meteorological Satellites' (EUMETSAT) Meteosat, and the United States' Geostationary Operational Environmental Satellites (GOES). These geostationary meteorological satellites provide the images for daily weather forecasts.

Molniya orbits. Used primarily in the Soviet Union and on rare occasions in post-Soviet Russia, Molniya orbits have been important because they require less energy to maintain in the area's high latitudes. These high latitudes cause low grazing angles, which indicate angles of incidence for a beam of electromagnetic energy as it approaches the surface of Earth. The angle of incidence specifically measures the deviation of this approach of energy from a straight line. As a result, geostationary satellites would orbit too low to Earth's surface and their signals would have significant interference. Because of Russia's high latitudes, Molniya orbits are more energy efficient than geostationary orbits. The word *Molniya* comes from the Russian word for "lightning," and these orbits have a period of twelve hours, instead of the twenty-four hours characteristic of geostationary orbits. Molniya orbits have a large amount of incline, with an angle of incidence of about 63 degrees.

Low-earth orbits. Low-earth orbit (LEO) refers to a satellite orbiting between 140 and 970 kilometers (about 87 to 602 miles) above Earth's surface. The periods are short, only about ninety minutes, which means that several of them are necessary to provide the type of uninterrupted communication characteristic of geostationary orbits, which have twenty-four-hour periods. Although a larger number of LEOs are needed, they have lower launching costs and require less energy for signal transmission because of how close to the earth they orbit.

APPLICATIONS AND PRODUCTS

Direct broadcast satellites. Direct broadcast satellite (DBS) television service is available in several countries through many commercial direct-to-home providers, including DISH Network and DirecTV in the United States, Freesat and Sky in the United Kingdom, and Bell TV in Canada. These satellites transmit using the upper portion of the microwave Ku band, which has a range of between 10.95 and 14.5 GHz. This range is divided based on the geographic regions requiring transmissions. Law enforcement also uses the frequencies of the electromagnetic spectrum to detect traffic-speed violators.

Fixed service satellites. Besides the DBS services, the other type of communication satellite is called a "fixed service satellite" (FSS), which is useful for cable television channel reception, distance learning applications for universities, videoconferencing applications for businesses, and local television stations for live shots during the news broadcasts. Fixed service satellites use the lower frequencies of the Ku bands and the C band for transmission. All of these frequencies are within the microwave region of the electromagnetic spectrum. The frequency range for the C band is about 4 to 8 GHz, and generally the C-band functions better when moisture is present, making it especially useful for weather communication.

Intercontinental telephone service. Traditional landline telephone calls are relayed to an Earth station via the public switched telephone network (PSTN). Calls are then forwarded to a geostationary satellite to allow intercontinental phone communication. Fiber-optic technology is decreasing the dependence on satellites for this type of communication.

Satellite internet. In the first decades of the twenty-first century, several companies offered satellite internet services to customers within the United States. Service providers operating within that field included DISH Network, Viasat, and HughesNet. Satellite internet services are particularly important in rural areas in which terrestrial forms of internet service, including digital subscriber line (DSL) and fiber internet, are not available.

Satellite phones. Satellites are useful for mobile phones when regular mobile phones have poor reception. These phones depend only on open sky for access to an orbiting satellite, making them very useful for ships on the open ocean for navigational purposes. Iridium Communications is one of the world's largest mobile satellite communications companies. Iridium manufactures several types of satellite phones, including the Iridium Extreme and Iridium 9555, and models that have water resistance, email, and USB data ports. Iridium faces competition from fellow satellite phone companies such as Immarsat and Globalstar.

Satellite trucks and portable satellites. Trucks equipped with electrical generators to provide the power for an attached satellite have found applications for mobile transmission of news, especially after natural disasters. Some of these portable satellites use the C-band frequency for the transmission of information via the uplink process, which requires rather large antennas, whereas other portable satellites were developed in the 1980s to use the Ku band for transmission of information.

Global positioning system (GPS). GPS makes use of communications satellite technology for navigational purposes. The GPS was first developed by the

US government for military applications but has become widely used in civilian applications in products such as cars and mobile phones.

CAREERS AND COURSEWORK

Careers working with communications satellite technology can be found primarily in the radio, television, and mobile phone industries. Specifically, these careers involve working with the wired telecommunications services that often include direct-to-home satellite television distributors as well as the newer wireless telecommunications carriers that provide mobile telephone, internet, satellite radio, and navigational services. Government organizations also need employees who are trained in working with communications satellite technology for weather forecasting and other environmental applications as well as communication of data between public-safety officials.

The highest salaries are earned by those with a bachelor's degree in avionics technology, computer engineering, computer science, computer information systems, electrical engineering, electronics engineering, physics, or telecommunications technology, although a degree in television broadcast technology can also lead to lucrative career after obtaining several years of on-the-job-training. The National Alliance for Communications Technology Education and Learning (NACTEL), the Communications Workers of America (CWA), and the Society of Cable Telecommunications Engineers (SCTE) are sources of detailed career information for anyone interested in communications satellite technology.

SOCIAL CONTEXT AND FUTURE PROSPECTS

Advances in satellite technology have accompanied the rapid evolution of computer technology to such an extent that some experts describe this media revolution as an actual convergence of all media (television, motion pictures, printed news, internet, and mobile phone communications). In 1979, Nicholas Negroponte of the Massachusetts Institute of Technology (MIT) began giving lectures describing this future convergence of all forms of media. As of the twenty-first century, this convergence seems to be nearly complete. Television shows can be viewed on the internet, as can news from cable television news stations such as CNN, Fox, and MSNBC. Hyperlinks provide digital connections between information that can be accessed from almost anywhere in the world instantly because of communications satellite technology. The result is that there is a twenty-four-hour news cycle, and the effects are sometimes positive but can also be negative if the wrong information is broadcast. The instantaneous transmission of political and social unrest by communications satellite technology can lead to further actions, as shown by the 2011 Arab Spring protests in Egypt, Iran, Yemen, Libya, and Bahrain.

—*Jeanne L. Kuhler, BS, MS, PhD*

Further Reading

Baran, Stanley J., and Dennis K. Davis. *Mass Communication Theory: Foundations, Ferment, and Future.* 8th ed., Oxford UP, 2020.

Buettner, Timothee, Atanas Tanev, Lars Pfotzer, Arne Roennau, and Ruediger Dillmann. "The Intelligent Computer Aided Satellite Designer iCASD—Creating Viable Configurations for Modular Satellites." *2018 NASA/ESA Conference on Adaptive Hardware and Systems (AHS)*, 2018, pp. 25-32.

Elbert, Bruce R. *Introduction to Satellite Communication.* 3rd ed., Artech House, 2008.

"EQUISat." *Brown Space Engineering*, 2020, brownspace.org/equisat/. Accessed 28 Nov. 2021.

Grant, August E., and Jennifer Meadows. *Communication Technology Update and Fundamentals.* 16th ed., Routledge, 2018.

Hesmondhalgh, David. *The Cultural Industries.* 4th ed., SAGE Publications, 2018.

Mattelart, Armand. *Networking the World: 1794-2000.* Translated by Liz Carey-Libbrecht and James A. Cohen. U of Minnesota P, 2000.

Minoli, Daniel. *Innovations in Satellite Communications and Satellite Technology.* John Wiley & Sons, 2015.

"Space Systems Computer-Aided Design Technology." *NASA*, ntrs.nasa.gov/citations/19840046682. Accessed 28 Nov. 2021.

Computer-aided Design (CAD) in Education

ABSTRACT
Already a major tool used by engineers, designers, researchers, manufacturers, urban planners, architects, landscapers, and technologists, computer-aided design (CAD) software has become increasingly important in education during the twenty-first century. Students at nearly all levels of education, from primary school to college, have been introduced to a wide array of CAD programs as well as related technology such as three-dimensional (3D) printers. When selecting a CAD software for use in a school environment, educators must determine which software best meets both student needs and the educator's own goals.

INTRODUCTION
Computer-aided design (CAD) appears at nearly all levels of education, from primary and middle school to high school and college. Its increased presence in schools provides considerable advantages to many students. Students planning a future in design or engineering will be better prepared for higher education and entry into the job market. In addition, students looking to enter fields such as art, medicine, landscaping, and manufacturing will have the necessary head start when 3D tools become more present in their fields.

HOW CAD SOFTWARE CONTRIBUTES TO EDUCATION
Whatever the level or goal of a student's education, CAD software is finding ways to adapt and serve students' needs. If students begin with simple programs designed for beginners, their early work can serve as a valuable foundation for more complex projects and software. When presented with CAD software with easily understandable instructions and friendly interfaces, many children quickly pick up the concepts. From there, children can design and draft any number of projects, either for school or personal satisfaction. Such projects encourage creativity and acting on inspiration, which can then, in turn, be applied to other areas of schooling. In addition, early introduction to CAD software helps students stay ahead and learn a skill that is becoming increasingly practical.

Even if a student has no interest in pursuing a career in a CAD-heavy field such as automotive or aerospace design, CAD knowledge can be valuable. General computer knowledge was once considered a skill applicable to only a narrow range of fields; by the early twenty-first century, however, computers had become an integral part of daily life. Those who grew up with little or no basic computer education thus found themselves at a distinct disadvantage in the professional world and everyday life. While knowledge in CAD may not be quite as far-reaching, CAD knowledge is still a helpful tool for any student to have at the ready. Numerous fields make use of 3D modeling and related functions. There are even practical applications for CAD knowledge in creative fields such as fashion design, sculpture, illustration, and film. With more CAD education available in schools, students are better equipped to develop creativity and take on the jobs of the future.

SELECTING CAD SOFTWARE FOR SCHOOLS
There are a number of factors that go into selecting the best CAD software for a particular school setting. These range from the age of the students to the academic and personal goals they have set.

CAD can be difficult to use at first for many people. Therefore, it is essential to choose software appropriate for students of a given age. Some tools have highly intuitive interfaces that allow students to learn and complete simple design tasks. As students

Photo via iStock/monkeybusinessimages. [Used under license.]

get older, they can be introduced to more functional software with full suites of editing tools. It is also important to select software that meshes with the projects the students will take on as well as the goals the individual educator has set for the students.

Cost can also be a factor. Some CAD software packages can be expensive, particularly those widely used in industry. However, there is a wealth of less expensive and sometimes free options. Many of these are available online for either download or in-browser use. Hardware may also be something to consider. CAD software that focuses more on detailed rendering can take up significant processing power and may not run efficiently on older computers. It can be beneficial for an educator to consult with an information technology (IT) professional to ensure that the computers available meet the desired CAD software's technical requirements.

CAD PROGRAMS FOR USE IN SCHOOLS

In the third decade of the twenty-first century, numerous software options are available to educators and schools seeking to incorporate CAD into their curricula.

Elementary school. For students on the elementary level, popular CAD programs available as of 2021 include the simple and versatile software 3D Slash and SolidWorks Apps for Kids, a software package that includes the applications Style It, Shape It, and Print It, among others. Other popular options include LeoCAD, which shows students how to build models using digital LEGO bricks.

Middle to high school. CAD options for use in middle schools and high schools as of 2021 include SculptGL, an intuitive 3D browser-based introduction to sculpting software, and SketchUp for Schools, which offers a full selection of CAD tools specifically designed for classrooms. Tinkercad, a product of the software developer Autodesk, likewise provides a strong introduction to CAD design.

High school to college. Options available to students on the college level, as well as advanced high school students, as of 2021 include BricsCAD, a complete CAD software that is free for students and schools, and Rhino3D, a software that is optimal for students looking to work in 3D design. Some students may also make use of AutoCAD, a professional and widely used CAD package, and SolidWorks for Students.

CONCLUSION

As CAD becomes increasingly important to a diverse range of fields, it is more important than ever to ensure that educators integrate CAD software into schools to prepare students for careers and encourage creativity and innovation. Affordable resources are more readily available than many think, and the benefits of CAD in education are immeasurable.

—*John Teehan*

Further Reading

Asperl, Andreas. "How to Teach CAD." *Computer-Aided Design & Applications*, vol. 2, no. 1-4, 2005, pp. 459-68.

Brown, William Christopher. "An Effective AutoCAD Curriculum for the High School Student." *CSUSB ScholarWorks*, 1999, scholarworks.lib.csusb.edu/etd-project/1791/. Accessed 16 Dec. 2021.

Duelm, Brian Lee. "Computer Aided Design in the Classroom." *LearnTechLib*, Dec. 1986, files.eric.ed.gov/fulltext/ED276885.pdf. Accessed 16 Dec. 2021.

Gaget, Lucie. "How to Learn CAD in Schools: Top 15 of the Best Educational Software." *Sculpteo*, 26 Dec. 2017, www.sculpteo.com/blog/2017/12/26/how-to-learn-cad-in-schools-top-15-of-the-best-educational-software/. Accessed 16 Dec. 2021.

Poggenpohl, Sharon, and Keiichi Sato. *Design Integration: Research and Collaboration*. Intellect, 2009.

Segura, Diana. "13 Best CAD Programs for Kids." *3DPrinterChat.com*, 8 Feb. 2020, 3dprinterchat.com/13-best-cad-programs-for-kids/. Accessed 16 Dec. 2021.

CAD Research and Theory

ABSTRACT

Research is an essential aspect of the development of computer-aided design (CAD) and the myriad ways it contributes to the modern world. Without research, there would be no improvements in manufacturing and no advantages gained in engineering, architecture, robotics, and even entertainment. Researchers and theorists explore the ways in which human users interact with CAD technology and the potential effects of such interactions on technology and society.

INTRODUCTION

While computer-aided design (CAD) technology is perhaps most commonly associated with its practical uses and benefits in fields such as manufacturing, the field is also one steeped in research and theory. CAD undergoes continuous study of the ways in which it is used and its potential in multiple facets of everyday life. From simulations to artificial intelligence, researchers and theorists examine and learn more about how human users interact with CAD to design and produce the modern world.

AREAS OF CAD RESEARCH

Constant advances are a defining characteristic of technology, and CAD technology is no exception. Software developers are always looking for ways to improve their current technology, how their technology interacts with a wide selection of industries, and how they can branch out into new sectors that would benefit from CAD technology. In the early twenty-first century, CAD research is underway in a wide range of industries.

Architecture, engineering, and construction. CAD developers study the ever-changing needs and considerations in architecture, engineering, and construction—collectively known as the AEC industries. Using CAD technology to create and develop designs, companies share their needs and processes with developers as they adapt to suit modern materials, energy requirements, and environmental concerns. Software developers gather these insights collaboratively to create software that better meets the unique and important needs of the AEC community.

Artificial intelligence. A developing feature of CAD software is knowledge-based engineering (KBE), a technology based in artificial intelligence that can improve the efficiency of product-development processes. Researchers are also exploring the intersections of CAD and machine learning and have developed data sets intended for use in training artificial intelligence systems to work with CAD models or drawings.

Human-computer interaction. Research in human-computer interaction (HCI) involves looking at how people and technology work together. This includes such concepts as intuitive interfaces and user friendliness. HCI research likewise considers the ways in which people respond to tools such as CAD technology and how human use, in turn, forms the development of the technology. CAD developers and researchers focusing on HCI look for novel ways humans and computers might interact and then design technologies that utilize that knowledge.

Manufacturing. When developing products for the manufacturing industry, CAD developers look into ways CAD can improve the entire manufacturing process, from initial design to final assembly. This research encompasses all areas of manufacturing, from the consumer products sector to aerospace manufacturing. By researching manufacturing processes and needs, CAD researchers can help create new, cutting-edge solutions to manufacturing challenges, improve efficiency, and cut down on waste.

Simulation. All fields stand to benefit from research into the intersections between CAD and simulation programs. Before going to the trouble of creating new manufacturing processes or products, researchers can test and optimize the different approaches possible for design and find the one most suited for a specific need. Simulations can consider physics, materials, sensors, environmental conditions, and other factors.

CAD THEORY

Like many other developing technologies, CAD raises important questions among researchers: Where do we go from here? How much has CAD significantly changed how humanity approaches design and engineering, and where will it end? What unforeseen challenges might arise out of such technology? What are the ethical implications of efforts to merge CAD technology with artificial intelligence and machine learning? These are some of the questions CAD theory explores.

Studying CAD theory means looking at all of the research conducted to help CAD serve various industries, determining how all the parts work together, and improving and applying CAD technology to ever-widening fields of creativity and industry. By working with industry leaders, CAD researchers and developers attempt to reimagine the role of technology and the workforce by postulating a sustainable future and developing a more coherent vision for a better world.

IMPACT

Much like any other process or field of study, CAD in a constant state of development and growth. When CAD technology was first introduced in the 1950s, it changed how many businesses approached design, engineering, and manufacturing, but it was limited to a small number of industries. In the twenty-first century, CAD has become a part of—or is actively becoming part of—nearly every facet of modern life. It is a valuable tool not only for engineers but also for artists, doctors, and entertainers. Researching how CAD interacts with different industries gives insight into how CAD can serve everyone better. Studying how CAD and humans interact and what they can produce provides developers with possible paths for future enhancements and greater opportunities.

—*John Teehan*

Further Reading

"Autodesk Research." *Autodesk*, 2021, www.autodesk.com/research/overview. Accessed 16 Dec. 2021.

Chang, Kuang-Hua. *Design Theory and Methods Using CAD/CAE*. Academic Press, 2014.

Jiang, Wenbo, and Yuan Zhang. "Application of 3D Visualization in Landscape Design Teaching." *International Journal of Emerging Technologies in Learning (JET)*, vol. 14, no. 6, 2019, pp. 53-62.

Johnson, Khari. "Researchers Seek to Advance Predictive AI for Engineers with CAD Model Data Set." *VentureBeat*, 21 July 2020, venturebeat.com/2020/07/21/researchers-seek-to-advance-predictive-ai-for-engineers-with-cad-model-data-set/. Accessed 16 Dec. 2021.

Mealing, Stuart, editor. *Computers and Art*. 2nd ed., Intellect, 2008.

Rowe, Jeff. "3D Model-Based Design: Setting the Definitions Straight." *MCADCafe*, 27 Sept. 2010, www10.mcadcafe.com/nbc/articles/2/867959/3D-Model-Based-Design-Setting-Definitions-Straight. Accessed 16 Dec. 2021.

Saran, Cliff. "How 3D Printing Is Growing One Step at a Time." *ComputerWeekly.com*, 26 Aug. 2021, www.computerweekly.com/news/252505878/How-3D-printing-is-growing-one-step-at-a-time. Accessed 16 Dec. 2021.

Computer-aided Engineering (CAE)

ABSTRACT

Computer-aided engineering (CAE), sometimes known as computer-assisted engineering, is a computational adjunct to computer-aided design (CAD). CAD programs are used to generate a detailed technical drawing or model that specifies the shape and dimensions of an object. CAE software is used to carry out computations of properties of the object in the CAD drawing. CAD and CAE applications are often part of the same program.

CAD, CAM, AND CAE

In 1957, Dr. Patrick Hanratty produced the first functional application of computer-controlled machine operation in the form of computer numerical control, or CNC. A programmable CNC controller uses a specified set of instructions based on data from the specifications in the appropriate technical drawing. CNC programming required a human user to compose the program, a step-by-step set of explicit instructions that direct the movement of machine parts in operation. This elementary step by Hanratty had the potential to be augmented and expanded, and as computer technology and software developed, the means was found to combine electronic drawing software with CNC controllers in such a way that specifications could be transferred directly from one to the other. The drawing software is the basis of computer-aided design (CAD) and, by extension, of computer-aided engineering (CAE).

The technical drawing is the first major step in the engineering of an actual product, as it documents the specifications to which the object is to conform. This is where computer-assisted engineering plays its role. Underlying the actual creation of the object in the technical drawing are a great many property values and engineering factors that must be computed based on the desired performance of the object and the specifications assigned to it. These include physical factors such as load distributions, strain, compression, tension, deformation under load, and many others. CAE software uses the CAD data, along with direct user input—such as material properties, thermal expansion rates, rotational speed, conductivity, and other properties that describe the object's response to the environment to which it will be exposed—to compute the object's expected behavior in operation. Computed values from the CAE software can, and often do, reveal weaknesses in the design of the object as its specifications were presented, which thus allows the designer to improve the design by adjusting various specifications.

ENGINEERING DESIGN

There are essentially four stages to the engineering process. The process begins with the definition of the particular engineering problem and a clear definition of what the engineered product is meant to achieve in order to solve the engineering problem. The second stage is the creative process, in which designers and engineers collaborate to ideate the form that the product might take. In the third stage of the process, the proposed product is subjected to critical analysis that may involve multiple product solutions and their evaluation, an area in which generative design software may be useful. This is the stage at which CAE software is used by engineers to evaluate the parameters and characteristics of the

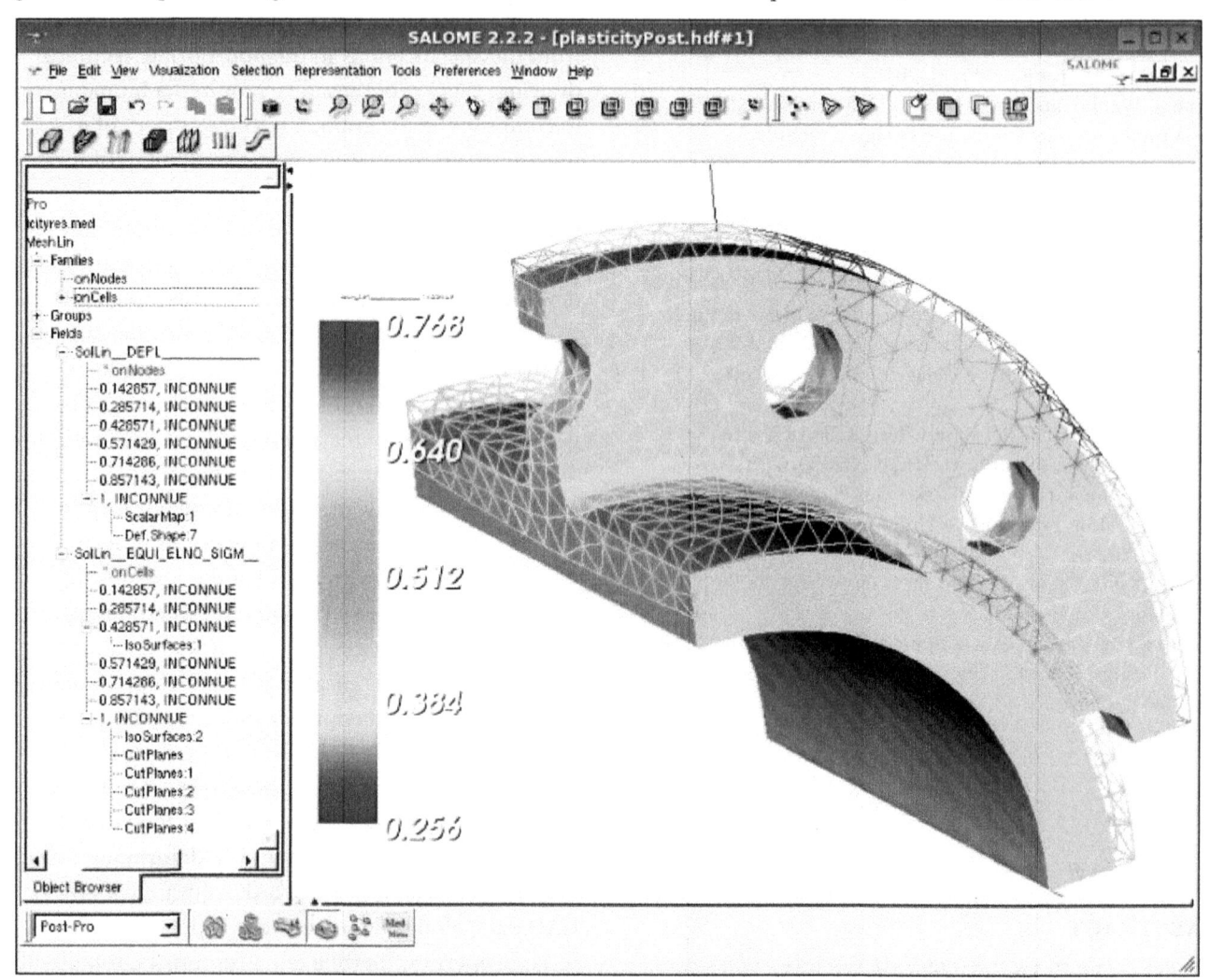

Nonlinear static analysis of a 3D structure subjected to plastic deformations. Image by Joël Cugnoni, via Wikimedia Commons.

proposed product. The fourth and final stage of the process is prototype development and testing. In many cases, a prototype object can be produced by three-dimensional (3D) printing or another method of rapid prototyping. The working prototype constitutes the proof of concept for the solution to the engineering problem defined in the first stage of the engineering process.

There are many branches of engineering: chemical, electrical, mechanical, architectural, automotive, aeronautical, and civil, to name just a few. There are also many subbranches within each discipline. Chemical engineering, for example, includes biochemical engineering, and electrical engineering includes computer and software engineering. CAE is an applicable technology in all branches of engineering, though it is more prevalent in some than in others. CAE itself can be broken down into distinct application sectors. Mechanical CAE (MCAE), for example, is software used to simulate the performance or production methodology of a mechanical component, assembly, or product, and enable improvement of those entities. Circuit design and virtual testing carried out with electronic computer-aided design (ECAD) software with the appropriate simulation capabilities qualifies as electrical, or electronic, CAE (ECAE). Similarly, CAE software that simulates the design and operation of a chemical or biochemical production facility and computes numerical values for the different stages of its operation corresponds to chemical CAE (CCAE). Accordingly, CAE software can be written specifically for a particular branch or subbranch of engineering without being generally applicable, although having specialized applications as modules within a general CAE software package is a more efficient approach.

A CLOSER LOOK AT MCAE AND CAE IN GENERAL

MCAE has the same basic purposes as all CAE programs: to simulate and improve the performance of concept designs, as well as of detailed designs; to confirm the performance of designs prior to prototyping and testing (a vitally important function, especially in architectural engineering); and to identify and address failure of a design as part of root cause analysis. Beyond this, specialized CAE software computes factors specific to its associated discipline. MCAE computes structural, kinematic and dynamic, vibrational, thermal, fluid, manufacturing, and multiphysics analyses of mechanical objects, each of which comprises a number of factors unique to the particular analysis. ECAE computes such factors as thermal response, gain fluctuation, hysteresis, magnetic susceptibility, and other factors affecting the performance of electronic circuitry. Other specific applied CAE software programs compute similar analyses corresponding to their particular fields of application. Not the least consideration, CAE software applications also compute cost analyses.

MCAE and other CAE software programs use preprocessor modules to carry out mathematical solutions of prepared simulation models that are termed solvers. A solver is a prewritten model that has been contrived specifically to be put through the solution process. The results of the solved simulations are then put through test modules called "postprocessors."

The performance of a design can be improved in a CAE program through automated functions. In a sensitivity study, for example, one component of a design such as a physical dimension or a material property is varied, and the effect of that variation on the performance of the design is monitored. This analysis measures how sensitive the performance of the design is to changes in a particular parameter. Thermal expansion, for example, changes the overall dimensions of an object in its working environment, and with the close tolerances allowed in engineered products, it is important to know just how a change in physical dimension would affect the performance of that product in real world applications.

Sensitivity analysis allows the design engineer to adjust parameters to improve and optimize the performance of the design.

In an optimization study, improvement of the design with respect to a particular goal is an automated process. The desired goal of an optimization study generally is to improve the overall performance of a design by automatically varying individual design parameters and comparing performance with each variation. In a design-of-experiment study, the software changes several variables in the design and records the analysis of each change. This type of study provides designers with a more comprehensive view of the design's performance than can be achieved by sensitivity or optimization studies.

There are related software units that can be applied in conjunction with CAE software and may be a simulation capability embedded within CAD software. Alternatively, the module may be associated with CAD software to allow automatic exchange of geometry between CAD and CAE. In another arrangement, changes to design geometry are exchanged indirectly using import and export capabilities of two different programs.

CAE software simulations involve the creation and use of a number of digital artifacts that are tracked by simulation data management (SDM) software. SDM software tracks and manages simulation changes throughout the design development process.

—*Richard M. Renneboog, MSc*

Further Reading

Bi, Zhuming, and Xiaoqin Wang. *Computer Aided Design and Manufacturing*. Wiley, 2020.

Chang, Kuang-Hua. *e-Design: Computer-Aided Engineering Design*. Academic Press, 2016.

Filipovic, Nenad. *Computational Modeling in Bioengineering and Bioinformatics*. Academic Press, 2020.

Jackson, Chad. "What Is Mechanical Computer Aided Engineering (MCAE)?" *Lifecycle Insights*, 2021, www.lifecycleinsights.com/tech-guide/mcae/. Accessed 16 Dec. 2021.

Kyratsis, Panagiotis, Konstantinos G. Kakoulis, and Angelos P. Markopoulos, editors. *Advances in CAD/CAM/CAE Technologies*. MDPI, 2020.

Udroiu, Razvan, editor. *Computer-Aided Technologies: Applications in Engineering and Medicine*. IntechOpen, 2016.

Um, Dugan. *Solid Modeling and Applications: Rapid Prototyping, CAD and CAE Theory*. Springer, 2016.

Computer-aided Mechanical Design (CAM)

ABSTRACT

More and more, industry professionals are turning to computer modeling software to help design machines, factories, assembly plants, and civil engineering projects in addition to the products and tools they manufacture. This paper will take a closer look at the growing field of computer-aided manufacturing (CAM) design, discussing the use of such technologies as well as their applications in the important arenas of architecture, manufacturing, and the medical device industry.

OVERVIEW

The modern world has become heavily dependent on computer technology, which has become vital for virtually every aspect of life in the twenty-first century—invaluable for commerce, education, government, health care, and even the simplification of household affairs. Computer technology has also become a key component in organizing and processing data. It is also being used increasingly in crafting a road to the future. Weather forecasters use computer modeling and imagery to better predict storm patterns, and economists use similar technologies to help understand market trends of the present and the near future. Computer modeling software is even used in hospital and medical research facilities, helping doctors and medical professionals track patient responses to medications as well as to better conduct surgical procedures. The manufacturing industry is no exception. More and more, industry professionals are turning to computer modeling software to help design machines in addition to the products and tools they manufacture.

A BRIEF HISTORY OF COMPUTER-AIDED DESIGN (CAD)

The practice of using computers for the purposes of designing complex machinery and systems began in the early 1960s, although it was conducted privately with specific design purposes in mind. Specifically, the automotive, electronics, and aerospace industries employed such design techniques through automated three-dimensional (3D) modeling programs.

Early computer-aided design (CAD) programs, however, were extremely complex and expensive, and they required massive computer hardware systems to conduct their calculations. Few industries could afford to support such systems. Among the companies that did utilize such systems were US automaker General Motors (GM), US aerospace giant Lockheed, and European automaker Renault. These applications stemmed from the 1963 program known as SKETCHPAD, which was created by Massachusetts Institute of Technology (MIT) scientist Ivan Sutherland. That system, for the first time, contained a feature that enabled the designer to interact with his or her computer through graphics. Such a graphical user interface (GUI) would ultimately become indispensable in CAD circles.

Particularly notable among these systems were the works of Dr. Peter J. Hanratty, who in 1964 introduced Design-Augmented by Computer (DAC-1) for GM. In 1971, Hanratty rolled out the program known as Automated Drafting and Machining (ADAM); not long after he started his own firm, Manufacturing and Consulting Services, Inc. Shortly thereafter, Hanratty began offering code to a number of companies outside of the three discussed above. Among the industry leaders who would adopt similar design programs were Computer Vision, baby food manufacturer and supplier Gerber, and McDonnell Douglas. Thanks to the work of such figures as Hanratty and Sutherland, early versions of CAD systems became increasingly

CAD is particularly useful to industries that manufacture large numbers of complex mechanical systems, such as airplanes and automobiles. Photo via iStock/sefa ozel. [Used under license.]

popular among large corporations. However, the size and cost of computer systems in general, along with the costs of systems specific to this purpose, left CAD applications largely beyond the reach of smaller businesses.

In the late 1970s, computer technology became more compact and affordable. With this came an evolution of CAD programs, which increased in terms of capability and versatility. By the early 1980s, CAD programs were able to create more complex, interlinked models as well as design in clearer 3D settings (previous incarnations utilized a simpler, two-dimensional [2D] format). Such modified systems led to greater interconnectivity among design models. By the late 1980s, CAD technology was considerably more sophisticated and more widespread in its use than it had been only two decades earlier. An example may be found in the introduction of PTC Pro/Engineer, a system that used parametric design programs, which allow for greater connectivity with other design models through the application of historical data. This "history-based" approach became, for a few years, popular among engineers who had previously used 3D modeling in their work.

Introduced in the 1970s, the personal computer (PC) saw a rapid evolution over the next two decades. The prevalence of smaller, multiple-unit computer terminals allowed a larger number of engineers, computer scientists, and design professionals to both use existing CAD programs as well as create modified versions for their own purposes. CAD systems became more common and had greater capabilities—some systems allowed the user to manipulate 3D shapes, while others created greater parametric connectivity that allowed for the development of extensive and more complex design models. In the twenty-first century, CAD systems are some of the most popularly used computer programs by corporations of all sizes and in all industries.

CAD IN MANUFACTURING

CAD has proven increasingly useful for fields that require the creation of models that connect complex systems. The development and construction of manufacturing facilities entails the establishment of a model that blends structural integrity, electrical capacity, and other vital yet intricate systems.

The heavy machinery and related systems that are part of a manufacturing facility require a similar design approach. Such machines have a wide range of parts, each of which entails careful definition. Many of these parts are geometric in origin; the design of the overall system involves the modeling of a number of geometric shapes. Computer programs have increasingly been utilized for the purposes of creating such models. The 3D and layering abilities (also known as "stereolithography") of an ever-increasing array of CAD programs have become central to this endeavor.

However, since CAD's applications to the manufacturing industry became evident in the 1970s, a persistent problem has arisen. While CAD software has long been adroit in reconciling and designing geometric shapes, they have historically been limited to known geographic shapes, unable to see beyond such contours. CAD developers have therefore worked to increase the learning capacity of such programs so that they are able to recognize shapes beyond their limited caches. Such efforts remain challenging, as computer systems must be programmed to recognize patterns and features, not just standard geometric shapes but their compositions as well. Put simply, in order to help CAD programs move beyond their original parameters, programmers have attempted to install an ability to operate with a degree of "intelligence."

While CAD has demonstrated its shortcomings in such arenas, it remains an important element of the manufacturing sector. Programmers, looking to remedy these issues, are increasingly looking to other software and hardware resources to fill in where CAD has come up short. One area, for example, was the introduction of virtual reality (VR) programs. VR employs a degree of human-computer interface that is considerably quicker than that seen in typical CAD programs. VR therefore injects into the design and modeling process the user's ability to see the entire environment, including the areas that CAD historically simply could not take into account.

Another issue revealed in the application of CAD to the manufacturing sector is one of process. Because it has had problems with recognition of nongeometric shapes, the process of manufacturing design has been slowed considerably. However, by applying another program to CAD systems, such as rule-based reasoning, these recognition problems may be circumvented. Other programs, such as the Standard for Exchange of Product Model Data (STEP), have been used as information resources for CAD, enabling the system to interconnect its database and link together complex processes or multiple groups.

Manufacturing of medical devices. The twenty-first-century global economy has had a major impact on how industries develop. The fact that so many markets are merging into a singular, international network means substantially increased competition. While this has so far caused only modest growth in competition for such established manufacturing industries as aerospace and automobiles, other growing industries are suddenly faced with much greater amounts of pressure. This places heightened emphasis not only on the quality of products manufactured (and the prices at which they are sold), but also requires that those products be produced in higher quantities at a much faster rate.

The product category of medical devices aptly demonstrates this phenomenon, in part due to the substantial demand for such devices within an aging population and the frequent need for such devices to be customized to meet the needs of their users. In light of such issues, medical device manufacturers are increasingly turning to CAD technologies to expedite the development of their products and to address the need for customization. CAD software has therefore come into high demand, following in the shoes of more established corporations in other industries that have long enjoyed the application of such software to their own manufacturing endeavors.

Initially, the traditional applications of CAD software and systems proved somewhat daunting for the many small companies that make up the medical device manufacturing industry. Such systems were historically confined to large and very expensive computer frameworks available typically to larger and more fiscally healthy organizations. Small medical device manufacturers typically have less financial stability and revenue growth, especially in a tight, highly competitive market. The growing demand among medical device manufacturers thus facilitated the evolution of CAD software: in order to enable a more cost- and space-effective application of CAD systems, program developers sought ways to make such technology more accessible for a broader contingent of industries. The rise of technology such as 3D printing, a manufacturing process that enables objects designed via CAD software to be produced in a relatively speedy and cost-effective manner, further broadened the opportunities available to medical device manufacturers as well as manufacturers in other industries.

CONCLUSIONS

Throughout history, a common pursuit has always been to use technology to benefit humanity. In the twenty-first century, this theme is particularly relevant. The global economy is one in which competition is increasing quickly. As a result, demand for efficient rates of production has risen significantly, and the use of cutting-edge technology remains the key to the acquisition of such projects.

It is for this reason that CAD systems were created. They offer many of the same capabilities that more traditional design tools create but usually at a much faster and usually more reliable rate. In its earliest stages, CAD was of particular use to those industries that sought to manufacture large numbers of complex mechanical systems, such as airplanes and automobiles. The speed at which CAD could process the intricate shapes and components that would ultimately comprise the product helped the automobile and aerospace manufacturers maintain a distant lead over competitors.

While the shortcomings of CAD programs, including their cost and computing requirements, were evident throughout much of their history, CAD programmers are constantly adapting to the demands of would-be consumers and therefore introducing evolved versions of CAD software and its applications. The enormous, expensive CAD systems of the past have given way to less expensive PC applications, which appeal to the smaller manufacturer. Additionally, much of this software is being improved to address its previous limitations as well as render it more adaptable to a variety of applications. CAD programs are being constantly upgraded and modified to suit the twenty-first-century global economy, making each software and system incarnation appealing to a growing number of industries.

—*Michael P. Auerbach, MA*

Further Reading

Bajaj, Varun, and G. R. Sinha, editors. *Computer-Aided Design and Diagnosis Methods for Biomedical Applications*. CRC Press, 2021.

Bi, Zhuming, and Xiaoqin Wang. *Computer Aided Design and Manufacturing*. Wiley-ASME Press, 2020.

"The History of Design, Model Making and CAD." *Creative Mechanisms*, 14 Dec. 2015, www.creativemechanisms.com/blog/the-history-of-design-model-making-and-cad. Accessed 28 Nov. 2021.

Krar, Steve, Arthur Gill, and Peter Smid. *Technology of Machine Tools*. 8th ed., McGraw-Hill, 2020.

O'Leary, Timothy, Linda O'Leary, and Daniel O'Leary. *Computing Essentials 2021*. McGraw-Hill, 2020.

Sarkar, Jayanta. *Computer Aided Design: A Conceptual Approach*. CRC Press, 2017.

"What Is the Difference between CAD, CAE, and CAM?" *Michigan State University*, 2 Apr. 2021, online.egr.msu.edu/articles/cad-vs-cae-vs-cam-what-is-the-difference/. Accessed 28 Nov. 2021.

CAD/CAM, Popularization of

ABSTRACT

The popular use of computers to design buildings and mechanical parts can be dated to the groundbreaking release in 1982 of the software product AutoCAD. Computer-aided design (CAD) and computer-aided manufacturing (CAM) enhanced flexibility in engineering design, leading to higher-quality products and reduced time for manufacturing.

OVERVIEW

Architects and mechanical parts designers once planned their buildings and machines with pencil and paper only, making elaborate blueprint drawings. Much of this method changed in 1982 with the groundbreaking introduction of computer software useful for vehicle design called "AutoCAD," released by a company called Autodesk. By the end of the twentieth century, many architects and mechanical designers were working on computers using specialty software that enables computer-aided design (CAD) and computer-aided manufacturing (CAM): CAD/CAM software.

Long before Autodesk released AutoCAD, the idea of using a computer to design buildings and mechanical parts was being explored by the military and the Massachusetts Institute of Technology (MIT). Semi-Automatic Ground Environment (SAGE), an air defense system, began testing in the 1950s; Sketchpad, a program created by MIT's Ivan Sutherland, focused on industrial uses. Sketchpad was revolutionary in its ease of use: the user entered a design into the computer simply by drawing on the computer's monitor with a light pen. Automobile manufacturer General Motors (GM) realized the importance of the technology to vehicle design and began to experiment with making software. Lockheed, Renault, and others followed suit. Many of these companies used software and code invented by the "father of CAD/CAM," Dr. Patrick J. Hanratty.

The momentum increased as computer memory grew and as computer monitors became larger. Thus, during the 1970s, when computers were becoming increasingly affordable, CAD software was used to make industrial tools and to do solid modeling. Computer design in two dimensions became augmented by design in three dimensions. In the 1980s, a three-dimensional (3D) program from Graphsoft and CAD for the Mac were released. The now-famous two-dimensional (2D) design software AutoCAD was developed by the firm Autodesk, which was started in 1982 by John Walker. The 1990s saw the introduction of hybrid modeling and template control from Unigraphics, and at the end of that decade, Think3's products allowed users to work simultaneously with wire frames, advanced surfacing, and parametric solids and to do other two-dimensional drafting tasks. In 1997, the CAD program computer-aided three-dimensional interactive application (CATIA) was used to design—on time and within budget—the spectacular Guggenheim Museum Bilbao in Spain, designed by Frank Gehry.

As CAD/CAM software grew increasingly prevalent, designers began to use such software to perform many different tasks, such as creating wire frames, solid models, and part assemblies. In addition to designing buildings and machine parts, designers applied that technology to other uses and products, such as textile design, milling, piping, hose and cable routing, heating and cooling units, welding, forging, engraving, laser use, shipbuilding, aerospace, electrical and biomechanical systems, printed electronic circuit boards, and even the design of tiny nano parts and intricate gardens.

Essential to any CAD/CAM user is the idea of geometric tolerancing. By using the principles of tolerancing, designers are able to make parts that exactly fit other parts, to make a whole unit. A CAD/CAM program can tell a designer if a part is matching its specifications; the program analyzes curves and checks assemblies for kinematics, interference, and clearance. A parts design operator can also manipulate the program to output the design to a rapid prototyping machine, to make a rough physical copy of the designed item.

Finite element analysis is an increasingly important part of CAD/CAM. This analysis uses linear algebra or nonlinear algebra and combines equations about compatibility, constitutive relations, and equilibrium. The method can refine how a complex model looks in CAD/CAM, and it is useful to determine stresses and solve problems in heat transfer, electromagnetism, fluid dynamics, and other types of reactions.

SIGNIFICANCE
Prior to CAD/CAM, designers worked with the basics—pencils, erasers, and rulers. The power of computers to help operators more easily create, alter, and store 3D designs has revolutionized the global marketplace. The software can allow a user to produce amazing walk-throughs, enabling a prospective client to examine a building from inside and outside. Operators can work more efficiently and can control a product from design to the end of the product's life. The software can even design standard parts automatically. Products can be designed for one purpose and can easily be redesigned to fit new purposes. Thus, the user can keep an immense library of designs, manage manufacturing processes, and control material waste.

CAD/CAM Software, Overview of

ABSTRACT

The term "CAD/CAM" is an acronym for "computer-aided design" and "computer-aided manufacturing." CAD/CAM refers collectively to a wide range of computer software products. Although CAD software and CAM software are considered two different types of programs, they are frequently used in concert and thus associated strongly with each other. Used primarily in manufacturing, CAD/CAM software enables users to design, model, and produce various objects—from prototypes to usable parts—with the assistance of computers.

APPLICATIONS OF CAD/CAM

Computer-aided design/computer-aided manufacturing (CAD/CAM) software originated in the 1960s, when researchers developed computer programs to assist professionals with design and modeling. Prior to that point, designing objects and creating three-dimensional (3D) models was a time-consuming process. Computer programs designed to aid with such tasks represented a significant time savings. By the late 1960s, CAD programs began to be used alongside early CAM software. CAM enabled users to instruct computer-compatible machinery to manufacture various objects according to digital designs. The use of CAD/CAM software became widespread over the following decades.

CAD and CAM are used in many industries to fulfill the same basic goals. 3D items are scanned and analyzed, new items are designed, and those designs can then be translated into manufactured items through CAM, which can develop the program necessary for machines to properly create the new item.

CAD/CAM is now a key part of the manufacturing process for numerous companies, from large corporations to small start-ups. Industries in which CAD/CAM can be particularly useful include the au-

This long-range control allows companies to cut waste and consider the environmental impacts of their products. Companies can more easily redesign products to be unique to the countries in which the products are to be sold, which is a big advantage in the global marketplace. Computers decrease the time needed from design to production, and new software even simulates stress tests. When CAD/CAM added communication features, staff in all areas of the business became much better connected.

For companies producing products in mass quantities, CAD/CAM technology is invaluable. In particular, machines run by computer numerical control (CNC) have been vastly improved in accuracy by CAD. CAM sometimes is part of a CNC machine, so that the CAM program operates the machine, with a person managing its work, to achieve such tasks as drilling holes into metal at precise intervals. The merger with CNC and CAD made the machines faster, cheaper to use, and much easier to monitor.

—*Jan Hall*

Further Reading

Andrews, Wen. *CAD Tools for Interior Design*. Autodesk Press, 2008.

Bi, Zhuming, and Xiaoqin Wang. *Computer Aided Design and Manufacturing*. Wiley-ASME Press, 2020.

Engle, Emily. "What Is CAD (Computer-Aided Design)?" *Autodesk*, 27 Apr. 2021, www.autodesk.com/products/fusion-360/blog/what-is-cad-computer-aided-design/. Accessed 28 Nov. 2021.

Green, Robert. *Expert CAD Management*. Sybex, 2007.

Kutz, Myer. *Environmentally Conscious Mechanical Design*. Wiley, 2007.

Lee, Ji-Hyun, editor. *Computer-Aided Architectural Design: "Hello, Culture."* Springer Nature Singapore, 2019.

Sarkar, Jayanta. *Computer Aided Design: A Conceptual Approach*. CRC Press, 2017.

Simpson, Timothy W., Zahed Siddique, and Jianxin Jiao, editors. *Product Platform and Product Family Design*. Springer, 2007.

tomotive and computer technology industries. However, CAM software has also been widely used in less obvious fields, including dentistry and textile manufacturing.

In addition to its use alongside CAM software, CAD software functions alone in a number of fields. CAD software allows users to create 3D models of objects or structures that do not need to be manufactured by machine. For instance, specialized CAD software is used in architecture to design floor plans and 3D models of buildings.

COMPUTER-AIDED DESIGN

Using CAD/CAM software is a two-part process that begins with design. In some cases, the user begins designing an object by using CAD software to create two-dimensional (2D) line drawings of the object. This process is known as "drafting." The user may then use tools within the CAD software to transform those 2D plans into a 3D model. As CAD/CAM is used to create physical objects, the modeling stage is the most essential stage in the design process. In that stage, the user creates a 3D representation of the item. This item may be a part for a machine, a semiconductor component, or a prototype of a new product, among other possibilities.

In some cases, the user may create what is known as a "wireframe model," a 3D model that resembles the outline of an object. However, such models do not include the solid surfaces or interior details of the object. Thus, they are not well suited for CAM, the goal of which is to manufacture a solid object. As such, those using CAD software in a CAD/CAM context often focus more on solid modeling. Solid modeling is the process of creating a 3D model of an object that includes the object's edges as well as its internal structure. CAD software typically allows the user to rotate or otherwise manipulate the created model. With CAD, designers can ensure that all the separate parts of a product will fit together as intended. CAD also enables users to modify the digital model. This is less time-consuming and produces less waste than modifying a physical model.

When designing models with the intention of manufacturing them through CAM technology, users must be particularly mindful of their key measurements. Precision and accurate scaling are crucial. As such, users must be sure to use vector images when designing their models. Unlike raster images, which are based on the use of individual pixels, vector images are based on lines and points that have defined relationships to one another. No matter how much a user shrinks or enlarges a vector image, the image will retain the correct proportions in terms of the relative placement of points and lines.

COMPUTER-AIDED MANUFACTURING

After designing an object using CAD software, a user may use a CAM program to manufacture it. CAM programs typically operate through computer numerical control (CNC). In CNC, instructions are transmitted to the manufacturing machine as a series of numbers. Those instructions tell the machine how to move and what actions to perform in order to construct the object. The types of machines used in that process vary and may include milling machines, drills, and lathes.

In the early twenty-first century, 3D printers, devices that manufacture objects out of thin layers of plastic or other materials, began to be used in CAM. Unlike traditional CNC machinery, 3D printers are typically used by individuals or small companies for whom larger-scale manufacturing technology is excessive.

SPECIALIZED APPLICATIONS

As CAD/CAM technology has evolved, it has come to be used for a number of specialized applications. Some CAD software, for instance, is used to perform four-dimensional (4D) building information modeling (4D BIM). This process enables a user to incorporate information related to time. For instance, the schedule for a particular project can be accounted for in the modeling process with 4D BIM.

Another common CAD/CAM application is rapid prototyping. In that process, a company or individual can design and manufacture physical prototypes of an object. This allows the designers to make changes in response to testing and evaluation and to test different iterations of the product. The resulting prototypes are often manufactured using 3D printers. Rapid prototyping results in improved quality control and a reduced time to bring a product to market.

—*Joy Crelin*

Further Reading
Bi, Zhuming, and Xiaoqin Wang. *Computer Aided Design and Manufacturing*. Wiley-ASME Press, 2020.
Chua, C. K., K. F. Leong, and C. S. Lim. *Rapid Prototyping: Principles and Applications*. World Scientific, 2010.
"Computer-Aided Design (CAD) and Computer-Aided Manufacturing (CAM)." *Inc.*, 6 Feb. 2020, www.inc.com/encyclopedia/computer-aided-design-cad-and-computer-aided-cam.html. Accessed 28 Nov. 2021.
Krar, Steve, Arthur Gill, and Peter Smid. *Technology of Machine Tools*. 8th ed., McGraw-Hill, 2020.
Sarkar, Jayanta. *Computer Aided Design: A Conceptual Approach*. CRC Press, 2017.

Computer Animation

ABSTRACT

Computer animation is the process of creating animated projects for film, television, or other media using any of a variety of specialized computer programs. As animation projects may range from short, simple clips to detailed and vibrant feature-length films, a wide variety of animation software is available, each addressing the particular needs of animators. The computer animation process includes several key steps, including modeling, adding lighting and special effects, and rendering, which are typically carried out by a team of animators.

HISTORY OF COMPUTER ANIMATION

Since the early twentieth century, the field of animation has been marked by frequent, rapid change. Innovation in the field has been far reaching, filtering into film, television, advertising, video games, and other media. It was initially an experimental method and took decades to develop. Computer animation revitalized the film and television industries during the late twentieth and early twenty-first centuries, in many ways echoing the cultural influence that animation had decades before.

Prior to the advent of computer animation, most animated projects were created using a process that later became known as "traditional," or "cel," animation. In cel animation, the movement of characters, objects, and backgrounds was created frame by frame. Each frame was drawn by hand. This time-consuming and difficult process necessitated the creation of dozens of individual frames for each second of film.

As computer technology developed, computer researchers and animators began to experiment with creating short animations using computers. Throughout the 1960s, computers were used to create two-dimensional (2D) images. Ed Catmull, who later founded the studio Pixar in 1986, created a three-dimensional (3D) animation of his hand using a computer in 1972. This was the first 3D computer graphic to be used in a feature film when it appeared in *Futureworld* (1976). Early attempts at computer animation were found in live-action films. The 1986 film *Labyrinth*, for instance, notably features a computer-animated owl flying through its opening credits. As technology improved, computer animation became a major component of special effects in live-action media. While cel animation continued to be used in animated feature films, filmmakers began to include some computer-generated elements in such works. The 1991 Walt Disney Studios film *Beauty and the Beast*, for instance, featured a ball-

Computer animated bee. Photo via iStock/julos. [Used under license.]

room in one scene that was largely created using a computer.

In 1995, the release of the first feature-length computer-animated film marked a turning point in the field of animation. That film, *Toy Story*, was created by Pixar, a pioneer in computer animation. Over the following decades, Pixar and other studios, including Disney (which acquired Pixar in 2006) and DreamWorks, produced numerous computer-animated films. Computer animation became a common process for creating animated television shows as well as video games, advertisements, music videos, and other media.

In the early twenty-first century, computer animation also began to be used to create simulated environments accessed through virtual reality equipment such as the head-mounted display Oculus Rift. Much of the computer-animated content created during this time featured characters and surroundings that appeared 3D. However, some animators opted to create 2D animations that more closely resemble traditionally animated works in style.

From designing the original animation model to creating algorithms that control the movement of fluids, hair, and other complex systems, computer software has drastically changed the art of animation. Through software that can manipulate polygons, a face can be rendered and further manipulated to create a number of images much more efficiently than with hand-drawn illustrations. Thus, the detail of the imaging is increased, while the time needed to develop a full animation is reduced.

THREE-DIMENSIONAL COMPUTER ANIMATION

Creating a feature-length computer-animated production is a complex and time-intensive process that is carried out by a large team of animators, working with other film-industry professionals. When creating a 3D computer-animated project, the animation team typically begins by drawing storyboards. Storyboards are small sketches that serve as a rough draft of the proposed scenes.

Next, animators transform 2D character designs into 3D models using animation software. They use animation variables (avars) to control the ways in which the 3D characters move, assigning possible directions of movement to various points on the characters' bodies. The number of avars used and the areas they control can vary widely. The 2006 Pixar film *Cars* reportedly used several hundred avars to control the characters' mouths alone. Using such variables gives animated characters a greater range of motion and often more realistic expressions and gestures. After the characters and objects are modeled and animated, they are combined with backgrounds as well as lighting and special effects. All of the elements are then combined to transform the 3D models into a 2D image or film. This process is known as 3D rendering.

TWO-DIMENSIONAL COMPUTER ANIMATION

Animating a 2D computer-animated work is somewhat different from its 3D counterpart, in that it does not rely on 3D modeling. Instead, it typically features the use of multiple layers, each of which contains different individual elements. This method of animating typically features keyframing. In this procedure, animators define the first and last frames in an animated sequence and allow the computer to fill in the movement in between. This process, which in traditionally animated films was a laborious task done by hand, is often known as "inbetweening," or "tweening."

TOOLS

Various animation programs are available to animators, each with its own strengths and weaknesses. Some animation software, such as Maya and Cinema 4D, are geared toward 3D animation. Others, such as Adobe Flash, are better suited to 2D animation. Adobe Flash has commonly been used to produce 2D cartoons for television, as it is considered a quick and low-cost means of creating such content. Animation studios such as Pixar typically use proprietary animation software, thus ensuring that their specific needs are met.

In addition to animation software, the process of computer animation relies heavily on hardware, as many steps in the process can be taxing for the systems in use. Rendering, for example, often demands a sizable amount of processing power. As such, many studios make use of render farms, large, powerful computer systems devoted to that task.

—*Joy Crelin*

Further Reading

"Computer Animator." *Art Career Project*, 15 July 2021, theartcareerproject.com/careers/computer-animation/. Accessed 28 Nov. 2021.

Glawion, Alex. "Building the Best PC for 3D Animation [2021 Guide]." *CGDirector*, 5 Oct. 2021, www.cgdirector.com/best-computer-for-animation/. Accessed 28 Nov. 2021.

Highfield, Roger. "Fast Forward to Cartoon Reality." *Telegraph*, 13 June 2006, www.telegraph.co.uk/technology/3346141/Fast-forward-to-cartoon-reality.html. Accessed 28 Nov. 2021.

"Our Story." *Pixar*, 2021, www.pixar.com/our-story-pixar. Accessed 28 Nov. 2021.

Parent, Rick. *Computer Animation: Algorithms and Techniques*. 3rd ed., Elsevier, 2012.

Sito, Tom. *Moving Innovation: A History of Computer Animation*. MIT Press, 2013.

Winder, Catherine, and Zahra Dowlatabadi. *Producing Animation*. Focal, 2011.

COMPUTER LANGUAGES, COMPILERS, AND TOOLS

ABSTRACT

Computer languages are used to provide the instructions for computers and other digital devices based on formal protocols. Low-level languages, or machine code, were initially written using the binary digits needed by the computer hardware, but since the 1960s, languages have evolved from early procedural languages to object-oriented high-level languages, which are more similar to English. There are many of these high-level languages, with their own unique capabilities and limitations, and most require some type of compiler or other intermediate translator to communicate with the computer hardware. Computer languages underlie the multitude of programs in use in the twenty-first century, from word-processing and computer-aided design (CAD) programs to data-analysis and simulation software. The popularity of the internet has created the need to develop numerous applications and tools designed to share data across the internet.

DEFINITION AND BASIC PRINCIPLES

The traditional process of using a computer language to write a program has generally involved the initial design of the program using a flowchart based on the purpose and desired output of the program, followed by typing the actual instructions for the computer (the code) into a file using a text editor, and then saving this code in a file (the source code file). A text editor is used because it does not have the formatting features of a word processor. An intermediate tool called a "compiler" then has been used to convert this source code into a format that can be run (executed) by a computer.

However, in the 2010s, a tool much faster and more efficient than compiler, called "interpreters," gained prominence and replaced most compilers. Larger, more complex programs have evolved that have required an additional step to link external files. This process is called "linking" and it joins the main, executable program created by the compiler to other necessary programs. Finally, the executable program is run and its output is displayed on the computer monitor, printed, or saved to another digital file. If errors are found, the process of debugging is followed to go back through the code to make corrections.

BACKGROUND AND HISTORY

Early computers such as ENIAC (Electronic Numerical Integrator and Computer), the first general-purpose computer, were based on the use of switches that could be turned on or off. Thus, the binary digits of 0 and 1 were used to write machine code. In addition to being tedious for a programmer, the code had to be rewritten if used on a different type of machine, and it certainly could not be used to transmit data across the internet, where different computers all over the world require access to the same code.

Assembly language evolved by using mnemonics (alphabetic abbreviations) for code instead of the binary digits. Because these alphabetic abbreviations of assembly language no longer used the binary digits, additional programs were developed to act as intermediaries between the human programmers writing the code and the computer itself. These additional programs were called compilers, and this process was initially known as compiling the code. This compilation process was still machine and vendor dependent, however, meaning, for example, that there were several types of compilers that were used to compile code written in one language. This was expensive and made communication of computer applications difficult.

The evolution of computer languages from the 1950s has accompanied technological advances that have allowed languages to become increasingly powerful, yet easier for programmers to use. FORTRAN and COBOL languages led the way for programmers to develop scientific and business application programs, respectively, and were dependent on a command-line user interface, which required a user to type in a command to complete a specific task. Several other languages were developed, including Basic, Pascal, PL/I, Ada, Lisp, Prolog, and Smalltalk, but each of these had limited versatility and various problems. The C and C++ languages of the 1970s and 1980s, respectively, emerged as the most useful and powerful languages and are still in use. These were followed by development tools written in the Java and Visual Basic languages, including integrated development environments with editors, designers, debuggers, and compilers all built into a single software package.

HOW IT WORKS

BIOS and Operating System. The programs within the BIOS are the first and last programs to execute whenever a computer device is turned on or off. These programs interact directly with the operating system (OS). The early mainframe computers that were used in the 1960s and 1970s depended on several different operating systems, most of which are no longer in usage, except for UNIX and DOS. DOS (disk operating system) was used on the initial microcomputers of the 1980s and early 1990s, and it is

Photo via iStock/matejmo. [Used under license.]

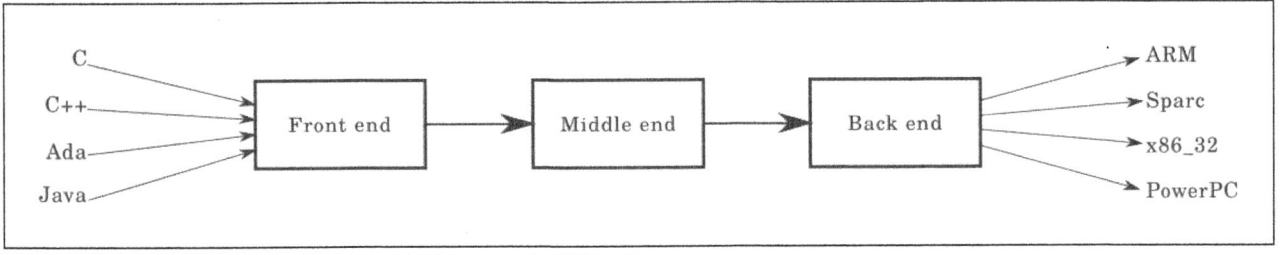

Three phase compiler structure design. Image by Pronesto, via Wikimedia Commons.

still used for certain command-line specific instructions.

Graphical User Interfaces (GUIs). Microsoft dominates the PC market with its many updated operating systems, which are very user-friendly with GUIs. These operating systems consist of computer programs and software that act as the management system for all of the computer's resources, including the various applications most taken for granted, such as Word (for documents), Excel (for mathematical and spreadsheet operations), and Access (for database functions). Each of these applications is a program itself, and there are many more that are also available.

Since the 1980s, many programming innovations increasingly have been built to involve the client-server model, with less emphasis on large mainframes and more emphasis on the GUIs for smaller microcomputers and handheld devices that allow consumers to have deep color displays with high resolution and voice and sound capabilities. However, these initial GUIs on client computers required additional upgrades and maintenance to be able to interact effectively with servers.

World Wide Web. The creation of the World Wide Web provided new means of accessing information, and the widespread use of the internet led to the creation of new programming languages and tools. The browser was developed to allow an end user (client) to be able to access web information, and hypertext markup language (HTML) was developed to display web pages. Because the client computer was manufactured by many different companies, the Java language was developed to include applets, which are mini-programs embedded into web pages that could be displayed on any type of client computer. This was made possible by a special type of compiler-like tool called the "Java Virtual Machine," which translated byte code.

APPLICATIONS AND PRODUCTS
FORTRAN and COBOL. FORTRAN (sometimes written as Fortran) was developed by a team of programmers at IBM and was first released in 1957 to be used primarily for highly numerical and scientific applications. It derived its name from formula translation. Initially, it used punched cards for input, because the text editors were not available in the 1950s. It has evolved but still continues to be used primarily in many engineering and scientific programs, including almost all programs written for geology research. Several updated versions have been released, including the 2018 revision Fortran 2018. FORTRAN77, released in 1980, had the most significant language improvements. COBOL (Common Business-Oriented Language) was released in 1959 with the goal of being used primarily for tracking retail sales, payroll, inventory control, and many other accounting-related activities.

C and C++. The C computer language was the predecessor to the C++ language. Programs written in C were procedural and based on the usage of functions, which are small programming units. As programs grew in complexity, more functions were added to a C program. The problem was that eventually it became necessary to redesign the entire program, because trying to connect all of the functions, which added one right after the other, in a procedural way, was too difficult. C++ was created in the 1980s based on the idea of objects grouped into classes as the building blocks of the programs, which meant that the order did not have to be procedural anymore. Object-oriented programming made developing complex programs much more efficient.

Microsoft.NET. In June 2000, Microsoft introduced a suite of languages and tools named Microsoft.NET along with its new language called "Visual C#." Later known simply as .NET, Microsoft.NET is a software infrastructure that consists of many programs that allow a user to write programs for a range of new applications such as server components and web applications by using new tools. Although programs written in Java can be run on any machine, as long as the entire program is written in Java, .NET allows various programs to be run on the Windows OS. Additional advantages of .NET involve its use of Visual C#. Visual C# provides services to help Web pages already in existence, and C# can be integrated with the Visual Basic and Visual C++ languages, which facilitate the work of web programmers by allowing them to update existing web applications, rather than having to rewrite them.

The .NET framework uses a common type system (CTS) tool to compile programs written in a variety of languages into an intermediate language. This common intermediate language (CIL) can then be compiled to a common language runtime (CLR). The result is that the .NET programming environment promotes interoperability to allow programs originally written in different languages to be executed on a variety of operating systems and computer devices. This interoperability is crucial for sharing data and communication across the internet.

SOCIAL CONTEXT AND FUTURE PROSPECTS

The internet continues to bring the world together at a rapid pace, which has both positive and negative ramifications. Consumers have much easier access to many services, such as online education and telemedicine, and can use free search tools to locate doctors, learn more about any topic, comparison shop and purchase, and immediately access software, movies, pictures, and music. However, along with this increase in electronic commerce involving credit card purchases, bank accounts, and additional financial transactions has been the increase of cybercrime. Thousands of dollars are lost each year to various internet scams and the accessing of private financial information by hackers. Some programmers even use computer languages to produce viruses and other destructive programs for purely malicious purposes, which have a negative impact on computer security. Such phenomena have given rise to the development of improved security features within computer languages and tools.

—*Jeanne L. Kuhler, BS, MS, PhD*

Further Reading

Das, Sumitabha. *Your UNIX: The Ultimate Guide*. 3rd ed., McGraw-Hill, 2012.

Dhillon, Gupreet. "Dimensions of Power and IS Implementation." *Information and Management*, vol. 41, no. 5, 2004, pp. 635-44.

Guelich, Scott, Shishir Gundavaram, and Gunther Birznieks. *CGI Programming with Perl*. 2nd ed., O'Reilly, 2000.

Horstmann, Cay. *Big Java: Early Objects*. 7th ed., John Wiley & Sons, 2018.

Lee, Kent D. *Foundations of Programming Languages*. Springer, 2014.

O'Leary, Timothy, Linda O'Leary, and Daniel O'Leary. *Computing Essentials 2021*. McGraw-Hill, 2020.

Sandals, Jonathan. "Top Programming Languages of 2021." *Coding Dojo*, 7 Feb. 2020, www.codingdojo.com/blog/top-7-programming-languages. Accessed 28 Nov. 2021.

Scott, Michael L. *Programming Language Pragmatics*. 4th ed., Morgan Kaufmann, 2016.

Computer Memory and Storage

ABSTRACT

There are different types of memory inside a computer, including temporary memory, read-only memory (ROM), random-access memory (RAM), and programmable read-only memory (PROM). Computer storage technologies include hard drives and cloud storage. Memory and storage are used for different purposes. Fast, temporary memory such as RAM is used to make quick calculations, while hard drives are used for long-term storage of programs and files. Without memory and storage, computers would not be able to function in any meaningful capacity.

HISTORY OF THE COMPUTER

In their earliest days, computers were strictly mechanical devices. They used punch cards for memory and output. These machines were developed for utility rather than for the multitude of tasks for which modern computers are designed. They were primarily used for complex calculations.

Alan Turing, a famous computer scientist, is credited with the idea for the first multipurpose computer. In the 1930s, J. V. Atanasoff created the first computer that contained no gears, cams, belts, or shafts. Atanasoff and his team then designed the first computer with functioning, nonmechanical memory devices. Primitive when compared to today's devices, Atanasoff's creation allowed the computer to solve up to twenty-nine equations simultaneously.

The next major leap in computing power was the usage of vacuum tubes. In 1994, professors John Mauchly and J. Presper Eckert built the first tube-powered electronic calculator. This is commonly considered the first digital computer. It was a massive machine, taking up the entirety of a large room. They soon began to market this computer to governments and businesses. However, tube computers became obsolete in 1947 with the invention of the transistor.

Ten years later, the transistor was used by Robert Noyce and Jack Kilby to create the first computer chip. This spurred the development of the first devices recognizable as modern computers. Computers took another leap forward with the graphical user interface (GUI), which projects options as images on a screen instead of requiring users to learn to code. Computers advanced further with the inventions of RAM in 1970 and floppy disks in 1971. Floppy disks were a form of permanent storage used in the early days of computers. They could easily be transferred

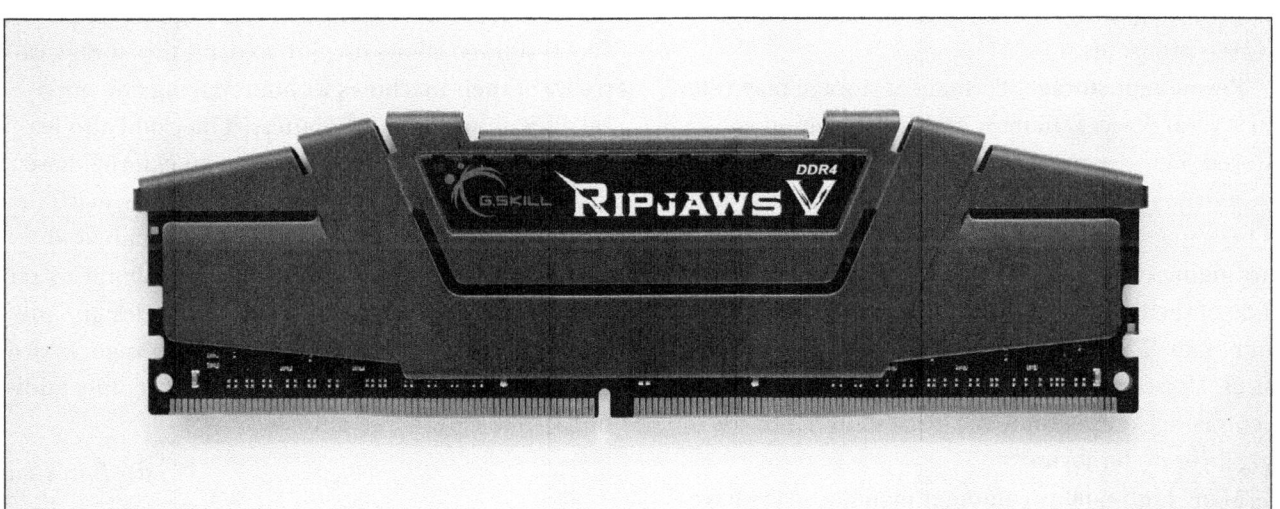

Modern DDR4 SDRAM module, usually found in desktop computers. Photo by ElooKoN, via Wikimedia Commons.

from one computer to another, making them ideal for transporting information. Floppy disks were made obsolete by CD-ROMs, which are small plastic disks that store large amounts of information.

Computer memory and storage are measured in binary digits, called "bits." One bit is an extremely small amount of information. Eight bits is the equivalent of one byte. 1,024 bytes is called a "kilobyte" (KB); 1,024 KB makes a megabyte (MB); 1,024 MB makes a gigabyte (GB); and 1,024 GB makes a terabyte (TB). Over time, the cost of large amounts of computer memory and storage has drastically fallen. However, the amount of memory and storage required by computers has also drastically increased.

TYPES OF MEMORY AND STORAGE

Temporary memory. Computers contain several types of memory. The most common type is temporary memory, which is designed to hold information for only a short period. Most of a computer's temporary memory is RAM. RAM is designed to quickly write and erase information. It performs calculations, runs scripts, and enacts most of the computer's functions. A computer with more RAM can perform more functions at once, making it more powerful and more capable of running resource-intensive programs, such as computer-aided design (CAD) programs.

Permanent storage. Permanent storage may refer to several devices. In most cases, information is stored on the computer's hard disk drive. Most hard disk drives use a spinning disk and an actuator arm. The actuator arm writes to the spinning disk by rearranging electrons. In this scenario, the entire inside of the hard disk drive is located inside an airtight seal. These hard drives can be found in many sizes. However, hard disk drives of the twenty-first century are often found in capacities of hundreds of gigabytes to terabytes.

Many high-quality computer manufacturers have begun replacing hard disk drives with solid-state drives. Solid-state drives contain no moving parts. In most instances, these drives can read and write data much faster than hard disk drives. Because they have no moving parts, solid-state drives are also much quieter than hard disk drives. However, solid-state drives are also significantly more expensive than hard disk drives. For this reason, if a device needs large quantities of storage, it may be more cost-effective to use hard disk drives. However, if the device needs to be able to access data quickly, be durable, or be compact in size, manufacturers may use a solid-state drive.

External storage. Some computers utilize external forms of storage. These are drives located outside the device. If it is connected to the device by a universal serial bus (USB) cable or other interface, it is called an "external hard drive." External hard drives are easily transferable from one device to another, making them useful for quickly moving large media files. They may also be used to back up large amounts of important files, protecting them from computer malfunction or viruses.

If the external memory is accessed through the internet, it is referred to as cloud storage. Many services offer large amounts of external storage for purchase. This may be used for server backups, media storage, or any number of other applications. Cloud storage allows users to expand the storage capacity of their machines without making any physical alterations to the computers. The cloud also features many of the same benefits as an external hard drive. Files can easily be relocated to a new machine in the event of a hardware or software failure and can likewise be shared among those collaborating on a group project, such as an engineering design. Additionally, renting space from a cloud storage service may be cheaper than purchasing and installing additional physical storage devices.

—Tyler Biscontini

Further Reading

"Data Measurement Chart." *University of Florida*, www.wu.ece.ufl.edu/links/dataRate/DataMeasurementChart.html. Accessed 28 Nov. 2021.

"Hard Drive." *Computer Hope*, 2 Aug. 2020, www.computerhope.com/jargon/h/harddriv.htm. Accessed 28 Nov. 2021.

"How Computers Work: The CPU and Memory." *University of Rhode Island*, homepage.cs.uri.edu/faculty/wolfe/book/Readings/Reading04.htm. Accessed 28 Nov. 2021.

"Introduction to Memory." *CCM Benchmark Group*, 22 Jan. 2021, ccm.net/contents/396-computer-introduction-to-memory. Accessed 28 Nov. 2021.

O'Leary, Timothy, Linda O'Leary, and Daniel O'Leary. *Computing Essentials 2021*. McGraw-Hill, 2020.

"Storage vs. Memory." *PCMag*, www.pcmag.com/encyclopedia/term/storage-vs-memory. Accessed 28 Nov. 2021.

"Timeline of Computer History." *Computer History Museum*, www.computerhistory.org/timeline/computers/. Accessed 28 Nov. 2021.

Watson, Catie. "What Are the Four Basic Functions of a Computer?" *Techwalla*, 21 Sept. 2018, www.techwalla.com/articles/what-are-the-four-basic-functions-of-a-computer. Accessed 28 Nov. 2021.

"What Goes into Meeting the Workstation Requirements for CAD Systems." *Infratech*, 13 Jan. 2019, www.infratechcivil.com/pages/Workstation-requirements-for-CAD-systems-for-autocad-revit. Accessed 28 Nov. 2021.

Computer Modeling

ABSTRACT

Computer modeling is the process of designing a representation of a particular system of interacting or interdependent parts in order to study its behavior. Models that have been implemented and executed as computer programs are called "computer simulations."

UNDERSTANDING COMPUTER MODELS

A computer model is a programmed representation of a system that is meant to mimic the behavior of the system. A wide range of disciplines, including meteorology, physics, astronomy, biology, and economics, use computer models to analyze different types of systems. When the program representing the system is executed by a computer, it is called a "simulation."

One of the first large-scale computer models was developed during the Manhattan Project by scientists designing and building the first atomic bomb. Early computer models produced output in the form of tables or matrices that were difficult to analyze. It was later discovered that humans can see data trends more easily if the data is presented visually. For example, humans find it easier to analyze the output of a storm-system simulation if it is presented as graphic symbols on a map rather than as a table of meteorological data. Thus, simulations that produced graphic outputs were developed.

Computer models are used when a system is too complex or hard to study using a physical model. For example, it would be difficult to create a physical model representing the gravitational effects of planets and moons on each other and on other ob-

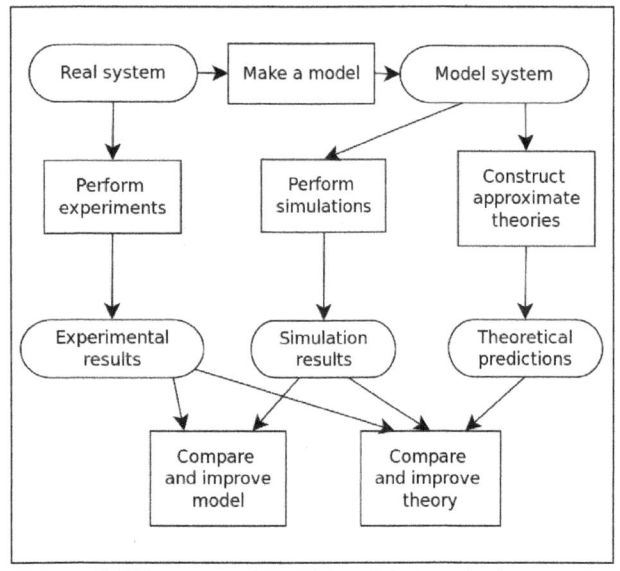

Process of building a computer model, and the interplay between experiment, simulation, and theory. Image by Danski14, via Wikimedia Commons.

jects in space, although the National Aeronautics and Space Administration (NASA) has done exactly that for the Voyager space probes.

There are several different types of models. Static models simulate a system at rest, such as a building design. Dynamic models simulate a system that changes over time. A dynamic model could be used to simulate the effects of changing ocean temperatures on the speed of ocean currents throughout the year. A continuous model simulates a system that changes constantly, while a discrete model simulates a system that changes only at specific times. Some models contain both discrete and continuous elements. A farming model might simulate the effects of both weather patterns, which constantly change, and pesticide spraying, which occurs at specified times.

HOW COMPUTER MODELS WORK

To create a computer model, one must first determine the boundaries of the system being modeled and what aspect of the system is being studied. For example, if the model is of the solar system, it might be used to study the potential effect on the orbits of the existing planets if another planet were to enter the solar system.

To create such a model, a computer programmer would develop a series of algorithms that contain the equations and other instructions needed to replicate the operation of the system. Variables are used to represent the input data needed. Examples of variables that might be used for the solar system model include the mass, diameter, and trajectory of the theoretical new planet. The values that define the system, and thus how the variables affect each other, are the parameters of the system. The parameters control the outputs of the simulation when it is run. Different values can be used to test different scenarios related to the system and problem being studied. Example parameters for the solar system model might include the orbits of the known planets, their distance from the sun, and the equations that relate an object's mass to its gravity. Certain parameters can be changed to test different scenarios each time a simulation is run. Because parameters are not always constant, they can be difficult to distinguish from variables at times.

WHY COMPUTER MODELS ARE IMPORTANT

Computer models have provided great benefits to society. They help scientists explore the universe, understand the earth, cure diseases, and discover and test new theories. They help engineers design buildings, transportation systems, power systems, and other items that affect everyday life. With the development of more powerful computer systems, computer models will remain an important mechanism for understanding the world and improving the human condition.

—*Maura Valentino, MSLIS*

Further Reading

Abbasov, Iftikhar B., editor. *Computer Modeling in the Aerospace Industry*. Wiley/Scrivener Publishing, 2020.

Agrawal, Manindra, S. Barry Cooper, and Angsheng Li, editors. *Theory and Applications of Models of Computation: 9th Annual Conference, TAMC 2012, Beijing, China, May 16-21, 2012*. Springer, 2012.

"Computational Modeling." *National Institute of Biomedical Imaging and Bioengineering*, May 2020, www.nibib.nih.gov/science-education/science-topics/computational-modeling. Accessed 28 Nov. 2021.

Edwards, Paul N. *A Vast Machine: Computer Models, Climate Data, and the Politics of Global Warming*. MIT Press, 2010.

Kojiæ, Miloš, et al. *Computer Modeling in Bioengineering: Theoretical Background, Examples and Software*. Wiley, 2008.

Law, Averill M. *Simulation Modeling and Analysis*. 5th ed., McGraw, 2015.

Mityushev, Vladimir, Wojciech Nawalaniec, and Natalia Rylko. *Introduction to Mathematical Modeling and Computer Simulations*. CRC Press, 2018.

Morrison, Foster. *The Art of Modeling Dynamic Systems: Forecasting for Chaos, Randomness, and Determinism*. 1991. Dover, 2008.

Seidl, Martina, et al. *UML@Classroom: An Introduction to Object-Oriented Modeling.* Springer, 2015.

Computer Numerical Control (CNC) Milling

ABSTRACT
Computer numerical control milling, commonly known as CNC milling, is a precision process used in industrial machining to create customized products or parts. It uses computer-programmed code to relay instructions to production machines, which then execute the instructions to yield objects with the desired physical and functional characteristics. CNC milling is compatible with numerous commonly used raw materials, including glass, metal, plastic, and wood. By definition, CNC milling alters the raw material, known as "workpieces," by removing substances from it via machine-powered cutting.

The systems and equipment used to program and control CNC milling machines work through computer interactions. Technicians use specialized software to enter numerical code, which is then relayed to the machine as Cartesian coordinates. The machine then uses those coordinates to carry out the assigned task. CNC milling is one of multiple types of precision computer numerical control machining, with others including CNC lathing, turning, grinding, lasering, waterjet cutting, plasma cutting, sheet metal stamping, and electrical discharging.

BRIEF HISTORY
Milling is an industrial process that deploys rotating cutting equipment to remove material from a workpiece and shape it into a finished product or part. During the early stages of the Industrial Revolution in the nineteenth century, workers performed milling tasks manually using a technique known as "hand-filing." Milling machines first appeared when rudimentary industrial technologies began to evolve during the early nineteenth century. Surveys of machining history note that it is not known exactly when the first milling machines were invented, as many independent industrial manufacturers developed and used their own systems on small scales. Machine-assisted milling became a common feature of industrial production beginning in the 1840s, and the earliest such machines capable of milling materials in three dimensions appeared in 1861 when the Providence, Rhode Island-based Brown & Sharpe company introduced its first Universal Milling Machine. The Universal Milling Machine quickly became a widely used standard, leading competitors to create refined systems capable of more precise movements.

CNC milling was preceded by a noncomputerized technology known as numerical control (NC) milling. NC milling arose to address persistent production errors arising from the high volume of input required of manual machinists. Its invention is credited to the American industrial developer John T. Parsons (1913-2007), who pioneered a system of using punched tape to relay instructions to automated machines in the late 1940s. The punched tape contained numerical data, which was interpreted by specialized tape readers and relayed to machines, which then carried out the assigned task according to the submitted instructions. NC machining was initially limited to the manufacture of aviation and aerospace equipment and products but slowly expanded into other industries over the course of the 1950s.

During the 1960s, improvements in data storage capabilities propelled significant advancements in emerging computer technologies and allowed automated tools to replace human workers in many processes. NC machining became computerized when the initial generations of computer-aided design (CAD) software became compatible with three-dimensional (3D) objects, an advancement attributed to the French engineer Pierre Bézier (1910-1999), who created an early CAD system known as

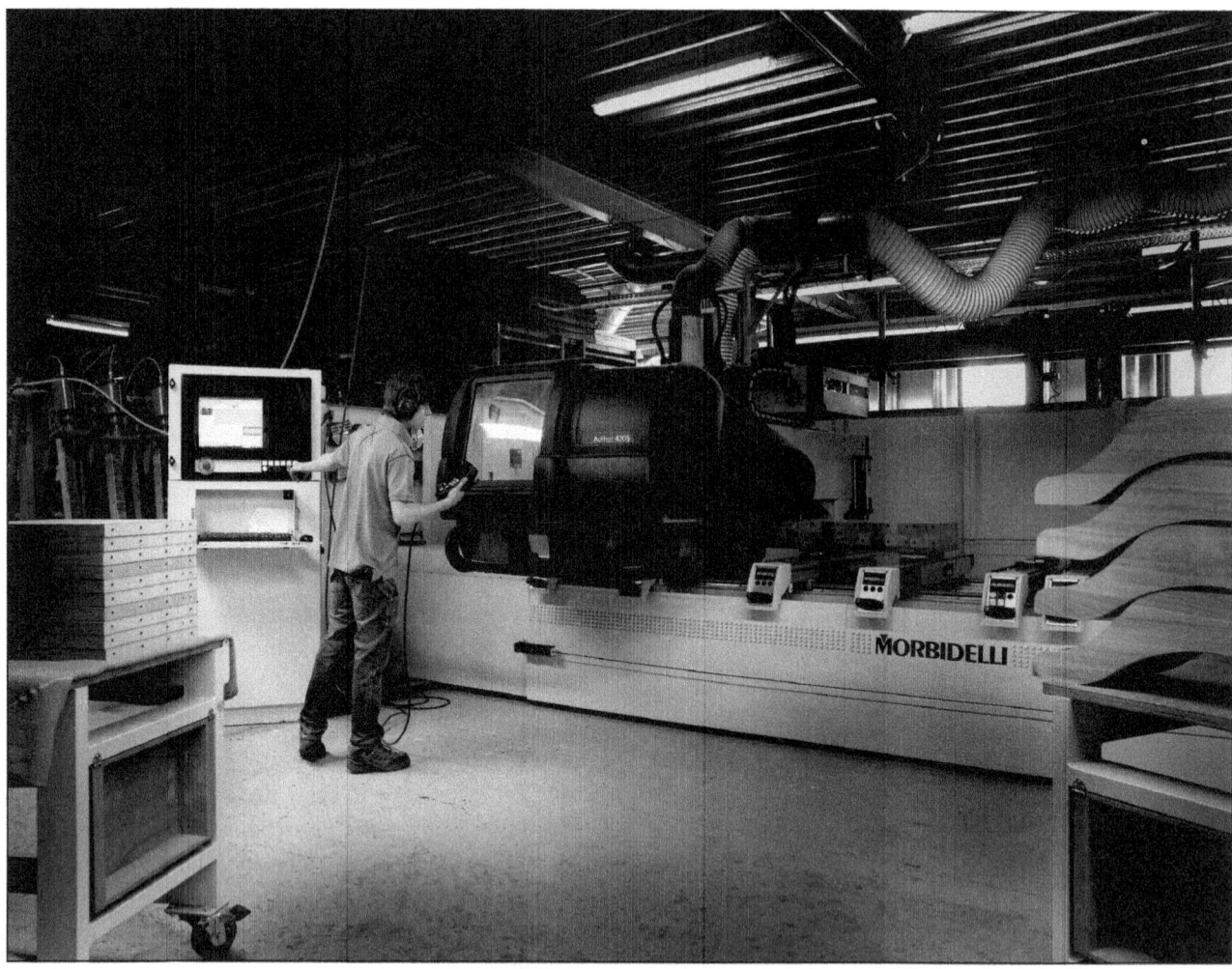

A CNC machine that operates on wood. Photo via Wikimedia Commons. [Public domain.]

UNISURF for the Renault automobile company in 1968. As the capabilities of CAD software continued to expand, it became able to interpret complex 3D blueprints and relay specifications to milling machines. CNC milling matured further during the 1970s, becoming a widely used technique in automated industrial production.

OVERVIEW

Contemporary CNC milling systems have the capability and data capacity to carry out highly complex and large-scale milling processes with extreme precision. Their basic structure links a computer running CAD software to a production machine with cutting tools affixed to rotating spindles. A technician places a workpiece of raw material into the cutting machine, and the CAD software then relays instructions that tell the machine exactly where, when, and how to cut the workpiece. The machine then carries out the commands, selectively removing material from the workpiece until it matches final specifications. Simple CNC milling systems operate on a single, flat plane, but more complex examples mount workpieces on tables, which then rise, tilt, or rotate at various angles to facilitate cutting on multiple planes.

Manufacturers can use CNC milling in many ways. It has become a common way to cut workpieces into specified shapes, but CNC milling systems also create holes, notches, pockets, slots, and other precision characteristics. Exact manufacturing instructions can be entered in two-dimensional (2D) or three-dimensional (3D) formats, which CAD software converts into a set of commands readable by the cutting machine. These commands are then exported, and the CNC machine selectively activates its cutting tools as needed to create a product or part that matches the original instructions. In shaping workpieces, the CNC milling machine's cutting tools spin at extremely fast rates, guiding raw materials into their final forms with great speed and efficiency.

Industrial manufacturers use four main types of CNC milling processes: plain, face, angular, and form milling. Plain milling, sometimes called "slab milling" or "surface milling," brings cutting tools into contact with workpieces at a flat, parallel angle. In face milling, the cutting tool's rotary axis is perpendicular to the workpiece. Angular milling straddles plain and face milling, positioning the cutting tool's rotary axis in positions that are neither parallel nor perpendicular. Form milling is the most complex type, yielding curved, concave, or convex products and parts with no flat surfaces. These four primary CNC milling techniques can be deployed to create many different types of manufactured goods, but they are most commonly used to make precision instruments or product components, furniture and cabinetry, sculpted objects, signage, and industrial prototypes.

Human operators still participate in various phases of the process. Some CNC milling machines have removable tools, allowing technicians to choose and place the specific implements necessary to complete the task at hand. Machinists also place and secure the unformed workpieces, then initiate the production process by manually enabling the programmed task with the CNC machine's interface. However, advancements in machine learning (ML), artificial intelligence (AI), and robotics technologies continue to drive CNC milling processes toward complete automation.

—*Jim Greene, MFA*

Further Reading

"The Complete Engineering Guide: CNC Machining." *Hubs*, 2021, www.hubs.com/guides/cnc-machining/. Accessed 28 Nov. 2021.

"Different Types of Machining Operations and the Machining Process." *Thomas*, 2021, www.thomasnet.com/articles/custom-manufacturing-fabricating/machining-processes/. Accessed 28 Nov. 2021.

Gupta, Kapil, and J. Paulo Davim, editors. *High-Speed Machining*. Academic Press, 2020.

"The History and Design of Milling Machines." *Plethora*, 8 Aug. 2017, www.plethora.com/insights/the-history-and-design-of-milling-machines. Accessed 28 Nov. 2021.

Jepson, Phil. "The CNC Milling Process Explained." *EGL Vaughan*, 4 Aug. 2020, eglvaughan.co.uk/cnc-milling-process-explained/. Accessed 28 Nov. 2021.

Kumar, Kaushik, Chikesh Ranjan, and J. Paulo Davim. *CNC Programming for Machining*. Springer Nature Switzerland, 2020.

Ronquillo, Romina. "Understanding CNC Milling." *Thomas*, 2021, www.thomasnet.com/articles/custom-manufacturing-fabricating/understanding-cnc-milling/. Accessed 28 Nov. 2021.

Computer Simulation

ABSTRACT

Computer simulation is the use of computer technology to make digital models that represent real-world elements, behaviors, and systems. Programmers and engineers can then use the computerized model in experiments, changing conditions and observing the effects on the model. By observing and analyzing the results of these experiments, people can draw inferences about how the elements might behave in the real world. Testing a simulated model in-

stead of a real-life object or scenario is generally much safer and less expensive, though simulated tests may prove to be less accurate. A type of applied mathematics, computer simulation is commonly used for a wide variety of purposes in fields such as science, politics, military studies, and entertainment.

USES AND TYPES

To perform a computer simulation, operators design a digital model of something to be tested. For instance, engineers may want to explore the feasibility of a new bridge linking two cities. In this case, operators program data about the proposed bridge—such as its dimensions, weight, construction style, and materials—into an appropriate simulation program. Other factors, such as the location, climate, water flow, and typical wind speed, are programmed as well to complete the simulated scenario.

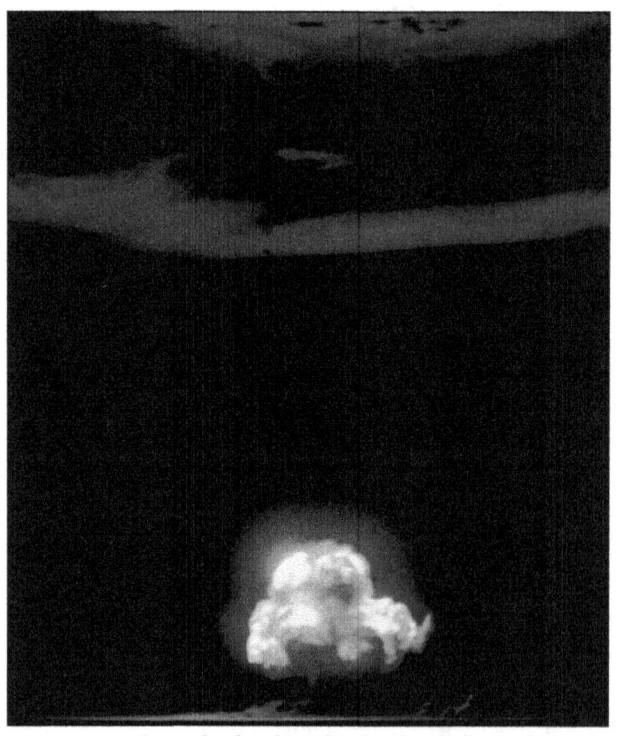

Computer simulation developed hand-in-hand with the rapid growth of the computer, following its first large-scale deployment during the Manhattan Project in World War II to model the process of nuclear detonation. Photo via Wikimedia Commons. [Public domain.]

Once the simulation begins, the program shows how the proposed bridge would likely fare in the prevailing conditions. If engineers need specific information, such as how a tornado would affect the bridge, they can manipulate the data to reflect tornado-speed winds. They may also want to test different designs for the bridge and may program different sizes or styles of bridge to test which works best in the given circumstances.

The simulation may run once or many times and may be programmed to reflect a short time, a single event, or potentially countless times or events. Operators study the data gathered by each simulation to help them gain better understanding of the dynamics of the system they have designed. Scientists with large quantities of data usually use statistics or other means of interpreting their findings, especially since simulations may not accurately reflect real-world possibilities.

People may use computer simulations to test proposed systems for many reasons. Sometimes the system being studied does not exist in the real world and cannot be easily or safely created, or it may even be impossible to create. Sometimes a system does exist, but operators want to simulate proposed changes to the system without actually altering the system in real life, which might involve serious expenses or dangers. In other cases, the simulation tests systems that have not occurred but may occur in the future—some examples of this are forecasting weather or predicting the spread of populations or diseases across a given area. Other simulations may test physical structures, economic principles, workplace practices, biological systems, or social trends.

There are three major kinds of computer simulations: continuous, Monte Carlo, and discrete. Continuous simulations show results of a system over time, with equations designed to show progressive changes. Monte Carlo simulations use random numbers and random events without regard for time. Finally, discrete simulations (sometimes classified as a subtype of Monte Carlo simulations) involve occasional events that break up otherwise uneventful blocks of time.

DEVELOPMENT AND MODERN IMPORTANCE

Although computer simulations are a relatively modern science, only arising after the dawn of the computer age in the twentieth century, the history of simulation reaches into ancient times. Before advanced science and technology were available to provide some accuracy to simulated results, people used mystical means to try to divine details of the future or hypothetical situations. Astrologers, oracles, prophets, and sorcerers were sought after in many lands for their purported abilities to gather information inaccessible to most.

As advances in science and technology replaced mysticism, people began creating computer programs that would use mathematical and scientific principles to create simulations. Some of the earliest computer-based simulations took place during World War II, when scientists such as John von Neumann and Stanislaw Ulam used early computerized devices to simulate the effects of atomic bombs. As the primitive computers of the 1940s became faster, stronger, and more reliable, their ability to create simulations developed as well.

Twenty-first-century computers are able to create comprehensive simulations for a wide range of different fields and applications. Simulation programs give operators more tools to customize the factors of their simulations, alter variables, and create animated digital displays to represent the simulated scenarios. As the efficiency of simulations increases, so too do demands on simulation programmers to make their products more efficient and free of errors.

Computer simulations are generally less costly and difficult to prepare than real-life demonstrations, enabling them to be performed more quickly and frequently, thus creating more usable data. Even the process of creating a simulation could result in benefits for an individual or organization. To design the simulation, operators must painstakingly plan the model, which means analyzing all aspects of the proposed design and sometimes gathering new information from other sources. During this process, flaws in the concept may appear, or new potential approaches may come to light. When the simulation is complete, it is generally easy to customize and modify, allowing operators to use their creativity to explore any different factors or approaches they have identified. In short, making a simulation may be like a trial run of creating a real-life project, and as such help to refine the final design.

At the same time, computer simulations are not without their faults. Complex simulations may require extensive costs for programming, training, software, and data analysis as well as a significant amount of preparation time. Additionally, data resulting from simulations are inexact, since simulations only approximately represents possibilities, not real-world happenings. Accepting simulation data as perfectly accurate can lead to serious risks.

—*Mark Dziak*

Further Reading

McHaney, Roger. *Computer Simulation: A Practical Perspective*. Academic Press, 1991.

"Monte Carlo Simulation." *IBM*, 24 Aug. 2020, www.ibm.com/cloud/learn/monte-carlo-simulation. Accessed 28 Nov. 2021.

Shih, Willy C. "Computer Simulations Are Better—and More Affordable—Than Ever." *Harvard Business Review*, 2 Oct. 2020, hbr.org/2020/10/computer-simulations-are-better-and-more-affordable-than-ever. Accessed 28 Nov. 2021.

"What Is Simulation Modeling (and How Does It Work)?" *Spatial*, 25 Mar. 2020, blog.spatial.com/simulation-in-cad. Accessed 28 Nov. 2021.

Winsberg, Eric. "Computer Simulations in Science." *Stanford Encyclopedia of Philosophy*, 26 Sept. 2019, plato.stanford.edu/entries/simulations-science/. Accessed 28 Nov. 2021.

———. *Science in the Age of Computer Simulation*. U of Chicago P, 2010.

Contract Manufacturing

ABSTRACT
Contract manufacturing is the process of hiring a manufacturing firm to produce one or more components, assemblies, or completed products. The manufacturing firm under contract may use any of a multitude of manufacturing technologies to produce the desired items, including computer-aided design (CAD) and computer-aided manufacturing (CAM) technologies.

OVERVIEW
Contract manufacturing is the process of hiring a manufacturing firm to produce one or more components, assemblies, or completed products. The hiring company is usually an original equipment manufacturer (OEM), which uses the products produced by the contract manufacturer (CM) as subassemblies for its own products, or to sell as is (perhaps with its own packaging) to its customers. OEMs usually provide the CM with completed designs, at times in the form of computer-aided design (CAD) files, and oftentimes a prototype, though CMs are increasingly providing even these services to the OEM.

An OEM's selection of a CM is generally based on cost, expertise, quality, and other factors related to the specific part or product to be produced. An OEM may negotiate a contract with a single manufacturer with which it has an existing relationship or may put out a request for proposal (RFP) to multiple CMs, depending on the need, the size and complexity of the project, and whether or not the OEM has a good relationship with a CM that has the capabilities needed. A typical OEM, depending on the size and breadth of its offerings, may use many different CMs for various purposes and products.

REASONS FOR CONTRACT MANUFACTURING
Expertise. One of the key reasons for outsourcing manufacturing is to obtain specific expertise. With the increasing complexity of equipment, some CMs are specializing in very narrow skill sets and capabilities. Rather than investing in expensive equipment and hiring the skill sets needed, it often makes sense for an OEM to outsource to the expert, gaining better quality, faster turnaround and very often a lower cost than manufacturing in-house.

Lower cost. Another reason for contracting manufacturing services is to achieve a lower production cost. This may be done by leveraging offshore manufacturers whose labor, land, and materials costs are very often much lower than in the United States. CMs also may get much better pricing from component suppliers, wherever they are based, since those suppliers typically buy the required materials in very large volumes.

Speed to market. Cost and specialization aside, speed to market is often the biggest driver. The ability to get an idea to market fast is often a critical success factor for profitability. CMs can ramp up much more quickly than the OEM, especially those that have widely diverse capabilities and have many factories that can handle spikes in demand. The ability to tap into this vast resource ensures OEMs a much quicker turnaround on products than would otherwise be feasible.

Innovation possibilities. Outsourcing also allows OEMs to focus on innovation, rather than production. This enables a company to expend its internal talent on identifying emerging market needs, developing new products to fill those needs, promoting the new products aggressively and creatively, and moving them rapidly from design into production and out to the market.

Some innovative products may have a more uncertain market than their more traditional or popular counterparts. Manufacturing outsourcing, in these cases, can be a much less risky alternative to in-house production. If the product does not perform at a profitable level, the OEM's losses are minimized, since it has not made investments in new factories, equipment, hiring, and training.

Lastly, contract manufacturing has enabled much smaller companies to bring new products to market. Without the need to invest in equipment and workers, new companies with minimal funding can now enter the manufacturing game, even producing to demand in many cases.

HISTORY

The electronics industry was the first to engage in contract manufacturing, with the outsourcing of circuit board assembly in the 1980s. IBM was the first to outsource an entire product when it contracted with SCI to build its personal computers.

Pharmaceuticals and medical devices were next to experience a boom in contract manufacturing. While lack of capacity had historically pushed outsourcing of specific product lines in the past, pressure to speed products to market has driven more outsourcing in these industries in recent years. Outsourcing has not only saved these companies money but has also enabled them to focus more on research and development (R&D) and brand building.

During the 1990s, outsourcing became a mainstream business topic, covered in business school curriculums and debated in business publications, including the pivotal paper "Make versus Buy: Strategic Outsourcing" by James Brian Quinn and Frederick G. Hilmer. While outsourcing had been around long before this period, these discussions drove it from a contingency practice to a strategic model, prompting businesses to focus on their core competencies and to consider outsourcing everything else. Also key to the growth of CM was the emerging internet and internet-related technologies that enabled real-time communication, collaboration, and data sharing. The ability to resolve issues quickly and communicate instantly regarding product and process design was critical to success.

Military and aerospace prime contractors became some of the next companies to delve into contract manufacturing beyond simple circuit boards. While there were more restrictions and encumbrances on these companies due to national security and accountability, they were increasingly finding CM is a cost-effective way of doing business for specialized parts and assemblies.

CHALLENGES

Such a market is never without significant challenges. OEMs, Brand owners and CMs alike have very real and diverse concerns. A 2007 Contract Manufacturing and Packaging (CM&P) study of 224 CMs and 150 brand owners showed that the key concerns of brand owners revolved around product quality, consistency, and brand protection, while CMs' concerns at that time were focused on customer loyalty and high energy prices. Such concerns persisted over the next years, and concerns about supply chain disruption likewise arose by the third decade of the twenty-first century. Time and cultural differences between the regions where the brand owners and CMs were based also prompted concerns, contributing further to the complexity of the contract manufacturing arena.

Quality control. One of the most obvious challenges in contract manufacturing is ensuring that the quality and consistency of the product is maintained. The OEM loses a great deal of control once manufacturing is moved to another entity, particularly to far-flung places. With this more limited oversight, and often beyond the reach of US product safety laws, any number of practices can negatively influence product quality.

Probably the largest impediments to quality are poor communications between the OEM and CM and insufficient collaboration in the design process. When product design and development take place apart from the manufacturing plant where the products will be produced, misunderstandings and lack of involvement in the design process can lead to faulty manufacturing processes and products that do not fully meet the design requirements. This can result in costly adjustments after production has begun.

More insidious than simple miscommunication issues, however, are purposeful practices by CMs or their suppliers to keep costs down, a primary attraction for hiring firms. A number of counterfeit activities have surfaced in overseas markets. These include passing off recycled parts as new, declaring components to be compliant with regulations when they are not, and producing parts with lower cost techniques that make for a less robust product. Another practice is re-marking a less expensive component to look like a more expensive version. Even worse, outright fakes have emerged that look, and even perform, exactly like their brand-name counterparts, complete with trademarks and logos, but without the guarantees of the real thing.

But beyond the danger of customers dissatisfied with a faulty or substandard product is the much greater issue of safety. Recalls of products such as toys featuring lead paint, poisonous pet food, and tainted toothpaste, among other products, made some consumers in the United States skittish about buying products manufactured overseas during the first decades of the twenty-first century. In addition to harming the reputation of the brand affected, such recalls can prove costly: recalls carried out by the toy company Mattel in 2007, for instance, racked up costs of $29 million. In light of those costs and the risk of harm to consumers, industries such as the toy industry expressed strong support for tightened safety regulations that would result in more rigorous testing of products.

More important than catching issues before products hit the market is to ensure that such issues do not arise at all. One way hiring firms are countering these issues is by involving the contract manufacturer earlier in the product life cycle. By being involved in the product and process design, the contract manufacturer has a better understanding of the product, can provide valuable input to ensure efficient and quality-focused manufacturing, and can set standards for testing and acceptance of the products.

IP theft. As the CMs get more involved in the design and development processes and increase their own capabilities as a result, many are moving beyond simple collaboration to provide full design services to their OEM customers. For example, a CM may offer CAD services, creating digital drawings and three-dimensional models based on the OEM's specifications. By leveraging investments in equipment, technology, and space, they can avoid the largest cost associated with design and prototyping. Furthermore, these manufacturers have the commitment to see design through and move towards manufacturing as quickly as possible, while also ensuring that the design will be manufacturing "friendly."

However, such deep involvement in design, along with the increasing practice by OEMs of contracting out entire products, creates a whole new set of problems in contract manufacturing. International laws do not provide the protections that the US market affords, and hiring firms have much less control over where the contract manufacturer sources its own parts and assemblies (with whom it shares information) and what it does with the knowledge and capabilities it develops through contract manufacturing.

Such an environment creates the opportunity for intellectual property (IP) theft, patent infringement, and copycat practices. These activities can seriously erode the revenue companies need to cover the costs of product innovation and development. This is particularly true in certain industries, such as pharmaceuticals, where it typically takes years to develop and test new products. There is often a fine line between IP theft and innovation through the application of knowledge gained, and it can be tremendously costly and frustrating for OEMs to seek redress in international courts, where laws are less rigid than in the United States.

OEMs can mitigate these threats to some degree by clearly and specifically identifying ownership rights in the contract. This includes identifying ownership of product designs, process designs, and manufacturing as well as the right to sell and to whom. Many OEMs are finding that truly innovative products are often best kept in-house to reduce the risk of copying.

CONCLUSION

Clearly, contract manufacturing can be fraught with risk, cost, and complexity. As such, there are circumstances where contract manufacturing may not make sense. If the component or product needs to be tightly integrated with components and products of the hiring firm, or if the component or product is a core competency, it may not make sense to outsource, unless the purpose is to focus the organization on innovation, marketing, and sales. In this case, communication and collaboration will become critical success factors, perhaps more so than in any other mode of contract manufacturing.

Given the growth of contract manufacturing worldwide, and its spread across multiple industries, it is clear that it is here to stay. While a myriad of issues still need to be worked out, this is not unusual in a still young industry. Earlier adopters have blazed a trail and unearthed the complexities and risks, suffering the typical and sometimes significant costs of the fallout but also reaping the biggest rewards. As the model matures, best practices and regulations will continue to emerge and the industry will no doubt stabilize, while continuing to enjoy strong global growth.

—*Joyce Gubata, MBA*

Further Reading

Arruñada, Benito, and Xosé H. Vázquez. "When Your Contract Manufacturer Becomes Your Competitor." *Harvard Business Review*, Sept. 2006, hbr.org/2006/09/when-your-contract-manufacturer-becomes-your-competitor. Accessed 28 Nov. 2021.

Baatz, E. "Rapid Growth Changes Rules for Purchasing." *Purchasing*, vol. 126, no. 10, 1999, pp. 33-35.

Brewer, Barry L., Bryan Ashenbaum, and Joseph R. Carter. "Understanding the Supply Chain Outsourcing Cascade: When Does Procurement Follow Manufacturing Out the Door?" *Journal of Supply Chain Management*, vol. 49, no. 3, 2013, pp. 90-110.

Britt, Hugo. "How to Produce an Effective Contract Manufacturing Agreement." *Thomas*, 28 July 2020, www.thomasnet.com/insights/contract-manufacturing-agreement/. Accessed 28 Nov. 2021.

Clarke, Peter. "Why Contract Manufacturing Is Getting into Design." *eeNews*, 11 Apr. 2017, www.eenewseurope.com/news/why-contract-manufacturing-getting-design. Accessed 28 Nov. 2021.

Collins, Michael. "The Long-Term Problem of Outsourcing." *IndustryWeek*, 18 Feb. 2021, www.industryweek.com/the-economy/competitiveness/article/21155621/the-longterm-problem-of-outsourcing. Accessed 28 Nov. 2021.

Palmeri, Christopher. "Mattel Takes the Blame for Toy Recalls." *Business Week*, 21 Sept. 2007, www.bloomberg.com/news/articles/2007-09-21/mattel-takes-the-blame-for-toy-recallsbusinessweek-business-news-stock-market-and-financial-advice. Accessed 28 Nov. 2021.

Penn, C. "Inquiring Minds Want to Know." *Private Label Buyer*, no. 21, 2007, pp. 36-37.

"6 Contract Manufacturing Issues (and How to Avoid Them)." *Smart Machine Technologies*, 26 Sept. 2019, www.smartmachine.com/6-contract-manufacturing-issues-how-to-avoid-them/. Accessed 28 Nov. 2021.

Control of Manufacturing Systems

ABSTRACT

Effective functioning requires that manufacturers control their operations through careful monitoring on a consistent basis. The operations that must be controlled include eight operations intrinsic to manufacturing: the sales function, ordering function, inventory management, product tracking, labor tracking, quality control, distribution, and overall planning and control. Good communication and effective tools are crucial elements for the control of manufacturing systems, regardless of the specific items being manufactured or the equipment in use.

OVERVIEW

Effective functioning requires that manufacturers control their operations through careful monitoring on a consistent basis. The following eight operations are intrinsic to manufacturing:

- Sales function
- Ordering function
- Inventory management
- Product tracking
- Labor tracking
- Quality control
- Distribution
- Overall planning and control

In order to control these eight operations in the manufacturing process (the "manufacturing systems") successfully, a manufacturer needs to employ a control strategy that capitalizes on two crucial elements: good communication and appropriate tools.

OPERATIONS INTRINSIC TO THE MANUFACTURING PROCESS

Eight operations are intrinsic to the manufacturing process. Although there may be additional operations within a manufacturing company, such as a separate purchasing or marketing department, the control of manufacturing systems can be considered to encompass the control of those eight operations.

Sales function. he first operation that is intrinsic to the manufacturing process is the sales function. Sales drive many subsequent functions in the manufacturing process including ordering, inventory management, product tracking, job control, distribution, and overall planning. A good sales team strikes the proper balance between selling a product and overselling. Overselling a product occurs when a salesperson promises a customer more than the manufacturer can comfortably deliver. For example, the customer agrees to purchase more products than can be produced or delivered within the agreed upon delivery date.

Ordering function. The second operation that is intrinsic to the manufacturing process is the ordering function. The ordering of the manufactured product for customers usually originates from the sales team. The ordering of the supplies and parts necessary to manufacture products usually originates from employees with a specific purchasing role. It is essential that orders—whether for products or parts and supplies—are accurately placed and tracked.

Inventory management. The third operation that is intrinsic to the manufacturing process is inventory management. Inventory management is central to controlling manufacturing systems. In fact, modern automation advances have resulted from lean manufacturing strategies for inventory management, such as just-in-time (JIT) and kanban techniques.

Product tracking. The fourth operation that is intrinsic to the manufacturing process is product tracking. Product tracking refers to methods for identifying the status and progression of all stages of a product from each step of manufacture to final distribution to the customer. The goal is to be able to quickly identify the product's stage at any time during the progression.

Labor tracking. The fifth operation that is intrinsic to the manufacturing process is labor tracking. Labor tracking refers to procedures for quickly determining the number and identities of employees who are performing specific job functions, on specific products, at specific times. Labor costs constitute a large part of a manufacturer's budget, and the availability of labor affects a manufacturer's production rate, so labor tracking is crucial to controlling manufacturing systems.

Quality control. The sixth operation that is intrinsic to the manufacturing process is quality control. Quality control refers to the methods that ensure the product is being manufactured meets the customer's specifications at a satisfactory cost to the manufacturer. Quality control can be initiated before the manufacturing process even begins through a process known as design for manufacturability (DFM). DFM involves the tailoring of product designs to eliminate manufacturing difficulties and minimize costs. Quality control can also be implemented by performing inspection and testing procedures during various stages of the manufacturing process. Manufacturers will usually employ more than one procedure for quality control.

Distribution. The seventh operation that is intrinsic to the manufacturing process is distribution. Distribution refers to delivery of the manufactured product from the manufacturing facility to the customer. Distribution might involve multiple distribution points. For example, the product may be moved by the manufacturer from the manufacturing facility to a warehouse. From there, an outside trucking company may move the product to a rail or airport terminal. After the rail or air journey, another truck may deliver the product to the customer.

Overall planning and control. The last operation that is intrinsic to the manufacturing process is overall planning and control. Overall planning and control is listed last not because it is the least important factor but because it includes the previous seven operations. Overall planning and control constitutes the master plan for controlling all the manufacturing systems. Frequently, the computerized mechanism for creating and managing the overall plan is achieved by utilizing a system that is labeled as either Enterprise Resource Planning (ERP) or Manufacturing Resource Planning (MRPII).

Enterprise resource planning (ERP). An ERP system integrates information from all the departments in the manufacturing company and is used by all the departments.

Manufacturing resource planning (MRPII). MRPII is a system for planning, controlling, and integrating all the resources associated with manufacturing, including finance and distribution. MRPII evolved from Material Requirements Planning (MRP), a system for planning all the material requirements in a company.

CONTROL OF MANUFACTURING SYSTEMS: TWO CRUCIAL ELEMENTS

The control of manufacturing systems depends upon two crucial elements: good communication and effective tools.

Good Communication

Good communication is the first crucial element for the control of manufacturing systems. Good communication within and across the departments of a company is absolutely essential to any strategy for effectively controlling manufacturing systems and will exhibit the following three characteristics: transparency, customer information exchange, and supplier partnerships.

Transparency. Transparency is the first characteristic of good communication. The goals, strategies, and methods of individual departments and the company as a whole need to be established and clearly communicated in writing to all employees who affect or are affected by the manufacturing systems. Any changes will be communicated as soon as possible and employees need to know who to contact quickly for questions or clarification. For example, the sales team needs to be notified immediately if there will be a delay in production that will affect delivery dates to current or potential customers.

Customer information exchange. Customer information exchange is the second characteristic of good communication. Relevant information will flow continuously between the manufacturer and customers. Manufacturers who institute a mechanism whereby customers are able to check on orders, initiate queries, or report problems will reap the double benefit of cultivating better customer relationships, while also maintaining better control of manufacturing systems.

Supplier partnerships. Supplier partnerships constitute the last characteristic of good communication. Relevant information will flow continuously between the manufacturer and suppliers. Manufacturers can encourage suppliers to be part of their success by freely exchanging suggestions and information about needs and problems as soon as they arise and, if possible, before they arise.

Effective Tools

Effective tools constitute the second crucial element for the control of manufacturing systems. The tools will vary in number and complexity depending upon the manufacturer's goals, budget, market base, and type and variety of products manufactured. However, the most effective tools for controlling manufacturing systems are often classified into three categories: technology, lean manufacturing techniques, and training.

Technology. The first category of effective tools is technology. Technology includes computer hardware and software as well as other automated devices. Examples of technology tools that are widely used for the control of manufacturing systems include flexible manufacturing system (FMS) and radio frequency identification (RFID).

Flexible manufacturing system (FMS). A flexible manufacturing system (FMS) is an automated system in which a central computer controls the functions of multiple linked manufacturing devices. Although FMS is well-suited for the manufacturing of multiple products simultaneously, or products that require changes, it is not appropriate for the manufacturing of single, repetitive items because simpler, less costly methods would be capable of handling that type of production.

Radio frequency identification (RFID). Radio frequency identification (RFID) is a means of tagging and tracking items through the use of a tag that communicates information to a reader device via radio waves. The advantage of RFID is that it allows manufacturers to track parts and items through the manufacturing process. However, there are also security flaws in RFID chips that allow breaches through a variety of methods including cloning, viruses, and attacks on encryption.

Lean manufacturing techniques. The second category of effective tools is lean manufacturing techniques. Lean manufacturing refers to an ongoing, systematic effort to eliminate the sources of waste in a production process. Two of the most prevalent lean manufacturing techniques, just-in-time (JIT) and kanban, were perfected in Japan.

Just-in-time (JIT). In a JIT manufacturing strategy, production and delivery take place only as products are needed. Toyota Motor Company is generally considered to have spearheaded modern lean manufacturing by implementing the JIT inventory system on a full-scale basis in 1938.

Kanban. Kanban is an integral part of the JIT production process; it is an information tool that specifies exactly which parts or items are needed during the production process and exactly when they are needed.

Lean manufacturing techniques are effective tools for controlling manufacturing systems because they depend upon careful planning and oversight of inventory and production operations.

Training. The last category of effective tools is training. The initial and ongoing training of employees in operations and goals is of course critical to any manufacturing operation. However, the cross-training of employees on more than one machine, process, or product goes a step further: It improves the control of manufacturing systems by increasing employee versatility and usefulness and limiting their potential for downtime. For example, cross-training allows the flexibility of easily replacing employees who are on vacation or of using them to help with other processes during a crunch or emergency. Also, training employees to broaden their skills improves morale by lessening the potential for boredom.

CONCLUSION

Astute manufacturers employ a variety of methods and strategies for integrating and controlling the operations that make up their manufacturing systems, depending upon their budgets and the type and complexity of products they manufacture. At a minimum, most manufacturers will employ strategies to control inventory, quality control, and distribution; most will implement an overall control such as and ERP or MRPII system to integrate and control all their operations.

—Sue Ann Connaughton, MLS

Further Reading

Alqahtan, Ammar Y., Elif Kongar, Kishore K. Pochampally, and Surendra M. Gupta, editors. *Responsible Manufacturing: Issues Pertaining to Sustainability*. CRC Press, 2019.

Chen, C. C., T. M. Yeh, and C. C. Yang, "The Establishment of Project-Oriented and Cost-Based NPD Performance Evaluation." *Human Systems Management*, vol. 25, no. 3, 2006, pp. 185-96.

Hendry, Linda C. "Applying World Class Manufacturing to Make-to-Order Companies: Problems and Solutions." *International Journal of Operations & Production Management*, vol. 18, no. 11, 1998, pp. 1086-1100.

Lee, S. M., R. Harrison, and A. A. West. "A Component-Based Control System for Agile Manufacturing." *Proceedings of the Institution of Mechanical Engineers—Part B—Engineering Manufacture*, vol. 219, no. 1, 2005, pp. 123-35.

Pinto, José Luís Quesado, João Carlos O. Matas, Carina Pimental, et al. *Just in Time Factory: Implementation through Lean Manufacturing Tools*. Springer International Publishing, 2018.

Productivity Press Development Team. *Kanban for the Shopfloor*. CRC Press, 2019.

D

DAC-1

ABSTRACT
The DAC-1 system began at General Motors (GM) as an evolved solution to the problem of having to use multiple types of diagrams in as many different divisions. It was a revolutionary file manipulation program in which one local type of drawing file could be stored, retrieved, translated to another local file type, and passed to another user.

GM'S DRAWINGS PROBLEM
In the late 1950s, General Motors (GM) was faced with a thorny problem, in that each step of their industrial design process used different types of diagrams. This required each division within GM to be supported by its own drawing department. Drawings that had to be moved from one department to another had to be redrawn in the format used by that department, resulting in the introduction of errors in copying and a considerable loss of time due to the requirements of the transaction. Retrieving diagrams from GM's engineering libraries added significantly to the amount of lost time. Even worse, any change that was made to a drawing required the entire sequence to be repeated, no matter how small the change. In 1959, the data processing department of GM began a program to develop a system for the storage, rapid retrieval, and simple modification of digitized diagrams. Computer technology was quite new at that time, and software resided on a mainframe computer that would not have had more than about 32 kilobytes of memory capacity and would have used punched cards or paper tape for input and storage of programming and data.

In GM's proposed system, digitized diagrams would be entered into the computer and displayed in an interactive way to allow operations such as scaling, rotation, and projection to be performed, and the resulting diagram could be saved and printed out on demand. Drawings were to be looked up via a punched card query. A rather elegant solution was found for printing the digitized drawings, by replacing the milling head of a computerized milling machine with a pen-holding device and using the mainframe computer to operate the milling machine. This effectively turned the milling machine into a plotter. Sectioning large diagrams into squares of 32 inches by 32 inches and then aligning the squares allowed them to be printed out on paper that was 96 inches wide. Digitizing existing drawings was accomplished by reprinting them on clear acetate sheets that were then placed in front of the display. A detection program running on the mainframe computer, operating a photomultiplier to detect light variations, was capable of detecting the lines and other markings on the drawing and recording the drawing into memory, thus digitizing preexisting plans and concept art.

GM's system was at first called "Digital Design" but was subsequently renamed to DAC-1 (for Design Augmented by Computer). The system was improved continually afterwards. Other software was used to convert the "scanned" drawing lines into a representation of a three-dimensional (3D) shape, which could then be output directly to milling machines as numerical control language instructions. As computers and software developed in the following years and the output technology improved, it became even easier for designers to generate a drawing and put it into use. In November 1963, the DAC-1 system was used to create a model of a trunk lid directly from an original sketch drawing through to the milling machine output of the object. By 1967, however, the rapidly advancing computer and peripheral technology had rendered the DAC-1 system obsolete due to the additional development that it would require to become competitive, and in that year the DAC-1 CAD/CAM system was terminated.

THE DAC-1 OPERATING SYSTEM

The operating system for the DAC-1 system, known as Monitor, was custom-made for that system. It was a batch processing system in which data was fed into channel controllers rather than directly from punched cards. The DAC-1 system was programmed in the FORTRAN-IV language at first but then was switched over to an ALGOL-58 derivative called "NOMAD" to make use of its graphics capabilities. A custom language similar to NOMAD was used to run the channel controllers. It was called "Maybe" and was used in the production DAC-1 systems sold to consumers. Another custom language called "Descriptive Geometry Language," or DGL, was also provided with the DAC-1 system. DGL allowed users to write programs that could then be input into DAC using punched cards, creating reusable program modules at the same time.

DAC-1 was one of the earliest of CAD/CAM systems to enter use for production operations. The system was commercialized by IBM in the early 1960s and in that form featured a graphics terminal designed for use with the IBM 360 computer. IBM's design used a capacitance screen with a metal pencil that enabled the user to interact with the screen, in a manner similar to using a stylus. Though effective, the use of a metal wand or pencil proved less efficient that developing technologies such as the computer mouse, which over the next decades would become a standard means of interacting with CAD/CAM software.

—*Richard M. Renneboog, MSc*

Further Reading

Chang, Kuang-Hua. *e-Design: Computer-Aided Engineering Design*. Academic Press, 2016.

Friedl, Gunther, and Horst J. Kayser, editors. *Valuing Corporate Innovation: Strategies, Tools and Best Practice from the Energy and Technology Sector*. Springer, 2018.

Gaboury, Jacob. *Image Objects: An Archaeology of Computer Graphics*. MIT Press, 2021.

Khan, Omera. *Product Design and the Supply Chain: Competing through Design*. Kogan Page, 2019.

Krull, Fred N. "The Origin of Computer Graphics within General Motors." IEEE Annals of the History of Computing, vol. 16, no. 3, 1994, pp. 40-56.

Smith, Alvy Ray. *A Biography of the Pixel*. MIT Press, 2021.

Deep Submergence Vehicle Design

ABSTRACT

Deep submergence vehicles (DSVs) are primarily designed to aid researchers in exploring the depths of Earth's oceans. Much is unknown about the suboceanic environment, and exploration of these depths requires transport vehicles that can withstand tremendous pressures. Submergence vehicles must be carefully designed to take into account undersea conditions. Twenty-first-century submergence vehicles cannot only dive to great depths but can also stay submerged for hours at length and are equipped with external lights and tele-operated robotic manipulators to gather deep sea samples for further research. Besides researching marine life, DSVs also play vital roles in the oil exploration and the telecommunications industries, where robotic submarine vehicles known as "autonomous underwater vehicles" detect faulty cables and help in oil field exploration.

HISTORY

English mathematician William Bourne may have been the first to record a design for an underwater navigation vehicle in 1578, but functional vehicles of that nature would not emerge until centuries later. The earliest deep-sea submersibles were known as

In 1960, Jacques Piccard and Don Walsh were the first people to explore the deepest part of the world's ocean, and the deepest location on the surface of the Earth's crust, in the bathyscaphe Trieste designed by Auguste Piccard. Photo via Wikimedia Commons. [Public domain.]

"bathyspheres" (from *bathys*, Greek for "deep"). They were raised in and out of the water by a cable. They were fitted with oxygen cylinders inside to provide air to the divers and had chemicals to absorb the expelled carbon dioxide. The early bathyspheres were not maneuverable—the only degree of freedom they had enabled them to go up and down.

The notable Swiss physicist Auguste Piccard (1884-1962) was influential in making the next design iteration to the bathysphere, called the "bathyscaph." The vessel was not suspended from a ship but instead attached to a free-floating tank filled with petroleum liquid. This tank made it buoyant (lighter than water). The bathyscaph had metal ballasts that, when released, allowed the vessel to surface. Auguste and his son Jacques designed the next-generation bathyscaph, the Trieste. The Trieste set a new world record when it reached the lowest point on Earth, the Mariana Trench (35,800 feet).

Improvements in electronics and materials engineering throughout the twentieth century led to the design of *Alvin*, a deep-sea vessel capable of accommodating up to three people and diving for up to ten hours. *Alvin* sports two robotic arms that can be customized depending on the mission it is undertaking. Operated by the National Deep Submergence Facility (NDSF) of the Woods Hole Oceanographic Institution (WHOI), Alvin became well known for its role in exploring the submerged wreck of the RMS *Titanic* during the 1980s. *Alvin* underwent numerous upgrades over its decades of operation and by 2021 featured a larger personnel sphere as well as additional viewports, among other new elements.

DESIGN CHALLENGES

The physical characteristics of the deep ocean present a host of challenges that designers of deep submergence vehicles (DSVs) must take into account when designing submergence vehicles and their components.

Pressure. At ρany given depth under the sea level, the pressure on a body can be calculated as $P = \rho \times g \times h$ where P is pressure, ρ is the density of the seawater, g is the acceleration because of gravity, and h is the depth at which the measurement is being taken.

The atmospheric pressure at sea level is about 100 kPa (~14.6 psi), the same amount of water pressure at about 10 meters (33 feet) below the surface, making the combined pressure experienced by a body at a 10-meter depth almost double of that at the surface.

Light. Most of the visible light entering the ocean is absorbed within 10 meters (33 feet) of the water's surface. Almost no light penetrates below 150 meters (490 feet). Solid particles, waves, and debris in the water affect light penetration. The longer wavelengths of light, red, yellow, and orange, penetrate to 15, 30, and 50 meters, respectively, while the shorter wavelengths—violet, blue, and green—can penetrate further. The depth of water where sunlight penetrates sufficiently for photosynthesis to take place is called the "Euphotic Zone": and is normally around 200 meters (655 feet) in the ocean. The zone where filtered sunlight only suffuses in the water is known as the "Disphotic Zone" and extends from the end of the Euphotic Zone to about a depth of 1,000 meters (3,280 feet). Below that, no sunlight ever penetrates, and this is known as the "Aphotic Zone."

Temperature. There is a significant difference in the temperatures between the Euphotic and Aphotic zones. However, in the Aphotic Zone, the temperature remains almost constant, hovering around 2 to 4° Celsius (about 35 to 39° Fahrenheit). The only exception occurs when deep-sea volcanoes or hydrothermal vents exist, which cause significant warming of the waters.

In light of such challenges, designers of crewed DSVs and autonomous remotely operated vehicles (ROVs) work to ensure that proposed vehicles and their components are capable of operating safely at the desired depths. Computer-aided design (CAD) software and simulation programs are crucial to creators of such vehicles, enabling them to design, model, modify, and test proposed vehicles prior to their fabrication.

—*Ashwin Mudigonda*

Further Reading

"*Alvin* Upgrade." *WHOI*, 2021, www.whoi.edu/what-we-do/explore/underwater-vehicles/hov-alvin/history-of-alvin/alvin-upgrade/. Accessed 28 Nov. 2021.

Arroyo, Sheri, and Rhea Stewart. *How Deep Sea Divers Use Math*. Chelsea House, 2009.

Hai, Yao, Bao Jinsong, Hu Xiaofeng, and Jin Ye. "Dynamics Simulation Research on Load Vehicle of Deep Submergence Rescue Vehicle (LV-DSRV)." *International Journal for Engineering Modelling*, vol. 22, no. 1, 2009, pp. 71-79.

Morse, Philip, and George Kimball. *Methods of Operations Research*. Kormendi Press, 2008.

Mosher, D. C., Craig Shipp, Lorena Moscardelli, Jason Chaytor, Chris Baxtor, Homa Lee, and Roger Urgeles, editors. *Submarine Mass Movements and Their Consequences*. Springer, 2009.

Parras, Toni. "Opening Our Eyes to the Deep: Molly Curran." *WHOI*, 12 Mar. 2020, www.whoi.edu/news-insights/content/opening-our-eyes-to-the-deep-molly-curran/. Accessed 28 Nov. 2021.

DENTISTRY

ABSTRACT

Dentistry involves the diagnosis, treatment, and prevention of disorders and diseases of the teeth, mouth, jaw, and face. Dentistry includes instruction on proper dental care, removal of tooth decay, teeth straightening, cavity filling, and corrective and reconstructive work on teeth and gums. Dentistry is recognized as an important component of overall health. Practitioners of dentistry are called "dentists." Dental hygienists, technicians, and assistants aid dentists in the provision of dental care.

DEFINITION AND BASIC PRINCIPLES

Dentistry is a branch of medicine that focuses on diseases and disorders of the teeth, mouth, face, and oral cavity. Dentistry includes examining the teeth, gums, mouth, head, and neck to evaluate dental health. The examination may include a variety of dental instruments, imaging techniques, and other diagnostic equipment. Dentistry involves diagnosing oral or dental diseases or disorders and formulating treatment plans. Dentistry is instrumental in teaching patients about the importance of maintaining oral health and instructing patients on proper oral hygiene techniques.

Although dentistry is an independent health-care field, it is not entirely detached from other health-care services and collaboration between dentistry and other health-care providers ensure positive outcomes for patients. Dentists often see patients more often than physicians and may be the first to diagnose systemic diseases, including inflammatory conditions, autoimmune diseases, and cardiovascular risk factors. Dentists also work with pharmacists to prescribe the best antibiotics or anesthetics for dental patients, as well as to understand how certain medications affect dental care and oral health.

Dentistry not only prevents and treats serious oral health disorders but also provides cosmetic services to enhance facial features and correct signs of aging. Dentistry strives to promote oral health as a part of overall health and applies principles of basic medicine, pharmacology, and psychology to dental care.

BACKGROUND AND HISTORY

Before the seventeenth century, dental care was crude, unrefined, and most often provided by physicians. Through the eighteenth and nineteenth centuries, dentistry emerged as its own medical discipline, and most dentists trained through apprenticeships.

Pierre Fauchard is credited as the founder of modern dentistry. In 1728, the French surgeon published *Le Chirurgien Dentiste: Ou, Traité des dents* (*The Surgeon Dentist: Or, Treatise on the Teeth*, 1946), which summarized all available knowledge of dental anatomy, diseases of the teeth, and the construction of dentures.

In 1840, Horace Hayden and Chapin Harris established the world's first dental school, the Baltimore College of Dental Surgery, in Baltimore, Maryland. In 1867, Harvard University became the first university to establish a university-affiliated dental school.

Several scientific milestones transformed dentistry in the nineteenth century. In 1844, Horace Wells administered nitrous oxide to a patient before a tooth extraction, becoming the first dentist to use anesthesia. In 1890, dentist Willoughby Dayton Miller connected microbes to the decay process, extending the germ theory to dental disease. In 1898, William Hunter introduced the term "oral sepsis" to the profession of dentistry and called attention to the contaminated practices and instruments used by dentists. In 1918, radiology was added to dental school curricula, and by the 1930s, most dentists in the United States were using X-rays as part of routine dental diagnostics.

Advances in science and technology, including the arrival of the digital age and the development of computer-aided design (CAD) and computer-aided manufacturing (CAM) software, have revolutionized dentistry, rendering it nearly unrecognizable when compared with nineteenth-century dentistry and improving the diagnostic and treatment capabilities within the field.

HOW IT WORKS

Dental tools. Many common dental tools are available for home use as part of a daily oral care routine. The most basic of dental tools is the toothbrush. Toothbrushes come in a variety of sizes, shapes, and stiffness. Patient age and oral condition determine the best toothbrush for each individual. Toothbrushes usually consist of a plastic handle with nylon bristles that remove food, bacteria, and plaque that can lead to tartar and dental caries. Toothpaste is usually added to a toothbrush to aid in cleaning the teeth and freshening the mouth. Toothpaste is available in a variety of flavors and compositions and may contain polishing or bleaching agents. Dental floss is another basic tool used to remove food and debris from between the teeth. Floss is available in waxed and unwaxed formulations and in a variety of widths and thicknesses. Mouthwash is a rinse that prevents gum disease. Mouthwash is available in many flavors, but all types reduce the number of germs in the mouth that cause gingivitis.

More sophisticated dental tools are used by dentists during dental examinations and procedures. A routine dental cleaning removes stains on the teeth, as well as tartar that brushing and flossing cannot remove. Polishing the teeth aids the dentist in visualizing the teeth and makes it more difficult for plaque to accumulate on the surface of the teeth. Mirrors, scrapers, scalers, and probes are essential in-office dental tools.

Dental therapy and devices. Countless therapies and devices are available to diagnose, prevent, and treat disorders and diseases of the teeth and mouth. Extraction, previously the mainstay of dentistry, involves simply removing the affected tooth. Fillings are used to replace a portion of a tooth that is missing or decayed. Fillings are often made of gold or silver but may also be made of composite resins or amalgam depending on the size and location of the filling. A dental implant is the extension or replacement of a tooth or its root by inserting a post made of metal or other material into the bone to support a new artificial tooth. Crownwork involves covering a damaged tooth with porcelain or other alloy to restore the tooth's original size and shape. A denture is a removable prosthetic appliance that replaces missing teeth. Dentures may replace all or just some teeth. In contrast, a bridge is a tooth-replacement device that cannot be removed. A bridge is made of one or more artificial crowns that are cemented to adjacent teeth.

Orthodontic appliances are necessary to correct and prevent irregularities in the alignment of the teeth, face, and jaw. Braces are among the most common orthodontic appliances, along with headgear and retainers. Conventional braces have metal brackets that are attached to the outer surfaces of the teeth. Wires are attached to the brackets, and manipulation of the wire allows movement and rotation of the teeth into the desired position. The braces may be attached to headgear to help move teeth or secure them into position. Retainers are often worn after braces are removed to maintain the new position of the teeth. Retainers may be permanent or removable. Removable retainers consist of a wire attached to a resin base that is worn at all times (except during meals) to hold the teeth in place for up to several years after braces are removed. A permanent retainer is a metal wire attached to the tongue side of the lower teeth that can maintain the desired position of severely crowded or rotated teeth.

By the mid-1980s, researchers within the field of dentistry began to use CAD/CAM technology as a means of designing and manufacturing dental devices, initially experimenting with computer-aided methods of designing and fabricating ceramic inlays. Over the next decades, dental devices such as crowns, bridges, and dentures were designed using CAD software and fabricated through a variety of CAM processes, including milling- and extrusion-based manufacturing techniques. CAD software likewise facilitated the design and manufacture of customized orthodontic appliances and their components. As of 2021, software companies such as 3Shape, exocad, and Benco offered specialized CAD programs intended for use in the dental and orthodontic fields.

APPLICATIONS AND PRODUCTS

Most dentists practice dentistry as general practitioners. In addition, a number of specialties exist within the field of dentistry, each of which requires additional education or training beyond dental school.

General dentistry. A general practitioner of dentistry deals with the overall maintenance of patients'

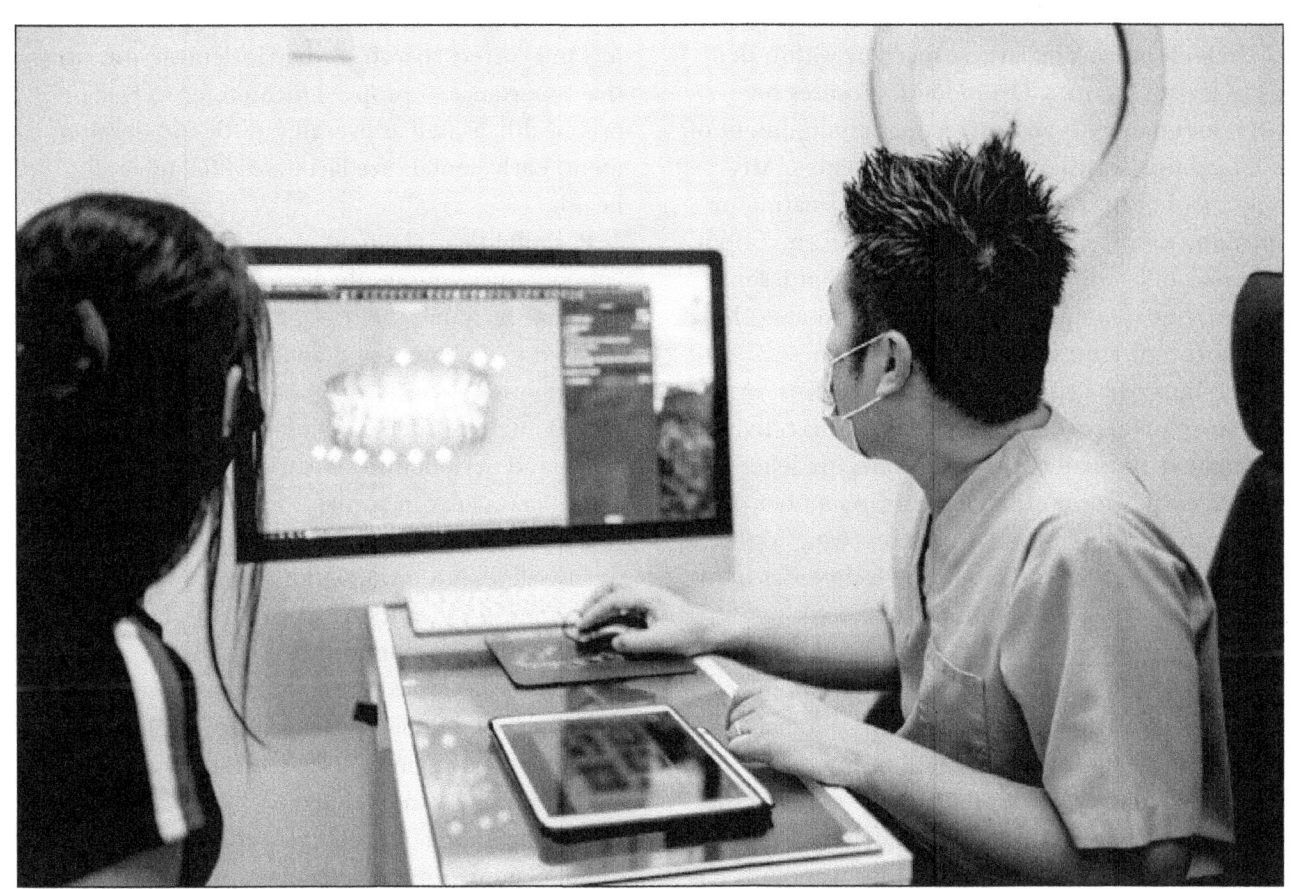

CAD and CAM software have revolutionized dentistry, improving diagnostic and treatment capabilities. Photo via iStock/Edwin Tan. [Used under license.]

teeth, gum, and mouth health. Ideally, general dentistry is preventive in nature, focusing on the maintenance of oral health and hygiene to avoid the occurrence of disorders and diseases of the mouth. Dentists who practice general dentistry encourage regular checkups to ensure proper functioning of the mouth and teeth. A general dentist will provide individualized treatment plans that include dental examinations, tooth cleanings, and X-rays or other diagnostic tests to prevent or treat disorders of the mouth as early as possible. General dentists also repair and restore injuries of the teeth and mouth that result from decay, disease, or trauma. All dentists are able to prescribe medicines and treatments to diagnose, prevent, or treat diseases of the mouth and teeth.

Orthodontics. The largest specialty within dentistry is orthodontics. Orthodontics focuses on straightening teeth and correcting misalignment of the bite, usually using braces and retainers. Misalignment of the teeth or bite can cause eating or speaking disorders, making orthodontics an important part of overall health. Also, orthodontics may be aesthetic in nature, focusing on improving the structure and appearance of the teeth, mouth, and face to improve a patient's self-esteem. Most orthodontic patients are children because corrective procedures of the teeth are most effective when started early. However, an increasing number of adults are seeking orthodontic care, owing to the development of new methods and techniques in orthodontics that allow minimal discomfort and improved healing.

Oral and maxillofacial surgery. Commonly referred to as oral surgery, oral and maxillofacial surgery is the application of surgical techniques to the diagnosis and treatment of disorders of the teeth, mouth, face, and jaw. An oral surgeon may remove damaged or decayed teeth under intravenous sedation or general anesthesia; place dental implants to replace missing or damaged teeth; repair facial trauma, including injuries to soft tissues, nerves, and bones; evaluate and treat head and neck cancers; alleviate facial pain; perform cosmetic surgery of the face; perform corrective and reconstructive surgery of the face and jaw; and correct sleep apnea.

Pedodontics. Also known as "pediatric dentistry," pedodontics focuses on dental care and oral hygiene of children and adolescents. Pediatric dentists apply the principles of dentistry to the growth and development of young patients, oral disease prevention, and child psychology. Some pediatric dentists also specialize in the treatment of patients with developmental or physical disabilities. Pediatric dentists emphasize proper oral hygiene, beginning with baby teeth, because healthy teeth allow for proper chewing and correct speech. Pediatric dentists also stress the importance of proper nutrition for its role in oral health, as well as overall growth and development. Early dental care facilitates lifelong oral health.

Periodontics. The field of dentistry called "periodontics" studies the bone and connective tissues that surround the teeth. Periodontics also involves the placement of dental implants. Periodontists prevent, diagnose, and treat periodontal disorders and infections, including gingivitis and periodontitis. Most periodontal diseases are inflammatory in nature, as are some cardiovascular diseases, and a connection between these two disease states has prompted physicians and periodontists to work together to treat patients at risk for either condition.

Prosthodontics. Also known as "prosthetic dentistry," prosthodontics is the specialized field of dentistry that focuses on restoring and replacing teeth with dental implants, bridges, dentures, and crowns. Although general dentists can perform simple restoration or replacement of teeth, prosthodontists handle severe or extreme cases of tooth loss because of trauma, disease, congenital defects, and age.

Endodontics. The field of dentistry that studies abnormal tooth pulp and focuses on the prevention, diagnosis, and treatment of diseases of the tooth pulp is called "endodontics." Endodontic treatment is also known as "root canal therapy." Endodontic therapy may also include surgery necessary to save a diseased tooth. Endodontists are often able to treat the diseased or damaged inside of a tooth instead of extracting it completely.

Oral and maxillofacial pathology. In oral and maxillofacial pathology, the principles of dentistry are applied to investigating the causes and effects of diseases of the mouth, head, and neck. Oral pathologists are trained to diagnose and treat such diseases, as well as to expose the connection between oral disease and systemic disease.

Oral and maxillofacial radiology. The use of advanced imaging techniques to diagnose and treat disorders of the mouth, teeth, head, and neck is known as "oral and maxillofacial radiology." An oral and maxillofacial radiologist is a dentist who uses radiographic images to diagnose disease and guide treatment plans. Radiologists may use X-rays, computed tomography (CT) scans, magnetic resonance imaging (MRI), ultrasound, and positron emission tomography (PET) to visualize the oral cavity or maxillofacial regions. Specialized sialography images the salivary glands. Intraoral radiographs are used routinely by general dentists as part of regular dental checkups.

Dental public health. The field of dental public health is involved in the epidemiology of dental diseases and applies the principles of dentistry to populations rather than individuals. Dental public health specialists have been involved in promoting fluoridation of drinking water and examining the links between commercial mouthwash and cancer. Dental health specialists assess the oral health needs of communities, develop programs to teach and promote oral health, and implement policies and regulations to address oral health issues.

GOVERNMENT INITIATIVES

In the United States, the government is increasingly involved in the provision and regulation of health care and medical services, including dentistry, in order to maintain the safety and health of patients, consumers, and workers within the industry.

The Occupational Safety and Health Administration (OSHA), a division of the United States Department of Labor, maintains workplace safety standards for the dentistry industry. Primarily, dental professionals may be exposed to toxic or harmful chemicals, materials, infectious substances, or medications as part of their professional duties. OSHA establishes guidelines to recognize and prevent situations that place workers in the dentistry industry at risk for exposure to harmful substances or pathogens. OSHA also provides safety training for all health-care workers.

The United States Department of Health and Human Services established the Health Insurance Portability and Accountability Act (HIPAA) in 1996, which, in part, protects the privacy and security of private health information. Dental care history is considered private health information and is, therefore, protected by HIPAA regulations. Dental practices must adhere to strict guidelines to maintain patient confidentiality and improve patient safety.

The National Institute of Dental and Craniofacial Research (NIDCR), part of the National Institutes of Health, is the government-sponsored research arm within the field of dentistry. The NIDCR conducts research covering the entire spectrum of dental-related diseases and disorders and encourages interdisciplinary approaches to oral health. The NIDCR is also a major contributor to the government's Healthy People program, the fifth incarnation of which, Healthy People 2030, began operations in 2020. Overall, the goals of the oral health arm of the program include preventing tooth decay and tooth loss by promoting oral hygiene and improving access to oral health care for underserved populations.

CONSUMER INITIATIVES

Consumer demand for oral health-care products is increasing as people recognize the importance of oral health in overall health and well-being. There are several major corporations that contribute to the worldwide market for dental products, but no single company dominates the landscape. The largest players include Colgate, Procter & Gamble, and Johnson & Johnson. Many consumer oral health-product manufacturers are involved in sponsoring dentistry research and education. In addition to educating dentistry scientists and professionals, these large corporations sponsor education programs for school-age children and the community at large to promote awareness of oral health and teach proper oral hygiene. Industry-supported programs also bring dental care to underserved patients.

Consumers demand safe and effective oral health products and rely on the Seal of Acceptance of the American Dental Association (ADA) to choose goods. All major manufacturers strive to receive the ADA seal, which denotes extensive clinical and laboratory research to ensure product safety and effectiveness. Although the Food and Drug Administration (FDA) establishes and enforces safety and effectiveness guidelines for the manufacture and use of health-care products, the ADA surpasses these guidelines to offer reassurance in product choice for consumers.

CAREERS AND COURSEWORK

All fifty states in the United States, plus the District of Columbia, require a license to practice dentistry. To obtain a license, applicants must graduate from an accredited school of dentistry and pass written and practical exams. There are more than fifty dental schools in the United States, offering either the doctor of dental surgery (DDS) or the doctor of dental medicine (DMD) degree, which are equivalent degrees.

To apply to dental school, students should be proficient in basic sciences, including biology, chemistry, physics, health science, and mathematics. A minimum of two years of college education is necessary to apply to dental school, but most applicants have completed an undergraduate degree in a science discipline. The Dental Admission Test is also required for applicants to dental school.

Dental school is a four-year program consisting of two years of didactic learning and two years of clinical training. Education in anatomy, microbiology, biochemistry, physiology, and pharmacology is essential to training in dentistry. Clinical practice experience takes place under the supervision of licensed dentists.

Dentists must possess superb diagnostic skills, supreme visual memory, and excellent manual dexterity. Most dentists work in private practice, either alone or with partners. Therefore, dentists also need business management talents, self-discipline, and communication skills.

Dental hygienists, assistants, and laboratory technicians are related professions within the field of dentistry. They each work closely with a dentist to perform the technical duties associated with oral care and teach patients about proper hygiene and good nutrition. The educational and licensing requirements for these dental careers vary by state, although formal education is encouraged and favorable in a competitive job market.

SOCIAL CONTEXT AND FUTURE PROSPECTS

The connection between oral health and overall health has led to an increase in oral home care as well as in professional dentistry services. Patients seek dental care for routine maintenance of oral health and cosmetic procedures to improve the appearance of the face and mouth. In the future, dentistry will increasingly play a fundamental role in people's overall health and wellness. From preventing childhood tooth decay and age-related tooth loss to improving self-esteem through a brighter, straighter smile, dentistry has evolved from a fearful, painful process of tooth extraction to a respected field of medicine that is associated with comfortable care and daily hygiene.

Dentistry of the future will emphasize less painful therapy and disease prevention. It will seek to identify at-risk groups and to provide services to underserved populations to improve dental public health, which will have lasting benefits in education and overall disease morbidity and mortality. Emerging research is focused on mouthwashes that prevent the buildup of plaque on teeth, vaccines that prevent decay and dental caries, and long-lasting pellets that deliver a continuous dose of fluoride to the teeth. Braces may soon be replaced or aided by small, battery-operated paddles that deliver an undetectable electric current to the gums to rearrange bone and tissue structures of the mouth. Lasers will replace existing surgical techniques, allowing for pain-free treatment of dental disease. Further, new enzymes and plastics are emerging as options for tooth restoration and dental diagnostics. Dentistry will continue to be a collaborative and interdisciplinary practice that meets the growing and changing needs of dental health.

—*Jennifer L. Gibson, BS, DP*

Further Reading

Kendall, Bonnie. *Opportunities in Dental Care Careers*. Rev. ed., McGraw-Hill, 2006.

"Oral Conditions." *Healthy People 2030*, health.gov/healthypeople/objectives-and-data/browse-objectives/oral-conditions. Accessed 28 Nov. 2021.

Picard, Alyssa. *Making the American Mouth: Dentists and Public Health in the Twentieth Century*. Rutgers UP, 2009.

Rossomando, Edward F., and Mathew Moura. "The Role of Science and Technology in Shaping the Dental Curriculum." *Journal of Dental Education*, vol. 72, no. 1, 2008, pp. 19-25.

Tamimi, Faleh, and Hiroshi Hirayama, editors. *Digital Restorative Dentistry: A Guide to Materials, Equipment, and Clinical Procedures*. Springer, 2019.

"What Is CAD/CAM Dentistry?" *Colgate*, 2021, www.colgate.com/en-us/oral-health/dental-visits/cad-cam-dentistry-what-is-it. Accessed 28 Nov. 2021.

Wynbrandt, James. *The Excruciating History of Dentistry: Toothsome Tales and Oral Oddities from Babylon to Braces*. St. Martin's Press, 1998.

DESIGN

ABSTRACT

Design is the development of a plan or process to achieve or create something. Designs include objects, events, and many other elements of daily life—anything that is created by humankind. Successful design is appealing to its intended audience for its appearance and usefulness. However, it must take into account practical matters, such as materials and engineering concerns. An attractive and innovative structure, for example, must be constructed to meet safety standards. Examples of design arenas include business and organization strategies; structures, such as buildings and bridges; websites; publications; interiors; vehicles; landscapes; tools, ranging from paper clips to robotic arms; clothing and footwear; and product packaging. While early designs were likely achieved through trial and error—people simply used what they had and adopted changes that seemed to work better—effort and expertise may be required for modern design efforts. An organization may employ a number of teams to research, provide input and expertise, and develop various aspects of a design project.

BACKGROUND

Archaeologists are unsure when early humans developed creativity. The earliest tools were likely spears and digging sticks made of wood, bone, and other materials. Humans used stone tools that did not vary for about 1.6 million years. The tools they crafted were designed with a purpose—to help them survive by performing tasks better than they could with their bare hands—even though tool design remained static.

Between forty thousand and ninety thousand years ago, during the Upper Paleolithic period, humans began painting cave walls and creating items with shell beads. They carved flutes and figures. Stone tools also began to evolve. This development indicates that as the human brain became larger, humans developed the ability to form ideas and design and create with a purpose.

Anthropologists call the human ability to take an idea and further develop and refine it cultural ratcheting. Design frequently involves looking at old ideas and finding new solutions. Anthropologists believe that as society developed and people lived in larger groups, the chances of individuals within the group having the ability to improve tools and processes increased.

Some aspects of design changed the course of human history. In agriculture, for example, early humans used primitive tools such as digging sticks and stone axes to cultivate crops. Eventually, a simple plow was created to dig more efficiently. As animals were domesticated, humans altered the plow to use animals to pull it. The development of metal tools allowed people to design a better tool for carving into soil. All of these design changes improved human living conditions. Humans who successfully raised crops had more and better food, which allowed them to develop their brains and continue to advance ideas.

While humans were changing physical aspects of their lives, they were also developing communication. Early pictographs likely developed from gestures and sounds people used to communicate. Humans designed writing systems to convey messages.

While early design was largely practical, eventually people became concerned about aesthetics. Early shelters gave way to decorative structures. Simple body coverings were replaced by clothing the wearer deemed attractive. By the third millennium BCE, civil design was evident in urban planning, such as the prehistoric city of Mohenjo Daro in Pakistan. By the late eighteenth century CE, design was recognized as a practice.

OVERVIEW

Design is an element of all human creations and plans. It encompasses practical and aesthetic concerns. In many cases, design begins with a need and desire to address the need. Designers may require expertise to help define the problem and desired goal.

In the visual arts, elements of design include color, direction, form, line, point, shape, space, texture, and value. Visual art design also includes design principles, such as balance, contrast, dominance, emphasis, gradation, harmony, movement, pattern, perspective, proportion, repetition, rhythm, unity, and variety. A skilled artist employs a variety of techniques to achieve an effect through drawing, painting, sculpting, carving, or molding. Many of these elements and principles are useful in other fields. For example, someone designing the interior of a car should consider placement of instruments from both an aesthetic perspective and a practical consideration. While the driver must be able to view the speedometer with ease, the designer may choose fonts or other elements to make the display visually pleasing.

Civil, transportation, and architectural design often involve engineering. Engineering addresses the practical elements of design. Computer-aided design (CAD) is increasingly central to the design process, allowing designers to create two-dimensional (2D) and three-dimensional (3D) models of projects. CAD also offers the benefit of simulating situations to test a design and evaluate its performance. Civil and transportation designers draft and scale drawings and maps, such as those used for the construction of bridges and roads. Civil engineers also design cities and other elements of human civilization. Designs take into consideration the community and human experiences, for example, by integrating green spaces and wide, walkable sidewalks into an urban environment. Access to highways and rivers should be designed for the benefit of citizens and industry. Civil engineers must also consider future expansion in a design and plan where and how growth will occur.

Universal design, or the design of items to be accessible to everyone, arose late in the twentieth century. The movement seeks to address communications, environments, and products to ensure no one is barred from access because of a disability or health condition. Universal design is prominent in building design and redesign. It is also important to infrastructure, such as sidewalks and streets to ensure all individuals can safely travel.

Business model design or strategy involves evaluation of a market and goals. Managers must consider both short-term and long-term goals. In designing a business model, one should consider the value of what the business has to offer; test it in the market; seek feedback and advice; and plan, execute, and evaluate a limited rollout.

Most businesses and organizations design a corporate structure. This may include departments, which have specific goals and responsibilities and may work with other departments on the same level or may function in a hierarchy. A small business may need only a few departments, such as finance, human resources, and production. The management and executive teams must be defined and their responsibilities and authority clearly stated. Job descriptions at all levels should include their places in the hierarchy of the organization and expectations for employees. A well-designed organizational structure helps members perform at their best.

—*Josephine Campbell*

Further Reading

Bi, Zhuming, and Xiaoqin Wang. *Computer Aided Design and Manufacturing*. Wiley-ASME Press, 2020.

DiChristina, Mariette. "How Human Creativity Arose." *Scientific American*, 1 Mar. 2013, www.scientificamerican.com/article/how-human-creativity-arose. Accessed 28 Nov. 2021.

Heller, Steven. "The Evolution of Design." *The Atlantic*, 9 Apr. 2015, www.theatlantic.com/entertainment/archive/2015/04/a-more-inclusive-history-of-design/390069. Accessed 28 Nov. 2021.

"History of Universal Design." *Centre for Excellence in Universal Design*, 2020, universaldesign.ie/what-is-universal-design/history-of-ud/. Accessed 28 Nov. 2021.

Margolin, Victor. *World History of Design: Two-Volume Set*. Bloomsbury, 2015.

Pringle, Heather. "The Origins of Creativity." *Scientific American*, Oct. 2016, www.scientificamerican.com/article/the-origins-of-creativity/. Accessed 28 Nov. 2021.

Sarkar, Jayanta. *Computer Aided Design: A Conceptual Approach*. CRC Press, 2017.

"What Do We Mean by Design?" *Design Council*, www.designcouncil.org.uk/news-opinion/what-do-we-mean-design. Accessed 28 Nov. 2021.

"What Is Design?" *University of Illinois at Chicago College of Architecture, Design, and the Arts*, design.uic.edu/what-is-design. Accessed 28 Nov. 2021.

Design for Manufacturability

ABSTRACT

Design for manufacturability (DFM) is the concept of creating a product that can be consistently manufactured without problems, at minimal cost. DFM generally relies upon standardization practices; it incorporates manufacturing processes that use standard parts, reduce the number of parts, and minimize handling during production. However, the most sophisticated DFM strategies allow for a range of product customization.

OVERVIEW

The manufacturability of a product refers to characteristics that make the product suitable for reproduction (manufacture), usually on a large-scale basis. Manufacturability is dependent upon two conditions: the ability to consistently manufacture a reliable product without problems and the ability to manufacture the product at minimal cost.

DESIGN FOR MANUFACTURABILITY (DFM)

When the two conditions for manufacturability—the ability to manufacture a reliable product without problems, and at minimal cost—are given foremost consideration during the design cycle of a product, the concept is known as design for manufacturability (DFM), also known as design for manufacture.

The principle behind DFM is to create the ability to economically manufacture a reliable product into its initial design rather than to fix problems later in the manufacturing process. This principle expands the idea of "do it right the first time" into "do it right the first time, but as inexpensively as possible."

DFM generally relies upon standardization practices; it incorporates manufacturing processes that use standard parts, reduce the number of parts, and minimize handling during production. However, the most sophisticated DFM strategies allow for a range of product customization.

DFM practices may result in both direct cost savings and indirect cost benefits for the manufacturer. Direct cost savings for the manufacturer using DFM practices may result from:
- Eliminating the extra materials and labor needed to correct mistakes
- Reducing the overhead associated with extra materials and labor
- Minimizing wear and tear on machinery
- Shortening the development and manufacturing cycles, thus hastening time-to-market of the product
- Lowering the number of product returns

Indirect cost benefits for the manufacturer using DFM practices may result from:
- Lowering employee turnover due to higher satisfaction with output
- Improving customer satisfaction due to offering a more reliable and economical product
- Gaining industry status as a manufacturer of reliable, economically priced products

Since manufacturers' success and profits usually rely upon producing reliable products at the lowest possible cost and in the shortest possible timeframe, the concept of DFM is an attractive one.

Depending upon the product or manufacturing process, DFM may incorporate one or more of the following solutions:
- Additive manufacturing (AM) technologies (also known as "rapid prototyping")
- Computer-aided design (CAD)
- Computer-aided engineering (CAE)
- Computer-aided manufacturing (CAM)
- Concurrent engineering
- Poka-yoke
- Product lifecycle management (PLM)

APPLICATIONS

DFM solutions generally involve computer technology. In addition, many of the computer technology solutions are used in combination, leading to such common practices and acronyms as CAD/CAE and CAD/CAM.

Additive manufacturing (AM) technologies. Additive manufacturing (AM) technologies, also known as rapid prototyping, allow a manufacturer to fabricate customizable parts of any shape from complex materials. "Rapid prototyping" refers to quicker-than-average production of models for the purpose of working out problems. Because of its intent to tackle the manufacturing issues involving the complexities of shape and materials, AM technologies have the potential to move beyond providing cost-cutting benefits to actually achieving new, higher manufacturing capabilities.

Computer-aided design (CAD) and computer-aided engineering (CAE). Computer-aided design (CAD) is routinely used by designers to produce digital drawings and designs. In manufacturing, digitally stored CAD designs are often the basis for computer-aided engineering (CAE), which is the analysis of a product's structural integrity and performance. Companies employ CAD/CAE to develop virtual prototypes of products; evaluate their suitability and effectiveness; and *determine their ability to be manufactured economically.*

Computer-aided manufacturing (CAM). Computer-aided manufacturing (CAM) uses computer technology to control the manufacturing process. CAM enables manufacturers to produce complex parts with precise specifications in a consistent manner.

Concurrent engineering. Concurrent engineering is a method of product or process design that includes simultaneous input from every individual with a stake or role, including engineers, salespersons, support personnel, vendors, and customers, throughout the entire design process. Because it removes communication and design barriers by engaging all the stakeholders throughout the design process, concurrent engineering results in the following benefits:

- Involvement of all functions and personnel
- Better processing considerations
- Improved manufacturing launch considerations
- Fewer product revisions after the manufacturing process begins
- A better product
- Improved worker involvement and satisfaction
- Management involvement and acceptance

Success in concurrent engineering initiatives relies upon constant communication and management of the language, facts, and product and process requirements by everyone involved in the initiative. For example, each group involved may use different jargon or may have a different perspective about what constitutes product requirements.

Poka-yoke. Poka-yoke is the concept of mistake-proofing the entire manufacturing process by preventing mistakes in the product design, the process, and from human actions. Poka-yoke refers to the mechanisms used throughout a manufacturing process to ensure that proper conditions exist before a process step is begun. If it is not possible to invoke poka-yoke before the process actually begins, then it is used to detect defects at the earliest point in the process.

Product lifecycle management (PLM). Product lifecycle management (PLM) integrates all the people, processes, and information related to a product in order to communicate information across the enterprise, from initial product concept to the end of its life. PLM takes the concept of concurrent engineering—people and process integration throughout the design cycle—further, by applying the principles throughout the product's life, from inception to disposal.

ADDITIONAL DFM SOLUTIONS

Manufacturers and the vendors who cater to them continue to develop DFM tools and technologies in their quest to solve the issue of manufacturing more reliable products, more quickly, at a lower cost. Additional DFM solutions that can be found in the manufacturing environment include:

- Spreadsheets
- Model-based design tools
- Dimensional measurement tools
- Manufacturing intelligence tools

Spreadsheets. The first additional DFM solution is the spreadsheet model. Spreadsheet models are the most basic of DFM tools. These are produced in-house by companies who are working through DFM issues but have not yet moved to more sophisticated technologies. While the use of spreadsheets as a DFM solution may seem primitive, it is often the impetus for a company's exploration of and desire for more advanced DFM solutions.

Model-based design solutions. The second additional DFM solution is the model-based design tool. DFM tools that manage all the aspects of variability that affect design have included OutPerform and InShape, both introduced in 2006 by Clear Shape Technologies. OutPerform was intended to be used during the physical design of the product to identify timing and leakage problems and calculate changes needed. InShape could be used to check each layer of a design to ensure that elements conform to the actual fabrication process model. It was capable of scanning an entire design and then automatically generating a set of "fixing guidelines" that designers could use to implement changes in third-party tools.

Dimensional measurement solutions. The third additional DFM solution is the dimensional measurement tool. Examples of such tools have included Optigo and OptiCell, produced by CogniTens. A portable tool for shop floor operators and engineers, Optigo came in several flexible platforms and offered high accessibility in a variety of engineering and manufacturing environments. OptiCell was a fully automated platform that provided recurring measurements of parts and assemblies on the shop floor. Both Optigo and OptiCell automatically transformed measurements into three-dimensional (3D) information that provided comprehensive measurement analysis.

Manufacturing intelligence solutions. The last DFM solution is the manufacturing intelligence tool. Software companies such as Aprio have produced DFM tools that enabled manufacturers of integrated circuits to inject manufacturing intelligence into existing design tools.

CONCLUSION

DFM practices offer many direct cost benefits for manufacturers, including cost savings in materials and labor, more reliable products, and faster time-to-market potential. They also offer indirect cost benefits, including lower employee turnover, higher customer satisfaction, and improved industry status. A variety of commercial DFM solutions are already available and manufacturers and the vendors who cater to them are developing new and more sophisticated solutions to meet the goals of consistently manufacturing reliable products, in the minimum amount of time, at minimal cost. Although DFM generally relies upon principles of standardization—it incorporates manufacturing processes that use standard parts, reduce the number of parts, and minimize handling during production—the most sophisticated DFM strategies allow for a range of product customization.

—*Sue Ann Connaughton, MLS*

Further Reading

Albert, Mark. "Always in the Learning Mode." *Modern Machine Shop*, 1 Mar. 2007, www.mmsonline.com/articles/always-in-the-learning-mode. Accessed 28 Nov. 2021.

Anderson, David M. *Design for Manufacturability*. 2nd ed., Routledge/Productivity Press, 2020.

"Design for Manufacturability: Reducing Costs through Design." *Aved*, 22 Sept. 2021, aved.com/design-for-manufacturability-the-economics-of-design/. Accessed 28 Nov. 2021.

Dillon, Andrew P., translator. *Zero Quality Control: Source Inspection and the Poka-Yoke System*. CRC Press, 2021.

Fantoni, G., C. Taviani, and R. Santoro. "Design by Functional Synonyms and Antonyms: A Structured Creative Technique Based on Functional Analysis." *Proceedings of the Institution of Mechanical Engineers, Part B: Journal of Engineering Manufacture*, vol. 221, no. 4, 2007, pp. 673-83.

Van Vliet, Hans Willem, and Kees van Luttervelt. "Development and Application of a Mixed Product/Process-Based DFM Methodology." *International Journal of Computer Integrated Manufacturing*, vol. 17, no. 3, 2007, pp. 224-34.

"What Is Design for Manufacturing (DFM)?" *TWI*, 2021, www.twi-global.com/technical-knowledge/faqs/faq-what-is-design-for-manufacture-dfm. Accessed 28 Nov. 2021.

Design Thinking

ABSTRACT
Design thinking is a thought process that depends on examining all sides of an issue from both a practical and a creative perspective before deciding what course of action is most likely to achieve the desired goal. Design thinking, which is a major tool within the business world, is a form of solution-focused thinking. The major aspects of design thinking are understanding the practical and emotional needs of a client, using prototypes or physical models to explore possible ways of achieving goals, and being willing to try different paths even though they may result in failure. Unlike the scientific method of thinking, which is based on a thorough analysis of a problem and involves both observation and experimentation, design thinking begins with a specific goal in mind and then investigates all possible paths that travel toward that goal. With design thinking, it is often necessary to redefine terms, repeat steps, and reexamine initial ideas before achieving the ultimate goal.

BACKGROUND
Design thinking arose out of the need to modernize existing businesses and government agencies as advances in technology continued to change the traditional ways that these entities carried out their activities. Choices were often restricted by financial parameters, and any solution was useless if it did not accomplish the client's desired goals. Thus, technical feasibility, economic viability, and user desirability became the chief tenets of design thinking. The groundwork for design thinking was established during and immediately after World War II as scientists, social scientists, and other researchers struggled to meet the needs of the government and military by developing new strategies such as operational research methods, which depended on thorough analysis of an issue, and management decision-making techniques that used spreadsheets to examine different aspects of an issue.

The concept behind design thinking was introduced by Herbert A. Simon, an American political scientist and economist, in *The Sciences of the Artificial* (1969). Simon identified three critical steps to engaging in decision-making: first, thoroughly investigate the issue to discover all relevant information; second, analyze the information and identify all possible courses of action; and finally, make a choice about which path should be taken. Simon was awarded the Nobel Prize in Economic Sciences in 1978 for his work. The concept of design thinking received a boost in 1973 with the publication of Robert H. McKim's *Experiences in Visual Thinking*, in which he outlines seeing, imaging, and idea sketching as steps to identifying and examining possible solutions to problems.

In the 1980s, L. Bruce Archer, a British engineer, began expanding on ways to engage in "designerly" thinking, noting that it was vastly different from methods used by scientists and scholars. Archer is credited with coining the term "design thinking." Over the course of the decade, other engineers, including those in Germany and Japan, adopted design thinking. Influential studies in the field were also produced by architect Bryan Lawson in *How Designers Think* (1980) and by Peter Rowe, a professor of design and architecture at Harvard University, in *Design Thinking* (1987). The popularity of design thinking led to an upsurge in the number of design journals being published. By the following decade, most university business schools were offering classes in design thinking, and the concept spread into other fields.

In the 2000s, the business press further popularized design thinking, offering articles that suggested that it was an important element in creative thinking. Design thinking also became increasingly popular with engineering schools.

OVERVIEW

Experts in design thinking usually agree that there are four rules that govern the process. First, one must maintain the emphasis on the needs of humans rather than simply engaging in technical experimentation. If choices are made without recognizing those needs, then the process of design thinking fails. Second, ambiguity is used to guide the search for possible solutions, preventing the designer from becoming limited by narrow ways of thinking. Third, design thinking must always involve redesign, which calls for retaining traditional tenets of design while employing new tools and innovative ways of thinking. The final rule of design thinking emphasizes the need to use tangible methods of improving communication as the design thinking process is carried out.

Many designers have discovered that design thinking is ideal for dealing with problems that have not been well defined. In cases where existing technology is incapable of finding a solution to a problem, design thinking may be used to clarify the issue and identify what needs to be done to deal with the issue at hand. One of the chief purposes of design thinking is to use visual thinking to clarify problems that may not be fully defined.

Design thinking may employ such strategies as synthesis, divergent thinking, analysis, and convergent thinking in order to arrive at a solution. Divergent thinking is the process of brainstorming all possible solutions to a problem or all options in a given situation, while convergent thinking applies rules and logic to a limited set of options to determine which is best. With synthesis and divergent

Photo via iStock/eclipse_images. [Used under license.]

thinking, the designer may offer a number of ideas while considering a single aspect of the situation. After doing this, analysis and convergent thinking can be used to reach a decision about what should be done.

While the phrases "design methods" and "design processes" are often used interchangeably, there are distinct differences in their meanings. The former refers to the techniques and strategies used within the field. Those techniques include interviewing interested parties, gathering data on product use, creating physical models, and analyzing the issue at hand. Design process, on the other hand, is more involved with determining how a project should be carried out and involves such actions as allotting tasks and identifying what equipment might be needed.

Design thinking is always concerned with examining all possible solutions to a problem. Solutions are possible only when they are based on the needs of stakeholders involved in the project. By examining all aspects of the situation, it is possible to arrive at creative solutions that address client needs while allowing a designer the freedom to explore and create.

—*Elizabeth Rholetter Purdy, PhD*
and Elena Popan, MA

Further Reading

Archer, L. Bruce. "Whatever Became of Design Methodology?" *Design Studies*, vol. 1, no. 1, 1979, pp. 17-20.

Ben Manmoud-Jouini, Sihem, Christophe Midler, and Philippe Silberzahn. "Contributions of Design Thinking to Project Management in an Innovation Context." *Project Management Journal*, vol. 47, no. 2, 2016, pp. 144-56.

Dijksterhuis, Eva, and Gilbert Silvius. "The Design Thinking Approach to Projects." *Project Management Development—Practices and Perspectives*, vol. 5, no. 6, 2016, pp. 67-81.

Kolko, Jon. "Design Thinking Comes of Age." *Harvard Business Review*, Sept. 2015, hbr.org/2015/09/design-thinking-comes-of-age. Accessed 28 Nov. 2021.

Kumar, Kaushik, Divya Zindani, and J. Paulo Davim. *Design Thinking to Digital Thinking*. Springer Nature Switzerland, 2020.

Leifer, Larry J., Christoph Meinel, and Hasso Plattner. *Design Thinking: Understand—Improve—Apply*. Springer, 2011.

Lewrick, Michael, Patrick Link, and Larry Leifer. *The Design Thinking Toolbox*. Wiley, 2020.

Liedtka, Jeanne. "Why Design Thinking Works." *Harvard Business Review*, Sept. 2018, hbr.org/2018/09/why-design-thinking-works. Accessed 28 Nov. 2021.

Retna, Kala S. "Thinking about 'Design Thinking': A Study of Teacher Experiences." *Asia Pacific Journal of Education*, vol. 36, suppl. 1, 2016, pp. 5-19.

Rowe, Peter G. *Design Thinking*. MIT Press, 1987.

Shearer, Allan W. "Abduction to Argument: A Framework of Design Thinking." *Landscape Journal*, vol. 34, no. 2, 2015, pp. 127-38.

Ecodesign

ABSTRACT

Ecodesign refers to the designing of products with economic sustainability in mind. In light of climate change, ecodesign has become more important than ever. Minimalizing the ecological impact of the manufacturing process, as well as products themselves, is an important endeavor now being undertaken by many companies. Successfully engaging in such practices could help slow the onset of global climate change.

Designing a product with ecodesign in mind involves every stage of product development. Factories should use resources efficiently, and products should include as many renewable resources as possible. Products should then be distributed in an efficient manner and use as little packing materials as needed to reach clients safely. Finally, designers should plan for the product's environmental impact after the product has fulfilled its intended use.

BACKGROUND

Engineers, inventors, and scientists are looking toward ecodesign for the sake of the planet. Nonsustainable designs, such as the use of fossil fuels and nonrenewable resources, endanger the planet. Additionally, many forms of pollutants that could be reduced by utilizing ecodesign principles are contributing to global climate change.

Global climate change, also called "global warming," is a gradual shift of Earth's climate. Temperatures are rising quickly, causing more ice to melt at Earth's poles. More melted ice causes higher sea levels, which may eventually severely alter the coastlines of the continents. Some coastal cities may become uninhabitable as the sea moves over their location. Additionally, warmer oceans will likely result in more common and more severe storms, further increasing the danger of living in coastal areas.

The scientific community believes that humans have contributed significantly to global climate change. Earth is naturally surrounded by an atmosphere, a protective layer of gases that keeps warmth trapped on the planet and protects Earth from solar radiation. Burning fossil fuels, spraying aerosols, and conducting many other activities can release greenhouse gases into the atmosphere. These gases excel at trapping heat, which leads to warmer temperatures for Earth. Other activities, such as removing large areas of forest, can also increase the amount of greenhouse gases in the atmosphere.

Because Earth is warming so much faster than it normally would during a climate shift, many species may be unable to adapt. If a species cannot adapt to a new environment, it will go extinct. For this reason, if global climate change continues, scientists expect large numbers of species to die out.

Humans have already caused climate change to progress considerably, and many of these changes may be irreversible. For example, the ice at the poles is melting more than ever before, and the Arctic may become ice-free for the first time in recorded human history. Because Earth is so slow to respond, even if humanity were to stop emitting greenhouse gasses immediately, global warming would continue to progress for decades or centuries. Despite this, it may still be possible for humanity to stop some of the worst effects of global climate change. However, avoiding the most severe consequences will require the global community to come together and act in a more sustainable manner.

OVERVIEW

Ecodesign refers to products that are intentionally designed for sustainability. Ecological sustainability refers to actions that can be continued long term without causing significant damage to the environment. For example, single-use plastics are not created with ecodesign. They are made from oil, a finite resource that will eventually run out, and do not biodegrade easily. This means that the plastics will sit in landfills for decades or more without breaking down. However, plastics that can be recycled efficiently may be a step towards better ecodesign. If such materials can be reused repeatedly, instead of being thrown into a landfill or the ocean, they can be turned into a new, usable objects.

One important principle of ecodesign is reducing the amount of wasted material used in everyday life. For example, because of the recent advances of the internet, humanity is shipping large numbers of packages every day. Utilizing recyclable cardboard boxes reduces the environmental impact of the massive amounts of resources required to manufacture so much packing material. Additionally, reducing such material to the minimum necessary to safely deliver the product is also an effective means of reducing environmental impact.

Ecodesign can be applied to any industry. Buildings, vehicles, books, and many other products can be designed in a manner that makes them more energy-efficient to produce. They may

Minimalizing the ecological impact of the manufacturing process, as well as products themselves, is an important endeavor. Photo via iStock/piyaset. [Used under license.]

also utilize more renewable resources and more recyclable parts.

Though it may be a difficult initial transition for some companies, shifting to ecodesign as a priority has the potential to increase the long-term profits of a company. For example, designing a product to use fewer resources during construction also lowers the amount of raw materials that the company must pay to procure, increasing the profit margin for the product. Designing factories in an energy-efficient manner lowers the constant cost of running the factory in addition to helping the environment. Finding more efficient means of shipping product can reduce the amount of fossil fuels released into the atmosphere while also reducing shipping costs. Finding the minimum amount of necessary packaging required to safely deliver the product to the consumer cuts down on waste and reduces the amount of packaging materials that companies need to purchase.

In most cases, ecodesign can be broken down into four phases. The first phase, adopting responsible procurement, means procuring the materials necessary for a product in an environmentally sustainable manner. The second phase, optimizing design, means designing and packaging a product in an ecologically sustainable and efficient manner. The third phase, improving end-of-life management, means minimizing the impact that the product will have on the environment after its primary purpose has ended. The fourth stage, communication, involves communicating effective practices with other companies so that they can be replicated.

—*Tyler Biscontini*

Further Reading

"Ecodesign." *Sustainability Guide*, 2018, sustainabilityguide.eu/ecodesign/. Accessed 28 Nov. 2021.

"Ecodesign." *Sustainable Minds*, 2021, www.sustainableminds.com/software/ecodesign-and-lca. Accessed 28 Nov. 2021.

"Environmental Sustainability." *Thwink.org*, 2014, www.thwink.org/sustain/glossary/EnvironmentalSustainability.htm. Accessed 28 Nov. 2021.

Gaha, Raoudha, Bernard Yannou, and Benamara Abdelmajid. "A New Eco-Design Approach on CAD Systems." *International Journal of Precision Engineering and Manufacturing*, vol. 15, no. 7, 2014, pp. 1443-51.

"Is It Too Late to Prevent Climate Change?" *NASA*, 2019, climate.nasa.gov/faq/16/is-it-too-late-to-prevent-climate-change/. Accessed 28 Nov. 2021.

Keivanpour, Samira. *Approaches, Opportunities, and Challenges for Eco-Design 4.0: A Concise Guide for Practitioners and Students*. Springer Nature Switzerland, 2022.

Kishita, Yusuke, Mitsutaka Matsumoto, Masato Inoue, and Shinichi Fukushige, editors. *EcoDesign and Sustainability I: Products, Services, and Business Models*. Springer Nature Singapore, 2021.

"What Is Global Climate Change?" *NASA*, 2019, climatekids.nasa.gov/climate-change-meaning/. Accessed 28 Nov. 2021.

Electric Automobile Technology

ABSTRACT

Electric vehicles have been around even longer than internal combustion engine cars. With health issues resulting from the modern use of internal combustion engines, the automotive industry is intensifying its efforts to produce novel machines that run on electricity. Many cars come with drivetrains that can accept electric propulsion, offering quieter, healthier transportation options.

DEFINITION AND BASIC PRINCIPLES

An electric vehicle is driven by an electric motor. The electricity for this motor can come from different sources. In vehicle technology, electrical power is usually provided by batteries or fuel cells. The main advantages of these devices are that they are silent, operate with a high efficiency, and do not have tailpipe emissions harmful to humans and the environment. In hybrid vehicles, two or more motors coexist in the vehicle. When large quantities of power are required rapidly, the power is provided by combusting fuels in the internal combustion engine; when driving is steady, or the car is idling at a traffic light, the car is entirely driven by the electric motor, thereby cutting emissions while providing the consumer with the normal range typically associated with traditional cars that would rely entirely on internal combustion engines. Electric vehicles make it possible for drivers to avoid having to recharge at a station. Recharging can occur at home, at work, and in parking structures, quietly, cleanly, and without involving potentially carcinogenic petroleum products.

BACKGROUND AND HISTORY

Electric vehicles have been around since the early 1890s. Early electric vehicles had many advantages over their combustion-engine competitors. They had no smell, emitted no vibration, and were quiet. They also did not need gear changes, a mechanical problem that made early combustion-engine cars cumbersome. In addition, the torque exhibited by an electric engine is superior to the torque generated by an equivalent internal combustion engine. However, battery technology was not yet sufficiently developed, and consequently, as a result of low charge, storage capacity in the batteries, and rapid developments in internal combustion engine vehicle technology, electric vehicles declined on the international markets in the early 1900s.

At the heart of electric vehicles is the electric motor, a relatively simple device that converts electric energy into motion by using magnets. This technology is typically credited to the English chemist and physicist Michael Faraday, who discovered electromagnetic induction in 1831. These motors require some electrical power, which is typically provided by batteries, as it was done in the early cars, or by fuel cells. Batteries were described as early as 1748 by one of the founding fathers of the United States, Benjamin Franklin. These devices can convert chemically stored energy into a flow of electrons by converting the chemicals present in the battery into different chemicals. Depending on the materials used, some of these reactions are reversible, which means that by applying electricity, the initial chemical can be re-created and the battery reused. The development of fuel cells is typically credited to the English lawyer and physicist Sir William Grove in 1839, who discovered that flowing hydrogen and air over the surfaces of platinum rods in sulfuric acid creates a current of electricity and leads to the formation of water. The devices necessary to develop an electric car had been around for many decades before they were first assembled into a vehicle.

A major circumstance that led to the commercial success of combustion-engine vehicles over electric vehicles was the discovery and mining of cheap and easily available oil. Marginal improvements in battery technology compared with internal combustion engine technology occurred during the twentieth century. As a result of stricter emissions standards near the end of the twentieth century, global battery research began to reemerge and significantly accelerated in the 2010s.

During the 1990s, oil was still very cheap, and consumers, especially in North America, demanded heavier and larger cars with stronger motors. During this decade, General Motors (GM) developed an electric vehicle called the "EV1," which gained significant, though brief, international positive attention before it was taken off the market shortly after its introduction. All produced new cars were destroyed, and the electric-vehicle program was shut down. The development of electric vehicles was then left to other companies.

Barely twenty years later, following a significant negative impact on the car manufacturing companies in North America from the 2009 financial crisis and their earlier abandonment of research and de-

Tesla Motors used CAD software to design its earliest vehicles, creating virtual schematics prior to creating prototypes. Photo via iStock/Studio Powers. [Used under license.]

velopment of electric car technology, North American companies tried to catch up with the electric vehicle technology of the global vehicle manufacturing industry. During the hiatus, global competitors surpassed North American companies by creating modern, fast, useful electrical vehicles such as the Nissan Cube from Japan and the BMW ActiveE models from Germany. GM, at least, has made a full turnaround after receiving government financial incentives to develop battery-run vehicles and actively pursued a new electric concept called "Chevrolet Volt." Similar to hybrid cars, the original Volt had a standard battery, but because early twenty-first century batteries were not yet meeting desired performance levels, the Volt also had a small engine to extend its range. Installing two different power sources in a vehicle, one electric and one combustion based, made sense in order to develop a product that has lower emissions but the same range as combustion engine-based vehicles.

Advances in computer technology, and especially computer-aided design (CAD) and computer-simulation programs, proved beneficial to the electric-automobile industry during the first decades of the twenty-first century. The electric vehicle manufacturer Tesla Motors, for instance, made significant use of CAD software while designing its earliest cars, creating virtual schematics of the company's designs prior to creating prototypes. In addition to using CAD technology to design complete vehicles, automotive manufacturers utilized the technology to design and modify individual components of their vehicles; Tesla Motors, for instance, made use of CAD software when designing the covers for its cars' seats.

HOW IT WORKS

Power source. Gasoline, which is mainly a chemical called "octane," is a geologic product of animals and plants that lived many millions of years ago. They stored the energy of the sun either directly from photosynthesis or through digestion of plant matter. The solar energy that is chemically stored in gasoline is released during combustion.

The storage of energy in batteries occurs through different chemicals, depending on the type of battery. For example, typical car-starter lead-acid batteries use the metal lead and the ceramic lead oxide to store energy. During discharge, both these materials convert into yet another chemical called "lead sulfate." When a charge is applied to the battery, the original lead and lead oxide are re-created from the lead sulfate. Over time, some of the lead and lead oxide are lost in the battery, as they separate from the main material. This can be seen as a black dust swimming in the sulfuric acid of a long-used battery and indicates that the battery can no longer be recharged to its full initial storage capacity. This happens to all types of batteries. Modern lithium-ion batteries used in anything from vehicles to mobile phones use lithium-cobalt/nickel/manganese oxide, and lithium graphite. These batteries use lithium ions to transport the charges around, while allowing the liberated electrons to be used in an electric motor. Other batteries use zinc to store energy—for example, in small button cells. Toxic materials such as mercury and cadmium have for some years been used in specific types of batteries but have mostly been phased out because of the potential leaching of these materials into groundwater after the batteries' disposal.

Fuel cells do not use a solid material to store their charge. Instead, low-temperature proton exchange membrane fuel cells use gases such as hydrogen and liquid ethanol (the same form of alcohol found in vodka) or methanol as fuels. These materials are pumped over the surface of the fuel cells, and in the presence of noble-metal catalysts, the protons in these fuels are broken away from the fuel molecule and transported through the electrolyte membrane to form water and heat in the presence of air. The liberated electrons can, just as in the case of batteries, be used to drive an electric motor. Other types of fuel cells, such as molten carbonate fuel cells and solid oxide fuel cells, can use fuels such as carbon in the form of coal, soot, or old rubber tires and operate at 800° Celsius with a very high efficiency.

Converting electricity into motion. Most electric motors use a rotatable magnet the polarity of which can be reversed inside a permanent magnet. Once electricity is available to an electric motor, electrons, traveling through an electric wire and coiled around a shaft that can be magnetized, generate an electrical field that polarizes the shaft. As a result, the shaft is aligned within the external permanent magnet, since reverse polarities in magnets are attracted to each other. If the polarity of the rotatable shaft is now reversed by changing the electron flow, the magnet reverses polarity and rotates 180 degrees. If the switching of the magnetic polarity is precisely timed, constant motion will be created. Changes in rotational speed can be achieved by changing the frequency of the change in polarization. The rotation generated by an electric motor can then be used like the rotation generated by an internal combustion engine by transferring it to the wheels of the vehicle.

Research and development. Many components of electric vehicles can be improved by research and development. In the electric motor, special magnetic glasses can be used that magnetize rapidly with few losses to heat, and the magnet rotation can occur in a vacuum and by using low-friction bearings. Materials research of batteries has resulted in higher storage capacities, lower overall mass, faster recharge cycles, and low degradation over time. Significant further improvements can still be expected from this type of research as the fundamental understanding of the processes occurring in batteries become better understood. Novel fuel cells are being developed with the goal of making them cheaper by using non-precious-metal catalysts that degrade slowly with time and are reliable throughout the lifetime of the electric motor. The US Department of Energy has set specific lifetime and performance targets to which all these devices have to adhere to be useful on the commercial market.

There are, however, disadvantages to all energy-conversion technologies. Internal combustion engines require large amounts of metals, including iron, chromium, nickel, manganese, and other alloying elements. They also require very high temperatures in forges during production. Additionally, the petroleum-based fuels contain carcinogenic chemicals, and the exhausts are potentially dangerous to humans and the environment, even when catalytic converters are used; to function well, these devices require large amounts of expensive and rare noble metals such as palladium and platinum. The highest concentrations of oil deposits have been found in politically volatile regions, and oil developments in those regions have been shown to increase local poverty and to cause severe local environmental problems.

Batteries require large quantities of rare-earth elements such as lanthanum. Most of these elements are almost exclusively mined in China, which holds a monopoly on the pricing and availability of these elements. Some batteries use toxic materials such as lead, mercury, or cadmium, although the use of these elements is being phased out in Europe. Lithium-ion batteries can rapidly and explosively discharge when short-circuited and are also considered a health risk. Electricity is required to recharge batteries, and it is often produced off-site in reactors whose emissions and other waste can be detrimental to human health and the environment.

Fuel cells require catalysts that are mostly made from expensive noble metals. Severe price fluctuations make it difficult to identify a stable or predictable cost for these devices. The fuels used in fuel cells, mostly hydrogen and methanol or ethanol, have to be produced, stored, and distributed. Hydrogen used is often derived via a water-gas shift reaction, where oxygen is stripped off the water molecules and binds with carbon molecules from methane gas, producing hydrogen with carbon dioxide as a byproduct; the process requires large quantities of natural gas. Methanol or ethanol can be derived from plant matter, but if it is derived from plants originally intended as food, food prices may increase, and arable land once used for food production then produces fuels instead.

Nevertheless, while the advantages and disadvantages of cleaner energy technologies such as fuel cells and batteries must be weighed against their ecological and economic impacts, it is important to remember that they are significantly cleaner than internal combustion engine technologies.

APPLICATIONS AND PRODUCTS
Batteries. Battery technology still needs to be developed to be lighter without reducing the available charge. This means that the energy density of the battery (both by mass and by volume) needs to increase in order to improve a vehicle's range. Furthermore, faster recharge cycles have to be developed that will not negatively impact the degradation of the batteries. Overnight recharge cycles are possible, and good for home use, but a quick recharge during a shopping trip should allow the car to regain a significant proportion of its original charge. Repeated recharge cycles at different charge levels as well as longtime operation with large temperature fluctuations should not detrimentally affect the

microstructure of the batteries, so the power density of the batteries will remain intact. Furthermore, operation in very cold environments, in which the charge carriers inside the battery are less mobile, should be realized for a good market penetration.

Personal vehicles. GM's EV1 was an attempt to market electric vehicles in North America in the 1990s. It was fast and lightweight and had all the amenities required by consumers but was discontinued by the manufacturer because it was not commercially viable. The 2011 edition of GM's Chevrolet Volt was almost indistinguishable from other GM station wagons, but the cost for the battery-powered car proved too high for a market that was used to very cheap vehicles with internal combustion engines. Electric vehicle technology at that time was arguably much more advanced in Asia. Asian vehicle manufacturers were up to ten years ahead of the rest of the world in producing hybrid-electric vehicles, and they were ahead in the manufacturing of completely electric vehicles as well, introducing battery-only vehicles such as the Toyota iQ and the Nissan Leaf during the first decade of the twenty-first century. In the North American market, major electric vehicles of the early twenty-first century included the Tesla Roadster, introduced in 2008, and the Tesla Model S, released in 2012.

Electric automobile technology continued to develop over the next decade, and an increasing number of automotive manufacturers introduced new electric vehicles for sale in the United States and abroad. Tesla Motors remained a major force in the market, and in 2021, its Model Y and Model 3 automobiles were the United States' best-selling and second-best-selling electric vehicles of the year, respectively. Other popular personal electric vehicles of that period included the electric Ford Mustang Mach-E, the Volkswagen ID.4, the Nissan Leaf, and the Audi e-tron.

Utility vehicles and trucks. To develop a green image, some municipalities considered switching their fleets to electric vehicles based on fuel cells or batteries. Ford created a model called "Transit Connect," which was an electrified version of its Ford Transporter, while Navistar developed an electric truck, the eStar. Smith Electric Vehicles developed several models, such as the Newton, for the expected demand in electric-utility vehicles. Additionally, there were many small companies producing small utility trucks during the early twenty-first century, such as the Italian manufacturer Alkè. The products of these companies are small, practical multipurpose vehicles for cities and municipalities. In 2021, the automotive manufacturers Volvo and Daimler opened preorders for electric semitrucks.

Other vehicles. Small electric motor-assisted bicycles and electric scooters have been in use since the early twentieth century. Other small electric vehicles include wheelchairs, skateboards, golf carts, lawnmowers, and other equipment that typically does not require much power.

In the United States and elsewhere, some public transit companies have tested the use of fuel-cell- or battery-powered electric buses. About 598,000 electric buses were in use by the end of 2020; however, 98 percent of those buses were located in China, and electric buses remained rare in countries such as the United States. Cities that used electric overhead lines to power trolley buses, trams, and trains had much higher impact in terms of actual transported passengers. All these systems constitute electric vehicles, but all of them are dependent on having electric wires in place before they can operate. On the other hand, once the wires are in place, the public transit systems can operate silently and cleanly, using electricity provided through an electric grid instead of a battery or a fuel cell.

CAREERS AND COURSEWORK

As gasoline prices increase, it becomes more important to have lighter vehicles that require less material during manufacturing, as these have to be mined and transported around the world and machined using energy coming primarily from fossil fuels. Additionally, vehicles should become more efficient, to reduce the operating cost for vehicle owners. All these issues are addressed by selecting and designing better, novel materials. Those interested in a career in electric vehicle manufacturing or design would do well studying materials, mechanical, chemical, mining, or environmental engineering for designing novel cars, highly efficient motors, better batteries, and cheaper, more durable fuel cells. The mathematical modeling of the electrochemistry involved in electric motors is also very important to understand how to improve electric devices, and studies in chemistry and physics may lead to improvements in the efficiency of vehicles.

After earning a bachelor's degree in one of the above-mentioned areas, an internship would be ideal. After an internship, one's career path can be extremely varied. In the research sector, for example, working on catalysts for batteries and fuel cells in a chemical company could include developing new materials that involve inexpensive, nontoxic, durable noble metals that are at least as efficient as traditional catalysts. This is only one example of many potential careers in the global electric vehicle market.

SOCIAL CONTEXT AND FUTURE PROSPECTS

Energy consumption per capita is increasing continuously. The majority of power production uses the combustion of fossil fuels with additional contributions from hydroelectric and nuclear energy conversion. These energy-conversion methods create varying kinds of pollution and dangers to the environment such as habitat destruction, toxic-waste production, or radiation, as seen in nuclear reactors hit by earthquakes, equipment malfunction, or operator errors. The increasing demand for a finite quantity of fossil fuels has the potential to increase the cost of these resources significantly. Another undesirable consequence of the thermochemical conversion of fossil fuels by combustion is environmental contamination. The reaction products from combustion can be harmful to humans on a local scale and have been cited as contributing to global climate change. The remaining ash of coal combustion contains heavy metals and radioactive isotopes that can be severely damaging to health, as seen in the 2008 Kingston Fossil Plant coal ash slurry spill in Tennessee. Furthermore, fossil fuel resources are unevenly distributed over the globe, leading to geopolitical unrest as a result of the competition for resource access.

Clearly, the energy demands of society need to be satisfied in a more appropriate, sustainable, and efficient way. Cleaner devices for energy conversion are batteries and fuel cells. They operate more efficiently, produce less pollution, are modular, and are less likely to fail mechanically since they have fewer moving parts than energy conversion based on combustion.

The advantages of electric vehicles are clear: a world in which all or most vehicles are quiet, with no truck engine brakes to rattle windows from a mile away and no lawnmowers disturbing the quiet or fresh air of a neighborhood; a society with no harmful local emissions from any of the machines being used, allowing people to walk by a leaf blower without having to hold their breath and to live next to major roads without risking chronic diseases from continually breathing in harmful emissions. All this could already be humanity's present-day reality if people were willing to change their habits and simply use electric motors instead of combustion engines.

—*Lars Rose, MSc, PhD*

Further Reading

Cancilla, Riccardo, and Monte Gargano, editors. *Global Environmental Policies: Impact, Management and Effects.* Nova Science Publishers, 2010.

Eckhouse, Brian, and Jennifer A. Dlouhy. "Electric Buses Are Poised to Get a US Infrastructure Boost." *Bloomberg*, 13 Aug. 2021, www.bloomberg.com/news/newsletters/2021-08-13/electric-buses-are-poised-to-get-a-u-s-infrastructure-boost. Accessed 28 Nov. 2021.

Hoel, Michael, and Snorre Kverndokk. "Depletion of Fossil Fuels and the Impact of Global Warming." *Resource and Energy Economics*, vol. 18, no. 2, 1996, pp. 115-36.

Husain, Iqbal. *Electric and Hybrid Vehicles: Design Fundamentals*. 3rd ed., CRC Press, 2021.

Pavey, Lisa. "Never a Dull Moment." *Tesla*, 22 Nov. 2006, www.tesla.com/blog/never-dull-moment. Accessed 28 Nov. 2021.

Ramey, Jay. "Electric Semi-Trucks Are on Their Way, at Last." *Autoweek*, 22 Apr. 2021, www.autoweek.com/news/green-cars/a36201258/electric-semi-trucks-arrive/. Accessed 28 Nov. 2021.

Root, Michael. *The TAB Battery Book: An In-Depth Guide to Construction, Design, and Use*. McGraw-Hill, 2011.

Stone, Sarah. "Textile Engineering Student Helping to Develop Tesla Seat Covers." *NC State University*, 11 Oct. 2021, textiles.ncsu.edu/news/2021/10/textile-engineering-student-helping-to-develop-tesla-seat-covers/. Accessed 28 Nov. 2021.

Taylor, Peter J., and Frederick H. Buttel. "How Do We Know We Have Global Environmental Problems? Science and the Globalization of Environmental Discourse." *Geoforum* vol. 23, no. 3, 1992, pp. 405-16.

White, Annie. "12 Best-Selling Electric Vehicles of 2021 (So Far)." *Car and Driver*, 29 Oct. 2021, www.caranddriver.com/features/g36278968/best-selling-evs-of-2021/. Accessed 28 Nov. 2021.

Electrical Engineering

ABSTRACT

Electrical engineering is a broad field ranging from the most elemental electrical devices to high-level electronic systems design. An electrical engineer is expected to have fundamental understanding of electricity and electrical devices as well as be a versatile computer programmer. All of the electronic devices that permeate modern living originate with an electrical engineer. Items such as garage-door openers and smartphones are based on the application of electrical theory. Even the computer tools, fabrication facilities, and math to describe it all is the purview of the electrical engineer. Within the field there are many specializations. Some focus on high-power analog devices, while others focus on integrated circuit design or computer systems.

DEFINITION AND BASIC PRINCIPLES

Electrical engineering is the application of multiple disciplines converging to create simple or complex electrical systems. An electrical system can be as simple as a light bulb, power supply, or switch and as complicated as the internet, including all its hardware and software subcomponents. The spectrum and scale of electrical engineering is extremely diverse. At the atomic scale, electrical engineers can be found studying the electrical properties of electrons through materials. For example, silicon is an extremely important semiconductive material found in all integrated circuit (IC) devices, and knowing how to manipulate it is extremely important to those who work in microelectronics.

While electrical engineers need a fundamental background in basic electricity, many (if not most) electrical engineers do not deal directly with wires and devices, at least on a daily basis. An important subdiscipline in electrical engineering includes IC design engineering: A team of engineers are tasked with using computer software to design IC circuit schematics. As of 2021, popular electrical computer-aided design (ECAD) programs included SolidWorks Electrical Professional, produced by Dassault Systèmes, and the AutoCAD Electrical Toolset offered by Autodesk. Schematics produced via such programs are then passed through a series of verification steps (also done by electrical engineers) before being assembled. Because computers are ubiquitous, and the reliance on good computer programs to perform complicated operations is so important, electrical engineers can be adept computer programmers as well. The steps would be the same in any of the subdisciplines of the field.

BACKGROUND AND HISTORY
Electrical engineering has its roots in the pioneering work of early experimenters in electricity in the eighteenth and nineteenth centuries, who lent their names to much of the nomenclature, such as French physicist André-Marie Ampère and Italian physicist Alessandro Volta. The title electrical engineer began appearing in the late nineteenth century, although to become an electrical engineer did not entail any special education or training, just ambition. After American inventor Thomas Edison's direct current (DC) lost the standards war to Croatian-born inventor Nicola Tesla's alternating current (AC), it was only a matter of time before AC power became standard in every household.

Vacuum tubes were used in electrical devices such as radios in the early twentieth century. The first computers were built using warehouses full of vacuum tubes. They required multiple technicians and programmers to operate because when one tube burst, computation could not begin until it had been identified and replaced.

The transistor was invented in 1947 by John Bardeen, Walter Brattain, and William Shockley, employees of Bell Laboratories. By soldering together boards of transistors, electrical engineers created the first modern computers in the 1960s. By the 1970s, integrated circuits were shrinking the size of computers and the purely electrical focus of the field.

Electrical engineers have dominated IC design and systems engineering, which include mainframes, personal computers, and cloud computing. There is still a demand for high-energy electrical devices, such as airplanes, tanks, and power plants, but because electricity has so many diverse uses, the field will continue to diversify as well.

HOW IT WORKS
In a typical scenario, an electrical engineer, or a team of electrical engineers, will be tasked with designing an electrical device or system. It could be a computer, the component inside a computer (such as a central processing unit, or CPU), a national power grid, an office intranet, a power supply for a jet, or an automobile ignition system. In each case, however, the electrical engineer's *grasp on the fundamentals of the field is crucial*.

Electricity. For any electrical application to work, it needs electricity. Once a device or system has been identified for assembly, the electrical engineer must know how it uses electricity. A computer will use low voltages for sensitive IC devices and higher ones for fans and disks. Inside the IC, electricity will be used as the edges of clock cycles that determine what its logical values are. A power grid will generate the electricity itself at a power plant, then transmit it at high voltage over a grid of transmission lines.

Electric power. When it is determined how the device or application will use electricity, the source of that power must also be understood. Will it be a

A replica of the first working transistor, a point-contact transistor. Photo via Wikimedia Commons. [Public domain.]

169

standard AC power outlet? Or a DC battery? To power a computer, the voltage must be lowered and converted to DC. To power a jet, the spinning turbines (which run on jet fuel) generate electricity, which can then be converted to DC and will then power the onboard electrical systems. In some cases, it is possible to design for what happens in the absence of power, such as the battery backup on an alarm clock or an office's backup generator. An interesting case is the hybrid motor of certain cars such as the Toyota Prius. It has both an electromechanical motor and an electric one. Switching the drivetrain seamlessly between the two is quite a feat of electrical and mechanical engineering.

Circuits. If the application under consideration has circuit components, then its circuitry must be designed and tested. To test the design, mock-ups are often built onto breadboards (plastic rows of contacts that allow wiring up a circuit to be done easily and quickly). An oscilloscope and voltmeter can be used to measure the signal and its strength at various nodes. Once the design is verified, if necessary, the schematic can be sent to a fabricator and mass manufactured onto a circuit board.

Digital logic. Often, an electrical engineer will not need to build the circuits themselves. Using computer design tools and tailored programming languages, an electrical engineer can create a system using logic blocks, then synthesize the design into a circuit. This is the method used for designing and fabricating application-specific integrated circuits (ASICs) and field-programmable gate arrays (FPGAs).

Digital signal processing (DSP). Since digital devices require digital signals, it is up to the electrical engineer to ensure that the correct signal is coming in and going out of the digital circuit block. If the incoming signal is analog, it must be converted to digital via an analog-to-digital converter, or if the circuit block can only process so much data at a time, the circuit block must be able to time slice the

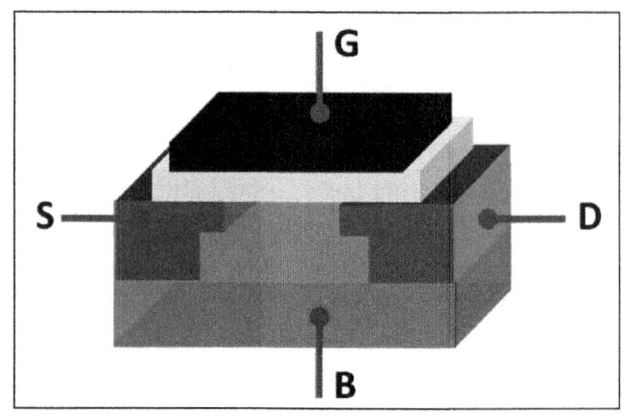

Metal–oxide–semiconductor field-effect transistor (MOSFET), the basic building block of modern electronics. Diagram is showing gate (G), body (B), source (S) and drain (D) terminals. The gate is separated from the body by an insulating layer. Image by Brews ohare, via Wikimedia Commons.

data into manageable chunks. A good example is an MP3 player: The data must be read from the disk while it is moving, converted to sound at a frequency humans can hear, played back at a normal rate, then converted to an analog sound signal in the headphones. Each one of those steps involves DSP.

Computer programming. Many of the steps above can be abstracted out to a computer programming language. For example, in a logical programming language such as Verilog, an electrical engineer can write lines of code that represent the logic. Another program can then convert it into the schematics of an IC block. A popular programming language called "SPICE" can simulate how a circuit will behave, saving the designer time by verifying the circuit works as expected before it is ever assembled.

APPLICATIONS AND PRODUCTS

The products of electrical engineering are an integral part of everyday life. Everything from cell phones and computers to stereos and electric lighting encompass the purview of the field.

For example, a cell phone has at every layer the mark of electrical engineering. An electrical engineer designed the hardware that runs the device. That hardware must be able to interface with the established communication channels designated for use. Thus, a firm knowledge of DSP and radio waves went into its design. The base stations with which the cell phone communicates were designed by electrical engineers. The network that allows them to work in concert is the latest incarnation of a century of study in electromagnetism. The digital logic that allows multiple phone conversations to occur at the same time on the same frequency was crafted by electrical engineers. The whole mobile experience integrates seamlessly into the existing landline grid. Even the preexisting technology (low voltage wire to every home) is an electrical engineering accomplishment—not to mention the power cable that charges it from a standard AC outlet.

One finds the handiwork of electrical engineers in such mundane devices as thermostats to the ubiquitous internet, where everything from the network cards to the keyboards, screens, and software are crafted by electrical engineers. Electrical engineers are historically involved with electromagnetic devices as well, such as the electrical starter of a car or the turbines of a hydroelectric plant. Many devices that aid artists, such as sound recording and electronic musical instruments, are also the inspiration of electrical engineers.

Below is a sampling of the myriad electrical devices that are designed by electrical engineers.

Computers. Computer hardware and often computer software are designed by electrical engineers. The CPU and other ICs of the computer are the product of hundreds of electrical engineers working together to create ever-faster and more miniature devices. Many products can rightfully be considered computers, though they are not often thought of as such. Smartphones, video-game consoles, and even the controllers in modern automobiles are computers, as they all employ a microprocessor. Additionally, the peripherals that are required to interface with a computer have to be designed to work with the computer as well, such as printers, copiers, scanners, and specialty industrial and medical equipment.

Test equipment. Although these devices are seldom seen by the general public, they are essential to keeping all the other electrical devices in the world working. For example, an oscilloscope can help an electrical engineer test and debug a failing circuit because it can show how various nodes are behaving relative to each other over time. A carpenter might use a wall scanner to find electrical wire, pipes, and studs enclosed behind a wall. A multimeter, which measures voltage, resistance, and current, is handy not just for electrical engineers but also for electricians and hobbyists.

Sound amplifiers. Car stereos, home theaters, and electric guitars all have one thing in common: They all contain an amplifier. In the past, these have been purely analog devices, but since the late twentieth century, digital amplifiers have supplanted their analog brethren due to their ease of operation and size. Audiophiles, however, claim that analog amplifies sound better.

Power supplies. These can come in many sizes, both physically and in terms of power. Most people encounter a power supply as a black box plugged into an AC outlet with a cord that powers electrical devices such as a laptop, radio, or television. Inside each is a specially designed power inverter that converts AC power to the required volts and amperes of DC power.

Batteries. Thomas Edison is credited with creating the first portable battery, a rechargeable box that required only water once a week. Batteries are an electrochemical reaction, that is the realm of chemistry, and demonstrate how far afield electrical engineering can seem to go while remaining firmly grounded in its fundamentals. Battery technology is entering a new renaissance as the charge life is extending and the size is shrinking. Edison first marketed his "A" battery for use in electric cars before they went out of fashion. Electric cars that run on batteries may be making a comeback, and their cousin, the hybrid, runs on both batteries and combustion.

The power grid. This is one of the oldest accomplishments of electrical engineering. A massive nationwide interdependent network of transmission lines delivers power to every corner of the country. The power is generated at hydroelectric plants, coal plants, nuclear plants, and wind and solar plants. The whole thing works such that if any one section fails, the others can pick up the slack. Wind and solar pose particular challenges to the field, as wind and sunshine do not flow at a constant rate, but the power grid must deliver the same current and voltage at all times of day.

Electric trains and buses. Many major cities have some kind of public transportation that involves either an electrified rail, or bus wires, or both. These subways, light rails, and trolleys are an important part of municipal infrastructure, built on many of the same principles as the power grid, except that it is localized.

Automobiles. There are many electronic parts in a car. The first to emerge historically is the electric starter, obviating the hand crank. Once there was a battery in the car to power the starter, engineers came up with all sorts of other uses for it: headlamps, windshield wipers, interior lighting, a radio (and later tape and compact disk [CD] players), and the car alarm, to name a few. The most important

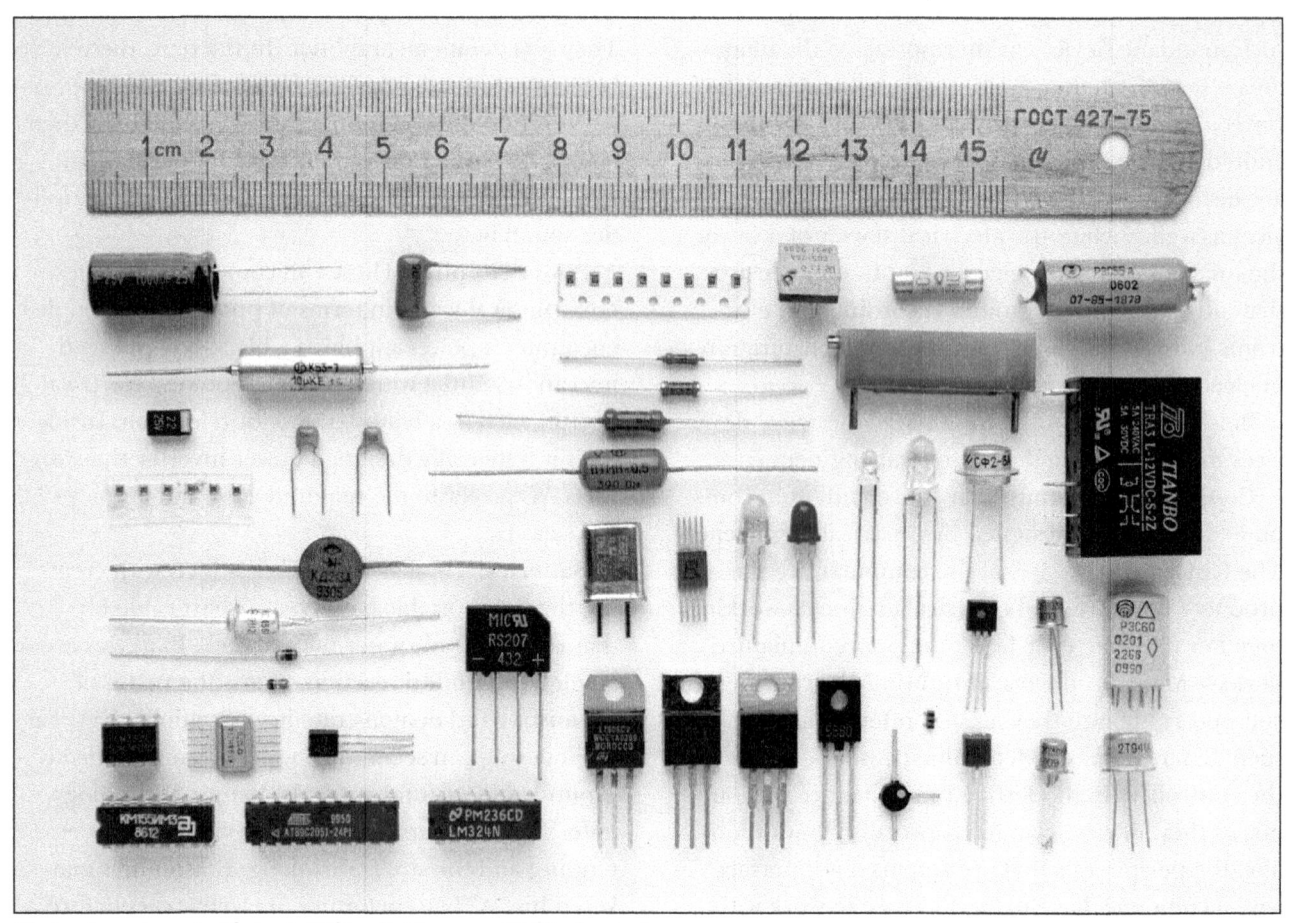

Electronic components. Photo via Wikimedia Commons. [Public domain.]

electrical component of modern automobiles is the computer-controlled fuel injector. This allows for the right amount of oxygen and fuel to be present in the engine for maximum fuel efficiency (or for maximum horsepower). The success of hybrids, and the emerging market of all-electric vehicles, means that there is still more electrical innovation to be had inside a century-old technology.

Medical devices. Though specifically the domain of biomedical engineering, many, if not most, medical devices are designed by electrical engineers who have entered this subdiscipline. Computed axial tomography (CAT) scanners, X-rays, ultrasound, and magnetic resonance imaging (MRI) machines all rely on electromagnetic and nuclear physics applied in an electrical setting (and controlled by electronics). These devices can be used to look into things other than human bodies as well. Researchers demonstrated that an MRI could determine if a block of cheese had properly aged.

Telecommunications. This used to be an international grid of telephone wires and cables connecting as many corners of the globe where wire could be strung. In the twenty-first century, however, even the most remote outposts can communicate voice, data, and video thanks to advances in radio technology. The major innovation in this field has been the ability for multiple connections to ride the same signal. The original cell phone technology picked a tiny frequency for each of its users, thus limiting the number of total users to a fixed division in that band. Mobile communication has multiple users on the same frequency, which opens up the band to more users.

Broadcast television and radio. These technologies are older but still relevant to the electrical engineer. Radio is as vibrant as ever, and ham radio is even experiencing a mini renaissance. While there may not be much room for innovation, electrical engineers must understand them to maintain them, as well as understand their derivative technologies.

Lighting. Light-emitting diodes (LEDs) are low-power alternatives to incandescent bulbs (the light bulb that Edison invented). They are just transistors, but as they have grown smaller and more colors have been added to their spectrum, they have found their way into interior lighting, computer monitors, flashlights, indicator displays, and control panels.

CAREERS AND COURSEWORK

Electrical engineering requires a diverse breadth of background coursework—math, physics, computer science, and electrical theory—and a desire to specialize while at the same time being flexible to work with other electrical engineers in their own areas of expertise. A bachelor of science degree in electrical engineering usually entails specialization after the general coursework is completed. Specializations include circuit design, communications and networks, power systems, and computer science. A master's degree would be required to enter academia or to gain a deeper understanding in the specialization. An electrical engineer wishing to work as an electrical systems contractor will probably require professional engineer (PE) certification, which is issued by the state after one has several years of work experience and has passed the certification exam.

Careers in the field of electrical engineering are as diverse as its applications. Manufacturing uses electrical engineers to design and program industrial equipment. Telecommunications employs electrical engineers because of their understanding of DSP. Many electrical engineers work in the microchip sector, which uses legions of electrical engineers to design, test, and fabricate ICs on a continually shrinking scale. Though these companies seem dissimilar—medical devices, smartphones, computers (any device that uses an IC)—they have their own staffs of electrical engineers that design, test, fabricate, and retest the devices.

Electrical engineers are being seen more and more in the role of computer scientist. The coursework has been converging since the twentieth century. University electrical engineering and computer science departments may share lecturers between the two disciplines. Companies may use electrical engineers to solve a computer-programming problem in the hopes that the electrical engineer can debug both the hardware and software.

SOCIAL CONTEXT AND FUTURE PROSPECTS

Electrical engineering may be the most underrecognized driving force behind modern living. Everything from the electrical revolution to the rise of the personal computer to the internet and social networking has been initiated by electrical engineers. This field first brought electricity into homes and then ushered in the age of transistors. Much of the new technology being developed is consumed as software and requires computer programmers. But the power grid, hardware, and internet that powers it were designed by electrical engineers and maintained by electrical engineers.

As the field continues to diversify and the uses for electricity expand, the need for electrical engineers will expand, as will the demands placed on the knowledge base required to enter the field. Electrical engineers have been working in the biological sciences, a field rarely explored by the electrical engineer. The neurons that comprise the human brain are an electrical system, and it makes sense for both fields to embrace the knowledge acquired in the other.

Other disciplines rely on electrical engineering as the foundation. Robotics, for example, merge mechanical and electrical engineering. As robots move out of manufacturing plants and into offices and homes, engineers with a strong understanding of the underlying physics are essential. Another related field, biomedical engineering, combines medicine and electrical engineering to produce lifesaving devices such pacemakers, defibrillators, and CAT scanners. As the population ages, the need for more advanced medical treatments and early-detection devices becomes paramount. Green power initiatives will require electrical engineers with strong mechanical engineering and chemistry knowledge. If recent and past history are our guides, the next scientific revolution will likely come from electrical engineering.

—*Vincent Jorgensen, BS*

Further Reading

Adhami, Reza, Peter M. Meenen III, and Dennis Hite. *Fundamental Concepts in Electrical and Computer Engineering with Practical Design Problems*. 2nd ed., Universal, 2005.

Ashby, Darren. *Electrical Engineering 101: Everything You Should Have Learned in School—But Probably Didn't*. 3rd ed., Newnes, 2012.

"Computer Aided Design (CAD) vs. Manual Drafting." *Electrical Engineering* 123, electricalengineering123.com/computer-aided-design-cad-vs-manual-drafting/. Accessed 28 Nov. 2021.

Davis, L. J. *Fleet Fire: Thomas Edison and the Pioneers of the Electric Revolution*. Arcade, 2003.

Dorr, Barry L. *Ten Essential Skills for Electrical Engineers*. Wiley-IEEE Press, 2014.

Fink, Zachary L. *Encyclopedia of Electrical Engineering Research*. Nova Science, 2013.

Ida, Nathan. *Engineering Electromagnetics*. 3rd ed., Springer, 2015.

Irwin, J. David, and R. Mark Nelms. *Basic Engineering Circuit Analysis*. 12th ed., Wiley, 2021.

McNichol, Tom. *AC/DC: The Savage Tale of the First Standards War*. Jossey-Bass, 2006.

Rauf, S. Bobby. *Electrical Engineering Fundamentals*. CRC Press, 2020.

Shurkin, Joel N. *Broken Genius: The Rise and Fall of William Shockley, Creator of the Electronic Age*. Macmillan, 2006.

"What Is Electrical CAD (ECAD)?" *Arena*, www.arenasolutions.com/resources/glossary/electrical-cad/. Accessed 28 Nov. 2021.

Electronic Design Automation (EDA)

ABSTRACT
Electronic design automation (EDA) refers to the various software programs used to design electronic circuitry such as printed circuit boards and integrated circuits. EDA is essential for the design of twenty-first-century computer chips, each of which may comprise billions of transistors.

BASIC ELECTRONICS CONCEPTS
An electric current is the flow of subatomic particles called "electrons" as they transfer from atom to atom in an electrically conducting material. The direction of that electrical current flow is from a point of higher electrical potential to a point of lower electrical potential. Every material has its own characteristic ability to conduct electrical current. Those that do it well are classed as conductors, and those that do not are classed as nonconductors or insulators. In between is a class of materials called "semiconductors," the most well-known being silicon.

An electrical circuit is the structure of conducting components such as wires that provide a path through which electricity can flow to provide power to various electrical devices, such as light bulbs and computers. An electronic circuit, on the other hand, refers to circuits composed of electronic devices such as transistors and diodes. The terms "electrical" and "electronic" are often used interchangeably, and while not exactly incorrect, this usage does lose the distinction between the two.

Both electrical and electronic devices function through the manipulation and control of electrical current. Prior to the invention of the semiconductor transistor, devices such as radios and televisions relied on vacuum tubes and standard circuit components such as resistors and capacitors for their operation. The vacuum tube components were the essential current control devices, with a variety of names depending on their function. A diode, for example, functioned to allow current flow in one direction only.

Vacuum tubes, though fairly robust in operation, were nevertheless subject to sudden failure if the wire filament structure it contained burned out. The evacuated glass bulb containing the filament structure was also prone to breakage if not handled carefully. Any such failure required replacement of the vacuum tube. Vacuum tube devices also consumed a lot of power and typically required a warm-up period before they could become fully functional, after which they also emitted a good deal of heat. Attempts to build a functional digital computer based on vacuum tubes in the 1940s were ultimately successful, but failures among the thousands of tubes it required were common, the amount of heat the units generated posed a real danger, and the computing ability of the units was very low compared even to the most basic modern calculator.

TRANSISTOR TECHNOLOGY
In 1947, the first transistor using a semiconductor was constructed. It required only a low direct current voltage to function and produced very little heat. In the following years, the electronic devices of vacuum tube technology were duplicated as much smaller semiconductor-based transistor devices that did not require an evacuated glass tube or a warm-up period for their operation. The differences in size and power consumption between vacuum tube and semiconductor devices were staggering. For example, a typical home radio required 120V house current to function, and took up significant space due to the size of the tubes and the speaker used in its operation. A radio of equal, and often greater, capability using semiconductor technology was powered by a small dry cell battery and could fit in the palm of one's hand, its required space now determined by the similarly smaller size of the speaker it could op-

PCB layout and schematic for connector design. Photo by Peter Clifton, via Wikimedia Commons.

erate. The use of headphones with microplug adapters allowed them to be even smaller.

As methods of production for semiconductor technology developed, the rate of miniaturization of electronic circuits increased rapidly. It is a topic of debate whether the rate of miniaturization drove the development of the production technology, or the rate of development of the production technology drove the rate of miniaturization. In the twenty-first century, both have progressed to the point where billions of transistor nanocircuits can be etched onto a silicon-based semiconductor chip such as those in the control processing units (CPUs) of personal computers and the micro-secure digital (SD) cards used in cell phones. The semiconductor chip inside a micro-SD card has a surface area comparable to that of the nail on an adult's little finger, and such chips can contain one terabyte or more of storage, each byte requiring a number of transistor nanocircuits.

A COMMONALITY

Both vacuum tube and transistor technology share one common requirement: their circuits must be designed to fit on a substrate. For vacuum tubes and other components this substrate is the printed circuit board (PCB), while for transistor nanocircuits it is the surface of the semiconductor chip. A printed circuit board typically consists of a fiberglass and resin sheet on which the appropriate electrical circuit has been "printed" by the application of thin copper conducting lines that connect the pinholes through which component-connecting pins will protrude. A soldering process is then used to connect the pins to the circuit lines. This method is conducive to mass-production methods, and manufacturers can use computer-controlled robotics for the placement of components into the circuit board.

The production of semiconductor devices such as computer chips is a much more complex, multistep operation. A single large crystal of pure silicon that has been alloyed with a small amount of germanium and phosphorus is cut into a number of thin slices, and each slice is polished to an extreme degree to provide a perfect surface. The slices that are deemed suitable after this operation are then sent through a multistage etching process in which a multitude of transistor nanocircuits are formed in and on the surface of each slice. Each slice may have multiple discrete chips etched into its surface, which are then very carefully separated.

In both cases, electronic design automation (EDA) software—part of the broader field of computer-aided design (CAD) software—can be used to design the layout of the electronic circuits.

CAD SOFTWARE

In the decades before the development of CAD software, all electrical and electronic circuitry was designed and drawn using standard technical drawing methods. The process was simplified by the use of standard symbols for different circuit components and features but was nonetheless labor and time consuming. The larger and more complex the desired circuit, the longer it would take to draw its optimum layout.

CAD software, and even the most basic graphics programs, facilitate the production of electronic circuit diagrams. But even these are restricted by the same types of time constraints that limit standard technical drawing methods. There are, however, CAD programs available that allow the user to design relatively simple electrical and electronic circuits and printed circuit board layouts quickly. Tools marketed by the software developer OrCAD, for example, allow the user to drag and drop standard device symbols onto a workspace. Changes can be made easily, and such programs can calculate voltages, resistances, currents, and other parameters according to the circuit design. More complex circuitry design, especially that involving complex semiconductor devices operating on Boolean logic principles, requires substantially more complex automated programs. Such automated programs are often designed to use computational parameters provided by a second program that is executing as a module inside the EDA program.

In the third decade of the twenty-first century, EDA software is available in a wide range of application levels, ranging from simple EDA for electronic hobbyists to cutting-edge EDA for high-end market chip designers and electronics researchers. EDA software is available for Linux, Windows, UNIX, and Mac operating systems and range from free open-source programs to high-priced proprietary programs. According to a 2021 report by Marqual IT Solutions, the global value of the EDA software market was increasing substantially each year and was projected to reach a total value of $16 billion by 2027.

—*Richard M. Renneboog MSc*

Further Reading
"Global Electronic Design Automation Software Market by Application, by End User, by Regional Outlook, Industry Analysis Report and Forecast, 2021-2027." *Research and Markets,* June 2021,

www.researchandmarkets.com/reports/5354457/global-electronic-design-automation-software. Accessed 16 Dec. 2021.

Lavagno, Luciano, Igor L. Markov, Grant Martin, and Louis K. Scheffer, editors. *Electronic Design Automation for IC Implementation, Circuit Design, and Process Technology*. 2nd ed., CRC Press, 2016.

Lienig, Jens, and Juergen Scheible. *Fundamentals of Layout Design for Electronic Circuits*. Springer, 2020.

Lou, Shuqin, and Chunling Yang. *Digital Electronic Circuits: Principles and Practices*. De Gruyter, 2019.

Maiti, Chinmay Kumar. *Computer Aided Design of Micro- and Nanoelectronic Devices*. World Scientific, 2017.

Martins, Ricardo, Nuno Lourenço, and Nuno Horta. *Analog Integrated Circuit Design Automation: Placement, Routing and Parasitic Extraction Techniques*. Springer, 2017.

Mitzner, Kraig, Bob Doe, Alexander Akulin, et al. *Complete PCB Design Using OrCAD Capture and PCB Editor*. 2nd ed., Academic Press, 2019.

Electronics and Electronic Engineering

ABSTRACT

A workable understanding of the phenomenon of electricity originated with proof that atoms were composed of smaller particles bearing positive and negative electrical charges. The modern field of electronics is essentially the science and technology of devices designed to control the movement of electricity to achieve some useful purpose. Initially, electronic technology consisted of devices that worked with continuously flowing electricity, whether direct or alternating current. Since the development of the transistor in 1947 and the integrated circuit in 1970, electronic technology has become digital, concurrent with the ability to assemble millions of transistor structures on the surface of a single silicon chip.

DEFINITION AND BASIC PRINCIPLES

The term "electronics" has acquired different meanings in different contexts. Fundamentally, "electronics" refers to the behavior of matter as affected by the properties and movement of electrons. More generally, electronics has come to mean the technology that has been developed to function according to electronic principles, especially pertaining to basic digital devices and the systems that they operate. The term "electronic engineering" refers to the practice of designing and building circuitry and devices that function on electronic principles.

The underlying principle of electronics derives from the basic structure of matter: that matter is composed of atoms composed in turn of smaller particles. The mass of atoms exists in the atomic nucleus, which is a structure composed of electrically neutral particles called "neutrons" and positively charged particles called "protons." Isolated from the nuclear structure by a relatively immense distance is an equal number of negatively charged particles called "electrons." Electrons are easily removed from atoms, and when a difference in electrical potential (voltage) exists between two points, electrons can move from the area of higher potential toward that of lower potential. This defines an electrical current.

Devices that control the presence and magnitude of both voltages and currents are used to bring about changes to the intrinsic form of the electrical signals so generated. These devices also produce physical changes in materials that make comprehensible the information carried by the electronic signal.

BACKGROUND AND HISTORY

Archaeologists have found well-preserved Parthian relics that are believed by some to have been rudimentary, but functional, batteries. It has been hypothesized that these ancient devices were used by the Parthians to plate objects with gold. The knowledge was lost until 1800, when Italian physicist Alessandro Volta reinvented the voltaic pile. Danish physicist and chemist Hans Christian Oersted demonstrated the relationship between electricity and magnetism in 1820, and in 1821, British physicist and chemist Michael Faraday used that relationship to demonstrate the electromagnetic principle on which all electric motors work. In 1831, he demonstrated the reverse relationship, inventing the electrical generator in the process.

Electricity was thought, by American statesman and scientist Benjamin Franklin and many other scientists of the eighteenth and nineteenth centuries, to be some mysterious kind of fluid that might be captured and stored. A workable concept of electricity was not developed until 1897, when English physicist J. J. Thomson identified cathode rays as streams of light electrical particles that must have come from within the atoms of their source materials. He arbitrarily ascribed their electrical charge as negative. Thomson also identified channel rays as streams of massive particles from within the atoms of their source materials that are endowed with the opposite electrical charge of the electrons that made up cathode rays. These observations essentially proved that atoms have substructures. They also provided a means of explaining electricity as the movement of charged particles from one location to another.

With the establishment of an electrical grid, based on the advocacy of alternating current by Serbian American engineer and inventor Nikola Tesla (1856-1943), a vast assortment of analog electrical devices were soon developed for consumer use, though initially these devices were no more than

The emergence of powerful computers and CAD software facilitated the digital design and testing of later electronic devices as well as crucial components such as printed circuit boards. Photo via iStock/scanrail. [Used under license.]

electric lights and electromechanical applications based on electric motors and generators.

As the quantum theory of atomic structure came to be better understood and electricity better controlled, electronic theory became much more important. Spurred by the success of the electromagnetic telegraph of American inventor Samuel Morse (1791-1872), scientists sought other applications. The first major electronic application of worldwide importance was wireless radio, first demonstrated by Italian inventor Guglielmo Marconi (1874-1937). Radio depended on electronic devices known as "vacuum tubes," in which structures capable of controlling currents and voltages could operate at high temperatures in an evacuated tube with external contacts. In 1947, American physicist William Shockley and colleagues invented the semiconductor-based transistor, which could be made to function in the same manner as vacuum tube devices, but without the high temperatures, electrical power consumption, and vacuum construction of those analog devices.

In 1970, the first integrated circuit "chips" were made by constructing very small transistor structures on the surface of a silicon chip. This gave rise to the entire digital technology that powers the modern world. Advances in digital technology themselves spurred on further advances: The emergence of powerful personal computers and advanced computer-aided design (CAD) software, for instance, facilitated the digital design and testing of later electronic devices as well as crucial components such as printed circuit boards (PCBs).

APPLICATIONS AND PRODUCTS

Electronics are applied in practically every conceivable manner in the twenty-first century, based on their utility in converting easily produced electrical current into mechanical movement, sound, light, and information signals.

Basic electronic devices. Transistor-based digital technology has replaced older vacuum tube technology, except in rare instances in which a transistorized device cannot perform the same function. Electronic circuits based on vacuum tubes could carry out essentially the same individual operations as transistors, but they were severely limited by physical size, heat production, energy consumption, and mechanical failure. Nevertheless, vacuum tube technology was the basic technology that produced radio, television, radar, X-ray machines, and a broad variety of other electronic applications.

Electronic devices that did not use vacuum tube technology, but which operated on electronic and electromagnetic principles, were, and still are, numerous. These devices include electromagnets and all electric motors and generators. The control systems for many such devices generally consisted of nothing more than switching circuits and indicator lights. More advanced and highly sensitive devices required control systems that utilized the more refined and correspondingly sensitive capabilities available with vacuum tube technology.

Circuit boards. The basic principles of electricity, such as Ohm's resistance law and Kirchoff's current law and capacitance and inductance, are key features in the functional design and engineering of analog electronic systems, especially for vacuum-tube control systems. An important application that facilitated the general use and development of electronic systems of all kinds is printed circuit board technology. A printed circuit board accepts standardized components onto a nonconducting platform made initially of compressed fiberboard, which was eventually replaced by a resin-based composite board. A circuit design is photoetched onto a copper sheet that makes up one face of the circuit board, and all nonetched copper is chemically removed from the surface of the board, leaving the circuit pattern. The leads of circuit components such as resistors, capaci-

Photo via iStock/sefa ozel. [Used under license.]

tors, and inductors are inserted into the circuit pattern and secured with solder connections.

Mass production requirements developed the flotation soldering process, whereby preassembled circuit boards are floated on a bed of molten solder, which automatically completes all solder connections at once with a high degree of consistency. This has become the most important means of circuit board production since the development of transistor technology, being highly compatible with mechanization and automation and with the physical shapes and dimensions of integrated circuit (IC) chips and other components.

Digital devices. Semiconductor-based transistors comprise the heart of modern electronics and electronic engineering. Unlike vacuum tubes, transistors do not work on a continuous electrical signal. Instead, they function exceedingly well as simple on-off switches that are easily controlled. This makes them well adapted to functions based on Boolean algebra. All transistor structures consist of a series of "gates" that perform a specific function on the electronic signals that are delivered to them.

Digital devices now represent the most common (and rapidly growing) application of electronics and electronic engineering, including relatively simple consumer electronic devices such as compact fluorescent light bulbs and motion-detecting air fresheners to the most advanced computers and analytical instrumentation. All applications, however, utilize an extensive, but limited, assortment of digital components in the form of IC chips that have been designed to carry out specific actions with electrical or electromagnetic input signals.

Input signals are defined by the presence or absence of a voltage or a current, depending upon the nature of the device. Inverter gates reverse the sense of the input signal, converting an input voltage (high input) into an output signal of no voltage (low output), and vice versa. Other transistor structures (gates) called "AND, NAND, OR, NOR, and X-OR" function to combine input signals in different ways to produce corresponding output signals. More advanced devices (e.g., counters and shift registers) use combinations of the different gates to construct various functional circuits that accumulate signal information or that manipulate signal information in various ways.

One of the most useful of digital IC components is the operational amplifier, or op-amp. Op-amps contain transistor-based circuitry that boosts the magnitude of an input signal, either voltage or current, by five orders of magnitude (100,000 times) or more, and are the basis of the exceptional sensitivity of the modern analytical instruments used in all fields of science and technology.

Electrical engineers are involved in all aspects of the design and development of electronic equipment. Engineers act first as the inventors and designers of electronic systems, conceptualizing the specific functions a potential system will be required to carry out. This process moves through the specification of the components required for the system's functionality to the design of new system devices. The design parameters extend to the infrastructure that must support the system in operation. Engineers determine the standards of safety, integrity, and operation that must be met for electronic systems.

Consumer electronics. For the most part, the term "electronics" is commonly used to refer to the electronic devices developed for retail sale to consumers. These devices include radios; television sets; digital video disk (DVD), Blu-ray, and compact disk (CD) players; cell phones and messaging devices; cameras and camcorders; laptops, tablets, and desktop computers; printers; fax and copy machines; cash registers; and scanners. Millions such devices are sold around the world each day, and numerous other businesses have formed to support their operation.

SOCIAL CONTEXT AND FUTURE PROSPECTS

It is difficult, if not impossible, to imagine modern society without electronic technology. Electronics has enabled the world of instant communication, wherein a person on one side of the world can communicate directly and almost instantaneously with someone on the other side of the world. As a social tool, such facile communication has the potential to bring about understanding between peoples in a way that has until now been imagined only in science fiction.

Consequently, this facility has also resulted in harm. While social networking sites, for example, bring people from widely varied backgrounds together peacefully to a common forum, hackers and other malicious individuals use electronic technology to steal personal data, disrupt financial markets, and spread misinformation.

Electronics itself is not the problem, for it is only a tool. Electronic technology, though built on a foundation that is unlikely to change in any significant way, will nevertheless be transformed into newer and better applications. New electronic principles will come to the fore. Materials such as graphene and quantum dots, for example, are expected to provide entirely new means of constructing transistor structures at the atomic and molecular levels. Compared with the 10- to 20-nanometer size of twenty-first-century transistor technology, these new levels would represent a difference of several orders of magnitude. Researchers suggest that this sort of refinement in scale could produce magnetic memory devices that can store as much as ten terabits of information in one square centimeter of disk surface. Although the technological advances seem inevitable, realizing such a scale will require a great deal of research and development.

—*Richard M. Renneboog, MSc*

Further Reading

Baker, R. Jacob. *CMOS: Circuit Design, Layout, and Simulation*. 4th ed., Wiley-IEEE Press, 2019.

"The Basics of Designing PCBs with CAD." *PCB Train*, 29 Sept. 2015, www.pcbtrain.co.uk/blog/the-basics-of-designing-pcbs-with-cad. Accessed 28 Nov. 2021.

Irwin, J. David, and R. Mark Nelms. *Basic Engineering Circuit Analysis*. 12th ed., Wiley, 2021.

Mughal, Ghulam Rasool. "Impact of Semiconductors in Electronics Industry." *PAF-KIET Journal of Engineering and Sciences*, vol. 1, no. 2, 2007, pp. 91-98.

Otte, Lea. "Computer-Aided-Design in Electronics Engineering." *Celus*, 25 June 2020, www.celus.io/en/blog/cad. Accessed 28 Nov. 2021.

Platt, Charles. *Make: Electronics*. 2nd ed., Maker Media, 2015.

Plonus, Martin. *Electronics and Communications for Scientists and Engineers*. 2nd ed., Butterworth-Heinemann, 2020.

Singmin, Andrew. *Beginning Digital Electronics through Projects*. Butterworth-Heinemann, 2001.

Tartakovskii, Alexander, editor. *Quantum Dots: Optics, Electron Transport and Future Applications*. Cambridge UP, 2012.

Thompson, Avery. "Scientists Have Made Transistors Smaller Than We Thought Possible." *Popular Mechanics*, 12. Oct. 2016, www.popularmechanics.com/technology/a23353/1nm-transistor-gate/. Accessed 28 Nov. 2021.

Engineering Design

ABSTRACT

Engineering design is a carefully regulated process to create optimal solutions for given problems. Steps in the process include idea generation, design selection, modeling, and testing. Engineers design everything from automobiles and bridges to prosthetic limbs and sporting equipment.

ENGINEERS

For engineers, designing is different than simply building in that it requires the adherence to a very systematic, yet iterative, process known as the "engineering design process." This process is to engineers what the scientific method is to scientists guiding steps that help ensure that the end result is the best it can be. When a new product is created without following the steps of the engineering design process, there is a higher likelihood that the product designed will lack some important aspect: the end product may not appropriately account for the needs of its users, it may cost too much to manufacture, or it may not have been tested to ensure safety. Accordingly, the term "designing" refers to the entire process, such that an engineer "does design." The use of the term "design" as a noun may be used at different points in the process but may have very different meanings depending on what phase of the process the engineer is in. Design may really mean "design idea" during the brainstorming phase of the process or "model or prototype of the design" during the building phase of the process.

The engineering design process requires the application of mathematics in many of the steps. Throughout the process, engineers use basic mathematics concepts, including addition and multiplication to calculate costs; geometry to calculate surface areas for material needs; and measurements to ensure appropriate dimensioning. However, more sophisticated projects may require the application of higher-level mathematics, such as calculus and differential equations, to solve the technical engineering problems certain designs pose.

THE ENGINEERING DESIGN PROCESS

The engineering design process refers to the steps that are required to create the best possible solution to a problem. It is a process often undertaken by a team of engineers who work together, though it can be performed by an individual trained or untrained as an engineer. Though there is no consensus as the exact breakdown and name of each step, the general design process is universally accepted.

In the first step of the engineering design process, the engineering team is presented with some type of problem or unmet societal need to be solved. Often, this problem is presented to the engineering team by a company that is trying to offer a product that better meets its customers' needs. The engineer must ask many questions to both the client and the user, as well as conduct background research, in an effort to establish the objectives and constraints of the design. The objectives are what the solution to the problem (the final designed product) should aim to accomplish. The constraints are the factors that limit the possible designs, such as time, money, or material restrictions. Time and money constraints are particularly important as they often drive the project and must be monitored throughout to ensure that the project is completed on time and within budget. At the end of this step of the design process, the engineering team fully understands the problem and has developed objectives and constraints to guide their possible solutions.

In the next step of the engineering design process, the engineers generate design ideas to solve the newly refined problem. Idea generation normally occurs through group brainstorming methods, with the goal of producing as many ideas as possible. There are a number of methods used to enhance the innovation and creativity of the ideas that come from the brainstorming session, including ensuring group diversity, drawing from existing stimulus and building off of each other's ideas. In this step of the process, some of the generated ideas will evolve into rough hand-drawn sketches. These sketches need to show perspective and relative size clearly.

The next step of the engineering design process is design selection. A method known as "decision analysis" is most commonly used for design selection. Decision analysis is a systematic process to objectively and logically choose the best idea to move forward with from the many generated through brainstorming. It is important because it reduces the likelihood of a designer's bias in selecting a design. As a first step, the brainstormed ideas must initially be narrowed down through discussion or other means to only the handful of ideas that appear to be most promising. These ideas are then compared through decision analysis. For the decision analysis, it is first necessary to create a list of design criteria and weight them based on their relative importance. As an example, as safety is paramount in design, the criteria of "safety" would be the most important criteria and would be weighted as 1.0 on a scale of 0-1. The criteria of "portability," on the other hand, might be desirable but not necessary, so it would be weighted as 0.5. There is no standard as to what weighting scale should be used but it is important to be consistent in its application. For each criterion, in addition to the determined weighted importance, a numerical range must also be established for rating each design with respect to the criterion. When possible, this range should be as objective and quantifiable as possible.

Each design being considered is then "scored" using the range for each criterion. The score is then multiplied by the relative criteria weight for a total score for each criterion and for each design. The total scores for each criterion are then summed for each design. The summed scores can be used to compare multiple designs, with the one scoring the highest being the one most likely to be successful.

After identifying a design to move forward with, refinement of the design is necessary. This step includes determining dimensions and materials that will be used to construct the chosen design. Detailed sketches, often drawn from multiple perspectives, are created and include the dimensions of each part to be made. Determining these dimensions often requires in-depth estimation and calculation. At the most simplistic level, dimensioning requires taking into account any necessary clearances or gaps in the design, especially when multiple parts need to be fitted together. It may also be necessary to determine the combinations of dimensions that ensure a specified surface area requirement is met, in which case algebra can be helpful. More in-depth designs may require that dimensions come from established tables of normative dimensions, such as anthropometric tables, providing typical measurements of different-sized people, or from engineering analysis, such as stress or buckling calculations. Deriving dimensions from engineering analysis methods often requires high-level mathematics and a technical background in engineering but ensures a stronger, safer product.

Once the design has been refined and the dimensions are known, building begins. For most designs, a scale model or a simplified prototype is created first to test for feasibility of the design before further time and money is invested. To create a scale model, all dimensions of the detailed sketches must be reduced by multiplying by some chosen scaling factor, often 1:2. In the case of a physical model, it is necessary to calculate the amount of each material that needs to be purchased to build the design. This requires thought and calculation, in particular when multiple parts could be cut from one piece of wood, metal, or fabric. Often, surface area is calculated according to the part's geometry to determine the total amount of material needed. Once material has been secured, building of the design can occur. Throughout building, it is essential to make careful measurements for all parts because almost all designs are made from multiple components that must fit together to function as one product. For example, if a piece of wood to be used for one leg of a chair is measured even a fraction of an inch shorter than the other legs, it will likely mean the finished chair will rock and wobble, and the design will be undesirable. In some cases, the models created may include three-dimensional virtual models built through the use of computer-aided design (CAD) software. Creating virtual rather than physical models can reduce costs, enable engineers working in different physical locations to collaborate on shared designs, and allow for more efficient revision and prototyping processes. However, physical models remain may remain preferable in some professional contexts.

As a next step in the engineering design process, the constructed design is experimentally tested to determine its performance. This step helps to identify design strengths and weaknesses, which can be used to make recommendations for future refinement of the product. The specific experimental test performed is determined by the type of product designed and the design objectives, and in some cases, virtual tests may be performed through the use of simulation software. Regardless of the type of test conducted, measurements are taken throughout the experiment to record some aspect of the design's performance. Often, multiple trials will be taken, generating many data points. The data obtained from these measurements are then used to draw conclusions about the success of the design. Statistical analysis may also be employed to further assist in the interpretation of the data.

Almost always, the data collected during testing will suggest that the design could perform better if refined in some way. As such, it is common for the engineering team to return to the building stage and then iteratively cycle between it and testing steps until satisfied. At times, it may also be necessary to return to earlier steps in the engineering design process. Once the team is satisfied with the final product, final documentation is prepared to explain the design and share it with others. This is often done through CAD drawings and written technical reports.

—*Kimberly Edginton Bigelow*

Further Reading

Bi, Zhuming, and Xiaoqin Wang. *Computer Aided Design and Manufacturing*. Wiley-ASME Press, 2020.

Dym, Clive L., and Patrick Little. *Engineering Design: A Project-Based Introduction*. 4th ed., John Wiley and Sons, 2013.

Eide, Arvid, Roland Jenison, Larry Northup, and Steven Mickelson. *Engineering Fundamentals and Problem Solving*. 7th ed., McGraw-Hill, 2018.

Pahl, Gerhard, Wolfgang Beitz, Jörg Feldhusen, and Karl-Heinrich Grote. *Engineering Design: A Systematic Approach*. 3rd ed., Springer, 2007.

Ulrich, Karl, Steven Eppinger, and Maria C. Yang. *Product Design and Development*. 7th ed., McGraw-Hill, 2020.

"What Is the Engineering Design Process?" *TWI*, www.twi-global.com/technical-knowledge/faqs/engineering-design-process. Accessed 28 Nov. 2021.

Engineering Tolerances

ABSTRACT

Technical drawings, including those created through the use of computer-aided design (CAD) software, depict objects that will be manufactured, typically to function with many other pieces in an overall assembly. All parts of the finished assembly must fit together closely, with little or no variation from their design specifications. The very small amount that sizes can be allowed to vary is the tolerance of the dimensions.

CUMULATIVE ERROR

How precisely can a particular physical dimension be determined? In practice, students in technical programs are taught that measurements using a graduated scale that is read by eye, such as that on a steel rule in a metalworking class or the side of a dispensing burette in a chemistry laboratory, can only be determined with accuracy to one-tenth of the smallest division on the scale. On a scale graduated in one-millimeter divisions, for example, a trained technician may determine a measurement on one part of an assembly to be 10.3 millimeters with an uncertainty of 0.05 millimeter. That is to say, the true value of the measurement is somewhere between 10.25 and 10.35 millimeters. For several such measurements of pieces in the assembly, these small variances accumulate for the overall dimension of an object made up of several parts. If the object is made of eleven such parts, the overall dimension of the object would nominally be 113.3 millimeters, but its actual dimension would be between 112.75 and 113.85 millimeters, a range of 1.1 millimeters. This is cumulative error. There is an upper and a lower limit of variance that can be tolerated in the assembly if it is to function properly in the purpose for which it was designed. Therefore, there are corresponding upper and lower limits on the variances of each part of the assembly. Those limits are the tolerance, the maximum and minimum amounts of variance from design specifications that can be tolerated.

The components of machines and structures are designed to very fine tolerances in order to fit together closely. The most familiar example is probably the piston and cylinder arrangement of internal combustion engines and compressors. The cylinders of a particular engine are machined to a specific diameter, and the associated piston must be machined to a diameter to match. The diameter of the piston cannot be even the slightest bit larger than the diameter of the cylinder, or it will not fit inside the cylinder. Nor can it be an exact match in size, or friction would quickly destroy both piston and cylinder. Therefore, the diameter of the piston must be smaller than the diameter of the cylinder. But how much smaller? The purpose of the piston is to compress the gases inside the cylinder, and if the diameter of the piston is much less than the diameter of the cylinder, the hot, compressed gases could escape between the rim of the piston and the wall of the cylinder and would eventually destroy both. Clearly, the tolerance of the fit between piston and cylinder must be small.

The piston and cylinder example demonstrates one level of tolerance, in that inconsistencies in the piston diameters that are within design tolerance can be compensated for by the use of metal spring rings and polymer O-rings to provide the necessary gas leakage seals. High-precision devices, however, demand much smaller tolerances, which become increasingly important as the physical size of the component pieces becomes smaller.

GEOMETRIC DIMENSIONING AND TOLERANCING

Technical drawings are used to depict accurately the design specifications of an object to be manufactured or constructed. Each view of the object or structure is accompanied by the appropriate dimensions and the tolerance range of those dimensions. A tolerance range sets the acceptable boundaries of deviation for the manufacture of the subject of the drawing. Materials and the components the materials are used to make will always have certain innate inconsistencies. Even the purest of materials will not have a perfectly homogeneous internal structure. Steel, for example, has internal microzones in which the iron atoms and the atoms of whatever other elements are in the steel alloy have crystallized in different patterns. Those zones have different strength properties and may be of a size that represents a flaw in the material itself, a potential point of failure in the manufactured product. Accordingly, the material itself is manufactured within a range of tolerances.

The macroscopic nature of the material being used is also a consideration of the production method. The specified material must be able to accept the tolerance range to which it is to be produced. A material that can only be machined to a tolerance of 0.1 millimeter, for example, would not be suitable for a design tolerance of 0.001 millimeter, a tolerance range that is readily achievable with twenty-first-century computer numerical control (CNC) and computer-aided manufacturing (CAM) machines. The engineering of a product thus includes all such relevant considerations in its inception and design. The technical drawing of the object therefore also includes the standards designations of the materials, as well as the drawing details.

ENGINEERING TOLERANCES IN HISTORICAL PERSPECTIVE

There is a definite relationship between tolerance and precision in engineering. In ancient times, stonework, woodwork, and metalwork were the epitome of engineering. All of the craft professions relied on the fitting together of materials formed to exacting specifications. In a Roman arch, for example, the keystone at the top of the arch had to be carefully shaped to the correct size and geometric dimensions in order to provide the necessary shape and strength in the arch. This was the handiwork of a master mason. In some ancient cities of Central and South America, the precision fit of huge blocks of stone in some structures continues to amaze. In Japan, an island nation subject to regular earthquakes and tremors, there are wooden buildings that have easily survived those environmental effects for many centuries. The key to their survival is a system of precision-made sliding beams that underlies each story of the structure. This allows each story to oscillate independently of the others, rather than the entire structure shaking back and forth as a single unit. Master woodworkers were responsible for their formation. Environmental effects and the passage of time have acted to obliterate much of the detailed work in most metal objects, but the surviving work of ancient goldsmiths often reveals a high degree of intricate metalwork.

Since the Industrial Revolution, metalworking has been the most important of these various craft professions and has passed through a number of stages in terms of tolerances and precision. The use of powered machinery is at the forefront of those technological changes. Though known since ancient times for use in woodwork, powered lathes for metalwork enabled the production of threaded bolts and nuts. Originally, these objects could only be made by a master machinist who could cut the threads on a bolt and those inside a nut to match. These were not interchangeable with other bolts and nuts. The development of standard bolt sizes and thread gauges became possible with the development of precision metal lathes that could be set to reproduce a specific thread gauge. Similarly, metallurgy produced steel alloys of sufficient hardness that taps and dies could be made to cut standard threads on softer steel and other metals.

Interchangeable parts are the basis of the assembly line method of production. The methodology was popularized in the early twentieth century by industrialist Henry Ford and adapted to the rapid production of the Ford Model T automobile. Threaded parts for these and other conveyances previously had required the work of a master machinist or metalsmith to produce a replacement part to match, but the use of interchangeable parts allowed anyone at all to provide the replacement. Interchangeable parts also requires that each part, whether the smallest of threaded nuts or the largest of structural beams in a superstructure, be made to the same geometric dimensions and tolerances.

—*Richard M. Renneboog, MSc*

Further Reading

Childs, P. R. N. *Mechanical Design: Theory and Applications*. 3rd ed., Butterworth-Heinemann, 2021.

Jensen, Cecil H., and Ed Espin. *Interpreting Engineering Drawings*. 7th Canadian ed., Nelson Education, 2015.

Leach, Richard, and Stuart T. Smith, editors. *Basics of Precision Engineering*. CRC Press, 2018.

Osakue, Edward E. *Introductory Engineering Graphics*. Momentum Press, 2018.

Plantenberg, Kirstie. *Engineering Graphics Essentials*. 5th ed., SDC Publications, 2016.

Winchester, Simon. *The Perfectionists: How Precision Engineers Created the Modern World*. HarperCollins, 2018.

Environmental Engineering

ABSTRACT

Environmental engineering is a field of engineering involving the planning, design, construction, and operation of equipment, systems, and structures to protect and enhance the environment. Major areas of application within the field of environmental engineering are wastewater treatment, water-pollution control, water treatment, air-pollution control, solid-waste management, and hazardous-waste management. Water-pollution control deals with physical, chemical, biological, radioactive, and thermal contaminants. Water treatment may be for the drinking water supply or for industrial water use. Air-pollution control is needed for stationary and moving sources. The management of solid and hazardous wastes includes landfill and incinerators for disposal of solid waste and identification and management of hazardous wastes.

DEFINITION AND BASIC PRINCIPLES

Environmental engineering is a field of engineering that split off from civil engineering as the importance of the treatment of drinking water and wastewater was recognized. This field of engineering was first known as "sanitary engineering" and dealt almost exclusively with the treatment of water and wastewater. As awareness of other environmental concerns and the need to do something about them grew, this field of engineering became known as "environmental engineering," with the expanded scope of dealing with air pollution, solid wastes, and hazardous wastes, in addition to water and wastewater treatment.

Environmental engineering is an interdisciplinary field that makes use of principles of chemistry, biology, mathematics, and physics, along with engineering sciences (such as soil mechanics, fluid mechanics, and hydrology) and empirical engineering correlations and knowledge to plan for, design, construct, maintain, and operate facilities for treatment of liquid and gaseous waste streams, for prevention of air pollution, and for management of solid and hazardous wastes.

The field also includes investigation of sites with contaminated soil and/or groundwater and the planning and design of remediation strategies. Environmental engineers also provide environmental impact analyses, in which they assess how a proposed project will affect the environment.

BACKGROUND AND HISTORY

When environmental engineering, once a branch of civil engineering, first became a separate field in the mid-1800s, it was known as sanitary engineering. Initially, the field involved the water supply, water treatment, and wastewater collection and treatment.

In the middle of the twentieth century, people began to become concerned about environmental quality issues such as water and air pollution. As a consequence, the field of sanitary engineering began to change to environmental engineering, expanding its scope to include air pollution, solid- and hazardous-waste management, and industrial hygiene.

Several pieces of legislation have affected and helped define the work of environmental engineers. Some of the major laws include the Clean Air Act of 1970, the Safe Drinking Water Act of 1974, the Toxic Substances Control Act of 1976, the Resource Recovery and Conservation Act (RCRA) of 1976, and the Clean Water Act of 1977.

HOW IT WORKS

Environmental engineering uses chemical, physical, and biological processes for the treatment of water, wastewater, and air, as well as in-site remediation processes. Therefore, knowledge of the basic sciences—chemistry, biology, and physics—is important along with knowledge of engineering sciences and applied engineering.

Chemistry. Chemical processes are used to treat water and wastewater, to control air pollution, and for site remediation. These chemical treatments include chlorination for disinfection of both water and wastewater, chemical oxidation for iron and manga-

Environmental engineering includes wastewater treatment, water-pollution control, water treatment, air-pollution control, solid-waste management, and hazardous-waste management. Photo via iStock/metamorworks. [Used under license.]

nese removal in water-treatment plants, chemical oxidation for odor control, chemical precipitation for removal of metals or phosphorus from wastewater, water softening by the lime-soda process, and chemical neutralization for pH (acidity) control and for scaling control.

The chemistry principles and knowledge that are needed for these treatment processes include the ability to understand and work with chemical equations, to make stoichiometric calculations for dosages, and to determine size and configuration requirements for chemical reactors to carry out the various processes.

Biology. The major biological treatment processes used in wastewater treatment are biological oxidation of dissolved and fine suspended organic matter in wastewater (secondary treatment) and stabilization of biological wastewater biosolids (sludge) by anaerobic digestion or aerobic digestion.

Biological principles and knowledge that are useful in designing and operating biological wastewater treatment and biosolids digestion processes include the kinetics of the biological reactions and knowledge of the environmental conditions required for the microorganisms. The required environmental conditions include the presence or absence of oxygen and the appropriate temperature and pH.

Physics. Physical treatment processes used in environmental engineering include screening, grinding, comminuting, mixing, flow equalization, flocculation, sedimentation, flotation, and granular filtration. These processes are used to remove materials that can be screened, settled, or filtered out of water or wastewater and to assist in managing some of the processes. Many of these physical treatment processes are designed on the basis of empirical loading factors, although some use theoretical relationships such as the use of estimated particle settling velocities for design of sedimentation equipment.

Soil mechanics. Topics covered in soil mechanics include the physical properties of soil, the distribution of stress within the soil, soil compaction, and water flow through soil. Knowledge of soil mechanics is used by environmental engineers in connection with design and operation of sanitary landfills for solid waste, in storm water management, and in the investigation and remediation of contaminated soil and groundwater.

Fluid mechanics. Principles of fluid mechanics are used by environmental engineers in connection with the transport of water and wastewater through pipes and open channels. Such transport takes place in water distribution systems, in sanitary sewer collection systems, in storm water sewers, and in wastewater-treatment and water-treatment plants. Design and sizing of the pipes and open channels make use of empirical relationships such as the Manning equation for open channel flow and the Darcy-Weisbach equation for frictional head loss in pipe flow. Environmental engineers also design and select pumps and flow measuring devices.

Hydrology. The principles of hydrology (the science of water) are used to determine flow rates for storm water management when designing storm sewers or storm water detention or retention facilities. Knowledge of hydrology is also helpful in planning and developing surface water or groundwater as sources of water.

Practical knowledge. Environmental engineers make use of accumulated knowledge from their work in the field. Theoretical equations, empirical equations, graphs, nomographs, guidelines, and rules of thumb have been developed based on experience. Empirical loading factors are used to size and design many treatment processes for water and wastewater. For example, the design of rapid sand filters to treat drinking water was based on a specified loading rate in gallons per minute of water per square foot of sand filter. Also, the size required for a rotating biological contactor to provide secondary treatment of wastewater was determined based on a loading rate in pounds of biochemical oxygen demand (BOD) per day per 1,000 square feet of contactor area.

Engineering tools. Tools such as engineering graphics, geographic information systems (GIS), and surveying are available for use by environmental engineers. Computer-aided design (CAD) software is likewise crucial to many engineering projects, and software developers such as Autodesk and Dassault Systèmes released specialized engineering CAD programs by the third decade of the twenty-first century. Such tools are used for working with plans and drawings and for laying out treatment facilities or landfills.

Codes and design criteria. Much environmental engineering work makes use of codes or design criteria specified by local, state, or federal government agencies. Examples of such design criteria are the storm return period to be used in designing storm sewers or storm water detention facilities and the loading factor for rapid sand filters. Design and operation of treatment facilities for water and wastewater are also based on mandated requirements for the finished water or the treated effluent.

APPLICATIONS AND PRODUCTS

Environmental engineers design, build, operate, and maintain treatment facilities and equipment for the treatment of drinking water and wastewater, air-pollution control, and the management of solid and hazardous wastes.

Air-pollution control. Increasing air pollution from industries and power plants as well as automobiles led to passage of the Clean Air Act of 1970. This law led to greater efforts to control air pollution. The two major ways to control air pollution are the treatment of emissions from fixed sources and from moving sources (primarily automobiles).

The fixed sources of air pollution are mainly the smokestacks of industrial facilities and power plants. Devices used to reduce the number of particulates emitted include settling chambers, baghouses, cyclones, wet scrubbers, and electrostatic precipitators. Electrostatic precipitators impart the particles with an electric charge to aid in their removal. They are often used in power plants, at least in part because of the readily available electric power to run them. Water-soluble gaseous pollutants can be removed by wet scrubbers. Other options for gaseous pollutants are adsorption on activated carbon or incineration of combustible pollutants. Because sulfur is contained in the coal used as fuel, coal-fired power plants produce sulfur oxides, particularly troublesome pollutants. The main options for reducing these sulfur oxides are desulfurizing the coal or desulfurizing the flue gas, most typically with a wet scrubber using lime to precipitate the sulfur oxides.

Legislation has greatly reduced the amount of automobile emissions, the main moving source of air pollution. The reduction in emissions has been accomplished through catalytic converters to treat exhaust gases and improvements in the efficiency of automobile engines.

Water treatment. The two main sources for the water supply are surface water (river, lake, or reservoir) and groundwater. The treatment requirements for these two sources are somewhat different.

For surface water, treatment is aimed primarily at removal of turbidity (fine suspended matter) and perhaps softening the water. The typical treatment processes for removal of turbidity involve the addition of chemicals such as alum or ferric chloride. The chemicals are rapidly mixed into the water so that they react with alkalinity in the water, then slowly mixed (flocculation) to form a settleable precipitate. After sedimentation, the water passes through a sand filter and finally is disinfected with chlorine. If the water is to be softened as part of the treatment, lime, $Ca(OH)_2$, and soda ash, Na_2CO_3, are used in place of alum or ferric chloride, and the water hardness (calcium and magnesium ions) is removed along with its turbidity.

Groundwater is typically not turbid (cloudy), so it does not require the type of treatment used for surface water. At minimum, it requires disinfection. Removal of iron and manganese by aeration may be needed, and if the water is very hard, it may be softened by ion exchange.

Wastewater treatment. The Clean Water Act of 1977 brought wastewater treatment to a new level by requiring that all wastewater discharged from municipal treatment plants must first undergo at least secondary treatment. Before the passage of the legislation, many large cities located on a river or along the ocean provided only primary treatment in their wastewater-treatment plants and discharged effluent with only settleable solids removed. All dissolved and fine suspended organic matter remained in the effluent. Upgrading treatment plants involved added a biological treatment to remove dissolved and fine suspended organic matter that would otherwise exert an oxygen demand on the receiving stream, perhaps depleting the oxygen enough to cause problems for fish and other aquatic life.

Solid-waste management. The main options for solid-waste management are incineration, which reduces the volume for disposal to that of the ash that is produced, and disposal in a sanitary landfill. Some efforts have been made to reuse and recycle materials to reduce the amount of waste sent to incinerators or landfills. A sanitary landfill is a big improvement over the traditional garbage dump, which was simply an open dumping ground. A sanitary landfill uses liners to prevent groundwater contamination, and each day, the solid waste is covered with soil.

Hazardous-waste management. The Resource Conservation and Recovery Act (RCRA) of 1976 provides the framework for regulating hazardous-waste handling and disposal in the United States. One very useful component of RCRA is that it specifies a very clear and organized procedure for determining if a particular material is a hazardous waste and therefore subject to RCRA regulations. If the material of interest is indeed a waste, then it is defined to be a hazardous waste if it appears on one of RCRA's lists of hazardous wastes, if it contains one or more hazardous chemicals that appear on an RCRA list, or if it has one or more of the four RCRA hazardous waste characteristics as defined by laboratory tests. The four RCRA hazardous waste characteristics are flammability, reactivity, corrosivity, and toxicity. The RCRA regulations set standards for secure landfills and treatment processes for disposal of hazardous waste.

Much work has been done in investigating and cleaning up sites that have been contaminated by hazardous wastes in the past. In some cases, funding is available for cleanup of such sites through the Comprehensive Environmental Response, Compensation, and Liability Act of 1980 (known as CERCLA or Superfund) or the Superfund Amendments and Reauthorization Act (SARA) of 1986.

CAREERS AND COURSEWORK

An entry-level environmental engineering position can be obtained with a bachelor's degree in environmental engineering or in civil or chemical engineering with an environmental specialization. However, because many positions require registration as an engineer in training or as a professional engineer, it is important that the bachelor's degree program is accredited by the Accreditation Board for Engineering and Technology (ABET). Students must first graduate from an accredited program before taking the exam to become a registered engineer in training. After four years of experience, the engineer in training can take another exam for registration as a professional engineer.

A typical program of study for an environmental engineering degree at the undergraduate level includes the chemistry, calculus-based physics, and mathematics that is typical of almost all engineering programs in the first two years of study. It also may include biology, additional chemistry, and engineering geology. The last two years of study will typically include hydrology, soil mechanics, an introductory course in environmental engineering, and courses in specialized areas of environmental engineering such as water treatment, wastewater treatment, air-pollution control, and solid- and hazardous-waste management.

Master's degree programs in environmental engineering fall into two categories: those designed primarily for people with an undergraduate degree in environmental engineering and those for people with an undergraduate degree in another type of engineering. Some environmental engineering positions require a master's degree. A doctoral degree in environmental engineering is necessary for a position in research or teaching at a college or university.

SOCIAL CONTEXT AND FUTURE PROSPECTS
Many major areas of concern in the United States and around the world are related to the environment. Issues such as water-pollution control, air-pollution control, global warming, and climate change all need the work of environmental engineers. These issues, as well as the need for environmental engineers, are likely to remain concerns for much of the twenty-first century. Water supply, wastewater treatment, and solid-waste management all involve infrastructure, needing repair, maintenance, and upgrading, which are all likely to need the help of environmental engineers.

—Harlan H. Bengtson, BS, MS, PhD

Further Reading
Darwin, David, and Charles Dolan. *Design of Concrete Structures*. 16th ed., McGraw-Hill, 2021.
Davis, Mackenzie L., and Susan J. Masten. *Principles of Environmental Engineering and Science*. 4th ed., McGraw-Hill, 2020.
Juuti, Petri S., Tapio S. Katko, and Heikki Vuorinen. *Environmental History of Water: Global Views on Community Water Supply and Sanitation*. IWA, 2007.
Leonard, Kathleen M. "Brief History of Environmental Engineering: 'The World's Second Oldest Profession.'" *ASCE Conference Proceedings*, vol. 265, no. 47, 2001, pp. 389-93.
Moaveni, Saeed. *Engineering Fundamentals: An Introduction to Engineering*. 6th ed., Cengage Learning, 2020.
Rogers, Jerry R., and Augustine J. Fredrich, editors. *Environmental and Water Resources History*. American Society of Civil Engineers, 2003.
Spellman, Frank R., and Nancy E. Whiting. *Environmental Science and Technology: Concepts and Applications*. 2nd ed., Government Institutes, 2006.
Yasmin, Nighat. *Introduction to AutoCAD 2022 for Civil Engineering Applications*. SDC Publications, 2021.

Epoxies and Resin Technologies

ABSTRACT
Epoxies and resins are chemical systems, as opposed to single compounds, that are used in a variety of applications. Their value derives from their polymerization into three-dimensional (3D) or cross-linked polymeric materials when the components are combined and allowed to react. Epoxies are so-named because the principal component is a reactive epoxide compound. The combination of the epoxy compound with a second material that promotes the polymerization reaction is called a "resin." The term also applies generally to any polymerizing combination of materials that is not epoxy based. Epoxies and resins are used primarily in structural composite applications, in which the combination of a reinforcement material (usually a specialized fiber) bound within a solid matrix of polymerized resin provides the advantages of high strength, low weight, and unique design capabilities. Resins are also used in injection molding and other molding operations, extrusion and pultrusion, prototype modeling, and 3D printing, and as high-strength adhesives.

DEFINITION AND BASIC PRINCIPLES

In the field of polymers, resin refers to the material or blend of materials that is specifically prepared to undergo a polymerization reaction. In this type of reaction, molecules add together sequentially to form much longer and larger molecules. A polymerization reaction can proceed in a linear manner to form long-chain single molecules whose bulk strength derives from physical entanglement of the molecules. It also can proceed with branching to form large, multiple-branch molecules that derive their bulk strength from their sheer size and complex three-dimensional (3D) interlinking bonds between the molecules.

The particular combination of materials used to prepare the resin for polymerization is chosen according to the extent and type of polymerization desired. Monomers containing only one reactive site or two functional groups can form only linear polymers. 3D polymers require the presence of three or more functional groups or reactive sites in at least one of the resin components. The polymerization reaction can proceed as a simple addition reaction, in which the single monomer molecules simply add together by forming chemical bonds between the reactive sites or functional groups on different molecules.

Polymerization reactions are generally driven to completion with heating, although the heat produced by exothermic reactions must be controlled to prevent overheating, decomposition, and dangerous runaway reactions from occurring. The polymeric product of the reaction may be thermoplastic—becoming soft, or plastic, with heating. Thermoplastics are characterized by this change of behavior at the glass transition temperature, Tg. Below this temperature, the material is solid and fractures in the characteristic conchoidal manner of glass rather than along any regular planes that would denote a regular crystal structure. At the Tg, the material begins to deform rather than to fracture. The Tg is always

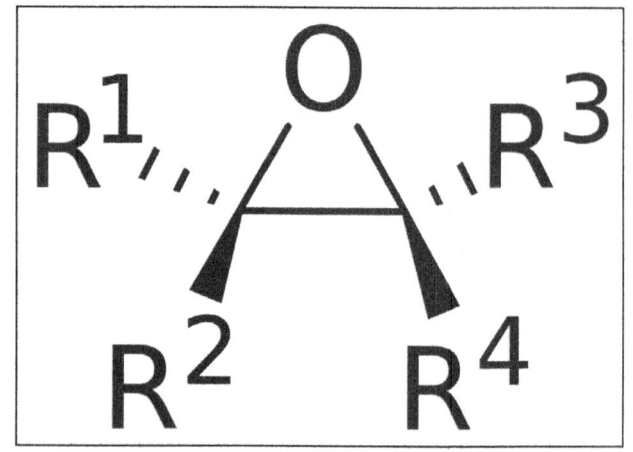

Structure of the epoxide group, a reactive functional group present in all epoxy resins. Image via Wikimedia Commons. [Public domain.]

stated as a fairly broad temperature range, and at its higher value, the material has no resistance to deformation that would result in fracture, although it may not yet be entirely liquefied.

A thermosetting resin produces a polymer that does not soften with further heating and exhibits conchoidal fracture behavior at all temperatures at which it is stable. Such polymers will undergo thermal decomposition (also called "thermolysis") when heated, as their Tg is at a higher temperature than the temperature at which they break down.

Epoxies are a specific type of resin in which one of the components is an epoxide compound. A second component, typically an amine, reacts irreversibly with the epoxide functional group, causing its three-membered ring structure to open up. The intermediate form produced reacts in a chainlike manner with other epoxide molecules to form complex, 3D polymeric molecules.

Various technologies, methods, and applications are encompassed by the field of epoxies and other resins. These range from molecular design and testing in the chemical and material sciences laboratory, to injection molding and hand layup of fiber-reinforced plastics, and the repair of structures made from resin-based materials. The production of specific resin formulations on an industrial scale is particularly exacting because of the regulations governing certification of the materials for specific critical uses and concomitant purity requirements throughout the handling of the product. Specialized training and equipment are required for the safe production and transportation of the materials.

BACKGROUND AND HISTORY

Resins and their property of solidifying have been known and used since ancient times. During explorations of the New World and Asia, European explorers such as Christopher Columbus and Hernán Cortés found the indigenous peoples playing sports with balls that bounced and wearing clothing and footwear that had been waterproofed. The indigenous peoples used natural latex materials derived from plants in the making of these and other objects.

In the mid-nineteenth century, as the industrial sciences, especially chemistry, blossomed in Europe, these marvelous natural latex materials, known as "caoutchouc" and "gutta percha," were imported and put to a variety of uses that capitalized on their unique properties. Gutta percha, for example, was used to make the corrosion-resistant coating and insulation for the first undersea telegraph cables laid across the English Channel between England and France. Other resins produced at this time were semisynthetic, chemical modifications of vegetable oils and latexes. The development of synthetic polymers such as Bakelite, especially after World War II, opened the way for untold applications. The unique and customizable properties of plastics and polymer resins served as the foundation of a very large and growing industry that has constantly sought new materials, new innovations, and new applications.

During the first decades of the twenty-first century, resins found a host of new applications within the realm of 3D printing. While 3D printers of that era used a range of materials for their additive-manufacturing processes, resin-based printers specifically manufactured objects through a process known as "stereolithography," in which thin layers of resin were extruded from the machine and were subsequently cured and hardened through the use of a specialized light. Resin-based 3D printers were used to manufacture a variety of items, including resin crowns and bridges used in the dental field.

HOW IT WORKS

Resins and chain reactions. The term "resin" was originally used to refer to secretions of natural origin that could be used in waterproofing. It has since come to mean any organic polymer that does not have a distinct molecular weight. Typically, organic polymers form through sequential addition reactions between small molecules that then form much larger molecules through a chain-reaction mechanism. Once initiated, the progress of such a reaction chain becomes entirely random. Any particular reaction chain will proceed and continue to add monomer molecules to the growing polymer molecule as long as it encounters them in an orientation that permits the additional step to occur. Typically, this happens several thousand times before a condition, such as an errant impurity, is encountered that terminates the series of reactions. The exact molecular and chemical identity of any individual polymer molecule is determined precisely by the number of monomer molecules that have been combined to produce that particular polymer molecule. However, within a bulk polymerization process, billions of individual reaction chains progress at the same time, in competition for the available monomers, and there is no way to directly control any of the individual reactions. As a result, any polymerized resin contains a variety of homologous molecules whose molecular weights follow a standard distribution pattern. In thermoplastic resins, this composition, consisting of what is technically a large number of different chemical compounds, is the main reason that the *Tg* is characterized by softening and gradual melting behavior over a range of temperatures rather than as the distinct melting point typical of a pure compound.

Polymerization reaction processes. Polymerization reactions occur in one of two modes. In one, monomer molecules add together in a linear head-to-tail manner in each single chain reaction. This occurs when only two atoms in the molecular structure function as reactive sites. In the other mode, there is more than one reactive site or functional group in each molecule. Polymerization reactions occur between reactive sites rather than between molecules. The presence of more than one reactive site in a molecule means that the molecule can take part in as many chain-reaction sequences, with the resulting polymer molecules being cross-linked perhaps thousands of times and to as many different polymer chains. The result can, in theory, be a massive block of solid polymeric material composed of a single, large molecule.

Epoxy resins and cross-linking. Polymerization and cross-linking bonds arise as the reactive site or sites of the molecules become connected by the formation of chemical bonds between them. As a bond forms from the atom at one end of a reactive site, the atom at the other end becomes able to form a bond to the reactive site of another molecule. When the reactive site is an epoxide ring structure, the resulting resin is called an "epoxy." Epoxy resins are two-part reaction systems, requiring the mixture and thorough blending of the epoxide compound and the catalyst, a second compound that initiates the ring opening of the epoxide. This is typically an amine, and the relative amount of amine to epoxide controls the rate at which the polymerization occurs. This represents essentially all the control that can be exercised over the progress of a polymerization reaction. It is therefore critical to control the relative amounts of epoxide and catalyst in an epoxy resin blend.

APPLICATIONS AND PRODUCTS

The value of epoxy and other resins is in their versatility; they are used in a wide variety of products and applications that have become central to twenty-first-century society. Without epoxy resins and technology, many products would not exist, and modern society would be very different. Epoxy resins cure to a tough, resilient, and very durable solid that has high resistance to impact breakage, fracturing, erosion, and oxidation. They are also reasonably good thermal conductors that tolerate rapid temperature changes very well.

Aircraft. An excellent example of resin application is in aircraft technology, particularly in modern fighter jets. The fuselage and wing structures of many aircraft are constructed of fiber-reinforced plastics. The materials used in aircraft production must be able to tolerate drastic changes in temperature and pressure. For example, an aircraft may be stationed on the ground in a desert with surface temperatures in excess of 60° Celsius (140° Fahrenheit), and less than one minute later, the aircraft may be in the air at altitudes where the air temperature is -35° C (-31° F) or colder. That the structural materials of such an aircraft can repeatedly withstand abrupt changes of temperature and physical stresses says a great deal about the strength, toughness, and thermal properties of the epoxy resins used in its construction.

Electronic devices. The thermal stability of epoxy resins is also evident in their use in the packaging material of modern integrated circuits, transistors, computer chips, and other electronic devices. The operation of these devices produces a great deal of heat because of the friction of electrons moving in the semiconductor material of the actual chip. Pushed to extremes, the devices can fail and burn out, but it is far more usual for the packaging material to adequately conduct and safely dissipate heat, allowing whatever process is running to continue uninterrupted. That may be something as trivial as some spare-time gaming, or as crucial as an emergency response call, the flight control program of an aircraft in the air, or an advanced medical procedure.

Structural composite applications. The applications of and the products produced from resins are numerous. The combinations of materials for the production of resins are essentially limitless, and each combination has specific qualities that make it suitable to particular applications. Thus, the varieties and possibilities in the field of epoxies and resin technologies are virtually limitless. A very significant area of application for epoxy resins and other types of resins is in the field of structural composites, particularly in fiber-reinforced plastics and as insulating or barrier foams. The particular application of a resin is determined as much by the desired properties of the product as by the properties of the polymerized resin. Resins that produce a hard, durable polymer such as those produced by epoxy resins are used in products of a corresponding nature. Resins that have good shape-retaining properties coupled with high compressibility, such as those used to produce urethane foams, are used in products such as furniture cushions, pillows, mattresses, floor mats, shoe insoles, and other applications in which the material provides protection from impact forces. Resins that exhibit high levels of expansion while forming a fairly rigid polymer with good thermal resistance are used in sealing and insulating applications, such as those for which urea-formaldehyde resin combinations are so useful. Some resins are also used in construction and in civil engineering. For example, a type of epoxies called "polyacrylates" are used for concrete patching and making traffic stripes on roads.

Resin production and supply. A completely different set of technologies and applications is related to the supply and material processing of the resins themselves. Chemists and chemical engineers expend a great deal of effort and time in the development and testing of resins in order to identify new commercially valuable materials or to customize the properties of existing materials. When the new product leaves the laboratory for commercial applications, the system must then be established for the production and safe transport of the material from the supplier to the user. Systems and methods must also be established for the end user to prepare the intended products from the material. Resins for low-volume use can be packaged in cans and other small containers, while those for high-volume use may be transported by rail or in other types of large containers. Production methods must produce the resin material in a sufficiently pure state so that it will not polymerize en route. Methods of transport must also be such that the resin is protected against any contamination that could result in initiation of polymerization. This requires specialized applications in transportation technology. The end user of the resins will require the means to manipulate the resin, typically in spray-on applications or molding operations. The equipment used in the various molding operations also requires the creation of molds and forms appropriate to the product design. There is accordingly a very large sector of skilled support workers in industries and applications for resin usage.

CAREERS AND COURSEWORK

The demand for products of resin technologies is likely to increase in accord with the expanding human population. The facility with which large quantities of objects can be produced by epoxy and resin technologies ensures the continued growth of the field as it keeps pace with the needs of the population. The need for new or improved qualities in the materials being used in resin products means a need for materials scientists with advanced training and knowledge in organic and physical chemistry.

An individual who chooses to make a career of resin technologies must learn the chemical principles of polymerization by taking courses in advanced organic chemistry, physical chemistry, analytical chemistry, reaction kinetics, and specialty polymer chemistry. He or she will also need courses in mathematics, statistics, and physics. Specialized fields of engineering related to epoxy and resin technologies include chemical engineering, mechanical engineering, and civil engineering (in regard to certain special infrastructure applications). Aircraft maintenance engineers and technicians must go through specific training programs in the use of resins and epoxies as they apply to aircraft structural maintenance standards. These are hands-on training programs focused on the physical use and applications of the materials rather than courses of instruction in chemical theory. No special training is required for the layperson to make use of the materials, which are sold in the automotive and marine supply sections of many retail outlets and by certain hobby and craft suppliers.

SOCIAL CONTEXT AND FUTURE PROSPECTS

A vast quantity of plastics is produced from resins. The strongest of these are the epoxy resins. In concert with the commercial and social benefits of epoxy and resin technologies are the logistical problems inherent in the materials themselves. The use of resin-based technologies carries with it the responsibility for the proper disposal of the used products. Thermoplastics are relatively easily managed because of their built-in ability to be reused. Because they can be rendered into a mobile fluid form simply by heating, used objects made from thermoplastic resins can be melted down and formed into new products. Thermosetting resins, however, cannot be reformed and must be processed for disposal in other ways. Thermoset plastics, such as the epoxy resins, are resistant to facile reprocessing as they are generally also impervious to solvents and all but the strongest oxidizing agents. Historically, and unfortunately, this has meant that the vast majority of goods made from thermosetting resins have been relegated to landfills or offshore dumps, or just left as litter and refuse. Beginning in the late twentieth century, efforts began to be made to put such materials to other uses, the most common being simply to grind them up for use as bulk filling materials.

Epoxy and resin technologies and the plastics industry in general have had a huge impact on life since their inception, becoming essential to the infrastructure of twenty-first-century society. Essentially every government and university research program, every industry and business sector, and every corporation that deals in material goods of any kind deals with resins and plastics in some way, and new ventures are established almost daily for the production of material goods designed specifically to be produced by epoxy or resin technologies.

—*Richard M. J. Renneboog, MSc*

Further Reading

Bi, Zhuming, and Xiaoqin Wang. *Computer Aided Design and Manufacturing*. Wiley-ASME Press, 2020.

Elias, Hans-Georg. *An Introduction to Plastics*. 2nd ed., Wiley-VCH, 2003.

Fenichell, Stephen. *Plastic: The Making of a Synthetic Century*. HarperBusiness, 1997.

Goodship, Vanessa. *Injection Moulding: A Practical Guide*. 3rd ed., De Gruyter, 2020.

Green, Mark M., and Harold A. Wittcoff. *Organic Chemistry Principles and Industrial Practice*. Wiley-VCH, 2006.

Grover, William H. "The Rise (and Risks) of Resin-Based 3D Printers." *Grover Lab*, 13 June 2021, groverlab.org/hnbfpr/2021-06-13-3d-printer-risks.html. Accessed 28 Nov. 2021.

"Guide to Stereolithography (SLA) 3D Printing." *Formlabs*, 2021, formlabs.com/blog/ultimate-guide-to-stereo-lithography-sla-3d-printing/. Accessed 28 Nov. 2021.

Kumar, Sudheer. "Recent Development of Biobased Epoxy Resins: A Review." *Polymer-Plastics Technology and Engineering*, vol. 57, no. 3, 2017, pp. 133-55.

Larrañaga, Michael D., Richard J. Lewis, and Robert A. Lewis. *Hawley's Condensed Chemical Dictionary*. 16th ed., John Wiley & Sons, 2016.

Scherer, Michael. "3D Printing Same-Day Permanent Crowns with a Desktop Printer and Helping Out a Patient at the Same Time!" *LearnDentistry*, learndentistry.com/3d-printing-same-day-permanent-crowns-with-a-desktop-printer/. Accessed 28 Nov. 2021.

Ergonomics

ABSTRACT

Ergonomics, a holistic multidisciplinary science, draws from the fields of engineering, psychology, physiology, computer science, occupational health, and environmental sciences. These sciences define ergonomics as optimizing effectiveness of human activities while improving the quality of life with safety, comfort, and reduced fatigue.

DEFINITION AND BASIC PRINCIPLES

The term "ergonomics" dates to the mid-1800s, but credit for applying it generally goes to Hywel Murrell, a British chemist. Ergonomics derives from the Greek words *ergon*, meaning "work," and *nomos*, meaning "law." Ergonomics studies work within the natural laws of the human body.

The International Ergonomics Association promotes a systematic approach to the ergonomic process, to incorporate human factors and human performance engineering and address problems in design of machines, environments, or systems. This can improve efficiency and safety of the human-machine relationship. The basic steps in the ergonomic process include organization of the process, identification and analysis the problem, development of a solution, implementation of the solution, and evaluation of the result.

BACKGROUND AND HISTORY

The types of work and settings have changed over the centuries. Humans have consistently been aware of the need for a good fit between work tools and the human body. While he was a medical student at Parma University in Italy, Bernardino Ramazzini recognized that workers suffered certain diseases. In 1682, he focused on worker health concerns. His scholarly collection of observations, *De Mortis Artificum Diatriba* (Diseases of Workers), published in 1700, detailed conditions associated with specific work environments and factors such as prolonged body postures and repetitive motion. His work earned him the title "father of occupational medicine."

The term "ergonomics" is attributed to Hywel Murrell, a chemist who worked with the British Army Operational Research Group during World War II. In 1949, he served as leader of the Naval Motion Study Unit. He invited people with like interests in human factors research to meet with him, forming the Ergonomics Research Society. He remained active in academia until his death in 1989 at age seventy-six. Murrell's specialties included skill development and use and fatigue and aging. He was interested in applications of psychology and ergonomics in day-to-day situations. Murrell authored the first textbook on ergonomics, *Ergonomics: Man in His Working Environment*.

In the industrial era, tools and machines were developed to increase productivity. These put a new strain on the relationship between work and the human body. Between World Wars I and II, classic work was accomplished by the British Industrial Fatigue Research Board on the impact of environmental factors and human work performance. By the time World War II had begun, worker safety became a primary concern, leading the way for the science of ergonomics.

The increasing prevalence of computer technology during the late twentieth century raised new concerns about the health of workers, who were at times subject to health problems such as eye strain and carpal tunnel syndrome linked to their extensive computer use. At the same time, advances in computer technology provided new opportunities within the field of ergonomic design. Computer-aided design (CAD) programs, for instance, enabled designers to design furniture and workstations that would meet individuals' ergonomic needs with greater efficiency. Some such programs further allowed designers to analyze and test their creations by placing a three-dimensional model of a human being into the virtual work environment being designed.

HOW IT WORKS

Ergonomics, the science of adapting the workplace environment to the work and workers, seeks to maintain worker safety. The goal of industry employers is to keep workers well and comfortable while functioning efficiently on the job. This can be best accomplished by providing safe working conditions to prevent work-related injuries.

National Institute for Occupational Safety and Health's seven-step approach. Businesses can assume a reactive or proactive approach. The National Institute for Occupational Safety and Health (NIOSH), part of the Centers for Disease Control and Prevention (CDC), has defined a seven-step program for evaluating and addressing potential musculoskeletal problems in the workplace. First is finding worker complaints of pains or aches and defining jobs that require repetitive movement or forceful exertion. Management must then commit to addressing the problem with input from the worker. Participatory ergonomics is important in encouraging workers to help define problems and solutions to work-related stress. Key is education and training about the potential work-related risks and musculoskeletal problems from defined jobs. Using attendance, illness, and medical records, management should investigate high-risk jobs, where injury is most common. Leadership must analyze job descriptions and functions to see if risky work-related tasks can be eliminated. Management should support health-care intervention that emphasizes early detection and treatment to avoid work-related impairment and disability. Finally, management should use this information to minimize work-related musculoskeletal risks when creating new jobs, policies, and procedures.

Physical ergonomics. Ergonomics can be subdivided into several disciplines: physical, cognitive, and organizational. Physical ergonomics is the body's response to physical workloads. It addresses physiological and anatomical characteristics of humans as related to physical activity. Biomechanics and anthropometrics fall into this category. This discipline is concerned with safety and health and en-

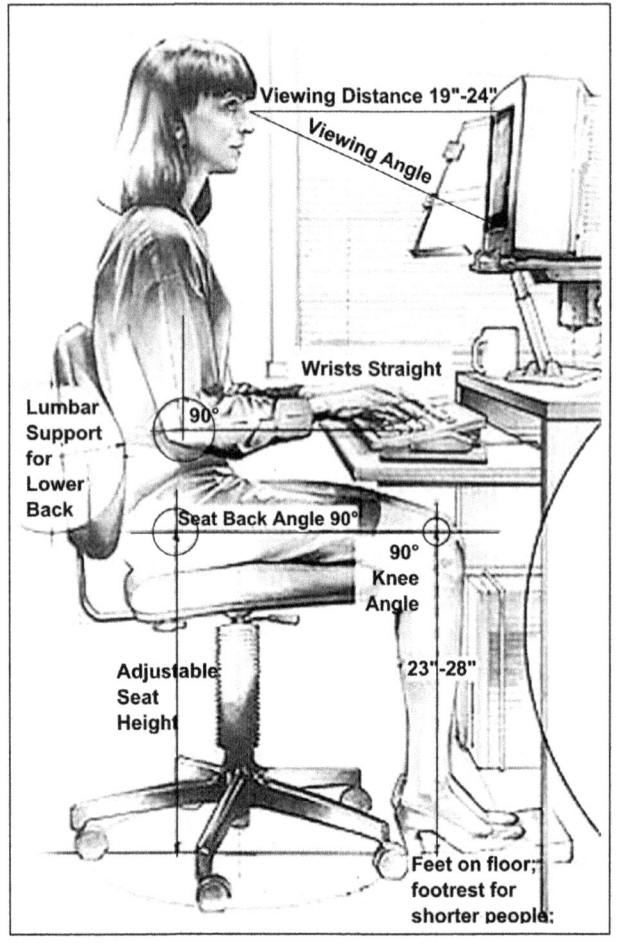

Physical ergonomics: the science of designing user interaction with equipment and workplaces to fit the user. Image via Wikimedia Commons. [Public domain.]

compasses work postures, repetitive movements, vibration, materials handling, posture, workspace layout, and work-related musculoskeletal disorders. Common injuries in an office setting result from computer use, such as carpal tunnel syndrome for using a keyboard and mouse and eye strain from viewing a monitor for prolonged periods of time.

Cognitive ergonomics. Cognitive ergonomics deals with human mental processes and capabilities at work, such as reasoning, perception, and memory, as well as motor response. Topics related to cognitive ergonomics include work stress and mental workload, decision-making, performance, and reliability. Computer-human interaction and human training are sometimes listed here.

Organizational ergonomics. Organizational ergonomics addresses sociotechnical systems of the organization and its policies, procedures, processes, and structures. Concepts in this subdiscipline could include work design and hours, job satisfaction, time management, telecommuting, ethics, and motivation, as well as teamwork, cooperation, participation, and communication.

APPLICATIONS AND PRODUCTS

Ergonomics can be applied to work in any setting with the goal of achieving efficiency and effectiveness while maintaining worker comfort and safety. The principles of ergonomics have been applied to many industries, including aerospace, health care, communications, geriatrics, transportation, product design, and information technology.

Office workers. Global industry requires office workers to use computers every day. Product orders are taken by workers via phone and the internet. Office workers spend time tied to phones and computers, while sitting in one place. These workers are subject to work-related injury and stress created by continuous computer and phone use.

Ergonomic experts have taken the principles of human factors engineering to improve the work environment for computer users. The placement and maintenance of the computer monitor will affect the user's eyes and musculoskeletal system. The monitor should be clean with brightness and contrast set for the comfort of the user. Placing the monitor directly in front of the user will minimize neck strain. The monitor should be set one arm's length away, tilted back by 10 to 20 degrees, and positioned away from windows or direct lighting to reduce glare.

Office workers often sit for extended periods while working, which is stressful on legs, feet, and the intervertebral discs of the spine. Pooling of the blood in the feet and ankles can cause swelling and place stress on the heart. Employers should encourage workers to alternate between standing and sitting. Many employers, in fact, offer the option of trading out a normal desk for a desk specially designed to be worked at while standing. Others might provide desks that feature both sitting and standing configurations. Ergonomic chairs are designed to relieve the pressure placed on the back while sitting for extended periods. Arm rests should be adjusted so arms rest at the side of the body, allowing the shoulder to drop to a natural, relaxed position.

Many ergonomic ailments occur in the soft tissues of the wrist and forearm, as continuous computer use subjects workers to repetitive motions and sometimes awkward positioning. Computer mouses are ergonomically designed to minimize worker injury, and the no-hands mouse uses foot pedals to navigate. Ergonomically friendly computer keyboards are also available.

Health care. In the health-care field, ergonomics is useful in designing products for conditions such as arthritis, carpal tunnel syndrome, and chronic pain. Ergonomic applications for persons with arthritis include appliances with larger dials that can be grasped more easily, levers rather than doorknobs, and cars with keyless entry and ignition. Larger controls on the dashboard and thicker steering wheels can be more easily grasped.

Health-care workers are at risk for work-related musculoskeletal injuries, such as back or muscle strain, without adequate ergonomics. This is true in nursing homes where nursing assistants must lift patients with impaired mobility. These workers can benefit from ergonomically designed patient-handling equipment and devices such as belts and portable hoists to lift patients.

Dentists are likewise at risk for work-related musculoskeletal disorders. They experience repetitive hand movements, vibrating tools, and fixed and awkward posturing. Neck, back, hand, and wrist injuries are common. Ergonomic equipment is available for dentists, including specially designed hand instruments, syringes and dispensers, lighting, magnification tools, and patient chairs.

Transportation. Ergonomics has applications useful to anthropometry. A study in the United Kingdom found the airline industry did not provide adequate space for passengers in the economy-class sections. The study focused on seating standards and the passengers' ability to make a safe emergency exit. They found that the economy-class seats did not have enough space to brace for an emergency landing and that even the seats themselves could delay a safe exit. The study also stated that the existing seating would accommodate only up to the 77th percentile of European travelers based on the buttock-knee length dimension.

Other applications include ergonomic food carts and passenger delivery, crew rest seats, and ergonomic design for first-class, business, and economy passenger seats. Cockpit design is important for pilot comfort and safety and to minimize fatigue.

Many competitive manufacturers in the automotive industry have employed ergonomics in designing cars for comfort, safety, and efficiency. Examples include options for driver seat position to accommodate variation in body size and allow the steering wheel and backrest to be ergonomically positioned. Also noted are passenger-seat comfort and safety, placement of controls, and an option for cell phone placement. These considerations can lessen work stress considerably when someone drives as part of his or her job.

Communication technology. Cell phones have been a plus for industry and individuals but can come at a price. Shoulder and neck pain may be related to cell phone use. Many people will attempt to cradle the phone between their head and shoulder when talking in order to free their hands. Ergonomic solutions exist to decrease user strain and pain. Headsets keep hands and head free of awkward posturing. Frequently changing sides can help if a headset is not available. Using cell phone technology with ergonomic design can reduce the daily and cumulative stress of cell phone use.

Aging. With an increasing aging population, industries are applying ergonomic solutions to meet senior needs. Gerontechnology addresses the need for work and leisure, comfort and safety in older adults. Some automobiles have larger and simple dashboard controls. Many tools for use in kitchen or garden have special adaptive handles for less strain on the hands and muscles. Phones are equipped with different levels of tone for varying hearing issues; digits are larger and easier to push. Bathrooms are equipped with safety handles and equipment that allow independence.

Employers need ergonomically designed workplaces to accommodate the physical and cognitive changes of normal aging. Seats may need to be firmer and higher to allow for decreased joint flexibility. Good lighting is important for safe work. Restrooms with modifications may be necessary. Flexible-schedule availability will assist with worker fatigue. By redesigning the work environment for aging workers, the risk of illness and injury can be diminished and performance improved.

CAREERS AND COURSEWORK

The health and safety of workers continues to be a primary concern for employers. The job opportunities for persons interested in ergonomics are varied and depend on the role desired. As with other professions, some jobs require formal education, while others provide on-the-job training. Other jobs require certification or special training in the area of interest.

Jobs related to ergonomics include the role of ergonomist, who has special knowledge and skills in the science of ergonomics, designing the workplace to fit the worker. Ergonomists typically have the minimum of a bachelor's degree in industrial engineering or mechanical engineering, industrial design, or health-care sciences and often a master's or doctoral degree in a related area such as human factors engineering. The International Ergonomics Association (IEA) encourages all ergonomists to become board certified. Other ergonomics professional groups include the Institute of Ergonomics and Human Factors, the International Society for Occupational Ergonomics and Safety, and the Human Factors and Ergonomics Society.

Health-care professionals such as occupational therapists have also become interested in the growing field of ergonomics.

SOCIAL CONTEXT AND FUTURE PROSPECTS

The IEA attests to the fact that ergonomics is an international concern that affects the global economy. As of 2021, the IEA is composed of more than fifty federated societies from around the world and run by a council with representatives from those groups. IEA supports ergonomic efforts in developing countries and keeps a directory of educational programs in various countries. The goals of the IEA include advancing ergonomics to the international level and enhancing the contribution of the discipline of ergonomics in a global society.

—*Marylane Wade Koch, MSN, RN*

Further Reading

Bhattacharya, Amit, and James D. McGlothin, *Occupational Ergonomics: Theory and Applications*. 2nd ed., CRC Press, 2019.

Dul, Jan, and Bernard Weerdmeester. *Ergonomics for Beginners: A Quick Reference Guide*. 3rd ed., CRC Press, 2008.

Eastman Kodak Company. *Kodak's Ergonomic Design for People at Work*. 2nd ed., Wiley, 2003.

Falzon, Pierre. *Constructive Ergonomics*. CRC Press, 2019.

Karwowsi, Waldemar, Marcelo Soares, and Neville A. Stanton, editors. *Handbook of Human Factors and Ergonomics in Consumer Product Design*. 2 vols. CRC Press, 2020.

Marras, William S., and Waldemar Karwowski, editors. *Interventions, Controls, and Applications in Occupational Ergonomics*. 2nd ed., CRC Press, 2019.

Soares, Marcelo M., and Francisco Rebelo. *Ergonomics in Design: Methods & Techniques*. CRC Press, 2017.

Stanton, Neville A., Paul M. Salmon, Laura A. Rafferty, et al. *Human Factors Methods: A Practical Guide for Engineering and Design*. 2nd ed., CRC Press, 2013.

"3-D Human CAD." *United States Ergonomics*, 2021, us-ergo.com/ergonomics-laboratory/measurement-technologies/human-cad-analysis/. Accessed 28 Nov. 2021.

Fossil Fuel Power Plants

ABSTRACT

Fossil fuels are the organic residues of geological processes and include the various grades of coal, natural gas, petroleum, and crude oil. By definition, all fossil fuels are nonrenewable resources. Fossil fuel power plants all function in fundamentally the same manner and rely on a principle that has not changed significantly since the earliest applications of steam power. In short, the fuel is combusted to generate heat, producing pressurized steam that in turn drives the turbines of large electric generators.

Coal was the first major fossil fuel to be exploited as an energy source for the steam-powered plants that drove the Industrial Revolution of the eighteenth and nineteenth centuries. When steam technology was applied to the large-scale generation of electricity, coal became the fuel of choice because of its ready availability. Coal remains the major fuel source for fossil fuel power plants, although natural gas and, to a much lesser extent, petroleum-based fuels are used as well.

Significant costs, both economic and environmental, have been identified in the use of fossil fuels for the production of electricity. Economically, the prices of fossil fuels have been driven upward by the market economy, and environmentally, the combustion of large quantities of carbon-based fossil fuels releases a great deal of carbon dioxide and other gases into the atmosphere.

DEFINITION AND BASIC PRINCIPLES

Fossil fuel power plants are generating stations that rely on the combustion of fossil fuels to produce electricity. Only three fossil fuels—coal, petroleum, and natural gas—are used for this purpose. The term "power plant" does not refer only to facilities that generate electricity but rather to any facility whose function is to produce usable power, whether electrical, mechanical, hydraulic, pneumatic, or another type. In common usage, however, power plant generally refers to those facilities that are used to generate electricity.

All fossil fuels are the remnants of organisms that existed, in most cases, many millions of years ago. Time and geologic processes involving heat and pressure chemically and physically altered the form of these organisms, turning them into mineralogical fossils (such as mineralized bones found in sedimentary rock formations) and the carbonaceous forms of coal, crude oil, and natural gas. When these carbonaceous materials are refined, they can be used as combustion fuels in fossil fuel power plants.

The combustion process is carried out in a variety of ways, from standard internal combustion engines using natural gas, gasoline, or diesel oil, to fluidized bed combustors using pulverized coal powder. Internal combustion engines are used to drive a generator directly, while other combustion methods are used to heat water and produce pressurized steam through heat exchange. The steam is then used to drive a turbine that in turn drives electric generators. The spent steam is generally recycled through the system. The exhaust steam from combustion is passed through a treatment process to reduce or eliminate contaminants formed from materials that were in the fuel.

Ideally, the combustion process would produce only carbon dioxide—from the combustion of coal—or carbon dioxide and water—from the combustion of hydrocarbon fuels such as natural gas and refined petroleum fuels. In practice, however, fossil fuels contain a percentage of materials other than carbon and hydrogen, such as sulfur, metals (including iron, mercury, and lead), and nonmetals (including phosphorus, silicon, and arsenic). In addition, air used to supply oxygen for combustion also contains about 78 percent nitrogen and about 1 percent of other gases. At the temperatures of combustion, these impurities can react with oxygen to produce a variety of pollutant byproducts such as sulfur dioxide, nitrogen oxides, and fly ash.

The combustion of fossil fuels results in a very large quantity of carbon dioxide being released into the atmosphere, where it can act as a greenhouse gas. A greenhouse gas traps heat that normally would be radiated out of the atmosphere and into space. Researchers have concluded that the carbon dioxide released by the burning of fossil fuels is a primary factor in global warming, which refers to an increase in the mean annual temperature of the planet.

BACKGROUND AND HISTORY

Coal has been used as a fuel for combustion for thousands of years. It was reportedly used by native North Americans when the first European settlers arrived, and it was undoubtedly used by other peoples throughout the world because of the ease with which it could be extracted from the ground in certain areas. It became the fuel of choice beginning in the eighteenth century and had almost completely replaced wood as the dominant fuel of industry by the early 1900s because of its more favorable energy density. Coal's increasing popularity as a fuel also drove the growth of the coal-mining industry, in turn increasing its availability.

Coal-fired power plants provide about 32 percent of consumed electricity in the United States (Sep. 2017). This is the Castle Gate Plant near Helper, Utah. Photo by David Jolley, via Wikimedia Commons.

With the development of the large-scale generation of electricity and its many applications, coal-fired power plants were used to drive electric generators where suitable water power, such as at voluminous waterfalls, was not available. The convenience and versatility of a common electric grid resulted in the growth of the electric generation industry. Small and localized generation systems ranging from low-output gasoline-powered home generators to large diesel-powered industrial generating stations can provide emergency and local service if the common grid is not available. Large generating stations using fossil fuels have been built and continue to be built in areas where coal or other fossil fuels are readily available.

HOW IT WORKS

Fossil fuels. Coal and petroleum are the remnants of plants and animals that lived millions of years ago. Over the years, geologic processes compressed and chemically altered the plants and animals in such a way that coal consists almost entirely of pure carbon, crude petroleum consists almost entirely of a vast assortment of hydrocarbons, and natural gas consists almost entirely of methane, ethane, and propane, which are simple hydrocarbon gases. Coal can be found at various depths in the earth's crust, in veins ranging from only a few centimeters to hundreds of meters thick. It is mined out as a solid, rocky, and relatively lightweight material and used in forms ranging from crude lump coal to a fine powder that is fluidlike in its behavior.

Crude oil and natural gas are found only at depths of hundreds and thousands of meters. As liquids or fluids, these materials have migrated downward through porous rock over a long period of time, until further progress is prevented by an impervious rock layer. There, they collect, often in large pools of oil and gas that can be recovered only after being found through careful exploration and deep borehole drilling. Natural gas requires no further processing before being used as a combustion fuel, unless it is classed as sour gas, meaning it contains an unacceptably large proportion of foul-smelling hydrogen sulfide and other poisonous gases that must be removed. Petroleum, or crude oil, must be heavily refined before it can be used as a fuel. The crude oil is subjected to thermal cracking, which breaks down and separates the various hydrocarbon components into usable portions from light petroleum ethers such as pentanes and hexanes to heavy tars such as asphalt. The most well-known fractions refined from petroleum are gasoline, kerosene, diesel fuel, and waxes, and various grades of lubricating oils and greases.

Combustion. Combustion is a chemical reaction between a material and oxygen. The reaction is an oxidation-reduction process in which one material becomes chemically oxidized and the other becomes chemically reduced. In the context of fossil fuels, the material that becomes oxidized is coal, fuel liquids, or natural gas. Combustion of these carbonaceous materials converts each atom of carbon in the fuel molecules to a molecule of carbon dioxide, according to the general equation: $C + O_2 = CO_2$.

This conversion (greatly simplified here) releases an amount of energy that can then be transferred to and captured by a moderator—typically water—through the use of heat exchangers (devices that facilitate the transfer of heat from one material to another material). Combustion of hydrocarbons also produces water as an output of the reaction, in which two atoms of hydrogen combine with one atom of oxygen to produce one molecule of water. Other reactions corresponding to the combustion of impurities in the fuel stream also take place, and their products are ejected in the exhaust flow from the combustion process.

Turbines and generators. Steam under pressure, produced by heating water via the combustion of fuels, is directed into a mechanical device called a "turbine." Turbines can basically be described as

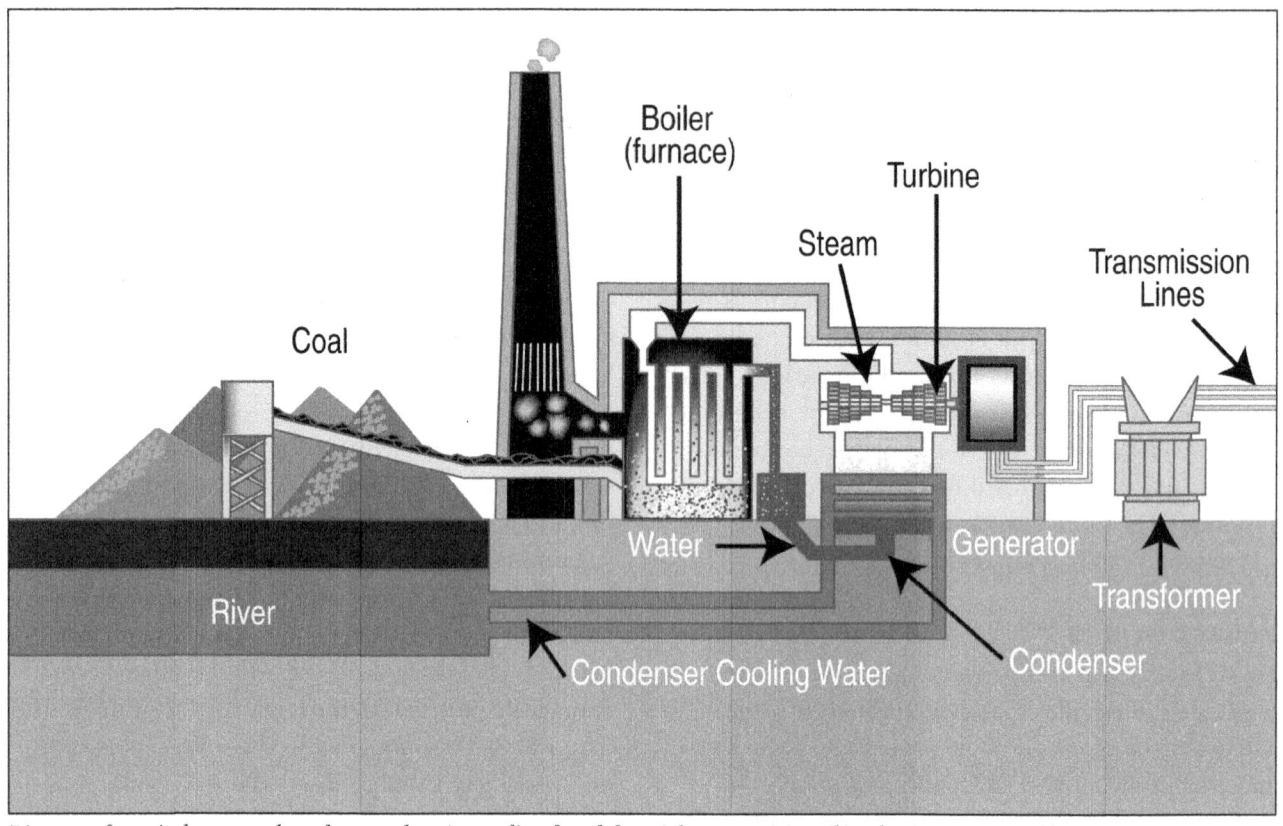

Diagram of a typical steam-cycle coal power plant (proceeding from left to right). Image via Wikimedia Commons. [Public domain.]

high-tech versions of the ancient water wheel. The pressure of the flowing gas (steam) pushes against a series of vanes attached to an armature (electric component) in the structure of the turbine, driving them to spin the armature with force. This converts the linear fluid motion of the steam into the rotary mechanical motion of the turbine. Turbines are coupled to an electric generator so that their rotation results in the generation of electricity.

A generator is another rotary device that, in its most basic concept, consists of a magnet spinning inside a cage of conducting wires. The magnetic field of the magnet also spins at the same rate that the magnet spins. The movement of the magnetic field through the conductors in the surrounding cage produces an electromotive force (EMF) in the conductors, which is measured in volts. If the generator is connected into a circuit, this EMF causes current to flow in the circuit. Strictly speaking, generators produce direct current (DC) electricity, while alternators produce alternating current (AC) electricity. AC electricity is the standard form of electricity used in national power grids around the world.

Both generators and alternators are available in various output capacities and are driven by many types of rotary engines, from small internal combustion engines to large industrial steam turbines.

APPLICATIONS AND PRODUCTS

Fossil fuel power plants, in the context of electric generating stations, produce only one product: electricity. Any and all other materials that come from them are considered ancillary or waste byproducts. The ultimate goal of operating a fossil fuel power plant is to maximize the output of electricity from each unit of fuel consumed, while also minimizing any and all undesirable outputs. To that end, the efficiencies of control design, the data feedback process, economics, fuel processing, and a host of other aspects of the electric power generation industrial complex are examined each year. Not the least of these considerations is the placement and construction of new facilities and the maintenance of older facilities.

Those responsible for the design of new power plants and the upgrading of existing facilities benefited significantly from advances in computing capabilities and in computer-aided design (CAD) software, which streamlined the design process for both individual plant components, such as turbines, and complete power-generation facilities. CAD was used extensively in the industry by the early 1990s; a paper presented at the 1993 POWER-GEN Asia conference, for instance, reported that a complex CAD system had been used in the design of the Shajiao C coal power plant in Guangdong Province, China. By the third decade of the twenty-first century, CAD software producers such as Bentley Systems offered a variety of software products specially intended for the design and analysis of fossil fuel power plants.

At one time, the competitive cost and the availability of natural gas and crude oil nearly spelled the demise of the coal-fired power plant. However, the prices of natural gas and crude oil were driven upward, both artificially and naturally, making these choices less attractive. Nuclear power plants were initially welcomed by the public, but their popularity declined because of radioactivity concerns. Because of these circumstances, the continuing demand for electricity caused fossil fuel power plants—especially coal-fired plants—to regain their position of prominence in electric power generation. The operation of fossil fuel plants spawned related industries: the development of coal-mining methods and machinery, oil and gas exploration and recovery, fossil fuel transportation and preprocessing, specialized construction and trades, environmental assessment and maintenance operations, financial and administrative companies, plant operations and control technology, industrial maintenance, and grid supply and service.

Concern about greenhouse gases resulted in the birth of an industry aimed at capturing and storing the carbon dioxide produced by the power plants. Different approaches are being developed, but among the most promising technologies is the sequestering of carbon dioxide in deep underground water formations. This has engendered a whole new area of research and development in regard to compression and recovery technology.

The operation of fuel fossil power plants generates chemicals, some of which have been recovered during preprocessing and exhaust gas scrubbing procedures. Sulfur recovered from preprocessing and from entrapment of sulfur dioxide in the exhaust gas stream is used to produce sulfuric acid, an important industrial chemical, as well as numerous other sulfur-containing compounds. Similarly, nitrogen oxides recovered from the combustion process provide nitric acid and other nitrogen-containing compounds. Interestingly, the entire plastics industry grew out of research to find uses for compounds recovered from coal tar, a byproduct of the coal processing industry in the nineteenth century. In modern times, however, essentially all plastics are derived from petroleum.

CAREERS AND COURSEWORK

Students undertaking any program that will lead them into a career related to fossil fuel power plants, whether directly or indirectly, will be required to exit high school with an understanding of physics, chemistry, mathematics, and business and technology. Biology will also be required if the career path chosen is directed toward environmental studies. College and university level coursework will depend greatly on the area of specialization chosen, as the range of options at this level is immense. At a minimum, students will continue studies in mathematics, physical sciences, industrial technologies (chemical, electrical, and mechanical), and business as undergraduates or as trade students. More advanced studies will take the form of specialist courses in a chosen field. In addition, as technologies and regulations change, those working in the field of fossil fuel power plants can expect to be required to upgrade their working knowledge on an almost continual basis to keep abreast of changes.

SOCIAL CONTEXT AND FUTURE PROSPECTS
Beginning around the turn of the twenty-first century, coal- and oil-fired power plants lost dominance to natural gas plants, as well as renewable electricity sources such as solar and wind power. Natural gas plants' combined-cycle generators recover and recycle waste heat, making them more efficient for producing electricity, and gas-fired turbines start up faster than coal-fired ones. Because of hydraulic fracturing innovations and the US shale oil boom in the late 2000s and early 2010s, natural gas dropped in price. Meanwhile, solar and wind power developed significantly, to the point of costing less than natural gas. Another threat to the fossil fuel power industry comes from increasing water stress, given the role of steam in running electric turbines.

The world's reliance on the ready availability of coal and the industrial convenience of fossil fuel power plants, especially in countries such as China and India, likely ensures that those facilities will be part of the landscape for many years to come, despite those intensive efforts to develop alternative power sources. Advances in existing technologies, such as pulverized coal combustion systems and new oxygen-separation and heat-recovery techniques for coal gasification, can improve the efficiency of fossil fuel power plants and thereby decrease greenhouse gas emissions. Technologies being developed, such as carbon dioxide capture and storage (CCS) and cogeneration power systems combining geothermal or biomass energy and fossil fuels, will require fossil fuel power plant workers to understand both the older and the newer technologies as fossil fuel power plants are managed toward a low-cost, high-efficiency, zero-emissions platform (ZEP). It may also become possible to recover carbon dioxide from fossil fuel power plants for use in plastics, petrochemicals, concrete, oil and gas extraction, or fuel cell generators. Another issue facing fossil fuel power plant workers is the wear and tear on fossil fuel power plants from increased cycling, load following, and ramping as these plants shift to providing backup to renewable energy sources.

Emission-abatement plans also include elimination of the heavy metals in fossil fuels, as the combustion of those materials has the effect of greatly concentrating any heavy metals, including radioactive trace elements such as uranium and thorium, in the ash residues. It is therefore not inconceivable that, in the future, work in a fossil fuel power plant will also require training in working with radioactive materials.

—*Richard M. J. Renneboog, MSc*

Further Reading
Borowitz, Sidney. *Farewell Fossil Fuels: Reviewing America's Energy Policy*. Plenum Trade, 1999.
Breeze, Paul. *Power Generation Technologies*. 3rd ed., Elsevier, 2019.
Cooper, J. F. "Computer Aided Design of Modern Power Plant." *ETDEWEB*, www.osti.gov/etdeweb/biblio/6912842. Accessed 28 Nov. 2021.
Droege, Peter, editor. *Urban Energy Transition: From Fossil Fuels to Renewable Power*. Elsevier, 2008.
"Electric Power Sector Consumption of Fossil Fuels at Lowest Level since 1994." *Today in Energy*, 29 May 2018, www.eia.gov/todayinenergy/detail.php?id=33543. Accessed 28 Nov. 2021.
Evans, Robert L. *Fueling Our Future: An Introduction to Sustainable Energy*. Cambridge UP, 2007.
Gonzalez-Salazar, Miguel Angel, et al. "Review of the Operational Flexibility and Emissions of Gas- and Coal-Fired Power Plants in a Future with Growing

Renewables." *Renewable and Sustainable Energy Reviews*, vol. 82, 2018, pp. 1497-1513.

Leyzerovich, Alexander S. *Steam Turbines for Modern Fossil-Fuel Power Plants*. River Publishers, 2020.

Zabihian, Farshid. *Power Plant Engineering*. CRC Press, 2021.

FUEL CELL TECHNOLOGIES

ABSTRACT

The devices known as fuel cells convert the chemical energy stored in fuel materials directly into electrical energy, bypassing the thermal-energy stage. Among the many technologies used to convert chemical energy to electrical energy, fuel cells are favored for their high efficiency and low emissions. Because of their high efficiency, fuel cells have found applications in spacecraft and show great potential as sources of energy in generating stations.

DEFINITION AND BASIC PRINCIPLES

Fuel cells provide a clean and versatile means to convert chemical energy to electricity. The reaction between a fuel and an oxidizer is what generates electricity. The reactants flow into the cell, and the products of that reaction flow out of it, leaving the electrolyte behind. As long as the necessary reactant and oxidant flows are maintained, they can operate continuously. Fuel cells differ from electrochemical cell batteries in that they use reactant from an external source that must be replenished. This is known as a "thermodynamically open system." Batteries store electrical energy chemically and are considered a thermodynamically closed system. In general, fuel cells consist of three components: the anode, where oxidation of the fuel occurs; the electrolyte, which allows ions but not electrons to pass through; and the cathode, which consumes electrons from the anode.

A fuel cell does not produce heat as a primary energy conversion mode and is not considered a heat engine. Consequently, fuel cell efficiencies are not limited by the Carnot efficiency. They convert chemical energy to electrical energy essentially in an isothermal manner.

Fuel cells can be distinguished by: reactant type (hydrogen, methane, carbon monoxide, methanol for a fuel and oxygen, air, or chlorine for an oxidizer); electrolyte type (liquid or solid); and working temperature (low temperature, below 120° Celsius [248° Fahrenheit]; intermediate temperature, 120 to 300° C [248 to 572° F]; or high temperature, more than 600° C [1,112° F]).

BACKGROUND AND HISTORY

The first fuel cell was developed by the Welsh physicist and judge Sir William Robert Grove in 1839, but fuel cells did not receive serious attention until the early 1960s, when they were used to produce water and electricity for the Gemini and Apollo space programs. These were the first practical fuel cell applications developed by Pratt & Whitney. In 1989, Canadian geophysicist Geoffrey Ballard's Ballard Power Systems and Perry Oceanographics developed a submarine powered by a polymer electrolyte membrane or proton exchange membrane fuel cell (PEMFC). In 1993, Ballard developed a fuel-cell-powered bus and later a PEMFC-powered passenger car. Also in the late twentieth century, United Technologies (UTC) manufactured a large stationary fuel cell system for the cogeneration power plant, while continuously developing the fuel cells for the US space program. UTC (later bought by ClearEdge Power) also worked on developing fuel cells for automobiles. Siemens Westinghouse successfully operated a 100-kilowatt (kW) cogeneration solid oxide fuel cell (SOFC) system, and development later began on 1-megawatt (MW) systems. Among other key tools, computer-aided design (CAD) programs proved particularly beneficial to fuel cell designers, enabling them to design, model, and prototype fuel cells in development. ClearEdge

Power, for example, used the Autodesk CAD software Inventor to design small fuel cells for residential use.

HOW IT WORKS

Polymer electrolyte membranes or proton exchange membrane fuel cells (PEMFCs). PEMFCs use a proton conductive polymer membrane as an electrolyte. At the anode, the hydrogen separates into protons and electrons, and only the protons pass through the proton exchange membrane. The excess of electrons on the anode creates a voltage difference that can work across an exterior load. At the cathode, electrons and protons are consumed and water is formed.

For PEMFC, the water management is critical to the fuel cell performance: Excess water at the positive electrode leads to flooding of the membrane; dehydration of the membrane leads to the increase of ohmic resistance. In addition, the catalyst of the membrane is sensitive to carbon monoxide poisoning. In practice, pure hydrogen gas is not economical to mass produce. Thus, hydrogen gas is typically produced by steam reforming of hydrocarbons, which contains carbon monoxide.

Direct methanol fuel cells (DMFCs). Like PEMFCs, DMFCs also use a proton exchange membrane. The main advantage of DMFCs is the use of liquid methanol, which is more convenient and less dangerous than gaseous hydrogen. The efficiency has been low for DMFCs, so they are used where the energy and power density are more important than efficiency, such as in portable electronic devices.

At the anode, methanol oxidation on a catalyst layer forms carbon dioxide. Protons pass through the proton exchange membrane to the cathode. Water is produced by the reaction between protons and oxygen at the cathode and is consumed at the anode. Electrons are transported through an external circuit from anode to cathode, providing power to connected devices.

Demonstration model of a direct-methanol fuel cell (black layered cube) in its enclosure. Photo via Wikimedia Commons. [Public domain.]

Solid oxide fuel cells (SOFCs). Unlike PEMFCs, SOFCs can use hydrocarbon fuels directly and do not require fuel preprocessing to generate hydrogen prior to utilization. Rather, hydrogen and carbon monoxide are generated in situ, either by partial oxidation or, more typically, by steam reforming of the hydrocarbon fuel in the anode chamber of the fuel cell. SOFCs are all-solid electrochemical devices. There is no liquid electrolyte with its attendant material corrosion and electrolyte management problems. The high operating temperature (typically 500-1,000° C) allows internal re-forming, promotes rapid kinetics with nonprecious materials, and yields high-quality byproduct heat for cogeneration. The total efficiency of a cogeneration system can be as high as 90 percent—far beyond the conventional power-production system—according to the European Commission.

The function of the fuel cell with oxides is based on the activity of oxide ions passing from the cathode region to the anode region, where they combine with hydrogen or hydrocarbons; the freed electrons flow through the external circuit. The ideal performance of an SOFC depends on the electrochemical reaction that occurs with different fuels and oxygen.

Molten carbonate fuel cells (MCFCs). MCFCs use an electrolyte composed of a molten carbonate salt mixture suspended in a porous, chemically inert ceramic matrix. Like SOFCs, MCFCs do not require an external reformer to convert fuels to hydrogen. Because of the high operating temperatures, these fuels are converted to hydrogen within the fuel cell itself by an internal re-forming process.

MCFCs are also able to use carbon oxides as fuel. They are not poisoned by carbon monoxide or carbon dioxide, thus MCFCs are advanced to use gases from coal so that they can be integrated with coal gasification.

APPLICATIONS AND PRODUCTS

Hydrogen fuel cell vehicles. In the early twenty-first century, both the automobile and energy industries displayed great interest in the fuel cell-powered vehicle as an alternative to internal combustion engine vehicles, which are driven by petroleum-based liquid fuels. Many automobile manufacturers, including Hyundai, Toyota, and Honda, began developing prototype hydrogen fuel cell vehicles. Energy industries also installed prototype hydrogen filling stations in large cities, including Los Angeles, California; Washington, DC; and Tokyo, Japan.

The first hydrogen fuel cell passenger vehicle for a private individual was leased by Honda in 2005. However, public buses provide better demonstrations of hydrogen fuel cell vehicles compared with passenger vehicles, since public buses are operated and maintained by professionals, and have more volume for the hydrogen fuel storage than passenger vehicles. Bus manufacturers such as Toyota, Man, and Daimler developed hydrogen fuel cell buses and they have been in service in Palm Springs, California; Nagoya, Japan; Vancouver, Canada; and Stockholm, Sweden.

Despite many advantages of hydrogen fuel cell vehicles, this technology faces substantial challenges such as high costs of novel metal catalyst, safety of hydrogen fuel, effective storage of hydrogen onboard, and infrastructure needed for public refueling stations.

Stationary power plants and hybrid power systems. Siemens Westinghouse and UTC produced a number of power plant units in the range of about 100 kW by using SOFCs, MCFCs, and phosphoric acid fuel cells (PAFCs). Approximately half of the power plants were MCFC-based plants. They showed that these fuel cell systems had exceeded the research-and-discovery level and already produced an economic benefit. These systems generate power with less fossil fuel and lower emissions of greenhouse gases and other harmful products. Just a small number PEMFC-based power plants were built as the cost of fuel cell materials was prohibitive. In many cases, the fuel-cell-based stationary power plants are used for heat supply in addition to power production, enabling so-called combined heat and power systems. Such systems increase the total efficiency of the power plants and offer an economic benefit.

Many efforts to develop hybrid power plants combining fuel cells and gas turbines have been made. While the high-temperature fuel cells, such as SOFCs and MCFCs, produce electrical power, the gas turbines produce additional electrical power from the heat produced by the fuel cells' operation. At the same time, the gas turbines compress the air fed into the fuel cells. The expected overall efficiency for the direct conversion of chemical energy to electrical energy is up to 80 percent.

Small power generation for portable electronic devices. At the end of the twentieth century, the demand for electricity continued to increase in many applications, including portable electronics. Batteries have seen significant advances, but their power density is still far inferior to combustion devices. Typically, hydrocarbon fuels have 50 to 100 times more energy storage density than commercially available batteries. Even with low conversion efficiencies, fuel-driven generators will still have superior energy density. There has been considerable interest in miniaturizing thermochemical systems for electrical power generation for remote sensors, microrobots, unmanned vehicles (UMVs), unmanned aerial vehicles (UAVs), and even portable electronic devices such as laptop computers and cell phones.

Much work on such systems has been developed by the military. The Defense Advanced Research Projects Agency (DARPA) has initiated and developed many types of portable power concepts using fuel cells. Corporations such as Samsung, Sony, NEC, Toshiba, and Fujitsu developed fuel cell-based portable power generation. Most devices were based on PEMFCs or DMFCs, which require lower operating temperatures than SOFC. However, development of SOFC-based portable power generation under the DARPA Microsystems Technology Office showed the feasibility of employing high-temperature fuel cells with appropriate thermal management.

The military. In addition to the portable power generation for foot soldiers, the military market has been interested in developing medium-size power plants (a few hundred watts) for recharging various types of storage batteries and high stationary power plants (more than a few kW) for the auxiliary power units.

Military programs in particular have been interested in the direct use of logistic fuel (e.g., Jet Propellant 8) for fuel cells, because of the complexities and difficulties of the re-forming processes. While the new and improved re-forming processes of logistic fuel were being developed to feed hydrogen into the fuel cells, direct jet-fuel SOFCs were also demonstrated by developing new anode materials that had a high resistance to coking and sulfur poisoning.

CAREERS AND COURSEWORK

Courses in chemistry, physics, electrochemistry, materials science, chemical engineering, and mechanical engineering make up the foundational requirements for students interested in pursuing careers in fuel cell research. Earning a bachelor of science degree in any of these fields would be appropriate preparation for graduate work in a similar area. In most circumstances, either a master's or doctorate degree is necessary for the most advanced career opportunities in both academia and industry.

Careers in the fuel cells field can take several different shapes. Fuel cell industries are the biggest employers of fuel cell engineers, who focus on developing and manufacturing new fuel cell units as well as maintaining or repairing fuel cell units. Other industries in which fuel cell engineers often find work include aviation, automotive, electronics, telecommunications, and education.

Many fuel cell engineers seek employment within the national laboratories and government agencies such as the Pacific Northwest National Laboratory, the National Renewable Energy Laboratory, the Argonne National Laboratory, the National Aeronautics and Space Administration (NASA), DOE, and DARPA. Others find work in academia. Such professionals divide their time between teaching university classes on fuel cells and conducting their own research.

SOCIAL CONTEXT AND FUTURE PROSPECTS

In the future, it is not likely that sustainable transportation will involve use of conventional petroleum.

Transportation energy technologies should be developed with the goal of providing an alternative to the petroleum-based internal combustion engine vehicles. People evaluate vehicles not only on the basis of fuel economy but also on the basis of performance. Vehicles using an alternative energy source should be designed with these parameters. One of the most promising energy sources for the future will be hydrogen. The hydrogen fuel cell vehicles face cost and technical challenges, especially the fuel cell stack and onboard hydrogen storage.

For the fuel cell power plants, the economic and lifetime-related issues hinder the acceptance of fuel cell technologies. Such problems were not associated with fuel cells but with auxiliary fuel cell units such as thermal management, reactant storage, and water management. Therefore, the auxiliary units of fuel cell systems should be further developed to address these issues. The fundamental problems of fuel cells related to electrocatalysis also need to be addressed for improvement in performance, as highly selective catalysts will provide better electrochemical reactions. Lastly, once the new fuel cell technologies are successfully developed and meet the safety requirements, the infrastructure to distribute and to recycle fuel cells will also be necessary.

—*Jeongmin Ahn, MS, PhD*

Further Reading

Bagotsky, Vladimir S. *Fuel Cells: Problems and Solutions*. 2nd ed., John Wiley & Sons, 2012.

"Designing Small Fuel Cells for Homes." *3D CAD World*, 14 Apr. 2009, www.3dcadworld.com/designing-small-fuel-cells-for-homes/. Accessed 28 Nov. 2021.

Dicks, Andrew L., and David A. J. Rand. *Fuel Cell Systems Explained*. John Wiley & Sons, 2018.

Hoogers, Gregor, editor. *Fuel Cell Technology Handbook*. CRC Press, 2003.

Kotas, T. J. *The Exergy Method of Thermal Plant Analysis*. Krieger Publications, 1995.

O'Hayre, Ryan, Suk-Won Cha, Whitney Colella, and Fritz B. Prinz. *Fuel Cell Fundamentals*. 3rd ed. John Wiley & Sons, 2016.

Reddy, Thomas B., editor. *Linden's Handbook of Batteries*. 4th ed., McGraw-Hill, 2011.

Sharifzadeh, Mahdi, editor. *Design and Operation of Solid Oxide Fuel Cells*. Academic Press, 2020.

Functional Design

ABSTRACT

Functional design is a paradigm of computer programming. Following functional design principles, computer programs are created using discrete modules that interact with one another only in very specific, limited ways. An individual module can be modified extensively with only minor impacts on other parts of the program. Functional design is also an important principle in manufacturing. Under that principle, a complex machine is separated into simple sections that can be individually produced, including through processes such as three-dimensional (3D) printing, and then assembled.

BENEFITS OF FUNCTIONAL DESIGN

Functional design is a concept most commonly associated with computer programming. However, it is also relevant to other fields, such as manufacturing and business management. At its core, the concepts underlying functional design are simple. Instead of designing a program in which the individual parts perform many different functions and are highly interconnected, modules should have low coupling. Modules—the individual parts of the program—should be designed to have the simplest possible inputs and outputs. When possible, each module should only perform a single function. Low coupling ensures that each module has a high degree of independence from other parts of the program. This makes the overall program easier to debug and maintain. Most of the labor that goes into programming is related to these two activities. Therefore, it makes sense to use a design approach that makes both of these tasks easier.

Functional design is preferable because when a program has a bug, if the modules perform many different functions and are highly coupled, it is difficult to make adjustments to the malfunctioning part without causing unintended consequences in other parts of the program. Some parts of a program do not easily lend themselves to functional design because their very nature requires that they be connected to multiple parts of the overall program. One example of this is the main loop of the program. By necessity, the main loop interacts with and modifies different modules, variables, and functions. Similarly, the interrupt vector table acts as a directory for interrupt handlers used throughout the program. Still, many other functions of a typical program can be designed in ways that minimize interdependencies.

INTERDEPENDENT COMPLICATIONS

Functional programming is a form of declarative programming. Declarative programs simply specify the end result that a program should achieve. In contrast, imperative programming outlines the particular sequence of operations a program should perform. Programmers must carefully consider how they design variables and functions. While functional design emphasizes modularity and independence between different program components, a number of design techniques rely on interconnections. For example, inheritance draws on the properties of one class to create another. With polymorphism, the same methods and operations can be performed on a variety of elements but will have specific, customized behaviors depending on the elements' class. With subtyping, a type is designed to contain one or more other variables types. While each of these techniques has advantages, their interdependence can cause issues when a change is made to other parts of the program. For example, consider a variable called "NUM" that can take on any numeric value. A second variable is defined as EVENNUM and can take on any NUM value divisible by 2 with no remainder. Because EVENNUM is defined in relation to NUM, if a programmer later makes a change to NUM, it could have unintended consequences on the variable EVENNUM. A program that is highly coupled could have a long chain reaction of bugs due to a change in one of its modules.

Functional design tries to avoid these issues in two ways. First, programmers specifically consider interrelations as they design a program and try to make design choices that will minimize complications. Second, once a program has been written, programmers will proofread the code to find any elements that have unnecessary complications. Some clues are the presence of language such as "and" or "or" in the descriptions of variables, classes, and types. This can suggest that multiple functions are being combined into one module. The programmer may then separate these functions into separate, less dependent modules if possible.

MANUFACTURING APPLICATIONS

Functional design also has applications in physical manufacturing. This has been facilitated by the advent of three-dimensional (3D) printing. 3D printing can make it easier to produce parts, components, and even whole pieces of machinery that would be expensive or impossible to manufacture using traditional methods. In this context, functional design conceptually separates a complex machine into simple sections that can be individually produced and then assembled.

Designers who approach a problem from the standpoint of functional design often observe that functional design is not simply an outcome but also a process. Functional design is a way of thinking about problems before any code is written or any component is manufactured. It asks how a design can be broken down into simpler steps and include only essential processes.

—*Scott Zimmer, MLS, MS, JD*

Further Reading

Bessière, Pierre, Emmanuel Mazer, Juan Manuel Ahuactzin, and Kamel Mekhnacha. *Bayesian Programming*. CRC Press, 2014.

Bi, Zhuming, and Xiaoqin Wang. *Computer Aided Design and Manufacturing*. Wiley-ASME Press, 2020.

Clarke, Dave, James Noble, and Tobias Wrigstad, editors. *Aliasing in Object-Oriented Programming: Types, Analysis and Verification*. Springer, 2013.

Lee, Kent D. *Foundations of Programming Languages*. Springer, 2014.

Neapolitan, Richard E. *Foundations of Algorithms*. 5th ed., Jones, 2015.

Streib, James T., and Takako Soma. *Guide to Java: A Concise Introduction to Programming*. Springer, 2014.

Wang, John, editor. *Optimizing, Innovating, and Capitalizing on Information Systems for Operations*. Business Science Reference, 2013.

G

Game Programming

ABSTRACT
Game programming is a type of software engineering used to develop computer and video games. Depending on the type of game under development, programmers may be required to specialize in areas of software development not normally required for computer programmers. These specialties include artificial intelligence, physics, audio, graphics, input, database management, and network management.

HOW GAME PROGRAMMING WORKS
While many video games are developed as homebrew projects by individuals working in their spare time, most major games are developed by employees of large companies that specialize in video games. In such a company, the process of creating a video game begins with a basic idea of the game's design. If enough people in the company feel the idea has merit, the company will create a prototype to develop the concept further. The prototype gives form to the game's basic story line, graphics, and programming. It helps developers decide whether the game is likely to do well in the marketplace and what resources are needed for its development.

Games that move past the prototyping stage proceed along many of the same pathways as traditional software development. However, video games differ from most other software applications in that elements of the game must continue to run in the absence of user input. Programmers must therefore create a game loop, which continues to run the program's graphics, artificial intelligence, and audio when the user is not active.

Game programmers often use object-oriented programming (OOP). This is an approach to software development that defines the essential objects of a program and how they can interact with each other. Each object shares attributes and behaviors with other objects in the same class. Because many video games run hundreds of thousands of lines of code, an object-oriented approach to game development can help make the code more manageable. OOP makes programs easier to modify, maintain, and extend. This approach can make it easier to plan out and repurpose elements of the game.

Large numbers of people are involved in writing the source code of a game intended for wide distribution. They are typically organized in teams, with each team specializing in certain aspects of the game's mechanics or certain types of programming. To facilitate collaboration, detailed comments and pseudocode are used to document features of the program and explain choices about coding strategies. Pseudocode is a combination of a programming language and a natural language such as English. It is not executable, but it is much easier to read and understand than source code.

GAME PROGRAMMING TOOLS
Game programmers use the same basic tools as most software developers. These tools include text editors, debuggers, and compilers. The tools used are often determined by the type of device the game is intended to run on. Games can be developed for a particular computer platform, such as Windows, macOS, or Linux. They can also be developed for a gaming console, such as the Nintendo Switch, the Xbox Series X, or the PlayStation 5. Finally, games

Developers of computer-graphics software and CAD offer software packages geared toward the creation of complex video game graphics. Photo via iStock/eclipse_images. [Used under license.]

may be developed for mobile platforms such as Apple's iOS or Google's Android operating system.

A wide variety of programming languages are used to create video games. Some of the most commonly used programming languages in game development are C++, C#, and Java. Many video games are programmed with a combination of several different languages. Assembly code or C may be used to write lower-level modules. The graphics of many games are programmed using a shading language such as Cg or HLSL.

Game developers often use application programming interfaces (APIs) such as OpenGL and DirectX. They also rely heavily on the use of libraries and APIs to repurpose frequently used functions. Many of these resources are associated with animation, graphics, and the manipulation of 3D elements. One driving force in game development has been the use of increasingly sophisticated visual elements. Prominent developers of computer-graphics software and computer-aided design (CAD) software offer software packages geared toward the creation of complex video game graphics; the Autodesk software Maya LT, for instance, was developed for use by independent game developers. Video games have come to rival motion pictures in their use of complex plotlines, dazzling special effects, and fully developed characters.

A POPULAR BUT DEMANDING CAREER

Game programming has been a popular career choice among young people. Due to the popularity of video games, it is not surprising that large numbers of people are interested in a career that will allow them to get paid to work on games. Becoming a game programmer requires the ability to code and a familiarity with several different programming languages. Game programmers can specialize in developing game engines, artificial intelligence, audio, graphics, user interfaces, inputs, or gameplay.

Game programmers regularly report high levels of stress as they are pressured to produce increasingly impressive games every year. There is intense competition to produce better special effects, more exciting stories, and more realistic action with each new title. Some game companies have been criticized for the high demands and heavy workloads placed upon game developers.

—*Scott Zimmer, MLS, MS, JD*

Further Reading

Halpern, Daniel Noah. *Becoming a Video Game Designer*. Simon & Schuster, 2020.
Harbour, Jonathan S. *Beginning Game Programming*. 4th ed., Cengage Learning, 2015.
Ingrassia, Michael. *Maya for Games*. Focal Press, 2009.
Kim, Chang-Hun, et al. *Real-Time Visual Effects for Game Programming*. Springer, 2015.
Madhav, Sanjay. *Game Programming Algorithms and Techniques: A Platform-Agnostic Approach*. Addison-Wesley, 2014.
Marchant, Ben. "Game Programming in C and C++." *Cprogramming.com*, www.cprogramming.com/game-programming.html. Accessed 28 Nov. 2021.
Tyler, Dustin. "Graphic Design vs Video Game Design: Which Career Match Your Skills?" *GameDesigning*, 25 June 2021, www.gamedesigning.org/learn/graphic-design-vs-game-design/. Accessed 28 Nov. 2021.
Yamamoto, Jazon. *The Black Art of Multiplatform Game Programming*. Cengage Learning, 2015.

Gas Turbine Technology

ABSTRACT

Gas turbine technology covers the design, manufacture, operation, and maintenance of rotary conversion engines that generate power from the energy of the hot, pressurized gas they create. Key components are air and fuel intake systems, compressor, combustor, the gas turbine itself, and an output shaft in those gas turbines that are not designed to provide thrust alone as jet engines. Primary applications of gas turbines are jet engines and generators for industrial power and electric utilities. Sea and land vehicles can also be propelled by gas turbines.

DEFINITION AND BASIC PRINCIPLES

Gas turbine technology concerns itself with all aspects of designing, building, running, and servicing gas turbines, which provide jet engines for airplanes and represent the heart of many contemporary power plants, among other uses. Strictly speaking, the gas turbine itself is only one part of a complex engine assembly commonly given this name.

A gas turbine employs the physical fact that thermal energy can be converted into mechanical energy. Its basic principle is often called the "Brayton cycle," named after George Brayton, the American engineer who developed it in 1872. The Brayton cycle involves compression of air, its heating by fuel combustion, and the release of the hot gas stream to expand and drive a turbine. The turbine creates both power for air compression and free power. The free power gained can be used either as thrust in traditional jet engines or as mechanical power driving another unit such as an electric generator, pump, or compressor.

The gas turbine is closely related to the steam turbine. The gas turbine got its name from the fact that it operates with air in gaseous form. A wide variety of fuel can be used to heat the gaseous air.

BACKGROUND AND HISTORY

The oldest known reference to an apparatus utilizing the physical principles of a gas turbine is a design by Leonardo da Vinci from 1550 for a hot-air-powered roasting spit. In 1791, British inventor John Barber obtained a patent for the design of a combined gas and steam turbine. However, the lack of suitable materials to withstand the heat and pressure needed for a working gas turbine impeded any practical applications for a long time.

In 1872, German engineer Franz Stolze designed a gas turbine, but driving its compressor used more energy than the turbine generated. In 1903, the first gas turbine with a surplus of power was built by Norwegian inventor Aegidius Elling. The idea to use gas turbines to build jet engines was pioneered by British aviation engineer and pilot Sir Frank Whittle by 1930. At the same time, German physicist Hans von Ohain developed a jet engine on his own. On August 27, 1939, the German Heinkel He 178 became the first flying jet airplane. That year, the first power plant using a gas turbine became operational in Switzerland.

Since the first half of the twentieth century, the twin use of gas turbine technology either to propel jet airplanes or serve as a source for generating power on the ground, particularly electricity, has been subject to many technological advances. Like many industries, the field of gas turbine design benefited from advances in computer-aided design (CAD) software and that technology's design, modeling, and evaluation functions. Over the course of the late twentieth and early twenty-first centuries, professionals in the field used CAD programs to design a host of relevant products, including gas turbine engines, rotors, blades, and combustion chambers.

HOW IT WORKS

Brayton cycle. A gas turbine engine is a device to convert fuel energy via the compression and subsequent expansion of air. Its working process is commonly known as the Brayton cycle. The Brayton cycle begins with the compression of air, in gaseous form, for which energy is expended. For this reason, a gas turbine assembly needs an air intake and a compressor where air is pressurized. Next, more energy is added to the compressed air through the heat from the combustion of fuel. Fuel is burned, most commonly, internally in the engine's combustor. However, in a variation called the "Ericsson cycle," the fuel is burned externally and

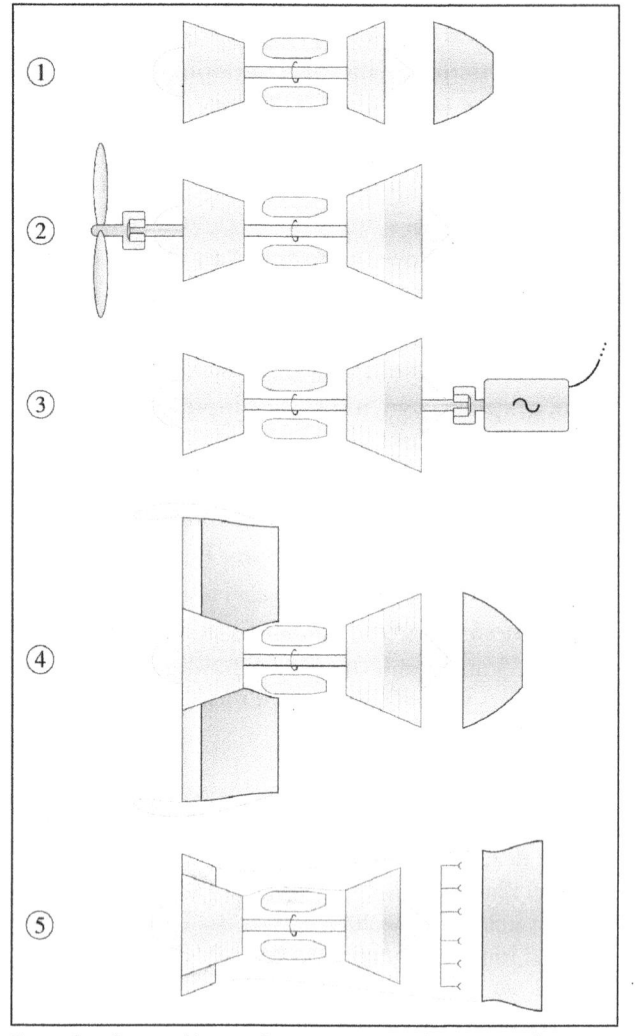

Examples of gas turbine configurations: (1) turbojet, (2) turboprop, (3) turboshaft (electric generator), (4) high-bypass turbofan, (5) low-bypass afterburning turbofan. Image by Olivier Cleynen, via Wikimedia Commons.

the generated heat is relayed to the compressed air. The third step of the cycle comes with the release of the heated gas stream through nozzles into the gas turbine proper. The gas expands as it loses some of its pressure and cools off. The energy released by gas expansion is captured by the gas turbine, which is driven in a rotary fashion as its blades are turned by the exiting hot gas stream. In the last step, the expanding air releases its leftover heat into the atmosphere.

Power generation. As the hot gas stream flows along stator vanes to hit the airfoil-shaped rotor blades arranged on a disk inside the gas turbine, it drives the blades in rotary fashion, creating mechanical power. This power is captured by one or more output shafts, called "spools." There are two uses for this power. The first is to drive the compressor of the gas turbine assembly, feeding power back to the first step of operations. Any free power remaining can be used to drive external loads or to provide thrust for jet engines, either directly through exhaust or by driving a fan or propeller.

The engineering challenge in gas turbine technology is to gain as much free power as possible. Attention has been focused both on materials used inside the gas turbine, looking for those that can withstand the most heat and pressure, and in arranging the individual components of the gas turbine to optimize its output. The metal of single-crystal cast alloy turbine blades can withstand temperatures of up to 1,940° Fahrenheit (1,060° Celsius). Ingenious air-cooling systems enable these blades to deal with gas as hot as 2,912° F (1,600° C). Top compressors can achieve a 40:1 ratio. At the same time, designing gas turbines with multiple shafts to drive low- and high-pressure compressors or adding a power turbine behind the first turbine used only to gather sufficient power for the compressor has also improved efficiency. While early gas turbines used between 66 and 75 percent of the power they generated from fuel to drive their own compressor, leaving only 25 to 34 percent of free power, contemporary gas turbines for industrial power can achieve up to 65 percent of free power.

Fuel. Fuel for gas turbines is variable and ranges from the hydrocarbon product kerosene for jet engines to coal or natural gas for industrial gas turbines. The engineering challenges have been to optimize fuel efficiency and to lower emissions, particularly of nitrogen oxides.

Operation maintenance. Gas turbines require careful operation as they are very responsive, and malfunctions in either the compressor or turbine can happen in fractions of a second. The primary control systems are handled by computer and are hydromechanical and electrical. From start and stop and loading and unloading the gas turbine, operating controls cover speed, temperature, load, surges, and output. The control regimen ranges from sequencing to routine operation and protection control.

Gas turbines have some accessories to facilitate their operation. These include starting and ignition systems, lubrication and bearings, air-inlet cooling and injection systems for water, and steam or technical gases such as ammonia to control nitrogen oxide emissions.

To facilitate maintenance, gas turbines used for aircraft and those modeled after these have a modular design so that the individual components such as compressor, combustor, and turbine can be taken out of the assembly individually. Those gas turbines allow also for a borescope inspection of their insides by an optical tube with lens and eyepiece. Heavy industrial gas turbines are not designed for borescope inspection and must be dismantled for inspection and maintenance. Preventive maintenance is very important for gas turbines.

APPLICATIONS AND PRODUCTS

Jet engines. The first jet engines were designed to use the free power of gas turbines exclusively for thrust. This gave them a speed advantage over piston- engine aircraft but at the price of very low fuel economy. As a result, gas turbine technology developed more economical alternatives. For helicopters and smaller commercial airplanes, the turboprop system was developed. Here, the gas turbine uses its free power to drive the propeller of the aircraft.

The turbofan jet engine is used in most contemporary medium to large commercial aircraft. Efficiency is increased by the addition of a fan that acts like a ducted propeller and that is driven by the free power of the gas turbine. In contemporary high-bypass turbofan jet engines in use since the 1970s and continuously improved since, much of the air taken in bypasses the compressor and is directly propelled into the engine by the turbine-driven fan. Only a smaller part of air is taken into a low- and then a high-pressure compressor, joined with fuel burned in the combustor and driving both a high- and low-pressure turbine. The net resulting thrust, primarily from the fan, is achieved with high fuel economy and relatively little noise.

Military aircraft, the only ones flying at supersonic speed, also use afterburners with their gas turbines. This is done by adding another combustor behind the turbine blades and before the exhaust nozzle, creating extra thrust at the expense of much fuel.

Aeroderivative turbines. Because of their relatively low weight, gas turbines based on jet engine design have been used on the ground for power generation and propulsion. Especially with the contemporary trend toward turbofan jet engines, an aeroderivative turbine that uses one or more spools, or output shafts, to provide a mechanical drive needs very little adaptation from air to ground use. There are also hybrid gas turbines that use an aeroderivative design but replace the jet engine's lighter roller and antifriction ball bearings with hydrodynamic bearings typical of the heavy industrial gas turbine.

With higher shaft speed but lower airflow through the turbine, aeroderivative turbines require less complex and shorter maintenance than other ground gas turbines. They are often used in remote areas, where they are employed to drive pumps and compressors for pipelines, for example. Because of their quicker start, stop, and loading times, aeroderivative gas turbines are also used for flexible peak load power generation and for ground propulsion.

Heavy industrial gas turbines. Gas turbines for use on the ground can be built more sturdily and larger than jet engines. These heavy units have been generally used for power generation or to drive heavy industrial pumps or compressors, with power generation increasingly important. Gas turbine technology has experimented with a variety of designs for these turbines. One decision is whether to place the output shaft (spool) at the "hot" end where the gas stream exits the turbine, or at the "cold" end in front of the air intake. "Cold" end drives are easier to access for service and do not have to withstand the hot environment at the turbine end, but their position has to be carefully designed so as not to disturb the air intake. If the output shaft would cause a turbulence or vortex in the air flowing into the compressor this could lead to a surge potentially destroying the whole engine.

There are also design differences regarding the numbers of shafts (spools) and turbines within a contemporary heavy industrial gas turbine. The basic form has one output shaft rotating at the speed of the compressor and turbine. At the output, this speed can be geared up or down depending on the speed desired for the application the gas turbine is driving. This design is almost exclusively used for power generation. An alternative to minimize gear losses is to put a second, free-power turbine behind the first gas turbine driving the compressor. This means that the speed of the free-power turbine can be regulated independently of the turbine speed needed to drive the compressor, which makes it an attractive design when pumps or compressors are driven by the gas turbine. This design is only possible with a "hot" end configuration. Finally, there are gas turbine designs that use more than one shaft (spool). A dual spool split output shaft gas turbine, for example, employs three output shafts to operate independently with a high-pressure and low-pressure turbine-compressor assembly as well as a free-power turbine.

Because a single-cycle, stand-alone gas turbine has a fuel efficiency of as little as 17 percent, meaning 83 percent of the energy created is used for the compressor, engineers have combined gas turbines for power generation in cogeneration or combined-cycle power plants. In a cogeneration plant, the remaining heat that exits the gas turbine is used for industrial purposes, such as heating steam for a refinery. In a combined-cycle power plant, the heat from typically two gas turbines fuels a steam turbine. This can create fuel efficiencies ranging from 55 to 65 percent or more. These gas turbines typically create about 250 to 350 megawatts of electrical power each.

Marine and tank propulsion. Aeroderivative gas turbines are also used to propel ships, particularly military vessels. Military requirements of high speed outweigh the fuel and construction cost disadvantages that make gas turbines too expensive for commercial ships. Gas turbines can also be used as tank engines, for example in the American M1A1 Abrams tank or the Russian T-80. However, their high fuel use provides an engineering challenge, particularly at idle speed. The M1A1 tanks have been retrofitted with batteries to use for idling, and the Russian T-80 was replaced by the diesel-engine-powered T-90.

Turbochargers. Their low fuel efficiency makes gas turbines unsuitable for car propulsion. However, small gas turbines working as turbochargers are commonly added to increase the power of diesel car engines. The power from the turbine is used to compress the air taken in by the diesel engine, increasing its performance.

CAREERS AND COURSEWORK

Gas turbine technology has been a key to two of the world's leading industries, power and aviation, so job demand in the field should remain very strong. Students interested in the field should take science courses in high school, particularly physics, as well as mathematics and computer science. An associate's degree in an engineering or science field (engineering or industrial technology) will provide a good entry.

A bachelor of science in an engineering discipline, particularly mechanical, electrical, or computer engineering, is excellent preparation for an advanced job. A BS in physics or mathematics would point to a more theoretically informed career, perhaps in design. A bachelor of arts in environmental studies is also useful, as emission control is becoming a major part of gas turbine technology. A minor in any science is always beneficial.

If one's career focus is on advanced work, a master of science in mechanical, electrical, and computer engineering, or in environmental science and management, could be chosen. For top scientific positions, a PhD in these disciplines, together with some postdoctoral work, is advisable.

Because of the global nature of the field, students should maintain a general openness to work abroad or in somewhat remote locations, with the exception of those purely interested in design. The field can also be attractive to students with expertise in support functions, including those who have earned a bachelor's degree in English, communications, economics, or biology. A master of business administration would serve as preparation for the business end of the field.

SOCIAL CONTEXT AND FUTURE PROSPECTS

As more nations industrialize and global development continues, the demand for power and mobility, including air travel, is expected to increase. Especially with the key applications of jet engines and gas turbines for power generation, the field of gas turbine technology is likely to keep its great relevancy. The quest for more efficient gas turbines that combust their fuel with as little emissions as possible will continue to motivate major developments in the field. If gas turbines can become an ever-more efficient and low-emission source of generating power they have the potential, like fuel cells, to become part of the next generation of power sources. There is also much promise linked to micro gas turbines as a source of efficient, affordable, clean, and decentralized power.

For jet engines, the design challenge is to reduce fuel consumption and noise and increase power. There is ongoing research to employ gas turbines in combination with electric hybrid car engines to lower overall carbon dioxide emissions from personal transport. This will grow in importance as more people in developing nations acquire cars.

—*R. C. Lutz, BA, MA, PhD*

Further Reading

Akhmedzyanov, D. A., A. E. Kishalov, and K. V. Markina. "Computer-Aided Design of Aircraft Gas Turbine Engines and Selection of Materials for Their Main Parts." *Vestnik*, vol. 14, no. 1, 2015, pp. 101-11.

Boyce, Meherwan P. *Gas Turbine Engineering Handbook*. 4th ed., Butterworth-Heinemann, 2012.

Dye, Christopher, Joseph B. Staubach, Diane Emmerson, and C. Greg Jensen. "CAD-Based Parametric Cross-Section Designer for Gas Turbine Engine MDO Applications." *Computer-Aided Design and Applications*, vol. 4, no. 1-4, 2007, pp. 509-18.

Giampaolo, Tony. *Gas Turbine Handbook: Principles and Practices*. 5th ed., River Publishers, 2013.

Gülen, S. Can. *Gas Turbines for Electric Power Generation*. Cambridge UP, 2019.

Kehlhofer, Rolf, et al. *Combined-Cycle Gas and Steam Turbine Power Plants*. 3rd ed., PennWell, 2009.

Peng, William W. *Fundamentals of Turbomachinery*. Wiley, 2008.

Rangwala, A. S. *Turbo-Machinery Dynamics: Design and Operation*. McGraw-Hill, 2005.

Schobeiri, Meinhard T. *Gas Turbine Design, Components and System Design Integration*. 2nd ed., Springer Nature Switzerland, 2019.

Soares, Claire. *Gas Turbines: A Handbook of Air, Land and Sea Applications*. 2nd ed., Butterworth-Heinemann, 2015.

Generative Design

ABSTRACT

Generative design is a software-based approach that renders the design parameters of a concept into the many different forms that conform to those parameters. The generated designs may be tested virtually, and a design engineer can then select the most appropriate form to suit the particular need.

DESIGN

All design processes begin with an idea, a concept or theory. Typically, a designer will be given concept data and then choose materials from which to construct a proof-of-concept object for real-world testing. This may prove to be something as simple as a small three-dimensional (3D) model or as complex as a fully functional device. All such things begin as technical drawings, generally as two (2D)- or three (3D)-dimensional representations produced by a draftsperson using the tools of technical drawing. However, computer-aided design (CAD) programs provide a means of testing a proof-of-concept object without actually building the prototype. Many CAD programs have the ability to create a "digital twin" of the object and test it virtually in simulation. There is also a type of CAD program that can use the principal data of a design concept to generate every design that conforms to the structural parameters. This is generative design.

A generative design CAD program can produce an unlimited number of different designs that correspond to the input design parameters. As a simple example, one can consider the dimensions of a cube as the principal design parameters. A cube can be described as a shape in which eight points in space are equidistant from each other. Conventionally, those eight points are the corners of the solid block form that everyone envisions as a cube. But what if there is no need for the solid block structure, as long as the eight points in space are equidistant and the strength requirements for the "cube" are met, nor for all the useless mass associated with the solid block of material? This is where generative design becomes useful, by generating different structural designs in which the spatial relationship of the eight corners is maintained and all other requirements are met. One such structure may have the corners connected by rods, with four longer rods connecting the diametrically opposed corners. Another equivalent structure may simply have four semicircular components connecting adjacent corners and coincident at the cube's center. Still another equivalent structure may have two conjoined semicircular components connecting the four corners of one face of the cube and a similar structure in the opposite face of the cube, both connected to a shaft passing through the center of the cube. Many other such possible structures for a "cube" can also be generated.

Samba, a piece of furniture created with generative design. Photo by Estudio Guto Requena, via Wikimedia Commons.

This principle of generative design is applicable in essentially all areas of engineering. One could ask, for example, how many different ways a hundred-unit apartment complex could be designed. Any number of architects would provide as many different architectural designs, in effect becoming the generative design software themselves.

GENERATIVE DESIGN IN ENGINEERING

The engineering process begins with defining how a particular engineered product is to perform in carrying out its function. The agitator spindle of a washing machine is a good example. This component is to be positioned on a central shaft that turns with reciprocating motion. The agitator spindle's purpose is to move laundry items in a random agitating motion within the wash and rinse waters. This is achieved by fins protruding from the agitator shaft. There are any number of ways to design the shape of both the spindle and the fins. Within a generative design program, an algorithmic function process uses the various input data, such as overall dimensions, required strengths, and weights, to generate designs that meet the necessary criteria. These different designs become the output of the program and are then presented to human design engineers who will select the most appropriate and desirable design for production. The method of production is also a consideration in the designs that were generated. These may range from machining the part from a solid block of material (subtractive manufacturing), to casting the part in a mold and finishing it off with standard finishing operations, to constructing the part by welding pieces together, or even creating the entire piece from scratch using 3D printing (additive manufacturing). Generative design software can also produce and test designs that are impossible to create physically, even though the design fits the required parameters. In addition to offering speed and versatility in generating designs, generative design programs are able to optimize materials and manufacturing methods for any particular design.

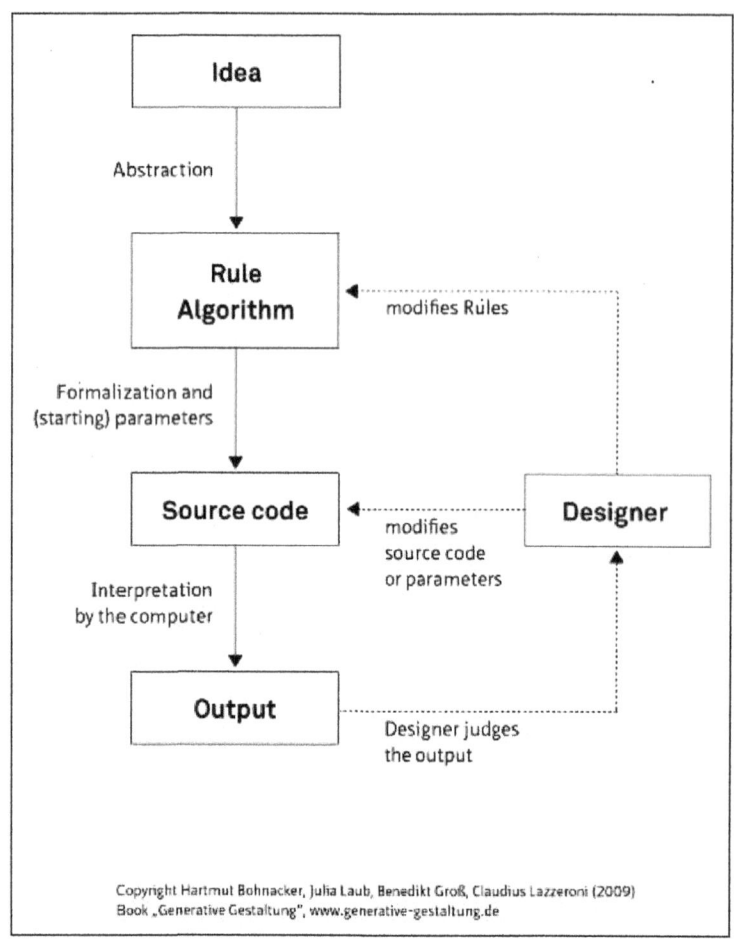

Schema of generative design as an iterative process. Image by Hartmut Bohnacker, via Wikimedia Commons.

ADVANTAGES OF GENERATIVE DESIGN

The capabilities of generative design software make it applicable to a wide range of engineering fields, especially manufacturing, and at all levels of the engineering process, from product ideation to the actual manufacturing of a particular product. A selected design from a generative design program can be output directly to an associated CAD program for rendering and to an associated computer-aided manufacturing (CAM) process for actual production. This is increasingly important for additive manufacturing, as more and more components are produced using 3D printing methodologies. A particular advantage of using a 3D printing process with generative design is that it allows production of a design output as a one-off prototype, without the need to commit to a full-scale production run. The ability to produce an engineered component in this way simplifies and encourages innovation. By simply adjusting the input parameters of a successful design output, the engineer can make the product lighter if weight is an issue, or more streamlined and efficient.

Generative design is used in the automotive industry to develop lighter parts and components as well as to optimize the overall design of vehicles in order to minimize materials costs and improve fuel economy. In the aerospace industry, weight determines how much fuel is used by an aircraft. From a purely commercial standpoint, reducing the weight of an aircraft effectively increases the amount of commercial product it can transport and therefore the profitability of the flight for a given amount of fuel. The same holds true for rail and truck transport. Similarly, goods that weight less cost less to transport. With regard to consumer goods, generative design that generates multiple CAD-ready, process-aware solutions to a particular design goal can encourage innovation and productivity. In architecture and construction, generative design enables exploration of goals and constraints that are not actually part of the manufacturing process. At the same time, it allows simplification of complex assemblies used in the building process.

DISADVANTAGES OF GENERATIVE DESIGN

There are essentially only three stages in the overall generative design process. The first is the data stage, in which requirements and constraints are defined. The second is the iterative cycle of generating a design, evaluating that design, and evolving it into a subsequent design. The third stage is the selection stage, in which a human engineer manually refines a selected design. The second stage effectively eliminates the labor-intensive and time-consuming act of manually producing multiple designs to suit the specified criteria. In many fields, this is a reasonable and effective method, depending on the particular goal or purpose to which generative design could be applied. There are those, however, who do not see generative design in a positive light. In a 2020 article detailing his misgivings about generative design, the technology and architecture researcher Daniel Davis presented several distinct disadvantages of generative design technology. The first is that there is no built-in, universal process for creating the multiple design possibilities. The user is required to produce the specific algorithm for design generation, and unless that user is a master programmer and knows every possible variable to include in the generative algorithm, there will be a limit to the program's ability to generate designs, even if it is capable of generating many. This ties into a second weakness, which is that such a large proportion of generated designs will be so similar as to be redundant and therefore useless. The quantity of designs does not reflect the quality of the designs; a large number of designs that are no good is not equivalent to a very small number of well-considered designs.

An additional drawback of generative design also derives from the number of possible designs. The program produces possible designs, but a human is tasked with selecting the best option from all of the possible choices. Comparing those designs can be difficult, especially when a significant aspect of the overall design goal, such as the visual appeal of a particular structural assembly, is not quantifiable. There is thus no absolute way of determining which possible design is the "best" possible design, and choosing to optimize a design solely on the basis of a feature that can be readily quantified can easily lead to optimizing a design that results in failure. There is also consideration to be given to the fact that the design process itself is subject to outside influences such as budgetary constraints, changing governing regulations, and a host of other external influences that no generative design algorithm can encompass. Although generative design software is effective in some applications and seemingly has great potential, arguments such as those presented by Davis suggest that it will require further development as a process itself before it can ever become a general standard of design applications.

—Richard M. Renneboog, MSc

Further Reading

Agkathidis, Asterios. *Generative Design: Form-Finding Techniques in Architecture*. Laurence King, 2015.

Bandyopadhyay, Amit, and Susmita Bose, editors. *Additive Manufacturing*. 2nd ed., CRC Press, 2020.

Davis, Daniel. "Generative Design Is Doomed to Fail." Daniel Davis, 20 Feb. 2020, www.danieldavis.com/generative-design-doomed-to-fail/. Accessed 16 Nov. 2021.

Generative Design Primer, 2021, generativedesign.org. Accessed 16 Nov. 2021.

Tremblay, Thom. *Fusion 360: Generative Design*. LinkedIn Learning, 2019.

Yu, Rongrong, Ning Gu, and Michael J. Ostwald. *Computational Design: Technology, Cognition and Environments*. CRC Press, 2021.

Geometry

ABSTRACT

Geometry, which literally means "earth measurement," is absolutely critical to most fields of physical science and technology and especially to any application that involves surfaces and surface measurement. The term applies on all scales, from nanotechnology to deep-space science, where it describes the relative physical arrangement of things in space. Although the first organized description of the principles of geometry is ascribed to the ancient Greek philosopher Euclid, those principles were known by others before him and had certainly been used by the Egyptians and the Babylonians. Euclidean, or plane, geometry deals with lines and angles on flat surfaces (planes), while non-Euclidean geometry applies to nonplanar surfaces and relationships.

DEFINITION AND BASIC PRINCIPLES

Geometry is the branch of mathematics concerned with the properties and relationships of points, lines, and surfaces and the space contained by those entities. A point translated in a single direction describes a line, while a line translated in a single direction describes a plane. The intersections and rotations of various identities describe corresponding structures that have specific mathematical relationships and properties. These include angles and numerous two (2D)- and three-dimensional (3D) forms. Geometric principles can also be extended into realms encompassing more than three dimensions, such as with the incorporation of time as a fourth dimension in Albert Einstein's space-time continuum. Higher-dimensional analysis is also possible and is the subject of theoretical studies.

The basic principles of geometry are subject to various applications within different frames of reference. Plane geometry, called "Euclidean geometry" after the ancient Greek mathematician Euclid, deals with the properties of 2D constructs such as lines, planes, and polygons. The five basic principles of plane geometry, called "postulates," were described by Euclid. The first four are accepted as they are stated and require no proof, although they can be proven. The fifth postulate differs considerably from the first four in nature, and attempts to prove or disprove it have consistently failed. However, it gave rise to other branches of geometry known as "non-Euclidean." The first four postulates apply equally to all branches of Euclidean and non-Euclid-

The CAD application can calculate the movements of robotic machines that will then use the program of instructions to produce a finished object from a piece of raw material. Image via iStock/lasagnaforone. [Used under license.]

ean geometry, while each of the non-Euclidean branches uses its own interpretation of the fifth postulate. These are known as: hyperbolic, elliptic, and spherical geometry.

The point, defined as a specific location within the frame of reference being used, is the common foundation of all branches of geometry. Any point can be uniquely and unequivocally defined by a set of coordinates relative to the central point or origin of the frame of reference. Any two points within the frame of reference can be joined with a single line segment, which can be extended indefinitely in that direction to produce a line. Alternatively, the movement of a point in a single direction within the frame of reference describes a line. Any line can be translated in any orthogonal direction to produce a plane. Rotation of a line segment in a plane about one of its end points describes a circle whose radius is equal to the length of that line segment. In any plane, two lines that intersect orthogonally produce a right angle (an angle of 90 degrees). These are the essential elements of the first four Euclidean postulates. The fifth, which states that nonparallel lines must intersect, could not be proved within Euclidean geometry, and its interpretation under specific conditions gives rise to other frames of reference.

BACKGROUND AND HISTORY

The Greek historian Herodotus soundly argued that geometry originated in ancient Egypt. During the time of the legendary pharaoh Sesostris, the farmland of the empire was apportioned equally among the people, and taxes were levied accordingly. However, the annual inundation of the Nile River tended to wash away portions of farmland, and farmers who lost land in this way complained that it was unfair for them to pay taxes equal to those whose farms were complete. Sesostris is said to have sent agents to measure the loss of land so that taxation could be made fair again. The agents' observations of the relationships that existed gave rise to an understanding of the principles of geometry.

It is well documented that the principles of geometry were known to people long before the ancient Greeks described them. The Rhind papyrus, an Egyptian document dating from 2000 BCE, contains a valid geometric approximation of the value of pi, the ratio of the circumference of a circle to its diameter. The ancient Babylonians were also aware of the principles of geometry, as is evidenced by the inscription on a clay tablet that is housed in Berlin. The inscription has been translated as an explanation of the relationship of the sides and hypotenuse of a right triangle in what is known as the "Pythagorean theorem," although the tablet predates Pythagoras by several hundred years.

From these early beginnings to modern times, studies in geometry have evolved from being simply a means of describing geometric relationships to encompassing a complete description of the workings of the universe. Such studies allow the behavior of materials, structures, and numerous processes to be predicted in a quantifiable way.

HOW IT WORKS

Geometry is concerned with the relationship between points, lines, surfaces, and the spaces enclosed or bounded by those entities.

Points. A point is any unique and particular location within a frame of reference. It exists in one dimension only, having location but no length, width, or breadth. The location of any point can be uniquely and unequivocally defined by a set of coordinate values relative to the central point of the particular reference system being used. For example, in a Cartesian coordinate system—named after French mathematician René Descartes, although the method was also described at the same time by Pierre de Fermat—the location of any point in a 2D plane is described completely by an x-coordinate and a y-coordinate, as (x, y), relative to the origin point at $(0, 0)$. Thus, a point located at $(3, 6)$ is 3 units away from the origin in the direction corresponding to positive values of x, and 6 units away from the origin in the direction corresponding to positive values of y. Similarly, a point in a 3D Cartesian system is identified by three coordinates, as (x, y, z). In Cartesian coordinate systems, each axis is orthogonal to the others. Because orthogonality is a mathematical property, it can also be ascribed to other dimensions as well, allowing the identification of points in theoretical terms in n-space, where n is the number of distinct dimensions assigned to the system. For the purposes of all but the most theoretical of applications, however, three dimensions are sufficient for normal physical representations.

Points can also be identified as corresponding to specific distances and angles, also relative to a coordinate system origin. Thus, a point located in a spherical coordinate system is defined by the radius (the straight-line distance from the origin to the point), the angle that the radius is swept through a plane, and the angle that the radius is swept through an orthogonal plane to achieve the location of the point in space.

Lines. A line can be formed by the translation of a point in a single direction within the reference system. In its simplest designation, a line is described in a 2D system when one of the coordinate values remains constant. In a 3D system, two of the three coordinate values must remain constant. The lines so described are parallel to the reference coordinate axis. For example, the set of points (x, y) in a 2D Cartesian system that corresponds to the form $(x,$

3)—so that the value of the y-coordinate is 3 no matter what the value of x—defines a line that is parallel to the x-axis and always separated from it by 3 units in the positive y direction.

Lines can also be defined by an algebraic relationship between the coordinate axes. In a 2D Cartesian system, a line has the general algebraic form $y = mx + b$. In 3D systems, the relationship is more complex but can be broken down into the sum of two such algebraic equations involving only two of the three coordinate axes.

Planes and surfaces. Planes are described by the translation of a line through the reference system, or by the designation of two of the three coordinates having constant values while the third varies. A plane can be thought of as a flat surface. A curved surface can be formed in an analogous manner by translating a curved line through the reference system, or by definition, as the result of a specific algebraic relationship between the coordinate axes.

Angles. Intersecting lines have the property of defining an angle that exists between them. The angle can be thought of as the amount by which one line must be rotated about the intersection point in order to coincide with the other line. The magnitude, or value, of angles rigidly determines the shape of structures, especially when the structures are formed by the intersection of planes.

Conic sections. A cone is formed by the rotation of a line at an angle about a point. Conic sections are described by the intersection of a plane with the cone structure. As an example, consider a cone formed in the 3D Cartesian system by rotating the line $x = y$ about the y-axis, forming both a positive and a negative cone shape that meet at the origin point. If this is intersected by a plane parallel to the x-z plane, the intersection describes a circle. If the plane is canted so that it is not parallel to the x-z plane and intersects only one of the cone ends, the result is an ellipse. If the plane is canted further and positioned so that it intersects the positive cone on one side of the y-axis and the negative cone on the other side of the y-axis, the intersection defines a hyperbola. If the plane is canted still further so that it intersects both cones on the same side of the y-axis, then a parabola is described.

APPLICATIONS AND PRODUCTS
It is impossible to describe even briefly more than a small portion of the applications of geometry because geometry is so intimately bound to the structures and properties of the physical universe. Every physical structure, no matter its scale, must and does adhere to the principles of geometry, since these are the properties of the physical universe. The application of geometry is fundamental to essentially every field, from agriculture to zymurgy.

GIS and GPS. Geographical information systems (GIS) and global positioning systems (GPS) have been developed as a universal means of location identification. GPS is based on a number of satellites orbiting the planet and using the principles of geometry to define the position of each point on Earth's surface. Electronic signals from the various satellites triangulate to define the coordinates of each point. Triangulation uses the geometry of triangles and the strict mathematical relationships that exist between the angles and sides of a triangle, particularly the sine law, the cosine law, and the Pythagorean theorem.

GIS combines GPS data with the geographic surface features of the planet to provide an accurate "living" map of the world. These two systems have revolutionized how people plan and coordinate their movements and the movement of materials all over the world. Applications range from the relatively simple GPS devices found in many modern vehicles and smartphones to precise tracking of weather systems and seismic activity. An application that is familiar to many through the internet is Google Earth, which presents a satellite view of essentially any place on the planet at a level of detail that once was available from only the most top secret of military reconnaissance satellites. The system also allows a user to view traditional map images in a way that allows them to be scaled as needed and to add overlays of specific buildings, structures, and street views. Anyone with access to the internet can quickly and easily call up an accurate map of almost any desired location on the planet.

GIS and GPS have provided a whole new level of security for travelers. They have also enabled the development of transportation security features such as General Motors' OnStar system, the European Space Agency's Satellite-Based Alarm and Surveillance System (SASS), and several other satellite-based security applications. They invariably use the GPS and GIS networks to provide the almost instantaneous location of individuals and events as needed.

CAD. Computer-aided design (CAD) is a system in which computers are used to generate the design of a physical object and then to control the mechanical reproduction of the design as an actual physical object. A computer drafting application such as AutoCAD is used to produce a drawing of an object in electronic format. The data stored in the drawing file include all the dimensions and tolerances that define the object's size and shape. At this point, the object itself does not exist; only the concept of it exists as a collection of electronic data. The CAD application can calculate the movements of ancillary robotic machines that will then use the program of instructions to produce a finished object from a piece of raw material. The operations, depending on the complexity and capabilities of the machinery being directed, can include shaping, milling, lathework, boring or drilling, threading, and several other procedures. The nature of the machinery ranges from basic mechanical shaping devices to advanced tooling devices employing lasers, high-pressure jets, and plasma- and electron-beam cutting tools.

The advantages provided by CAD systems are numerous. Using the system, it is possible to design and produce single units, or one offs, quickly and precisely to test a physical design. Adjustments to production steps are made very quickly and simply by adjusting the object data in the program file rather than through repeated physical processing steps with their concomitant waste of time and materials. Once perfected, the production of multiple pieces becomes automatic, with little or no variation from piece to piece.

Metrology. Closely related to CAD is the application of geometry in metrology, particularly through the use of precision measuring devices such as the measuring machine. This is an automated device that uses the electronic drawing file of an object, as was produced in a CAD procedure, as the reference standard for objects as they are made in a production facility. Typically, this is an integral component of a statistical process control and quality assurance program. In practice, parts are selected at random from a production line and submitted to testing for the accuracy of their construction during the production process. A production piece is placed in a custom jig or fixture, and the calibrated measuring machine then goes through a series of test measurements to determine the correlation between the features of the actual piece and the features of the piece as they are designated in the drawing file. The measuring machine is precisely controlled by electronic mechanisms and is capable of highly accurate measurement.

Game programming and animation. Basic and integral parts of both video-game design and computer-generated animation for films are described by the terms "polygon," "wireframe," "motion capture," and "computer-generated imagery" (CGI). Motion capture uses a series of reference points attached to an actor's body. The reference points become data points in a computer file, and the motions of the actor are recorded as the geometric translation of one set of data points into another in a series. The data points can then be used to generate a wireframe drawing of a figure that corresponds to the character whose actions have been imitated by the actor during the motion-capture process. The finished appearance of the character is achieved by using polygon constructions to provide an outward texture to the image. The texture can be anything from a plain, smooth, and shiny surface to a complex arrangement of individually colored hairs. Perhaps the most immediately recognizable application of the polygon process is the generation of dinosaur skin and aliens in video games and films.

The movements of the characters in both games and films are choreographed and controlled through strict geometric relationships, even down to the play of light over the character's surface from a single light source. This is commonly known as "ray tracing" and is used to produce photorealistic images.

CAREERS AND COURSEWORK

Geometry is an essential and absolutely critical component of practically all fields of applied science. A solid grounding in mathematics and basic geometry is required during secondary school studies. In more advanced or applied studies at the postsecondary level, in any applied field, mathematical training in geometrical principles will focus more closely on the applications that are specific to that field of study. Any program of study that integrates design concepts will include subject-specific applications of geometric principles. Applications of geometric principles are used in mechanical engineering, manufacturing, civil engineering, industrial plant operations, agricultural development, forestry management, environmental management, mining, project management and logistics, transportation, aeronautical engineering, hydraulics and fluid dynamics, physical chemistry, crystallography, graphic design, and game programming.

The principles involved in any particular field of study can often be applied to other fields as well. In economics, for example, data mining uses many of the same ideological principles that are used in the mining of mineral resources. Similarly, the generation of figures in electronic game design uses the same geometric principles as land surveying and topographical mapping. Thus, a good grasp of geometry and its applications can be considered a transferable skill usable in many different professions.

SOCIAL CONTEXT AND FUTURE PROSPECTS

Geometry is set to play a central role in many fields. Geometry is often the foundation on which decisions affecting individuals and society are made. This is perhaps most evident in the establishment and construction of the most basic infrastructure in every country in the world, and in the most high-tech advances represented by the satellite networks for GPS and GIS. It is easy to imagine the establishment of similar networks around the moon, Mars, and other planets, providing an unprecedented geological and geographical understanding of those bodies. In between these extremes that indicate the most basic and the most advanced applications of geometry and geometrical principles are the typical everyday applications that serve to maintain practically all aspects of human endeavor. The scales at which geometry is applied cover an extremely broad range, from the ultrasmall constructs of molecular structures and nanotechnological devices to the construction of islands and buildings of novel design and the ultralarge expanses of interplanetary and even interstellar space.

—*Richard M. J. Renneboog, MSc*

Further Reading
Acheson, David. *The Wonder Book of Geometry*. Oxford UP, 2020.
Bar-Lev, Adi. "Big Waves: Creating Swells, Wakes and Everything In-Between." *Game Developer*, Feb. 2008, pp. 14-24.

Bi, Zhuming, and Xiaoqin Wang. *Computer Aided Design and Manufacturing*. Wiley-ASME Press, 2020.

Boyer, Carl B. *History of Analytic Geometry*. Dover, 2004.

Darling, David. *The Universal Book of Mathematics: From Abracadabra to Zeno's Paradoxes*. Castle, 2007.

Ellenberg, Jordan. *Shape: The Hidden Geometry of Information, Biology, Strategy, Democracy, and Everything Else*. Penguin Press, 2021.

Heilbron, J. L. *Geometry Civilized: History, Culture, and Technique*. Oxford UP, 2000.

Herz-Fischler, Roger. *A Mathematical History of the Golden Number*. Dover, 1998.

Holme, Audun. *Geometry: Our Cultural Heritage*. 2nd ed., Springer, 2010.

West, Nick. "Practical Fluid Dynamics: Part 1." *Game Developer*, Mar. 2007, pp. 43-47.

Graphical User Interface (GUI)

ABSTRACT

Graphical user interfaces (GUIs) are human-computer interaction systems. In these systems, users interact with the computer by manipulating visual representations of objects or commands. GUIs are part of common operating systems such as Windows and macOS. They are also used in other applications.

GRAPHICS AND INTERFACE BASICS

A user interface is a system for human-computer interaction. The interface determines the way that a user can access and work with data stored on a computer or within a computer network. Interfaces can be either text-based or graphics-based. Text-based systems allow users to input commands. These commands may be text strings or specific words that activate functions. By contrast, graphical user interfaces (GUIs) are designed so that computer functions are tied to graphic icons such as folders, files, and drives. Manipulating an icon causes the computer to perform certain functions.

HISTORY OF INTERFACE DESIGN

The earliest computers used a text-based interface. Users entered text instructions into a command line. For instance, typing "run" in the command line would tell the computer to activate a program or process. One of the earliest text-based interfaces for consumer computer technology was known as a "disk operating system" (DOS). Using DOS-based systems required users to learn specific text commands, such as "del" for deleting or erasing files or "dir" for listing the contents of a directory. The first GUIs were created in the 1970s as a visual "shell" built over a DOS system.

GUIs transform the computer screen into a physical map on which graphics represent functions, programs, files, and directories. In GUIs, users control an onscreen pointer, usually an arrow or hand symbol, to navigate the computer screen. Users activate computing functions by directing the pointer over an icon and "clicking" on it. For instance, GUI users can cause the computer to display the contents of a directory (the "dir" command in DOS) by clicking on a folder or directory icon on the screen. One of the earliest known GUIs was the interactive interface provided in Sketchpad, an early computer-aided design (CAD) program created in the 1960s. Twenty-first-century GUIs combine text-based icons, such as those found in menu bars and movable windows, with linked text icons that can be used to access programs and directories.

ELEMENTS OF GUIS AND OTHER OBJECT INTERFACES

Computer programs are built using coded instructions that tell the computer how to behave when given inputs from a user. Many different programming languages can be used to create GUIs. These include C++, C#, JavaFX, XAML, XUL, among others. Each language offers different advantages and disadvantages when used to create and modify GUIs.

User-centered design focuses on understanding and addressing user preferences, needs, capabilities, and tendencies. According to these design principles, interface metaphors help make GUIs user friendly. Interface metaphors are models that represent real-world objects or concepts to enhance user understanding of computer functions. For example, the desktop structure of a GUI is designed using the metaphor of a desk. Computer desktops, like actual desktops, might have stacks of documents (windows) and objects or tools for performing various functions. Computer folders, trash cans, and recycle bins are icons whose functions mirror those of their real-world counterparts.

GUIs became popular in the early 1980s. Early uses of a GUI included analog clocks, simple icons, charts, and menus.

Object-oriented user interfaces (OOUIs) allow a user to manipulate objects onscreen in intuitive ways based on the function that the user hopes to achieve. Most modern GUIs have some object-oriented functionality. Icons that can be dragged, dropped, slid, toggled, pushed, and clicked are "objects." Objects include folders, program shortcuts, drive icons, and trash or recycle bins. Interfaces that use icons can also be direct manipulation interfaces (DMI). These interfaces allow the user to adjust onscreen objects as though they were physical objects to get certain results. Resizing a window by dragging its corner is one example of direct manipulation used in many GUIs.

CURRENT AND FUTURE OF INTERFACE DESIGN

GUIs have long been based on a model known as WIMP. WIMP stands for "windows, icons, menus, and pointer objects," which describes the ways that users can interact with the interface. Modern GUIs are a blend of graphics-based and text-based functions, but this system is more difficult to implement on modern handheld computers, which have less space to hold icons and menus. Touch-screen interfaces represent the post-WIMP age of interface design. With touch screens, users more often interact directly with objects on the screen, rather than using menus and text-based instructions. Touch-screen design is important in a many application-specific GUIs. These interfaces are designed to handle a single process or application, such as self-checkout kiosks in grocery stores and point-of-sale retail software.

Computer interfaces of the early twenty-first century typically require users to navigate through files, folders, and menus to locate functions, data, or programs. However, voice activation of programs or functions is also available on many computing devices. As this technology becomes more common and effective, verbal commands may replace many functions that have been accessed by point-and-click or menu navigation.

—*Micah L. Issitt*

Further Reading

"Graphical User Interface (GUI)." *Techopedia*, 28 May 2021, www.techopedia.com/definition/5435/graphical-user-interface-gui. Accessed 28 Nov. 2021.

"Ivan Sutherland Creates the First Graphical User Interface." *Historyofinformation.com*, historyofinformation.com/detail.php?id=805. Accessed 28 Nov. 2021.

Johnson, Jeff. *Designing with the Mind in Mind*. 2nd ed., Morgan Kaufmann, 2014.

Long, Simon. *An Introduction to C & GUI Programming*. Raspberry Pi Press, 2019.

Reimer, Jeremy. "A History of the GUI." *Ars Technica*, 5 May 2005, arstechnica.com/features/2005/05/gui/. Accessed 28 Nov. 2021.

Tidwell, Jenifer, Charles Brewer, and Aynne Valencia. *Designing Interfaces: Patterns for Effective Interaction Design*. 3rd ed., O'Reilly Media, 2020.

"User Interface Design Basics." *Usability.gov*, www.usability.gov/what-and-why/user-interface-design.html. Accessed 28 Nov. 2021.

Wood, David. *Interface Design: An Introduction to Visual Communication in UI Design*. Fairchild Books, 2014.

Graphics Formats

ABSTRACT

Graphics formats are standardized forms of computer files used to transfer, display, store, or print reproductions of digital images. Digital image files are divided into two major families, vector and raster files. They can be compressed or uncompressed for storage. Each type of digital file has advantages and disadvantages when used for various applications.

DIGITAL IMAGING

A digital image is a mathematical representation of an image that can be displayed, manipulated, and modified with a computer or other digital device. It can also be compressed. Compression uses algorithms to reduce the size of the image file to facilitate sharing, displaying, or storing images. Digital images may be stored and manipulated as raster or vector images. A third type of graphic file family, called "metafiles," uses both raster and vector elements.

The quality and resolution (clarity) of an image depend on the digital file's size and complexity. In raster graphics, images are stored as a set of squares, called "pixels." Each pixel has a color value and a color depth. This is defined by the number of "bits" allocated to each pixel. Pixels can range from 1 bit per pixel, which has a monochrome (two-color) depth, to 32-bit, or "true color." 32-bit color allows for more than four billion colors through various combinations. Raster graphics have the highest level of color detail because each pixel in the image can have its own color depth. For this reason, raster formats are used for photographs and in image programs such as Adobe Photoshop. However, the resolution of a raster image depends on size because the image has the same number of pixels at any magnification. For this reason, raster images cannot be magnified past a certain point without losing resolution.

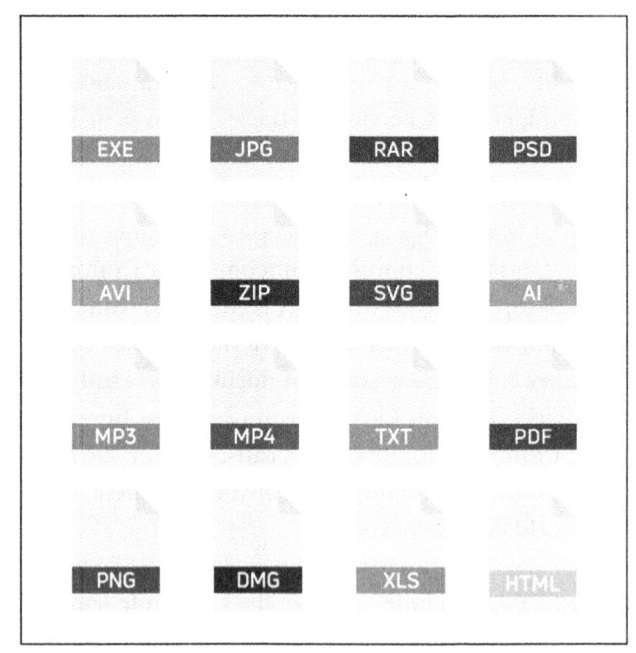

Photo via iStock/Olena Horbatiuk. [Used under license.]

Vector graphics store images as sets of polygons that are not size-dependent and look the same at any magnification. For relatively simple graphics, such as logos, vector files are smaller and more precise than raster images. However, vector files do not support complex colors or advanced effects, such as blurring or drop shadows. Depending on the image format, data may be lost after compression and restoration. Loss of image data reduces the quality of the image.

Two basic color models are used to digitally display various colors. The RGB color model, also called "additive color," combines red, green, and blue to create colors. The CMYK model, also called "subtractive color," combines the subtractive primary colors cyan, magenta, yellow, and black to absorb certain wavelengths of light while reflecting others.

IMAGE COMPRESSION

Image compression reduces the size of an image to enable easier storage and processing. Lossless compression uses a modeling algorithm that identifies repeated or redundant information contained within an image. It stores this information as a set of instructions can be used to reconstruct the image without any loss of data or resolution. One form of lossless compression commonly used is the LZW (Lempel-Ziv-Welch) compression algorithm developed in the 1980s. The LZW algorithm uses a "code table" or "dictionary" for compression. It scans data for repeated sequences and then adds these sequences to a "dictionary" within the compressed file. By replacing repeated data with references to the dictionary file, space is saved but no data is lost. Lossless compression is of benefit when image quality is essential but is less efficient at reducing image size. Lossy compression algorithms reduce file size by removing less "valuable" information. However, images compressed with lossy algorithms continue to lose resolution each time the image is compressed and decompressed. Despite the loss of image quality, lossy compression creates smaller files and is useful when image quality is less important or when computing resources are in high demand.

COMMON GRAPHIC FORMATS

JPEG (joint photographic experts group) is a type of lossy image compression format developed in the early 1990s. JPEGs support RGB and CMYK color and are most useful for small images, such as those used for display on websites. JPEGs are automatically compressed using a lossy algorithm. Thus, some image quality is lost each time the image is edited and saved as a new JPEG.

GIF (graphics interchange format) files have a limited color palette and use LZW compression so that they can be compressed without losing quality. Unlike JPEG, GIF supports "transparency" within an image by ignoring certain colors when displaying or printing. GIF files are open source and can be used in a wide variety of programs and applications. However, most GIF formats support only limited color because the embedded LZW compression is most effective when an image contains a limited color palette. PNGs (portable network graphics) are open-source alternatives to GIFs that support transparency and 24-bit color. This makes them better at complex colors than GIFs.

SVGs (scalable vector graphics) are an open-source format used to store and transfer vector images. SVG files lack built-in compression but can be compressed using external programs. In addition, there are "metafile" formats that can be used to share images combining both vector and raster elements. These include PDF (Portable Document Format) files, which are used to store and display documents, and the Encapsulated PostScript (EPS) format, which is typically used to transfer image files between programs.

—*Micah L. Issitt*

Further Reading

Brown, Adrian. "Graphics File Formats." *National Archives*, Aug. 2008, www.nationalarchives.gov.uk/documents/information-management/graphic-file-formats.pdf. Accessed 28 Nov. 2021.

Costello, Vic, Susan Youngblood, and Norman E. Youngblood. *Multimedia Foundations: Core Concepts for Digital Design*. 2nd ed., Routledge, 2017.

Dale, Nell, and John Lewis. *Computer Science Illuminated*. 6th ed., Jones & Bartlett Learning, 2016.

Gambetta, Gabriel. *Computer Graphics from Scratch*. No Starch Press, 2021.

"Introduction to Image Files Tutorial." *Boston University Information Services and Technology*, www.bu.edu/tech/support/research/training-consulting/online-tutorials/imagefiles/image101-1/. Accessed 28 Nov. 2021.

Marschner, Steve, et al. *Fundamentals of Computer Graphics*. 4th ed., CRC Press, 2016.

Prust, Z. A., and Peggy B. Deal. *Graphic Communications: Digital Design and Print Essentials*. 6th ed., Goodheart-Willcox, 2019.

Graphics Technologies

ABSTRACT
Graphics technology, which includes computer-generated imagery, has become an essential technology of the motion picture and video-gaming industries, of television, and of virtual reality. The production of such images, and especially of animated images, is a complex process that demands a sound understanding of not only physics and mathematics but also anatomy and physiology.

DEFINITION AND BASIC PRINCIPLES
While graphics technologies include all of the theoretical principles and physical methods used to produce images, the term more specifically refers to the principles and methods associated with digital or computer-generated images. Digital graphics are displayed as a limited array of colored picture elements (pixels). The greater the number of pixels that are used for an image, the greater the resolution of the image and the finer the detail that can be portrayed. The data that specifies the attributes of each individual pixel are stored in an electronic file using one of several specific formats. Each file format has its own characteristics with regard to how the image data can be manipulated and utilized.

Because the content of images is intended to portray real-world objects, the data for each image must be mathematically manipulated to reflect real-world structures and physics. The rendering of images, especially for photorealistic animation, is thus a calculation-intensive process. For images that are not produced photographically, special techniques and applications are continually being developed to produce image content that looks and moves as though it were real.

BACKGROUND AND HISTORY
Imaging is as old as the human race. Static graphics have historically been the norm up to the invention of the devices that could make a series of still pictures appear to move. The invention of celluloid in the late nineteenth century provided the material for photographic film, with the invention of motion picture cameras and projectors to follow. Animated films, commonly known as "cartoons," have been produced since the early twentieth century by repeatedly photographing a series of hand-drawn "cels." With the development of the digital computer and color displays in the second half of the twentieth century, it became possible to generate images without the need for hand-drawn intermediaries.

Computer graphics in the twenty-first century can produce images that are indistinguishable from traditional photographs of real objects. The methodology continues to develop in step with the development of new computer technology and new programming methods that make use of the computing abilities of the technology.

HOW IT WORKS
Images are produced initially as still or static images. Human perception requires about one-thirtieth of a second to process the visual information obtained through the seeing of a still image. If a sequential series of static images is displayed at a rate that exceeds the frequency of thirty images per second, the images are perceived as continuous motion. This is the basic principle of motion pictures, which are nothing more than displays of a sequential series of still pictures. Computer-generated still images (now indistinguishable from still photographs since the advent of digital cameras) have the same relationship to computer animation.

Images are presented on a computer screen as an array of colored dots called "pixels" (an abbreviation of "picture elements"). The clarity, or resolution, of the image depends on the number of pixels that it contains within a defined area. The more pixels within a defined area, the smaller each pixel must be and the finer the detail that can be displayed. In the 2010s, digital cameras typically captured image data in an array of between eight and fifty megapixels, though some specialty digital cameras manufactured later in the decade were capable of capturing that data in one hundred megapixels or more. The electronic data file of the image contains the specific color, hue, saturation, and brightness designations for each pixel in the associated image, as well as other information about the image itself.

To obtain photorealistic representation in computer-generated images, effects must be applied that correspond to the mathematical laws of physics. In still images, computational techniques such as ray tracing and reflection must be used to imitate the effect of light sources and reflective surfaces. For the virtual reality of the image to be effective, all of the actual physical characteristics that the subject would have if it were real must be clearly defined as well so that when the particular graphics application being used renders the image to the screen, all of the various parts of the image are displayed in their proper positions.

To achieve photorealistic effects in animation, the corresponding motion of each pixel must be coordinated with the defined surfaces of the virtual object, and their positions must be calculated for each frame of the animation. Because the motions of the objects would be strictly governed by the mathematics of physics in the real world, so must the motions of the virtual objects. For example, an animated image of a round object bouncing down a street must appear to obey the laws of gravity and Newtonian mechanics. Thus, the same mathematical equations that apply to the motion and properties of the real object must also apply to the virtual object.

Other essential techniques are required to produce realistic animated images. When two virtual objects are designed to interact as though they are real, solid objects, clipping instructions identify where the virtual solid surfaces of the objects are located; the instructions then mandate the clipping of any corresponding portions of an image to prevent the objects from seeming to pass through each other. Surface textures are mapped and associated with underlying data in such a way that movement corresponds to real body movements and surface responses. Image animation to produce realistic skin and hair effects is based on a sound understanding of anatomy and physiology and represents a specialized field of graphics technology.

APPLICATIONS AND PRODUCTS

Software. The vast majority of products and applications related to graphics technology are software applications created specifically to manipulate electronic data so that it produces realistic images and animations. The software ranges from basic paint programs installed on most personal computers (PCs) to full-featured programs that produce wireframe structures, map surface textures, coordinate behaviors, movements of surfaces to underlying structures, and 360-degree, three-dimensional (3D) animated views of the resulting images.

Other types of software applications are used to design objects and processes that are to be produced as real objects. Computer-assisted design (CAD) is commonly used to generate construction-specification drawings and to design printed circuit boards, electronic circuits and integrated circuits, complex machines, and many other real-world constructs. The features and capabilities of individual applications vary.

The simplest applications produce only a static image of a schematic layout, while the most advanced are capable of modeling the behavior of the system being designed in real time. The latter are increasingly useful in designing and virtually testing such dynamic systems as advanced jet engines and industrial processes. One significant benefit that has accrued from the use of such applications has been the ability to refine the efficiency of systems such as production lines in manufacturing facilities.

Hardware. The computational requirements of graphics can quickly exceed the capabilities of any particular computer system. This is especially true of PCs. Graphics technology in this area makes use of separate graphics processing units (GPUs) to handle the computational load of graphics display. This allows the PC's central processing unit (CPU) to carry out the other computational requirements of the application without having to switch back and forth between graphic and nongraphic tasks.

Many graphics boards also include dedicated memory for exclusive use in graphics processing. This eliminates the need for large sectors of a PC's random-access memory (RAM) to be used for storing graphics data, a requirement that can render a computer practically unusable.

Another requirement of hardware is an instruction system to operate the various components so that they function together. For graphics applications, with the long periods of time they require to carry out the calculations needed to render a detailed image, it is essential that the computer's operating system (OS) be functionally stable. The main operating systems of PCs are Microsoft Windows, the Apple macOS, the open-source OS Linux, and Google's Chrome OS. Some versions of other operating systems, such as Oracle Solaris, have been made available but do not account for a significant share of the PC market.

The huge amounts of graphics and rendering required for large-scale projects such as motion pictures demand the services of mainframe computers. The operating systems for these units have a longer history than do PC operating systems. Mainframe computers function primarily with the UNIX operating system, although many run under some variant of the Linux operating system. UNIX and Linux are similar operating systems, the main difference being that UNIX is a proprietary system whereas Linux is open source.

Motion pictures and television. Graphics technology is a hardware- and software-intensive field. The motion picture industry of the twenty-first century would not be possible without the digital technology that has been developed since 1980. While live-action images are often recorded on standard photographic film in the traditional way, motion picture special effects and animation have become the exclusive realm of digital graphics technologies. The use of computer-generated imagery (CGI) in motion pictures has driven the development of new technology and continually raised the standards of image quality. Amalgamating live action with CGI through digital processing and manipulation enables filmmakers to produce motion pictures in which live characters interact seamlessly with virtual characters, sometimes in entirely fantastic environments. Examples of such motion pictures are numerous in the science-fiction and fantasy film genres, but the technique is finding application in all areas, especially in educational programming. In addition, motion capture technology combines graphics with recorded human movement to create animated characters.

Video gaming and virtual training. The most graphics-intensive application is video gaming. All video games, in all genres, exist only as the graphic representation of complex program code. The variety of video game types ranges from straightforward computer versions of simple card games to complex 3D virtual worlds.

Many graphics software applications are developed for the use of game designers, but they have also made their way into many other imaging uses. The same software that is used to create a fictional virtual world can also be used to create virtual copies of the real world. This technology has been adapted for use in pilot- and driver-training programs in all aspects of transportation. Military, police, and security personnel are given extensive practical and scenario training through the use of virtual simulators. A simulator uses video and graphic displays of actual terrain to give the person being trained hands-on experience without endangering either personnel or actual machinery.

SOCIAL CONTEXT AND FUTURE PROSPECTS
Graphics technology is inextricably linked to the computer and digital electronics industries. Accordingly, graphics technology changes at a rate that at minimum equals the rate of change in those industries. Since 1980, graphics technology using computers has developed from the display of just sixteen colors on color television screens, yielding blocky image components and very slow animation effects, to photorealistic full-motion video, with the capacity to display more colors than the human eye can perceive and to display real-time animation in intricate detail. The rate of change in graphics technology exceeds that of computer technology because it also depends on the development of newer algorithms and coding strategies. Each of these changes produces a corresponding new set of applications and upgrades to graphic technology systems, in addition to the changes introduced to the technology itself.

Each successive generation of computer processors has introduced new architectures and capabilities that exceed those of the preceding generation, requiring that applications update both their capabilities and the manner in which those capabilities are performed. At the same time, advances in the technology of display devices require that graphics applications keep pace to display the best renderings possible. All of these factors combine to produce the unparalleled value of graphics technologies in modern society and into the future. With advances in 3D computer graphics and products such as smart glasses in the 2010s, graphics technologies have become even more immersive, allowing for a continually growing range of functions from education to game play.

—*Richard M. Renneboog, MSc*

Further Reading
Bi, Zhuming, and Xiaoqin Wang. *Computer Aided Design and Manufacturing*. Wiley-ASME Press, 2020.
Brown, Eric. "True Physics." *Game Developer*, vol. 17, no. 5, 2010, pp. 13-18.
Jimenez, Jorge, et al. "Destroy All Jaggies." *Game Developer*, vol. 18, no. 6, 2011, pp. 13-20.
Marschner, Steve, et al. *Fundamentals of Computer Graphics*. 4th ed., CRC Press, 2016.
Prust, Z. A., and Peggy B. Deal. *Graphic Communications: Digital Design and Print Essentials*. 6th ed., Goodheart-Willcox, 2019.
Wang, Yongtian, Xueming Li, and Yuxin Peng, editors. *Image and Graphics Technologies and Applications*. Springer Singapore, 2020.
Zhao, Pengfei, et al., editors. *Advanced Graphic Communications and Media Technologies*. Springer Singapore, 2017.

Heat-Exchanger Technologies

ABSTRACT
A heat exchanger transfers thermal energy from one flowing fluid to another. A car radiator transfers thermal energy from the engine-cooling water to the atmosphere. A nuclear power plant contains very large heat exchangers called "steam generators," which transfer thermal energy out of the water that circulates through the reactor core and makes steam that drives the turbines. In some heat exchangers, the two fluids mix together, while in others, the fluids are separated by a solid surface such as a tube wall.

DEFINITION AND BASIC PRINCIPLES
There are three modes of heat transfer. Conduction is the method of heat transfer within a solid. In closed heat exchangers, conduction is how thermal energy moves through the solid boundary that separates the two fluids. Convection is the method for transferring heat between a fluid and a solid surface. In a heat exchanger, heat moves out of the hotter fluid into the solid boundary by convection. That is also the way it moves from the solid boundary into the cooler fluid. The final mode of heat transfer is radiation. This is how the energy from the sun is transmitted through space to Earth.

The simplest type of closed heat exchanger is composed of a small tube running inside a larger one. One fluid flows through the inner tube, while the other fluid flows in the annular space between the inner and outer tubes. In most applications, a double-pipe heat exchanger would be very long and narrow. It is usually more appropriate to make the outer tube large in diameter and have many small tubes inside it. Such a device is called a "shell and tube" heat exchanger. When one of the fluids is a gas, fins are often added to heat-exchanger tubes on the gas side, which is usually on the outside.

Plate heat exchangers consist of many thin sheets of metal. One fluid flows across one side of each sheet, and the other fluid flows across the other side.

BACKGROUND AND HISTORY
Boilers were probably the first important heat exchangers. One of the first documented boilers was invented by Hero of Alexandria in the first century. This device included a crude steam turbine, but Hero's engine was little more than a toy. The first truly useful boiler may have been invented by the Marquess of Worcester in about 1663. His boiler provided steam to drive a water pump. Further developments were made by British engineer Thomas Savery and British blacksmith Thomas Newcomen, though many people mistakenly believe that James Watt invented the steam engine. Watt invented the condenser, another kind of heat exchanger. Combining the condenser with existing engines made them much more efficient. Until the late nineteenth century, boilers and condensers dominated the heat-exchanger scene. The invention of the diesel engine in 1897 by Bavarian engineer Rudolf Diesel gave rise to the need for other heat exchangers: lubricating oil coolers, radiators, and fuel oil heaters.

During the twentieth century, heat exchangers grew rapidly in number, size, and variety. Plate heat exchangers were invented. The huge steam generators used in nuclear plants were produced. Highly specialized heat exchangers were developed for use in spacecraft. As heat exchangers grew increasingly specialized and complex, tools such as computer-aided design (CAD) software became useful resources for engineers working in that field, offering new methods of designing and modeling multiple types of heat exchanger. By pairing CAD software with simulation programs, engineers could likewise perform virtual tests of the modeled equipment in order to assess the functionality of new heat exchangers and troubleshoot problems with existing systems.

HOW IT WORKS

Thermal calculations. There are two kinds of thermal calculations: design calculations and rating calculations. In design calculations, engineers know what rate of heat transfer is needed in a particular application. The dimensions of the heat exchanger that will satisfy the need must be determined. In rating calculations, an existing heat exchanger is to be used in a new situation. The rate of heat transfer that it will provide in this situation must be determined.

In both design and rating analyses, engineers must deal with the following resistances to heat transfer: the convection resistance between the hot fluid and the solid boundary, the conduction resistance of the solid boundary itself, and the convection resistance between the solid boundary and the cold fluid. The conduction resistance is easy to calculate. It depends only on the thickness of the boundary and the thermal conductivity of the boundary material. Calculation of the convection resistances is much more complicated. They depend on the velocities of the fluid flows and on the properties of the fluids such as viscosity, thermal conductivity, heat capacity, and density. The geometries of the flow passages are also a factor.

Because the convection resistances are so complicated, they are usually determined by empirical methods. This means that research engineers have conducted many experiments, graphed the results, and found equations that represent the lines on their graphs. Other engineers use these graphs or equations to predict the convection resistances in their heat exchangers.

In liquids, the convection resistance is usually low, but in gases, it is usually high. In order to compensate for high convection resistance, fins are often installed on the gas side of heat-exchanger tubes. This can increase the amount of heat transfer area on the gas side by a factor of ten without significantly increasing the overall size of the heat exchanger.

Hydraulic calculations. Fluid friction and turbulence within a heat exchanger cause the exit pressure of each fluid to be lower than its entrance pres-

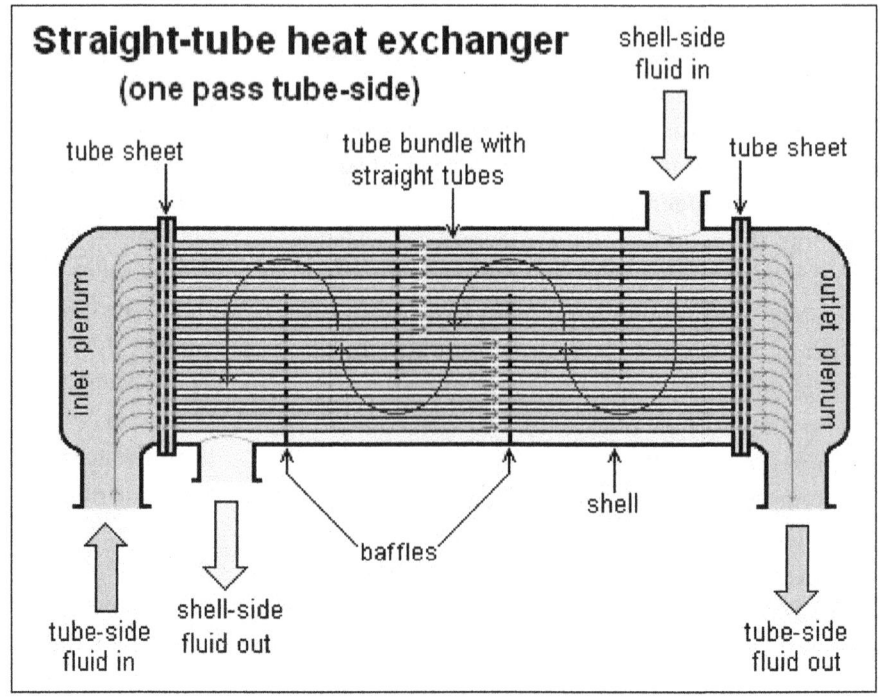

A shell and tube heat exchanger. Image by H Padleckas, via Wikimedia Commons.

sure. It is desirable to minimize this pressure drop. If a fluid is made to flow by a pump, increased pressure drop will require more pumping power. As with convection resistance, pressure drop depends on many factors and is difficult to predict accurately. Empirical methods are again used. Generally, design changes that reduce the convection resistance will increase the pressure drop, so engineers must reach a compromise between these issues.

Strength calculations. The pressure of the fluid flowing inside the tubes is often significantly different from the pressure of the fluid flowing around the outside. Engineers must ensure that the tubes are strong enough to withstand this pressure difference so the tubes do not burst. Similarly, the pressure of the fluid in the shell (outside the tubes) is often significantly different from the atmospheric pressure outside the shell. The shell must be strong enough to withstand this.

Fouling. In many applications, one or both fluids may cause corrosion of heat-exchanger tubes, and they may deposit unwanted material on the tube surfaces. River water may deposit mud. Seawater may deposit barnacles and other biological contamination. The general term for all these things is "fouling." The tubes may have a layer of fouling on the inside surface and another one on the outside. In addition to the two convection resistances and the conduction resistance, there may be two fouling resistances. When heat exchangers are designed, a reasonable allowance must be made for these fouling resistances.

APPLICATIONS AND PRODUCTS

Heat exchangers come in an amazing variety of shapes and sizes. They are used with fluids ranging from liquid metals to water and air. A home with hot-water heat has a heat exchanger in each room. They are called "radiators," but they rely on convection, not radiation. A room air conditioner has two heat exchangers in it. One transfers heat from room air to the refrigerant, and the other transfers heat from the refrigerant to outside air. Cars with water-cooled engines have a heat exchanger to get rid of engine heat. It is called a "radiator," but again it relies on convection.

Boilers. Boilers come in two basic types: fire tube and water tube. In both cases, the heat transfer is between the hot gases produced by combustion of fuel and water that is turning to steam. As the name suggests, a fire-tube boiler has very hot gas, not actually fire, inside the tubes. These tubes are submerged in water, which absorbs heat and turns into steam. In a water-tube boiler, water goes inside the tubes and hot gases pass around them. Water-tube boilers often include superheaters. These heat exchangers allow the steam to flow through tubes that are exposed to the hot combustion gases. As a result, the final temperature of the steam may reach 1,000° Fahrenheit (538° Celsius) or higher. An important and dangerous kind of fouling in boilers is called "scale." Scale forms when minerals in the water come out of solution and form a layer of fouling on the hot tube surface. Scale is dangerous because it causes the tube metal behind it to get hotter. In high-performance boilers, this can cause a tube to overheat and burst.

Condensers. Many electric plants have generators driven by steam turbines. As steam leaves a turbine it is transformed back into liquid water in a condenser. This increases the efficiency of the system, and it recovers the mineral-free water for reuse. A typical condenser has thousands of tubes with cooling water flowing inside them. Steam flows around the outsides, transfers heat, and turns back into liquid water. The cooling water may come from a river or ocean. When a source of a large amount of water is not available, cooling water may be recirculated through a cooling tower. Hot cooling water leaving the condenser is sprayed into a stream of atmospheric air. Some of it evaporates, which lowers the temperature of the remaining water. This remaining

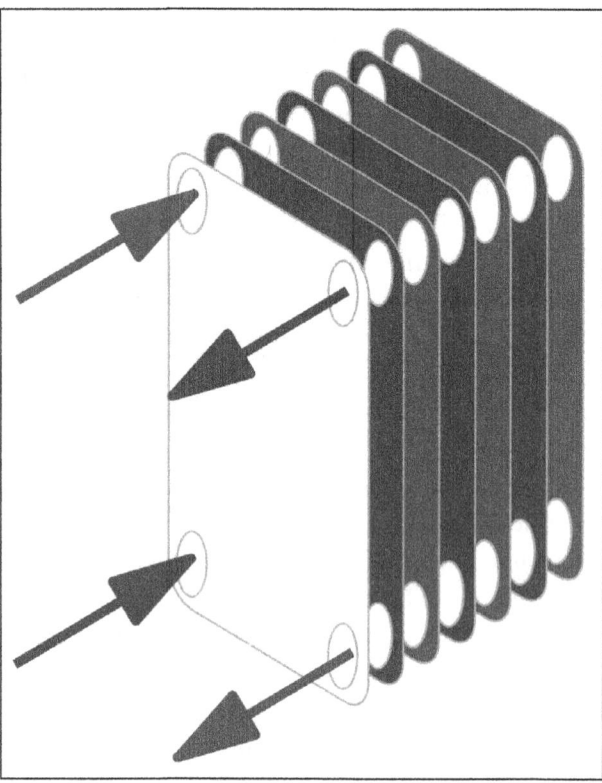

Conceptual diagram of a plate and frame heat exchanger. Image by Malyszkz, via Wikimedia Commons.

water can be reused as cooling water in the condenser. The water that evaporates must be replaced from some source, but the quantity of new water needed is much less than when cooling water is used only once. When river water or seawater is used for cooling, there may be significant fouling on the insides of the tubes. Because the steam leaving a turbine contains very small droplets of water moving at high speed, erosion on the outsides of the tubes is a problem. Eventually a hole may develop, and cooling water, which contains dissolved minerals, can leak into the condensing steam.

Steam generators. In a pressurized-water nuclear power plant, there is a huge heat exchanger called a "steam generator." The primary loop contains water under high pressure that circulates through the reactor core. This water, which does not boil, then moves to the steam generator, where it flows inside a large number of tubes. Secondary water at lower pressure surrounds these tubes. As the secondary water absorbs heat it turns into steam. This steam is used to drive the turbines. Steam generators are among the largest heat exchangers in existence.

Deaerators. Because the condensers in steam systems operate with internal pressures below one atmosphere, air may leak in. Some of this air dissolves in the water that forms as steam condenses. If this air remained in the water as it reached the boiler, rapid rusting of boiler surfaces would result. To prevent this, an open heat exchanger, called a "deaerator," is installed. Water is sprayed into the deaerator as a fine mist, and steam is also admitted. As the steam and water mix, the water droplets are heated to their boiling point but not actually boiled. The solubility of air in water goes to zero as the water temperature approaches the boiling point, so nearly all air is forced out of solution in the deaerator. Once the air is in gaseous form, it is removed from the system.

Feedwater heaters. Leaving the deaerator, the water in a steam plant is on its way to the boiler. The system can be made more efficient by preheating the water along the way. This is done in a feedwater heater. Steam is extracted from the steam turbines to serve as the heat source in feedwater heaters. Feedwater flows inside the tubes and steam flows around the tubes. Feedwater heaters are often multipass heat exchangers. This means that the feedwater passes back and forth through the heat exchanger several times. This makes the heat exchanger shorter and fatter, which is a more convenient shape.

Intercoolers. Many diesel engines have turbochargers that pressurize the air being fed to the cylinders. As air is compressed, its temperature rises. It is desirable to lower the temperature of the air before it enters the cylinders, because that means a greater mass of air can occupy the same space. More air in the cylinder means more fuel can be burned, and more power can be produced. An intercooler is a closed heat exchanger between the turbocharger and the engine cylinders. In this device, air passes around the tubes, and cooling water passes inside them. There are usually fins on the outsides of the tubes to provide increased heat transfer area.

Industrial air compressors also have intercoolers. These compressors are two-stage machines. That means air is compressed part way in one cylinder and the rest of the way in another. As with turbochargers, the first compression raises the air temperature. An intercooler is often installed between the cylinders. Compressed air flows through the intercooler tubes. Either atmospheric air or cooling water flows around the outside. Cooling the air before the second compression reduces the power required there.

CAREERS AND COURSEWORK

Heat exchangers are usually designed by mechanical engineers who hold bachelor of science (BS) or master of science (MS) degrees in this field. Students of mechanical engineering take courses in advanced mathematics, mechanics of materials, thermodynamics, fluid mechanics, and heat transfer. An MS degree provides advanced understanding of the physical phenomena involved in heat exchangers. Research into the theory of heat transfer is normally carried out by mechanical engineers with doctoral degrees. They conduct research in laboratories, at universities, private research companies, or large corporations that build heat exchangers. Convection heat transfer calculations rely on equations that are derived from extensive experiments, and much research work continues to be devoted to improving the accuracy of these equations.

Construction of heat exchangers is executed by companies large and small. The work is carried out by skilled tradespeople using precise machine tools and other equipment. Machinists, welders, sheet-metal, and other highly trained workers are involved. Students who pursue such careers may begin with vocational-technical training at the high school level. They become apprentices to one of these trades. During apprenticeship, the workers receive formal training in classrooms and on-the-job training. As their skills develop, they become journeymen and then master mechanics.

Workers who operate, maintain, and repair heat exchangers have a variety of backgrounds. Some have engineering or engineering technology degrees. Others have vocational-technical and on-the-job training. At nuclear power plants, the Nuclear Regulatory Commission requires a program of extensive testing of the vital heat exchangers. This is carried out by engineers with BS or MS degrees, assisted by skilled tradespeople.

SOCIAL CONTEXT AND FUTURE PROSPECTS

Although heat exchangers are not glamorous, they are an essential part of people's lives. Most homes have several, as do all cars and trucks. Without heat exchangers, people would still be heating their homes with fireplaces, and engines of all types and sizes would not be possible. Heat exchangers are essential in all manner of industries. In particular, they play a key role in the generation of electricity.

The design of heat exchangers is based on empirical methods rather than basic principles. While empirical methods are reasonably effective, design from basic principles would be preferred. In the first half of the twenty-first century, extensive research projects are under way with the goal of solving the very complicated equations that represent the basic principles of heat transfer. These projects make use of very powerful computers. As the cost of computers continues to drop and their power continues to increase, heat exchangers may come to be designed from basic principles.

—Edwin G. Wiggins, BS, MS, PhD

Further Reading

Babcock and Wilcox Company. *Steam: Its Generation and Use*. Kessinger, 2010.

Blank, David A., Arthur E. Bock, and David J. Richardson. *Introduction to Naval Engineering*. 2nd ed., Naval Institute Press, 2005.

"Computational Fluid Dynamics in Heat Exchanger Design and Analysis." *HRS Heat Exchangers*, www.hrs-heatexchangers.com/us/resource/computational-fluid-dynamics-in-heat-exchanger-design-and-analysis/. Accessed 28 Nov. 2021.

Hesselgreaves, J. E., Richard Law, and David Reay. *Compact Heat Exchangers: Selection, Design and Operation*. 2nd ed., Butterworth-Heinemann, 2016.

McGeorge, H. D. *Marine Auxiliary Machinery*. 7th ed., Butterworth, 1995.

Ranganayakulu, C., and K. N. Seetharamu. *Compact Heat Exchangers: Analysis Design and Optimization Using FEM and CFD Approach*. Wiley-ASME Press, 2018.

HYBRID VEHICLE TECHNOLOGIES

ABSTRACT

Hybrid vehicle technologies use shared systems of electrical and gas power to create ecologically sustainable industrial and passenger vehicles. With both types of vehicles, the main goals are to reduce hazardous emissions and conserve fuel consumption.

DEFINITION AND BASIC PRINCIPLES

As the word "hybrid" suggests, hybrid vehicle technology seeks to develop an automobile (or, more broadly defined, any power-driven mechanical system) using power from at least two different sources. During the late twentieth and early twenty-first centuries, hybrid technology emphasized the combination of an internal combustion engine working with an electric motor component.

BACKGROUND AND HISTORY

Before technological development of what is now called a "hybrid vehicle," the automobile industry, by necessity, had to have two existing forms of motor energy to hybridize—namely internal combustion in combination with some form of electric power. Early versions of cars driven with electric motors emerged in the 1890s and seemed destined to compete very seriously with both gasoline (internal combustion engines) and steam engines at the turn of the twentieth century.

Although development of commercially attractive hybrid vehicles would not occur until the middle of the twentieth century, the Austrian engineer Ferdinand Porsche made a first-series hybrid automobile in 1900. Within a short time, however, the commercial attractiveness of mass-produced internal combustion engines became the force that dominated the automobile industry for more than a half century. Experimentation with hybrid technology as it could be applied to other forms of transport, especially motorcycles, however, continued throughout this early period.

By the 1970s the main emerging goal of hybrid car engineering was to reduce exhaust emissions; conservation of fuel was a secondary consideration. This situation changed when, in the wake of the 1973 Arab-Israeli War, many petroleum-producing countries supporting the Arab cause cut exports drastically, causing a nationwide gas shortage and worldwide fears that oil would be used as a political weapon. Until 1975, government support for research and development of hybrid cars was tied to the Environmental Protection Agency (EPA). In that year (and after at least two unsatisfactory results of EPA-supported hybrid car projects), this role was shifted to the Energy Research and Development Administration, which later became the US Department of Energy (DOE).

During the decade that followed the introduction of Honda's Insight hybrid car in 1999, the most widely recognized commercially marketed hybrid automobile was Toyota's Prius, a vehicle first sold in Japan in 1997 but not released outside of that country until 2000. Despite some setbacks in sales following major recalls connected with (among other less dangerous problems) the malfunctioning antilock braking system and accelerator devices, Prius models remained popular among drivers and represented 8 percent of hybrid car sales in the United States in 2020. Other popular hybrid vehicles during that period included Toyota's hybrid RAV4 and Highlander models, the hybrid incarnation of the Honda CRV, and the hybrid Ford Escape. As with other sectors of the automotive industry, the hybrid vehicle sector of the late twentieth and early twenty-first centuries benefited significantly from advances in computer-aided design (CAD) software, which enabled designers to create digital drawings and three-dimensional (3D) models of in-development vehicles throughout the design process.

HOW IT WORKS

"Integrated motor assist," a common layperson's engineering phrase borrowed from Honda's late-1990s technology, suggests a simple explanation of how a hybrid vehicle works. The well-known relationship between the electrical starter motor and the gas-driven engine in an internal combustion engine (ICE) car provides a (technically incomplete) analogy: The electric starter motor takes the load needed to turn the crankcase (and the wheels if gears are engaged) until the ICE itself kicks in. This overly general analogy could be carried further by including the alternator in the system, since it relieves the battery of the job of supplying constant electricity to the running engine (recharging the battery at the same time).

In a hybrid system, however, power from the electric motor (or the gas engine) enters and leaves the drivetrain as the demand for power to move the vehicle increases or decreases. To obtain optimum results in terms of carbon dioxide emissions and overall fuel efficiency, the power train of most hybrid vehicles is designed to depend on a relatively small internal combustion engine with various forms of rechargeable electrical energy. Although petroleum-driven ICEs are commonly used, hybrid car engineering is not limited to petroleum. Ethanol, biodiesel, and natural gas have also been used.

The Toyota Prius is the world's best selling hybrid car, with cumulative global sales of almost 4 million units up until January 2017. Photo by Vauxford, via Wikimedia Commons.

In a parallel hybrid, the electric motor and ICE are installed so that they can power the vehicle either individually or together. These power sources are integrated by automatically controlled clutches. For electric driving, the clutch between the ICE and the gearbox is disengaged, while the clutch connecting the electric motor to the gearbox is engaged. A typical situation requiring simultaneous operation of the ICE and the electric motor would be for rapid acceleration (as in passing) or in climbing hills. Reliance on the electric motor would happen only when the car is braking, coasting, or advancing on level surfaces.

It is extremely important to note that one of the most vital challenges for researchers involved in hybrid-vehicle technology has to do with variable options for supplying electricity to the system. It is far too simple to say that the electrical motor is run by a rechargeable battery, since a wide range of batteries (and alternatives to batteries) exists. A primary and obvious concern, of course, will always be reducing battery weight. To this aim, several carmakers, including Ford, have developed highly effective first-, second-, and even third-generation lithium-ion batteries. Many engineers predict that, in the future, hydrogen-driven fuel cells will play a bigger role in the electrical components of hybrids.

Selection of the basic source of electrical power ties in with corollary issues such as calculation of the driving range (time elapsed and distances covered before the electrical system must be recharged) and optimal technologies for recharging. The simplest scenario for recharging, which is an early direct borrowing from pure-electric car technology, involves plugging into a household outlet (either 110 volt or 220 volt) overnight. However, hybrid-car engineers have developed several more sophisticated methods. One is a "subhybrid" procedure, which uses very lightweight fuel cells in combination with conventional batteries (the latter being recharged by the fuel cells while the vehicle is underway). Research engineers continue to look at any number of ways to tweak energy and power sources from different phases of hybrid vehicle operation. One example, which has been used in Honda's Insight, is a process that temporarily converts the motor into a generator when the car does not require application of the accelerator. Other channels are being investigated for tapping kinetic-energy recovery during different phases of simple mechanical operation of hybrid vehicles.

APPLICATIONS AND PRODUCTS

Some countries, especially Japan, have begun to use the principle of the hybrid engine for heavy-duty transport or construction-equipment needs, as well as hybrid systems for diesel road graders and new forms of diesel-powered industrial cranes. Hybrid medium-power commercial vehicles, especially urban trolleys and buses, have been manufactured, mainly in Europe and Japan. Important for broad ecological planning, several countries, including China and Japan, have incorporated hybrid (diesel combined with electric) technology into their programs for rail transport. The biggest potential consumer market for hybrid technology, however, is probably in the private automobile sector.

By the third decade of the twenty-first century, a wide variety of commercially produced hybrid automobiles had been introduced into the market. Among US manufacturers, Ford developed the increasingly popular Escape, and General Motors produced models ranging from Chevrolet's economical Volt to Cadillac's more expensive Escalade. Japanese manufacturers Nissan, Honda, and Toyota introduced several standard hybrid models, to which one should add Lexus's RX semi-luxury and technologically more advanced series of cars. Korea's Hyundai Elantra and Germany's Volkswagen Golf also competed for some share of the market.

At the outset of 2011, Lexus launched an ambitious campaign to attract attention to what it called its "full hybrid technology" (as compared with mild hybrid) in its high-end RX models. A main feature of the full hybrid system, according to Lexus, is a combination of both series and parallel hybrid power in one vehicle. Such a combination aims at transferring a variable but continuously optimum ratio of gas-engine and electric-motor power to the car. Another advance claimed by Lexus's full hybrid over parallel hybrids is its reliance on the electric motor only at lower speeds.

As fuel alternatives continue to be added to the ICE components of hybrid electric vehicles (HEVs), advanced fuel-cell technology could transform the technological field that supplies electrical energy to the combined system.

CAREERS AND COURSEWORK

Academic preparation for careers tied to HEV technology is, of course, closely tied to the fields of electrical and mechanical engineering and, perhaps to a lesser degree, chemistry. All of these fields demand coursework at the undergraduate level to develop familiarity not only with engineering principles but with basic sciences and mathematics used, especially those used by physicists. Beyond a bachelor's degree, graduate-level preparation would include continuation of all of the above subjects at more advanced levels, plus an eventual choice for specialization, based on the assumption that some subfields of engineering are more relevant to HEV technology than others.

The most obvious employment possibilities for engineers interested in HEV technology is with actual manufacturers of automobiles or heavy equipment. Depending on the applicant's academic background, employment with manufacturing firms can range from hands-on engineering applications to more conceptually based research and design functions.

Employment openings in research may be found with a wide variety of private-sector firms, some involving studies of environmental impact, others embedded in actual hybrid-engineering technology. One outstanding example of a major private firm that is engaged on an international level in environmentally sustainable technology linked to hybrid vehicle research is ABB. ABB grew from late-nineteenth-century origins in electrical lighting and generator manufacturing in Sweden (ASEA), merging in 1987 with the Swiss firm Brown Boveri. ABB carries on operations in many locations throughout the world.

Internationally known US firm Argonne National Laboratory not only produces research data but also serves as a training ground for engineers who either move on to work with smaller ecology-sensitive engineering enterprises or enter government agencies and university research programs. Finally, employment with government agencies, especially the EPA, the DOE, and Department of Transportation, represents a viable alternative for applicants with requisite advanced engineering and managerial training.

SOCIAL CONTEXT AND FUTURE PROSPECTS

Although obvious ecological advantages can result as more and more buyers of new vehicles opt for hybrid cars, a variety of potentially negative socioeconomic factors could come into play, certainly over the short to medium term. The higher sales price of hybrids that were available during the first decades of the twenty-first century already raised the question of consumer ability (or willingness) to pay more at the outset for fuel-economy savings that would have to be spread out over a fairly long time frame—possibly even longer than the owner kept the vehicle. It is nearly impossible to predict the number of potential buyers whose statistically lower purchasing ability prevents them from paying higher prices for hybrids. Continued unwillingness or inability to purchase hybrids would mean that a proportionally large number of used older-model ICE's (or brand-new models of older-technology vehicles) would remain on the roads. This socioeconomic potentiality remains linked, of course, to any investment strategies under consideration by industrial producers of cars.

—Byron D. Cannon, MA, PhD

Further Reading

"Alternative Fuels Data Center: Hybrid Electric Vehicles." *Energy Efficiency & Renewable Energy*, US Department of Energy, 28 Sept. 2016, www.afdc.energy.gov/vehicles/electric_basics_hev.html. Accessed 28 Nov. 2021.

Bethscheider-Kieser, Ulrich. *Green Designed: Future Cars*. Avedition, 2008.

Clemens, Kevin. *The Crooked Mile: Through Peak Oil, Hybrid Cars and Global Climate Change to Reach a Brighter Future*. Demontreville Press, 2009.

Fish, Tom. "The 10 Most Popular Hybrid Car Models in America." *Newsweek*, 14 May 2021, www.newsweek.com/most-popular-hybrid-car-models-america-1590402. Accessed 28 Nov. 2021.

Hirz, Mario, Patrick Rossbacher, and Jana Gulanová. "Future Trends in CAD—From the Perspective of Automotive Industry." *Computer-Aided Design and Applications*, vol. 14, no. 6, 217, pp. 734-41.

"How 3D Modeling Software Meet the Requirements of the Automotive Industry." *ZWSoft*, 28 May 2021, www.zwsoft.com/news/zwschool/how-3d-modeling-software-meet-the-requirements-of-the-automotive-industry. Accessed 28 Nov. 2021.

Lim, Kieran. *Hybrid Cars, Fuel-Cell Buses and Sustainable Energy Use*. Royal Australian Chemical Institute, 2004.

Motoyama, Yasuyuki. *Global Companies, Local Innovations: Why the Engineering Aspects of Innovation Making Require Co-Location*. Routledge, 2016.

Hydraulic Engineering

ABSTRACT

Hydraulic engineering is a branch of civil engineering concerned with the properties, flow, control, and uses of water. Its applications are in the fields of water supply, sewerage evacuation, water recycling, flood management, irrigation, and the generation of electricity. Hydraulic engineering is an essential element in the design of many civil and environmental engineering projects and structures, such as water distribution systems, wastewater management systems, drainage systems, dams, hydraulic turbines, channels, canals, bridges, dikes, levees, weirs, tanks, pumps, and valves.

DEFINITION AND BASIC PRINCIPLES

Hydraulic engineering is a branch of civil engineering that focuses on the flow of water and its role in civil engineering projects. The principles of hydraulic engineering are rooted in fluid mechanics. The conservation of mass principle (or the continuity principle) is the cornerstone of hydraulic analysis and design. It states that the mass going into a control volume within fixed boundaries is equal to the rate of increase of mass within the same control volume. For an incompressible fluid with fixed boundaries, such as water flowing through a pipe, the continuity equation is simplified to state that the inflow rate is equal to the outflow rate. For unsteady flow in a channel or a reservoir, the continuity principle states that the flow rate into a control volume minus the outflow rate is equal to the time rate of change of storage within the control volume.

Energy is always conserved, according to the first law of thermodynamics, which states that energy can neither be created nor be destroyed. Also, all forms of energy are equivalent. In fluid mechanics, there are mainly three forms of head (energy expressed in unit of length). First, the potential head is equal to the elevation of the water particle above an arbitrary datum. Second, the pressure head is proportional to the water pressure. Third, the kinetic head is proportional to the square of the velocity. Therefore, the conservation of energy principle states that the potential, pressure, and kinetic heads of water entering a control volume, plus the head gained from any pumps in the control volume, are equal to the potential, pressure, and kinetic heads of water exiting the control volume, plus the friction loss head and any head lost in the system, such as the head lost in a turbine to generate electricity.

Hydraulic engineering deals with water quantity (flow, velocity, and volume) and not water quality, which falls under sanitary and environmental engineering. However, hydraulic engineering is an essential element in designing sanitary engineering facilities such as wastewater-treatment plants.

Hydraulic engineering is often mistakenly thought to be petroleum engineering, which deals with the flow of natural gas and oil in pipelines, or the branch of mechanical engineering that deals with a vehicle's engine, gas pump, and hydraulic braking system. The only machines that are of concern to hydraulic engineers are hydraulic turbines and water pumps.

Hydraulic flood retention basin. Photo by Qinli Yang/ Will McMinn, via Wikimedia Commons.

BACKGROUND AND HISTORY

Irrigation and water supply projects were built by ancient civilizations long before mathematicians defined the governing principles of fluid mechanics. In the Andes Mountains in Peru, remains of irrigation canals were found, radiocarbon dating from the fourth millennium BCE. The first dam for which there are reliable records was built before 4000 BCE on the Nile River in Memphis in ancient Egypt. Egyptians built dams and dikes to divert the Nile's floodwaters into irrigation canals. Mesopotamia (now Iraq and western Iran) has low rainfall and is supplied with surface water by two major rivers, the Tigris and the Euphrates, which are much smaller than the Nile but have more dramatic floods in the spring. Mesopotamian engineers, concerned about water storage and flood control as well as irrigation, built diversion dams and large weirs to create reservoirs and to supply canals that carried water for long distances. In the Indus Valley civilization (now Pakistan and northwestern India), sophisticated irrigation and storage systems were developed.

One of the most impressive dams of ancient times is near Marib, an ancient city in Yemen. The 1,600-foot-long dam was built of masonry strengthened by copper around 600 BCE. It holds back some of the annual floodwaters coming down the valley and diverts the rest of that water out of sluice gates and into a canal system. The same sort of diversion dam system was independently built in Arizona by the Hohokam civilization around the second or third century CE. In the Szechuan region of ancient China, the Dujiangyan irrigation system was built around 250 BCE and still supplies water in modern times. By the second century CE, the Chinese used chain pumps, which lifted water from lower to higher elevations, powered by hydraulic waterwheels, manual foot pedals, or rotating mechanical wheels pulled by oxen.

The Minoan civilization developed an aqueduct system in 1500 BCE to convey water in tubular conduits in the city of Knossos in Crete. Roman aqueducts were built to carry water from large distances to Rome and other cities in the empire. Of the 800 miles of aqueducts in Rome, only 29 miles were above ground. The Romans kept most of their aqueducts underground to protect their water from enemies and diseases spread by animals.

The Muslim agricultural revolution flourished during the Islamic golden age in various parts of Asia and Africa, as well as in Europe. Islamic hydraulic engineers built water management technological complexes, consisting of dams, canals, screw pumps, and *norias*, which are wheels that lift water from a river into an aqueduct.

The Swiss mathematician Daniel Bernoulli published *Hydrodynamica* (1738; Hydrodynamics by Daniel Bernoulli, 1968), applying the discoveries of Sir Isaac Newton and Gottfried Wilhelm Leibniz in mathematics and physics to fluid systems. In 1752, Leonhard Euler, Bernoulli's colleague, developed the more generalized form of the energy equation.

In 1843, Adhémar Jean Claude Barré de Saint Venant developed the most general form of the differential equations describing the motion of fluids, known as the "Saint Venant equations." They are sometimes called "Navier-Stokes equations" after Claude-Louis Navier and Sir George Gabriel Stokes, who were working on them around the same time.

The German scientist Ludwig Prandtl and his students studied the interactions between fluids and solids between 1900 and 1930, thus developing the boundary layer theory, which theoretically explains the drag or friction between pipe walls and a fluid.

Much like other branches of civil engineering, the field of hydraulic engineering benefited significantly from the development of computer-aided design (CAD) technology throughout the late twentieth and early twenty-first centuries. By 2021, CAD software such as Autodesk's Civil 3D enabled hydraulic engineers to design and model infrastructure such as dams and irrigation systems as well as to perform hydraulic analysis, among other tasks.

HOW IT WORKS

Properties of water. Density and viscosity are important properties in fluid mechanics. The density of a fluid is its mass per unit volume. When the temperature or pressure of water changes significantly, its density variation remains negligible. Therefore, water is assumed to be incompressible. Viscosity, on the other hand, is the measure of a fluid's resistance to shear or deformation. Heavy oil is more viscous than water, whereas air is less viscous than water. The viscosity of water increases with reduced temperatures. For instance, the viscosity of water at its freezing point is six times its viscosity at its boiling temperature. Therefore, a flow of colder water assumes higher friction.

Hydrostatics. Hydrostatics is a subdiscipline of fluid mechanics that examines the pressures in water at rest and the forces on floating bodies or bodies submerged in water. When water is at rest, as in a tank or a large reservoir, it does not experience shear stresses; therefore, only normal pressure is present. When the pressure is uniform over the surface of a body in water, the total force applied on the body is a product of its surface area times the pressure. The direction of the force is perpendicular (normal) to the surface. Hydrostatic pressure forces can be mathematically determined on any shape. Buoyancy, for instance, is the upward vertical force applied on floating bodies (such as boats) or submerged ones (such as submarines). Hydraulic engineers use hydrostatics to compute the forces on submerged gates in reservoirs and detention basins.

Fluid kinematics. Water flowing at a steady rate in a constant-diameter pipe has a constant average velocity. The viscosity of water introduces shear stresses between particles that move at different velocities. The velocity of the particle adjacent to the wall of the pipe is zero. The velocity increases for particles away from the wall, and it reaches its maximum at the center of the pipe for a particular flow rate or pipe discharge. The velocity profile in a pipe has a parabolic shape. Hydraulic engineers use the average velocity of the velocity profile distribution, which is the flow rate over the cross-sectional area of the pipe.

Bernoulli's theorem. When friction is negligible and there are no hydraulic machines, the conservation of energy principle is reduced to Bernoulli's equation, which has many applications in pressurized flow and open-channel flow when it is safe to neglect the losses.

APPLICATIONS AND PRODUCTS

Water distribution systems. A water distribution network consists of pipes and several of the following components: reservoirs, pumps, elevated storage tanks, valves, and other appurtenances such as surge tanks or standpipes. Regardless of its size and complexity, a water distribution system serves the purpose of transferring water from one or more sources to customers. There are raw and treated water systems. A raw water network transmits water from a storage reservoir to treatment plants via large pipes, also called "transmission mains." The purpose of a treated water network is to move water from a water-treatment plant and distribute it to water retailers through transmission mains or directly to municipal and industrial customers through smaller distribution mains.

Some water distribution systems are branched, whereas others are looped. The latter type offers more reliability in case of a pipe failure. The hydraulic engineering problem is to compute the steady velocity or flow rate in each pipe and the pressure at each junction node by solving a large set of continuity equations and nonlinear energy equations that characterize the network. The steady solution of a branched network is easily obtained mathematically; however, the looped network initially offered challenges to engineers. In 1936, American structural engineer Hardy Cross developed a simplified method that tackled networks formed of only pipes. In the 1970s and 1980s, three other categories of numerical methods were developed to provide solutions for complex networks with pumps and valves. In 1996, engineer Habib A. Basha and his colleagues offered a perturbation solution to the nonlinear set of equations in a direct, mathematical fashion, thus eliminating the risk of divergent numerical solutions.

Hydraulic transients in pipes. Unsteady flow in pipe networks can be gradual; therefore, it can be modeled as a series of steady solutions in an extended period simulation, mostly useful for water-quality analysis. However, abrupt changes in a valve position, a sudden shutoff of a pump because of power failure, or a rapid change in demand could cause a hydraulic transient or a water hammer that travels back and forth in the system at high speed, causing large pressure fluctuations that could cause pipe rupture or collapse.

The solution of the quasi-linear partial differential equations that govern the hydraulic transient problem is more challenging than the steady network solution. The Russian scientist Nikolai Zhukovsky offered a simplified arithmetic solution in 1904. Many other methods—graphical, algebraic, wave-plane analysis, implicit, and linear methods, as well as the method of characteristics-were introduced between the 1950s and 1990s. In 1996, Basha and his colleagues published another paper solving the hydraulic transient problem in a direct, noniterative fashion, using the mathematical concept of perturbation.

Open-channel flow. Unlike pressure flow in full pipes, which is typical for water distribution systems, flow in channels, rivers, and partially full pipes is called "gravity flow." Pipes in wastewater evacuation and drainage systems usually flow partially full with a free water surface that is subject to atmospheric pressure. This is the case for human-built canals and channels (earth or concrete lined) and natural creeks and rivers.

The velocity in an open channel depends on the area of the cross section, the length of the wetted perimeter, the bed slope, and the roughness of the channel bed and sides. A roughness factor is estimated empirically and usually accounts for the material, the vegetation, and the meandering in the channel.

Open-channel flow can be characterized as steady or unsteady. It also can be uniform or varied flow, which could be gradually or rapidly varied flow. A famous example of rapidly varied flow is the hydraulic jump.

When high-energy water, gushing at a high velocity and a shallow depth, encounters a hump, an obstruction, or a channel with a milder slope, it cannot sustain its supercritical flow (characterized by a Froude number larger than 1). It dissipates most of its energy through a hydraulic jump, which is a highly turbulent transition to a calmer flow (subcritical flow with a Froude number less than 1) at a higher depth and a much lower velocity. One way to solve for the depths and velocities upstream and downstream of the hydraulic jump is by applying the conservation of momentum principle, the third principle of fluid mechanics and hydraulic engineering. The hydraulic jump is a very effective energy dissipater that is used in the designs of spillways.

Hydraulic structures. Many types of hydraulic structures are built in small or large civil engineering projects. The most notable by its size and cost is the dam. A dam is built over a creek or a river, forming a reservoir in a canyon. Water is released through an outlet structure into a pipeline for water supply or into the river or creek for groundwater recharge and environmental reasons (sustainability of the biological life in the river downstream). During a large flood, the reservoir fills up and water can flow into a side overflow spillway—which protects the integrity of the face of the dam from overtopping—and into the river.

The four major types of dams are gravity, arch, buttress, and earth. Dams are designed to hold the immense water pressure applied on their upstream face. The pressure increases as the water elevation in the reservoir rises.

Hydraulic machinery. Hydraulic turbines transform the drop in pressure (head) into electric power. Also, pumps take electric power and transform it into water head, thereby moving the flow in a pipe to a higher elevation.

There are two types of turbines, impulse and reaction. The reaction turbine is based on the steam-powered device that was developed in Egypt in the first century CE by Hero of Alexandria. A simple example of a reaction turbine is the rotating lawn sprinkler.

Pumps are classified into two main categories, centrifugal and axial flow. Pumps have many industrial, municipal, and household uses, such as boosting the flow in a water distribution system or pumping water from a groundwater well.

CAREERS AND COURSEWORK

Undergraduate students majoring in civil or environmental engineering usually take several core courses in hydraulic engineering, including fluid mechanics, water resources, and fluid mechanics laboratory. Advanced studies in hydraulic engineering lead to a master of science or a doctoral degree. Students with a bachelor's degree in a science or another engineering specialty could pursue an advanced degree in hydraulic engineering, but they may need to take several undergraduate level courses before starting the graduate program.

Graduates with a bachelor's degree in civil engineering or advanced degrees in hydraulics can work for private design firms that compete to be chosen to work on the planning and design phases of large governmental hydraulic engineering projects. They can work for construction companies that bid on governmental projects to build structures and facilities that include hydraulic elements, or for water utility companies, whether private or public. Some common areas for hydraulic engineers to work in are stormwater management, sediment transport, and creation of canals for irrigation and transportation.

To teach or conduct research at a university or a research laboratory requires a doctoral degree in one of the branches of hydraulic engineering.

SOCIAL CONTEXT AND FUTURE PROSPECTS

In the twenty-first century, hydraulic engineering has become closely tied to environmental engineering. Reservoir operators plan and vary water releases to keep downstream creeks wet, thus protecting the biological life in the ecosystem. Hydraulic engineers can also be involved in coastal engineering, which includes fighting erosion through sediment delivery, and in flood management; their skills can also be applied to various other conservation projects involving rivers or oceans.

Clean energy is the way to ensure sustainability of the planet's resources. Hydroelectric power generation is a form of clean energy. Energy generated by ocean waves is a developing and promising field, although wave power technologies still face technical challenges.

—*Bassam Kassab, BEng, MEng, MSc*

Further Reading
Boulos, Paul F., Kevin E. Lansey, and Bryan W. Karney. *Comprehensive Water Distribution Systems Analysis Handbook for Engineers and Planners*. 2nd ed., MWH Soft Press, 2006.
Chow, Ven Te. *Open-Channel Hydraulics*. 1959. Blackburn, 2008.
Finnemore, E. John, and Joseph B. Franzini. *Fluid Mechanics with Engineering Applications*. 10th International ed., McGraw-Hill, 2009.
Julien, Pierre Y. "Our Hydraulic Engineering Profession." *Journal of Hydraulic Engineering*, vol. 143, no. 5, 2017.
Lindell, James E. *Handbook of Hydraulics*. 8th ed., McGraw Hill Professional, 2017.
Walski, Thomas M. *Advanced Water Distribution Modeling and Management*. Methods, 2003.
Yasmin, Nighat. *Introduction to AutoCAD 2022 for Civil Engineering Applications*. SDC Publications, 2021.

Hydroponics

ABSTRACT

Hydroponics uses varied scientific and technological processes to cultivate plants without soils usually associated with agriculture. Throughout history, humans have delivered nutrients directly to plant roots with water. Based on that principle, modern hydroponics has diverse applications for commercial and utilitarian agriculture. Hydroponics supplies food to military personnel in places where agricultural resources are limited because of climate and terrain. Astronauts eat fresh vegetables grown with hydroponics in space. Food security is bolstered by the availability of substantial yields year-round assured by hydroponics, providing people access to nutrients and relief from hunger. Agribusinesses sell hydroponic crops and equipment to consumers. Many scientific educational curricula incorporate hydroponic lessons.

DEFINITION AND BASIC PRINCIPLES

Hydroponics is the scientific use of chemicals, organic and inorganic materials, and technology to grow plants independently of soil. Solutions composed of water and dissolved minerals and elements provide essential macronutrients and micronutrients and supplement oxygen and light necessary for plant growth. Plant roots absorb nutrients that are supplied through various methods. Some hydroponic systems involve suspending roots into liquid solutions. Other hydroponic techniques periodically wash or spray roots with solutions. Methods also utilize containers filled with substrates, such as gravel, where roots are flooded with nutrient solutions. Hydroponics is practiced both in greenhouses, where temperatures and lighting can be regulated, and outdoors, where milder climates pose few natural detriments to plants.

Hydroponics enables agriculturists to grow crops continually without relying on weather, precipitation, and other factors associated with natural growing seasons. These systems permit agricultural production in otherwise unsuitable settings for crop cultivation such as congested cities, deserts, and mountains. Hydroponics is convenient, producing foods in all seasons. Plants can be grown closely together because root growth does not spread like soil-based plant roots extending to seek nutrients and water. Agriculturists can grow crops that are not indigenous to areas, such as tropical fruits. Growth typically occurs more quickly with hydroponics than in soil, because plants invest energy in maturing rather than competing for resources, resulting in large yields. Many hydroponic systems recycle water not absorbed by roots to use for other purposes. Crops cultivated with hydroponic systems are usually safer for consumers than field-grown crops because their exposure to soil-transmitted diseases has been minimized.

Negative aspects of hydroponics include costs associated with acquiring equipment and supplies. Automation and computerized systems require substantial investments in machinery, software, and training personnel to operate them. Advances in computer-aided design (CAD) and three-dimensional (3D) printing technology, however, have made designing, fabricating, and operating small-scale hydroponics systems more feasible for some individuals, particularly hobbyists and students. As of 2021, open-source projects such as 3Dponics offered downloadable CAD models of a host of components to individuals and groups interested in manufacturing and assembling their own hydroponics systems.

NASA researcher checking hydroponic onions (center), Bibb lettuces (left), and radishes (right). Photo via NASA/Wikimedia Commons. [Public domain.]

BACKGROUND AND HISTORY

Records indicate people cultivated plants using water instead of soil in ancient Mesopotamia, Egypt, and Rome. Aztecs in Mexico innovated floating barges, *chinampas*, for growing food because they lacked suitable agricultural land. In the mid-nineteenth century, German botanist Julius von Sachs and German agrochemist Wilhelm Knop experimented with combining minerals with water to nourish plants.

During the 1920s, University of California, Berkeley, plant nutrition professor Dennis R. Hoagland studied how roots absorb nutrients. William F. Gericke, also a professor at the University of California, Berkeley, cultivated tomatoes in tanks of mineral-rich solution and discussed his research in a February 1937 *Science* article, noting colleague William A. Setchell referred to that process as hydroponics, representing Greek vocabulary: *hydro* (water) and *ponos* (work).

In the 1940s, the United States military utilized hydroponics to provide sustenance to World War II soldiers in the Pacific. Oil companies built hydroponic gardens on Caribbean islands to feed employees extracting natural resources in that region. The United States Army established a hydroponics branch to supply troops serving in the Korean War in the early 1950s, growing 8 million pounds of food.

By mid-century, researchers began incorporating plastic equipment in hydroponic systems. Engineers innovated better pumps and devices, automating some hydroponic processes with computers. By the 1970s new methods included drip-irrigation systems and the nutrient film technique (NFT) created by English scientist Allen Cooper, which helped commercial hydroponics expand globally. The United Nations' Food and Agriculture Organization (FAO) funded hydroponic programs in areas experiencing food crises. Scientists continued devising new techniques, such as aerohydroponics, in the late twentieth and early twenty-first centuries.

HOW IT WORKS

Hydroponics. Hydroponic processes represent examples of controlled environment agriculture in which plant cultivation involves technology such as greenhouses enabling growers to stabilize conditions. Most hydroponic systems function with basic components that supply oxygen and nutrients necessary to sustain plants until they have matured for harvest. Electrical or solar-powered lights, fans, heaters, and pumps regulate temperatures, ventilation for plant respiration, water flow, and photosynthesis impacting plant growth. Each hydroponic system incorporates variations of equipment and methods according to growers' resources and goals. Styrofoam, wood, glass, and plastic are materials used to construct hydroponic systems.

Basic hydroponic procedures involve placing seeds in substrates that consist of organic materials such as coconut fibers, rice hulls, sawdust, peat moss or inorganic mediums including gravel, pumice, perlite, rock wool, or vermiculite. After roots emerge during germination, growers keep seedlings in substrates or remove them depending on which hydroponic method is selected for cultivation. Roots undergo varying durations of exposure to nutrient solutions to absorb macronutrients and micronutrients. Most hydroponic processes utilize either an open, or nonrecirculating, system, or a closed system, referred to as recirculating, depending on whether nutrient solution contacts roots once and is discarded or is kept for consistent or repeated use.

Water-culture techniques. These hydroponic methods, which are frequently used to cultivate plants that quickly attain maturity, involve roots constantly being suspended in a nutrient solution. Water-culture hydroponic techniques are often utilized to grow lettuce crops. For the raft culture technique, growers place plants on platforms drilled with holes to pull roots through so roots can be submerged in pools of nutrient solution on which the platforms float. In the dynamic root floating technique, roots closest to the plant are kept dry so they can supply oxygen to the plant. The lower roots are constantly exposed to nutrient solutions and absorb those minerals and elements to nourish the plant.

Pumps and air stones oxygenate nutrient solutions so that roots are aerated. Lighting is essential for plants to undergo photosynthesis above the solution surface. Growers monitor nutrient solutions' pH levels and the presence of any algae, which might harm roots, interfere with their adsorption of nutrients, and impede plant growth. Growers also replenish fluids lost to evaporation.

Nutrient solution culture (NSC) methods. Several forms of NSC are utilized to feed plants. Continuous-flow NSC involves nutrient solutions being poured into a trough and constantly moving through roots. Nutrient solutions contact roots less frequently in intermittent-flow NSC. The drip NSC technique delivers nutrient solutions through tubing and emitters that dispense water on the substrate near roots. Some drip systems recycle nutrient solution. The wick system utilizes strings that extend from substrates to a reservoir filled with nutrient solution.

In the ebb-and-flow method, nutrient solution contacts roots in cycles after flooding trays containing roots and substrates then draining and returning to a tank to store for additional delivery. Timers control pump mechanisms, which move nutrient solutions. Aquaponics systems transport water from ponds or greenhouses where fish tanks are kept to greenhouses where plants are grown so that wastes from the fish can provide nutrients for plants.

Nutrient film technique (NFT). This closed system continually pumps nutrient solutions into a channel placed at an angle in which roots hang under plants supported from above by platforms or other equipment. No substrates are used. The solution contacting roots is delivered as a watery film to assure roots will receive sufficient oxygen. The hydroponic trough system uses a reservoir, which includes a filtering device to strain contaminants from nutrient solutions. Resembling NFT methods, aeroponics does not rely on substrates. Sprayers attached to timers continually dispense nutrient solutions on roots suspended in air below plants.

APPLICATIONS AND PRODUCTS

Nutrition. Hydroponics enables ample production of food supplies that meet nutritional needs for vitamins, antioxidants, and amino acids crucial for maintaining people's bodies. These techniques aid hunger relief in arid regions where climate change is associated with expanding desertification and loss of arable land, threatening food security. Hydroponic cultivation provides both rural and urban populations access to affordable, fresh, healthy food despite loss of access to traditional agricultural supplies due to political, economic, or military crises; natural disasters; or famines. Various hydroponic techniques can be applied to produce crops with increased levels of calcium, potassium, and other elements essential to sustain health. Hydroponic processes can be designed to grow food with appealing tastes, textures, and appearances.

Agribusiness. Hydroponics generates profits for commercial sellers of crops, manufacturers of hydroponic equipment, nutrient solutions, and supplies and wholesalers and retailers that distribute hydroponic merchandise to consumers. Agribusinesses create and market hydroponic greenhouses of varying sizes, including small growing containers such as AeroGarden for use inside homes, to consumers. Many florists grow stock cultivated with hydroponics at their stores. Internationally, the number of hydroponic businesses has expanded on all continents except Antarctica, contributing to countries' economies. Some hydroponic companies develop and sell smartphone applications to perform hydroponic functions, such as calculators for preparing nutrient solutions.

Education. Students at various levels, from elementary through graduate school, often study hydroponics in science classes. Some courses may discuss hydroponics to explain basic scientific principles such as how roots absorb nutrients, while others may focus on special topics such as genetics. Students frequently investigate aspects of hydroponics for science-fair competitions or projects for the Future Farmers of America. Teachers instructing Advanced Placement biology courses often encourage students to develop hydroponic systems to comprehend concepts associated with plant growth and nutrition. Some school cafeterias use foods grown on their campuses or students sell products cultivated with hydroponic techniques for fund-raisers. Universities sometimes award funds to students' innovative hydroponic projects, especially those with humanitarian applications.

Military and exploration. Military troops benefit from the establishment of hydroponic systems near bases and battlefields to produce fresh vegetables for rations regardless of soil and climate conditions in those areas. Hydroponic applications for military usage enable crews on vessels undergoing lengthy sea voyages to grow foods when they are between ports. Veterans with hydroponic experience or who complete Veterans Sustainable Agriculture Training or similar programs are often sought out for employment in that field. The ability to grow foods without soil nourishes people traveling by submarine, whether for military or scientific reasons. Workers in remote locations, such as offshore oil and natural-gas rigs, eat meals incorporating hydroponic produce grown at those sites.

Scientists conducting research at Antarctic stations rely on hydroponics for sustenance and as a method to recycle, purify, and store water. The South Pole Food Growth Chamber, designed by the Controlled Environment Agriculture Center at the University of Arizona, uses NFT methods and is automated with an Argus climate-control system. The National Aeronautics and Space Administration (NASA) has funded projects such as Controlled Ecological Life Support Systems (CELSS), in which hydroponic plants remove carbon dioxide and pollutants while producing food on spacecraft. Researchers are investigating using hydroponics for future missions of long duration.

Urban planning. Some twenty-first-century architecture incorporates hydroponics as a strategy to feed increasing populations, particularly in urban areas. Rooftops are popular sites for hydroponic systems in places where land is unavailable for gardens. These urban farms grow large yields of basic vegetable crops and supply fresh produce to residents who might otherwise not have access to those foods. Some proponents of hydroponics have argued that by establishing more hydroponic gardens on rooftops located in close proximity to supermarkets, produce could reach consumers in a much fresher and less damaged state than having to be shipped across distances from traditional farms. Vertical farming techniques also inspired proposals applying hydroponics, and by 2021, hydroponics and the water-misting technique known as "aeroponics" became the primary growing techniques used in the more than two thousand indoor vertical farms operating in the United States.

CAREERS AND COURSEWORK

Students interested in professions associated with hydroponics can complete diverse educational programs to pursue their career goals. Many entry-level hydroponic positions are available to people with high school educations or associate's degrees. Some employers seeking qualified workers to build and maintain hydroponic systems expect candidates to have completed basic horticultural courses at technical schools, community colleges, or universities, preparing them to cultivate plants and assemble equipment. Experience working for landscaping businesses, farms, or other positions that involve tending plants enhances one's employability. One can sometimes find available positions at gardening businesses that use hydroponics to grow crops and ornamental plants to sell to consumers and markets. Resorts, botanical gardens, and theme parks hire people with educational and work experience to establish and maintain hydroponic gardens.

Government, academic, and industrial employers that staff scientific and technological positions focusing on hydroponics usually require the minimum of a bachelor of science degree in a related field. Candidates can acquire basic knowledge for plant cultivation by studying horticulture, botany, agriculture, or subjects applicable to hydroponics. Those seeking research positions typically need to earn advanced degrees—a master's or doctorate—in relevant subjects, acquiring expertise that will benefit the quality of their employers' services and hydroponic products. Agricultural engineering, computer science, or robotics courses prepare employees for positions designing hydroponic structures, machinery, and automation software. Candidates with advanced education or hydroponic experience have credentials for many positions as administrators or educators in schools, experiment stations, extension services, or government agencies.

SOCIAL CONTEXT AND FUTURE PROSPECTS

Throughout the twenty-first century, hydroponics will continue to provide humanitarian benefits. Industry experts suggest that hydroponics, universal to diverse cultures, will continue to expand for several reasons, including depletion of arable lands caused by natural disasters and global warming, expenses associated with machinery and operation of conventional agriculture; and public disapproval of bioengineering associated with field crops. Hydroponics presents food-security solutions to the increasing global population, which as of 2020 was estimated to reach nearly 10 billion people by 2050. Some experts speculate that hydroponics will eventually surpass mainstream agriculture to produce the most food worldwide. The hydroponics industry is likewise expected to offer commercial benefits: a 2021 report by the market-research firm Grand View Research, for instance, projected that the value of the global hydroponics market would increase from $2.6 billion in 2021 to $9.76 billion in 2028.

Hydroponics, while beneficial for numerous reasons, has also been the source of continued debate in the community of organic farmers; while some believe that the hydroponic process should be considered organic, others have argued that, due to the lack of the use of soil, products resulting from the process should not be called "organic." In an effort to settle the debate, in late 2015, the US Department of Agriculture (USDA) announced that it would be assigning a task force to analyze the procedure and determine whether hydroponic products should qualify as organic according to USDA standards. However, when the task force released its report in the summer of 2016, commentators noted that the issue remained unresolved, as the advisory group had not taken a definitive stance either way. At the same time, the report did indicate that the standards could potentially be interpreted to also include such soilless methods. The USDA subsequently specified in a 2018 statement that hydroponic, aquaponic, and aeroponic farming operations could be certified as organic under existing regulations, and a 2021 ruling by the United States District Court for the Northern District further affirmed that policy.

—*Elizabeth D. Schafer, PhD*

Further Reading

"Court Rules USDA Authorized to Certify Soil-less Hydroponic Operations as Organic." *Center for Food Safety*, 22 Mar. 2021, www.centerforfoodsafety.org/press-releases/6314/court-rules-usda-authorized-to-certify-soilless-hydroponic-operations-as-organic. Accessed 28 Nov. 2021.

Despommier, Dickson. *The Vertical Farm: Feeding the World in the Twenty-First Century*. St. Martin's Press, 2010.

"Gardening without Soil." *U of California at Berkeley Wellness Letter*, vol. 28, no. 4, 2012, p. 4.

Giacomelli, Gene A., et al. "CEA in Antarctica: Growing Vegetables on 'the Ice.'" *Resource: Engineering & Technology for a Sustainable World*, vol. 13, no. 1, 2006, pp. 3-5.

Grand View Research. "Hydroponics Market Size, Share & Trends Analysis Report by Type (Aggregate Systems, Liquid Systems), by Crops (Tomatoes, Lettuce, Peppers, Cucumbers, Herbs), by Region, and Segment Forecasts, 2021-2028." *Research and Markets*, Oct. 2021, www.researchandmarkets.com/reports/5457654/hydroponics-market-size-share-and-trends. Accessed 28 Nov. 2021.

Grossman, Elizabeth. "If Your Veggies Weren't Grown in Soil, Can They Be Organic?" *Civil Eats*, 28 July 2016, civileats.com/2016/07/28/if-your-veggies-were-grown-hydroponic-can-they-be-organic/. Accessed 28 Nov. 2021.

Hansen, Robert, et al. "Development and Operation of a Hydroponic Lettuce Research Laboratory." *Resource: Engineering & Technology for a Sustainable World*, vol. 17, no. 4, 2010, pp. 4-7.

Jones, J. Benton, Jr. *Hydroponics: A Practical Guide for the Soilless Grower*. 2nd ed., CRC Press, 2005.

Lloyd, Marion. "Gardens of Hope on the Rooftops of Rio." *Chronicle of Higher Education*, vol. 52, no. 8, 2005, p. A56.

Walsh, Bryan. "Indoor Vertical Farming Grows Up." *Axios*, 26 May 2021, www.axios.com/vertical-farming-e6137f78-6a73-46e6-9277-5f8d22b6a2fc.html. Accessed 28 Nov. 2021.

"What Is 3Dponics?" *3Dponics*, 2021, www.3dponics.com/what-is-3dponics/. Accessed 28 Nov. 2021.

"World Population to Reach 9.9 Billion by 2050." *IISD*, 6 Aug. 2020, sdg.iisd.org/news/world-population-to-reach-9-9-billion-by-2050/. Accessed 28 Nov. 2021.

INTEGRATED-CIRCUIT DESIGN

ABSTRACT

The integrated circuit (IC) is the essential building block of modern electronics. Each IC consists of a chip of silicon upon which has been constructed a series of transistor structures, typically MOSFETs, or metal oxide semiconductor field effect transistors. The chip is encased in a protective outer package whose size facilitates use by humans and by automated machinery. Each chip is designed to perform specific electronic functions, and the package design allows electronics designers to work at the system level rather than with each individual circuit. The manufacture of silicon chips is a specialized industry, requiring the utmost care and quality control.

DEFINITION AND BASIC PRINCIPLES

An integrated circuit, or IC, is an interconnected series of transistor structures assembled on the surface of a silicon chip. The purpose of the transistor assemblages is to perform specific operations on electrical signals that are provided as inputs. All IC devices can be produced from a structure of four transistors that function to invert the value of the input signal, called "NOT gates" or "inverters." Digital electronic circuits are constructed from a small number of different transistor assemblages, called "gates," that are built into the circuitry of particular ICs. The individual ICs are used as the building blocks of the digital electronic circuitry that is the functional heart of twenty-first-century digital electronic technology.

The earliest ICs were constructed from bipolar transistors that function as two-state systems, a system high and a system low. This is not the same as "on" and "off," but is subject to the same logic. All digital systems function according to Boolean logic and binary mathematics.

Twenty-first-century ICs are constructed using metal oxide semiconductor field effect transistor (MOSFET) technology, which has allowed for a reduction in size of the transistor structures to the point in which millions of them can be constructed per square centimeter (cm^2) of silicon chip surface. The transistors function by conducting electrical current when they are biased by an applied voltage. ICs such as the central processing units (CPUs) of personal computers can operate at gigahertz frequencies, changing that state of the transistors on the IC billions of times per second.

BACKGROUND AND HISTORY

Digital electronics got its start in 1906, when American inventor Lee de Forest constructed the triode vacuum tube. Large, slow, and power-hungry as they were, vacuum tubes were nevertheless used to construct the first analog and digital electronic computers. In 1947, American physicist William Shockley and colleagues constructed the first semiconductor transistor junction, which quickly developed into more advanced silicon-germanium junction transistors.

Through various chemical and physical processes, methods were developed to construct small transistor structures on a substrate of pure crystalline silicon. In 1958, American physicist and Nobel laureate Jack Kilby first demonstrated the method by constructing germanium-based transistors as an IC chip, and American physicist Robert Noyce constructed the first silicon-based transistors as an IC chip. The transistor structures were planar bipolar in nature, until the CMOS (complementary metal oxide semiconductor) transistor was invented in 1963. Methods for producing CMOS chips efficiently were not developed for another twenty years.

Transistor structure took another developmental leap with the invention of the field effect transistor (FET), which was both a more efficient design than that of semiconductor junction transistors and easier to manufacture effectively. The MOSFET structure also is amenable to miniaturization and has allowed designers to engineer ICs that have 1 million or more transistor structures per centimeters squared.

In addition to facilitating advances in computing technology, efforts to utilize ICs in electronics have benefited from such advances, particularly within the realm of computer-aided design (CAD) software. Used by electronics designers since as early as the 1980s, CAD programs relevant to that field came to encompass twenty-first-century software products such as Autodesk's Eagle. Among other capabilities, Eagle enables users to create schematics and design the layout of components such as ICs within printed circuit boards (PCBs).

HOW IT WORKS

The electronic material silicon is the basis of all transistor structures. It is classed as a pure semiconductor. It is not a good conductor of electrical current, nor does it insulate well against electrical current. By adding a small amount of some impurity to the silicon, its electrical properties can be manipulated such that the application of a biasing voltage to the material allows it to conduct electrical current. When the biasing voltage is removed, the electrical properties of the material revert to their normal semiconductive state.

Silicon manufacture. Integrated-circuit design begins with the growth of single crystals of pure silicon. A high-purity form of the material, known as "polysilicon," is loaded into a furnace and heated to melt the material. At the proper stage of melt, a

Engineer using an early IC-designing workstation to analyze a section of a circuit design cut on rubylith, circa 1979. Photo via Wikimedia Commons. [Public domain.]

seed crystal is attached to a slowly turning rod and introduced to the melt. The single crystal begins to form around the seed crystal and the rotating crystal is "pulled" from the melt as it grows. This produces a relatively long, cylindrical, single crystal that is then allowed to cool and set.

Wafers. From this cylinder, thin wafers or slices are cut using a continuous wire saw that produces several uniform slices at the same time. The slices are subjected to numerous stages of polishing, cleaning, and quality checking, the end result of which is a consistent set of silicon wafers suitable for use as substrates for integrated circuits.

Circuitry. The integrated circuit itself begins as a complex design of electronic circuitry to be constructed from transistor structures and "wiring" on the surface of the silicon wafer. The circuits can be no more than a series of simple transistor gates (such as invertors, AND-gates, and OR-gates), up to and including the extremely complex transistor circuitry of advanced CPUs for computers.

Graphics technology is extremely important in this stage of the design and production of integrated circuits, as the entire layout of the required transistor circuitry must be imaged. The design software also is used to conduct virtual tests of the circuitry before any ICs are made. When the theoretical design is complete and imaged, the process of constructing ICs can begin.

Because the circuitry is so small, a great many copies can be produced on a single silicon wafer. The actual chips that are housed within the final polymer or ceramic package range in size from two to five cm². The actual dimensions of the circa 1986 Samsung KS74AHCT240 chip, for example, are just 1 cm x 2 cm. The transistor gate sizes used in this chip are 2 micrometers (μm) (2 x 10^{-6} meters [m]), and each chip contains the circuitry for two octal buffers, constructed from hundreds of transistor gate structures. Transistor construction methods have become much more efficient, and transistor

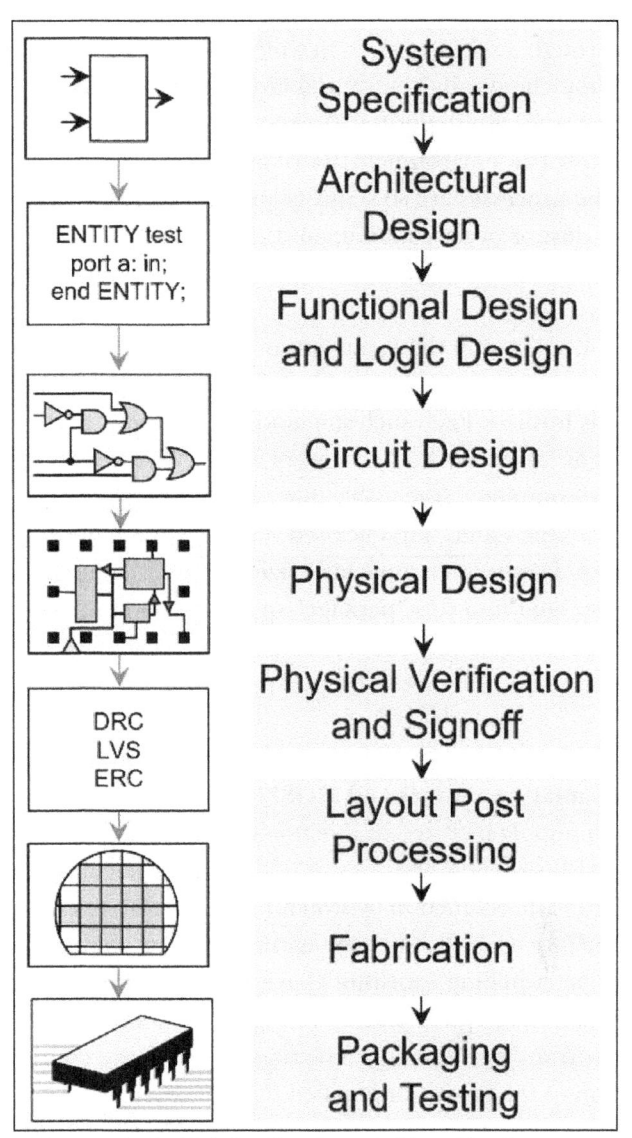

Major steps in the IC design flow. Image by Linear77, via Wikimedia Commons.

gate sizes are measured in nanometers (10^{-9} m) rather than μm, so that actual chip sizes have also become much smaller, in accord with Moore's law. The gate structures are connected through the formation of aluminum "wires" using the same chemical vapor deposition methodology used to form the silicon oxide and other layers needed.

Photochemical etching. The transistor structures of the chip are built up on the silicon wafer substrate through a series of steps in which the substrate is photochemically etched and layers of the necessary materials are deposited. Absolute precision and an ultraclean environment are required at each step. The processes are so sensitive that any errant speck of dust or other contaminant that finds its way to the wafer's surface renders that part of the structure useless.

Each step in the formation of the IC chip must be tested to identify the functionality of the circuitry as it is formed. Each such step and test procedure add significantly to the final cost of an IC. When the ICs are completed, the viable ones are identified, cut from the wafer, and enclosed within a protective casing of resin or ceramic material. A series of leads are also built into this "package" so that the circuitry of the IC chip can be connected into an electronic system.

APPLICATIONS AND PRODUCTS

Bipolar transistors and MOSFETS. Transistors are commonly pictured as functioning as electronic on-off switches. This view is not entirely correct. Transistors function by switching between states according to the biasing voltages that are applied. Bipolar switching transistors have a cut-off state in which the applied biasing voltage is too low to make the transistor function. The normal operating condition of the transistor is called the "linear state." The saturation state is achieved when the biasing voltage is applied to both poles of the transistor, preventing them from functioning. MOSFET transistors use a somewhat different means, relying on the extent of an electric field within the transistor substrate, but the resulting functions are essentially the same.

The transistor structures that form the electronic circuitry of an IC chip are designed to perform specific functions when an electrical signal is introduced. For simple IC circuits, each chip is packaged to perform just one function. An inverter chip, for example, contains only transistor circuitry that inverts the input signal from high to low or from low to high. Typically, six inverter circuits are provided in each package through twelve contact points. Two more contact points are provided for connection to the biasing voltage and ground of the external circuit. It is possible to construct all other transistor logic gates using just inverter gates. All ICs use this same general package format, varying only in their size and the number of contact points that must be provided.

MOSFETS have typical state switching times of something less than 100 nanoseconds and are the transistor structures of choice in designing ICs, even though bipolar transistors can switch states faster. Unlike bipolars, however, MOSFETS can be constructed and wired to function as resistors and can be made to a much smaller scale than true resistors in the normal production process. MOSEFTS are easier to manufacture than are bipolars as they can be made much smaller in VLSI (very large-scale integration) designs. MOSFETS also cost much less to produce.

NOTs, ANDs, ORs, and other gates. All digital electronic devices comprise just a few basic types of circuitry—called "logic elements"—of which there are two basic types: decision-making elements and storage elements. All logic elements function according to the Boolean logic of a two-state (binary) system. The only two states that are allowed are "high" and "low," representing an applied biasing voltage that either does or does not drive the transistor circuitry to function. All input to the circuitry is binary, as is all output from the circuitry.

Decision-making functions are carried out by logic gates (the AND, OR, NOT gates and their constructs) and memory functions are carried out by combination circuitry (flip-flops) that maintains certain input and output states until it is required to change states. All gates are made up of a circuit of interconnected transistors that produces a specific output according to the input that it receives.

A NOT gate, or inverter, outputs a signal that is the opposite of the input signal. A high input produces a low output, and vice versa. The AND gate outputs a high signal only when all input signals are high, and a low output signal only if any of the input signals are low. The OR gate functions in the opposite sense, producing a high output signal if any of the input signals are high and a low output signal only when all of the input signals are low. The NAND gate, which can be constructed from either four transistors and one diode or five diodes, is a combination of the AND and NOT gates. The NOR gate is a combination of the OR and NOT gates. These, and other gates, can have any number of inputs, limited only by the fan-out limits of the transistor structures.

Sequential logic circuits are used for timing, sequencing, and storage functions. The flip-flops are the main elements of these circuits, and memory functions are their primary uses. Counters consist of a series of flip-flops and are used to count the number of applied input pulses. They can be constructed to count up or down, as adders, subtracters, or both. Another set of devices called "shift registers" maintains a memory of the order of the applied input pulses, shifting over one place with each input pulse. These can be constructed to function as series devices, accepting one pulse (one data bit) at a time in a linear fashion, or as parallel devices, accepting several data bits, as bytes and words, with each input pulse. The devices also provide the corresponding output pulses.

Operational amplifiers, or OP-AMPs, represent a special class of ICs. Each OP-AMP IC contains a self-contained transistor-based amplifying circuit that provides a high voltage gain (typically 100,000 times or more), a very high input impedance and low output impedance, and good rejection of common-mode signals (i.e., the presence of the same signal on both input leads of the OP-AMP).

Combinations of all of the gates and other devices constructed from them provide all of the computing power of all ICs, up to and including the most cutting-edge CPU chips. Their manufacturing process begins with the theoretical design of the desired functions of the circuitry. When this has been determined, the designer minimizes the detailed transistor circuitry that will be required and develops the corresponding mask and circuitry images that will be required for the IC production process. The resulting ICs can then be used to build the electronic circuitry of all electronic devices.

SOCIAL CONTEXT AND FUTURE PROSPECTS
IC technology is on the verge of extreme change, as new electronic materials such as graphene and carbon nanotubes are developed. Research with these materials indicates that they will be the basic materials of molecular-scale transistor structures, which will be thousands of times smaller and more energy-efficient than VLSI technology based on MOSFETs. The computational capabilities of computers and other electronic devices are expected to become correspondingly greater as well.

Such devices will utilize what will be an entirely new type of IC technology, in which the structural features are actual molecules and atoms, rather than what are by comparison mass quantities of semiconductor materials and metals. As such, future IC designers will require a comprehensive understanding of both the chemical nature of the materials and of quantum physics to make the most effective use of the new concepts.

The scale of the material structures as well will have extraordinary application in society. It is possible, given the molecular scale of the components, that the technology could even be used to print ultrahigh resolution displays and computer circuitry that would make even the lightest and thinnest of twenty-first-century appliances look like the ENIAC

(Electronic Numerical Integrator and Computer) of 1947, which was the first electronic computer.

The social implications of such miniaturized technology are far-reaching. The RFID (radio-frequency identification) tag is becoming an important means of embedding identification markers directly into materials. RFID tags are tiny enough to be included as a component of paints, fuels, explosives, and other materials, allowing identification of the exact source of the material, a useful implication for forensic investigations and other purposes. Even the RFID tag, however, would be immense compared with the molecular scale of graphene and nanotube-based devices that could carry much more information on each tiny particle. This would make computers smaller, faster, and more powerful. Graphene transistors were successfully created in a laboratory setting at the University of Florida in 2017, while researchers at the Massachusetts Industry of Technology (MIT) succeeded in building a sixteen-bit microprocessor using carbon nanotube transistors in 2019. However, such experimental technologies were still, at that time, not expected to be used in commercial products in the near future.

The ultimate goal of electronic development for some researchers is the quantum computer, a device that would use single electrons, or their absence, as data bits. The speed of such a computer would be unfathomable, taking seconds to carry out calculations that would take traditional supercomputers billions of years to complete. The ICs used for such a device would bear little resemblance, if any, to the MOSFET-based ICs used during the first decades of the twenty-first century.

—*Richard M. Renneboog, MSc*

Further Reading

Brown, Julian R. *Minds, Machines, and the Multiverse: The Quest for the Quantum Computer*. New York: Simon & Schuster, 2000.

Daniel, M. E., and C. W. Gwyn. "CAD Systems for IC Design." *IEEE Transactions on Computer-Aided Design of Integrated Circuits and Systems*, vol. 1, no. 1, 1982, pp. 2-12.

"Graphene Transistor Could Mean Computers That Are 1,000 Times Faster." *Science Daily*, 13 June 2017, www.sciencedaily.com/releases/2017/06/170613145144.htm. Accessed 28 Nov. 2021.

Kurzweil, Ray. *The Age of Spiritual Machines: When Computers Exceed Human Intelligence*. Penguin, 2000.

Mahdoum, Ali. *CAD of Circuits and Integrated Systems*. Wiley-ISTE, 2020.

Marks, Myles H. *Basic Integrated Circuits*. Tab Books, 1986.

Matheson, Rob. "MIT Engineers Build Advanced Microprocessor Out of Carbon Nanotubes." *MIT News*, 28 Aug. 2019, news.mit.edu/2019/carbon-nanotubes-microprocessor-0828. Accessed 28 Nov. 2021.

O'Leary, Timothy, Linda O'Leary, and Daniel O'Leary. *Computing Essentials 2021*. McGraw-Hill, 2020.

Pavlidis, Vasilis F., Ioannis Savidis, and Eby Friedman. *Three-Dimensional Integrated Circuit Design*. 2nd ed., Morgan Kaufman, 2017.

Rafiquzzaman, M. *Fundamentals of Digital Logic and Microcontrollers*. 6th ed., John Wiley & Sons, 2014.

International System of Units

ABSTRACT

The International System of Units (Le Système International d'Unités, or SI) is the internationally accepted standard system of measurement in use throughout the world. The development of the metric system, which served as the basis of the International System of Units, occurred during the French Revolution in the mid-eighteenth century. This coincided with the beginning of the age of modern science, especially chemistry and physics, as the value of physical measurements in the conduct of those pursuits became apparent. As scientific activities became more precise and founded on sound theory, the common nature of science demanded an equally consistent system of units and measurements. The units in the SI have been defined by international accord to provide consistency in all fields of endeavor. The basic units are defined for only seven fun-

damental properties of matter and two supplementary properties. These are length, mass, time, electric current, thermodynamic temperature, the amount of a substance, luminous intensity, and the magnitude of plane and solid angles. All other consistent units are derived as functions of these seven fundamental units.

DEFINITION AND BASIC PRINCIPLES

The International System of Units (SI) is the internationally accepted standard system of measurement in use throughout the world. The units of the SI are ascribed to seven fundamental physical properties and two supplementary properties. These are length, mass, time, electric current, thermodynamic temperature, the amount of a substance, luminous intensity, and the magnitude of plane and solid angles.

Length is the extent of some physical structure or boundary in two dimensions, such as the distance from one point to another, how tall someone is, or the distance between nodes of a sinusoidal wave. The SI base unit associated with length is the meter, which in 1983 was officially defined as the distance light travels in 1/299,792,458 of a second when in a vacuum.

Mass refers to the amount of material in a bulk quantity. The term is often used interchangeably with weight, although the mass of any object remains constant while its weight varies according to the strength of the gravitational field to which it is subject. The SI base unit for mass is the kilogram, which is defined in terms of the Planck constant (h).

Time is a rather more difficult property to define outside of itself, as it relates to the continuous progression of existence of some state through past, present, and future stages. The SI base unit of time is the second, defined based on the radiation cycles of the cesium-133 atom.

Electric current is the movement of electronic charge from one point to another, and it is ascribed by the SI base unit of the ampere. One ampere is defined in relation to the elementary charge constant (e) as the movement of one coulomb of charge, as one mole of electrons, for a period of one second.

Thermodynamic temperature refers to the measurement of temperature in relation to absolute zero. The SI base unit used is the kelvin, which is expressed in relation to the Boltzmann constant (k) of 1.380649×10^{-23}. It was previously based on the triple point of water, or the temperature and pressure in which water's three phases are in thermodynamic equilibrium.

The amount of a substance is defined by an SI base unit called the "mole." The term is essentially never used outside of the context of atoms, molecules, and certain subatomic particles such as electrons. A mole of any substance is the quantity of that substance containing $6.02214129 \times 10^{23}$ of these elementary entities; that number is known as the "Avogadro constant."

The term "luminous intensity" refers to the brightness, or the quantity, of light or other forms of

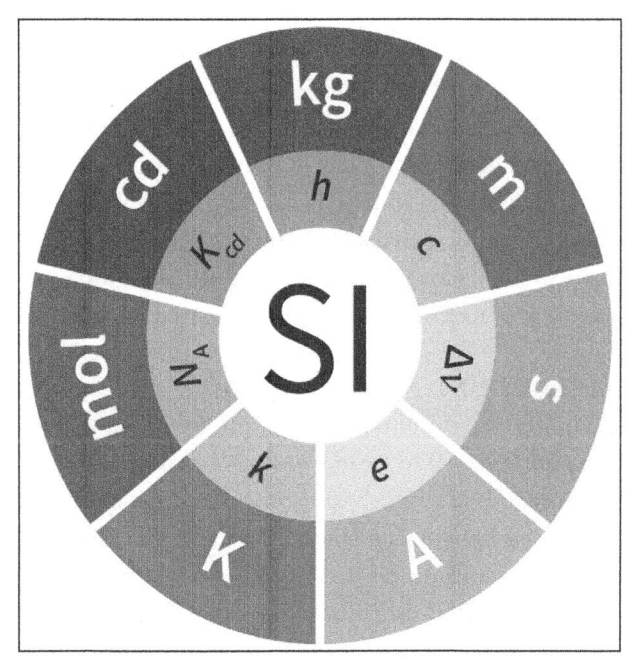

The SI logo, produced by the BIPM, showing the seven SI base units and the seven defining constants. Image via Wikimedia Commons. [Public domain.]

electromagnetic energy being emitted from a source. Initially luminous intensity was referred to by comparison to the light of a candle flame, but the variability of such a source is not conducive to standardization. The SI base unit for luminous intensity is the candela. This is about the amount of light emitted by a candle flame, but it has been standardized to mean an electromagnetic field strength of 0.00146 watts.

The derived unit known as the "plane angle" refers to the angular separation of two lines from a common point in a two-dimensional (2D) plane. The SI derived unit for plane angles is the radian. A complete rotation about a point origin is an angular displacement of 2π radians. The extension of this into three dimensions is known as the "solid angle" and is measured by the SI derived unit called the "steradian."

Measurement of any property or quantity is accomplished by comparing the particular amount of the property or quantity to the amount represented by the standard unit. For example, an object that is 3.62 times as long as the distance defined as 1 meter is said to be 3.62 meters long. Similarly, an object that is proportionately 6,486 times as massive as the quantity defined as 1 kilogram is said to weigh or to have a mass of 6,486 kilograms. The use of standard reference units such as the SI units ensures that measurements and quantities have the same meaning in all places where that system is used.

BACKGROUND AND HISTORY

Traditionally, systems of measurement employed units that related to various parts or proportions of the human body. Ready and convenient measuring tools in earlier times included the hand, the foot, the thumb, and the pace. Because these human measures tend to vary somewhat from person to person, no work that depended on measurements could be repeated exactly, even if the same person carried it out. Specialization in tasks eventually led to the realization that standard units of measurement would be beneficial, and determination of certain units were established by royal decree as long ago as the signing of the Magna Carta.

The Industrial Revolution in Europe and the growth of science as a common international pursuit drove the need for a unified system of measurement that would be independent of human variability and consistent from place to place. The International System of Units was developed and first put to use in about 1799. It represents the first real standardized system of measurements. Prior to this time, a broad variety of measurement systems were in use because many countries had developed their own measuring standards for use internally and in any territories that it held.

A need for a standardized system of measurement had been recognized by various luminaries and was proposed in 1670 by French scientist Gabriel Mouton. The incompatibility and variability of the many measurement systems in use at that time often resulted in unfair trade practices and power struggles. In 1790, the French Academy of Sciences was charged with developing a system of measurement that would be fixed and independent of any inconsistencies arising from human intervention. On April 7, 1795, the French National Assembly decreed the use of the meter as the standard unit of length. It was defined as being equal to one ten-millionth part of one quarter of the terrestrial meridian, specified by measurements undertaken between Dunkirk and Barcelona. The liter was later defined as being a unit of volume equal to the volume of a cube that is one-tenth of a meter on a side, and the kilogram as being equal to the mass of 1 liter of pure water. Larger and smaller quantities than these are indicated by the use of increasing and decreasing prefixes, all indicating units that were some power of ten times greater or lesser than the base units.

Standard reference models of the metric units were made and kept at the Palais-Royale, and it was then required that measuring devices being used for trade and commerce be regularly checked for accuracy against the official standard versions. Eventually, as methods of measurement became far more precise, it became clear that even these rigorously maintained reference models were susceptible to physical change over time, disrupting consistency. While adjustments were occasionally made, a movement to connect the definitions of the base units to more universally stable properties began.

HOW IT WORKS

All measurement practices relate the actual properties and proportions of something to a defined standard that is relevant to that property or proportion. For example, two-dimensional linear quantities are related to a standard of length, and the mass of an object is proportionately related to a standard unit of mass. In the measurement of length, for example, the standard SI unit is the meter. An object that is determined to be, for example, 6.3 times longer than the base unit of 1 meter is therefore said to be 6.3 meters long. Similarly, an object that is 5.5 times heavier than the base unit of 1 kilogram is said to weigh 5.5 kilograms, and something that has a volume of 22.4 times that of the base unit of 1 liter is said to have a volume of 22.4 liters.

The modern metric system is simple to use, especially when compared with its most common predecessor systems, the British Imperial and the US customary systems. Whereas these predecessor systems use units such as inches, feet, yards, ounces, and pounds that relate to one another irregularly, the metric system has always used the simple relation of factors of ten for all of its units. For example, the decameter is equal to 10 meters (10 x 1 meter), while the decimeter is equal to one-tenth of a meter (0.1 x 1 meter). A complete series of prefixes indicates the size of the smaller and larger units that are being used in a measurement. Thus, a decimeter is ten times smaller than a meter, a centimeter is a hundred times smaller than a meter, a millimeter is a thousand times smaller, and so on. Correspondingly, there are 10 millimeters in a centimeter, 10 centimeters in a decimeter, and 10 decimeters in a meter. There are 1,000 milliliters in a liter, 100 liters in a hectoliter, 1,000 grams in a kilogram, and 1,000 milligrams in a gram. The uniformity of the system readily allows one to visualize and estimate relative sizes and quantities.

The basic units of the SI have always been defined with the intention of relating to some universal and unalterable standard. In some cases, the definitions have been changed to relate the unit to a more permanent universal feature or a more accurately known property. For example, as the accuracy of time measurement greatly improved, the definition of the meter was changed from being a specific fraction of the distance between two fixed terrestrial points to "the length of the path traveled by light in vacuum during a time interval of 1/299792458 of a second."

A major turning point along these lines came in November 2018, when sixty countries participating in the General Conference on Weights and Measures unanimously voted to revise the definitions of the SI base units so that all seven would be based on universal constants. While the meter, candela, and second already conformed to this requirement, the kilogram, kelvin, mole, and ampere were officially redefined in terms of constants (and the definitions of the other three units were made more rigorous), effective May 2019. Widely hailed as a major development in science despite little impact on daily measurements for most people, the decision meant that the seven base units would be tied to the most stable properties known.

APPLICATIONS AND PRODUCTS

Applications and products related to the metric system essentially fall into two categories: educational devices and training to promote familiarity with the system and metric versions of existing products and the tools required for their maintenance.

Educational devices and training. The long history of independent measurement systems has served to entrench those systems in common usage. Therefore, a very large body of materials, products, and devices have been constructed using nonmetric measurements. More significantly, those independent systems have been so deeply entrenched in the education systems of many nations, including the United States, that several generations of people have grown up using no other system. The familiarity gained through a lifetime of using a particular system generally gives individuals the ability to visualize and estimate quantities in terms of that measurement system. Making the change to a different measurement system (such as US efforts to introduce the metric system in the 1970s) represents a paradigm shift that leaves many individuals unable to associate the new measurement units with even the most familiar dimensions. Such a change, however, can be accommodated in a number of ways as the world continues to adopt the metric system of measurement as its universal standard.

The most basic method of replacing one system with another is to incorporate the new system into the basic education system, teaching it in such a manner that it becomes the entrenched measurement system as children progress through school. It is, therefore, important that teachers are educated in the use of the metric system and they can actively replace their own reliance on any former system they have used. This guarantees that, in time, the older system is completely displaced from the public lexicon and the metric system becomes the primary measurement system over a period of essentially one generation.

Those who have already left the school system can learn the metric system through training programs. Training in the metric system can be incorporated into professional development programs at the workplace or take the shape of formal training programs offered by local educational institutions or third-party providers.

Metric versions of existing devices. The vast majority of goods and devices produced in countries that have not adopted the metric standard must be maintained using their original component dimensions because metric values and nonmetric values are not generally interchangeable. The fundamental difference between the two bases of measurement ensures that any coincidence of size from one system to the other is exactly that: coincidental. Therefore, switching to metric goods and devices requires that complete new lines of products be made with metric rather than nonmetric dimensions. This requirement places an odd sort of constraint on the situation because nonmetric parts and tools must still be produced in order to maintain existing nonmetric devices. At the same time, new devices to replace those that fail are produced in metric dimensions. This means that tradespeople, such as automobile mechanics, maintenance workers, and engineers, must obtain double sets of tools, and supply stores must maintain double sets of components and supplies. In addition, tools for taking measurements must be capable of using both metric and nonmetric dimensions, although the incorporation of electronic capabilities into many tools has greatly minimized the difficulties that arise from this dual requirement.

CAREERS AND COURSEWORK

The International System of Units is not broad enough to provide a field of study or advanced coursework and, by itself, is unlikely to form the basis of a career. However, during the process of converting from a nonmetric measurement system to a metric system, opportunities will arise for those familiar with SI to create and provide training to facilitate understanding and use of the metric system.

Anyone entering a technical or scientific field must become familiar with the metric system, as this has been the standard system of measurement in those areas since the SI was developed. As the metric system becomes more and more widely adopted and accepted in the United States, students and others should expect to carry out measurements and calculations using the appropriate metric system units.

Careers that depend specifically on measurement include quality-control engineering and most branches of scientific research and physical engineering. Specific examples of measurement-based careers include civil engineering, medical and biochemical analysis, analytical chemistry, metrology, mechanical engineering, and industrial chemical engineering.

SOCIAL CONTEXT AND FUTURE PROSPECTS

The 2018 redefinition of the SI base units represented a significant moment in history for the scientific community. It marked the first time that all the measurements within the metric system would be based on fundamental natural properties rather than physical characteristics. While most individuals' use of the metric system was unchanged by the redefinition, it was hailed by scientists for its potential to spark new theoretical and technological innovations. In addition, it was expected to cut down on the complexity and cost of calibration for precision devices in laboratories and industrial applications. However, the changes were criticized by some members of the scientific community who questioned the specifics of the new definitions and even debated the legitimacy of some of the base units.

Efforts continue to make the metric system the standard system of measurement in the United States, as it already is in most of the rest of the world. As international trade and offshore manufacturing increase, the necessity for American industry to adopt the SI increases. In addition, educational systems have increased their focus on science and technology, making metric systems more familiar to children in American schools. However, resistance to abandoning the US customary system of measures remains widespread, and metric adoption is subject to changing political and social attitudes.

In the meantime, development of other measurement systems and hybrids of measuring systems progresses. For example, the manufacturing community adopted a standard unit called the "metric inch," which is the standard inch divided into hundredths, to be used on visual measuring devices. There is some logic to this adoption, as this measurement apparently corresponds with the limits of differentiation of which the human eye is capable to a better degree than does the millimeter division of the metric system. However, such developments are likely to delay and otherwise interfere with the adoption of the metric system.

—*Richard M. J. Renneboog, MSc*

Further Reading

Butcher, Kenneth S., Linda D. Crown, and Elizabeth J. Gentry, editors. *The International System of Units (SI): Conversion Factors for General Use*. National Institute of Standards and Technology, 2006.

De Courtenay, Nadine, Olivier Darrigol, and Oliver Schlaudt, editors. *The Reform of the International System of Units (SI): Philosophical, Historical and Sociological Issues*. Routledge, 2019.

Göbel, Ernst O., and Uwe Siegner. *The New International System of Units (SI): Quantum Metrology and Quantum Standards*. Wiley VCH, 2019.

Himbert, M. E. "A Brief History of Measurement." *European Physical Journal Special Topics*, vol. 172, 2009, pp. 25-35.

Isakov, Edmund. *International System of Units (SI): How the World Measures Everything, and the People Who Made It Possible*. Industrial Press, 2013.

"The Redefinition of the SI Units." *NPL*, www.npl.co.uk/si-units/the-redefinition-of-the-si-units. Accessed 28 Nov. 2021.

"SI Redefinition." *NIST*, www.nist.gov/si-redefinition. Accessed 28 Nov. 2021.

Isometric Drawing

ABSTRACT

Isometric drawing is the process of representing a physical or conceptual object as a three-dimensional (3D) view. Isometric drawings are traditionally prepared using graphing paper in which the grid lines are angled at 30 degrees, and height, width, and depth scales use identical dimension scales. Hence, they are isometric. Manual conversion of a two-dimensional (2D) drawing into an isometric drawing requires point-to-point transfer of features. Computer graphics programs are capable of rendering 2D views into 3D views, an essential feature of computer-generated imagery in many applications.

INTRODUCTION

Isometric drawing is the process of representing a physical or conceptual object as a three-dimensional (3D) view. Isometric drawings are traditionally prepared using graphing paper in which the grid lines are angled at 30 degrees, and height, width, and depth scales use identical dimension scales. Hence, they are isometric. Using different scales on the depth axis results in a perspective drawing that is not isometric. Manual conversion of a two-dimensional (2D) drawing into an isometric drawing requires point-to-point transfer of features. This allows the 2D, or orthographic, drawing to be transferred in a one-to-one manner from regular square-grid graphing paper to the 3D, or isometric, graphing paper. The isometric paper itself does not have to be on the same scale as the orthographic drawing, which allows the isometric drawing to be larger or smaller than the orthographic drawing as desired.

Computer graphics programs can render 2D views into 3D views, an essential feature of computer-generated imagery (CGI) used in animations, films, video games, motion-based simulators, and many other applications.

BASIC DRAFTING

The simplest manual drafting techniques that are taught to students use a set of basic drafting tools: a precision-made drafting table, very sharp pencils, a T-square, a 30-60 triangle template, a 45-90 triangle template, and a gum eraser. Typically, the drafting instructor will present an object with a specific shape and specific dimensions and task the students to produce an accurate orthographic drawing consisting of the front, side, and top views of the object. Beginners often face some confusion at first regarding the three different views and may even attempt to represent the object's three dimensions in a single view before catching on to the correct method. Part of the problem in this is that from birth, people see the world in perspective view due to the phenomenon of visual parallax. One's left and right eyes see slightly different images of the same thing due to their separation from each other, and these different views are combined into a single perspective image by the visual processing center of the brain. It requires some training to overcome this tendency and understand orthographic imaging. For example, a person who looks at one side of a cube understands the cube's overall shape, and the brain expects to see that shape. However, an orthographic view of one side of a cube is a simple 2D square and nothing more. It takes a degree of focus to remove the brain's expectation of the cube's shape. The same principle applies to every 3D object seen in an orthographic view, no matter how complex the structure of the object may be.

The basic principle of orthographic drawing is that the draftsperson draws only the features that are visible on the object when looking directly at it along one of its length, width, or depth axes. If a cube had a hole drilled through it from one side to the other, that hole would not be visible in the front and top views, only in the side view. The side view of this perforated block would therefore appear simply as a square with a circle in it at the relative location of the hole. In keeping with drafting conventions such as the use of dashed lines to show such hidden features of an object, the front and top views could have dashed lines extending from one side to the other to show the dimensions of the hole.

With the front view of the object determined, the remainder of the orthographic drawing can then be completed. The drafters will draw barely visible "construction lines" vertically and horizontally from pertinent features of the front view to transfer those dimensions to the top and side views, then draw 45-degree construction lines to complete the transfer of structural details between the top and side views.

THE ISOMETRIC DRAWING

In basic drafting, an isometric drawing is generated from the orthographic drawing using isometric graphing paper that is scaled to represent the 3D axes (x, y, and z, corresponding to length, width, and depth) at mutual angles of 120 degrees. This results in a view that declines at a 15-degree angle for the length and inclines at a 15-degree angle for width and depth. It is important to note that an isometric drawing therefore has no horizontal lines, except in the rare case that an angular feature of the object being represented coincidentally falls horizontally in the isometric drawing. In essence, an isometric drawing represents the object as it would appear orthographically if it had been tilted 15 degrees clockwise and then rotated 15 degrees toward the viewer.

To transfer an orthographic drawing to isometric graphing paper, the draftsperson chooses an appropriate starting point, often the lower left corner of the front view. A corresponding starting point is then chosen on the isometric graphing paper. Each scale point on the orthographic drawing is then transferred to the corresponding point on the isometric

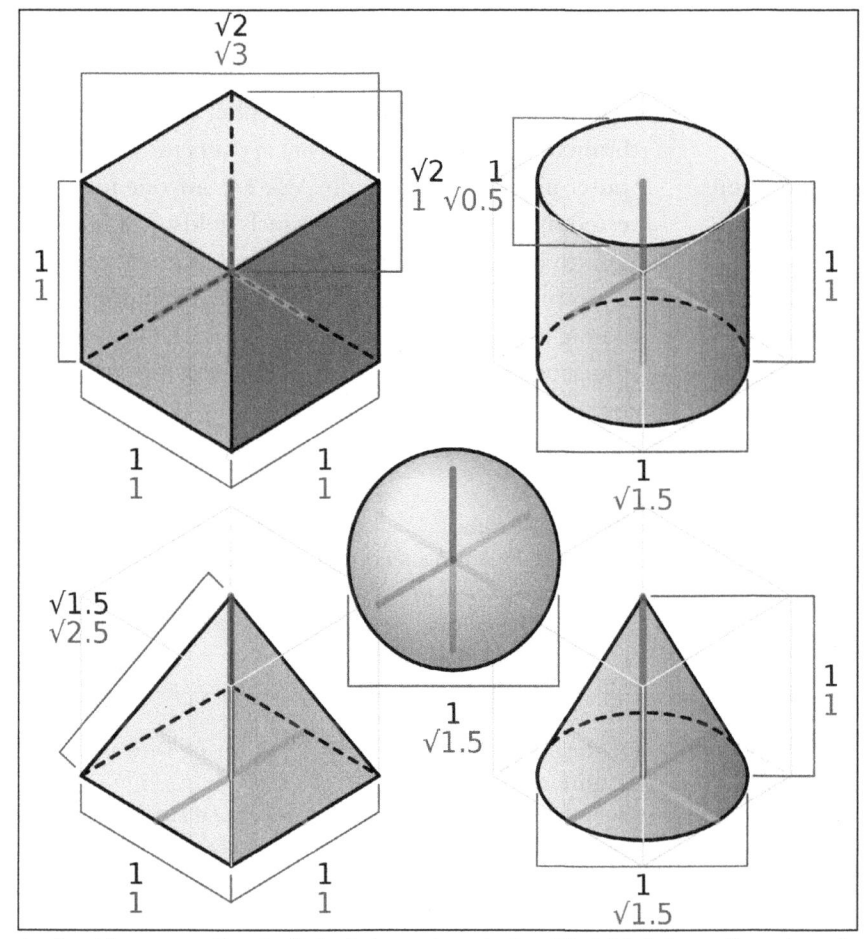

A cube, sphere, pyramid and cylinder in isometric projection. Black labels denote dimensions of the 3D object, while red labels denote dimensions of the 2D projection (drawing). Image by Cmglee, via Wikimedia Commons.

279

graphing paper and connected by drawing lines accordingly. This produces a 3D view of the object much as it would appear in reality. Naturally, certain features and shapes will have a different appearance in an isometric view than they have in an orthographic view. For example, a circle that is transformed from its perfectly round orthographic shape will become an ellipse in an orthographic view. Similarly, an equilateral triangle will transform into an isosceles triangle, all the while retaining its relative location in the overall proportions of the drawing.

ISOMETRIC DRAWING IN COMPUTER GRAPHICS

Conversion of an orthographic drawing to an isometric drawing is equivalent to rotating the object in the drawing slightly about its depth and length axes. Mathematically, coordinates are transformed rotationally using transformation matrix operations. The exact form of the transformation matrix uses the location of the point being rotated and the angle through which it is to be transformed. For static isometric renderings of an object, this transformation is carried out just once for each point to generate the 3D view of the object. Repeated, or iterative, rotational transformations allow for the 3D view to be rotated dynamically and manipulated in various ways to view potential changes in shape and function without first having to create the actual physical object. Many examples of the capability of this process can be seen in the supplementary material included on many Blu-ray Disks of films that contain significant CGI footage.

Similarly, dynamic isometric rendering is a staple of video games and motion simulators, especially those that employ a 360-degree world view. In such applications, however, the rendering is termed axonometric (of which isometric is a subset) to maintain the perspective view by using different scales on the 3D axes. In such games, as well as in advanced simulators (flight simulators, driving simulators, and others), the player's point of view is able to turn in any direction and see the surroundings in the appropriate perspective. It requires a considerable amount of dedicated graphics processing power to achieve this, but the capability to do so increases almost daily with advances in computer technology.

ISOMETRIC DRAWING IN HISTORY

While dynamic manipulation of isometry is a relatively recent development in historical terms, the principle of isometric drawing is not. Isometric drawings appeared in Chinese art as early as the twelfth century CE, and many examples of isometric drawings of machinery construction emerged by the early 1800s. Since the mid-nineteenth century, isometric drawing has been an essential feature of all branches of engineering, from architecture to computer-aided engineering (CAE). For anyone interested in pursuing a career in such fields, it is important to learn the computational and mathematical concepts that are the basis of both static and dynamic isometric drawing and rendering, although the actual calculations are now the province of computers.

—*Richard M. Renneboog, MSc*

Further Reading

Congdon-Fuller, Ashleigh, Antonio Ramirez, and Douglas Smith. *Technical Drawing 101 with AutoCAD 2022: A Multidisciplinary Guide to Drafting Theory and Practice*. SDC Publications, 2021.

Marschner, Steve, and Peter Shirley. *Fundamentals of Computer Graphics*. 4th ed., CRC Press, 2016.

Rathnam, K. A First Course in Engineering Drawing. Springer, 2018.

Sexton, Timothy J. *A Concise Introduction to Engineering Graphics Including Worksheet Series B*. 6th ed., SDC Publications, 2019.

Singh, Lakhwinder Pal, and Harwinder Singh. *Engineering Drawing: Principles and Applications*. Cambridge UP, 2021.

Jet Engine Technology

ABSTRACT

Jet engines are machines that add energy to a fluid stream and generate thrust from the increase of momentum and pressure of the fluid. Jet engines, which usually include turbomachines to raise the pressure, vary greatly in size. Applications include microelectromechanical gas turbines for insect-sized devices; mid-sized engines for helicopters, ships, and cruise missiles; giant turbofans for airliners; and scramjets for hypersonic vehicles. Jet engine development pushes technology frontiers in materials, chemical kinetics, measurement techniques, and control systems. Born in the desperation of World War II, jet engines have come to power twenty-first-century modern aircraft.

DEFINITION AND BASIC PRINCIPLES

The term "jet engine" is typically used to denote an engine in which the working fluid is mostly atmospheric air, so that the only propellant carried on the vehicle is the fuel used to release heat. Typically, the mass of fuel used is only about 2 to 4 percent of the mass of air that is accelerated by the vehicle.

BACKGROUND AND HISTORY

British engineer Frank Whittle and German engineer Hans Pabst von Ohain independently invented the jet engine, earning patents in Britain in 1932 and in Germany in 1936, respectively. Whittle's engine used a centrifugal compressor and turbine. The gas came in near the axis, was flung out to the periphery, and returned to the axis through ducts. Ohain's engine used a combination of centrifugal and axial-flow turbomachines. The gas direction inside the engine was mostly aligned with the axis of the engine, but it underwent small changes as it passed through the compressor and turbine. The axial-flow engine had higher thrust per unit weight of the engine and smaller frontal area than the centrifugal machine. Initially, the axial-flow machine, which had a large number of stages and blades, was much more prone to failure than the centrifugal machine, which had sturdier blades and fewer moving parts. However, these problems were resolved, and most modern jet engines use purely axial flow.

Several early experiments with jet engines ended in explosions. Ohain's engine was successfully used to power a Heinkel He 178 aircraft on August 27, 1939. Ohain's engine led to the Junkers Jumo 004 axial turbojet engine, which was mass-produced to power the Messerschmitt Me 262 fighter aircraft in 1944. The British Gloster E.28/39, which contained one of Whittle's engines, flew in 1941. In September 1942, a General Electric engine powered the Bell XP-59 Airacomet, the first American jet fighter aircraft.

The de Havilland Comet jet airliner service began in 1952, powered by the Rolls-Royce Avon. In 1958, a de Havilland Comet jet operated by British Overseas Airways Corporation flew from London to New York, initiating transatlantic passenger jet service. In the mid-1950s, the Rolls-Royce Conway became the first turbofan in airliner service when it was used for the Boeing 707. The Rolls-Royce Olympus afterburning turbofan powered the supersonic Concorde in 1969.

The majority of aircraft have come to be powered by jet engines, including commercial jetliners such as the Boeing 777, the first such aircraft to be designed entirely through digital means. As in the broader field of aerospace design, computer-aided design (CAD) software proved beneficial to the field of jet engine design during the late twentieth and early twenty-first centuries, providing designers with the opportunity to design, model, and virtually test crucial components such as turbine blades.

HOW IT WORKS

Jet engines operate by creating thrust through the Brayton thermodynamic cycle. In a process called "isentropic compression," a mixture of working gases is compressed, with no losses in stagnation pressure. Heat is chemically released or externally added to the fluid, ideally at constant pressure. A turbine extracts work from the expanding gases. This work runs the compressor and other components such as a fan or propeller, depending on the engine type and application. The gas leaving the turbine expands further through a nozzle, exiting at a high speed.

Jet engine developers try to maximize the pressure and temperature that the engine can tolerate. The thermal efficiency of the Brayton cycle increases with the overall pressure ratio; therefore, designers try to get the highest possible pressure at the end of the compression. However, the temperature rise accompanying the pressure rise limits the amount of heat that can be added before the temperature limit of the engine is reached. Thrust is highest when the greatest net momentum increase is added to the flow. The propulsive efficiency of the engine is highest when the speed of the jet exhaust is close to the flight speed of the vehicle. These considerations drive jet engine design in different directions depending on the ap-

A Pratt & Whitney F100 turbofan engine for the F-15 Eagle being tested in the hush house at Florida Air National Guard base. Photo via Wikimedia Commons. [Public domain.]

plication. For very-high-speed applications (typically military engines), engine mass and frontal area must be kept low, so a smaller amount of air is ingested and accelerated through a large speed difference. For engines such as those used on airliners, a large amount of air is ingested using a large diameter intake and accelerated through a small speed difference for best propulsive efficiency. The major components of a jet engine are the inlet, diffuser, compressor, fan, propeller, combustor, turbine, afterburner, nozzles, and gearbox.

Inlet diffuser. The engine inlet is designed to capture the required airflow without causing flow separation. An aircraft flying at supersonic speeds has a supersonic inlet in which a series of shocks slows down the flow to subsonic speeds with minimal losses in pressure. Once the flow is subsonic, it is slowed further to the Mach number of about 0.4 needed at the face of the compressor or fan. A supersonic inlet and diffuser may lose 5 to 10 percent of the stagnation pressure of the incoming flow when used with aircraft flying in excess of Mach 2.

Compressor, fan, and propeller. In 1908, René Lorin patented a jet engine in which a reciprocating piston engine compressed the fluid. In 1913, he patented a supersonic ramjet engine in which enough compression would occur simply by slowing the flow down to subsonic speeds. In 1921, Maxime Guillaume patented a jet engine with a rotating axial-flow compressor and turbine. Most modern engines use the turbomachine in some form. The compressor is built in several stages, with the pressure ratio of each stage limited to prevent flow separation and stall. A centrifugal compressor stage consists of a rotor that imparts a strong radial velocity to the flow, and the flow is flung out at the periphery of the blades with added kinetic energy. The flow is then turned and brought back near the axis by a diffuser stage in which the static pressure rises and the flow speed decreases. In an axial compressor, work is added to the flow in several stages, as many as fifteen in some engines. In each stage, a spinning rotor wheel with many blades that act as lifting wings, imparts a swirl velocity to the flow. This added energy is then converted to a pressure rise in stator blade passages, bringing the flow back to being axial, but with increased pressure. Some newer compressors have counterrotating wheels in each stage instead of a rotor and a stator. Shock-in-rotor stages use blades moving at supersonic speed relative to the flow to create large pressure rise because of shocks. Supersonic through-flow compressor designs are being developed for future high-speed engines.

The fans of most engines are extensions of the first, or low-pressure, compressor stages. Fans have only one or two stages, and fewer, larger blades than the compressor stages.

Propellers are used in turboprop engines to produce a portion of the engine's thrust.

Combustor. The combustor is designed to mix and react the fuel with the air rapidly and to contain the reaction zone within an envelope of cooling air. At the exit of the combustor, these flows are mixed to ensure the most uniform temperature distribution across the gases entering the turbine. Older combustors were either several cans connected by tubes, arranged around the turbomachine shaft, or an annular passage. Some modern combustors are arranged in a reverse-flow geometry to enable better mixing and reaction. Ideally, a jet engine combustor must add all the heat that can be released from the fuel, at a constant pressure, with minimal pressure losses because of flow separation and turbulence. Heat addition must also be done at the lowest flow Mach number possible.

Turbine. The critical limiting temperature in a jet engine is the temperature at the inlet to the first turbine stage. This is usually tied to the strength of the blade material at high temperatures. A turbine has only a few stages, typically four or fewer. The highest mass flow rate through the engine is limited to the flow rate at which the passages at the final turbine stage are choked, in other words, when the Mach number reaches 1 at these passages. Turbine stage disks and blades are integrated into blisks and can be made as a single piece, with cooling passages inside the blades, using powder metallurgy.

The turbine is directly attached to the compressor through a shaft. To enable starting the compressor and better matching the requirements of the different stages, a twin-spool or three-spool design is used, where the outer (low-pressure, lower rotation speed) stages of the compressor, fan, and turbine are connected through an inner shaft, and the inner (high-pressure) stages are connected through a concentric, outer shaft.

Afterburner. Older military engines use an afterburner (also known as "reheat") duct attached downstream of the turbine, where more fuel is added and burned, with temperatures possibly exceeding the turbine inlet temperature. Afterburners are highly inefficient but produce a large increment of thrust for short durations. Therefore, afterburners are used at takeoff, in supersonic dashes, or in combat situations.

Nozzles. For jet engines without afterburners, the exit velocity is at most sonic and the nozzle is just a converging duct. If the exhaust is expanded to supersonic speeds, the nozzle has a convergent-divergent contour. Thrust-vectoring nozzles either rotate the whole nozzle, as in the case of the Harrier or the F-22, or use paddles in the exhaust, as in the case of the Sukhoi-30.

Gearbox. When the engine must drive a rotor, propeller, or counterrotating fan, a gearbox is used to reduce the speed or change the direction of rotation. This usually adds considerable weight to the engine.

APPLICATIONS AND PRODUCTS

Ramjets and scramjet. Ramjets are used to power vehicles at speeds from about Mach 0.8 to 4. The diffuser slows the flow down to subsonic speeds, increasing the pressure so much that thrust can be generated without a mechanical compressor or turbine. Beyond Mach 4, the pressure loss in slowing down the flow to below Mach 1 is greater than the loss due to adding heat to a supersonic flow. In addition, if such a flow were decelerated to subsonic conditions, the pressure and temperature rise would be too high, either exceeding engine strength or leaving too little room for heat addition. In this regime, the supersonic combustion ramjet, or scramjet, becomes a better solution.

Turbojet. The turbojet is the purest jet engine, with a compressor and turbine added to the components of the ramjet. The turbojet can start from rest, which the pure ramjet cannot. However, since the turbojet converts all its net work into the kinetic energy of the jet exhaust, the exhaust speed is high. High propulsive efficiency requires a high flight speed, making the turbojet most suitable near Mach 2 to 3. Because jet noise scales as the fifth or sixth power of jet speed, the turbojet engine was unable to meet the noise regulations near airports in the 1970s and was rapidly superseded by the turbofan for airliner applications.

Turbofan. The turbine of the turbofan engine extracts more work than that required to run the compressor. The remaining work is used to drive a fan, which accelerates a large volume of air, albeit through a small pressure ratio. The air that goes through the fan may exit the engine through a separate fan nozzle or mix with the core exhaust that goes through the turbine before exiting. Because the overall exhaust speed of the turbofan is much lower than that of the turbojet, the propulsive efficiency is high in the transonic speed range where airliner flight is most efficient, yet airport noise levels are far lower than with a turbojet. Turbofan engines are used for most civilian airliner applications and even for fighter and business jet engines.

Turboprop. In the turboprop engine, a separate power turbine extracts work to run a propeller instead of a fan. The propeller typically has a larger diameter than a fan for an engine of comparable thrust. However, the rotating speed of a propeller, constrained by the Mach number at the tip, is only on the order of 3,000 to 5,000 revolutions per minute, as opposed to turbomachine speeds, which may be three to ten times higher. Therefore, a gearbox is required.

Turboshaft. Instead of a propeller, a helicopter rotor or other device may be driven by the power turbine. Automobile turbochargers, turbopumps for rocket propellants, and gas turbine electric power generators are all turboshaft engines.

Propfan. Propfans are turbofans in which the fan has no cowling, so that it resembles a propeller and has a larger capture area, but the blades are highly swept and wider than propeller blades.

Air liquefaction. The high pressures encountered in high-speed flight make it possible to liquefy some of the captured and compressed air at lower altitudes, using heat transfer to cryogenic fuels such as hydrogen. The oxygen from this liquid can be separated out and stored for use as the vehicle reaches the edge of the atmosphere and beyond. Turboramjet engines using this technology could enable routine travel to and from space, with fully reusable, single-stage vehicles.

CAREERS AND COURSEWORK

Jet engine development and manufacturing are parts of a highly specialized industry. Those interested in jet engine technology must have a very good basic understanding of thermodynamics and dynamics and can specialize in combustion, turbomachine aerodynamics, gas dynamics, or materials engineering. Airlines operate engine test cells and employ many technical workers to diagnose and repair problems and ensure proper maintenance and operating procedures. The National Aeronautics and Space Administration (NASA) and the US Department of Defense (DoD) offer many opportunities in all aspects of jet engine technology.

Engine developers include the very large corporations that supply airliner engines and the smaller companies that develop engines for business jets, cruise missiles, and other applications. Companies doing research, development, and manufacture of jet engines are located primarily in the United States, Europe, Russia, Japan, and China. Many other nations also produce jet engines under license.

SOCIAL CONTEXT AND FUTURE PROSPECTS

Jet engines have developed rapidly since the 1940s and have come to dominate the propulsion market for atmospheric flight vehicles. Because the air that makes up more than 95 percent of the working fluid is free and does not have to be carried up from the ground, air-breathing propulsion offers a huge increase in specific impulse over rocket engines for flight in the atmosphere. As technology advances to enable rotating machinery to tolerate higher temperatures, pressures, and stresses, jet engines can become substantially lighter and more efficient per unit of thrust. Hydrogen-fueled engines can operate much more efficiently than hydrocarbon-fueled engines. Turbo-ramjet engines may one day enable swift and inexpensive access to space. Helicopter engines and the lift fans developed for vertical-landing fighter planes bring personal air vehicles closer to reality. Supersonic airline travel using hydrogen fuel is much closer to becoming routine. At the other extreme, micro jet engines are finding use in devices to power actuators for many applications, including surgical tools and devices to control stall on wings and larger engines. A major area of jet engine research in the twenty-first century is the search for a quieter, more fuel-efficient method of jet propulsion; many companies are looking into electric-powered turbofans rather than the traditional gas-powered ones, for example.

—Narayanan M. Komerath, PhD

Further Reading

Akhmedzyanov, D. A., A. E. Kishalov, and K. V. Markina. "Computer-Aided Design of Aircraft Gas Turbine Engines and Selection of Materials for Their Main Parts." *Vestnik*, vol. 14, no. 1, 2015, pp. 101-11.

Constant, Edward W. *The Origin of the Turbojet Revolution*. Johns Hopkins UP, 1980.

Conway, Erik M. *High-Speed Dreams: NASA and the Technopolitics of Supersonic Transportation, 1945-1999*. 2005. Johns Hopkins UP, 2008.

Hill, Philip Graham, and Carl R. Peterson. *Mechanics and Thermodynamics of Propulsion*. 2nd ed., Addison-Wesley, 2010.

Martin, Richard. "The Race for the Ultra-Efficient Jet Engine of the Future." *MIT Technology Review*, 23 Mar. 2016, www.technologyreview.com/s/601008/the-race-for-the-ultra-efficient-jet-engine-of-the-future/. Accessed 28 Nov. 2021.

Mattingly, Jack. *Elements of Gas Turbine Propulsion*. 1996. American Institute of Aeronautics and Astronautics, 2005.

Rolls Royce. *The Jet Engine*. 5th ed., Wiley, 2015.

Schaberg, Christopher. "The Jet Engine Is a Futuristic Technology Stuck in the Past." *The Atlantic*, 11 Feb. 2018, www.theatlantic.com/technology/archive/2018/02/engine-failure/552959/. Accessed 28 Nov. 2021.

Schobeiri, Meinhard T. *Gas Turbine Design, Components and System Design Integration*. 2nd ed., Springer Nature Switzerland, 2019.

"777 Commercial Transport." *Boeing*, www.boeing.com/history/products/777.page. Accessed 28 Nov. 2021.

JUST-IN-TIME MANUFACTURING

ABSTRACT

Manufacturing is the process of combining raw materials or assemblies for the creation of new products, which may be consumer ready or which may be used in other manufacturing processes. One of the most studied areas of manufacturing is the efficient and cost-effective flow of materials through the supply chain. Popularized in the twentieth century through the Toyota Production System (TPS), just-in-time (JIT) manufacturing encompasses practices and methods such as small lot production, group technology, kanban, and 5S. In the twenty-first century, JIT has applications in many industries.

OVERVIEW

The process of combining raw materials or assemblies for the creation of new products, the manufacturing process is simple in theory but complex in practice. One of the most studied areas is the efficient and cost-effective flow of materials through the supply chain. The supply chain refers to the process of bringing an end product to market, from the production of raw materials to the consumer. Historically, this was a long path with materials, parts, and products stockpiled in warehouses and other storage facilities and drawn upon as needed by each entity in the chain. Producers of raw materials would keep producing and filling up their warehouses in anticipation of orders. Manufacturers would produce parts, assemblies, and finished goods in large quantities to attain economies of scale and reduce the number of machine setups. Retailers would then buy in quantities sufficient to meet expected consumer demand over weeks and even months.

Just-in-time (JIT) manufacturing turns this traditional supply chain on its head. It has its roots in a very simple idea, espoused succinctly by industrialist Henry Ford: "If transportation were perfect and an even flow of materials could be assured, it would not be necessary to carry any stock whatsoever." Why does it matter? In one phrase—cost reduction.

Beyond the obvious costs of the warehouse itself (lease or mortgage, utilities, and property taxes), are the labor costs involved with managing the inventory—receiving, storing, picking, and transporting. Add to that the equipment and systems needed to support these processes. Lastly, one must consider the opportunity cost of money that is tied up in inventory that is not being used immediately.

Development of JIT manufacturing. While Ford understood the value and concept of JIT, it was in the 1950s that the automobile manufacturer Toyota first fully implemented the concept and expanded it with the total quality management (TQM) system to create the Toyota Production System (TPS), also known more generically as "lean manufacturing." The founder of Toyota, Toyoda Kiichiro, after observing that American automobile factories were nine times more productive than Toyota, challenged his chief engineer, Taiichi Ohno, to catch up with American automakers in three years. Ohno not only did that but also created a system that was to be an enduring model for efficient manufacturing the whole world over.

Ohno identified eight wastes that account for up to 95 percent of all costs in traditional manufacturing:

- *Overproduction*: Producing more than a customer needs incurs heavy warehousing, equipment, and labor costs.
- *Waiting*: Any machine or human in a wait state, no matter what they are waiting for, represents lost money and opportunity.
- *Transportation*: Materials that are transported from the supplier to any location (e.g., a warehouse) other than the point-of-use creates unnecessary transportation costs in time and money.
- *Non-value-added processing*: Quality control (traditional processes of inspecting completed products and fixing defects after production is complete) is unnecessary in a manufacturing environment where products are produced without defects (quality assurance).
- *Excess inventory*: Carrying more inventory than is needed, from raw materials to finished goods, incurs expensive warehouse space and labor.
- *Defects*: Product defects incur labor, space, equipment, and time costs.
- *Excess motion*: Incurring more motion than is necessary to carry out a task wastes time and labor.
- *Underutilized people*: Failure to leverage the skills, creativity, time, and other attributes of people results in wasted opportunities for organizational, team, and individual efficiency improvements.

TPS was developed to address each of these wastes and is centered on a set of guiding principles that must be adopted in order for specific methods and techniques to succeed. Indeed, many implementations of JIT practices have failed due to a failure to adopt organization-wide policies and practices that support JIT.

Spread of JIT/TQM manufacturing. After Toyota's outstanding success with TPS in meeting and exceeding American manufacturing production at significantly lower costs, manufacturers around the globe rapidly adopted and emulated TPS-based practices throughout the 1980s and beyond. A 2006 survey of US manufacturers by *IndustryWeek* and the Manufacturing Performance Institute for the 2006 Census of Manufacturers showed that just-in-time supplier deliveries were at the top of the list of most commonly used methods for managing inventories, with over 43 percent of respondents reporting its use in their operations. JIT remained popular among US manufacturers over the next years: by 2020, according to a survey conducted by RapidRatings, 59 percent of US companies surveyed reported that they would run out of stock within two weeks if they had to halt production, a statistic that industry commentators linked to those companies' use of JIT.

JIT has enabled a different world. The twenty-first-century supply chain increasingly moves small amounts of product at a time, delivered directly onto the factory floor or retail shelves, rather than into warehouses. Manufacturing has been revolutionized with investments that focus on improved flexibility in volume, product, and delivery; increased production speed; and waste reduction. All this has worked to provide faster product to market rates at reduced costs.

Importance of JIT systems. A JIT system is important to manufacturers for several reasons. First, and most obvious, it saves the cost of warehouses, related equipment, and the people needed to manage the inventory in those warehouses. Second, it eliminates the need to predict far in advance how much material will be needed, thereby reducing wasted materials. It also enables the manufacturer to respond to customer requests in a fraction of the time previously required. In a world of aggressive cost competition, JIT enables a highly cost-effective way to manufacture if it is well implemented.

One can imagine, however, just how tricky this process can be. Materials planning must be highly accurate and efficient; suppliers must able to produce small lots of materials efficiently, quickly, and cost-effectively; and effective contingency plans must be in place to counter disruptions in the supply chain, such as natural disasters, accidents, or union strikes. Thus, there is considerable risk, and that risk has a demonstrated inverse relation to profitability. Yet, even so, companies utilizing the JIT model are generally more profitable than those that are not, even adjusting for the increased risk involved.

IMPLEMENTATION OF JIT SYSTEMS

JIT manufacturing implementation is typically made up of a group of programs, each contributing specific methods for achieving a JIT model. Some of the common programs implemented are as follows:

Focused factory. The "focused factory," a term coined by Wickham Skinner in a 1974 article for the *Harvard Business Review*, is the philosophy of allowing a factory (or self-contained production unit within a physical plant) a limited product mix for a particular market. Rather than expanding a factory's capabilities when adding new products and markets, the focused factory model dictates the creation of new factories. Manufacturers that have implemented this model have consistently shown reduced cycle times and improved on-time deliveries.

Small lots. Small lots production refers to the proactive reduction of batch sizes to the smallest lot possible. This reduces inventory carrying costs and facilitates reduced lead and cycle times, which enables faster turn-around time for customers.

Reduced setup times (the elapsed time between production runs used to change over machines) aid the JIT process by making it more feasible for manufacturers to produce small lots. The longer the setup time, the costlier it is to produce small lots of the product. In the JIT world is the Single Minute Exchange of Dies (SMED) method, also often referred to as "quick changeover." This was introduced in TPS and was applied to the changeover of dies but later found much wider applications. Simplistically, SMED is the practice of completing as many steps in the changeover process as possible while a production run is still in process, and reducing and improving the efficiency of the steps that must be completed during the changeover.

By the second decade of the twenty-first century, developing technologies such as three-dimensional (3D) printing likewise facilitated small lot production, enabling manufacturers to print small machine parts and other products in small batches.

Group technology. Group technology involves grouping parts that have physical similarities or are used for similar manufacturing processes to reduce work-in-progress and lead times. Instead of the traditional factory layout with similar machines grouped together and work-in-progress moving from area to area, individual factory cells (cell manufacturing) are created with all the machines necessary to complete the production of a particular product or group of products.

Kanban. Kanban is a Japanese word meaning sign and refers to a signaling system that is in wide use in JIT manufacturing to ensure the just-in-time delivery of parts and materials, as they are needed.

Kanban is a "pull" system—when a product or material is needed, a signal is sent to replenish the product or material. This flows all the way up the supply chain, with each entity in the chain sending a signal up the chain for its own replenishment after responding to a signal further down in the chain.

On the factory floor, this has historically been done with cards—when a cart or bin is empty, the card at the bottom is used to signal for more material. A good analogy is a checkbook. The kanban would be the ticket slipped in at the point where replenishments should be ordered.

Many systems, especially those spanning companies or plants, now use electronic kanban. A good example is in retail, where the checkout system creates the signal to suppliers when an inventory item reaches the reorder point.

5S. 5S is a methodology for eliminating wasted time by having an organized workplace where everything is in its place. The five Ss are:

- *Seiri* (or separating): Storing or discarding any materials or tools not needed for the task at hand.
- *Seiton* (or sorting): Having tools and materials arranged for efficient workflow.
- *Seiso* (or cleaning): Keeping the workplace clean and neat.
- *Seiketsu* (or standardizing): Doing the same tasks in the same way every time.
- *Shitsuki* (or sustaining): Maintaining the standards and practices developed with the first four Ss.

Total productive maintenance (TPM). TPM focuses on keeping all equipment in top condition to avoid breakdowns and delays in the manufacturing process.

Other concepts. Visual control is based on the premise that information presented visually is comprehended far faster than words.

The concept of the multifunctional employee is related to cell manufacturing, where employees are trained in multiple facets of the cell's technologies. Even outside of cell manufacturing, employees with multiple skill sets create organizational adaptability.

Uniform plant loading is a method of planning production so that the manufacturing processes throughout the factory are fully utilized, avoiding idling and overloads.

A quality circle is a TQM method used to minimize or eliminate rework due to defects. Comprising a team of workers, its purpose is to identify improvements to processes that will reduce errors.

Key success factors. In order to implement JIT successfully, operations must be highly integrated and synchronized, with empowered workers who can resolve problems on the spot to keep production moving and who are enabled to influence the production process to eliminate waste and improve productivity. This foundation is typically provided in a TQM environment, discussed further later in this article.

Also critical to success is the readiness and willingness of one's suppliers to work with the JIT system. When a company along the supply chain is unable or unwilling to implement JIT policies and practices, inventory must be stored somewhere. Either the supplier will stockpile it and pass the cost on to the manufacturer implicitly or explicitly or the manufacturer will store the inventory. Either way, the manufacturer has lost the key benefit of JIT—reduced inventory and subsequently lower costs.

Marriage of JIT and quality. American quality guru W. Edwards Deming introduced quality management to Japan in the 1950s. Total Quality Management (TQM) was well implemented before the introduction of JIT and provided an environment in which JIT could thrive. When US manufacturing companies began implementing JIT in the 1980s, TQM had not yet taken hold, and JIT met with mixed success. Once these companies realized the importance of TQM in the success of JIT, a TQM revolution began that continues in virtually every industry.

TQM is a management philosophy and practice that continuously improves the quality of products and processes in order to achieve customer satisfaction. TQM operates at all levels of the organization—everyone in the company has responsibility for quality. Because TQM has broader application in the organization and because it unifies the organizational entities by providing a cross-departmental philosophy for quality and process improvement, it lays a foundation upon which JIT programs can succeed.

APPLICATIONS

Successful integrations of JIT systems. There have been some notable successes, small and large, with implementations of JIT in the United States. Through implementation of JIT, and with some pro bono consulting support from Toyota, the Louisville, Kentucky-based American Printing House for the Blind Inc. was able to produce an IRS publication in one week with five people that had previously required twelve people and three weeks to produce.

After implementing JIT, Austin, Texas-based Factory Logic Software increased its production volume of fastener systems to 300,000 units annually with slightly more than 50 backorders per month. Prior to its implementation, it was producing about 200,000 units with an average of 800 backorders per month.

JIT has applications from production of raw materials all the way to the consumer markets. Walmart brought JIT to its retail stores to create one of the most cost-efficient retail supply chains in the world, requiring its suppliers to provide just-in-time inventory to its shelves, and going even further to vendor managed inventory (VMI), which puts the responsibility of its inventory management in the hands of its suppliers.

The principles of JIT are also being applied to other areas. In a survey conducted in 2005, Mohammad Z. Meybodi, associate professor of operations management in the School of Business at Indiana University Kokomo, found that organizations that applied JIT principles (empowered teams and quality practices, specifically) to new product development (NPD) developed significantly better-quality products in a much shorter time span and with significantly less cost.

But even beyond the supply chain, JIT principles have been applied to a host of other applications. "Just-in-time learning" technologies have been introduced to provide the right information at the right time for a host of applications—from figuring out how to fix a leaky faucet to making the best diagnosis in a complex medical case. The most effective technologies focus on the immediate need (just as in manufacturing), zeroing in on the right information based on the specific problem at hand.

DISCOURSE

Risks of JIT manufacturing. One of the key risks with JIT is that the world is not a perfect place. While JIT is an accepted standard for manufacturing, it is not without its risks and is not necessarily for every business application. The success of JIT depends on the ability of the supplier to avoid disruptions to its production, correctly predict demand, and achieve reliable, fast transportation. All manner of events can disrupt the supply of materials, from natural disasters to union strikes, which can have devastating effects on production if the company is not properly equipped to adjust or has little control over its supply chain. Beginning in 2020, the COVID-19 pandemic and the resulting lockdowns, which in some cases required factories and shipping companies to cease operations temporarily, disrupted global supply chains and led to shortages of crucial medical equipment as well as household essentials. While supply chains later normalized, the pandemic period drew attention to the risks of relying solely on JIT.

JIT constraints. In a 2006 paper, Dr. Tony Polito of East Carolina University and Dr. Kevin Watson of the University of New Orleans identified five major constraints on JIT practices that should be considered before a company decides to pursue JIT.

The first is customer-driven and economic conditions. Successful JIT requires a relatively stable pricing model for supplies, reasonably level customer demand, and a reliable supply of material. When materials pricing and consumer demand fluctuate significantly or scarcity issues are common, traditional manufacturing processes perform better.

The second constraint is logistics. There must be a reliable means for getting the materials from the supplier to the manufacturer. Transportation strikes, natural disasters, or remote locations with unreliable transportation can all adversely impact the supply chain. Generally speaking, the riskier the logistics, the more inventory the company should keep on hand.

Third, organizational culture and conditions can affect JIT practices. It goes without saying that a culture with poor worker and/or supplier relationships or with practices that are contrary to the worker empowerment model needed to support JIT must resolve these issues prior to implementing JIT.

The fourth constraint is intractable accounting and finance practices. Traditional companies typically focus on improvement of measures—inventory turns, sales, machine efficiency, etc.—rather than improvement of processes, which is at the core of JIT. Without a willingness and ability to change this, companies will be unsuccessful with JIT.

The fifth and last constraint is small supplier difficulties. Small suppliers generally lack the customers their high-volume counterparts possess. They must purchase in smaller quantities and lack the clout with their own suppliers to push JIT practices.

CONCLUSION

JIT has clearly had a radical impact on manufacturing paradigms the world over, and Toyota continues to lead the charge, practicing its TPS and achieving continued success and profitability in the auto industry. More and more manufacturers are implementing JIT and, if they are careful about how they are applying it and embedding organization-wide philosophies, are succeeding with it. However, disruptions to global supply chains have put increasing strain on JIT, and it is yet unclear how JIT will adapt to them. Undoubtedly, the world will continue to watch companies such as Toyota to get the answer to that question.

—*Joyce Gubata, MBA*

Further Reading

Callen, Jeffrey L., Mindy Morel, and Chris Fader. "The Profitability-Risk Tradeoff of Just-in-Time Manufacturing Technologies." *Managerial & Decision Economics*, vol. 24, no. 5, 2003, pp. 393-402.

Cox, Cody R., and Jeffrey M. Ulmer. "Lean Manufacturing: An Analysis of Process Improvement Techniques." *Franklin Business and Law Journal*, vol. 2015, no. 2, 2015, pp. 70-77.

Crone, Mark. "Are Global Supply Chains Too Risky?" *Logistics Management*, vol. 46, no. 4, 2007, pp. 37-40.

Eitel, Elisabeth. "3D Printing Goes Big-Time for Small Production Runs." *Machine Design*, 15 July 2014, www.machinedesign.com/3d-printing-cad/article/21831798/3d-printing-goes-bigtime-for-small-production-runs. Accessed 28 Nov. 2021.

Forde, Morgan. "Survey: 59% of US Companies Would Have 2 Weeks of Stock after Halting Production." *Supply Chain Dive*, 27 Mar. 2020, www.supplychaindive.com/news/coronavirus-survey-us-companies-shipments-after-production-stops/575026/. Accessed 28 Nov. 2021.

Hoss, Marcelo, and Carla Schwengber ten Caten. "Lean Schools of Thought." *International Journal of Production Research*, vol. 51, no. 11, 2013, pp. 3270-82.

Husby, Paul. "Becoming Lean." *Material Handling Management*, vol. 62, no. 8, 2007, pp. 42-45.

McClenahen, J. S. "JIT Tops Management Practices." *Industry Week/IW*, vol. 255, no. 12, 2006, p. 13.

McLachlin, Ron. "Internal Plant Environment and Just-in-Time Manufacturing." *International Journal of Manufacturing Technology & Management*, vol. 6, no. 1/2, 2004, pp. 112-24.

Pinto, José Luís Quesado, João Carlos O. Matas, Carina Pimental, et al. *Just in Time Factory: Implementation through Lean Manufacturing Tools*. Springer International Publishing, 2018.

Polito, Tony, and Kevin Watson. "Just-in-Time under Fire: The Five Major Constraints upon JIT Practices." *Journal of American Academy of Business, Cambridge*, vol. 9, no. 1, 2006, pp. 8-13.

Skinner, Wickham. "The Focused Factory." *Harvard Business Review*, May 1974, hbr.org/1974/05/the-focused-factory. Accessed 28 Nov. 2021.

Thakur-Weigold, Bublu, Stephan Wagner, and Tee Bin Ong. "The Challenging Business of Nuts and Bolts." *ISE Magazine*, Nov. 2016, pp. 44-48.

"Toyota Production System." *Toyota*, 2021, global.toyota/en/company/vision-and-philosophy/production-system/. Accessed 28 Nov. 2021.

K

KINEMATICS

ABSTRACT

Kinematics is the branch of classical mechanics concerned with the motion of particles or objects without explicit consideration of the masses and forces involved. Kinematics focuses on the geometry of motion and the relationship between position, velocity, and acceleration vectors of particles as they move. Kinematics is a subfield of classical mechanics, along with statics (the study of physical systems for which the forces are in equilibrium) and dynamics (the study of objects in motion under the influence of unequilibrated forces). In practice, kinematic equations appear in fields as diverse as astrophysics (e.g., to describe planetary orbits and the motion of other celestial bodies) and robotics (e.g., to describe the motion of an articulated arm on an assembly line).

MOTION OF A PARTICLE IN ONE DIMENSION

Kinematics focuses on the geometry of the motion of a particle, or point-like object, by investigating the relationship between position, velocity, and acceleration vectors of a particle without involving mass or force.

To describe mathematically the motion of a particle, it is first necessary to define a reference frame, or coordinate system, relative to which the motion of the particle is measured. For a particle moving in one dimension, a coordinate frame would be a number line.

The position, at time t, of a particle moving on a straight line can be described by its distance, $x(t)$, from a fixed point on the coordinate number line identified as the origin ($x = 0$).

The velocity $v(t)$ of the particle is the rate of change of its position with respect to time. Velocity is a vector quantity, which includes both the speed of the particle and its direction of motion. In one dimension, the speed of the particle is given by absolute value of the velocity, $|v(t)|$. The direction of motion is given by the sign of $v(t)$, with negative and positive values corresponding to motion to the left and right, respectively.

In general, the velocity is the first derivative, or rate of change, of the particle's position with respect to time: $v = dx/dt$.

In the special case of a particle moving at constant velocity v in one dimension, the position of the particle is given by $x(t) = vt + x_0$, where x_0 is the initial position of the particle at time $t = 0$.

The acceleration $a(t)$ of a particle is the rate of change of its velocity vector with respect to time. Acceleration is also vector quantity and includes both magnitude and direction. In one dimension, the absolute value $|a(t)|$ indicates the strength of the acceleration, or how quickly the velocity is changing. Note that the sign of $a(t)$ is the direction of the acceleration, not of the particle itself. When the sign of the acceleration and velocity are opposite, the speed of the particle will decrease.

In general, the acceleration is the time rate of change of the particle's velocity: $a = dv/dt$. Since velocity $v = dx/dt$, the acceleration is, equivalently, the second derivative of the particle's position with respect to time: $a = d^2x/dt^2$.

In the special case of a particle moving with constant acceleration a in one dimension, the velocity of the particle is given by $v(t) = at + v_0$, where v_0 is the initial velocity of the particle at time $t = 0$, and the position of the particle is given by $x(t) = \frac{1}{2}at^2 + v_0 t + x_0$, where x_0 is the initial position of the particle.

MOTION OF A PARTICLE IN TWO OR THREE DIMENSIONS

The position of a particle moving in two dimensions is a vector quantity. The position vector $\boldsymbol{p}$ is given by its coordinates (x, y) with respect to a coordinate reference frame. Together, the coordinate functions, $x(t)$ and $y(t)$, give the position of the particle at time t.

The *trajectory*, or path, $\boldsymbol{p}(t) = (x(t), y(t))$ of the particle is the curve in the plane defined parametrically by the coordinate functions.

Note that magnitude of the position vector, $\boldsymbol{p} = |\boldsymbol{p}| = \sqrt{x^2 + y^2}$, measures the distance from the particle to the origin.

As in one dimension, the velocity of a particle moving in two dimensions is the rate of change of its position with respect to time: $v(t) = d/dt\,\boldsymbol{p}(t)$, where the derivative is performed component wise. Thus, at time t, the velocity vector has x component $v(t) = d/dt\,x(t)$ and y component $v(t) = d/dt\,y(t)$.

Of key importance is the fact that the velocity vector $v(t) = d/dt\,\boldsymbol{p}(t)$ always points in the direction tangent to the trajectory $\boldsymbol{p}(t)$ of the particle, as the instantaneous velocity of the particle points in the direction the particle is moving at that instant.

The acceleration of a particle moving in two dimensions is the rate of change of its velocity vector with respect to time: $a(t) = d/dt\,v(t)$, where the derivative is again performed component wise. Thus, at time t, the acceleration vector has x component $a_x(t) = d/dt\,v_x(t)$ and y component $a_y(t) = d/dt\,v_y(t)$.

Since velocity is, in turn, the time-derivative of position, the components of the acceleration vector are the second derivatives of the coordinate functions. That is, $a_x(t) = d^2/dt^2\,x(t)$ and $a_y(t) = d^2/dt^2\,y(t)$.

In three dimensions, the motion of a particle is described similarly, with the trajectory of the particle given parametrically by $\boldsymbol{p}(t) = (x(t), y(t), zy(t))$ and the distance to the origin by $\boldsymbol{p} = |\boldsymbol{p}| = \sqrt{x^2 + y^2 + z^2}$.

The velocity, $v(t)$, and acceleration, $a(t)$, vectors gain z components as well; namely, $vz(t) = d/dt\,z(t)$ and $a_z(t) = d^2/dt^2 z(t)$.

OTHER TYPES OF KINEMATIC MOTION

Kinematic considerations can be extended to particles that are rotating about an axis and the motion of a particle with respect to another particle.

A point on a rotating circle of fixed radius is also constrained to move in one dimension. The kinematic equations of a rotating particle have the same form as above, with the linear quantities x, v, and a replaced by their rotational counterparts, angular position, angular velocity, and angular acceleration α.

The position of a particle may be defined with respect to a point other than the origin. The relative position of a particle with position vector $\boldsymbol{p}$ with respect to the point $\boldsymbol{q}$ is simply the vector difference, $\boldsymbol{p}$–$\boldsymbol{q}$. For speeds much less than the speed of light c, the relative velocity and relative acceleration are the first and second time-derivatives of the relative position vector. However, at speeds approaching c, the relative motion of two particles is dictated by the laws of special relativity.

—*Anne Collins*

Further Reading

Bi, Zhuming, and Xiaoqin Wang. *Computer Aided Design and Manufacturing*. Wiley-ASME Press, 2020.

Cohen, Michael. *Classical Mechanics: A Critical Introduction*. University of Pennsylvania, 2013, live-sas-physics.pantheon.sas.upenn.edu/sites/default/files/Classical_Mechanics_a_Critical_Introduction_0_0.pdf. Accessed 28 Nov. 2021.

"The Kinematic Equations." *Physics Classroom*, www.physicsclassroom.com/class/1DKin/Lesson-6/Kinematic-Equations. Accessed 28 Nov. 2021.

"What Is a Projectile?" *Physics Classroom*, www.physicsclassroom.com/class/vectors/Lesson-2/What-is-a-Projectile. Accessed 28 Nov. 2021.

Lean Manufacturing

ABSTRACT
Lean manufacturing refers to a company's ongoing, systematic effort to eliminate the sources of waste in a production process. Popularized by the Toyota Motor Company in the mid-twentieth century, lean manufacturing became a widely implemented manufacturing strategy and by the early twenty-first century encompassed a number of distinct tools, including cellular manufacturing and just-in-time (JIT) manufacturing.

OVERVIEW
Lean manufacturing refers to a company's ongoing, systematic effort to eliminate the sources of waste in a production process. The seeds of lean manufacturing in mass production were planted as early as the eighteenth century, when a French gunmaker, Honoré Blanc, implemented the time and resource-saving practice of using interchangeable parts for the assembly of guns. However, Toyota Motor Company is generally considered to have spearheaded modern lean manufacturing by implementing the just-in-time (JIT) inventory system on a full-scale basis in 1938.

THE MAJOR CAUSES OF WASTE IN THE PRODUCTION PROCESS
While there are many minor causes of waste in the production process, the major causes can be grouped into eight areas:
- Overproduction
- Waiting
- Conveyance
- Processing
- Inventory
- Unnecessary motion
- Processing failures
- Space

Overproduction. Overproduction waste refers to the practice of making something for which there is no customer. This was a very common practice before widespread adoption of lean manufacturing principles and is called "stockpiling." Many manufacturers still overproduce as a safety measure.

Waiting. Waiting waste results from searching for tools, or from waiting for machine setup, materials, or information. Whenever production workers are idle due to waiting for necessary parts, equipment, or information, the efficiency of the production process is compromised.

Conveyance. Conveyance waste involves the unnecessary moving of parts or information.

Processing. Processing waste occurs when more work is done to an item than is required by the customer's specifications, or when data must be entered into multiple locations.

Inventory. Inventory waste happens when assets are used to stock parts or products that have not been ordered by a customer.

Unnecessary motion. Waste from unnecessary motion includes time spent from performing extra movements, such as walking to get the parts needed for assembly. Unnecessary motion is similar to conveyance waste but generally applies to workers, while conveyance waste applies to extra movements of parts and data.

Processing failures. Waste from processing failure refers to any time spent reworking defective components or products.

Space. Space is wasted when more real estate is used than is required. Extra space also means more utilities and overhead required to manage the space.

LEAN MANUFACTURING TOOLS

Any technique or tool that reduces waste in a production process—whether it is developed in-house, copied from another company, or purchased from a supplier or consultant—can be considered part of a lean manufacturing strategy. However, the following five tools for reducing waste are commonly associated with lean manufacturing:

- Cellular manufacturing
- Just-in-time (JIT)
- Kaizen
- Kanban
- Poka-yoke

Cellular manufacturing. Cellular manufacturing involves the arrangement of production work stations and equipment in a sequence that supports a smooth flow of materials and components through the production process with minimal transport or delay. Cellular manufacturing minimizes the time required to manufacture a single product by moving the product through the entire production process one-piece at a time, at a rate determined by a customer's needs. Cellular manufacturing is in direct contrast to batch-and-queue (also known as "large-lot") production which involves processing multiple parts before sending them on to the next machine or process.

Just-in-time (JIT). The practice of JIT refers to the supplying of parts or items at the time that they are needed and not before. JIT can apply to parts or items supplied to the manufacturer or to the items that the manufacturer produces for its customers. In either scenario, JIT directly contrasts with the practice of building up inventory by stockpiling items.

Kaizen. Kaizen is a Japanese term that refers to the process of continuous improvement, often in small, incremental steps. To be effective, kaizen must involve the entire workforce in its philosophy and practice.

Kanban. Kanban is an integral part of the JIT production process; it is an information tool that specifies exactly which parts or items are needed during the production process and exactly when they are needed.

Poka-yoke. Poka-yoke refers to error-proofing the production process during the design phase to eliminate faulty products altogether or, if that is not possible, to detect defects at the earliest possible moment in the production process.

VIEWPOINTS

Lean manufacturing practices offer many advantages for the manufacturers who practice them. After all, most manufacturers want to eliminate waste from their production processes. However, depending upon the manufacturer and type of product manufactured, there can also be disadvantages to lean manufacturing.

Advantages of lean manufacturing practices. The advantages of lean manufacturing practices include the following benefits:

- The use of interchangeable and as-needed parts leads to savings in cost and storage.
- JIT inventory yields savings in parts costs and storage.
- JIT production results in savings in cost, storage, and labor.
- JIT delivery to customers saves on customer storage and provides more efficient customer service.
- Intrinsic principles of lean manufacturing, such as kaizen, promote more efficient, error-free processes and higher quality products.

- Lean manufacturing is more environmentally friendly because it saves space, utilities, and waste from overproduction and scraps.
- The transparency of process generated by lean manufacturing principles enables better communication with suppliers and customers.

Disadvantages of lean manufacturing practices. The disadvantages of lean manufacturing include the following drawbacks:

- JIT deliveries from suppliers can be disrupted due to natural or other disasters, thus holding up the production process.
- JIT deliveries from manufacturers to customers can be disrupted due to natural or other disasters, thus holding backing up the manufacturers' inventory and causing storage problems.
- Because lean manufacturing maintains an as-needed system of inventory and production, emergency orders are difficult to fulfill.
- Going lean may require the purchase of expensive new equipment.
- The adoption of new lean manufacturing techniques usually requires the retraining of employees.
- Preventive maintenance of machines is absolutely critical to ensure that all necessary equipment is utilized for lean, efficient production.
- Lean manufacturing depends upon constant, consistent quality control of all processes. Any slack in quality control can render the process ineffective.
- A lean manufacturing strategy can be ineffective if a manufacturer's suppliers do not also practice lean strategies.

CONCLUSION

In the decades after Toyota implemented full-scale JIT production of automobiles in 1938, many manufacturers adopted techniques of lean manufacturing strategies on a small- or large-scale basis. The advantages of lean manufacturing practices are plentiful and include cost savings, increased quality, a lower impact on the environment, and higher customer satisfaction. However, there are also disadvantages such as a lack of inventory of parts or products for emergencies, the possibility of distribution problems due to natural or other disasters, and the potential for ineffectiveness unless suppliers are also practicing lean strategies. Generally, though, the advantages of lean manufacturing outweigh the disadvantages. Each manufacturer must choose and cultivate a lean manufacturing strategy that is appropriate for its company, products, and customers.

—*Sue Ann Connaughton, MLS*

Further Reading

Amin, M., and M. A. Karim. "A Time-Based Quantitative Approach for Selecting Lean Strategies for Manufacturing Organisations." *International Journal of Production Research*, vol. 51, no. 4, 2013, pp. 1146-67.

Blanchard, Dave. "When Not to Go Lean." *Industry Week*, 10 Apr. 2007, www.industryweek.com/operations/continuous-improvement/article/21935329/when-not-to-go-lean. Accessed 28 Nov. 2021.

Brown, Charles B., Terry R. Collins, and Edward L. McCombs. "Transformation from Batch to Lean Manufacturing: The Performance Issues." *Engineering Management Journal*, vol. 18, no. 2, 2006, pp. 3-14.

Dillon, Andrew P., translator. *Zero Quality Control: Source Inspection and the Poka-Yoke System*. CRC Press, 2021.

"Lean Manufacturing and the Environment." *EPA*, 17 Mar. 2021, www.epa.gov/sustainability/lean-manufacturing-and-environment. Accessed 28 Nov. 2021.

Pinto, José Luís Quesado, João Carlos O. Matas, Carina Pimental, et al. *Just in Time Factory: Implementation through Lean Manufacturing Tools*. Springer International Publishing, 2018.

Productivity Press Development Team. *Kanban for the Shopfloor*. CRC Press, 2019.

Syddell, M. "Going Lean Can Mean Plump Profits." *Manufacturers' Monthly*, Mar. 2005, pp. 19-20.

Taylor, Andrew, Margaret Taylor, and Andrew McSweeney. "Towards Greater Understanding of

Success and Survival of Lean Systems." *International Journal of Production Research*, vol. 51, no. 22, 2013, pp. 6607-30.

"Toyota Production System." *Toyota*, 2021, global.toyota/en/company/vision-and-philosophy/production-system/. Accessed 28 Nov. 2021.

Manufacturing, Energy Use in

ABSTRACT
Industrial processes consume a significant portion of world energy each year. In the United States, much of that energy goes to the basic production industries of iron, steel, aluminum, paper, chemicals, and nonmetallic minerals (cement, brick, glass, and ceramics).

BACKGROUND
The sophistication of a society's technology can be judged by what it can make and how efficiently it can make those items. In ancient civilizations, rock and wood yielded to metal, fired pottery, and glass. Bronze and brass weapons swept aside stone. Then iron and steel replaced the softer metals.

Muscle power was sporadically aided by water power in antiquity, but the intensive use of water power began in Europe in the Middle Ages. Besides grinding flour, water mills supplied power for large-scale weaving, for sawmills, and for blowing air onto hot metal and hammering the finished metals. The gearing required to modify the motion and move it throughout a workshop also applied to wind power, and Dutch mills led manufacturing in the late Middle Ages.

A series of inventions led to James Watt's improved steam engine in 1782. The immediate goal was pumping water out of coal mines, but steam engines also allowed factory power to be located anywhere. Steam-powered locomotives allowed materials to be more easily moved to those locations.

At the beginning of the twentieth century, small electric motors allowed a further decentralization of industry. A small shop required only a power cable, the necessary equipment, and a flick of a switch rather than a large engine and the inconvenient (often dangerous) belts used to transfer power to various pieces of equipment.

Energy efficiency and materials efficiency grow as technology evolves. Often, increased efficiency is simply a byproduct of increased production or quality. Each doubling of cumulative production tends to drop production costs, including energy costs, by 20 percent. These improvements are connected to control of heat, control of motion, and the development of entirely new processes.

HEAT
Heat is the greatest component of manufacturing energy use. Heat (or the removal of heat) involves the same issues that space conditioning of a home does. One can add more fuel or reduce losses through increased efficiency. Efficiency can be increased by having more insulation in the walls, a furnace that burns more completely, a furnace that uses exhaust gases to preheat air coming into it, a stove with a lighter rather than a pilot light, and controls that shut off heat to unused areas.

Manufacturing has the additional option of selling excess heat or buying low-grade heat for cogeneration. Often a manufacturing plant only needs low-grade heat of several hundred degrees for drying or curing materials. This heat production does not fully use the energy of the fuel. An electrical power plant running at 600° Celsius (1112° Fahrenheit) can generate electricity and then send its waste heat on to the industrial process.

CAM technology can improve the precision of milling machines, routers, lathes, and other tools, ensuring that only essential motion occurs. Photo via iStock/petmal. [Used under license.]

A manufacturing plant also applies energy to materials, and in this process there are many choices. Heat may be applied in an oven (large or small). Some energy may also be applied directly. For instance, oven curing of paint on car parts has been replaced by infrared (heat lamp) radiation for quicker production. Some high-performance aerospace alloys are heated by microwave radiation in vacuum chambers.

There are a variety of other energy-saving approaches. Automated process controls are a major energy saver. In chemical industries, separating materials by their different boiling points with distillation columns requires much less steam than other methods. Also, the continuous safety flames at refineries are being replaced by automated lighters.

Another energy-efficient technique is to combine processes. For instance, steelmaking often comprises three separate heating steps: refining ore into blocks of pig iron, refining that into steel, and then forming the steel into products, such as beams or wire. An integrated steel mill heats the materials only once to make the finished product. A steel mini mill tends to be smaller, uses expensive electricity, and goes only a short distance in the production process, from iron scrap to steel. On the other hand, the mini mill is recycling a resource, thereby saving both energy and materials. The recycling of paper, plastics, and some metals typically requires one-half the energy needed to produce virgin materials. The fraction for aluminum is about one-fourth.

MOTION

Cutting, grinding, pumping, moving, polishing, compressing, and many other processes control the motion of materials and of heat. They use less energy than heating, but they often represent the high-grade energy in electricity.

The majority of the electricity used by industry is used for motors. Motors can be made efficient in many ways, including controllers that match power use to the actual load, metal cores that drop and take electric charges more easily, and windings with more turns of wire. Easing the tasks of industrial motors requires many disciplines. For example, fixing nitrogen into ammonia (NH_3) is typically done with streams of nitrogen and hydrogen passing over a catalyst. An improved catalyst pattern increases the reaction rate and thus decreases the hydrogen and nitrogen pumping. Automated controls again can control pumping, using it only where and when it is needed.

Energy consumption in the manufacturing industry can also be reduced by eliminating unnecessary motion. The use of computer-aided manufacturing (CAM) technology, for instance, can improve the precision of milling machines, routers, lathes, and other tools in use, ensuring that only essential motion occurs. Such manufacturing methods can likewise reduce waste in terms of materials, thus contributing further to the sustainability of the manufacturing process.

REDUCING ENERGY USE

Several additional processes can reduce energy use. For example, a lower pressure in manufacturing process for making polyethylene plastic uses one-fourth of the energy used in the previous process. Plastics have replaced energy-intensive metals in many commercial products. Silica in fiber-optic cables is replacing copper for communications. Composites, made with plastics and glass, metal, or other plastic fibers, not only require less energy to fabricate than all-metal materials but also have greater capabilities. Composites in railroad cars and airplanes reduce weight and thus energy costs of operation.

Vacuum deposition of metals, ceramics, and even diamond provide cheaply attained materials that multiply savings throughout industry. Diamond-edged machine tools operate significantly faster or longer before replacement. Rubidium-coated heat exchangers withstand sulfuric acid formed when the exhaust from the burning of high-sulfur coal drops below the boiling point, which allows both harnessing that lower heat and recovering the sulfur.

Other new processes have been contingent on developments in entirely new, even radical, fields. Advances in nanotechnology, for example, have led to improvements in data storage and processing speed within the electronics industry. Genetic engineering reduces energy costs in the chemical industry. Parasitic bacteria on legumes (such as peanuts and soy beans) fix atmospheric nitrogen into chemicals the plants can use. Breeding similar bacteria for other crops can largely eliminate the need for ammonia fertilizer and thereby decrease nitrate runoff.

ECONOMICS AND EFFICIENCY

Costs are the biggest factor affecting energy efficiency in manufacturing. When the price of natural gas was fixed by law at a low rate, for example, steam lines in some chemical plants had no insulation; it simply was not cost-effective to insulate.

Even after prices rise, there is often a long time lag. For example, the use of larger pipes in a chemical plant means lower pumping costs, but the cost of installing large pipes is not justified when energy costs are low. When energy costs rise, new plants being built might use the larger pipes, but old plants might well run for many years before replacement or a major refit.

Similarly, highly efficient electrical motors are typically more costly than conventional motors but can be capable of returning the extra cost and beginning to generate profit within several years. However, rebuilt conventional motors are available for a far lower price than new motors. Thus, companies might choose not to invest in efficient new motors, preferring the immediate cost savings.

Finally, social and political factors affect the adoption of energy-efficient technologies. Government policies have often discouraged recycling by granting tax subsidies to raw materials production and establishing requirements for their use rather than recycled materials. Tax policies have not allowed enough depreciation to encourage long-term investments in energy efficiency.

Government policies and programs can lead the way to decreased energy use in manufacturing. The US Department of Energy, for example, has supported initiatives such as the Save Energy Now program, through which the department partnered with companies and provided energy-use assessments at no cost. This resulted in recommendations for how the participating companies could reduce their energy consumption in the manufacturing process as well as their energy use in the workplace. Such programs on a global scale could make industry adopt a more energy-efficient manufacturing process.

—Roger V. Carlson

Further Reading

"Aspects of Energy Efficiency in Machine Tools." *Heidenhain*, 5 Oct. 2011, www.heidenhain.us/resources-and-news/aspects-of-energy-efficiency-in-machine-tools/. Accessed 28 Nov. 2021.

Beer, Jeroen de. *Potential for Industrial Energy-Efficiency Improvement in the Long Term.* Kluwer Academic, 2000.

Dean, Marti. "What Is CAM (Computer-Aided Manufacturing)?" *Autodesk*, 17 Mar. 2021, www.autodesk.com/products/fusion-360/blog/computer-aided-manufacturing-beginners/. Accessed 28 Nov. 2021.

Drexler, K. Eric. *Engines of Creation: The Coming Era of Nanotechnology.* Anchor Books, 1990.

Kenney, W. F. *Energy Conservation in the Process Industries.* Academic Press, 1984.

Kutz, Myer. *Environmentally Conscious Manufacturing.* Wiley, 2007.

Larson, Eric D., Marc H. Ross, and Robert H. Williams. "Beyond the Era of Materials." *Scientific American*, vol. 254, no. 6, 1986, p. 34.

National Research Council. *Decreasing Energy Intensity in Manufacturing: Assessing the Strategies and Future Directions of the Industrial Technologies Program.* National Academies Press, 2004.

Ross, Marc H., and Daniel Steinmeyer. "Energy for Industry." *Scientific American*, vol. 263, no. 3, 1990, p. 89.

"Save Energy Now LEADER." *US Department of Energy*, Feb. 2011, www1.eere.energy.gov/manufacturing/tech_assistance/pdfs/leaderpledgefaq.pdf. Accessed 28 Nov. 2021.

"Use of Energy Explained." *US Energy Information Administration*, 2 Aug. 2021, www.eia.gov/energyexplained/use-of-energy/industry.php. Accessed 28 Nov. 2021.

Manufacturing Processes

ABSTRACT

Manufacturing processes vary according to the type of product manufactured. This article discusses the issues unique to the processes of three manufacturing subsectors: apparel manufacturing, chemical manufacturing, and transportation equipment manufacturing, and describes two technological tools to aid in the manufacturing process.

OVERVIEW

In 2020, according to the National Institute of Standards and Technology, the manufacturing sector contributed 10.8 percent of value to the gross domestic product (GDP) of the United States. The manufacturing sector, as defined by the US Census Bureau, includes those establishments that are "engaged in the mechanical, physical, or chemical transformation of materials, substances, or components into new products."

Under the 2017 revision of the North American Industry Classification System (NAICS), the Census Bureau breaks down the manufacturing sector into twenty-one broad subsectors, each labeled by a three-number code. Subsectors include food manufacturing (NAICS 311), wood product manufacturing (NAICS 321), and primary metal manufacturing (NAICS 331). The Census Bureau breaks down each subsector further into multiple, more detailed segments with four-, five-, and six-number NAICS codes. For example, the transportation manufacturing subsector, NAICS 336, is further broken down into segments such as motor vehicle manufacturing (NAICS 3361) and ship and boat building (NAICS 3366). Each subsector reflects specific production methods associated with material inputs, production equipment, and employee skills.

This article will consider the manufacturing processes of three subsectors within the manufacturing sector:
- Apparel manufacturing
- Chemical manufacturing
- Transportation equipment manufacturing

These three subsectors will provide the framework for a discussion of some of their unique manufacturing processes.

APPLICATIONS

This section will define the basic processes for apparel manufacturing, chemical manufacturing, and transportation equipment manufacturing. These are crucial, but general processes; each process may include multiple subprocesses that are unique to the industry or product.

Apparel manufacturing process. The apparel manufacturing sector consists of establishments that turn fabric into clothing. The process of turning fabric into clothing is relatively straightforward and requires five main actions:
- Designing the clothing item
- Creating a pattern for the clothing item
- Purchasing fabric and materials for the clothing item
- Preparing the fabric and materials for construction into the clothing item
- Constructing the clothing item

An apparel manufacturing company may complete all or some of the actions in-house. For example, some companies might also weave their own fabric. Others may purchase patterns and fabrics. Others might contract out certain facets, such as the design of products, while still others may employ outsourcing for part of the process, such as pattern making or the sewing of the clothing item, to one or more persons or organizations outside the company.

Chemical manufacturing process. The chemical manufacturing subsector consists of establishments that transform organic and inorganic raw materials through a chemical process that allows for the formation of new products. The process for manufacturing chemicals requires controlled manufacturing conditions and highly skilled personnel with a knowledge of chemicals, their melting and boiling points, and reactive properties.

The process for manufacturing a chemical includes the following steps:
- Identifying the chemical to manufacture and establish the quantity needed
- Identifying the type and quantities of raw materials required to make the chemical
- Gathering information about the chemical properties of the raw materials, their reactive qualities, their melting and boiling points, and any byproducts that will result from the synthesizing and manufacturing processes

- Creating a manufacturing process flow document that details the process, equipment, and safety conditions required
- Following the process flow document to manufacture the chemical

Transportation equipment manufacturing process. The transportation equipment manufacturing subsector consists of establishments that produce certain tools that facilitate the transportation of people and products. One major segment of that subsector is automobile manufacturing. Of all the manufacturing subsectors, the process for manufacturing automobiles is probably the one that usually comes to mind when we think of large-scale manufacturing operations or factory production.

Once an automobile model has been designed; tested for safety, performance, and cost-effectiveness; and confirmed for production, the process for manufacturing it includes a series of highly automated operations. These operations include:

- The procurement of parts and materials
- The setup of the assembly line in one or more physical or geographical locations
- The assembly of the individual components of the automobile
- The joining of all the individual components into a complete automobile

ISSUES

Manufacturing processes are primarily driven by nine factors:

- Legal regulations
- Safety regulations
- Time-to-market of product
- Availability of raw materials
- Price of raw materials
- Geographic location of raw materials
- Availability of skilled workers
- Wages of workers
- Supply chain

Of course, legal and safety regulations are prominent concerns for every US manufacturer. However, the issues associated with each of the nine factors vary in prominence, complexity or level of difficulty to achieve, depending upon the manufacturing industry or subsector.

For each of the three subsectors discussed in this article, manufacturing presents a variety of unique issues. The following discussions are not comprehensive but rather highlight the variety of constraints in manufacturing processes.

Apparel Manufacturing Processes—Issues

The following four issues greatly affect the manufacturing process for apparel:

- Time to market
- Latency
- Fair labor practices by manufacturers
- Fair labor practices by organizations within the manufacturer's supply chain

Apparel manufacturing process issue 1—time to market. Time to market is a major driver in the manufacturing process of the apparel subsector. Fashion has a limited shelf life, and the competition is determined to be the first apparel company to bring the next best clothing item to the end customer. Even apparel manufacturers of products that are viewed as less trend conscious, such as uniforms, are driven by time-to-market factors, or they risk losing their customer base to competitors. Therefore, all other issues associated with the apparel manufacturing process are tackled with the goal of shortening the time to market.

Apparel manufacturing process issue 2—latency. Latency, or the amount of time that passes while a unit of work progresses from one step to the next, greatly affects time to market. Apparel manufacturers usually construct their items on a piece work basis. For example, each part for multiple numbers of the same shirt is made in separate operations: All the sleeves are constructed in one operation, and all the collars are constructed in another operation. When each part is completed, all the parts are sewn together into completed shirts. To minimize latency, there must always be shirt parts ready and waiting for the final operation of sewing them into complete garments.

Apparel manufacturing process 3—fair labor practices by manufacturers. Like other manufacturers, those in the apparel subsector are legally subject to fair labor practices that promote the payment of living wages and avoid the use of child and undocumented immigrant labor. The US Department of Labor oversees compliance of fair labor practices, including fair wages and benefits, safe working conditions, work authorization of non-US citizens, and equal opportunity standards. The US Occupational Safety and Health Administration (OSHA), an agency within the Department of Labor, enforces the federal laws and regulations concerning safe working conditions. In addition, OSHA encourages individual states to set up their own occupational safety and health programs, which OSHA monitors after approving them.

The apparel subsector has been closely monitored for its compliance with fair labor standards by the government and the media because of three practices that are historically common in its manufacturing process and make it more vulnerable to noncompliance: the prevalence of piece work construction, the use of work-from-home labor, and the outsourcing of operations both domestically and overseas.

Apparel manufacturing process 4—fair labor practices by organizations within the manufacturer's supply chain. The organizations within a manufacturer's supply chain—from suppliers to transporters to wholesalers to retail merchants—are also subject to the same fair labor practices as the manufacturer. However, an interesting twist to this fact is that a manufacturer is also expected to confirm that the members of its supply chain are indeed compliant with fair labor practices.

Chemical Manufacturing Processes—Issues

Two issues that particularly affect the manufacturing process for chemicals are:
- Legal and environmental requirements
- Working conditions

Chemical manufacturing process issue 1—legal and environmental requirements. In the chemical manufacturing subsector, legal and environmental requirements are usually intertwined due to the nature of the product and oversight by the Environmental Protection Agency (EPA). In 1976, Congress passed the Toxic Substances Control Act, which authorized the EPA to follow industrial chemicals that are created by or imported into America. The EPA has the power to ban the manufacture and import of chemicals that offer an unreasonable risk to humans or the environment. The EPA devises and enforces a comprehensive set of laws and regulations that companies which manufacture or store large quantities of chemicals are required to follow. The EPA requirements include the formation of an emergency response plan and adherence to multiple EPA laws and regulations that cover the handling, transport, and disposal of materials that are hazardous to humans, animals, or the environment.

Chemical manufacturers are also subject to any state or local laws governing their activities. For example, in 1989, the state of Massachusetts passed the Toxics Use Reduction Act (TURA) to encourage a reduction in the amount of toxics used in Massachusetts and the amount of toxic byproducts generated. Federal law requires companies to report toxic chemical releases, but TURA is stricter than the federal law because it requires companies to report on their toxic chemical usage and to also prepare a Toxics Use Reduction Plan.

Chemical manufacturing process issue 2—working conditions. It is crucial that persons involved in a chemical manufacturing process are highly trained in the knowledge of chemical properties, the handling of chemicals, and emergency responses. All chemical manufacturing facilities and storage facilities must meet federal, state, and local safety requirements and be equipped with emergency response and communication equipment. In addition, all transport vehicles must be labeled with the contents and Department of Transportation registration/identification numbers.

Automobile Manufacturing Processes—Issues

Factors that affect the manufacturing process for automobiles include the following four issues:
- Time to market
- Working conditions
- Environmental requirements
- Supply chain management

Automobile manufacturing process issue 1—time to market. In the automobile manufacturing subsector, time to market is a major consideration. The entire process from designing an automobile to ultimately getting it to the end customer is a lengthy process and automobile manufacturers strive to shorten it by devising a variety of strategies, including streamlining assembly techniques, improving facilities layouts, and designing parts that fit more than one automobile model.

Henry Ford was the first automobile manufacturer to grasp the financial and marketing benefits of the time-to-market concept. In 1913, after operating his company for ten years, Ford introduced the assembly line to one of his automotive plants in Michigan. The assembly line model, in which an individual worker stayed in one spot to perform the same task on multiple vehicles, proved so efficient that it allowed Ford Motor Company to far surpass the production levels of its competitors and therefore sell the vehicles at lower cost.

Automobile manufacturing process issue 2—working conditions. Like all US employers, automobile manufacturers are required to provide workers with safe working conditions according to OSHA laws and regulations. Elements of safe working conditions in the automobile manufacturing process include:
- Ongoing training to teach workers new skills and the safest and most efficient methods for performing their jobs
- Equipment that is regularly inspected
- Limited exposure to hazardous materials
- Effective emergency response plans in place in every facility

Automobile manufacturing process issue 3—environmental requirements. Automobile manufacturers and owners are subject to federal and state regulations for emissions, disposal, and storage. Automobile manufacturers can also be assessed a tax if their new automobiles do not meet federal fuel efficiency standards. In addition, many cities and towns have "junk car" laws or regulations that limit the visible storage of unlicensed or unregistered motor vehicles. Besides decreasing environmental and other safety hazards, these laws are intended to enhance the aesthetics of neighborhoods.

Automobile manufacturing process issue 4—supply chain management. The management of the intricate network of suppliers, distributors, transporters, and retailers that make up the supply chain for an automobile manufacturer is of utmost importance. Although distributors, transporters, and retailers are not part of the actual manufacturing process, their actions and efficiencies or inefficiencies are integral to the operations of an automobile manufacturer. To keep down the cost of purchasing and warehousing, automobile manufacturers are more likely to utilize the just-in-time (JIT) approach to inventory rather than stockpiling parts or finished products. The JIT approach requires proper management of the entire supply chain so that production has the parts needed at the time needed and that ultimately, retailers receive the automobiles exactly when they need them.

FURTHER DISCOURSE

Manufacturers and those who provide services to them are continuously seeking innovative methods to cut costs by speeding up the efficiency of the manufacturing processes while maintaining or improving the quality of the products. Two effective tools that are being employed to improve the processes for manufacturers are product lifecycle management (PLM) and process analytical technology (PAT).

Product lifecycle management (PLM). Product lifecycle management (PLM) is, as its name suggests, the process of managing and documenting the movement of a product through all stages of its lifecycle. PLM is an excellent tool for all manufacturers but particularly for those with complex or distributed supply chains who are driven by time-to-market issues, such as apparel manufacturers and automobile manufacturers. Web-based PLM technology allows a manufacturer to create an at-a-glance central product information repository that provides visibility into its inventory, sales, and distribution figures, and enables communication with all members of the supply chain.

Process analytical technology (PAT). Process analytical technology (PAT) is particularly useful for manufacturers of pharmaceutical products. PAT is a system in which the manufacturer ensures that the final product will meet all relevant quality standards by assessing whether the raw materials and partially completed product meet certain standards at various points throughout the manufacturing process.

—*Sue Ann Connaughton, MLS*

Further Reading

Ayhan, Mustafa Batuhan, Ercan Öztemel, Mehmet Emin Aydin, and Yong Yue. "A Quantitative Approach for Measuring Process Innovation: A Case Study in a Manufacturing Company." *International Journal of Production Research*, vol. 51, no. 11, 2013, pp. 3463-75.

Baukh, Oleksandra. "Pre-production Processes in Garment Manufacturing." *Techpacker*, 14 Oct. 2020, techpacker.com/blog/manufacturing/pre-production-processes-in-garment-manufacturing/. Accessed 28 Nov. 2021.

"Chemical Manufacturing." *US Environmental Protection Agency*, 20 Feb. 2020, archive.epa.gov/sectors/web/html/chemical.html. Accessed 28 Nov. 2021.

Cook, Jacob. "The Five Steps to Starting PAT." *PharmTech*, 1 Mar. 2007, www.pharmtech.com/view/five-steps-starting-pat. Accessed 28 Nov. 2021.

Kim, Chulhan, and Tae-Eog Lee. "Modelling and Simulation of Automated Manufacturing Systems for Evaluation of Complex Schedules." *International Journal of Production Research*, vol. 51, no. 12, 2013, pp. 3734-47.

"Manufacturing Industry Statistics." *National Institute of Standards and Technology*, 2 Nov. 2021, www.nist.gov/el/applied-economics-office/manufacturing/manufacturing-industry-statistics. Accessed 28 Nov. 2021.

"Manufacturing: NAICS 31-33." *US Bureau of Labor Statistics*, 28 Nov. 2021, www.bls.gov/iag/tgs/iag31-33.htm. Accessed 28 Nov. 2021.

McClenahen, J. S. "Factory of the Future." *Industry Week*, vol. 256, no. 2, 2007, pp. 21-22.

Mondal, S. C., J. J. Maiti, and P. K. Ray. "Modelling Robustness in Serial Multi-Stage Manufacturing Processes." *International Journal of Production Research*, vol. 51, no. 21, 2013, pp. 6359-77.

Seibert, B. "Design Agility Achieved with PDM/PLM." *Apparel Magazine*, May 2005, pp. 22-26.

Sherman, Don. "How a Car Is Made: Every Step from Invention to Launch." *Car and Driver*, 18 Nov. 2015, www.caranddriver.com/news/a15350381/how-a-car-is-made-every-step-from-invention-to-launch/. Accessed 28 Nov. 2021.

Manufacturing Strategies

ABSTRACT
Manufacturing strategies are the plans and methods that are particular to furthering the goals of a company that makes products. Strategies that are frequently used by manufacturing companies include strategic management, design for manufacturability, lean manufacturing, Six Sigma, and manufacturing for a sustainable society.

WHAT ARE MANUFACTURING STRATEGIES?
Manufacturing strategies are the plans and methods that are particular to furthering the goals of a company that makes products. One or more of the following five strategies are frequently used by manufacturing companies:
- Strategic management
- Design for manufacturability
- Lean manufacturing
- Six Sigma
- Manufacturing for a sustainable society

Some of the strategies overlap with others. For example, the first strategy examined, strategic management, may incorporate the remaining four strategies. Similarly, lean manufacturing may incorporate design for manufacturability and Six Sigma. Together with this overlap, the concept of flexible manufacturing systems (FMS), in which the system is designed to adapt to any changes it encounters, allows companies to evolve their strategies as needs or conditions require.

STRATEGIC MANAGEMENT
Strategic management revolves around devising and following a detailed plan for capturing and maintaining a competitive advantage in the marketplace. Presumably, most manufacturers would have some sort of plan for competing in the marketplace, so how does strategic management elevate that plan to "strategy" level? A strategic management plan does the following:
- Determines broad concepts of mission and goals
- Defines long and short-term objectives
- States the specific details of analysis and decision-making
- Assigns roles and responsibilities for implementing the plan
- Establishes timelines for accomplishing each aspect of the plan

Strategic management is comprehensive and is characterized by a clear, detailed plan for competing in the marketplace; it is this detailed plan that elevates strategic management to "strategy" level.

DESIGN FOR MANUFACTURABILITY
The manufacturability of a product refers to characteristics that make the product suitable for reproduction (manufacture), usually on a large-scale basis. Manufacturability is dependent upon two conditions: the ability to consistently manufacture a reliable product without problems and the ability to manufacture the product at minimal cost. When these two conditions for manufacturability are given foremost consideration during the design cycle of a product, the concept is known as "design for manufacturability" (DFM), also known as "design for manufacture."

The principle behind DFM is to create the ability to economically manufacture a reliable product into an initial design rather than to fix problems later in the manufacturing process. This principle expands the idea of "do it right the first time" into "do it right the first time, but as inexpensively as possible."

DFM generally relies upon standardization practices; it incorporates manufacturing processes that use standard parts, reduce the number of parts, and minimize handling during production. However, the most sophisticated DFM strategies allow for a range of product customization.

Depending upon the product or manufacturing process, DFM may incorporate a variety of tools to reach its goal.

Additive manufacturing (AM) technologies. Additive manufacturing (AM) technologies, also known as "rapid prototyping technologies," allow a manufacturer to fabricate customizable parts of any shape from complex materials. Rapid prototyping refers to quicker-than-average production of models for the purpose of working out problems. Because of its intent to tackle the manufacturing issues involving the complexities of shape and materials, AM technologies have the potential to move beyond providing cost-cutting benefits to actually achieving new, higher manufacturing capabilities.

Concurrent engineering. Concurrent engineering is a method of product or process design that includes simultaneous input from every individual with a stake or role in the final product, including engineers, salespersons, support personnel, vendors, and customers, throughout the entire design process.

Poka-yoke. Poka-yoke is the concept of mistake-proofing the entire manufacturing process by preventing mistakes in the product design, the process, and from human actions. Poka-yoke refers to the mechanisms used throughout a manufacturing process to ensure that proper conditions exist before a process step is begun. If it is not possible to invoke poka-yoke before the process actually begins, then it is used to detect defects at the earliest point in the process. Poka-yoke is also frequently employed as part of a lean manufacturing strategy.

Product lifecycle management (PLM). Product Lifecycle Management (PLM) integrates all the people, processes, and information related to a product in order to communicate information across the enterprise, from initial product concept to the end of its life. PLM takes the concept of concurrent engineering (people and process integration throughout the design cycle) further by applying the principles throughout the product's life, from inception to disposal.

LEAN MANUFACTURING

Lean manufacturing refers to a company's ongoing, systematic effort to eliminate the sources of waste in a production process. Notable sources of waste include overproduction, inventory problems, and processing failures. To combat the major causes of waste, companies that follow lean-manufacturing methodologies implement any of a number of tools.

Cellular manufacturing. One major lean manufacturing tool is cellular manufacturing. This strategy involves the arrangement of vital equipment in such a way that products being produced move smoothly and swiftly through the production process. Cellular manufacturing minimizes the time required to manufacture a single product by moving the product through the entire production process one piece at a time, according to a rate determined by a customer's needs. Cellular manufacturing is in direct contrast to batch-and-queue (also known as "large-lot") production, which involves processing multiple parts before moving them onto the next machine or process.

Just-in-time (JIT). The practice of JIT refers to the supplying of parts or items at the time that they are needed and not before. JIT can apply to parts or items supplied to the manufacturer or to the items that the manufacturer produces for its customers. In either scenario, JIT directly contrasts with the practice of building up inventory by stockpiling items.

Kaizen. Kaizen is a Japanese term that refers to the process of continuous improvement, often in small, incremental steps. To be effective, kaizen must involve the entire workforce in its philosophy and practice.

Kanban. Kanban is an integral part of the JIT production process; it is an information tool that specifies exactly which parts or items are needed during the production process and exactly when they are needed.

Poka-yoke. Just as in DFM contexts, poka-yoke in lean manufacturing refers to error-proofing the production process during the design phase to eliminate faulty products altogether or, if that is not possible, to detect defects at the earliest possible moment in the production process.

Outsourcing. When a manufacturer hires another company to manufacture parts or perform services (such as testing of products) instead of doing it in-house, this is called "outsourcing." Products or services are usually outsourced because it is less expensive than doing so in-house or because the hiring company does not have the expertise in-house. While products or services are sometimes outsourced to companies within the United States, they are often outsourced to foreign countries with cheaper labor rates for skilled workers. Outsourcing to foreign countries is known as "offshoring." While such practices can be efficient and cost-effective, they have also been criticized for various alleged economic and social impacts.

SIX SIGMA

Six Sigma is a tightly managed, statistical quality control methodology that is used to detect and eliminate defects or variations in the manufacturing process. Six Sigma involves a process that is named DMAIC after its five steps:

- Define
- Measure
- Analyze
- Improve
- Control

The control chart, a significant feature of Six Sigma methodology, is used to plot and graph a process over time in order to detect variations.

MANUFACTURING FOR A SUSTAINABLE SOCIETY

A sustainable society is one that meets current environmental, economic, and community needs without compromising those needs in the future. There are three main categories of issues that affect a sustainable society.

- Environmental issues
- Economic issues
- Community issues

A manufacturer that intends to incorporate a strategy that embraces and contributes to a sustainable society may incorporate a variety of practices that tackle those three categories of issues, including the following initiatives:

Environmental Issues: Initiatives

- Design products that are recyclable or biodegradable.
- Purchase products from companies that employ sustainable packaging.
- Offer financial incentives to employees who travel to work by bicycle, public transportation, and hybrid or electric motor vehicles.
- Operate facilities during non-peak utility and travel hours.
- Offer to remanufacture products when appropriate. (Remanufacturing is the process of restoring a worn or broken piece of equipment by repairing or replacing its component parts.)

Economic Issues: Initiatives

- Streamline costs and processes in order to offer goods and services at a fair price.
- Pay employees fair wages.
- Promote and enforce equal opportunity for employees.
- Refuse to do business with companies that engage in child labor or other human rights violations.

- Refuse to invest in companies or countries that engage in child labor or other human rights violations.

Community Issues: Initiatives

- When building or developing facilities, provide additional community benefits such as burying utilities, improving existing roads, or bringing in high-speed internet access.
- Contribute funds for fire, police, and social service organizations.
- Contribute funds and manpower to projects that provide free or low-cost medical care, food, and housing to low-income persons.
- Volunteer funds and manpower for community service projects, such as beautification programs, arts programs, community gardens, playgrounds, and afterschool programs.
- Set aside a percentage of new housing for affordable housing. If building or developing on land that will displace low-income persons, fund suitable alternative living arrangements for them.

—*Sue Ann Connaughton, MLS*

Further Reading

Alqahtan, Ammar Y., Elif Kongar, Kishore K. Pochampally, and Surendra M. Gupta, editors. *Responsible Manufacturing: Issues Pertaining to Sustainability*. CRC Press, 2019.

Amin, M., and M. A. Karim. "A Time-Based Quantitative Approach for Selecting Lean Strategies for Manufacturing Organisations." *International Journal of Production Research*, vol. 51, no. 4, 2013, pp. 1146-67.

Bird, Frederick, and Joseph Smucker. "The Social Responsibilities of International Business Firms in Developing Areas." *Journal of Business Ethics*, vol. 73, no. 1, 2007, pp. 1-9.

"Design for Manufacturability: Reducing Costs through Design." *Aved*, 22 Sept. 2021, aved.com/design-for-manufacturability-the-economics-of-design/. Accessed 28 Nov. 2021.

"DMAIC vs. DMADV." *Purdue University*, 28 May 2021, www.purdue.edu/leansixsigmaonline/blog/dmaic-vs-dmadv/. Accessed 28 Nov. 2021.

Kim, Minkyun, Nallan C. Suresh, and Canan Kocabasoglu-Hillmer. "An Impact of Manufacturing Flexibility and Technological Dimensions of Manufacturing Strategy on Improving Supply Chain Responsiveness: Business Environment Perspective." *International Journal of Production Research*, vol. 51, no. 18, 2013, pp. 5597-5611.

Leseure, Michel. "Trust in Manufacturing Engineering Project Systems: An Evolutionary Perspective." *Journal of Manufacturing Technology Management*, vol. 26, no. 7, 2015, pp. 1013-30.

Manivannan, Subramaniam. "Lean Error-Proofing for Productivity Improvement." *Forging*, 27 Apr. 2007, www.forgingmagazine.com/issues-and-ideas/article/21922032/lean-errorproofing-for-productivity-improvement. Accessed 28 Nov. 2021.

Pinto, José Luís Quesado, João Carlos O. Matas, Carina Pimental, et al. *Just in Time Factory: Implementation through Lean Manufacturing Tools*. Springer International Publishing, 2018.

Productivity Press Development Team. *Kanban for the Shopfloor*. CRC Press, 2019.

Pyzdek, Thomas, and Paul Keller. *The Six Sigma Handbook*. 5th ed., McGraw-Hill Education, 2018.

Syddell, M. "Going Lean Can Mean Plump Profits." *Manufacturers' Monthly*, Mar. 2005, pp. 19-20.

Taylor, Andrew, Margaret Taylor, and Andrew McSweeney. "Towards Greater Understanding of Success and Survival of Lean Systems." *International Journal of Production Research*, vol. 51, no. 22, 2013, pp. 6607-30.

"What Is Design for Manufacturing (DFM)?" *TWI*, 2021, www.twi-global.com/technical-knowledge/faqs/faq-what-is-design-for-manufacture-dfm. Accessed 28 Nov. 2021.

Manufacturing Systems Design

ABSTRACT

Manufacturing systems design is the art and science of developing, building, and implementing the methods by which products are manufactured. Manufacturing systems design is a broad field that involves a variety of different disciplines, including engineering, design, technology development, labor relations, organizational behavior, marketing, and business development. The history of manufacturing systems design has its roots in the quest to develop a system for manufacturing guns using a series of interchangeable parts that was pursued by Eli Whitney and other American inventors and manufacturers in the late 1700s and early 1800s. In the early 1900s, the American engineer Frederick Winslow Taylor developed and promoted a popular theory of manufacturing systems design called "scientific management." The scientific management system sought to maximize productivity and profitability in factories by using scientific methods to determine how each step in the manufacturing process could be performed at maximum efficiency. Twenty-first-century manufacturing systems design continues to employ some of the theories developed by Taylor, but more frequently focuses on the development and implementation of lean manufacturing techniques, "greener" methods that emphasize speed, versatility, and the elimination of all waste in the production process. Lean manufacturing methods were primarily developed and refined by the Toyota Motor Company in Japan. The application of lean methods to US industries has helped to strengthen and diversify the country's manufacturing base and has paid dividends in both economic and environmental terms.

ELI WHITNEY, JOHN HALL, AND THE AMERICAN SYSTEM OF MANUFACTURE

Up until the beginning of the nineteenth century, most products were made on a small scale by skilled craftsmen following their own individual systems and standards. This method of manufacturing called for specialized workers who were often trained through apprenticeships with accomplished craftsmen. It was not a system that was designed to manufacture products on a large scale, or to a consistent standard.

Since individual goods were handmade, the craftsmen system made it difficult to repair broken products, as replacement pieces had to be hand-crafted specifically to match the piece that was broken. This was an expensive, difficult and time-consuming process.

The history of modern manufacturing systems design is often linked to efforts of American inventor Eli Whitney and other industrialists to create a system of manufacturing guns using interchangeable parts in the late 1700s and early 1800s. The thinking of Whitney and others was that if guns were all made to the same set of standards, then it would be possible to produce identical replacement parts, thus making it easier to repair a broken gun.

Most historians agree that the idea of creating products with interchangeable parts dates far back beyond Whitney, however. The French gunsmith Honoré Blanc is credited with presenting the same idea to the French court years before Whitney brought the idea to American government officials. In fact, it is thought that Thomas Jefferson saw a presentation by Blanc while he was in France and brought the idea back with him to the United States.

Though Whitney was attempting to build guns with a standardized process as early as 1798, his early attempts produced mixed results. The inventor John H. Hall is credited with creating the first truly successful interchangeable system at the Harper's Ferry armory in Virginia between 1820 and 1840. Over this twenty-year period, Hall developed a series of machines that were able to create metal parts to match exact specifications.

The advances that Hall, Whitney, and other manufacturers made in the early 1800s helped to usher in the American system of manufacture, a system in which most products went from being made by hand in small, individual batches to being made in larger batches by using a series of machines.

THE INDUSTRIAL REVOLUTION AND THE RISE OF THE MACHINE

The Industrial Revolution of the 1800s and early 1900s produced another significant change in the manufacturing process, in which products went from being produced by machines on a relatively small scale to being produced by machines on a much larger scale using large machines powered by new sources of energy such as iron, steel, electricity, coal, and gasoline. The Industrial Revolution also led to new developments in transportation and communication, including the invention and use of the steam locomotive, the steamship, and later the automobile, airplane, telegraph, and radio.

The Industrial Revolution created changes in the social fabric as well. It helped to usher in the development of new cities, created a new middle class of factory workers, devalued the skilled work of artisans, and led to the creation of large industrial complexes around large centers of resources.

FREDERICK TAYLOR AND SCIENTIFIC MANAGEMENT

Perhaps the first prominent thinker to approach the manufacturing process as a science was Frederick Winslow Taylor, who published his theories in the book *Principles of Scientific Management* in 1911. In this book, Taylor set out to prove that the country's workplaces were suffering a great loss through worker inefficiency, both intentional and unintentional, in almost every daily task. Taylor also argued that the remedy for this inefficiency could be found in the systematic or scientific management of workers, rather than trying to locate or create workers with superhuman abilities.

As outlined by Taylor in his book, the theory of scientific management contends that there is a scientifically correct method to perform nearly any task to the greatest level of efficiency, and that this method can be determined through careful scientific analysis of worker practices. The theory further states that these scientifically determined methods should be used to replace the traditional "rule of thumb" work methods that employees have learned through on-the-job training and observing their co-workers.

Taylor claimed that his principles of scientific management would be able to increase worker output significantly while at the same time make workers happier. This idea is based on the assumption that working more efficiently will lead to an increase in production, which will in turn make the factory more profitable. With production and profitability up, factory managers can afford to pay workers more money, which makes them happier and helps to encourage them to continue working at maximum efficiency.

Taylor felt that such a large improvement in productivity was possible due to the "systematic soldiering" that he identified as endemic among American workers. Taylor defined soldiering as the practice of doing just enough work to get by, without actually working anywhere near full capacity. It is a practice, Taylor wrote, that is heavily encouraged by peer-pressure from co-workers.

When it comes to sporting events such as baseball or cricket, Taylor noted, it is fully expected for a man to give his best effort at all times. If he gave only a half-hearted effort, Taylor noted, then he would likely be criticized by his teammates. Taylor said that when a man is working, however, he does as little as he possibly can over the course of the day. If he tried too hard, he would be abused by his fellow workers for making them look bad, and he would also be worried that his increase in productivity might lead to others losing their jobs.

To correct this practice of soldiering, Taylor's theory calls for a harmonious relationship between workers and management, one in which managers select and train the right workers for the right jobs and then help them achieve their goals by setting out tasks for them to complete each day and directing them to use scientifically proven methods to complete the work at each step in the process.

In an effort to validate his theories on scientific management, Taylor spent time working with the pig iron handlers at the Bethlehem Steel Company in Bethlehem, Pennsylvania. As recounted in his book, when Taylor and his team first arrived at the steel company, they found a gang of seventy-five workers who were loading 90-pound pieces of pig iron at a rate of 12 tons per man per day.

Taylor attempted to prove through his theories of scientific management that a first-class pig iron handler should be able to handle much more than that—between 47 and 48 tons of iron per day—without becoming exhausted or burnt out. Taylor arrived at this ideal loading rate through an extensive series of tests that were designed to determine how long a man could reasonably be expected to bear weight during the course of the workday. The Taylor team determined that it was possible for men to increase their lifting capacity if they correctly balanced periods of rest with periods of exertion.

Taylor's first step was to observe the workmen in action to determine which of the crew members were physically capable of increasing their workload to 47 to 48 tons per day. Then he talked to each man separately. The first subject was told that he would earn more money if he did exactly what he was told to do by one of Taylor's team members, exactly when he was told to do it.

A member of Taylor's team then directed the man through a day's work, telling him when to work and when to rest. The result was that the man was able to lift 47.5 tons per day. Several other members of the team were subsequently approached by the Taylor team, and they each agreed to unquestionably follow direction in return for higher pay. Each of the men was in turn able to subsequently increase his workload.

While Taylor's book paints a rosy picture of factory life under the scientific management system, he also acknowledges that it will not always work as

Manufacturing systems design involves engineering, design, technology development, labor relations, organizational behavior, marketing, and business development. Photo via iStock/NanoStockk. [Used under license.]

planned. "It is not here claimed that any single panacea exists for all of the troubles of the working-people or of employers," he writes. "As long as some people are born lazy or inefficient, and others are born greedy and brutal, as long as vice and crime are with us, just so long will a certain amount of poverty, misery, and unhappiness be with us also."

Taylor can also be fairly criticized for taking a dim view of the laboring class, a view which may have resulted from his own clashes with workers as a factory manager. Taylor assumes that workers are dull people who will be motivated to work harder solely by the possibility of making more money. He also assumes that workers are not bright enough to grasp the principles of scientific management on their own and thus have to mindlessly follow orders from managers of superior intellect.

In their book *A Perfect Mess,* authors Eric Abrahamson and David Freedman note that strict Taylorism was discredited in 1920 by a series of studies at the Hawthorne Electrical Plant. The so-called Hawthorne Effect said that work tended to improve no matter what changes were made, so long as the workers were being observed by management.

The Hawthorne studies determined that a change as innocuous as adjusting the intensity of the lights could increase worker productivity if managers were seen to be observing workers in action, thereby calling into question Taylor's assertions that his "scientifically correct" methods of performing tasks were responsible for the increase in productivity.

Nevertheless, Taylor's theories about the importance of finding efficient ways to perform tasks, and of doing things faster, neater, and more efficiently continues to play a major part in systems of manufacturing design.

LEAN MANUFACTURING

The lean manufacturing system (closely related to the Toyota Production System or just-in-time [JIT] manufacturing) differs from scientific management in that the focus is not to produce as much product as possible using the most efficient methods, but to produce only what is needed, when it is needed: in other words, making only what has been ordered by customers in order to reduce the amount of capital that is tied up (or lost) in unnecessary labor, material, storage, or transportation costs.

The lean manufacturing system emphasizes a proactive, ever-evolving approach to manufacturing design, where workers and management are always looking for ways to improve the process and to eliminate problems as they occur. These efforts help to significantly reduce the number of faulty products that are created due to errors in the production process. The goal is to produce a high-quality product, when—and only when—it is needed. The company that has been most responsible for developing and codifying lean production techniques is Toyota Motors. The Toyota Production System, or TPS, is based on the identification and elimination of all waste and requires all aspects of the production process to concentrate on achieving this goal.

CONCLUSION

Updates to manufacturing systems and ways of thinking about them are, at least in part, driven by consumers. In the twenty-first century, consumers are increasingly focused on environmental concerns, and that interest may drive further adoption of manufacturing systems designed to limit the environmental ramifications of the manufacturing process. In the United States, there are a number of government agencies at the state and federal levels that work to encourage the adoption of lean manufacturing for that reason. The Environmental Protection Agency (EPA), an advocate of lean production methods for their environmental benefits, calls particular attention to lean manufacturing's emphasis on cost reduction. While cutting down on costs makes sense from a business perspective, it also makes sense environmentally, the EPA points out, as lean techniques help to make the manufacturing process as efficient as possible, cutting down on the amount of natural resources used, energy expended, and waste created by the production process.

—Brian Burns

Further Reading

Abrahamson, Eric, and David H. Freedman. *A Perfect Mess: The Hidden Benefits of Disorder*. Little, Brown, 2006.

Eli Whitney Museum and Workshop, www.eliwhitney.org/. Accessed 28 Nov. 2021.

"John H. Hall." *National Park Service*, www.nps.gov/hafe/learn/historyculture/john-h-hall.htm. Accessed 28 Nov. 2021.

Joyappa, P. "Lean and Green Manufacturing." *Flexible Packaging*, vol. 14, 2012, pp. 42-45.

"Lean Manufacturing and the Environment." *EPA*, 17 Mar. 2021, www.epa.gov/sustainability/lean- manufacturing-and-environment. Accessed 28 Nov. 2021.

Ocak, Z. "Streamlining Waste." *Industrial Engineer: IE*, vol. 43, no. 5, 2011, pp. 38-40.

Rempel, Gerhard. "The Industrial Revolution." *University of Delaware*, www1.udel.edu/fllt/faculty/aml/201files/IndRev.html. Accessed 28 Nov. 2021.

Taylor, Frederick Winslow. *The Principles of Scientific Management*. Harper & Brothers, 1913.

MEASUREMENT AND UNITS

ABSTRACT

Measurement is the act of quantifying a physical property, an effect, or some aspect of them. Seven fundamental properties are recognized in measurements: length, mass, time, electric current, thermodynamic temperature, amount of a substance, and luminous intensity. In addition, two supplementary or abstract fundamental properties are defined: plane and solid angles. The base units for the seven fundamental properties can be manipulated to produce derived units for other quantities that are the effect of combinations of these fundamental properties. For instance, a Newton is a derived unit measuring force and weight, and a square meter is a derived unit used to measure area.

Historically, a number of units representing different amounts of the same properties have been used in various cultures around the world. For example, the United States traditionally uses the US customary system (miles, cups, pints, ounces, and so on), while most other industrialized nations use the metric system (kilometer, milliliter, liters, grams, and so on). The metric system, developed in France in the late eighteenth century, represents the first true standard measurement system. The theory and physical practice of measurement is constant no matter what system of units is being used.

DEFINITION AND BASIC PRINCIPLES

Measurement has the purpose of associating a dimension or quantity proportionately with some fixed reference standard. Such an association is intended to facilitate the communication of information about a physical property in a manner that allows it to be reproduced in concept, or in actuality if needed. The function of an assigned unit that is associated with a definite dimension is to provide the necessary point of reference for someone to comprehend the exact dimensions that have been communicated. For example, a container may be described as having a volume of 8 cubic feet. Such a description is incomplete, however, because it does not state the shape or relative proportions of the container. The description applies equally well to containers of any shape, whether they be cubic, rectangular, cylindrical, conical, or some other shape. At a more basic level, however, there is the assumption that the person who receives the description has the same understanding of what is meant by "cubic feet" as does the person who provided the description. This is the fundamental principle of any measurement system: to provide a frame of reference that is commonly understood by a large number of people and that indicates exactly the same thing to each of them.

A measurement system, no matter what its basic units, must address a limited group of fundamental

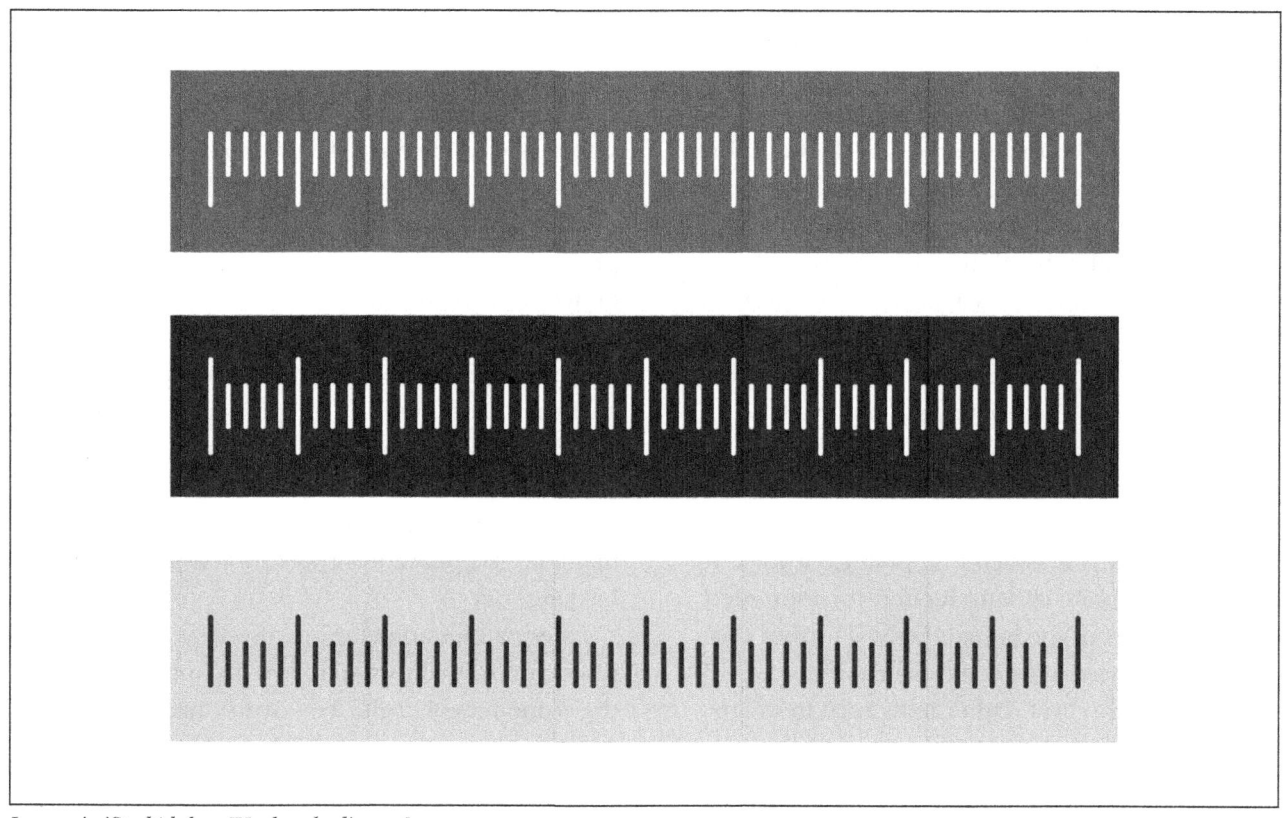

Image via iStock/ckybes. [Used under license.]

properties. These are length, mass, temperature, time, electric current, amount of a substance, and luminous intensity. In addition, it must also be able to describe angles. All other properties and quantities can be described or quantified by a combination of these fundamental properties.

In practice, any of these fundamental properties can be defined relative to any randomly selected relevant object or effect. Logically, though, for a measurement system to be as effective as possible, the objects and effects that are selected as the defined units of fundamental properties must be readily available to as many people as possible and readily reproducible. If, for example, a certain king were to decree that the "foot" to be used for measurement was the human foot, a great deal of confusion would result because of the variability in the size of the human foot from person to person and from a person's left foot to right foot. Should he instead decree that the "foot" would correspond to his own right foot and no other, the unit of measurement becomes significantly more precise, but at the same time, the decree raises the problem of how to verify that measurements being taken are in fact based on the decreed length of the foot. A physical model of the length of the king's right foot must then be made available for comparison. The same logic holds true for any and all defined properties and units. All measurements made within the definitions of a specific system of measurement are therefore made by comparing the proportional size of an effect or property to the defined standard units.

BACKGROUND AND HISTORY

Historically, measurement systems were generally based on various parts of the human body, and some of these units have remained in use in the modern world. The height of horses, for example, is generally given as being so many hands high. In many languages, the word for "thumb" and the word for "inch" are closely related, if not identical: In French, both words are *pouce*; in Norwegian, *tomme* and *tommelfinger*; and in Swedish, *tum* and *tumme*. Although using the thumb as a basis for measurement is convenient in that almost everyone has one, in practice, the generally accepted thumb size tended to vary from city to city, making it impossible to interchange parts made in different locations by separate artisans.

Units of measurement traditionally have been defined by a decree issued by a political leader. In ancient times, units of length often corresponded to certain parts of the human body: The foot was based on the human foot and the cubit on the length of the forearm. Other units used to weigh various goods were based on the weight of commonly available items. Examples include the stone (still used widely but not officially in Britain) and the grain. Invariably, the problem with such units lay in their variability. A stone weight may be defined as equivalent to the size of a stone that a grown man could enclose by both arms, but grown men come in different sizes and strengths, and stones come in different densities. A grain of gold may be defined as equivalent to the weight of a single grain of wheat; however, in drier years, when grains of wheat are smaller and lighter, the worth of gold is significantly different from its worth in years of good rainfall, when grains of wheat are larger and heavier.

HOW IT WORKS

Measurements and units are most useful when they are standardized so that measurements mean the same thing to everyone and are comparable. One method of solving the problem of variability in measurement is to establish a standard value for each unit and to regularly compare all measuring devices to this standard.

Historically, many societies required that measuring devices be physically compared with and calibrated against official standards. Physical representations of measuring units were made as precisely as possible and carefully stored and maintained to serve as standards for comparison. In ancient Egypt, the standard royal cubit was prepared as a black granite rod and most likely kept as one of the royal treasures by the pharaoh's chief steward. That simple stone object would have been accorded such a status because of its economic value to trade and construction and because it helped maintain the pharaoh's reputation as the keeper of his kingdom.

Later nations and empires also kept physical representations of most standard units appropriate to the economics of trade. The British made and kept definitive representations of the yard and the pound, just as the French made and kept definitive representations of the meter and the kilogram after developing the metric system in the late 1700s. Early on, countries recognized that the representative of the unit must not be subject to change or alteration. The Egyptian standard royal cubit was made of black granite; the standard meter and the kilogram, as well as the foot and the pound, were made from a platinum alloy so that they could not be altered by corrosion or oxidation.

France adopted the metric system as its official measuring system in 1795, and that system was standardized in 1960 as the International System of Units (*Le Système International d'Unités*, known as SI). The units of the metric system were defined based on unchanging, readily reproducible physical properties and effects rather than any physical object. For example, the standard SI unit of length, the meter, was originally defined to be one ten-millionth of the distance from the equator to the north polar axis along the meridian of longitude that passed through

Paris, France. In 1960, for greater accuracy, the definition of the meter was based on wavelengths of light emitted by the krypton-86 isotope. In 1983, it was changed to the length traveled by light in a vacuum during 1/299,792,458 of a second. Similarly, the length of a standard second of time had been defined as a fraction of one rotation of the earth on its axis, until it was realized that the rate of rotation was not constant but rather was slowly decreasing, so that the length of a day is increasing by 0.0013 second per hundred years. In 1967, it was formally redefined as a duration of 9,192,631,770 periods of the radiation corresponding to the transition between the two hyperfine levels of the ground state of the cesium-133 atom. As technology develops, it becomes possible to measure smaller quantities with finer precision. This capability has been the principal that permits ever more precise definitions of the basic units of measurement.

The application of measuring procedures is of fundamental importance in the economics of trade, especially in the modern global economy. In manufacturing, engineering, the sciences, and other fields, the accuracy and precision of measurement are essential to statistical process control and other quality-control techniques. All such measurement is a process of comparing the actual dimensions or properties of an item with its ideal or design dimensions or properties. The definition of a standard set of measuring units greatly facilitates that process.

APPLICATIONS AND PRODUCTS

It is quite impossible to calculate the economic effects that various systems of measurement, both good and bad, have had throughout history. Certainly, commonly understood and accepted units of weight, distance, and time have played a major role in facilitating trade between peoples for thousands of years. In many ways, all human activity can be thought of as dependent on measurement.

The study of measurement and measurement processes is known as "metrology." In essence, metrology is the determination and application of more precise and effective means of measuring quantities, properties, and effects. The value in metrology derives from how the information obtained is used. This is historically and traditionally tied to the concepts of fair trade and of well-made products. Measurement serves to ensure that trade is equitable, that people get exactly what they are supposed to get in exchange for their money, services, or other trade goods, and that as little goes to waste as possible.

By far, the largest segment of metrology deals with the design, production, and calibration of the various products and devices used to perform measurements. These devices range from the simplest spring scale or pan balance to some of the most sophisticated and specialized scientific instruments ever developed. In early times, measurements were restricted to those of mass, distance, and time because these were the foremost quantities used in trade. The remaining fundamental properties of electric current, amount of a substance, temperature, and luminous intensity either remained unknown or were not of consequence.

Weight determination. Originally, weights were determined with relative ease by the use of the pan balance. In the simplest variation of this device, two pans are suspended from opposite ends of a bar in such a way that they are at equal heights. The object to be weighed is placed in one of the pans and objects of known weights are placed in the other pan until the two pans are again at equal heights. The precision of the method depends on the ability of the bar to pivot as freely as possible about its balance point; any resistance will skew the measurement by preventing the pans from coming into proper balance with each other.

Essentially, all balances operate on the principle of comparing the weight of an unknown object against the weight of an accurately known counterweight, or some property such as electric current that can in turn be measured very accurately and precisely. The counterweight may not actually be a weight but rather an electronic pressure sensor or something that can be used to indicate the weight of an object such as the tension of a calibrated spring or a change in electrical resistance. Scales used in commercial applications, such as those in grocery stores, grain depots, and other trade locations, are inspected and calibrated on a regular basis according to law and regulations that govern their use.

Length determination. For many practical purposes, a linear device such as a scale ruler or tape measure is all that is needed to measure an unknown length. The device used should reflect the size of the object being measured and have scale markings that reflect the precision with which the measurement must be known. For example, a relatively small dimension being measured in a machine shop would be measured by a trained machinist against a precision steel scale ruler with dimensional markings of high precision. Training in the use of graduated scale markings typically enables the user to read them accurately to within one-tenth of the smallest division on the scale. High-precision micrometers are generally used to make more precise measurements of smaller dimensions, and electronic versions of such devices provide the ability to measure dimensions to extremely precise tolerances. Smaller dimensions, for which the accuracy of the human eye is neither sufficient nor sufficiently reproducible, are measured using microscope techniques and devices. Accurate measurements of larger dimensions have always been problematic, especially when the allowable tolerance of the measurement is very small. This has been overcome in many cases by the measuring machine, a semirobotic device that uses electronic control and logic programming to determine the distance between precise points on a specific object.

The 1960 definition of the meter was achieved through the use of a precision interferometer, a device that uses the interference pattern of light waves such that the number of wavelengths of a specific frequency of light can be counted. Using this device, the meter was precisely defined as the distance equal to 1,650,763.73 wavelengths of the $2p_{10}$-$5d_5$ emission of krypton-86 atoms. In 1983, however, the meter was defined as the distance traveled by light in vacuum in 1/299,792,548 of a second.

Time measurement. Essentially, the basic unit of time measurement in all systems is the second. This is a natural consequence of the fact that the length of a day is the same everywhere on the planet. The natural divisions of that period of time according to the observed patterns of stars and their motions almost inevitably results in twenty-four equal divisions. A natural result of the metric system is that a pendulum that is one meter in length swings with a period of one second. Pendulum clockworks have been used to measure the passage of time, coordinated to the natural divisions of the day, for thousands of years. More precise time measurements have become possible as better technology has become available. With the development of the metric system, the unit duration of one second was defined to correspond to the appropriate fraction of one rotation of the planet. Until the development of electronic methods and devices, this was a sufficient definition. However, with the realization that the rotation of the planet is not constant but is slowly decreasing, the need to redefine the second in terms that remain constant in time led to its redefinition in 1967. According to the new definition, a second is the time needed for a cesium-133 atom to perform 9,192,631,770 complete oscillations.

Temperature determination. Of all properties, measurement of thermodynamic temperature is perhaps the most relative and arbitrary of all. The thermometer was developed before any of the commonly used temperature scales, including the

Fahrenheit, Celsius, Kelvin, and Rankine scales. All are based on the freezing and boiling points of water, the most readily available and ubiquitous substance on the planet. The Fahrenheit scale arbitrarily set the freezing point of saturated salt water as 0 degrees. The physical dimensions of the scale used on Fahrenheit's thermometer resulted in the establishment of the boiling point of pure water as 212 degrees. The Celsius scale designated the freezing point of pure water to be 0 degrees and the boiling point of pure water to be 100 degrees. The relative sizes of Fahrenheit and Celsius degrees are thus different by a factor of 5 to 9. Conversion of Fahrenheit temperature to Celsius temperature is achieved by subtracting 32 degrees and multiplying the result by 5/9; to convert from Celsius to Fahrenheit, first multiply by 9/5, then add 32 degrees to the result. The temperature of -40 degrees is the same in both scales.

Each temperature scale recognizes a physical state called "absolute zero," at which matter contains no thermal energy whatsoever. This must physically be the same state regardless of whether Fahrenheit or Celsius degrees are being used. Because of this, two other scales of temperature were developed. The Rankine scale, established as part of the school of British engineering, uses the Fahrenheit degree scale, beginning at 0 degrees at absolute zero. The Kelvin scale uses the Celsius degree scale, beginning at 0 degrees at absolute zero.

Temperature is accurately measured electronically by its effect on light in the infrared region of the electromagnetic spectrum, although less accurate physical thermometers remain in wide use.

Amount of a substance. Of all the fundamental properties, amount of a substance is the least precisely known. The concept is intimately linked to the modern atomic theory and atomic weights, although it predates them by almost one hundred years. Through studies of the properties of gases in the early 1800s, Italian Amedeo Avogadro concluded that a quantity of any pure material equal to its molecular weight in grams contained exactly the same number of particles. This number of particles came to be referred to as the Avogadro constant. Thus, 2 grams of hydrogen gas (molecular weight = 2) contains exactly the same number of molecules as does 342 grams of sucrose (common white table sugar, molecular weight = 342) or 18 milliliters of water (molecular weight 18, density = 1 gram per milliliter). Calculations have determined the value of the Avogadro constant to be about 6.02214×10^{23}. Because all twenty-three decimal places are not known, the absolute value has not yet been determined, and therefore amount of a substance is the least precisely known unit of measurement.

The amount of material represented by the Avogadro constant (of atoms or molecules) is termed the "mole," a contraction from "gram molecular weight." The number is constant regardless of the system of measurement that is used, as a result of the indivisibility of the atom in modern chemical theory. Thus, a gram molecular weight of a substance and a pound molecular weight of a substance both contain a constant number of molecules.

Electric current. Of course, atoms are not indivisible in fact. They consist of a nucleus of protons and neutrons, surrounded by a cloud of electrons. The electrons can move from atom to atom through matter, and such movement constitutes an electric current. More generally, any movement of electronic charge between two different points in space defines an electric current. Although some controversial evidence suggests that electricity may have been known in ancient times, any serious study of electricity did not begin until the eighteenth century, after the discovery of the electrochemical cell. At that time, electricity was thought to be a mysterious fluid that permeated matter. With the discovery of subatomic particles (electrons and protons) in 1898 and the subsequent development of the modern atomic theory, the nature of electric currents came to be better understood. The ampere, named after one of the foremost investigators of electrical phenomena, is the basic unit of electric current and corresponds to the movement of one mole of electrons for a period of one second.

The development of the transistor—and the electronic revolution that followed—made it possible to measure extremely small electric currents as well as corresponding values of voltage, resistance, induction, and other electronic functions. This made it possible to precisely measure fundamental properties by electronic means rather than physical methods.

Measurement of luminous intensity. Until it became important and necessary to know precisely the intensity of light being emitted from a light source, particularly in the fields of astronomy and physics, there was no need for a fundamental unit of luminous intensity. Light intensities were generally compared, at least in post-Industrial Revolution Europe, to the intensity of light emitted from a candle. This sufficed for general uses such as light bulbs, but the innate variability of candle flames made them inadequate for precision measurements. The candela was set as the standard unit of luminous intensity and corresponds to the output of energy of 0.00146 watts. Modern light bulbs typically are rated at a certain number of watts, but this is a measure of the electric power that they consume and not of their luminous intensity.

CAREERS AND COURSEWORK

Measurement and units, as they apply to metrology, are part of every technical and scientific field. The student planning on a career in any of these areas can expect to learn how to use the metric system and the many ways in which measurement is applied in a specific field of study. Because measurement is related to the fundamental properties of matter, a good understanding of the relationships between measurements and properties will be essential to success in any chosen field. In addition, the continuing use of multiple measuring systems, such as the metric, US customary, and British Imperial systems, in the production of goods means that an understanding of those systems and how to convert between them will be necessary in many careers.

Specific courses that involve measurement include geometry and mathematics, essentially all of the physical science and technology courses, and design and technical drawing courses. Geometry, which literally means "earth measurement," is the quintessential mathematics of measurement and is essential for careers in land surveying, architecture, agriculture, civil engineering, and construction. Gaining an understanding of trigonometry and angular relationships is particularly important. The physical sciences, such as physics, chemistry, and geology, employ analytical measurement at all levels. Specializations in which measurement plays a prominent role are analytic chemistry and forensic research. Technology programs such as mechanical engineering, electronic design, and biomedical technology all rely heavily on measurement and the application of metrological techniques in the completion of projects that the engineer or technologist undertakes.

SOCIAL CONTEXT AND FUTURE PROSPECTS

Measurement and an understanding of the units of measurement are an entrenched aspect of modern society, taught informally to children from early childhood and formally throughout the course of their schooling. They are fundamental to the continued progress of technology and essential to the determination of solutions to problems as they arise, as well as to the development of new ideas and concepts. The need for individuals who are trained in metrology and who understand the relationship and use of measurements and units will be of increasing importance in ensuring the viability of both new and established industries.

Particular areas of growth and continuing development include the fields of medical research and analysis, transportation, mechanical design, and aerospace. The accuracy and precision of measurement in these fields is critical to the successful outcome of projects.

In 2017, it was announced that the kilogram, an SI base unit, would be redefined by the General Conference on Weights and Measures in November 2018, as a constant rather than based on a physical object. Three other SI base units were also under consideration for redefinition. In November 2018, the sixty countries participating in the conference unanimously voted to redefine the kilogram, kelvin, mole, and ampere in terms of constants. The new definitions came into effect in May of the following year.

—Richard M. J. Renneboog, MSc

Further Reading

Butcher, Kenneth S., Linda D. Crown, and Elizabeth J. Gentry, editors. *The International System of Units (SI): Conversion Factors for General Use*. National Institute of Standards and Technology, 2006.

Cardarelli, Francois. *Encyclopedia of Scientific Units, Weights and Measures: Their SI Equivalences and Origins*. Springer, 2003.

De Courtenay, Nadine, Olivier Darrigol, and Oliver Schlaudt, editors. *The Reform of the International System of Units (SI): Philosophical, Historical and Sociological Issues*. Routledge, 2019.

Kuhn, Karl F. *In Quest of the Universe*. 6th ed., Jones and Bartlett, 2010.

"The Redefinition of the SI Units." *NPL*, www.npl.co.uk/si-units/the-redefinition-of-the-si-units. Accessed 28 Nov. 2021.

"SI Redefinition." *NIST*, www.nist.gov/si-redefinition. Accessed 28 Nov. 2021.

Tavernor, Robert. *Smoot's Ear: The Measure of Humanity*. Yale UP, 2007.

Microscale 3D Printing

ABSTRACT

Microscale three-dimensional (3D) printing is a type of 3D printing that makes it possible to construct objects at an extremely small scale. Some processes can create objects as small as 100 micrometers. 3D printing at this scale has a number of applications for computing and medicine. It makes it possible to produce microscopic structures out of organic materials for biomedical applications.

A REVOLUTIONARY TECHNOLOGY

Three-dimensional (3D) printing is a relatively new technology. However, it has already revolutionized manufacturing. It takes its name from traditional computer printers that produce pages of printed images. Regular printers operate by depositing small amounts of ink at precise locations on a piece of paper. Instead of ink, a 3D printer uses a material, such as a polymer, metallic powder, or even organic material. Following a digital design, it builds an object by depositing small amounts of that material in successive layers; this process is also known as additive manufacturing (AM). In some cases, 3D printing fastens materials to a substrate using heat, adhesives, or other methods. 3D printing can produce incredibly intricate objects that would be difficult or impossible to create through traditional manufacturing methods.

Microscale 3D printing advances the innovation of standard 3D printing to create microscopic structures. The potential applications for microscale 3D printing are still being explored.

However, microscale 3D printing presents the possibility of creating tissue for transplant. For example, full-scale 3D printing has already produced some types of tissue, such as muscle, cartilage, and bones. One problem is the printed tissue sometimes did not survive because it had no circulatory system to bring blood and nutrients to the new tissue.

Microscale 3D printing makes it possible to create the tiny blood vessels needed in living tissue, among other potential applications.

3D PRINTING METHODS

The basic approach used by 3D printing is to build an object by attaching tiny amounts of material to each other at precise locations. Some materials are melted before they are deposited. Material extrusion heats polymer filament. The melted plastic material is then extruded through nozzles and deposited in a layer. The materials then harden into place, and another layer is added. With vat photopolymerization, a light-sensitive liquid polymer is printed onto a platform within a vat of liquid resin. An ultraviolet (UV) laser then hardens a layer of resin. More liquid polymer is then added, and the process is repeated. With material jetting, a printer head deposits liquefied plastic or other light-sensitive material onto a platform. The material is then hardened with UV light.

Other methods melt or fuse materials after they have been deposited. In powder bed fusion, the printer heats a bed of powdered glass, metal, ceramic, or plastic until the materials fuse together in the desired locations. Another layer of powder is then added and fused onto the first. Binder jetting uses a printer head to deposit drops of glue-like liquid into a powdered medium. The liquid soaks into and solidifies the medium. Sheet lamination fuses together thin sheets of paper, metal, or plastic with an adhesive. The layers are then cut with a laser into the desired shape. In directed energy deposition, a metal wire or powder is deposited in thin layers before being melted with a laser.

The method used depends on the physical properties of the material being printed. Metal alloys, for example, cannot easily be liquefied for vat polymerization, material jetting, or material extrusion. Instead, they are printed using binder jetting, powder bed fusion, or sheet lamination.

MICROSCALE METHODS

Microscale 3D printing requires more exact methods to create objects that are just a few micrometers wide. Microscopic objects require tiny droplets of materials and precise locations of deposition. One microscale 3D printing technique is optical lithography. This technique uses light to create patterns in a photosensitive resist, where material is then deposited. Optical transient liquid molding (TLM) uses UV light patterns and a custom flow of liquid polymer to create objects that are smaller than the width of a human hair. Optical TLM combines a liquid polymer, which will form the structure of the printed object, with a liquid mold in a series of tiny pillars. The pillars are arranged based on software that determines the shape of the liquids' flow. Patterned UV light then cuts into the liquids to further shape the stream. The combination of the liquid mold and the UV light pat-

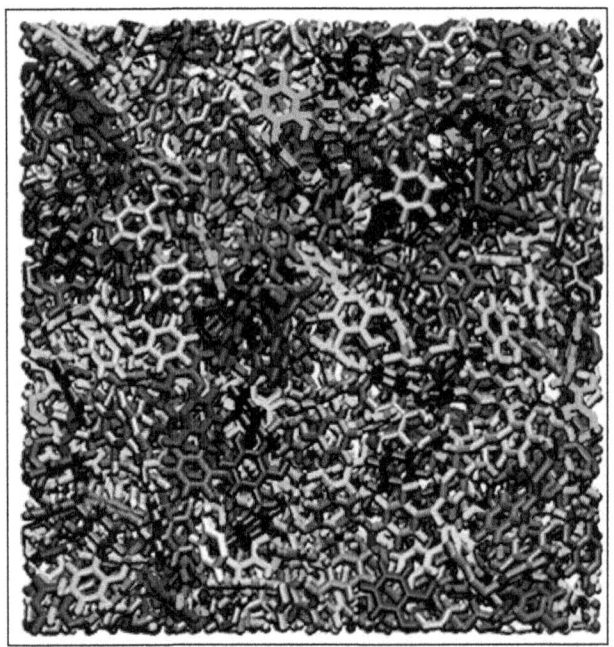

Material engineers can use microscale 3-D printing to develop unique materials for use in a wide range of fields, including bioengineering, architecture, and electronics. The combination and arrangement of particular molecules allows engineers to develop materials with the necessary characteristics to fulfill specific needs, such as the polymers used to build the entry heat shields for NASA. Image by Alexander Thompson and John Lawson, NASA Ames Research Center.

tern allow the creation of highly complex structures that are just 100 micrometers in size.

Microscale 3D printing makes it possible to create extremely small circuits. This will enable the creation of new devices, such as "smart clothing" that can sense the wearer's body temperature and adjust its properties based on this information. Microscale 3D printing may also revolutionize the creation of new medicines. Because drug uptake by cells is shape-dependent, the precision of microscale 3D printing may allow researchers to design custom drugs for specific brain receptors.

A NEW TYPE OF "INK"

Some refer to the build materials used in 3D printing as "inks" because they take the place of ink as it is used in regular document printers. This can stretch the definition of "ink." Most people think of ink as either the liquid in a pen or the toner of a computer printer. In microscale 3D printing, the ink might be human cells used to create an organ or metallic powder that will be fused into tiny circuits.

—*Scott Zimmer, MLS, MS, JD*

Further Reading

"About Additive Manufacturing." *Additive Manufacturing Research Group*, 2021, www.lboro.ac.uk/research/amrg/about/. Accessed 28 Nov. 2021.

Bernier, Samuel N., Bertier Luyt, Tatiana Reinhard, and Carl Bass. *Design for 3D Printing: Scanning, Creating, Editing, Remixing, and Making in Three Dimensions*. Maker Media, 2014.

Bitonti, Francis. *3D Printing Design: Additive Manufacturing and the Materials Revolution*. Bloomsbury, 2019.

Brockotter, Robin. "Key Design Considerations for 3D Printing." *HUBS*, www.hubs.com/knowledge-base/key-design-considerations-3d-printing/. Accessed 28 Nov. 2021.

Horvath, Joan. *Mastering 3D Printing: Modeling, Printing, and Prototyping with Reprap- Style 3D Printers*. Apress, 2014.

Hoskins, Stephen. *3D Printing for Artists, Designers and Makers*. Bloomsbury, 2013.

Lipson, Hod, and Melba Kurman. *Fabricated: The New World of 3D Printing*. Wiley, 2013.

V., Carlotta. "What Is the Current State of Microscale 3D Printing?" *3DNatives*, 16 Apr. 2020, www.3dnatives.com/en/what-is-the-current-state-of-microscale-3d-printing/. Accessed 28 Nov. 2021.

Naval Architecture and Marine Engineering

ABSTRACT

The process of designing a ship involves two complementary disciplines: naval architecture and marine engineering. Naval architecture has two subdivisions: hydrodynamics and ship structures. Hydrodynamics is concerned with the interaction between the moving ship hull and the water in which it floats. Ship structures is concerned with building a hull that has the strength needed to withstand the forces to which it is subject. Marine engineering is concerned with all the machinery that goes into the ship. The machinery must perform the following tasks: propulsion and steering, electric power generation and distribution, and cargo handling.

DEFINITION AND BASIC PRINCIPLES

A ship is a very complex object. Some ships must be able to load and unload themselves, while others depend on facilities in ports of call. A ship must propel itself from place to place and control its direction of motion. It must produce its own electricity and freshwater. In addition to the space devoted to cargo, a ship must provide space for fuel, freshwater, living accommodations for crew and perhaps passengers, propulsion, and related machinery. A ship must float, and it must remain upright in all sorts of sea conditions. There are many different kinds of ships: aircraft carriers, submarines, container ships, tankers, passenger ships, ferries, and ships that transport liquefied natural gas, to name a few. The size of a ship is chosen based on cargo-carrying capacity, but it is limited by channel depth, pier length, and other characteristics of the ports it must enter. Most ships are part of a transportation business. To maximize profit, the costs of construction and operation must be minimized, while the income from transporting cargo must be maximized. Working together, naval architects and marine engineers design each ship to satisfy the requirements mentioned above. A design team is assembled that represents the needed areas of expertise. The team may work for a year or more to produce the complete design. When the design work is finished, one or more shipyards may be invited to submit bids for construction.

BACKGROUND AND HISTORY

One of the earliest well-documented ships is the funeral ship of Pharaoh Cheops that was built in about 2600 BCE. The Greeks and the Romans built large oar-powered ships called "biremes" and "triremes." Bartholomew Diaz sailed three caravels around the tip of Africa in 1488, and Christopher Columbus reached the Americas in 1492. All these ships were built by artisans who knew no theory of ship design. Scientific ship design began in France and Spain in the late 1600s. Steam was first used to propel watercraft in the late 1700s, and the first successful steam powered vessel, *Charlotte Dundas*, made its first voyage on the River Clyde in Scotland in 1802. By 1816, steam-powered passenger ships sailed regularly between Brighton, England, and Le Havre, France. William H. Webb designed and built clipper ships along the East River in New York City in the years before the Civil War. Webb and his contemporaries and predecessors called themselves "shipbuilders," but they designed their ships, too.

During the twentieth century, the functions of designing ships and building them became separate. As computer technology developed throughout the late twentieth and early twenty-first centuries, engineers working within the field of ship design began to make use of digital tools that aided in the design of boats and other water vehicles. Marine engineers benefited particularly from computer-aided design (CAD) and computer-aided engineering (CAE) software products, which facilitated the design and modeling of ships. Other valuable tools included simulation programs, which enabled engineers to test the effects of relevant forces on virtual models of the crafts they designed.

HOW IT WORKS

The two principal issues in designing the hull of a ship are its structural strength and the force required to push it through the water at the desired speed. Other issues include stability and the way the ship moves up and down and side to side in waves.

Designing the hull. Forces on a ship's hull may be divided into static (constant) forces and dynamic (variable) forces. There are two static forces: the force of gravity pulling down on the ship and its contents and the upward force exerted by the water on the hull.

Wave action is responsible for the dynamic forces, but some of these forces are direct results of the waves and some are indirect. When the ship's bow meets a wave, the wave exerts an upward force, lifting the bow. As the ship passes through the wave, the upward force moves along the ship from bow to stern. When the bow reaches the low point between two wave crests, the bow drops and the stern rises. Wave action causes the ship to flex, like a board that is supported at its ends does when someone jumps up and down at the middle.

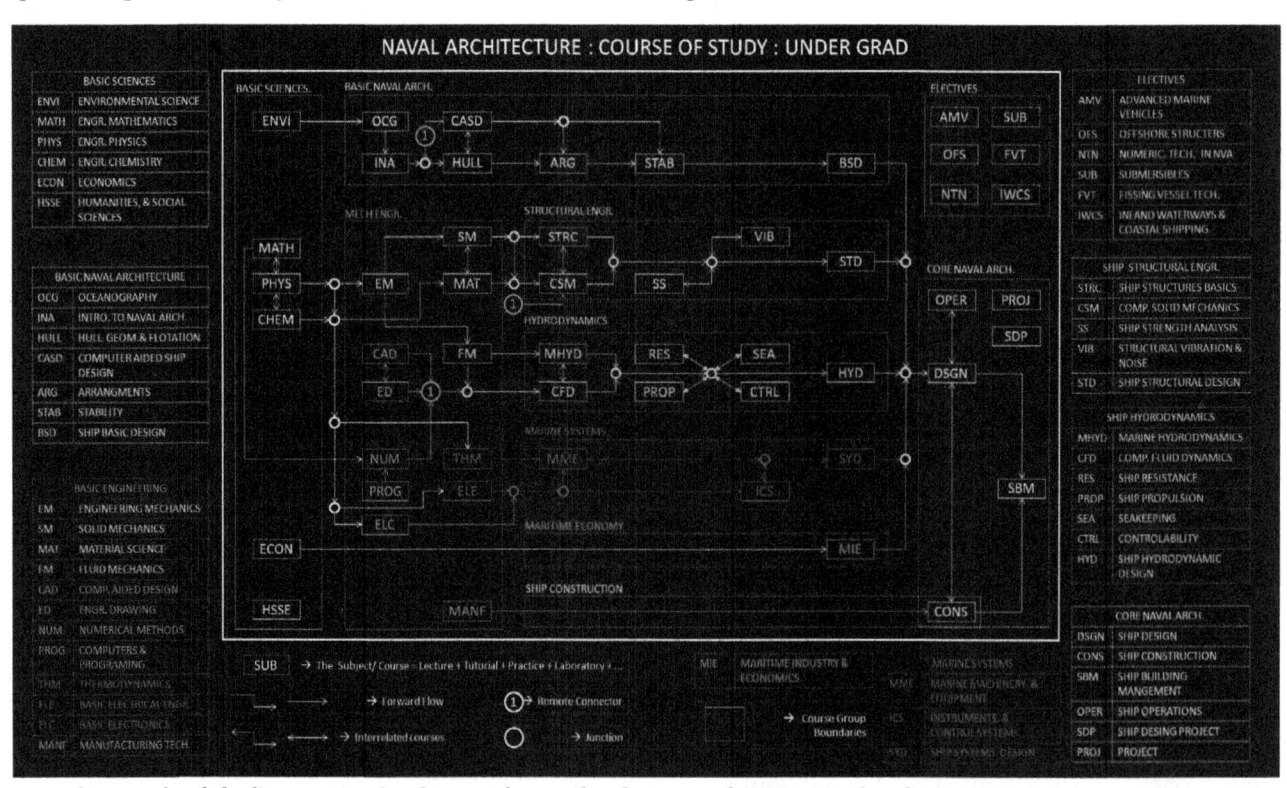

General course of study leading to a Naval Architecture degree. Photo by Praveench1888, via Wikimedia Commons.

The aircraft carrier USS Kitty Hawk (CV-63) at Naval Station Pearl Harbor. Photo via Wikimedia Commons. [Public domain.]

Wave action also causes the ship to roll from side to side. As the ship rolls, liquids in its tanks slosh from side to side. This causes dynamic forces on the walls of the tanks. Waves may slap against the sides of the ship, and sometimes waves put water onto the decks.

Resistance and stability. As a ship moves through the water, it must push aside the water ahead of it. This water moves away from the ship as waves. Water flowing along the sides of the ship exerts a friction force on the hull. The combination of these forces is called the "resistance." The propulsion force provided by a ship's propeller must overcome the resistance. Naval architects can accurately predict the friction resistance, but the resistance associated with pushing the water aside is usually determined by testing a scale model.

A ship must be stable. This means it must float upright in still water, and it must return to an upright position after waves cause it to tilt. A naval architect must perform detailed calculations to ensure that the ship being designed meets requirements for stability.

Propulsion and auxiliary machinery. It is the responsibility of the marine engineer to select the machinery that will provide the required power. There are ships powered by steam turbines, gas turbines, and diesel engines. The propeller may be driven directly by the engine, it may be driven through a speed-reducing gear, or the engine may drive an electric generator that provides power to a motor that drives the propeller.

The marine engineer must also select pumps, piping, oil purifiers, speed-reducing gears, heat exchangers, and many other pieces of auxiliary machinery. The marine engineer designs the systems that connect all of the components and allow them to work together. A ship must generate its own electricity and produce freshwater from seawater. Machinery must be provided to control the direction of motion of the ship.

APPLICATIONS AND PRODUCTS

Naval architects and marine engineers are called on to design many different types of ships. Each ship type has its own unique design requirements. The designers must consider many factors, including how deep the channels are in the intended ports of call, what type of cargo will be carried, and how time sensitive it is.

Passenger ships. Passenger ships may be liners or cruise ships. Liners are used to transport people from one place to another. Before air travel became common, this is how people traveled across oceans. In the early twenty-first century, most passenger ships are cruise ships. They embark passengers at a port, take them to visit interesting places, and return them to the same port where they embarked. Cruise ships have extensive passenger-entertainment facilities, which may range from rock-climbing walls to casinos. Most cruise ships are propelled by diesel engines. These engines may drive the propellers directly, or they may drive electric generators. In the latter case, the propellers are driven by electric motors.

Container ships. Shipping of cargo in standard rectangular containers has revolutionized the shipping business. At specialized container ship ports, a ship can be loaded or unloaded in twelve hours or less by large container cranes mounted on the dock. The largest container ships can carry more than ten thousand 20-foot-long containers. Containers can hold all manner of cargo, from cameras and televisions to food and cut flowers. Container ships are typically the fastest category of merchant ships. Speeds between 20 and 25 knots are common because these ships carry time-sensitive cargo.

Tankers. Tankers range from ultralarge crude-oil carriers that carry more than 300,000 long tons of crude to small coastal tankers that carry 10,000 long tons or less. Ultralarge crude-oil ships transport large amounts of crude oil from sources in the Persian Gulf to refineries in Europe and North America. There are many other categories of tankers. The most specialized are chemical tankers, which are equipped to carry corrosive cargo such as sulfuric acid and highly flammable cargo such as gasoline.

LNG ships. These tankers are designed to carry liquefied natural gas (LNG). Natural gas, which is mainly methane, changes from gas to liquid at -160° Celsius (-256° Fahrenheit). Although the tanks are heavily insulated, some heat does leak into the LNG. This causes a small amount of LNG to vaporize. One of the major decisions in designing an LNG ship is how to handle this gas. Many LNG ships are propelled by steam turbines, and the gas that boils off from the tanks is burned in the boilers. Other LNG ships are propelled by diesel engines. In some cases, the boil-off gas (BOG) is burned in the engines. On other diesel-powered ships the BOG is condensed and returned to the tanks. Many LNG ships operate at about 19 knots. Depending on their size, they may require as much as 50,000 horsepower for propulsion.

Naval surface ships. Naval surface ships range from huge aircraft carriers—which may weigh 100,000 long tons or more—to much smaller destroyers and frigates, which may weigh 4,000 long tons. Aircraft carriers and cruisers are often nuclear powered. Destroyers and frigates are often powered by gas turbines. On an aircraft carrier the main weapons are the aircraft. Other warships are armed with guns, missiles, and torpedoes. The ships must have the capability to locate and track enemy targets and to launch weapons at them. They must also be able to defend themselves against weapons launched by enemy ships and aircraft.

Submarines. Submarines range from one-person research vessels powered by batteries to the US Navy's large, nuclear-powered missile submarines. Two things make submarines different from other ships: First, they must be able to operate without access to the atmosphere, and second, their hulls must withstand the pressure of the sea at the depths where they operate. Navy submarines are powered by nuclear reactors so that they do not need air for the combustion of fuel. The oxygen required to support human life aboard a submarine is produced by using electricity to split water molecules into hydrogen and oxygen, a process called "electrolysis."

There are many other types of ships: ferries, roll-on/roll-off ships, heavy lift ships, fishing vessels, dredges, tugboats, and yachts of all shapes and sizes. Two very interesting specialized ships are hovercraft and hydrofoils. Hovercraft ride on a cushion of air that is trapped between the hull and the surface of the sea. Hydrofoils are supported by "wings" that are submerged in the water. Both hovercraft and hydrofoils are capable of much higher speeds than conventional ships.

CAREERS AND COURSEWORK

A small number of colleges and universities in the United States offer degrees in naval architecture, marine engineering, or a combination of the two. Similar programs are offered in Canada, Europe, and Asia. Students of naval architecture take courses in strength of materials, ship structures, hydrodynamics, ship resistance, and propeller design. Marine engineering programs include thermodynamics, heat transfer, and machine design. Advanced mathematics is a part of both programs. A bachelor of science degree is the minimum requirement, and many working professionals in these fields have master of science degrees.

Naval architect at work. Photo by Lucy Elizabeth Collins, via Wikimedia Commons.

Most ship design is performed by companies that produce only the plans and specifications for a ship. The would-be shipowner takes these documents to one or more shipyards and invites bids for the actual construction. Shipyards also employ naval architects and marine engineers who deal with design issues that arise during the construction of a ship.

SOCIAL CONTEXT AND FUTURE PROSPECTS

When cargo must be transported across large bodies of water, such as the Atlantic and Pacific oceans, there are only two possible ways to do it—ships and airplanes. Lightweight, high-value, time-sensitive cargo goes by air, but more mundane cargo goes by ship. Ships are slow, but in many cases, time is not of the essence. Crude oil and natural gas are abundant in a part of the world where demand for these materials is low. A steady stream of large tankers carries crude oil nearly halfway around the world. LNG ships do the same. It is hard to imagine an alternative. Although it is possible to transport cargo from France to Algeria by road, it is not practical to do so.

Transportation by ship is far less expensive than by air. Among other factors, the fuel consumed to move a given amount of cargo a given distance is much less. Shipping products in standard rectangular containers has drastically reduced the cost and time required for handling cargo at both ends of its travel by sea. As such, it appears that cargo transportation by ship will remain an important business for the foreseeable future.

—*Edwin G. Wiggins, BS, MS, PhD*

Further Reading

Benford, Harry. *Naval Architecture for Non-Naval Architects*. Society of Naval Architects and Marine Engineers, 1991.

Ferreiro, Larrie D. *Ships and Science: The Birth of Naval Architecture in the Scientific Revolution, 1600-1800*. MIT Press, 2007.

Gardiner, Robert, editor. *The Earliest Ships: The Evolution of Boats into Ships*. Conway Maritime, 2004.

Keane, Phillip. "Shipbuilding Sets Sail with CAD." *Engineers Rule*, 30 Aug. 2018, www.engineersrule.com/shipbuilding-sets-sail-cad/. Accessed 28 Nov. 2021.

Kemp, John F., and Peter Young. *Ship Construction Sketches and Notes*. 2nd ed., Butterworth, 1997.

Papanikolaou, Apostolos, editor. *A Holistic Approach to Ship Design: Volume 1; Optimisation of Ship Design and Operation for Life Cycle*. Springer Nature Switzerland, 2019.

Rowen, Alan L., et al. *Introduction to Practical Marine Engineering*. Society of Naval Architects and Marine Engineers, 2005.

"Ship Design Computer Laboratory." *University of New Orleans*, 2020, www.uno.edu/academics/coe/name/facilities/ship-design-computer-laboratory. Accessed 28 Nov. 2021.

Van Dokkum, Klaas. *Ship Knowledge: Ship Design, Construction and Operation*. 10th ed., Dokmar Maritime Publishers, 2020.

Zubaly, Robert B. *Applied Naval Architecture*. Cornell Maritime, 1996.

NX

ABSTRACT

NX is an advanced computer-aided design (CAD), manufacturing, and engineering program offered by Siemens. Products marketed under the NX for Design and NX for Manufacturing designations include a host of tools for drafting, building three-dimensional (3D) models, creating computer numerical control manufacturing programs, and validating designs, among others.

CAD, CAM, AND CAE

The three disciplines of computer-aided design (CAD), computer-aided engineering (CAE), and computer-aided manufacturing (CAM) are closely related technologies that have increasingly overlapped since their emergence in the mid-twentieth century. CAD specifically refers to the use of software to create two (2D)- and three-dimensional (3D) illustrations and models of objects to be engineered, ranging from tiny transistor structures on integrated circuit chips to gigantic buildings and structures. CAE uses computation software to simulate the response of a designed object or system to the various conditions it is expected to encounter and endure. As may be expected, CAE software is much more computational than CAD software. It can be, and is, routinely used to carry out analyses of CAD designs with regard to load and stress distributions, power consumption or output, and any number of other engineering computations. CAM software is used to direct the operation of manufacturing equipment. CAM software generally takes dimensional specifications and other data directly from CAE or CAD output and then performs numerous computational operations to determine tool paths, cutting and turning speeds and depths, and milling operations, as well as the order in which those operations must be carried out to produce the desired object precisely and repetitively.

As computer capabilities have evolved and grown, every new development of software and the technology to use it has blurred the boundaries of CAD, CAE, and CAM. As such, industry-leading software packages of the early twenty-first century often seek to meet the needs of professionals working in all three disciplines, offering tools crucial to each step of the design, engineering, and manufacturing processes. Such software packages include NX, also referred to as Siemens NX, a popular CAD/CAE/CAM option within fields such as the automotive industry.

SIEMENS NX

A precursor to NX, Integrated Design and Engineering Analysis System (I-DEAS), was a CAD package developed by the Structural Dynamics Research Corporation (SDRC) in 1982. It was primarily used for automotive design, including by prominent companies such as General Motors (GM). In 2001, SDRC and its I-DEAS software were acquired by Electronic Data Systems (EDS). EDS subsequently combined I-DEAS and the program Unigraphics, acquired during the company's previous purchase of the UGS Corporation, under the new name of NX. After Siemens acquired EDS in 2007, that company took charge of the development and marketing of NX, which would sometimes be referred to as Siemens NX.

Siemens NX is proprietary software and must be licensed for use. As of 2021, several different subscription options were available to individuals or businesses seeking to make use of Siemens's cloud-connected NX products, which included the packages NX Core Designer, NX Advanced Designer, and NX Drafting and Layout. The monthly subscription fees for such packages varied based on the tools and features included, which likewise varied widely. NX Drafting and Layout, for example, primarily featured drawing tools that could be used to create 2D- or 3D-engineering drawings and had a lower subscription fee than NX Core Designer, which offered more extensive modeling tools. As its name suggested, NX Advanced Designer offered all features included in the NX Core Designer package as well as advanced modeling and analysis tools, among others. In addition to such design-oriented packages, Siemens offered NX for Manufacturing solutions that included tools designed specifically for CAM processes such as turning and milling. Such procedures are considered forms of subtractive manufacturing because their function subtracts mass from the workpiece.

SIMULATION AND VALIDATION

Previously included in the dedicated NX CAM Integrated Simulation and Verification (ISV) software and later integrated into Siemens's cloud-connected NX offerings, simulation features are key to many of the design and manufacturing tools included in the NX software. NX CAD products can integrate with Siemens CAE software such as Simcenter 3D, which enables users to test the effects of motion on mechanical systems, analyze the durability of proposed designs, and simulate fluid dynamics, among other functions. NX also offers a variety of design-validation tools, including the automated feature NX Check-Mate, which checks designs in progress for their compliance with the relevant existing or custom standards. Available tools can also assist in the design of parts intended to be manufactured through specific processes. For example, integrated tools can assess whether using the process of injection molding to create a specific plastic part will have the desired results.

ADDITIVE MANUFACTURING

In addition to computer-aided subtractive-manufacturing methods such as milling and turning, NX supports the increasingly prominent process of additive manufacturing. In additive manufacturing, 3D objects are formed by depositing layers of material and joining them to create a desired shape. The most familiar type of additive manufacturing is probably 3D printing, which has quickly become a household term. 3D printing methodology has been extended from designs in plastics and resins to metals and other materials that can be made to flow through a position-controlled nozzle, even structural concrete. Other methods include powder bed fusion, in which the desired structure is constructed by applying and fusing successive layers of the appropriate powdered material. NX tools facilitate design for additive manufacturing, enabling users to create designs suitable for a number of 3D printing processes and validate those designs to ensure their suitability for printing. As of 2021, NX was capable of connecting directly with a number of 3D printers, including both industrial and smaller scale devices, and was also able to export CAD files for use with 3D printers that are not officially supported.

—*Richard M. Renneboog, MSc*

Further Reading

Anderl, Reiner, and Peter Binde. *Simulations with NX/Simcenter 3D: Kinematics, FEA, CFD, EM and Data Management*. 2nd ed., Hanser Publications, 2018.

"NX." Siemens, 2021, www.plm.automation.siemens.com/global/en/products/nx/. Accessed 16 Nov. 2021.

Qin, Zheng, Huidi Zhang, Xin Qing, et al. *Fundamentals of Software Culture*. Springer, 2018.

Shih, Randy. *Parametric Modeling with Siemens NX*. Spring 2020 ed., SDC Publications, 2020.

Tickoo, Sham. *Siemens NX 2020 for Designers*. 13th ed., CADCIM Technologies, 2020.

Open-Source CAD Software

ABSTRACT
Computer-aided design (CAD) software is used to design physical objects in a wide range of industries. High-end CAD programs are proprietary in nature and cannot be altered by the end user. Open-source CAD programs, however, are often free to use, and end users are allowed to alter or enhance the source code of the programs to suit their particular needs.

UNDERSTANDING CAD SOFTWARE

Software, generally, consists of computer programs designed to perform specific functions for computer users. Their real purpose is to allow a human user to communicate with the machine in a way that the machine can understand. A program is written in a code language the human user understands, as a series of instructional steps. These human-language steps are then translated and assembled into machine language that the computer understands. Machine language consists of a series of high- and low-electrical signals that specify operating procedures and memory locations where the corresponding instructions for those procedures are stored. As the program is executed, these stepwise instructions are carried out as required.

Computer-aided design (CAD) software is used by designers and engineers to develop technical drawings, and sometimes three-dimensional (3D) models, of devices and structures that are to be manufactured. Many CAD programs are designed with the ability to interface with machine control programs and provide the data a machine control program uses to operate the machines to which it is allied. The data may be used by the control program to determine the order of operations it must carry out and the parameters of those operations, such as the order in which features are to be machined and the depth of cuts to be made during the machining operations. In other applications, the data may be used to generate a technical drawing on an interfaced printer or to control the operation of a 3D printer.

The most powerful CAD software packages are proprietary intellectual properties owned by a parent company or organization and, though often initially developed for the needs of that particular entity, can be licensed for use by other companies and operations. The copyright of the application being licensed, however, remains with the proprietor of the software, and only the proprietor is legally allowed to alter the program code.

OPEN-SOURCE SOFTWARE

A proprietary software program, no matter how comprehensive and capable, can never meet the needs of everyone who would use it. There will always be someone somewhere who has a particular need that the software does not satisfy. It can also be the case that the software does satisfy that particular need, but much of the rest of the program itself is not needed, and running it in its entirety just to meet the limited need consumes computer time and space that is better spent in other operations.

To remedy this situation, a proprietary software may be offered with reduced functionality or with an open-source designation that allows end users to alter the program source code in a way that suits their needs. This generally carries the proviso that the core program code is not to be altered. Blocks of

A proprietary software may be offered with an open-source designation that allows end users to alter the source code to suit their needs. Photo via iStock/Imilian. [Used under license.]

program code that are not needed can be deactivated so they do not run in the application, and new modules of program code may be developed and inserted for specific purposes and functions that are not provided for in the program.

Alternatively, an entire software may be developed as an open-source application with no restrictions and distributed freely or for a small fee to anyone who would want to use it. There is an advantage peculiar to open-source software generally, in that it will quickly acquire a following of users and developers who will seek to find and correct any flaws in the programming, or to improve and enhance the program's usability. The group of developers who originally produced the software and who oversee its further development may choose to include modifications it receives in a release update, while other developers may choose to provide their modified version of the software as an open-source application with a different name. The many different versions of the Linux operating system are perfect examples of this. If the software happens to be an open-source version of proprietary software, however, the proprietor organization may incorporate functions from the open-source community into the software and then market it as a new or updated version with its own new licensing requirement.

OPEN-SOURCE CAD PROGRAMS

By 2021, numerous open-source CAD software options were available for use by designers of varying skill levels. Popular options included FreeCAD,

LibreCAD, and NanoCAD. Perhaps the best-known proprietary CAD software is AutoCAD, and the functionality of many open-source CAD applications is designed to be comparable to AutoCAD or parts of that software. Some open-source CAD software options offer only 2D graphics capability suitable for 2D representations such as orthographic drawings, floor plans, and other such renderings. Others offer full 3D representation and the ability to interface with computer-aided engineering (CAE) and computer-aided manufacturing (CAM) programs for full functionality. In some cases, the developer of an open-source CAD software offers a free version with functionality limits as well as a more advanced version to which users may upgrade for a small fee; the 2D CAD software QCAD, for instance, as of 2021 offered both a free, open-source "community edition" as well as a paid version known as QCAD Professional.

Open-source CAD tools are often supported by a community of developers and a parent website dedicated to the support of users and developers. Developer support may therefore be provided by thousands of users/developers around the world, as opposed to the in-house support staff tasked with supporting a proprietary CAD software.

—*Richard M. Renneboog, MSc*

Further Reading
Bi, Zhuming, and Xiaoqin Wang. *Computer Aided Design and Manufacturing.* Wiley-ASME Press, 2020.
Brito, Allan. *FreeCAD for Architectural Drawing: Create Technical Drawings with a Free and Open-source CAD.* Brito, 2020.
Gohde, Justin, and Marius Kintel. *Programming with OpenSCAD. A Beginners Guide to Coding 3D-Printable Objects.* No Starch Press, 2021.
Herstatt, Cornelius, and Daniel Ehls, editors. *Open-Source Innovation: The Phenomenon, Participant's Behavior, Business Implications.* Routledge, 2015.
Kaye, Naomi. "Best Open-Source CAD Software of 2021." *ALL3DP*, 16 July 2021, all3dp.com/2/best-open-source-cad-software/. Accessed 16 Dec. 2021.

Porterfield, Jason. *Creating with Milling Machines.* Rosen, 2017.

Optics

ABSTRACT
Optics is the study of light. It includes the description of light properties that involve refraction, reflection, diffraction, interference, and polarization of electromagnetic waves. Most commonly, the word "light" refers to the visible wavelengths of the electromagnetic spectrum, which is between 400 and 700 nanometers (nm). Lasers use wavelengths that vary from the ultraviolet (100 nm to 400 nm) through the visible spectrum into the infrared spectrum (greater than 700 nm). Optics can be used to understand and study mirrors, optical instruments such as telescopes and microscopes, vision, and lasers used in industry and medicine.

DEFINITION AND BASIC PRINCIPLES
Optics is the area of physics that involves the study of electromagnetic waves in the visible-light spectrum, between 400 and 700 nm. Optics principles also apply to lasers, which are used in industry and medicine. Each laser has a specific wavelength. There are lasers that use wavelengths in the 100-400 nm range, others that use a wavelength in the visible spectrum, and some that use wavelengths in the infrared spectrum (greater than 700 nm).

Light behaves as both a wave and a particle. This duality has resulted in the division of optics into physical optics, which describes the wave properties of light; geometric optics, which uses rays to model light behavior; and quantum optics, which deals with the particle properties of light. Optics uses these theories to describe the behavior of light in the form of refraction, reflection, interference, polarization, and diffraction.

When light and matter interact, photons are absorbed or released. Photons are a specific amount of energy described as the sum of Planck's constant h (6.626×10^{-34}), and the wavelength of the light. The formula to describe the energy of photons is $E = hf$. Photons have a constant speed in a vacuum. The speed of light is $c = 2.998 \times 10^8$ meters/second. The constant speed of light in a vacuum is an important concept in astronomy. The speed of light is used in the measurement of astronomic distances in the unit of light-years.

BACKGROUND AND HISTORY

Optics dates back to ancient times. The three-thousand-year-old Nimrud lens is crafted from natural crystal, and it may have been used for magnification or to start fires. Early academics such as Euclid in 300 BCE theorized that rays came out of the eyes in order to produce vision. Greek astronomer Ptolemy later described angles in refraction. In the thirteenth century CE, English philosopher Roger Bacon suggested that the speed of light was constant and that lenses might be used to correct defective vision.

By the seventeenth century, telescopes and microscopes were being developed by scientists such as Hans Lippershey, Johannes Kepler, and Galileo Galilei. During this time, Dutch astronomer Willebrord Snellius formulated the law of refraction to describe the behavior of light traveling between different media, such as from air to water. This is known as "Snell's law," or the "Snell-Descartes law," although it was previously described in 984 by Persian physicist Ibn Sahl.

Sir Isaac Newton was one of the most famous scientists to put forward the particle theory of light. Dutch scientist Christiaan Huygens was a contemporary of Newton's who advocated the wave theory of light. This debate between wave theory and particle theory continued into the nineteenth century. French physicist Augustin-Jean Fresnel was influential in the acceptance of the wave theory through his experiments in interference and diffraction.

The wave-particle debate continued into the next century. The wave theory of light described many optical phenomena; however, some findings, such as the emission of electrons when light strikes metal, can be explained only using a particle theory. In the early twentieth century, German physicists Max Planck and Albert Einstein described the energy released when light strikes matter as photons with the development of the formula $E = hv$, which states that the photon energy equals the sum of the wavelength and Planck's constant.

In the early twenty-first century, it is generally accepted that both the wave and the particle theories are correct in describing optical events. For some optical situations, light behaves as a wave, and for others, the particle theory is needed to explain the situation. Quantum physics tries to explain the wave-particle duality, and it is possible that future work will unify the wave and particle theories of light.

HOW IT WORKS

Physical optics. Physical optics is the science of understanding the physical properties of light. Light behaves as both a particle and a wave. According to the wave theory, light waves behave similarly to waves in water. As light moves through the air the electric field increases, decreases, and then reverses direction. Light waves generate an electric field perpendicular to the direction the light is traveling and a magnetic field that is perpendicular both to the direction the light is traveling and to the electric field.

Interference and coherence refer to the interactions between light rays. Both interference and coherence are often discussed in the context of a single wavelength or a narrow band of wavelengths from a light source. Interference can result either in an increased intensity of light or a reduction of intensity to zero. The optical phenomenon of interference is used in the creation of antireflective films.

Coherence occurs when light is passed through a narrow slit. This produces waves that are in phase with the waves exactly lined up or waves that are out of phase but have a constant relationship with one another. Coherence is an important element to the light emitted by lasers and allows for improved focusing properties necessary to laser applications.

Polarization involves passing light waves through a filter that allows only wavelengths of a certain orientation to pass. For example, polarized sunglasses allow only vertical rays to pass and stop the horizontal rays, such as light reflected from water or pavement. In this way, polarized sunglasses can reduce glare.

Diffraction causes light waves to change direction as light encounters a small opening or obstruction. Diffraction becomes a problem for optical systems of less than 2.5 millimeters (mm) for visible light. Telescopes overcome the diffraction effect by using a larger aperture, however, for very large-diameter telescopes the resolution is then limited due to atmospheric conditions. Space telescopes such as the Hubble are unaffected by these conditions as they are operating in a vacuum.

Scattering occurs when light rays encounter irregularities in their path, such as dust in the air. The increased scattering of blue light due to particles in the air is responsible for the blue color of the sky.

Illumination is the quantitative measurement of light. The watt is the measurement unit of light power. Light can also be measured in terms of its luminance as it encounters the eye. Units of luminance include the lumen and the candela.

The photoelectric effect that supports the particle theory of light was discovered by German physicist Heinrich Rudolph Hertz in 1887 and later by Albert Einstein. When light waves hit a metallic surface, electrons are emitted. This effect is used in the generation of solar power.

Geometric optics. Geometric optics describes optical behavior in the form of rays. In most ordinary situations, the ray can accurately describe the movement of light as it travels through various media such as glass or air and as it is reflected from a surface such as a mirror.

Geometric optics can describe the basics of photography. The simplest way to make an image of an object is to use a pinhole to produce an inverted image. When lenses and mirrors are added to the pinhole a refined image can be produced.

Reflection and refraction are two optical phenomena in which geometric optics applies. Reflections from plane (flat) mirrors, convex mirrors, and concave mirrors can all be described using ray diagrams. A plane mirror creates a virtual image behind the mirror. The image is considered virtual because the light is not coming from the image but only appears to because of the direction of the reflected rays. A convex mirror can create a real image in front of the lens or a virtual image behind the lens depending on where the object is located. If an object is past the focal point of the convex mirror, then the image is real and located in front of the mirror. If the object is between the focal point and the convex mirror then the image is virtual and located behind the mirror. A convex lens will create a virtual image. Geometric optics involves ray diagrams that will allow the determination of image size (magnification or minification), location of the image, and if it is real or virtual.

Refraction of light happens when light passes between two different substances such as air and glass or air and water. Snell's law expresses refraction of light as a mathematical formula. One form of Snell's law is: $n_1 \sin\theta_1 = n_2 \sin\theta_2$ where n_1 is the refractive index of the incident medium, θ_1 is the angle of incidence, n_2 is the refractive index of the refracted medium, and θ_2 is the angle of transmission. This formula, along with its variations, can be used to describe light behavior in nature and in various applications such as manufacturing corrective lenses. Refraction also occurs as light travels from the air into the eye and as it moves through the various structures inside the eye to produce vision.

Magnification or minification can be a product of refraction and reflection. Geometric optics can be applied to both microscopes and telescopes, which use lenses and mirrors for magnification and minification.

Quantum optics. Quantum optics is a division of physics that comes from the application of mathematical models of quantum mechanics to the dual wave and particle nature of light. This area of optics has applications in meteorology, telecommunications, and other industries.

APPLICATIONS AND PRODUCTS

Vision and vision science. There is a vast network of health-care professionals and industries that study and measure vision and vision problems as well as correct vision. Optometrists measure vision and refractive errors in order to prescribe corrective spectacles and contact lenses. Ophthalmologists are medical doctors who specialize in eye health and vision care. Some ophthalmologists specialize in vision-correction surgery, which uses lasers to reduce the need for glasses or contact lenses. In order to perform vision-correction surgeries there are a number of optical instruments, including wave-front mapping analyzers, that may be used.

The industries that support optometry and ophthalmology practices include laser manufacturers, optical diagnostic instruments manufacturers, and lens manufacturers. Lenses are used for diagnosis of vision problems as well as for vision correction.

Development of new lens technology in academic institutions and industry is ongoing, including multifocal lens implants and other vision-correction technologies.

Research. Many areas of research, including astronomy and medicine, use optical instruments and optics theory in the investigation of natural phenomena. In astronomy, distances between planets and galaxies are measured using the characteristics of light traveling through space and expressed as light-years. Meteorological optics is a branch of atmospheric physics that uses optics theory to investigate atmospheric events. Both telescopes and microscopes are optimized using optical principles. Many branches of medical research use optical instruments in the investigations of biological systems.

Medicine. Lasers have become commonplace in medicine, from skin-resurfacing and vision-correction procedures to the use of carbon-dioxide lasers in general surgery.

Industry. As noted above, there is an industry sector that is dedicated to the manufacture and development of vision-correction and diagnostic lenses and tools. Optics is an important part of the telecommunications industry, which uses fiber optics to transmit images and information. Photography, from the manufacture of cameras and lenses to their use by photographers, involves applied optics.

Lasers are also used for precision manufacturing of a variety of products. Computer-aided laser cutters, for example, can be used to cut or etch a wide range of materials, often following schematics created with computer-aided design (CAD) software. CAD software can likewise be used to design the layouts of optical telecommunications networks as well as to design and model components of other optics-based technologies, including sensors.

CAREERS AND COURSEWORK

A career in an optics field can be as varied as the applications. An interest in optics might lead to a career in physics, astronomy, meteorology, vision care, or photography. Depending on the specific position desired, the training may range from a high school diploma and on the job training to a university degree and postgraduate work.

Optics involves a combination of math and physics. An understanding of human eye anatomy is also essential for a career in vision care. For all of optics-related fields it is important to have a strong background in high school mathematics. For occupations in allied health care such as opticians or ophthalmic technicians, a high school diploma and technical training is required post high school. Photographers may pursue formal training through a university or art school or might develop skills through experience or an apprenticeship.

Many careers in physics, astronomy, and meteorology require at least a bachelor's degree and most require a master's or doctoral degree. University coursework in these fields includes mathematics and physics. To become an optometrist, a bachelor's degree plus a doctor of optometry degree is required. An ophthalmologist will need a bachelor's degree, a degree in medicine, and residency training.

SOCIAL CONTEXT AND FUTURE PROSPECTS

Advancements in optics theory and application have changed the fabric of life in industrialized countries, from the way people communicate to how the universe is understood. An increased understanding of optics has brought profound changes in photography, medicine, astronomy, manufacturing, and a number of other fields.

As wireless technology advances, it seems possible that this technology may replace some of the millions of miles of fiber-optic telecommunications cables in use. Because of their reliability, however, fiber optics will continue to be used for the foreseeable future. Existing lasers will continue to be optimized, and new lasers will likely be developed.

Refinements in optical systems will aid in research in a variety of fields. For example, oceanographers already apply optics theory to the study of low-light organisms and to the development of techniques for conducting research in low light. Improved optical systems will likely have a positive impact on this and other research.

Quantum computers using photonic circuits are a possible future development in the field of optics. A quantum computer that takes advantage of the photoelectric effect may be able to increase the capacity of computation over conventional computers. Optics and photonics may also be applied to chemical sensing, imaging through adverse atmospheric conditions, and solid-state lighting.

Some scientists have commented that the wave and particle theories of light are perhaps a temporary solution to the true understanding of light behavior. The area of quantum optics is dedicated to furthering the understanding of this duality of light. It is possible that in the future a more unified theory will lead to applications of optics and the use of light energy in ways that have not yet been imagined.

—*Ellen E. Anderson Penno,*
BS, MS, MD, FRCSC, Dip ABO

Further Reading

Azar, Dimitri T. *Clinical Optics, 2014-2015*. American Academy of Ophthalmology, 2014.

Garbovskiy, Yuriy A., and Anatoliy V. Glushchenko. *A Practical Guide to Experimental Geometrical Optics*. Cambridge UP, 2017.

Meschede, Dieter. *Optics, Light and Lasers: The Practical Approach to Modern Aspects of Photonics and Laser Physics*. 2nd ed., Wiley, 2007.

Pedrotti, Frank L., Leno M. Pedrotti, and Leno S. Pedrotti. *Introduction to Optics*. 3rd ed., Cambridge UP, 2017.

Siciliano, Antonio. *Optics: Problems and Solutions*. World Scientific, 2006.

Sun, Haiyin. *Basic Optical Engineering for Engineers and Scientists*. SPIE, 2019.

Tipler, Paul A., and Gene Mosca. *Physics for Scientists and Engineers*. 6th ed., extended version, Macmillan Learning, 2020.

Wolfe, William J. *Optics Made Clear: The Nature of Light and How We Use It*. SPIE, 2007.

Plastics Engineering

ABSTRACT

Plastics engineering functions on two principal fronts. The first is the application of the material properties of plastics to the solution of specific engineering problems. Examples in this aspect of the field include the application of Bakelite (a phenol-formaldehyde polymer) to the production of electric insulators and of epoxy-based fiber-reinforced polymers (FRPs) to the remediation of infrastructure. The second principal function of plastics engineering is the design and application of methods to produce the material objects desired. Typical examples of this aspect of plastics engineering include the design and manufacture of molding devices and of other machines to produce plastic materials and objects. These two fronts can be thought of as engineering with plastics and engineering of plastics.

DEFINITION AND BASIC PRINCIPLES

The term "plastics engineering" can be taken to mean both engineering with plastics and engineering of plastics. In the first sense, plastics engineering refers to the use of plastics in engineering applications. In the second, plastics engineering is the development of plastic materials and applications or methods for their formation and manipulation.

Plastics in engineering applications. Traditional engineering materials such as metals and wood often provide structural strengths and weights that are excessive or have a negative impact on the product. They also pose problems in regard to production, energy consumption, and the degree to which they can be recycled. In many cases, traditional materials have been replaced by plastics because of their strength and lower manufacturing costs. The replacement of a metal gear by a corresponding plastic gear is a prime example. Metal gears require individual machining processes at each and every stage of production. Some of these processes include producing a die, boring center holes and setscrew holes, milling in keyways, and shaping each gear tooth. In many applications, only metal gears can provide the necessary physical strength the product needs. In many other applications, however, metal gears, which are more expensive and labor intensive to create, can be substituted with gears made from plastic. A plastic gear made from high-density nylon can be injection molded by the thousands from a single die at a fraction of both the cost and the time required to produce a single machined metal gear. The plastic gear is strong enough to withstand the strain placed on it in use, is much less massive—which means it requires fewer support mechanisms than metal—and is usually recyclable.

Plastic materials, especially thermoplastics, are also easily machined using standard woodworking and metalworking tools. They do not require the high-strength materials that are needed for machining metals, and they can be machined to close tolerances. Thermoplastics have the property of softening when heated. The heat generated by the cutting tool at the point of contact weakens their physical structure and makes them easier to machine. They are also much softer materials than the cutting tools used on them, so they can be cut easily in machining operations. Thermosetting plastics, however, are harder to work with as they do not soften with heating but become brittle and prone to fracture. The localized heating at the cutting edges in machining operations tends to make the surface of the material more brittle, requiring other steps such as sanding and polishing to produce a finished surface. Thermosets also tend to be considerably harder materials than thermoplastics, compounding the problems encountered in machining operations carried out on the materials. This is because thermosetting polymers tend to have highly cross-linked, three-dimensional (3D) structures at the molecular level. They are used primarily as matrix materials in fiber-reinforced polymers and composite structures for that reason.

The use of fiber-reinforced polymers allows the manufacture of structures that could not otherwise be made. A fiber-reinforced polymer consists of a fibrous material such as woven glass or carbon fibers, consolidated and bound into a solid polymer matrix. Fiber-reinforced polymer structures are typically laid up by hand, consolidated (compressed together) with the polymer resin matrix material, and cured with heat and pressure. This method is capable of producing uniquely shaped, strong, and lightweight structural pieces. Fiber-reinforced polymers can also be used in mass-production methods; thermoplastic materials can be employed to produce many relatively simple shapes that do not call for high strength. Variations on these methods, such as extrusion and pultrusion, represent combinations of these methodologies.

Development of plastic materials. Plastics engineering also relates to the development of the plastics themselves for specific properties and to the industrial methods of preparing, handling, and manipulating the materials. Plastics begin as monomers, which are compounds whose molecules can add to themselves repeatedly in a chain reaction to form very large polymer molecules. Each polymer

Plastics engineering can refer to both engineering with plastics and engineering of plastics. Photo via iStock/Fahroni. [Used under license.]

molecule may be made up of several hundreds or thousands of monomer units. Thermoplastic polymers are almost always linear polymers, in which the monomers form a single head-to-tail chain from beginning to end. Thermosetting polymers are almost always made up of branched polymer molecules, in which monomer molecules have a structure that allows them to take part in more than one polymerization chain reaction. This results in a highly interconnected 3D molecular structure. Plastics engineering at this level involves the molecular design and synthesis of the monomeric material and subsequent chemical and physical tests of the polymeric material. After the design of the molecule has been engineered, the method of producing the material in quantity must be devised. This involves the design, construction, and operation of processes from which the monomeric material is obtained in a stable state of sufficient purity that it will not undergo polymerization prematurely.

To get the material from the point of manufacture to the point of use, appropriate packaging and handling methods must be determined or devised. Once at the point of use, the materials must be manipulated to turn them into the desired products. Plastics engineering, at this point, deals with the design and preparation of the machinery and processes that are required for product formation. This includes any machining processes and an assortment of molding methods.

BACKGROUND AND HISTORY

The history of plastics engineering extends back several centuries. European explorers of the New World and Asia found the indigenous peoples using natural latexes and resins for such purposes as waterproofing clothing, bouncing balls, and other everyday objects. From the late eighteenth to the mid-nineteenth centuries, many efforts were made to adapt those materials to the purposes of European industry. This meant that methods to manipulate the materials had to be developed. At the time, chemistry did not include atomic theory, and practicing chemists were restricted to experimenting through trial and error. The first significant advance in the manipulation of natural plastics was the masticator, a device that could cut and recut a raw rubber mass. The process permitted the rubber to be calendered, or rolled out in thin sheets, without crumbling. Calendering could also be used to bind fabric and plastic together to form a waterproof material.

Industrial applications of plastic materials were limited to the use of natural resins until the accidental discovery of nitrocellulose. A semisynthetic resin formed by the nitration of cellulose (from cotton), nitrocellulose exhibited many of the properties of thermoplastic polymers and eventually became the basis of the celluloid industry. In 1884, George Eastman, founder of the Eastman Kodak Company, began to mechanically produce celluloid in thin flexible sheets through a process invented by Belgian chemist Leo Hendrik Baekeland. This celluloid film became the basis for the photography industry.

Further development of plastics was greatly assisted by the realization of a workable, predictive atomic theory. Rapidly developing understanding of molecular interactions led Baekeland to create the first fully synthetic polymer, Bakelite, a formulation of phenol and formaldehyde, in 1907. Bakelite was developed to fill a specific need: a material for electric insulators. It proved to be much more than that, as its properties made it an excellent replacement for many natural materials that were in ever-decreasing supply. One of its earliest applications was as a substitute for elephant ivory, used for making billiard balls. Bakelite was the first engineered thermosetting plastic and was developed simultaneously with the method of production. This method involved heating a mass of the component mixture, or prepolymer, to drive the polymerization reaction to completion while confining it under pressure within a shaped die or mold.

The many ways of modifying nitrocellulose, combined with an advancing comprehension of the polymerization process within the context of atomic theory, resulted in the development of numerous new materials. Between 1930 and 1939, for example, polymer research resulted in the production of an average of one new polymeric material per day; this necessitated the creation of new methods for turning those materials into products and of applying their properties to engineering problems. These factors were crucial to the outcome of World War II, and research and development in these areas has continued unabated.

The very properties that make plastics so useful also make them environmentally problematic, especially because the primary source of raw materials for plastics production has shifted from coal tar residues to petroleum. Many recyclable thermoplastics have been discarded in landfills and garbage heaps. By the early twenty-first century, plastics engineering had developed a more circumspect view of plastic applications and focused on developing methods of recycling discarded plastic goods, including thermoset plastics, which historically had not been recyclable.

HOW IT WORKS
Polymerization. To understand the principles of plastics engineering, one should have an appreciation of the basic principles of polymerization. Polymers begin with specific molecules that are referred to as monomers. These contain a functional structure that allows them to form chemical bonds successively between individual molecules in a chain reaction. In a chain reaction, a molecule forms a bond to a second molecule, enabling the second to bond to a third, the third to bond to a fourth, and so on. Successive bond-forming reactions typically occur several thousand times before some condition is encountered that terminates the progress of the reaction chain. In linear polymers, this reaction process forms molecules that have a structure essentially as simple as that of their monomers but are much larger in size.

If the monomer molecules are selected in such a way that at least some of the molecules in the prepolymer can take part in more than one chain reaction at the same time, the reaction process produces a 3D polymeric structure. In this structure, the linear molecular chains become bonded to each other, or cross-linked, as the monomer molecules become bonded to each other in the chain reactions. This results in a structure in which the polymers are intimately intertwined in a 3D network that spans the entire mass. In principle, this can turn an entire multiton mass of resin into a single, very large molecule, although in practice this never happens because of the various and many ways in which polymerization chain reactions are terminated during the process.

Linear and 3D polymers. Linear polymers are generally thermoplastic in nature, becoming pliable when heated and eventually melting. 3D polymers, on the other hand, are generally thermosetting in nature, becoming brittle, breaking down, and decomposing when heated instead of becoming pliable and melting.

Thermosetting materials. Thermosetting plastics, also known as "thermoset," cannot be reformed once they have been polymerized, except through mechanical machining methods. As such, thermosetting materials are typically used in on-the-spot production methods such as injection molding and extrusion molding. Thermosetting plastics are stronger than thermoplastics because they are formed from rigid 3D bonds.

Thermoplastic materials. Thermoplastic materials can be reformed (and therefore recycled) when heated to a pliable state. They are capable of quick conversion from raw material to finished product and from waste material to new finished product. Plastics engineering at this stage begins with research and development of the molecular structure of the monomeric material to assess and characterize the properties of the polymeric material that it will produce. Such activity often includes chemically modifying and functionalizing the monomer molecules in specific ways to obtain desired properties in the resulting polymer. Once the molecular structure has been established, the engineering focus shifts from production of the material in the laboratory to production of the material in bulk. As plastics are typically produced on a scale of many millions of tons annually, continuous-flow methods of production are preferred, although some specialty plastics are best prepared by batch processes. The plastics engineer has the task of identifying and adapting or developing the most suitable process for the production of the material and of optimizing the process in practice. The processes used typically produce thermosetting resins for transshipment and use in polymerization reactions at other locations. Thermoplastics are produced by methods that make them easily transportable in solid form. A variety of process types are used in the subsequent processing and production of plastic objects.

APPLICATIONS AND PRODUCTS

Fiber-reinforces polymers. Plastics engineering involving fiber-reinforced polymers, particularly their use in advanced composite materials, begins with engineering the design of the desired finished component. This includes the nature and form of the reinforcing materials, often polymeric materials, that will be employed in the composite structure and their distribution pattern within the finished structure. Because the shape and form of a thermosetting plastic cannot be altered after polymerization is complete, any particular object made from such materials must be prepared in that final shape. The plastics engineer uses molds and forms made specifically for that purpose. The active surfaces of the molds and forms correspond exactly in shape to the desired final shape of the object being made. The reinforcing material, impregnated with the thermosetting resin, is laid into the mold or form according to the design specifications, and the resulting stack is enclosed in special containment fabrics. Next, the contents are subjected to reduced pressure, usually by use of a vacuum pump. This permits an even distribution of atmospheric pressure that will compress and consolidate the stack and remove any extraneous gases that could interfere with the structural integrity of the product. The application of heat at this point completes the polymerization reaction while assisting with the elimination of gaseous wastes. The resulting composite structure, once cooled, is then removed from the mold, and if the part is of suitable quality, it is sent on to the next stage in the manufacturing process.

Pultrusion. Another method by which thermoplastic fiber-reinforced polymers are produced is pultrusion. In pultrusion, an appropriately designed bundle of continuous fiber strands is drawn through a die along with a molten thermoplastic matrix material. The die serves to consolidate the material combination, and as the matrix material solidifies on exiting the die, a continuous fiber-reinforced structure is produced. Examples of pultruded products include fiberglass rods and reinforced water hoses.

Injection molding. Both thermosetting and thermoplastic polymers can be used in the injection-molding process, though the practical requirements are very different for the two types of polymers. In injection molding, a cavity in the shape of the desired object is filled with molten thermoplastic or a thermosetting prepolymer resin. When the solid polymer has formed, the object is removed from the mold and the process repeated. When a thermoplastic material is being used, the plastic material is fed into the mold under pressure from a heated hopper. If a thermosetting resin is being used, precautions must be taken to ensure that the polymerization reaction takes place only within the mold cavity and after the cavity has been filled. The process can rapidly produce a large quantity of objects of intricate design that would require many independent machining operations if the object were being made from traditional materials such as wood or metal. Successive molding steps enable the production of multicolored objects.

Thermoforming. The thermoforming process is applicable only to thermoplastic materials. In this process, a sheet of solid thermoplastic material, such as Plexiglas (polymethylmethacrylate) or polystyrene, is placed in a mold or form and heated to a temperature at which the material becomes highly pliable but does not melt. This allows the sheet to deform and adopt the shape of the mold, assisted by changing the pressure on one side of the sheet of material. The method is most suitable for designs that are relatively flat or low profile.

Blow molding. The process of blow molding also applies only to thermoplastics. It is similar to thermoforming in that it uses a difference in pressure to force softened thermoplastic material to adopt the shape of a mold. Blow molding uses 3D molds, however, and is typically used to produce open structures such as plastic bags, bottles, and other similar objects. In blow molding, a metered quantity of plastic material is set into a mold, where it is then blown outward by a sudden blast of heated air to the shape of the mold. The method is most suitable for open, three-dimensional shapes having little or no surface detail.

Extrusion. The process of extrusion is closely related to pultrusion. In extrusion, the plastic material is pushed through a die under pressure rather than drawn through with continuous fiber-reinforcement materials. Random-oriented fiber-reinforcement materials can be used in the extrusion process if they are blended with the molten plastic before entering the die. Extrusion can be used only to produce structures that have a constant cross-sectional profile along their entire length, as determined by the die profile. Quite complex cross-sectional designs can be produced in this way, but they are essentially only two-dimensional (2D).

Compression and transfer molding. Both compression and transfer molding are used primarily for thermosetting resins and rely on heating a filled mold to drive the cross-linking reactions in the polymer body to completion. The processes use either a powdered resin or a preformed plug that will be set into a final desired form. Compression molding is the process that was developed by Baekeland for the production of Bakelite objects, and it uses heat and pressure to restrict the material to the final form of the product throughout the polymerization process. In transfer molding, the resinous material is first preheated and liquefied in a separate chamber before being transferred to the object mold and undergoing polymerization.

Rotational molding. The process of rotational molding uses centrifugal force to distribute the plastic material within a spinning or rotating mold. The material may be injected as a liquid or added as a finely ground powder that is fused within the mold. The process is used exclusively for the production of hollow objects.

Foams. Various methods and treatments of resins, typically thermosetting resins, result in the formation of foams. The forceful addition or release of gas within the bulk polymer structure expands the material by pushing the component molecules apart. The gases may be produced as a byproduct of the polymerization reaction or added as an extraneous component. Urea-formaldehyde foams are typically produced by the first method, as the polymerization reaction produces quantities of water vapor. Expanded foams such as Styrofoam are generally produced by adding a low-boiling liquid such as pentane to be absorbed by the solid plastic material. Subsequent rapid heating quickly vaporizes the liquid, and the resulting pressure of the vapor acts to expand the solid material. In other applications, combinations of materials such as urea and formaldehyde solutions react quickly to produce a solidified foam structure. Such materials are generally applied as sprays to provide an insulating and sealing layer on flat surfaces.

Casting and encapsulation. Casting and encapsulation are essentially simple molding procedures in which a liquefied plastic material is introduced into a mold without the application of increased or decreased pressure, forming a specific shape as the material solidifies.

Calendering. Thermoplastic materials can be formed into thin sheets by calendering, a process by which the material is pressed between heated rollers. The process can be used to laminate a cloth insert layer with a plastic material and to impart various surface textures to the resulting sheet.

Mechanical machining methods. The inherent pliability and shear properties of plastics, particularly of thermoplastics, makes them highly amenable to shaping with traditional tools such as saws, drills, planes, shapers, lathes, sanders, and millers. The materials are easily cut by steel tools, which are harder than any plastic. For this reason, mock-up designs are often initially constructed as plastic models rather than as metal constructs, allowing design engineers to test various physical properties, such as aerodynamic stability and wind resistance, that are directly related only to the shape of the structure and not to the materials used.

Plastics and computer-aided technologies. By the third decade of the twenty-first century, the engineering of products made from plastic was closely linked to the fields of computer-aided design (CAD), computer-aided engineering (CAE), and computer-aided manufacturing (CAM). Such technologies enabled engineers to design virtual models of plastic products—or plastic prototypes of products that would eventually be manufactured in other materials—and to manufacture those products through the use of multiple CAM processes. Computer-aided injection molding and extrusion processes, for example, could be used to produce plastic products. The development of 3D printing technology was likewise deeply relevant to the plastics industry, as such devices often made use of plastic filament as a printing material.

CAREERS AND COURSEWORK

A career in plastics engineering requires a solid foundation in general and applied mathematics and in chemistry and physics, beginning in high school and continuing into postsecondary education. In college, students interested in a plastics engineering career should study organic chemistry, analytical chemistry, physical chemistry, physics, and applied mathematics, and take specialized courses in polymer chemistry, reaction kinetics, and industrial chemistry. This will guide the student into postgraduate academic programs and positions in industry. Those interested in careers related to the engineering of plastics materials for industrial applications should study chemistry, physics, applied mathematics, and engineering principles. Specialized coursework will be determined by the chosen branch of engineering: mechanical, chemical, civil, industrial, or polymer.

The many applications of engineered plastics guarantee that many careers will involve training in the uses and applications of plastics. Civil engineering technologists and technicians can expect to encounter applications of fiber-reinforced polymers, forms, and molded plastics in the course of their work. Aircraft maintenance engineers will be required to undertake training in the use and repair of fiber-reinforced polymers and advanced composite structures as a regulated licensing requirement. Automotive technicians have the opportunity to specialize in repair techniques using engineered plastic components.

SOCIAL CONTEXT AND FUTURE PROSPECTS

Plastics have become so entrenched in the workings of the modern world that careers involving plastics engineering seem destined to be as persistent as the materials themselves. The great strength of plastics, their chemical stability, is also their greatest failing. Plastic goods were never designed with the conservation of resources in mind. Rather, they have historically been produced as ultimately disposable items. The negative impact of this practice was realized only considerably after the use of plastics became widespread, at which time, the management of used plastics became an issue. The increasing price of plastics, tied to the ever-increasing price of the petroleum that is their source, has led to the consideration of mining landfill sites for their plastic content, particularly nylon. Scientists have also turned to developing methods of reusing and recycling plastics.

The plastics industry has continued to search for and devise new materials and products to maintain a constant supply of cheap, convenient, and ultimately disposable plastic products for consumer demand. At the same time, consumers increasingly demand that the plastics industry be more circumspect with and accountable for its use of plastics as a commodity. The long-term effects of the plastics industry include the accumulation of highly toxic and possibly carcinogenic materials in the environment, as well as problems resulting from the presence of leached monomers and other plastics-related chemicals.

The future of plastics engineering, therefore, appears to be developing along three distinct fronts, each offering broad opportunity as career choices. One is the traditional production and support base of the plastics industry. The second, and potentially the most significant, is the growing industry of plastics abatement, which involves the recovery of used plastics and the mitigation of plastic residues in the environment. The third front, only beginning to emerge, is the field of bioplastics, or plastics produced by living organisms through biological processes instead of through chemical alteration of petroleum sources. All three will require the services of plastics engineers in many different aspects.

—*Richard M. J. Renneboog, MSc*

Further Reading

Ashter, Syed Ali. *Introduction to Bioplastics Engineering*. Elsevier, 2016.

Crawford, Roy J., and Peter Martin. *Plastics Engineering*. 4th ed., Butterworth-Heinemann, 2020.

Geng, Hwaiyu. *Manufacturing Engineering Handbook*. 2nd ed., McGraw-Hill Professional, 2015.

Fenichell, Stephen. *Plastic: The Making of a Synthetic Century*. HarperBusiness, 1996.

Margolis, James M., editor. *Plastics Engineering Handbook*. McGraw-Hill, 2006.

Rosato, Dominick V., Donald V. Rosato, and Matthew V. Rosato. *Plastic Product Material and Process Selection Handbook*. Elsevier, 2004.

Stokes, Vijay K. *Introduction to Plastics Engineering*. Wiley-ASME Press, 2020.

Strong, A. Brent. *Plastics: Materials and Processing*. 3rd ed., Pearson Prentice Hall, 2006.

"3D Modeling and CAD Design in Plastic Manufacturing." *Advanced Plastiform, Inc.*, 2021, advancedplastiform.com/process/3d-modeling-and-cad-drawings/. Accessed 28 Nov. 2021.

Troughton, Michael J. *Handbook of Plastics Joining: A Practical Guide*. 2nd ed., William Andrew, 2008.

Van der Zwaag, Sybrand, editor. *Self-Healing Materials: An Alternative Approach to Twenty Centuries of Materials Science*. Springer, 2007.

"What Can You 3D Print with Plastics?" *3D Systems*, 2021, www.3dsystems.com/what-can-you-3d-print-with-plastics. Accessed 28 Nov. 2021.

POLYMER SCIENCE

ABSTRACT

Polymer science is a specialized field concerned with the structures, reactions, and applications of polymers. Polymer scientists generate basic knowledge that often leads to various industrial products such as plastics, synthetic fi-

bers, elastomers, stabilizers, colorants, resins, adhesives, coatings, and many others. A mastery of this field is also essential for understanding the structures and functions of polymers found in living things, such as proteins and deoxyribonucleic acid (DNA).

DEFINITION AND BASIC PRINCIPLES

Polymers are very large and often complex molecules constructed, either by nature or by humans, through the repetitive yoking of much smaller and simpler units. This results in linear chains in some cases and in branched or interconnected chains in others. The polymer can be built up of repetitions of a single monomer (homopolymer) or of different monomers (heteropolymer). The degree of polymerization is determined by the number of repeat units in a chain. No sharp boundary line exists between large molecules and the macromolecules characterized as polymers. Industrial polymers generally have molecular weights between ten thousand and one million, but some biopolymers extend into the billions.

Chemists usually synthesize polymers by condensation (or step-reaction polymerization) or addition (also known as "chain-reaction polymerization"). A good example of chain polymerization is the free-radical mechanism in which free radicals are created (initiation), facilitating the addition of monomers (propagation), and ending when two free radicals react with each other (termination). A general example of step-reaction polymerization is the reaction of two or more polyfunctional molecules to

CAD technology applied to the design of polymers is known as computer-aided polymer design (CAPD). Photo via iStock/imaginima. [Used under license.]

produce a larger grouping, with the elimination of a small molecule such as water, and the consequent repetition of the process until termination.

Besides free radicals, chemists have studied polymerizations utilizing charged atoms or groups of atoms (anions and cations). Physicists have been concerned with the thermal, electrical, and optical properties of polymers. Industrial scientists and engineers have devoted their efforts to creating such new polymers as plastics, elastomers, and synthetic fibers. These traditional applications have been expanded to include such advanced technologies as biotechnology, photonics, polymeric drugs, and dental plastics. Other scientists have found uses for polymers in such new fields as photochemistry and paleogenetics.

BACKGROUND AND HISTORY

Nature created the first polymers and, through chemical evolution, such complex and important macromolecules as proteins, deoxyribonucleic acid (DNA), and polysaccharides. These were pivotal in the development of increasingly multifaceted life-forms, including *Homo sapiens*, who, as this species evolved, made better and better use of such polymeric materials as pitch, woolen and linen fabrics, and leather. Pre-Columbian Indigenous Americans used natural rubber, or *cachucha*, to waterproof fabrics, as did Scottish chemist Charles Macintosh in nineteenth-century Britain.

The Swedish chemist Jöns Jakob Berzelius coined the term "polymer" in 1833, though his meaning was far from a modern chemist's understanding. Some scholars argue that the French natural historian Henri Braconnot was the first polymer scientist since, in investigating resins and other plant products, he created polymeric derivatives not found in nature. In 1836, the Swiss chemist Christian Friedrich Schönbein reacted natural cellulose with nitric and sulfuric acid to generate semisynthetic polymers. In 1843 in the United States, hardware merchant Charles Goodyear accidentally discovered "vulcanization" by heating natural rubber and sulfur, forming a new product that retained its beneficial properties in cold and hot weather. Vulcanized rubber won prizes at the London and Paris Expositions in 1850, helping to launch the first commercially successful product of polymer scientific research.

In the early twentieth century, the Belgian American chemist Leo Baekeland made the first totally synthetic polymer when he reacted phenol and formaldehyde to create a plastic that was marketed under the name Bakelite. The nature of this and other synthetic polymers was not understood until the 1920s and 1930s, when the German chemist Hermann Staudinger proved that these plastics (and other polymeric materials) were extremely long molecules built up from a sequential catenation of basic units, later called "monomers." This enhanced understanding led the American chemist Wallace Hume Carothers to develop a synthetic rubber, neoprene, that had numerous applications, and nylon, a synthetic substitute for silk. Synthetic polymers found wide use in World War II, and in the postwar period the Austrian American chemist Herman Francis Mark founded the Polymer Research Institute at Brooklyn Polytechnic, the first such facility in the United States. It helped foster an explosive growth in polymer science and a flourishing commercial polymer industry in the second half of the twentieth century. By the early twenty-first century, researchers had begun to investigate the possibility of applying computer-aided design (CAD) technology to the design of polymers; this field of study became known as computer-aided polymer design (CAPD).

HOW IT WORKS

After more than a century of development, scientists and engineers have discovered numerous techniques for making polymers, including a way to make them using ultrasound. Sometimes these techniques depend on whether the polymer to be synthesized is inorganic or organic, fibrous or solid, plastic or elastomeric, crystalline or amorphous. How various polymers function depends on a variety of properties, such as melting point, electrical conductivity, solubility, and interaction with light. Some polymers are fabricated to serve as coatings, adhesives, fibers, or thermoplastics. Scientists have also created specialized polymers to function as ion-exchange resins, piezoelectrical devices, and anaerobic adhesives. Certain new fields have required the creation of specialized polymers like heat-resistant plastics for the aerospace industry.

Condensation polymerization. Linking monomers into polymers requires the basic molecular building blocks to have reaction sites. Carothers recognized that most polymerizations fall into two broad categories, condensation and addition. In condensation, which many scientists prefer to call step, step-growth, or stepwise polymerization, the polymeric chain grows from monomers with two or more reactive groups that interact (or condense) intermolecularly, accompanied by the elimination of small molecules, often water. For example, the formation of a polyester begins with a bifunctional monomer, containing a hydroxyl group (OH, oxygen bonded to hydrogen) and a carboxylic acid group (COOH, carbon bonded to an oxygen and an OH group). When a pair of such monomers reacts, water is eliminated and a dimer formed. This dimer can now react with another monomer to form a trimer, and so on. The chain length increases steadily during the polymerization, necessitating long reaction times to get "high polymers" (those with large molecular weights).

Addition polymerization. Many chemists prefer to call Carothers's addition polymerization chain, chain-growth, or chain-wise polymerization. In this process, the polymer is formed without the loss of molecules, and the chain grows by adding monomers repeatedly, one at a time. This means that monomer concentrations decline steadily throughout the polymerization, and high polymers appear quickly. Addition polymers are often derived from unsaturated monomers (those with a double bond), and in the polymerization process the monomer's double bond is rearranged in forming single bonds with other molecules. Many of these polymerizations also require the use of catalysts and solvents, both of which have to be carefully chosen to maximize yields. Important examples of polymers produced by this mechanism are polyurethane and polyethylene.

APPLICATIONS AND PRODUCTS

Since the start of the twentieth century, the discoveries of polymer scientists have led to the formation of hundreds of thousands of companies worldwide that manufacture thousands of products, including plastic and rubber products. These and other products exhibit phenomenal variety, from acrylics to zeolites. Chemists in academia, industry, and governmental agencies have discovered many applications for traditional and new polymers, particularly in such modern fields as aerospace, biomedicine, and computer science.

Elastomers and plastics. From its simple beginnings manufacturing Bakelite and neoprene, the plastic and elastomeric industries have grown rapidly in the quantity and variety of the polymers their scientists and engineers synthesize and market. Some scholars believe that the modern elastomeric industry began with the commercial production of vulcanized rubber by Goodyear in the nineteenth century. Such synthetic rubber polymers as styrene-butadiene, neoprene, polystyrene, polybutadiene, and butyl rubber (a copolymer of butylene and isoprene) began to be made in the first half of the twentieth century, and they found extensive applications in the automotive and other industries in the second half.

Although an early synthetic plastic derived from cellulose was introduced in Europe in the nineteenth century, it was not until the twentieth century that the modern plastics industry was born, with the introduction of Bakelite, which found applications in the manufacture of telephones, phonograph records, and a variety of varnishes and enamels. Thermoplastics, such as polyethylene, polystyrene, and polyester, can be heated and molded, and billions of pounds of them are produced in the United States annually. Polyethylene, a low-weight, flexible material, has many applications, including packaging, electrical insulation, housewares, and toys. Polystyrene has found uses as an electrical insulator and, because of its clarity, in plastic optical components. Polyethylene terephthalate (PET) is an important polyester, with applications in fibers and plastic bottles. Polyvinyl chloride (PVC) is one of the most massively manufactured synthetic polymers. Its early applications were for raincoats, umbrellas, and shower curtains, but it later found uses in pipe fittings, automotive parts, and shoe soles.

Carothers synthesized a fiber that was stronger than silk, and it became known as "nylon" and led to a proliferation of other artificial textiles. Polyester fibers, such as PET, have become the world's principal synthetic materials for fabrics. Polyesters and nylons have many applications in the garment industry because they exceed natural fibers, including cotton and wool, in such qualities as strength and wrinkle resistance. Less in demand are acrylic fibers, but, because they are stronger than cotton, they have had numerous applications by manufacturers of clothing, blankets, and carpets.

Optoelectronic, aerospace, biomedical, and computer applications. As modern science and technology have expanded and diversified, so, too, have the applications of polymer science. For example, as researchers explored the electrical conductivity of various materials, they discovered polymers that have exhibited commercial potential as components in environmentally friendly battery systems. Transparent polymers have become essential to the fiber optics industry. Other polymers have had an important part in the improvement of solar-energy devices through products such as flexible polymeric film reflectors and photovoltaic encapsulants. Newly developed polymers have properties that make them suitable for optical information storage. The need for heat-resistant polymers led the US Air Force to fund the research and development of several such plastics, and one of them, polybenzimidazole, has achieved commercial success not only in aerospace but also in other industries as well.

Following the discovery of the double-helix structure of DNA in 1953, a multiple of applications followed, starting in biology and expanding into medicine and even to such fields as criminology. Nondegradable synthetic polymers have had multifarious medical applications as heart valves, catheters, prostheses, and contact lenses. Other polymeric materials show promise as blood-compatible linings for cardiovascular prostheses. Biodegradable synthetic polymers have found wide use in capsules that release drugs in carefully controlled ways. Dentists regularly take advantage of polymers for artificial teeth, composite restoratives, and various adhesives. Polymer scientists have also contributed to the acceleration of computer technology since the 1980s by developing electrically conductive polymers, and, in turn, computer science and technology have enabled polymer scientists to optimize and control various polymerization reactions as well as to design and manufacture polymer-based products.

CAREERS AND COURSEWORK

Building on a base of advanced courses in chemistry, mathematics, and chemical engineering, undergraduates generally take an introductory course in polymer science. Graduate students in polymer science usually take courses in line with their chosen career goal. For example, students aspiring to positions in the plastics industry would need to take advanced courses in macromolecular synthesis and the chemical engineering of polymer syntheses. Students interested in biotechnology or bioengineering would need to take graduate courses in molecular biology, biomolecular syntheses, and so on.

Many opportunities are available for those with undergraduate or graduate degrees in polymer science. The field is expanding, and careers in research can be forged in government agencies, academic institutions, and various industries. Chemical, pharmaceutical, biomedical, cosmetics, plastics, and petroleum companies hire polymer scientists and engineers. Because of concerns raised by the twenty-first-century environmental movement, many companies are hiring graduates with expertise in biodegradable polymers. The rapid development of the computer industry has led to a need for graduates with an understanding of electrically charged polymeric systems. In sum, traditional and new careers are accessible to polymer scientists and engineers both in the United States and many other countries.

SOCIAL CONTEXT AND FUTURE PROSPECTS

Barring a total global economic collapse or a cataclysmic environmental or nuclear-war disaster, the trend of expansion in polymer science and engineering, well-established in the twentieth century, should continue throughout the twenty-first. As polymer scientists created new materials that contributed to twentieth-century advances in such areas as transportation, communications, clothing, and health, so they are well-positioned to meet the challenges that will dominate the twenty-first century in such areas as energy, communications, and the health of humans and the environment. Many observers have noted the increasing use of plastics in automobiles, and polymer scientists will most likely help to create lightweight-plastic vehicles of the future. The role of polymer science in biotechnology will probably exceed its present influence, with synthesized polymers to monitor and induce gene expression or as components of nanobots to monitor and even improve the health of vital organs in the human body. Environmental scientists have made the makers of plastics aware that many of their products end up as persistent polluters of the land and water, thus fostering a search that will likely continue throughout the twenty-first century for biodegradable polymers that will serve both the needs of advanced industrialized societies and the desire for a sustainable world.

—*Robert J. Paradowski, MS, PhD*

Further Reading

Adams, Nico, and Peter Murray-Rust. "Engineering Polymer Informatics: Towards the Computer-Aided Design of Polymers." *Macromolecular Rapid Communications*, vol. 29, no. 8, 2008, pp. 615-32.

Al-Maadeed, Mariam, Deepalekshmi Ponnamma, and Marcelo Carignano, editors. *Polymer Science and Innovative Applications: Materials, Techniques, and Future Developments*. Elsevier, 2020.

Carraher, Charles E., Jr. *Giant Molecules: Essential Materials for Everyday Living and Problem Solving*. 2nd ed., John Wiley & Sons, 2003.

———. *Introduction to Polymer Chemistry*. 4th ed., CRC Press, 2017.

Ebewele, Robert O. *Polymer Science and Technology*. CRC Press, 2000.

Fried, Joel R. *Polymer Science and Technology*. 3rd ed., Prentice Hall, 2014.

Liang, Xinyuan, Xiang Zhang, Lei Zhang, et al. "Computer-Aided Polymer Design: Integrating Group Contribution and Molecular Dynamics." *Industrial & Engineering Chemistry Research*, vol. 58, no. 34, 2019, pp. 15542-52.

Morawetz, Herbert. *Polymers: The Origins and Growth of a Science*. Dover, 2002.

Painter, Paul C., and Michael M. Coleman. *Essentials of Polymer Science and Engineering*. DEStech Publications, 2009.

Seymour, Raymond B., editor. *Pioneers in Polymer Science: Chemists and Chemistry.* Kluwer Academic Publishers, 1989.

Wypych, George. *Handbook of Polymers.* 3rd ed., ChemTec, 2022.

Process Management for Manufacturing

ABSTRACT

Businesses want to get their products to the buyer quickly. Manufacturing process management electronically bridges product design and production and allows complex products to go to market faster. Manufacturing processes are complex, as are product designs and the schedules that control production. Information systems play a key role in tracking and monitoring activity as well as in planning and coordinating. The manufacturing and production of complex products falls into three phases: the design phase, the manufacturing process management phase, and the scheduling phase. Information systems for the design and scheduling phases have been used for a long time and are mature; information systems for the manufacturing process management phase, however, are a more recent development. Information systems have long supported product design with tools such as computer-aided design (CAD) and product data management (PDM). In the twenty-first century, digital manufacturing (another name for manufacturing process management) offers similar tools for manufacturing.

OVERVIEW

On a daily basis, organizations must manage the processes that run a business. This is called "process management." Operational business processes are those that are performed by organizations in the context of their day-to-day operations, as opposed to strategic decision-making processes that are performed by the top-level management of an organization. Nowhere are operational processes more applicable than in a manufacturing environment.

Manufacturers acquire and process raw materials through a specific set of operations to yield a finished product that is either complete on its own or a subassembled component of another product.

BENEFITS OF PROCESS MANAGEMENT

Firms can make more money if they respond to what the market wants. This responsiveness to the market can result in better and more innovative products as well as better customer service and support. Process management can include management of internal processes as well as external ones that affect a product. Other benefits that firms receive from process management include the ability to develop and deliver complex products, reduced time to market, and lower product cost. Researchers in the field have linked manufacturing process management to the ability of manufacturers to deliver complex products and have likewise suggested that process management can improve information quality and reduce time to market by helping to electronically link product design to production. Manufacturing process management can provide ways to identify and act upon areas where growth and productivity are possible.

PHASES OF PRODUCT MANUFACTURING

Manufacturing process management is a field that allows technology to support a product's full lifecycle, from design and engineering through production. Researchers have identified three phases needed to bring the twenty-first-century's complex products to market. The first phase is product design, in which the manufacturer defines what will be done. The second phase is manufacturing process management, in which the manufacturer defines how products will be manufactured and assembled. The third phase is the inventory schedule, in which the manufacturer has to come up with a production schedule and determine when these design and process management activities will take place.

THE CHARACTERISTICS OF INFORMATION IN MANUFACTURING

Correct and timely information is critical to the manufacturing process. There are many different types of information that are managed in manufacturing. The information type and flow are governed by the product lifecycle. The product lifecycle tracks a product from the design of the product through production, sales, service, use, and ultimate disposal. The ability to share information with others in the supply chain is critical to the ability of the manufacturer to improve productivity and to increase speed to market. Information can range from specifications about the product's size or composition to compatibility with other products.

COMPLEXITY OF INFORMATION AND PROCESS MANAGEMENT

There are many reasons information management and process management are complex in manufacturing. First, there is a great deal of information in various formats available in different systems that may or may not be compatible. Second, access to the information may not be seamless or easily integrated among systems. In addition, the manufacture of products, even mature products, is not stagnant. There are constant changes to production based on any number of variables, from a design change to customer requests to a variation in materials. The ability to respond to changes quickly is another expectation that manufacturers must meet. Government regulations may place another burden on manufacturers to quickly adapt new processes. For example, the federal government may require car manufacturers to make modifications to their vehicles in order to comply with new clean air regulations. The manufacturers have to create new designs, conduct testing, and retool their production environment to adhere to these regulations while still producing vehicles daily.

INFORMATION NEEDED BY FIRMS

What information does a firm need? In a 2006 paper published in the *Journal of Small Business Management*, Bret Golann examines the information needs of firms related to the marketplace and categorizes those information needs into three areas:

- Generating market intelligence
- Disseminating intelligence
- Responsiveness

Firms must collect information on their competition and customers: This is called "market intelligence." This information must be spread throughout the organization and create activity based on market intelligence. This process is referred to as disseminating intelligence and responding to market intelligence. The ability to access information seamlessly and integrate it into the manufacturing process using technology is valuable to companies that want to grow and capitalize on the changes in the market and in customers.

PROCESSES THAT MUST BE MANAGED

According to Golann, the processes that must be managed fall into three categories: outside-in, inside-out, and spanning. Outside-in processes emphasize gathering outside information about customers, channels, and markets through market research, customer feedback, or processes for ordering products. Inside-out processes collect information on how to create more value through manufacturing, financial controls, technology development, and human resources. Spanning processes link internal value creation to customers and markets and ultimately influence long-term strategy. Spanning processes cover both inside and outside processes such as order fulfillment, manufacturing processes, order delivery, customer service, and product development.

MANAGING MANUFACTURING PROCESSES

The management of manufacturing processes is dependent upon the manager's ability to consistently improve on methods of strategy and decision-making. Traditionally, manufacturing managers excelled according to how well they came to know processes and how adept they were at adjusting processes to fit production needs. The introduction of information technology into the management of manufacturing allowed managers to balance their ability to intuitively make changes and decisions that compare to historical data and projected information. The growth of competition and the application of best practices have increased the urgency for manufacturers to fine tune the methods of managing processes.

LEAN MANUFACTURING PROCESSES

In the view of some researchers, visual process management tools have the benefit of improving communication and helping companies realize the goals of lean manufacturing. Lean manufacturing principles ensure that companies do not waste materials, labor, or time on processes that are not efficient and on products the customers do not want. Obtaining the best results from lean principles comes from a combination of process management and people management. People management ensures that the most expensive resource that a company invests in, labor, is trained and deployed effectively. The combination works because people are not efficient when required to use poor processes, and processes that are optimized still depend on effective people resources to provide value to the company.

Information technology can be a powerful tool in creating lean manufacturing processes. As a result, manufacturers can find value in information technology to manage, analyze and improve processes instead of viewing the investment as wasteful.

CONFLICTS BETWEEN LEAN MANUFACTURING AND TRADITIONAL IT PRODUCTS

An inherent conflict exists between lean manufacturing and traditional information technology (IT) products such as enterprise resource planning (ERP). For example, ERP supports push manufacturing, while lean suggests pull manufacturing. Pull manufacturing allows customer requests to dictate manufacturing, while push manufacturing "pushes" product into the market. Traditional ERP supports a centralized enterprise view with knowledge managed by a few. Lean supports decentralization with information available to as many as possible. For process management, lean concentrates on how to collect and put together all information about creating the product and how to keep track of the information about that product that changes along the way. The ideal method of keeping track of information is through an integrated IT system that cuts across the enterprise, including manufacturing but going beyond. Despite the conflicts between IT and lean, enabling the two to coexist could bring productivity to all parts of an organization.

IMPORTANCE OF IT USERS AND BUSINESS USERS

Visual process management software allows for the visual representation of processes and facilitates communication between IT users and process management users. IT users are the designers of information systems and process management users are the ones who understand the business functions and processes that need to be managed. Both IT and business users are important if process management is to work well in organizations. The benefits of letting IT and business users visualize processes is best seen when the need for process management is across multiple applications. In this way, the team of business and IT users can identify where problems may migrate from one area to another. From a management point of view, it is most important to understand what each type of user knows best. Business users tend to understand functionality and the importance of processes. IT users tend to understand data integrity, security, and mission-critical processes and applications.

HOW TO IMPROVE FIRM PERFORMANCE

How do firms improve their performance? Sharing information among different managers is the key. As reported by Alden M. Hayashi for the *MIT Sloan Management Review* in 2004, researcher Jonathon N. Cummings observed various organizational teams, including those that were responsible for process management, and found that teams that shared information were more likely to exhibit better performance. Cummings also found that teams that are diverse tend to share information more and to perform better. Managers of teams who must make decisions about process management and process management tools may want to keep this information in mind to create teams where individuals with different functional responsibilities and backgrounds work together.

VIEWPOINT

Information systems that support process management in manufacturing. As with most functional applications of information technology, manufacturing has seen various subsets of its processes automated as information technology has become available and has improved. Initial efforts did not take into account the entire enterprise view of manufacturing. As a result, manufacturers, like their counterparts in health care and other industries, have had to piece together disparate systems that are only a part of the puzzle. In the first decades of the twenty-first century, companies began to realize the benefits of integrated systems that spanned across the functions of their organizations. However, many companies continued to use separate information systems to control, manage, and automate various parts of manufacturing process management.

Visual product representation. Visual representation of the process has been extremely effective. In the design phase, product engineers are able to create renderings of a product in three-dimensional (3D) views through the use of computer-aided design (CAD) software. This brings the product to life allowing engineers to discover and set the design specifications, sizes, tolerances, and product characteristics. From this information comes the bill of materials (BOM), which guides manufacturing by indicating all of the component parts that make up the product. A BOM can be considered as taking at least two forms: a product engineering version and a manufacturing engineering version. The product engineering version (engineering bill of materials, or eBOM) is used to design and envision all sorts of product innovation, while the bill of materials for manufacturing (mBOM) has one goal: to make sure the product can be made to specifications.

The reasons for computerizing the BOM are similar to most reasons for automating processes with information systems: reduced complexity and errors and increased efficiency. A single product can be made up of many parts and subcomponents. These subcomponents and parts may be provided by various suppliers. The ability to track part numbers and their source in a product is a natural application for computerization. Information systems can map the bill of materials for this purpose. Having such a system in place can be particularly crucial in times of crisis. If there is a catastrophic product failure, the manufacturer may isolate the failure to a particular part. If the part can be traced to the supplier, additional investigation can determine the actual source of the problem and whether or not it can be fixed with changes from that supplier or by switching suppliers.

Information system parts for the manufacturing process. Multiple information systems and application contribute to successful manufacturing process management. These include computer-aided production engineering (CAPE) and computer-aided process planning (CAPP) systems, among others. Other systems could include manufacturing execution system (MES) applications that create production plans from work orders; enterprise requirements planning (ERP) systems that track financials, inventory, distribution, and customer information; and material requirements planning (MRP) systems, which focus on controlling the ordering and use of materials in products. The ability to perform these tasks automatically is a large step forward for manufacturers and a huge improvement in manufacturing workflow. Computerized manufacturing process management systems allow for the seamless transit of information between applications and can reduce errors, increase speed, and allow more complex modeling of what-if scenarios.

Manufacturing process management software. Manufacturing process management (MPM) software can be considered to cover two specific functions. First, MPM software manages data for complex manufacturing processes, including multistep processes. Second, MPM software validates whether or not the processes are effective. Using software to manage manufacturing processes can aid in easing complexity, managing complexity, and making adjustments in a complex environment. The future for MPM software is limitless. An emerging MPM software function includes a program of plant automation.

One problem with software that manages processes is the high failure rate. The sources of failure tend to be either the growing pains of being an early adopter or the inability of the systems to meet expectations. Sometimes firms can obtain some benefits from process management software that does not completely address all of their problems. In a 2006 article published in *InfoWorld*, Ephraim Schwartz presented a case study of how business process management software was used in antiterror technology that was being evaluated by the Institute for Defense Analysis (IDA). The benefit of business process management software for the IDA was to free up the time of specialists who tracked activity on spreadsheets instead of through automated systems. The IDA also reduced the number of people engaged in tracking activity. The software helped the organization identify where the processes needed modification because of problems tracking the number and type of steps in a process, although actually making those modifications was a difficult process due to the limitations of the existing technology.

GOALS OF PROCESS MANAGEMENT IN MANUFACTURING

The goals of process management in manufacturing are to improve productivity and output of the process, provide adequate and accurate information about the product, and respond quickly and efficiently to requests. While improving the productivity and output of the processes is at times the most visible goal, there is also a specific informational need to make adequate and accurate information available for any functional, organizational purpose. This could also include functional purposes external to the organization, since manufacturers in a global environment must often cooperate with others. While the focus of manufacturing processes is often to meet the needs of manufacturing and production personnel, salespeople, customer service representatives, and other professionals likewise have a need for manufacturing information, and such information must thus be integrated into the complete record about a product.

—*Marlanda English, PhD*

Further Reading
Astall, Chris. "Lean Manufacturing and IT: No Oxymoron." *Manufacturers' Monthly*, Apr. 2006, p. 20.

Bosch-Mauchand, Magali, Farouk Belkadi, Matthieu Bricogne, and Benoît Eynard. "Knowledge-Based Assessment of Manufacturing Process Performance: Integration of Product Lifecycle Management and Value-Chain Simulation Approaches." *International Journal of Computer Integrated Manufacturing*, vol. 26, no. 5, 2013, pp. 453-73.

Cleaverland, Peter. "Building a Better Manufacturing Future." *Product Design & Development*, vol. 61, no. 8, 2006, pp. 8-9.

Courtnell, Jane. "What Is Business Process Management: For Industrial Companies." *Thomas Industrial Marketing and Manufacturing Blog*, 25 Nov. 2019, blog.thomasnet.com/what-is-business-process-management-for-industrial-companies?hs_amp=true. Accessed 28 Nov. 2021.

Essex, David. "Manufacturing Process Management (MPM)." *SearchERP*, Feb. 2017, searcherp.techtarget.com/definition/manufacturing-process-management-MPM. Accessed 28 Nov. 2021.

Golann, Bret. "Achieving Growth and Responsiveness: Process Management and Market Orientation in Small Firms." *Journal of Small Business Management*, vol. 44, no. 3, 2006, pp. 369-85.

Hayashi, Alden M. "Building Better Teams." *MIT Sloan Management Review*, 15 Jan. 2004, sloanreview.mit.edu/article/knowledge-management-building-better-teams/. Accessed 28 Nov. 2021.

Parry, G. C., and C. E. Turner. "Application of Lean Visual Process Management Tools." *Production Planning & Control*, vol. 17, no. 1, 2006, pp. 77-86.

Psomas, Evangelos L., Christos V. Fotopoulos, and Dimitrios P. Kafetzopoulos. "Core Process Management Practices, Quality Tools and Quality Improvement in ISO 9001 Certified Manufacturing Companies." *Business Process Management Journal*, vol. 17, no. 3, 2011, pp. 437-60.

Schwartz, Ephraim. "Evaluating Anti-Terror Technology." *InfoWorld*, 20 Feb. 2006, www.infoworld.com/article/2656261/evaluating-anti-terror-technology.html. Accessed 28 Nov. 2021.

Shukla, Arun. "Proactive People Management One Key to Lean Success." *Plant Engineering*, 1 July 2006, www.plantengineering.com/articles/proactive-people-management-one-key-to-lean-success/. Accessed 28 Nov. 2021.

Slack, Nigel. *Operations and Process Management: Principles and Practice for Strategic Impact*. 5th ed., Pearson, 2018.

Sly, David. "Manufacturing Process Management." *Technology Trends in PLM*, 17 June 2004, www.proplanner.com/media/cms/MPM_Whitepaper_Tech_Trend_PDF_CDF4B29897EE8.pdf. Accessed 28 Nov. 2021.

Product Design

ABSTRACT

Product design is a business process by which new products and models are conceptualized and developed before being introduced to the market. Product design brings together the fields of art, engineering, psychology, and marketing to improve upon the design of everyday products and to develop new products.

OVERVIEW

The product design process begins with the analysis of existing products to identify areas of improvement or with the completion of market research to identify consumer needs not yet met by available products on the market. This step involves consumer interviews and surveys, business metrics, market reviews, and goal mapping to clarify user needs and market competition.

Once designers have identified opportunities in the market for new products or improvements upon earlier designs, they can begin to define the content functions and determine the structure interface of the new design. Using sketches, blueprints, content outlines, and/or computer-aided design (CAD) software, designers begin to conceptualize and map out the product design. This stage of the product design process also typically involves the initial development of marketing messages and materials.

Once a draft of the product design has been completed, designers typically produce several iterations of prototypes. This stage of the design process requires the development of an integration plan to clarify how the product will be produced, with designers taking into consideration all budgetary and environmental constraints in the manufacturing process. The basic design of a product will influence all of its future costs, so designers are under pressure to select the most sustainable materials, processes, and systems to create their products.

Once a valid prototype has been developed, the product undergoes user testing to ensure that the designers' expectations play out in real life. Designers have a clear understanding of how their products work and how they want their audience to engage with their product, but the product's design is often not as evident or intuitive to new users. The designers' bias prevents them from seeing the problems and pitfalls of the product that become evident during user testing. Product designers must consider all the details, even anticipating how users will misuse or damage products and how to update or adapt the product for new uses. Once usability flaws have been identified in the product design, the designers return to the drawing board to correct these problems for the next round of user testing. When the user test results validate the designers' expectations, the product design process can move forward to the manufacturing stage. Once the product has been introduced to market, designers typically resume user testing and market analytics to start the design process again.

—Mary Woodbury Hooper

Further Reading

Bi, Zhuming, and Xiaoqin Wang. *Computer Aided Design and Manufacturing*. Wiley-ASME Press, 2020.

Cagan, Marty. *Inspired: How to Create Products Customers Love*. SVPG, 2008.

Chang, Kuang-Hua. *Product Design Modeling Using CAD/CAE*. Academic Press, 2014.

Lobos, Alex, and Callie W. Babbitt. "Integrating Emotional Attachment and Sustainability in Electronic Product Design." *Challenges*, vol. 4, no. 1, 2013, pp. 19-33.

Medina, Lourdes A., Gul E. Okudan Kremer, and Richard A. Wysk. "Supporting Medical Device Development: A Standard Product Design Process Model." *Journal of Engineering Design*, vol. 24, no. 2, 2013, pp. 83-119.

Metta, Haritha, and Fazleena Badurdeen. "Integrating Sustainable Product and Supply Chain Design: Modeling Issues and Challenges." *IEEE Transactions on Engineering Management*, vol. 60, no. 2, 2013, pp. 438-46.

Milton, Alex, and Paul Rodgers. *Product Design*. Laurence King, 2011.

Morris, Richard. *The Fundamentals of Product Design*. 2nd ed., Fairchild Books, 2016.

Norman, Donald A. *The Design of Everyday Things*. New York: Basic, 2002.

Tang, C. Y., et al. "Product Form Design Using Customer Perception Evaluation by a Combined Superellipse Fitting and ANN Approach." *Advanced Engineering Informatics*, vol. 27, no. 3, 2013, pp. 386-94.

Ulrich, Karl, Steven Eppinger, and Maria C. Yang. *Product Design and Development*. 7th ed., McGraw-Hill, 2020.

Product Lifecycle Management (PLM)

ABSTRACT

All products, whether artificial or natural, have a lifecycle that begins with the inception of the product and ends with the end-of-life disposal of the product. Project lifecycle management (PLM) software is designed to track a product throughout its lifecycle and allow different segments of that lifecycle to communicate with each other and coordinate their respective activities while monitoring and controlling the product's progress through its lifecycle.

WHAT IS A LIFECYCLE?

The term lifecycle applies to both natural and artificial products. A lifecycle typically involves several stages. In agriculture, for example, the natural product is the crop grown in a particular field. The lifecycle of that product begins when the farmer decides what crop will be planted in that field in a particular growing season. It progresses through the stages of soil preparation, planting, crop maintenance, and harvesting and ends when the farmer returns the crop residues to the soil.

The process is somewhat different for artificial products. Strictly speaking, the complete lifecycle of an artificial product begins with obtaining the raw materials from which the product will be made and ends when the product is either recycled or destroyed. For simplification, however, an artificial product's lifecycle is generally considered to progress from the point of its inception and design, through all stages of its production, and to the point of delivery to its end user. This is the definition of product lifecycle management (PLM) on which almost all PLM software is based.

THE ROLE OF PLM

Prior to the development of digital communications networks there was the telephone, and before that the telegraph. Before that, there was the postal service, which at the time was essentially the fastest means of communicating with geographically separated managers of segments of a product lifecycle. The time involved in regular communication by this means for the control of a product's lifecycle effectively prohibited any practice of product lifecycle management, especially if the lifecycle segments were separated by an ocean, as was the case between Europe and the North American continent.

The development of computer technology and the digital communications networks of the twenty-first century, however, has enabled product lifecycle management to take place in real time and between widely separated segments of a product's lifecycle. A product's design team in one location can almost instantaneously communicate its design concepts to a parent company halfway around the world. The parent company can similarly communicate its decisions and needs to production companies in different parts of the world and arrange delivery of the required parts of the product to an assembly plant somewhere else, which can then contact delivery and distribution services to transport the assembled product to various points of sale. There, consumers—the product's end users—are able to take ownership of the product. The company's involvement in the product's lifecycle often ends there; unless the producer of the product ensures the return and proper disposal of the product at the end of its useful life, the end user bears the responsibility for ensuring the proper disposal of the spent product.

PLM SOFTWARE

All of the interconnectedness of these processes, including real-time data acquisition, is provided by PLM software in conjunction with different computer-aided design (CAD), computer-aided manufacturing (CAM), computer-aided engineering (CAE), and project management applications. PLM software was historically used first by the aerospace and automobile industries due to the scope and size of their respective operations and needs. Large organizations developed PLM software specific to their needs in-house as a means of coordinating and controlling their operations. While in-house PLM tools initially are applicable only to the particular company that has developed them, and perhaps only to one location within that company, it can be to the company's benefit to develop the software to be generally useful in all locations and across a broad range of applications. This allows for the PLM software to remain useful as the company grows and diversifies both its product lines and its methods of production.

When a PLM software has been developed to a certain point of general usability, it can then be licensed for use by a wide range of companies. Apart from returning licensing fees to the proprietor of the PLM software, this grants the licensee companies the ability to optimize relationships across different organizations and throughout the product lifecycle. Some PLM software products are open source, meaning that its users are free to alter the source code of the application. Proprietary software cannot be altered by its licensee users, and all changes to its coding can be made only by the proprietor of the software, who may then market the revised application as a new or upgraded version with its own licensing requirements. Open-source PLM software, on the other hand, may be modified by its users and adapted to their particular needs.

Whether proprietary or open source, PLM software provides a single system of record that supports diverse data needs and applications. From a business standpoint, PLM software tends to maximize the lifetime value of the company's product portfolio by minimizing features that may have a negative effect on the product's performance or availability, thus acting to maintain its commercial value. By enabling the repeatability of processes throughout the product's lifecycle, primarily as a production consideration, PLM software also tends to drive revenue to the company by ensuring that a high level of quality is maintained. PLM software can also increase the speed with which new products can be brought into the marketplace.

—Richard M. Renneboog, MSc

Further Reading

Elangovan, Uthayan. *Product Lifecycle Management (PLM): A Digital Journey Using Industrial Internet of Things (IIoT)*. CRC Press, 2020.

"Product Lifecycle Management (PLM) Software." *Siemens*, 2021, www.plm.automation.siemens.com/global/en/our-story/glossary/product-lifecycle-management-plm-software/12506. Accessed 16 Dec. 2021.

Stark, John. *Product Lifecycle Management (Volume 2): The Devil is in the Details*. 3rd ed., Springer, 2016.

Tyulin, Andrey, and Alexander Chursin. *The New Economy of the Product Life Cycle: Innovation and Design in the Digital Era*. Springer, 2020.

Udroin, Azvan, and Paul Bere, editors. *Product Lifecycle Management: Terminology and Applications*. IntechOpen, 2018.

"What Is PLM (Product Lifecycle Management)?" Oracle, 2021, oracle.com/scm/product-lifecycle-management/what-is-plm/. Accessed 16 Dec. 2021.

Propulsion Technologies

ABSTRACT

The field of propulsion deals with the means by which aircraft, missiles, and spacecraft are propelled toward their destinations. Subjects of development include propellers and rotors driven by internal combustion engines or jet engines, rockets powered by solid- or liquid-fueled engines, spacecraft powered by ion engines, solar sails or nuclear reactors, and matter-antimatter engines. Propulsion system metrics include thrust, power, cycle efficiency, propulsion efficiency, specific impulse, and thrust-specific fuel consumption. Advances in this field have enabled humanity to travel across the world in a few hours, visit space and the moon, and send probes to distant planets.

DEFINITION AND BASIC PRINCIPLES

Propulsion is the science of making vehicles move. The propulsion system of a flight vehicle provides the force to accelerate the vehicle and to balance the other forces opposing the motion of the vehicle. Most twenty-first-century propulsion systems add energy to a working fluid to change its momentum and thus develop force, called "thrust," along the desired direction. A few systems use electromagnetic fields or radiation pressure to develop the force needed to accelerate the vehicle itself. The working fluid is usually a gas, and the process can be described by a thermodynamic heat engine cycle involving three basic steps: First, do work on the fluid to increase its pressure; second, add heat or other forms of energy at the highest possible pressure; and third, allow the fluid to expand, converting its potential energy directly to useful work, or to kinetic energy in an exhaust.

In the internal combustion engine, a high-energy fuel is placed in a small closed area and ignited by compression. This produces expanding gas, which drives a piston and a rotating shaft. The rotating shaft drives a transmission whose gears transfer the work to wheels, rotors, or propellers. Rocket and jet engines operate on the Brayton thermodynamic cycle. In this cycle, the gas mixture is compressed adiabatically (no heat added or lost during compression). Heat is added externally or by chemical reaction to the fluid, ideally at constant pressure. The expanding gases are exhausted, with a turbine extracting some work. The gas then expands out through a nozzle.

A remote camera captures a close-up view of an RS-25 during a test firing at the John C. Stennis Space Center in Hancock County, Mississippi. Photo via NASA/Wikimedia Commons. [Public domain.]

BACKGROUND AND HISTORY

Solid-fueled rockets developed in China in the thirteenth century achieved the first successful continuous propulsion of heavier-than-air flying machines. In 1903, Orville and Wilbur Wright used a spinning propeller driven by an internal combustion engine to accelerate air and develop the reaction force that propelled the first human-carrying heavier-than-air powered flight.

As propeller speeds approached the speed of sound in World War II, designers switched to the gas turbine or jet engine to achieve higher thrust and speeds. German Wernher von Braun developed the V-2 rocket, originally known as the A-4 for space travel, but in 1944, it began to be used as a long-range ballistic missile to attack France and England. The V-2 traveled faster than the speed of sound, reached heights of 83 to 93 kilometers, and had a range of more than 320 kilometers. The Soviet Union's 43-ton Sputnik rocket, powered by a LOX/RP2 engine generating 3.89 million Newtons of thrust, placed a 500-kilogram satellite in low-Earth orbit (LEO) on October 4, 1957.

The United States' three-stage, 111-meter-high Saturn V rocket weighed more than 2,280 tons and developed more than 33.36 million Newtons at launch. It could place more than 129,300 kilograms into an LEO and 48,500 kilograms into lunar orbit, thus enabling the first human visit to the moon in July 1969. Later rocket designs emphasized not only power but also reusability. The reusable Falcon 9 rocket, introduced by the private aerospace company SpaceX in 2010, was capable of generating more than 1.7 million pounds of thrust at launch, while the partially reusable Falcon Heavy, introduced in 2018, could reach more than 5 million pounds of thrust.

HOW IT WORKS

Rocket. The rocket is conceptually the simplest of all propulsion systems. All propellants are carried on board, gases are generated with high pressure, heat is added or released in a chamber, and the gases are exhausted through a nozzle. The momentum of the working fluid is increased, and the rate of increase of this momentum produces a force. The reaction to this force acts on the vehicle through the mounting structure of the rocket engine and propels it.

Jet propulsion. Although rockets certainly produce jets of gas, the term "jet engine" typically denotes an engine in which the working fluid is mostly atmospheric air, so that the only propellant carried on the vehicle is the fuel used to release heat. Typically, the mass of fuel used is only about 2 to 4 percent of the mass of air that is accelerated by the vehicle. Types of jet engines include the ramjet, the turbojet, the turbofan, and the turboshaft.

Propulsion system metrics. The thrust of a propulsion system is the force generated along the desired direction. Thrust for systems that exhaust a gas can come from two sources. Momentum thrust comes from the acceleration of the working fluid through the system. It is equal to the difference between the momentum per second of the exhaust and intake flows. Thrust can also be generated from the product of the area of the jet exhaust nozzle cross section and the difference between the static pressure at the nozzle exit and the outside pressure. This pressure thrust is absent for most aircraft in which the exhaust is not supersonic, but it is inevitable when operating in the vacuum of space. The total thrust is the sum of momentum thrust and pressure thrust. Dividing the total thrust by the exhaust mass flow rate of propellant gives the equivalent exhaust speed. All else being equal, designers prefer the highest specific impulse, though it must be noted that there is an optimum specific impulse for each mission. Air-breathing engines achieve very high values of specific impulse because most of the working fluid does not have to be carried onboard.

The higher the specific impulse, the lower the mass ratio needed for a given mission. To lower the mass ratio, space missions are built up in several stages. As each stage exhausts its propellant, the propellant tank and its engines are discarded. When all the propellant is gone, only the payload remains. The relation connecting the mass ratio, the delta-v, and specific impulse, along with the effects of gravity and drag, is called the "rocket equation."

Propulsion systems, especially for military applications, operate at the edge of their stable operation envelope. For instance, if the reaction rate in a solid propellant rocket grows with pressure at a greater than linear rate, the pressure will keep rising until the rocket blows up. A jet engine compressor will stall, and flames may shoot out the front if the blades go past the stalling angle of attack. Diagnosing and solving the problems of instability in these powerful systems has been a constant concern of developers since the first rocket exploded.

APPLICATIONS AND PRODUCTS

Many kinds of propulsion systems have been developed or proposed. The simplest rocket is a cold gas thruster, in which gas stored in tanks at high pressure is exhausted through a nozzle, accelerating (increasing momentum) in the process. All other types of rocket engines add heat or energy in some other form in a combustion (or thrust) chamber before exhausting the gas through a nozzle.

Solid-fueled rockets are simple and reliable, and can be stored for a long time, but once ignited, their thrust is difficult to control. An ignition source decomposes the propellant at its surface into gases whose reaction releases heat and creates high pressure in the thrust chamber. The surface recession rate is thus a measure of propellant gas generation. The thrust variation with time is built into the rocket grain geometry. The burning area exposed to the hot gases in the combustion chamber changes in a preset way with time. Solid rockets are used as boosters for space launch and for storable missiles that must be launched quickly on demand.

Liquid-fueled rockets typically use pumps to inject propellants into the combustion chamber, where the propellants vaporize, and a chemical reaction releases heat. Typical applications are the main engines of space launchers and engines used in space, where the highest specific impulse is needed.

Hybrid rockets use a solid propellant grain with a liquid propellant injected into the chamber to vary the thrust as desired. Electric resistojets use heat generated by currents flowing through resistances. Though simple, their specific impulse and thrust-to-weight ratio are too low for wide use. Ion rocket engines use electric fields or, in some cases, heat to ionize a gas and a magnetic field to accelerate the ions through the nozzle. These are preferred for long-duration space missions in which only a small level of thrust is needed but for an extended duration because the electric energy comes from solar photovoltaic panels. Nuclear-thermal rockets generate heat from nuclear fission and may be coupled with ion propulsion. Proposed matter-antimatter propulsion systems use the annihilation of antimatter to release heat, with extremely high specific impulse.

Pulsed detonation engines are being developed for some applications. A detonation is a supersonic shock wave generated by intense heat release. These engines use a cyclic process in which the propellants come into contact and detonate several times a second. Nuclear-detonation engines were once proposed, in which the vehicle would be accelerated by shock waves generated by nuclear explosions in space to reach extremely high velocities. However, international law prohibits nuclear explosions in space.

In light of the complexity of many propulsion systems, professionals working in that field make use of a number of computer-based tools, including computer-aided design (CAD) software, when developing propulsion systems and their components. CAD software and related technologies such as simulation programs enable engineers to design, model, and virtually test their proposed systems prior to beginning the fabrication and physical testing processes.

Ramjets and turbomechanics. Ramjet engines are used at supersonic speeds and beyond, where the deceleration of the incoming flow is enough to generate very high pressures, adequate for an efficient heat engine. When the heat addition is done without slowing the fluid below the speed of sound, the engine is called a "scramjet," or "supersonic combustion ramjet." Ramjets cannot start by themselves from rest. Turbojets add a turbine to extract work from the flow leaving the combustor and drive a compressor to increase the pressure ratio. A power turbine may be used downstream of the main turbine. In a turbofan engine, the power turbine drives a fan that works on a larger mass flow rate of air bypassing the combustor. In a turboprop, the power is taken to a gearbox to reduce revolutions per minute, powering a propeller. In a turboshaft engine, the power is transferred through a transmission as in the case of a helicopter rotor, tank, ship, or electric generator. Many applications combine these concepts, such as a propfan, a turboramjet, or a rocket-ramjet that starts off as a solid-fueled rocket and becomes a ramjet when propellant consumption opens enough space to ingest air.

Gravity assist. A spacecraft can be accelerated by sending it close enough to another heavenly body (such as a planet) to be strongly affected by its gravity field. This swing-by maneuver sends the vehicle into a more energetic orbit with a new direction, enabling surprisingly small mass ratios for deep space missions.

Tethers. Orbital momentum can be exchanged using a tether between two spacecraft. This principle has been proposed to efficiently transfer payloads from Earth orbit to lunar or Martian orbits and even to exchange payloads with the lunar surface. An extreme version is a stationary tether linking a point on Earth's equator to a craft in geostationary Earth orbit, the tether running far beyond to a countermass. The electrostatic tether concept uses variations in the electric potential with orbital height to induce a current in a tether strung from a spacecraft. An electrodynamic tether uses the force that is exerted on a current-carrying tether by the magnetic field of the planet to propel the tether and the craft attached to it.

Solar and plasma sails. Solar sails use the radiation pressure from sunlight bounced off or absorbed by thin, large sails to propel a craft. Typically, this works best in the inner solar system where radiation is more intense. Other versions of propulsion sails, in which lasers focus radiation on sails that are far away from the sun, have been proposed. In mini magnetospheric plasma propulsion (M2P2), a cloud of plasma (ionized gas) emitted into the field of a magnetic solenoid creates an electromagnetic bubble around 30 kilometers in diameter, which interacts with the solar wind of charged particles that travels at 300 to 800 kilometers per second. The result is a force perpendicular to the solar wind and the (controllable) magnetic field, similar to aerodynamic lift. This system has been proposed to conduct fast missions to the outer reaches of the solar system and back.

CAREERS AND COURSEWORK

Propulsion technology spans aerospace, mechanical, electrical, nuclear, chemical, and materials science engineering. Aircraft, space launcher, and spacecraft manufacturers and the defense industry are major customers of propulsion systems. Workplaces in this industry are distributed over many regions in the United States and near many major airports and National Aeronautics and Space Administration (NASA) centers. The large airlines operate engine testing facilities. Propulsion-related work outside the United States, France, Britain, and Germany is usually in companies run by or closely related to the government. Because propulsion technologies are closely related to weapon-system development, many products and projects come under the International Traffic in Arms Regulations.

Students aspiring to become rocket scientists or jet engine developers should take courses in physics, chemistry, mathematics, thermodynamics and heat transfer, gas dynamics and aerodynamics, combustion, and aerospace propulsion.

Machinery operating at thousands to hundreds of thousands of revolutions per minute requires extreme precision, accuracy, and material perfection. Manufacturing jobs in this field include specialist machinists and electronics experts. Because propulsion systems are limited by the pressure and temperature limits of structures that must also have minimal weight, the work usually involves advanced materials and manufacturing techniques. Instrumentation and diagnostic techniques for propulsion systems are constantly pushing the boundaries of technology and offer exciting opportunities using optical and acoustic techniques.

SOCIAL CONTEXT AND FUTURE PROSPECTS

Propulsion systems have enabled humanity to advance beyond the speed of ships, trains, balloons, and gliders to travel across the oceans safely, quickly, and comfortably and to venture beyond Earth's atmosphere. The result has been a radical transformation of global society since the early 1900s. Jet engine reliability has become so established that jetliners with only two engines routinely fly across the Atlantic and Pacific oceans. However, jet engines are not very energy efficient, which makes them expensive to operate and detrimental to the environment. As such, addressing this problem is a major area of jet engine research in the twenty-first century; one method under investigation is the use of electricity-powered rather than gas-powered turbines.

Propulsion technologies are just beginning to grow in their capabilities. During the early twenty-first century, specific impulse values were at best a couple of thousand seconds; however, concepts using radiation pressure, nuclear propulsion, and matter-antimatter promise values ranging into hundreds of thousands of seconds. Air-breathing propulsion systems promise specific impulse values of greater than 2,000 seconds, enabling single-stage trips by reusable craft to space and back. As electric propulsion systems with high specific impulse come down in system weight because of the use of specially tailored magnetic materials and superconductors, travel to the outer planets may become quite routine. Spacecraft with solar or magnetospheric sails, or tethers, may make travel and cargo transactions to the moon and inner planets routine as well. These technologies are at the core of human aspirations to travel far beyond their home planet.

—*Narayanan M. Komerath, PhD*

Further Reading

Faeth, G. M. *Centennial of Powered Flight: A Retrospective of Aerospace Research*. American Institute of Aeronautics and Astronautics, 2003.

Hays, Kevin. "What CAD Software Does SpaceX Use?" *Departing Earth*, departingearth.com/what-cad-software-does-spacex-use/. Accessed 28 Nov. 2021.

Henry, Gary N., Wiley J. Larson, and Ronald W. Humble. *Space Propulsion Analysis and Design*. McGraw-Hill 1995.

Martin, Richard. "The Race for the Ultra-Efficient Jet Engine of the Future." *MIT Technology Review*, 23 Mar. 2016, www.technologyreview.com/s/601008/the-race-for-the-ultra-efficient-jet-engine-of-the-future/. Accessed 28 Nov. 2021.

Norton, Bill. *STOL Progenitors: The Technology Path to a Large STOL Aircraft and the C-17A*. American Institute of Aeronautics and Astronautics, 2002.

Peebles, C. *Road to Mach 10: Lessons Learned from the X-43A Flight Research Program*. American Institute of Aeronautics and Astronautics, 2008.

Schaberg, Christopher. "The Jet Engine Is a Futuristic Technology Stuck in the Past." *The Atlantic*, 11 Feb. 2018, www.theatlantic.com/technology/archive/2018/02/engine-failure/552959/. Accessed 28 Nov. 2021.

Shepherd, D. *Aerospace Propulsion*. Elsevier, 1972.

SpaceX, 2021, www.spacex.com/. Accessed 28 Nov. 2021.

Sutton, George P., and Oscar Biblarz. *Rocket Propulsion Elements*. 9th ed., Wiley, 2016.

Prosthetics

ABSTRACT

Prosthetics is the branch of medicine focused on the replacement of missing body parts with artificial substitutes so that an individual can function and appear more natural. Prostheses are commonly used to replace hands, arms, legs, and feet; however, examples of other prosthetic devices developed to improve one's quality of life are heart valves, pacemakers, and components of the ear. Some prosthetic devices, including eye and breast implants, are developed primarily for cosmetic reasons. Several health-care professions work together as a team in this process, and teams include a surgeon, a nurse, a prosthetist, and physical and occupational therapists.

DEFINITION AND BASIC PRINCIPLES

"Prosthetics" is the science of developing and fitting substitute body parts. This branch of medicine is devoted to assisting patients in regaining as much function as possible after they have lost a body part from trauma, a birth defect, or illness. The replacement of a limb or other impaired or lost body part involves fitting an individual with an artificial leg, arm, or other body part to allow him or her to perform the activities of daily living.

A "prosthesis" is a device that replaces a missing body part or augments a partial one; an individual who measures, fits, and modifies the prosthesis is referred to as the "prosthetist." Legs, arms, feet, and hands are the most commonly known artificial devices.

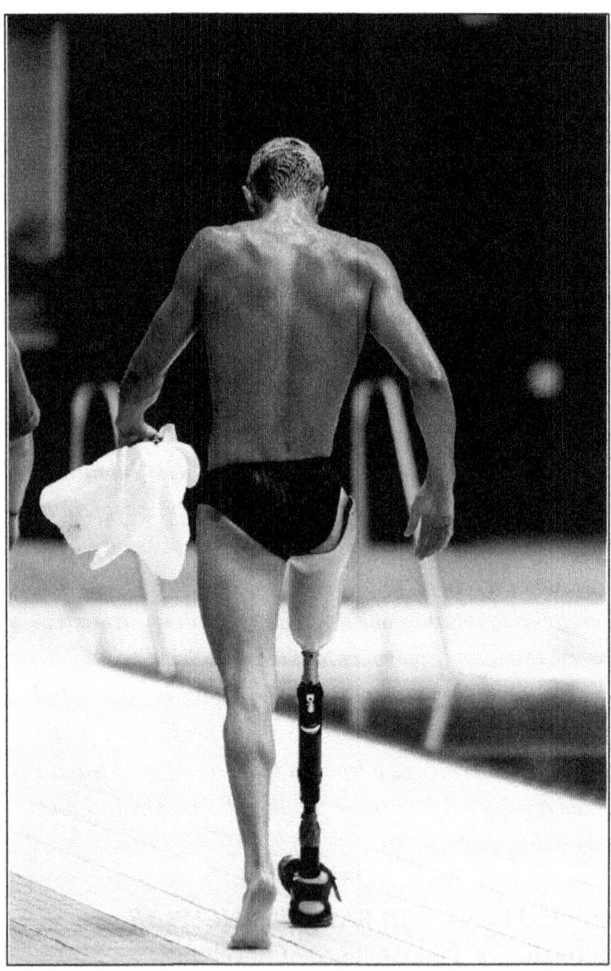

A man with a lower-extremity prosthesis. Photo by Australian Paralympic Committee, via Wikimedia Commons.

Although closely related to the field of prosthetics, the term "orthotics" is not identical in meaning. Orthotics usually focuses on the management of impairment, but the treatment may be more temporary, whereas prosthetics concerns permanent artificial replacements of body parts. An orthotist designs and fits surgical appliances; this process is referred to as "orthosis." Orthotic devices include braces, neck collars, and splints. Such devices are designed to support the patient's limbs or spine while relieving pain and helping movement. They also may be designed to restrict movement and provide an environment of protection and healing.

BACKGROUND AND HISTORY

The use of prosthetic devices can be traced back to sixteenth-century knights. A German knight known as Götz of the Iron Hand may have been the first to apply the science of prosthetics. He developed and used an appliance with movable fingers to help him hold a sword (hence, his nickname).

Until the twentieth century, most prosthetic devices were made of wood, but because of the large number of amputees produced by World Wars I and II, these devices began to be made of metals and fibers. The devices were designed to increase function and therefore incorporated mechanical devices and elastic materials to allow individuals to move their artificial limbs more effectively and easily.

In the late twentieth and early twenty-first centuries, advances in biomechanics and bioengineering resulted in prosthetic devices such as hydraulic knees and computer-programmable hands that sense the slightest muscle movement. Such technology has led to advances in prosthetic devices for other body parts, including the heart and the ear. Advances in computer technology likewise facilitated the creation of advanced prosthetic devices tailored to the individual user: specialized scanners, for instance, enabled the creation of digital images and models of an individual's body, and a three-dimensional (3D) model of a prosthetic device customized for that individual could be created through the use of computer-aided design (CAD) software. Related technology such as 3D printers could subsequently be used to manufacture prototypes or even fully functional prosthetic devices.

HOW IT WORKS

Prosthetics is often defined as a branch of surgery involving a team approach comprising such professionals as surgeons, nurses, prosthetists, physical and occupational therapists, prosthetic technicians and assistants, rehabilitation counselors, and social workers. By combining medical science with technology, rehabilitation engineering assists in the design and development of devices to meet each individual's needs.

Interaction with the patient begins well before any surgery, with the physician determining if replacement of the natural body part is required. If a surgical procedure such as amputation is required, the physician, nurse, and social workers must prepare the patient emotionally and physically. The prosthetist, physician, and physical therapist consult with the patient to determine the size, shape, and material most appropriate for the appropriate device. The physical therapist evaluates factors such as strength and ability to wear the prosthesis and works with the patient to increase physical strength as appropriate for the device involved.

Prosthetists and technicians work with their hands and high-tech machinery to make molds or casts of the amputated area to create the desired device. This process may include casting molds, using sewing machines, heating plastics in a special oven, or utilizing a specialized scanner. Rehabilitation engineers apply their expertise as well; for example, depending on the needs of the individual patient, they may suggest a prosthetic foot that offers a more natural spring to help push off from the floor from a standing start, or they may help design a prosthetic knee to facilitate stair climbing that avoids rubbing the foot on the steps, which could result in a fall.

Most prosthetists and related health-care team members often work in a combination of environments that are inspected and regulated by the American Board for Certification in Orthotics and Prosthetics. Later stages of rehabilitation engage an occupational therapist, who focuses on helping the patient complete everyday tasks independently with the new prosthesis and suggests activities to strengthen weakened muscles.

APPLICATIONS AND PRODUCTS

The products of prosthetics are primarily the physical devices used to replace lost body parts. The most common prosthetic devices replace limbs, but other, less familiar devices are also considered to be prostheses. The users of these products include a broad range of individuals, from children born with missing limbs to military personnel who have been injured during battle. The largest population of amputees in the United States are those individuals who have lost a limb from either diabetes or peripheral vascular disease. Trauma victims, such as those who have experienced motor vehicular accidents, make up another group of users, since accidents account for many lost limbs.

Prosthetic limbs. Over the years, prosthetic limbs consisted of combinations of springs and hinges to increase motion and function. Prosthetic limbs use a socket to fit over the remaining part of the limb and provide a link between the body and the prosthesis. Additional straps and belts are often used to attach the device to the body with soft, sock-like material used in between to protect the area of contact from excessive pressure and friction. The main body of the prosthesis is often made from material such as carbon fiber, popular for its light weight, strength, and durability. These properties require less exertion of effort by the patient, and the device appears more natural.

Prosthetic legs are generally of two types: transtibial and transfemoral. A transtibial prosthesis replaces the leg below the knee, which allows the knee joint to remain functional. A transfemoral prosthesis replaces the entire leg, including above the knee joint. Traditionally, the force needed to move either type of device has come from the patient's remaining muscles, including the momentum from using his or her entire body. Newer technology has brought the use of myoelectric limbs, which respond by converting muscle movement to an electric signal to move the device. This technology has allowed patients with leg and arm prostheses to have better control of the limb.

Prosthetic devices for the hip are made from materials similar to those used for prosthetic legs to provide strength, comfort, and support. A prosthetic hip joint is designed to support and link the patient to the prosthetic leg by way of a socket fitted to the body's torso and pelvis using a system of straps. Some artificial hip joints use a roller system to convey forces from the socket directly to the prosthetic leg.

Prosthetic arms and hands have advanced, using stronger and lighter materials that also look more like skin. The biomechanics of these devices has improved: Once anchored to the opposite shoulder with straps across the back, these devices have come to use electrical signals from the patient's nearby muscles to move specific fingers. A technique known as targeted muscle reinnervation (TMR), whereby the arm or hand will respond to signals from the brain to specific remaining muscles, has also gained promise. Patients potentially are able to manipulate a prosthetic hand as naturally as they once could move their own hand.

By 2015, the online nonprofit group e-NABLE began making affordable prosthetic hands—mainly for children—using 3D printers. After a customized hand was designed based on the future user's measurements, a volunteer could download the design and 3D print the components for the prosthetic hand, which would then be donated to the individual in need. Between 2015 and 2019, e-NABLE volunteers printed about seven thousand prosthetic devices.

Prosthetic applications for the foot have been primarily rigid in design, with little if any movement. Traditionally prosthetic feet were made from leather, metal, plastic, or a combination of such materials. Modern foot prostheses have improved, with computer-controlled components designed to handle the user's weight and the return of his or her momentum. Such products have been reported to be comfortable enough for participation in recreational sports. Further improvements have occurred with the use of a carbon fiber, compression springs, and telescoping tubes that help the prosthetic foot move more naturally without inducing pain or discomfort.

Nonlimb prosthetic devices. Other prosthetic devices include artificial eyes, breasts, heart valves, and pacemakers. The body's natural heart valve may need to be surgically replaced if it no longer functions properly because of disease, aging, or a birth defect. This vital prosthetic heart component is made from plastic, metal, or pig tissue. Calcification of the prosthetic heart valves is the major cause of product problems, and efforts have been aimed at constructing artificial valves with surfaces that resist calcification. Technological advancements in the durability of the tissue heart valves are also an area of research and could be more applicable to younger patients.

Prosthetic eyes are traditionally made from hard materials such as acrylic, gold, ceramics, and glass. When an individual loses an eye, it is replaced with a temporary implant that is positioned toward the back of the eye socket to allow proper room for the prosthetic eye. With the use of an impression, a wax model is made, followed by a mold for casting the prosthetic eye. Components of the eye, such as the pupil and the iris, are painted on a round plastic base and eventually inserted on the prosthetic eye. Some prosthetic eyes can even be designed to allow for the attachment of eye muscles. One of the trends in design is to develop an ocular system that allows for more natural movement.

A popular product for women who have had a mastectomy, prosthetic breasts are made of various materials, including lightweight silicone, soft gel, and a variety of fabrics. Breast prosthetics are often engineered using a cast of the body shape and other parameters. The prosthetic breast needs to be lightweight to avoid strain on the back and shoulders. Cosmetics—shape and contour—is a concern in the design and development of this form of prosthesis, as is comfort. For example, one breast prosthesis has at its center a climate control pad made of a soft gel that absorbs body heat, creating a cooling sensation. Future breast prostheses are expected to be developed with some type of climate-control technology.

Pacemakers are a complex form of prosthetic devices whose design and development require high-tech electric and computer expertise. These units are manufactured by the biomedical industry and have progressed significantly to keep up with advances in medicine. Originally stimulating the heart to beat at a standard rate of around 70 beats per minute, pacemakers can now interpret signals from the patient to change the rate of the heart. The latest device can take the electrical impulses from the heart's natural pacemaker, the sinoatrial node, and increase the heart rate during activity as needed.

Less well known but gaining in popularity are ear components, specifically the cochlea. Artificial cochleas are able to duplicate the function of converting sound waves into electronic chemical impulses.

Neuroprosthetics. Neuroprosthetics, a subspecialty of prosthetics, aims to integrate body, mind, and machine. One example is the development of a system that can decipher brain waves and translate them into computer commands. A young science, this specialty promises to allow quadriplegic individuals to gain sufficient function to operate household electric appliances and computers by using their thoughts, transmitted by an implant.

Tissue engineering. The concept of tissue engineering to complement prosthetics promises to play a key role in twenty-first-century prosthetic devices. Surgical techniques are being developed that could lengthen the bone in a residual limb to fit artificial limbs more effectively. Problems associated with anchoring methods can be solved with tissue engineering by way of the developing technology of attaching prosthetic legs to a titanium bolt directly in the bone, a process known as "osseointegration."

CAREERS AND COURSEWORK

The need for prosthetists, prosthetics assistants, and technicians is expected to increase as a result of an aging population, increases in obesity and diabetes, and the medical demands of war-related amputees.

A bachelor's degree in prosthetics is usually required from a program accredited by the American Board for Certification in Orthotics and Prosthetics. Following a period of supervised clinical internship, college graduates are eligible to take examinations given by its governing board. Another route to the profession has been designed for other members of the health-care team, such as surgeons, nurses, and physical therapists. These professionals may receive training in prosthetics while studying to achieve certification in their respective specialties.

Another avenue is to become certified by earning an associate's degree in any field, then completing a certificate program in orthotics and prosthetics, followed by working for four years in the field and eventually passing certification exams. Programs for prosthetics assistants and technicians range from six months to two years of study, and internships and are offered by the American Academy of Orthotists and Prosthetists, which also offers continuing education courses and forums so that those in the prosthetics industry can learn about new developments.

Because some patients will require both prosthetic devices and orthotics, many programs offer degrees and certificates in both disciplines. Individuals with education and experience in both disciplines will possess much more knowledge and therefore be more employable, compared with those with degrees or certificates in only one of the disciplines.

SOCIAL CONTEXT AND FUTURE PROSPECTS

Prosthetic devices can restore independence to people who have lost limbs or function through the impairment of body parts. With the use of a prosthesis, people can return to such fundamental activities as walking, writing with a pen, feeding themselves with a fork or spoon, receiving a handshake, holding a newborn, and playing sports. Such abilities, which most people take for granted, are dramatic to the person who has lost function and may mean the difference between independent living and institutionalization.

—*Jeffrey Larson, PT, ATC*

Further Reading

"About Us." *Enabling the Future*, 2019, enablingthefuture.org/about/. Accessed 28 Nov. 2021.

Chau, Brian. "iMedicalApps: CAD Beats Casting for Prosthetic Limbs." *MedPageToday*, 29 Aug. 2017, www.medpagetoday.com/opinion/iltifathusain/67598. Accessed 28 Nov. 2021.

Hawkins, Amanda, and Sam Aquillano. *Bespoke Bodies: The Design & Craft of Prosthetics*. Design Museum Press, 2020.

"How Proswith AutoCAD Training Design Prosthetics." *Digital School*, www.digitalschool.ca/pros-autocad-training-design-prosthetics/. Accessed 28 Nov. 2021.

Lusardi, Michelle M., and Caroline C. Nielsen, editors. *Orthotics and Prosthetics in Rehabilitation*. 3rd ed., Elsevier, 2013.

May, Bella J., and Margery A. Lockard. *Prosthetics and Orthotics in Clinical Practice: A Case Study Approach*. Davis, 2011.

Ott, Katherine, et al., editors. *Artificial Parts, Practical Lives: Modern Histories of Prosthetics*. New York UP, 2002.

Pitkin, Mark R. *Biomechanics of Lower Limb Prosthetics*. Springer, 2010.

Shurr, Donald G., and John W. Michael. *Prosthetics and Orthotics*. 2nd ed., Prentice Hall, 2002.

Smith, Marquard, and Joanne Morra, editors. *The Prosthetic Impulse: From a Posthuman Present to a Biocultural Future*. MIT, 2006.

Prototyping

ABSTRACT

Prototyping is a methodology that focuses on the use of working models that are repeatedly refined based on feedback from stakeholders. The creation of prototypes is a common strategy in a host of industries, including manufacturing and software development. In manufacturing, prototyping often includes the rapid manufacturing and testing of models of the item or component being designed. In software development, prototyping is most often used to develop systems that include significant end-user interaction and complex user interfaces.

UNDERSTANDING PROTOTYPING

Prototyping is a methodology that involves making working models of a product or application as it is being developed. These working models, or prototypes, are repeatedly refined and improved based on feedback from users and other stakeholders. Prototyping is an iterative development method in which prototypes are designed, built, evaluated, and refined repeatedly until the product or system functions as required. Prototypes are working models, but they are not complete. They include only partial functionality and are intended to be revised, expanded, and improved during each cycle in the development process.

A process common within the field of computer-aided design and computer-aided manufacturing (CAD/CAM) is that of rapid prototyping. In rapid prototyping, a company or individual uses technology such as three-dimensional (3D) printing to manufacture physical prototypes quickly and inexpensively. This enables the designers to test and evaluate the prototypes and create new iterations as needed. In addition to manufacturing, prototyping is commonly carried out in fields such as software development, which likewise benefits from the creation and testing of partially functional working models.

PROTOTYPING STEPS

Prototyping typically consists of four main steps: requirements identification, prototype development, user evaluation, and prototype revision. In the first

Prototypes are working models, but they are intended to be revised, expanded, and improved during each cycle in the development process. Image via iStock/PCH-Vector. [Used under license.]

step, the basic requirements that the product must fulfill are determined. The focus at this stage is on the users' needs, not on developing comprehensive and detailed requirements, as would be the case in traditional methodologies such as waterfall development. In the second step, the prototype is created, based on the project's initial requirements and on feedback received during any previous prototyping cycles. In the evaluation phase, stakeholders test the prototype and provide feedback. The fourth step involves revision or enhancement of the prototype based on that feedback. Steps two through four are then repeated until the product meets the needs of the users and other stakeholders.

SOFTWARE PROTOTYPING

There are different types of prototyping, several of which are commonly used in the field of software development. Choosing the correct approach to prototyping will depend on how much time is invested up front to define system requirements, whether or not the system will be available for use throughout development, and whether or not the prototype will be used to validate or fulfill a requirement during the development process.

In throwaway prototyping, also known as rapid or close-ended prototyping, the first prototype is created very early in the process, after only basic requirements have been determined. The creation of this preliminary prototype allows developers and stakeholders to further understand and refine the requirements. The prototype is then discarded, and work begins on the actual system. This method is often used to quickly test a small portion of a larger software system. Once the throwaway prototype has been used to verify that this small portion functions correctly, its functionality is incorporated into the final system. This process of incorporating functionality is called "integration."

Another type is called "evolutionary prototyping." In evolutionary prototyping, the first prototype is based only on those requirements that are well defined and clearly understood at the outset. The initial prototype is not discarded. Instead, new functionality is added to it as more requirements are clarified and understood. This process is repeated until the initial, minimally functional prototype has been expanded into the final, fully functional system.

In incremental prototyping, multiple prototypes are built for each of the various system components. These components are developed separately and then integrated to form the completed application.

Extreme prototyping is a three-step method commonly used for web development. First, a static, typically hypertext markup language (HTML)-based prototype of the entire website or application is developed. Next, a second prototype that simulates the complete user interface is developed. This prototype does not contain the underlying functionality required for the application to be operational. Actual functionality is added in the final step by integrating the prototypes from the first two steps.

BENEFITS AND DOWNSIDES

Prototyping offers several advantages over other design methodologies. In particular, the creation of working models and emphasis on evaluation allow for the early detection of design flaws and missing functionality. This increases the chance that the final product will meet the real-world needs of the end user.

While prototyping offers considerable benefits, there are also downsides to this methodology. Failure to determine detailed specifications at the beginning of the design process can result in constantly changing specifications and the inclusion of additional features that have a negative impact on project costs and scheduling. The system being developed may grow in size and complexity, causing stakeholders to lose sight of the project's original objectives. In addition, projects developed using prototyping must be managed to ensure that resources are used efficiently when building multiple prototypes.

—*Maura Valentino, MSLIS*

Further Reading

Bell, Michael. *Incremental Software Architecture: A Method for Saving Failing IT Implementations*. John Wiley & Sons, 2016.

Friedman, Daniel P., and Mitchell Wand. *Essentials of Programming Languages*. 3rd ed., MIT Press, 2008.

Jayaswal, Bijay K., and Peter C. Patton. *Design for Trustworthy Software: Tools, Techniques, and Methodology of Developing Robust Software*. Prentice Hall, 2007.

McElroy, Kathryn. *Prototyping for Designers*. O'Reilly Media, 2017.

Seliger, Günther, Marwan K. Khrasheh, and I. S. Jawahir, editors. *Advances in Sustainable Manufacturing*. Springer-Verlag, 2011.

Van Roy, Peter, and Seif Haridi. *Concepts, Techniques, and Models of Computer Programming*. MIT Press, 2004.

"What Is Rapid Prototyping?-Definition, Methods and Advantages." *TWI*, www.twi-global.com/technical-knowledge/faqs/faq-manufacturing-what-is-rapid-prototyping. Accessed 28 Nov. 2021.

Wysocki, Robert K. *Effective Project Management: Traditional, Agile, Extreme*. 7th ed., John Wiley & Sons, 2014.

Q

Quality Control

ABSTRACT

In its broadest sense, the concept of quality control refers to a process that ensures that the physical result of one's work matches the design concept of the work as closely and as consistently as possible. As goods began to be produced in large quantities, the importance of standardization, which creates easily interchangeable parts, and quality control, which ensures that goods are produced according to those standards, became apparent. The ideas, concepts, and practices for achieving quality control are readily transferable from one field to another. Thus, quality control as a working concept applies equally well to the preparation of drug compounds in a laboratory as to the manufacture of cast magnesium engine parts in a factory.

DEFINITION AND BASIC PRINCIPLES

Quality control can be defined as any process or procedure that has the purpose of maintaining an established or stated standard of quality for a product or process. The central aims of quality control are to ensure the consistent nature of the product or process of interest, to reduce costs and losses inherent in the process, and to maximize client satisfaction. These are generally embodied in the descriptive term "total quality management" (TQM).

TQM is an all-encompassing program designed to manage every aspect of the process of production of a good or service, from start to finish, and at all levels of a company. Generally, a TQM program includes thorough documentation of every stage through which the good or service passes and implementation of up-to-date processes and procedures designed to ensure quality. A TQM program always has a quality-control function. However, the converse is not always true, as quality-control activities and functions can be and often are employed on their own and not as an integral part of any TQM program.

Quality-control methods depend on the nature of the process involved. Methods employed, for example, in a manufacturing facility that turns out hundreds of identical machine parts per day will be very different from those used to ensure that teachers are performing to designated standards in their classrooms or that a complicated computer program performs to expectation without difficulty. All methods share the same purpose, however, which is to ensure that the output of the process meets the conditional criteria placed on its successful production.

In many instances, quality control consists of little more than visual inspection of a product to check for defects. This is a general and useful starting point for any quality-control function. Quality control is first and foremost a feedback process. When quality control is used to detect errors in the output stream, the information that it provides is used to adjust the manner in which the particular process treats the input stream. Determining the quality of the product (the output stream of the process) requires the creation of a product-specific system of quality-control testing and unequivocal methods of measuring designated features of the product, which can be compared with the ideal or standard features.

Metrology, the study and application of methods for the measurement of properties, plays an important role in quality control, which depends on measurement to obtain specific information about individual components of an output stream. Also critical

Photo via iStock/NicoElNino. [Used under license.]

in quality-control processes is the use of statistics, which determines and uses standard methods of obtaining generalized information relevant to specific aspects of the entire output stream. For example, metrology would be used to determine the achievement level of a particular student as a percentage mark on a specific test, while statistics would be used to determine the percentage mark typically achieved by a large number of students of the same age on the same test. In another setting, metrology would be used to accurately measure the distance between two features of individual machined parts in a factory, and statistics would be used to monitor how well, as a group, the parts being manufactured conform to the essential design criteria. The use of such statistical information as the basis for regulating and adjusting the manner in which the machine process is carried out is called "statistical process control" (SPC).

BACKGROUND AND HISTORY

People have always sought to create products that are satisfactory to others. Such workmanship generally attracts consumers and generates profits. In ancient times, most likely hunters preferred their arrowheads and spear points to come from the best flintknappers in the village because the best quality objects were the most effective; efficacy of the goods produced directly correlated with survival. Similarly, farmers who grew the best crops or craftspeople who made the best goods generally were able to sell or trade them more readily, thereby making a better living than those who produced goods of lesser quality.

With the development of skilled trades, the guild system developed. In a guild system, skilled tradespeople became represented in self-governing groups according to their specific type of trade. Each guild ensured that its members were able to perform the tasks associated with a specific trade to the guild standard. The guild system represents the first systematic approach to quality control. Quality control in the modern sense came about through the Industrial Revolution and the development of mass-production methods. In the late eighteenth century, the idea that machine components that were nominally the same should be interchangeable was put forward by American inventor Eli Whitney. Production methods, however, relied more on the machinist's art than anything else, and true interchangeability of parts was difficult to attain.

The number of standardized parts needed increased tremendously in the mid-twentieth century, largely because of the United States' involvement in World War II. Quality-control methods based on the statistical work of Walter Shewhart—often referred to as the father of statistical quality control—and American statistician W. Edwards Deming were developed as a means of ensuring absolute interchangeability of parts, eliminating waste, minimizing (or eliminating) liability issues, and maximizing return on investment in materials. Quality-control methods that were developed in the late twentieth century provided ongoing feedback that allowed processes to be adjusted as needed to allow for essentially continuous production of components.

HOW IT WORKS

Quality-control processes range from the exceedingly simple method of visual inspection and measurement typically used for parts produced in low quantities to the sophisticated automatic inspection and measurement systems employing advanced analytical techniques often used for parts produced in large quantities. All quality-control systems, however, refer to an ideal or design standard. The purpose of any quality-control technique is to determine how well the output item conforms to the ideal or design standard. Acceptable outputs are those that fall within a specific set of limiting values. Depending on the nature of the product, outputs may be subjected to several stages of examination before use and to ongoing inspection during use.

For example, in the production of cast magnesium rotors, the design standard for acceptable cast parts calls for uniform material distribution. Each part produced must pass a preliminary visual inspection. Those observed to have defects are rejected and recycled. The remaining parts proceed to the next stage, where they are checked for internal defects. Defective parts are sent to recycling, and acceptable parts are sent to the next stage. If a machining stage is required, the machined parts are checked for the correct dimensions. The quality checks continue until the parts are finished and acceptable.

Quality assessments are recorded as statistical data, which are used to maintain or control the specific process from which they were obtained. In the cast magnesium rotor example, if casting flaws frequently occurred in a specific location on the rotor, the casting process would be adjusted to eliminate the flaw or reduce the frequency of its occurrence. In other processes with high throughput (output over an extended period of time), it is not feasible to examine every single unit. In such cases, a random selection of individual outputs is tested and their conformance to the ideal is extrapolated to the entire output. This method relies on the output history as the basis for comparison, and variances in the output are tracked very closely to ensure that, overall, the individual components of the output stream remain within the parameters set in the design standard.

APPLICATIONS AND PRODUCTS
The value of quality-control processes and procedures is widely recognized. The quality-control process has been integrated into virtually all aspects of human activity, from the simplest of mechanical production operations to the most insubstantial of services. Human activities themselves are subject to the application of quality-control measures.

The quality-control process is a feedback control system. The ultimate purpose of determining the quality of any output is to ascertain what aspect of the procedure is not performing adequately so that it can be corrected and the subsequent output of the process improved or at least maintained within the design standard. This applies equally to physical objects being assembled or manufactured in a factory and to services provided to customers in the retail environment. In essence, quality control ensures that work is being done in an optimal manner that produces the most output with the least waste.

Standardization. Standardization is key to achieving optimal quality control in the international economy. The International Organization for Standardization (ISO) and other organizations provide internationally recognized industrial and commercial standards. For example, the ISO provides standards regarding the magnetic stripe on credit cards. The ISO also offers a family of quality management standards, which includes ISO 9000, 9001, and 14000. Other quality-control programs include the Motorola Corporation's Six Sigma and lean manufacturing (derived from the Toyota Production System). Such programs are generally not intended as stand-alone quality-control systems but instead define an overall management approach in which quality control is an integral component and tool of the project manager.

Quality-management programs. Quality-control programs determine how standardization is achieved. To obtain certification from any program, a company must first commit to organizing its operations in accordance with the standards specified by the program. These standards govern most aspects of operations, including the documentation of supplies and other inputs, detailed procedures for each step of the manufacturing process, and the storage and internal delivery of materials. The accrediting body rigorously inspects the organization's operations and, if the operations are satisfactory, grants certification to the particular standard. The organization must continue to operate within the specific guidelines of the accreditation standard and undergo periodic checks and assessments to retain the accreditation. Note that certification to an ISO standard means that the company is following formalized business standards created by the ISO; it does not mean that the finished products have been tested. ISO certification represents a significant investment of resources for an organization and can cost tens of thousands of dollars per year to maintain. Much of this money goes to train key personnel and purchase equipment, especially if the certification program is focused on quality control itself. The value of such programs is in the return on this investment. Companies often report that using a quality management program such as Six Sigma has saved the organization hundreds of thousands of dollars per project.

Quality-control processes. A typical quality-control function consists of assessing the output of a process using a representative sample. This quality check can be qualitative (observing employee-customer interactions to gauge customer satisfaction) or based on physical measurements (comparing measurements to evaluate the consistency of a machining operation in a factory). Assessments based on actual physical measurements have spawned an entire industry and science based on metrology.

Simply, if the design standard of a particular piece of work calls for accuracy to within 0.0001 inch, then devices must be available that can be used by a trained individual to check the measurements of the product pieces. Precision mechanical devices such as micrometers, scales, and gauges have been largely replaced by programmable digital electronic devices that automatically carry out dimensional analyses on specific parts. These devices are capable of far more precise measurement than even the most skilled of human artisans and have much greater consistency and reliability.

CAREERS AND COURSEWORK

Specialization in quality-control procedures is a growing and very viable career option. Careers range from support and maintenance of quality-control programs to advanced project management in practical applications. Academic careers in quality control are available for those who wish to work on statistical procedures and models for the development of quality-control algorithms and procedures.

Because quality control is a universal concept, it has applications in careers in many fields. Quality-control procedures are used in both simple mechanical production processes and complex computer programming operations. The student who considers a career in quality control will be expected to acquire a sound grounding in mathematics and statistics in order to understand the basic principles of sampling, variance, and other particular features relevant to quality-control procedures. In postsecondary education, the student will be able to specialize in a particular field of study. Many community colleges offer two-year programs designed to prepare a student to become a quality-control specialist. Following completion of the program, the practicing quality assurance technician would be expected to maintain certification through an appropriate association such as the American Society for Quality and to master new and emerging quality-control procedures.

Quality control plays a significant role in many other postsecondary fields of study. Those pursuing a career in one of these fields must acquire a basic understanding of not only quality control but also the specific methodologies used in the particular field. For example, biochemical laboratory procedures require that the practitioner has intimate knowledge of biochemistry as well as the analytical procedures and sampling methods that are used in maintaining the quality standard of the tests being carried out. Similarly, a computer science specialist needs intimate knowledge of computer programming as well as the specific methods that are used to ensure the functional quality of software applications.

SOCIAL CONTEXT AND FUTURE PROSPECTS

Quality control is more an application of knowledge than a tangible product. Sound quality-control practices are founded on the basic human desire to have access to the same goods and services that are available to others. The response of suppliers of those goods and services has been the development of methods to ensure that each unit of a good or service is as uniform as possible. These methods make it possible for sellers to offer virtually identical products to all customers.

The effects and value of quality control are far-reaching, and the absence or failure of quality control has equally far-reaching consequences. One can readily imagine the economic costs if the dependability of products were to decline. The cost per unit produced would rise as the proportion of unusable products increased. In the marketplace, more products would prove to be defective or fail, resulting in greater repair and replacement costs for the producer and consumer. If quality-control mechanisms affected service, resulting in less effective services, consumer satisfaction would also decline.

Quality-control procedures most likely will become an increasingly prominent component of production as more effective methods are developed.

—*Richard M. J. Renneboog, MSc*

Further Reading

Allen, Theodore T. *Introduction to Engineering Statistics and Six Sigma: Statistical Quality Control and Design of Experiments and Systems.* 2nd ed., Springer-Verlag, 2010.

Chorafas, Dimitris N. *Quality Control Applications.* Springer, 2012.

Chua, Chee Kai, Chee How Wong, and Wai Yee Yeong. *Standards, Quality Control, and Measurement Sciences in 3D Printing and Additive Manufacturing.* Academic Press, 2017.

Deming, W. Edwards. *Out of the Crisis.* 1982. MIT Press, 2006.

Ott, Ellis R., Edward G. Schilling, and Dean V. Neubauer. *Process Quality Control: Troubleshooting and Interpretation of Data.* 4th ed., American Society for Quality, 2005.

"Quality Assurance & Quality Control." *ASQ,* asq.org/quality-resources/quality-assurance-vs-control. Accessed 28 Nov. 2021.

Wheeler, Donald J., and David S. Chambers. *Understanding Statistical Process Control.* 3rd ed., Statistical Process Controls Press, 2010.

Ziliak, Stephen T., and Deidre N. McClosky. *The Cult of Statistical Significance: How the Standard Error Costs Us Jobs, Justice, and Lives.* U of Michigan P, 2008.

R

Random-Access Memory (RAM)

ABSTRACT

Random-access memory (RAM) is a form of memory that allows the computer to retain and quickly access program and operating system data. RAM hardware consists of an integrated circuit chip containing numerous transistors. Most RAM is dynamic, meaning it needs to be refreshed regularly, and volatile, meaning that data is not retained if the RAM loses power. However, some RAM is static or nonvolatile.

HISTORY OF RAM

The speed and efficiency of computer processes are among the most areas of greatest concern for computer users. Computers that run slowly (lag) or stop working altogether (hang or freeze) when one or more programs are initiated are frustrating to use. Lagging or freezing is often due to insufficient computer memory, typically random-access memory (RAM). RAM is an essential computer component that takes the form of small chips. It enables computers to work faster by providing a temporary space in which to store and process data. Without RAM, this data would need to be retrieved from direct-access storage or read-only memory (ROM), which would take much longer.

Computer memory has taken different forms over the decades. Early memory technology was based on vacuum tubes and magnetic drums. Between the 1950s and the mid-1970s, a form of memory called "magnetic-core memory" was most common. Although RAM chips were first developed during the same period, they were initially unable to replace core memory because they did not yet have enough memory capacity.

A major step forward in RAM technology came in 1968, when IBM engineer Robert Dennard patented the first dynamic random-access memory (DRAM) chip. Dennard's original chip featured a memory cell consisting of a paired transistor and capacitor. The capacitor stored a single bit of binary data as an electrical charge, and the transistor read and refreshed the charge thousands of times per second. Over the following years, semiconductor companies such as Fairchild and Intel produced DRAM chips of varying capacities, with increasing numbers of memory cells per chip. Intel also introduced DRAM with three transistors per cell, but over time the need for smaller and smaller computer components made this design less practical. By the 2010s, commonly used RAM chips incorporated billions of memory cells.

There are two major categories of random-access memory: static RAM (SRAM) and dynamic RAM (DRAM). Static RAM may be asynchronous SRAM (ASRAM) or synchronous SRAM with a burst feature (SBSRAM). Dynamic RAM may come in one of four types: fast page mode DRAM (FPMDRAM), extended data out DRAM (EDODRAM), extended data out DRAM with a burst feature (BEDODRAM), or synchronous DRAM (SDRAM).

TYPES OF RAM

Although all RAM serves the same basic purpose, there are a number of different varieties. Each type has its own unique characteristics. The RAM most often used in personal computers is a direct descendant of the DRAM invented by Dennard and popularized by companies such as Intel. DRAM is dynamic, meaning that the electrical charge in the memory cells, and thus the stored data, will fade if it is not refreshed often. A common variant of DRAM is speed-focused double data rate synchronous DRAM (DDR SDRAM), the fifth generation of which entered the market in 2020.

RAM that is not dynamic is known as static random-access memory (SRAM). SRAM chips contain many more transistors than their DRAM counterparts. They typically use six transistors per cell: two to control access to the cell and four to store a single bit of data. As such, they are much more costly to produce. A small amount of SRAM is often used in a computer's central processing unit (CPU), while DRAM performs the typical RAM functions.

Just as the majority of RAM is dynamic, most RAM is also volatile. Thus, the data stored in the RAM will disappear if it is no longer being supplied with electricity—for instance, if the computer in which it is installed has been turned off. Some RAM, however, can retain data even after losing power. Such RAM is known as nonvolatile random-access memory (NVRAM).

USING RAM

RAM works with a computer's other memory and storage components to enable the computer to run more quickly and efficiently, without lagging or freezing. Computer memory should not be confused with storage. Memory is where application data is processed and stored. Storage houses files and programs. It takes a computer longer to access program data stored in ROM or in long-term storage than to access data stored in RAM. Thus, using RAM enables a computer to retrieve data and perform requested functions faster. To improve a com-

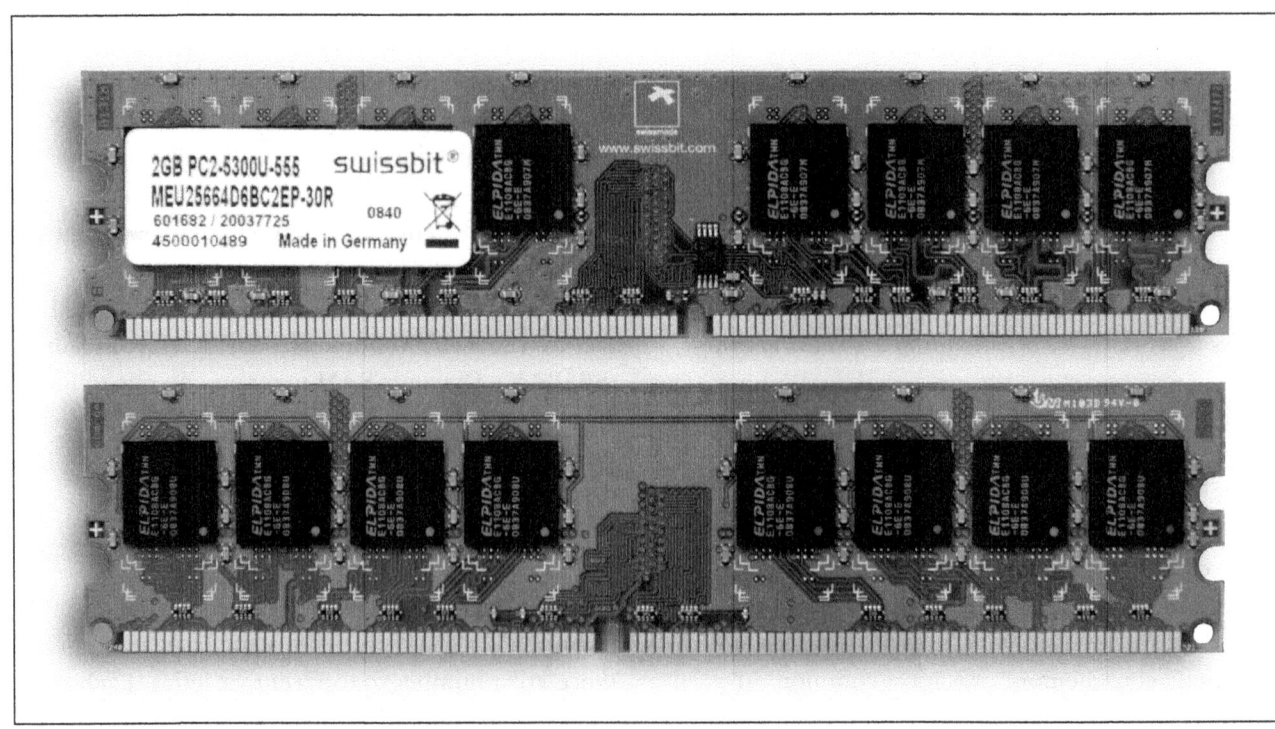

Example of writeable volatile random-access memory: Synchronous Dynamic RAM modules, primarily used as main memory in personal computers, workstations, and servers. Photo by An-d, via Wikimedia Commons.

puter's performance, particularly when running resource-intensive programs such as computer-aided design (CAD) software, a user may replace its RAM with a higher-capacity chip so the computer can store more data in its temporary memory.

SHADOW RAM

While RAM typically is used to manage data related to the applications in use, at times it can be used to assist in performing functions that do not usually involve RAM. Certain code, such as a computer's basic input/output system (BIOS), is typically stored within the computer's ROM. However, accessing data saved in ROM can be time consuming. Some computers can address this issue by copying data from the ROM and storing the copy in the RAM for ease of access. RAM that contains code copied from the ROM is known as shadow RAM.

—*Joy Crelin*

Further Reading

Dieny, Bernard, Ronald B. Goldfarb, and Kyung-Jin Lee. *Introduction to Magnetic Random-Access Memory*. IEEE Press/John Wiley & Sons, 2017.

Hey, Tony, and Gyuri Pápay. *The Computing Universe: A Journey through a Revolution*. Cambridge UP, 2015.

McLoughlin, Ian. *Computer Systems: An Embedded Approach*. McGraw-Hill, 2018.

O'Leary, Timothy, Linda O'Leary, and Daniel O'Leary. *Computing Essentials 2021*. McGraw-Hill, 2020.

Siddiqi, Muzaffer A. *Dynamic RAM: Technology Advancements*. CRC Press, 2013.

"SK Hynix Launches World's First DDR5 DRAM." *HPC Wire*, 7 Oct. 2020, www.hpcwire.com/off-the-wire/sk-hynix-launches-worlds-first-ddr5-dram/. Accessed 28 Nov. 2021.

"What Goes into Meeting the Workstation Requirements for CAD Systems." *Infratech*, 13 Jan. 2019, www.infratechcivil.com/pages/Workstation-requirements-for-CAD-systems-for-autocad-revit. Accessed 28 Nov. 2021.

Reconfigurable Agile Manufacturing

ABSTRACT

The forces of globalization and competition are driving the need for manufacturing companies to be agile in order to stay competitive. The technological enablers of agility, which share a common reconfigurability, include enterprise management systems, engineering systems, manufacturing systems, and manufacturing planning and control systems. The use of computer technology to schedule work in the manufacturing environment, to manage workflow, and to coordinate the movement of materials is essential for many companies that prioritize agility.

OVERVIEW

Prior to the late twentieth century, manufacturers had greater control over the supply chain because they controlled the pace at which products were manufactured and thus when they entered the supply chain. By the first decades of the twenty-first century, however, globalization, competition, and technology converged to the point where manufacturers no longer set the pace and customers rule the markets through their buying power and willingness to purchase from competing manufacturers or suppliers. Many manufacturers scrambled to meet customer demands for options, styles, and features as well as quick fulfillment and fast delivery. Companies that learned how to improve management of their production systems to meet demand, and changes in demand, developed a competitive advantage and worked hard to maintain that advantage.

Amid such changes, the concepts of "lean" and "agile" became increasingly important to industry in the United States and elsewhere. Lean focuses on eliminating or reducing any activity or expenditure that does not add value to a company's operations. Lean worked well enough in high volume, low variety, and predictable environments Agility was born out of necessity to deal with the issues of volatile markets and irregular demand patterns. Manufacturing automation and computer-aided design (CAD) helped to drive the lean and agile movement by allowing reusability of designs and processes and to provide faster reconfiguration of manufacturing systems.

A reconfigurable manufacturing system (RMS) is designed for easy and fast changes in system configuration, including rearrangement of equipment, reallocation of workers, or retooling of machines. To maximize the competitive advantage of an RMS, the manufacturing environment as a whole must be easily upgradeable and have the ability to assimilate new products and rapidly adjust system capacity as market demands change. The manufacturing environment should also have the ability to absorb new process technologies as well as new managerial practices.

Computer technology has enabled the agile movement by allowing reusability of designs and processes and to provide faster reconfiguration of manufacturing systems. Agility and reconfigurable technology allow companies to produce customized products in a short time at low cost. The various computer technologies that improve efficiency and accuracy in manufacturing are becoming ubiquitous in manufacturing industries.

AGILE MANUFACTURING

One of the major goals of agile manufacturing is to produce customized products in a short time at low cost. Agility in manufacturing helps to reduce material costs, maximize expenditures for human resources, minimize idle inventory, and improve facility or machine utilization. Flexibility is the key to productivity in reconfigurable agile manufacturing systems compared to previous designed manufacturing systems.

Agile manufacturing requires control of manufacturing systems as well as a design process that supports a modular manufacturing operation. Thus, to realize the benefits of an RMS and to achieve high levels of agility, consideration must be given to the design of products and components and how that design can best be manufactured in an agile environment.

Design for agility and agile manufacturing requires product grouping which allows for concurrent design and development of product families as well as faster and less expensive manufacturing and assembly systems and processes. The level of agility achieved in a manufacturing environment can thus be improved by addressing the interrelationships between manufacturing components and the design of the items being manufactured.

Another key factor in maximizing the success of agile reconfigurable manufacturing is the scheduling, or delaying of product differentiation in the machining and assembly process. With a delayed product differentiation strategy, common and simple parts are created at the machining stage and put in queue for the assembly stage. This allows the assembly of different or customized products to be grouped and assembly postponed until the schedule requires or when a large enough number of customized products has accumulated so that reconfiguration is convenient or more cost effective. Manufacturing scheduling helps to control costs and maintains profit margin, which is absolutely necessary because, simply put, achieving agility without achieving profit is not a sustainable competitive strategy.

The basic axiom underlying the concept of agility is the ability to respond to change by implementing necessary reconfigurations of manufacturing systems and processes. Some changes can be anticipated such as the need to reconfigure for delayed assembly management. In other cases, a company may plan or create change when installing new technologies. However, some changes such as disruptions in operations cannot be predicted because of supply problems or natural disasters. There are also circumstances that may not only be unpredictable but can also be unprecedented, such as widespread economic downturns, terrorist attacks, or pandemics that cause extensive physical, economic, or social damages.

APPLICATIONS

Building a reconfigurable agile manufacturing system. Agility just does not happen by itself. An agile manufacturing firm needs information systems that inherently support agile business processes as well as agile manufacturing systems. The use of computer numerical control (CNC) manufacturing equipment of all types eases reconfiguration of equipment and helps to minimize the cost of reconfiguration. In addition, the use of technologies that improve efficiency and accuracy can help reduce waste caused by defects in manufacturing, underutilization of resources, or overproduction caused by poor planning.

Agile manufacturing companies rely heavily on automation, including:

- Enterprise information systems that are readily capable of supporting an agile manufacturing environment, most commonly achieved through the use of enterprise resource planning (ERP) software suites
- Computerization of the design and manufacturing process through computer-aided design (CAD), computer-aided manufacturing (CAM), and computer-aided engineering (CAE) software
- Computer numerical control (CNC) of individual pieces of equipment as well as groups of equipment
- Computer integrated manufacturing (CIM) systems that connect and integrate the various machines and systems within the manufacturing process
- Supply chain management systems that tie together all of the companies in a supply chain

ERP software. Enterprise resource planning (ERP) systems are integrated software suites that allow data to be used by various different modules within the system. ERP systems are constantly evolving, and functionality has been expanded throughout the early twenty-first century. The ultimate goal of an ERP system is to provide cross-functional support to any department within an organization without that department needing to create new, smaller systems to meet its information processing needs. The implementation of an ERP system often requires standardizing terminology across an organization so that enterprise-wide databases can be established and maintained.

Over a period of several decades, material requirements planning (MRP) systems for inventory control and later manufacturing resource planning (MRPII) technology for shop-floor scheduling and coordination evolved and were integrated into large software suites that could help manage an entire enterprise. The newer ERP systems can help control and manage an entire manufacturing facility, including production, purchasing, finance, human resources, engineering, and logistics.

Computer-aided design and engineering technology. The major technologies driving changes in manufacturing processes during the late twentieth and early twenty-first centuries have been computer-aided design (CAD), computer-aided manufacturing (CAM), and computer-aided engineering (CAE). These systems support the manufacturing process from the engineering phase through production. CAD/CAM workstations provide designers with the ability to use libraries of stored designs as well as information about parts, materials, tooling, and production. These systems help to achieve and maintain modularity, scalability, integrability, and convertibility, which helps streamline design and manufacturing in an economically reusable manner, enabling manufacturers to be more agile.

CAE systems help engineers design a wide variety of products, while CAD systems can help designers document and present their designs using three-dimensional (3D) models and parametric drawings. CAD systems provide specialized support for architects, civil engineers, controls designers, mechanical engineers, manufacturing environments, and fabrication shops. There are also systems that simulate and help to optimize part, mold, and tool designs before manufacturing begins, including designing factory layouts.

CAM systems can translate the designs and specifications created with CAE and CAD systems into production processes using computer numerical control (CNC) features and technologies, which control individual as well as groups of machines that are required to produce an item. These systems can have a positive impact on manufacturing cost, quality, and delivery time. The deployment of equipment with an open architecture design eases system migration, allowing new control features to be added as the equipment and the control technology evolves. CNC technology also provides greater accuracy, and equipment can be operated at higher speeds.

The computers that run the control software for manufacturing machines can also be networked, allowing manufacturing personnel to update systems software or change control programs over the network as opposed to one machine at a time. The CNC systems can also be set up to run self-diagnostics and provide error logs for problems that occur during operation.

CIM systems. Computer-integrated manufacturing (CIM) systems are combinations of hardware and software products that are used to integrate and control manufacturing activities. These systems help to bring together the abilities in CAD and CAM software, CNC machine tools, and material handling equipment. As with CAD and CAM systems, a CIM system must provide flexibility and ease in reconfiguration in order to keep an enterprise agile.

In addition to controlling and scheduling configuration of manufacturing equipment, CIM systems can provide manufacturing support by electronically managing bill of materials, process flow, and bill of process for associated tools, consumables, and components. Materials flow can be managed for each job or product and with materials scheduled and routed to production stations and devices.

Plugging the enterprise into the supply chain. In a supply chain environment, the competitive success of a firm depends on how agile the whole chain is compared to those of competitors. To compete, all of the companies in a supply chain must be agile and deliver products that customers want at competitive price. Data business communication plays a key role in the modern supply chain system by supporting business-to-business (B2B) applications. Supply chain management systems (SCMS) are digitally enabled interfirm processes that integrate information flow, physical flow, and financial flow. Such systems require reliable networks capable of spanning the globe. Implementation of information technology (IT)-based supply chain management systems has been shown to have a positive effect on procurement of materials for production as well as distribution, marketing, and sales after production.

ISSUES

Developing manufacturing standards. Achieving agility in a manufacturing company requires both managers and production workers to understand the goal of agility and develop adaptable philosophies and attitudes towards business strategies as well as day-to-day operations. In addition, most aspects of a twenty-first-century manufacturing environment are digital. Thus, it is essential that both managers and production workers are trained in the use of appropriate technology that can reduce costs and improve quality, especially CAD, CAM, CAE, and CNC systems.

The other necessary element is to understand and adhere to standards that can be used in information exchange, design, and manufacturing and can ease processes, reduce costs, and enable a company to neatly fit into the global manufacturing infrastructure. Managing and utilizing product information and knowledge in the production process enables companies to move faster and be more agile.

Standard for the exchange of product model date (STEP). The standard for the exchange of product model data (STEP) is an International Standards Organization (ISO) standard (ISO 10303) that specifies processes and structures to represent and exchange digital product information. STEP is structured in a way that all essential information about a product can be exchanged between users, including CAD files and product data. The standard has a library of engineering definitions used for the product models in a wide range of industries. The common library covers geometry, topology, tolerances, relationships, attributes, assemblies, configuration and other characteristics. After STEP was developed, the next phase of the standards development process included the addition of STEP NC, which enabled data from CAD systems to be used to input into CNC tools.

STEP replaced an older system, Initial Graphics Exchange Specification (IGES), a system that was used for over thirty years and primarily aided in exchanging data in graphics CAD files. However, early CAD systems used different operating systems and file structures, and CAD files could thus not be used by companies that did not have the same type of equipment that the creator of the CAD work had used.

There are several advantages in using STEP for exchanging and maintaining product data. The use of a standard format supports long-term archiving of technical data for products that have a long life, including heavy equipment such as that used in construction or by the military. In addition, when everyone who works on or provides parts for the equipment receives the same technical data in a standard format, each individual knows where to look for the specific type of information needed to fulfill the relevant role in maintenance or repair.

Structuring the product development and manufacturing process. Another aspect of manufacturing that contributes to agility is implementing a structured product development process. As STEP was implemented, product planning and modeling systems started to use it as a core set of product data to support design and manufacturing.

Product development models are generally broken down into phases. These phases allow designers and producers to structure the development process and enable data management for all of the parts and steps in the manufacturing process. Phases generally include modularization, basic modeling objects, establishing relationship and attributes, identification and completion of constraints, and finally integrating all of the various modules that comprise a product.

Workflow management in the manufacturing process is also essential for smooth operations as well as cost control. Agility in workflow management is achieved by using a dynamic scheduling process for determining when to reconfigure a system or when to use a specific machine on a job in order to meet deadlines and satisfy customer needs. To improve workflow the manufacturing process must be planed, including determination of subprocesses, machining stages, machine and cutting tool selection, and the sequencing of machining operations.

Workflow planning and tool selection has become automated in many companies through the use of simulations and workflow management software. Workflow analysis provides a map of individual tasks that when combined result in a finished product.

When executed in proper sequence, they result in efficiencies and cost savings.

Material flows in a factory are also an important part of efficiency and cost control. One of the primary goals when designing material handling systems is that all work centers are provided with methods to move materials to and from the work center. Material handling systems can include ground conveyors, overhead conveyors, or automated monorails. Many of these systems are integrated into production scheduling systems or workflow management systems.

The development of standards for product data and structured product development models have reduced cost and eased some of the inherent problems that manufacturers face in the design and production processes. These standards and models also enable companies to fit more readily into the global scheme of manufacturing and support their drive to be agile and more competitive.

—*Michael Erbschloe*

Further Reading

Abdi, M. Reza, and Ashraf Labib. "Grouping and Selecting Products: The Design Key of Reconfigurable Manufacturing Systems (RMSs)." *International Journal of Production Research*, vol. 42, no. 3, 2004, pp. 521-46.

Aravind Raj, S., A. Sudheer, S. Vinodh, and G. Anand. "A Mathematical Model to Evaluate the Role of Agility Enablers and Criteria in a Manufacturing Environment." *International Journal of Production Research*, vol. 51, no. 19, pp. 5971-84.

Benyoucef, Lyes, editor. *Reconfigurable Manufacturing Systems: From Design to Implementation*. Springer Nature Switzerland, 2020.

Calvo, R., R. Domingo, R., and M. A. Sebastián. "Systemic Criterion of Sustainability in Agile Manufacturing." *International Journal of Production Research*, vol. 46, no. 12, 2008, pp. 3345-58.

Cummins, Fred. *Building the Agile Enterprise*. Elsevier, 2016.

Doheny, Mike, Venu Nagali, and Florian Weig. "Agile Operations for Volatile Times." *McKinsey and Company*, 1 May 2012, www.mckinsey.com/business-functions/operations/our-insights/agile-operations-for-volatile-times. Accessed 28 Nov. 2021.

Farish, M. "Our Flexible Friends [factory automation]." *Engineering & Technology*, vol. 3, no. 8, 2008, pp. 62-67.

Harris, A. "Reaping the Rewards of Agile Thinking." *Manufacturing Engineer*, vol. 83, no. 6, 2004, pp. 24-27.

Hwang, H. C., and B. K. Choi. "Workflow-Based Dynamic Scheduling of Job Shop Operations." *International Journal of Computer Integrated Manufacturing*, vol. 20, no. 6, 2007, pp. 557-66.

Pham, D., and A. Thomas, A. "Fighting Fit Factories: Making Industry Lean, Agile and Sustainable." *Manufacturing Engineer*, vol. 84, no. 2, 2005, pp. 24-29.

"The STEP Standard." *STEP Tools, Inc.*, 2021, www.steptools.com/stds/step/. Accessed 28 Nov. 2021.

Toller, Jonathan. "The History of Agile Manufacturing." *Kloeckner Metals*, 26 May 2020, www.kloecknermetals.com/blog/agile-manufacturing/. Accessed 28 Nov. 2021.

RECONFIGURABLE MANUFACTURING SYSTEMS

ABSTRACT

Manufacturing organizations need to be able to respond both fully and quickly to the demands of today's rapidly changing marketplace. To enable their production facilities to do this, an increasing number of manufacturing organizations are investing in technology for reconfigurable manufacturing systems. These systems are designed from the outset so that their structure, hardware, and software components can be rapidly changed to adjust production capacity in response to changing market needs.

Reconfigurable manufacturing systems have five key characteristics: modularity, integrability, convertibility, diagnosability, and customization. Research into practical ways to approach the designing of reconfigurable manufacturing systems is underway in many industrialized nations. These approaches include the analytical hierarchical process and the virtual production system approach.

CHANGING DEMANDS FOR MANUFACTURERS

The term "globalization" brings with it thoughts of wider marketplaces and greater opportunities. However, on the heels of such thoughts is the concomitant realization of greater competition. This is compounded by the fact that technology affects virtually every aspect of life, both at home and at the workplace. However, this technology is not static: Technological advances continue to proliferate, and businesses must stay abreast—or even ahead—of the needs of the marketplace in order to not only offer the goods and services that customers want, but also to be able to provide these goods and services at all. In short, technology not only offers opportunities to businesses but challenges as well.

One of the places where this fact is readily seen is in manufacturing companies. Long gone are the days of Henry Ford, when one could have a car in any color "as long as it is black." Contemporary customers want options and alternatives. If one company is unwilling or unable to offer it, its competitors typically are. In some cases, this means that an organization needs to expand its product line or offer new services. In other cases, however, this means that an organization needs to be flexible so that it can meet the demands of a changing marketplace and stay ahead of the competition. For an organization that primarily deals in services, this can be a challenging enough situation requiring the reengineering of business processes or changing of a marketing approach. However, in manufacturing organizations where there is a tangible product, this often means not only that the product needs to be changed, but also that the equipment used to manufacture it must be changed as well. As the twenty-first century progresses, manufacturing organizations will face increasing challenges, including the high frequency introduction of new products and innovations, new product demand and mix, new parts for exiting products, new government regulations, and new process technology. To maintain their competitiveness in this rapidly changing environment, manufacturing organizations will need to be able to respond both fully and quickly to the demands of any of these variables.

MANUFACTURING PARADIGMS AND CLASSIFICATIONS

There are a number of generic paradigms for traditional and conventional manufacturing systems. The dedicated manufacturing system is designed for a fixed process technology in stable market conditions. This manufacturing approach allows the company to manufacture a single product. The flexible manufacturing and cellular manufacturing systems are designed to produce limited product types under predictable market conditions and using an adaptable process.

Manufacturing systems are also often categorized broadly into four major classifications: job shops, mass and continuous production facilities, batch production, and traditional cellular manufacturing. Virtual manufacturing combines the features of jobs shops and traditional cellular manufacturing.

RECONFIGURABLE MANUFACTURING SYSTEMS

Because of the changing demands of the marketplace, an increasing number of manufacturing organizations are investing in technology for reconfigurable manufacturing systems that are designed from the outset so that their structure, hardware, and software components can be rapidly changed to adjust production capacity in response to new market circumstances or alter their functionality to produce a new part of the same part family. Using this philosophy, manufacturing systems will be able to provide organizations with exactly the functionality and capacity needed, exactly when it is needed in response to such rapidly evolving circumstances as changing product demand, the need to produce a new prod-

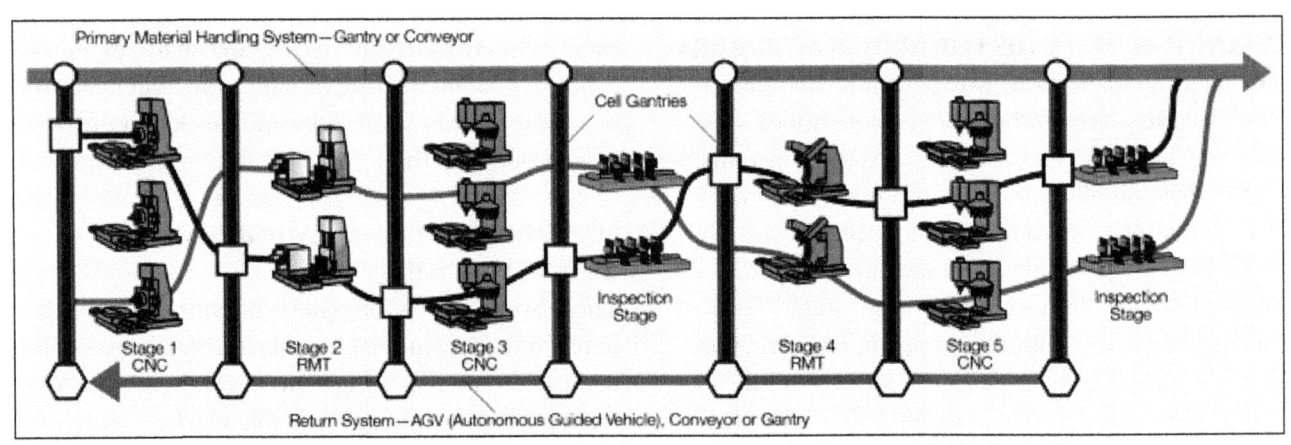

A schematic diagram of a RMS. Image by Rod Hill/University of Michigan, via Wikimedia Commons. [Public domain.]

uct on an existing system, or the need to integrate new process technology into an existing system.

Components that might be changed in a reconfigurable manufacturing system include individual machines, conveyors within a system or mechanisms in individual machines, new sensors, or new controller algorithms. To be useful, reconfigurable manufacturing systems need to be open ended so that they can be improved or upgraded rather than replaced. This approach to system design enables reconfigurable systems to be flexible both for producing a variety of products and for changing the system itself. One of the keys to building this kind of flexibility into the system is to do so from the onset using a modular design for both the hardware and the software that allows the system to be quickly and reliably rearranged to meet changing requirements.

THE ENGINEERING RESEARCH CENTER FOR RECONFIGURABLE MACHINING SYSTEMS

One of the leaders in research on reconfigurable manufacturing systems in the late twentieth and early twenty-first centuries has been the Engineering Research Center for Reconfigurable Machining Systems at the University of Michigan. The center has worked on the development of a type of evolving factory that is designed using a system that allows for reconfiguration of both controls and machines.

The development philosophy for this system has several goals.

- First, the system is being designed to reduce lead time and ramp up time for both the new and later reconfigured systems.
- Second, the system allows for rapid incremental changes to manufacturing capacity to accommodate changing needs of the marketplace.
- Third, the system design allows existing manufacturing systems to be quickly reconfigured to produce new products and parts.
- Finally, the system allows new process technology to be integrated into existing production systems.

CHARACTERISTICS OF RECONFIGURABLE MANUFACTURING

Reconfigurable manufacturing systems have five key characteristics: modularity, integrability, convertibility, diagnosability, and customization. Modularity is required in both the product and process design states to enable the system to produce different product families using common resources related by means of different configurations. A true reconfigurable manufacturing system is rapidly integrated from product to process design and can be rapidly upgraded in process technology to meet new operational requirements. To do this, reconfigurable manufacturing systems replace an existing module with a new module when requirements change and the old configuration is no longer sufficient to meet the demands. In addition, reconfigurable manufacturing systems can be converted to produce new products within a product family or quickly adjusted to produce different predictable or unpredictable capacities.

APPLICATIONS

Research into practical ways to approach designing reconfigurable manufacturing systems is underway in many industrialized nations. Two of these approaches—the analytical hierarchical process and the virtual production system approach—are discussed in the following sections.

Analytical Hierarchical Process

The analytical hierarchical process is a multicriteria decision-making approach that deconstructs a complex problem into a hierarchy that shows the relative importance of each manufacturing alternative using pairwise comparisons. This approach can be applied to select an optimal plant layout configuration (e.g., group technology, transfer lines, functional layout) vis à vis defined objectives and their preferences. As discussed in a 2003 paper published in the *International Journal of Production Research*, researchers M. Reza Abdi and Ashraf Labib performed a research study utilizing an analytical hierarchical process to deconstruct the decision-making process for determining the relative importance of manufacturing alternatives. Design parameters included both conventional considerations (e.g., cost, quality) as well as newer concerns (e.g., responsiveness). A strategy for a reconfigurable manufacturing system was achieved by making trade-offs between the relevant objectives, criteria, and alternatives. This approach was intended to support management strategies for planning and designing systems over their planning horizons.

Process steps. Specifically, the approach comprised six steps:
- First, the strategic objectives and criteria for the evaluation of the manufacturing system were set.
- Second, the decision hierarchy was set that could be used to determine the manufacturing choices that were both feasible and best suited to the nature of the manufacturing system.
- Third, the weight (relative importance) of each attribute was determined using the inputs of the organization's upper-level management.
- Fourth, the criteria, subscriptions, and alternatives were rated vis à vis the next higher objectives or criteria.
- Fifth, the preferred alternatives (i.e., those with the higher ratings) were identified and the solution analyzed with respect to the criteria.
- Finally, a strategy was developed to determine the most viable manufacturing systems across the criteria for the appropriate planning horizon.

Process success. The resultant model was validated in a case study in an actual manufacturing company that produces a large variety of spare parts for the automotive industry. The existing manufacturing system of the company was based on production lines. In the existing system, each line was dedicated to a particular customer. However, the company found that this approach does not provide the flexibility necessary to respond adequately to changes in product designs. In the past, the company tried to increase flexibility by standardizing similar products of different customers at the design stage in an attempt to maintain the existing system without increasing functionality of the product lines.

The use of the analytical hierarchical process helped management of the company better understand the process needed for future investments in manufacturing technology. The process also provided a realistic method to evaluate qualitatively and quantitatively the various aspects of the system options. The authors attributed the strength of the analytical hierarchical process to its use of multiple periods, actors, and criteria. The analytical hierarchical process approach of dividing a far planning horizon into multiple periods (e.g., short-term, medium-term, long-term) both decreases uncertainty and risk over time and also facilitates analysis of the model from the point of view of the various actors. The model is flexible, although not necessarily applicable to all situations.

Virtual Production Systems

There are a number of traditional and conventional approaches to the design of manufacturing systems. These vary on a number of characteristics, including their flexibility toward a changing market. Of these approaches, mass production and batch production manufacturing systems tend to be fairly inflexible and, therefore, less appropriate to many of the constantly changing products in the twenty-first-century marketplace. Two other conventional approaches—the job shop and traditional cellular manufacturing system—do have the potential to meet the demands of a quickly changing marketplace.

Job shops are an approach to manufacturing characterized by irregular material flow patterns, long material handling times, high flexibility, frequent machine set-up times, and low production efficiency. In a job shop, machines are grouped by functions to form departments. Job shops are used to produce a wide variety of products in relatively small volumes.

Traditional cellular manufacturing systems are another approach to manufacturing system design that groups together machines required to produce a family of parts, allowing jobs in the same part family to share machine set-up, thereby reducing overall set-up time for the jobs and reducing travel distance. However, cellular manufacturing also tends to require redundant machines among the various cells.

A cross between these two systems is offered by the virtual manufacturing approach. This is a more recent approach to cellular manufacturing in which the cells are logical rather than physical. Virtual cells are also adaptable and allow the sharing of machines and cells. Because the cells are virtual rather than physical, machines within a virtual cell are not necessarily collocated on the shop floor. Virtual manufacturing combines the features of jobs shops and traditional cellular manufacturing.

Procedure for adapting to product mix changes. As reported in a 2004 paper published in the *International Journal of Production Research*, academics Kuo-Cheng Ko and Pius J. Egbelu researched the reconfiguration of existing job shop and batch manufacturing systems in order to develop a systematic procedure to adapt operations in response to changes in the product mix. Their research indicated that there are efficiencies to be gained in using the virtual manufacturing system philosophy even when it was not possible to rearrange the shop layout.

To apply the virtual cell approach to an existing system, one must first define the initial job shop and the initial traditional cellular manufacturing configurations including machine locations. To develop a new product mix, the next step is to form virtual cells and form a transport network. An appropriate scheduling method is next developed to schedule the jobs through the cells and the machines.

When this has been done, the next step is to compute the total machine set-up time and travel distance for each configuration. This information is used to combine the processing system and network system configurations to form the basis of various possible manufacturing system configurations.

The weighted performance for each configuration is then computed using a distance-to-time conversion factor, and the configuration with the minimum weighted performance is used until a new product mix is launched. At that point, the system is reconfigured using the same steps.

CONCLUSION

Continuing advances in technology, coupled with the demands of a global marketplace, mean that an organization needs to be flexible in order to quickly adapt to the changing needs of the customer and gain or maintain a competitive advantage. One of the ways that this can be done in manufacturing firms is through the approach of reconfigurable manufacturing systems. These systems are designed so that their structure, hardware, and software components can be rapidly changed to adjust production capacity in response to new market circumstances or alter their functionality to produce a new part of the same part family. This is done through the key characteristics of modularity, integrability, convertibility, diagnosability, and customization. Although research continues to determine better approaches to the design of reconfigurable manufacturing systems, the results to date show this to be a viable approach to meeting the ever-changing needs of the twenty-first-century marketplace.

—*Ruth A. Wienclaw, PhD*

Further Reading

Abdi, M. Reza, and Ashraf Labib. "A Design Strategy for Reconfigurable Manufacturing Systems (RMSs) Using Analytical Hierarchical Process (AHP): A Case Study." *International Journal of Production Research*, vol. 41, no. 10, 2003, pp. 2273-99.

Benyoucef, Lyes, editor. *Reconfigurable Manufacturing Systems: From Design to Implementation*. Springer Nature Switzerland, 2020.

Cazares, A. "Reconfigurable Manufacturing Systems." *Production and Manufacturing Management*, World Technologies, 2012, pp. 101-6.

Ferreira, Paulo, Victoria Reyes, and João Mestre. "A Web-Based Integration Procedure for the Development of Reconfigurable Robotic Work-Cells." *International Journal of Advanced Robotic Systems*, vol. 10, no. 7, 2013, journals.sagepub.com/doi/full/10.5772/54641. Accessed 28 Nov. 2021.

Ko, Kuo-Cheng, and Pius J. Egbelu. "Reconfiguration of a Job Shop to Respond to Product Mix Changes Based on a Virtual Production System Concept." *International Journal of Production Research*, vol. 42, no. 22, 2004, pp. 4641-72.

Malhotra, Vasdev, Tilak Raj, and Ashok Arora. "Evaluation of Barriers Affecting Reconfigurable Manufacturing Systems with Graph Theory and Matrix Approach." *Materials and Manufacturing Processes*, vol. 27, no. 1, 2012, pp. 88-94.

NSF ERC for Reconfigurable Manufacturing Systems, 2021, erc.engin.umich.edu/. Accessed 28 Nov. 2021.

ROBOTICS

ABSTRACT

Robotics is an interdisciplinary scientific field concerned with the design, development, operation, and assessment of electromechanical devices used to perform tasks that would otherwise require human action. Robotics applications can be found in almost every arena of modern life. Robots, for example, are widely used in industrial assembly lines to perform repetitive tasks. They have also been developed to help physicians perform difficult surgeries and are essential to the operation of many advanced military vehicles. Among the most promising robot technologies are those that draw on biological models to solve problems, such as robots whose limbs and joints are designed to mimic those of insects and other animals.

DEFINITION AND BASIC PRINCIPLES

Robotics is the science of robots—machines that can be programmed to carry out a variety of tasks independently, without direct human intervention. Although robots in science fiction tend to be androids or humanoids (robots with recognizable human forms), most real-life robots, especially those designed for industrial use, do not resemble humans physically. Robots typically consist of at least three parts: a mechanical structure (most commonly a robotic arm) that enables the robot to affect either itself or its task environment physically; sensors that gather information about physical properties such as sound, temperature, motion, and pressure; and some kind of processing system that transforms data from the robot's sensors into instructions about what actions to perform. Some devices, such as the search-engine bots that mine the internet daily for data about links and online content, lack mechanical components. However, they are nevertheless often considered robotic because they can perform repeated tasks without supervision.

Shadow Dexterous Robot Hand holding a lightbulb. Photo by Richard Greenhill and Hugo Elias/The Shadow Robot Company, via Wikimedia Commons.

Many robotics applications also involve the use of artificial intelligence (AI). This is a complex concept with a shifting definition, but in its most basic sense, a robot with AI possesses features or capabilities that mimic human thought or behavior. For example, one aspect of AI involves creating parallels to the human senses of vision, hearing, or touch. The friendly voices at the other ends of customer-service lines, for example, are increasingly likely to be robotic speech-recognition devices capable not merely of hearing callers' words but also of interpreting their meanings and directing the customers' calls intelligently.

More advanced AI applications give robots the ability to assess their environmental conditions, make decisions, and independently develop efficient plans of action for their situations—and then modify these plans as circumstances change. Chess-playing robots do this each time they assess the state of the chessboard and make a new move. The ultimate goal of AI research is to create machines whose responses to questions or problems are so humanlike as to be indistinguishable from those of human operators. This standard is the so-called Turing test, named after the British mathematician and computing pioneer Alan Turing.

BACKGROUND AND HISTORY

The word "robot" comes from a Czech word for "forced labor" that the Czech writer Karel Èapek used in his 1921 play *R.U.R.* about a man who invents a humanlike automatic machine to do his work. During the 1940s, as computing power began to grow, the influential science-fiction writer Isaac Asimov began applying "robotics" to the technology behind robots. The 1950s saw the development of the first machines that could properly be called "robots." These prototypes took advantage of such new technologies as transistors (compact, solid-state devices that control electrical flow in electronic equipment) and integrated circuits (complex systems of

CAD programs have become crucial to the design of innovative robots with a range of applications. Photo by Steve Jurvetson, via Wikimedia Commons.

electronic connections stamped onto single chips) to enable more complicated mechanical actions. In 1959, an industrial robot was designed that could churn out ashtrays automatically. Over the ensuing decades, public fascination with robots expanded far beyond their actual capabilities. It was becoming clear that creating robots that could accomplish seemingly simple tasks—such as avoiding obstacles while walking—was a surprisingly complex problem.

During the late twentieth century, advances in computing, electronics, and mechanical engineering led to rapid progress in the science of robotics. These included the invention of microprocessors, single integrated circuits that perform all the functions of computers' central processing units; production of better sensors and actuators; and developments in AI and machine learning, such as a more widespread use of neural networks. (Machine learning is the study of computer programs that improves their performance through experience.)

In the twenty-first century, cutting-edge robotics applications are being developed by an interdisciplinary research cohort of computer scientists, electrical engineers, neuroscientists, psychologists, and others, and combine a greater mechanical complexity with more subtle information processing systems than were once possible. Digital tools such as computer-aided design (CAD) programs have become crucial to the design of innovative robots with a range of applications, while industrial robots themselves could be considered to fall within the broad field of computer-aided manufacturing (CAM).

Homes may not be populated with humanoid robots with whom one can hold conversations, but mechanical robots have become ubiquitous in industry. Also, unmanned robotic vehicles and planes are essential in warfare, search-engine robots crawl the World Wide Web every day collecting and analyzing data about internet links and content, and robotic surgical tools are indispensable in health care. All this is evidence of the extraordinarily broad range of problems robotics addresses.

HOW IT WORKS

Sensing. To move within and react to the conditions of task environments, robots must gather as much information as possible about the physical features of their environments. They do so through a large array of sensors designed to monitor different physical properties. Simple touch sensors consist of electric circuits that are completed when levers receive enough pressure to press down on switches. Robotic dogs designed as toys, for example, may have touch sensors in their backs or heads to detect when they are being petted and signal them to respond accordingly. More complex tactile sensors can detect properties such as torque (rotation) or texture. Such sensors may be used, for example, to help an assembly-line robot's end effector control the grip and force it uses to turn an object it is screwing into place.

Light sensors consist of one or more photocells that react to visible light with decreases in electrical resistance. They may serve as primitive eyes, allowing unmanned robotic vehicles, for example, to detect the bright white lines that demarcate parking spaces and maneuver between them. Reflectance sensors emit beams of infrared light, measuring the amounts of that light that reflect back from nearby surfaces. They can detect the presence of objects in front of robots and calculate the distances between the robots and the objects—allowing the robots either to follow or to avoid the objects. Temperature sensors rely on internal thermistors (resistors that react to high temperatures with decreases in electrical resistance). Robots used to rescue human beings trapped in fires may use temperature sensors to navigate away from areas of extreme heat. Similarly, altimeter sensors can detect changes in elevation, allowing robots to determine whether they are moving up or down slopes.

Other sensor types include magnetic sensors, sound sensors, accelerometers, and proprioceptive sensors that monitor the robots' internal systems and tell them where their own parts are located in space. After robots have collected information through their sensors, algorithms (mathematical processes based on predefined sets of rules) help them process that information intelligently and act on it. For example, a robot may use algorithms to help it determine its location, map its surroundings, and plan its next movements.

Motion and manipulation. Robots can be made to move around spaces and manipulate objects in many different ways. At the most basic level, a moving robot needs to have one or more mechanisms consisting of connected moving parts, known as links. Links can be connected by prismatic or sliding joints, in which one part slides along the other, or by rotary or articulated joints, in which both parts rotate around the same fixed axis. Combinations of prismatic and rotary joints enable robotic manipulators to perform a host of complex actions, including lifting, turning, sliding, squeezing, pushing, and grasping. Actuators are required to move jointed segments or robot wheels. Actuators may be electric or electromagnetic motors, hydraulic gears or pumps (powered by compressed liquid), or pneumatic gears or pumps powered by pressurized gas. To coordinate the robots' movements, the actuators are controlled by electric circuits.

Motion-description languages are a type of computer programming language designed to formalize robot motions. They consist of sets of symbols that can be combined and manipulated in different ways to identify whole series of predefined motions in which robots of specified types can engage. Motion-description languages were developed to simplify the process of manipulating robot movements by allowing different engineers to reuse common sets of symbols to describe actions or groups of actions, rather than having to formulate new algorithms to describe every individual task they want robots to perform.

Control and operation. A continuum of robotic control systems ranges from fully manual operation to fully autonomous operation. On the one hand, a human operator may be required to direct every movement a robot makes. For example, some bomb disposal robots are controlled by human operators working only a few feet away, using levers and buttons to guide the robots as they pick up and remove the bombs. On the other side of the spectrum are robots that operate with no human intervention at all, such as the KANTARO—a fully autonomous robot capable of navigating through sewer pipes while inspecting them for damage and obstructions. Many robots have control mechanisms lying somewhere between these two extremes.

Robots can also be controlled from a distance. Teleoperated systems can be controlled by human operators situated either a few centimeters away, as in robotic surgeries, or millions of miles away, as in outer space applications. "Supervisory control" is a term given to teleoperation in which the robots themselves are capable of performing the vast majority of their tasks independently; human operators are present merely to monitor the robots' behavior and occasionally offer high-level instructions.

Artificial intelligence. Three commonly accepted paradigms, or patterns, are used in AI robotics: hierarchical, reactive, and hybrid. The hierarchical paradigm, also known as a top-down approach, organizes robotic tasks in sequence. For example, a robot takes stock of its task environment, creates a detailed model of the world, uses that model to plan a list of tasks it must carry out to achieve a goal, and proceeds to act on each task in turn. The performance of hierarchical robots tends to be slow and disjointed since every time a change occurs in the environment, the robot pauses to reformulate its plan. For example, if such a robot is moving forward to reach a destination and an obstacle is placed in its way, it must pause, rebuild its model of the world, and begin lurching around the object.

In the reactive (or behavioral) paradigm, also known as a bottom-up approach, no planning occurs. Instead, robotic tasks are carried out spontaneously in reaction to a changing environment. If an obstacle is placed in front of such a robot, sensors can quickly incorporate information about the obstacle into the robot's actions and alter its path, causing it to swerve momentarily.

The hybrid paradigm is the one most commonly used in AI applications being developed during the twenty-first century. It combines elements of both the reactive and the hierarchical models.

APPLICATIONS AND PRODUCTS

Industrial robots. In the twenty-first century, almost no factory operates without at least one robot—more likely several—playing some part in its manufacturing processes. Welding robots, for example, consist of mechanical arms with several degrees of movement and end effectors in the shape of welding guns or grippers. They are used to join metal surfaces together by heating and then hammering them, and produce faster, more reliable, and more uniform results than human welders. They are also less vulnerable to injury than human workers. Another common industrial application of robotics is silicon-wafer manufacturing, which must be performed within meticulously clean rooms so as not to contaminate the semiconductors with dirt or oil. Humans are far more prone than robots to carry contaminants on them.

Six major types of industrial robots are defined by their different mechanical designs. Articulated robots are those whose manipulators (arms) have at least three rotary joints. They are often used for vehicle assembly, die casting (pouring molten metal into molds), welding, and spray painting. Cartesian robots, also known as gantry robots, have manipulators with three prismatic joints. They are often used for picking objects up and placing them in different locations, or for manipulating machine tools. Cylindrical robots have manipulators that rotate in a cylindrical shape around a central vertical axis. Parallel robots have both prismatic and rotary joints on their manipulators. Spherical robots have manipulators that can move in three-dimensional (3D) spaces shaped like spheres. SCARA (Selective Compliant Assembly Robot Arm) robots have two arms connected to vertical axes with rotary joints. One of their arms has another joint that serves as a wrist. SCARA robots are frequently used for palletizing (stacking goods on platforms for transportation or loading).

Service robots. Unlike industrial robots, service robots are designed to cater to the needs of individual people. Robopets, such as animatronic dogs, provide companionship and entertainment for their human owners. The Sony Corporation's AIBO (Artificial Intelligence roBOt) robopets use complex systems of sensors to detect human touch on their heads, backs, chins, and paws, and can recognize the faces and voices of their owners. They can maintain their balance while walking and running in response to human commands and also function as home-security devices. Consumer appliances, such as iRobot Corporation's robotic vacuum cleaner, the Roomba, and the robotic lawn mower, the Robomow, developed by Friendly Robotics, use AI approaches to safely and effectively maneuver around their task environments while performing repetitive tasks to save their human users time.

Even appliances that do not much resemble public notions of what robots should look like often contain robotic components. For example, digital video recorders (DVRs) such as TiVos, contain sensors, microprocessors, and a basic form of AI that enable them to seek out and record programs that conform to their owners' personal tastes. Some cars can assist their owners with driving tasks such as parallel parking. An example is the Toyota Prius, which offers an option known as Intelligent Parking Assist. Other cars have robotic seats that can lift elderly passengers or passengers with disabilities inside. In the 2010s, many companies actively explored technologies for autonomous cars (self-driving vehicles), with the goal of making mass-produced models available to the public that would function flawlessly on existing roads. Several prototypes were introduced, although much controversy surrounded the potential hazards and liabilities of such technology, including during the testing stage.

Many companies or organizations rely on humanoid robots to provide services to the public. The Smithsonian National Museum of American History, for example, has used an interactive robot named Minerva to guide visitors around the museum's exhibits, answering questions and providing information about individual exhibits. Other professional roles filled by robots include those of receptionists, floor cleaners, librarians, bartenders, and secretaries. At least one primary school in Japan even experimented with a robotic teacher developed by a scientist at the Tokyo University of Science. However, an important pitfall of humanoid robots is their susceptibility to the uncanny valley phenomenon. This is the theory that as a robot's appearance and behavior becomes more humanlike, people will respond to it more positively—but only up to a point. On a line graph plotting positive response against degree of human likeness, the response dips (the "uncanny valley") as the likeness approaches total realism but does not perfectly mimic it. In other words, while people will prefer a somewhat anthropomorphic robot to an industrial-looking one, a highly humanlike robot that is still identifiably a machine will cause people to feel revulsion and fear rather than empathy.

Medical uses. Robotic surgery has become an increasingly important area of medical technology. In most robotic surgeries, a system known as a master-slave manipulator is used to control robot movements. Surgeons look down into electronic displays showing their patients' bodies and the robots' tool tips. The surgeons use controls attached to consoles to precisely guide the robots' manipulators within the patients' bodies. A major benefit of robotic surgeries is that they are less invasive—smaller incisions need to be made because robotic manipulators can be extremely narrow. These surgeries are also safer because robotic end effectors can compensate for small tremors or shakes in the surgeons' movements that could seriously damage their patients' tissues if the surgeons were making the incisions themselves. Teleoperated surgical robots can even allow surgeons to perform operations remotely, without the need to transport patients over long distances. Surgical robots such as the da Vinci system are used to conduct operations such as prostatectomy, cardiac surgery, bariatric surgery, and various forms of neurosurgery.

Humanoid robots are also used as artificial patients to help train medical students in diagnosis and procedures. These robots have changing vital signs such as heart rates, blood pressure, and pupil dilation. Many are designed to breathe realistically, express pain, urinate, and even speak about their conditions. With their help, physicians-in-training can practice drawing blood, performing cardiopulmonary resuscitation (CPR), and delivering babies without the risk of harm to real patients.

Other medical robots include robotic nurses that can monitor patients' vital signs and alert physicians to crises and smart wheelchairs that can automatically maneuver around obstacles. Scientists are also working on developing nanorobots the size of bacteria that can be swallowed and sent to perform various tasks within human bodies, such as removing plaque from the insides of clogged arteries.

Robot exploration and rescue. One of the most intuitive applications of robotic technology is the concept of sending robots to places too remote or too dangerous for human beings to work in—such as outer space, great ocean depths, and disaster zones. The six successful crewed moon landings of the Apollo program carried out during the late 1960s and early 1970s are dwarfed in number by the unmanned robot missions that have set foot not only on the moon but also on other celestial bodies, such as planets in the solar system. The wheeled robots Spirit and Opportunity, for example, began analyzing material samples on Mars and sending photographs back to Earth in 2004. Roboticists have also designed biomimetic robots inspired by frogs that take advantage of lower gravitational fields, such as those found on smaller planets, to hop nimbly over rocks and other obstacles.

Robots are also used to explore the ocean floor. The Benthic Rover, for example, operates by dragging itself along the seabed at depths up to 2.5 miles below the surface. It measures oxygen and food levels, takes soil samples, and sends live streaming video up to the scientists above. The rover is operated by supervisory control and requires very little intervention on the part of its human operators.

Rescue robots seek out, pick up, and safely carry injured humans trapped in fires, under rubble, or in dangerous battle zones. For example, the US Army's Bear (Battlefield Extraction-Assist Robot) is a bipedal robot that can climb stairs, wedge itself through narrow spaces, and clamber over bumpy terrain while carrying weights of up to three hundred pounds.

Military robots. Militaries have often been among the leading organizations pioneering robotics, as robots have the potential to complete many military tasks that might otherwise prove dangerous to humans. While many projects, such as bomb-removal robots, have proven highly useful and have been widely accepted, other military applications have proven more controversial. For example, many observers and activists have expressed concern over the proliferation of drones, particularly unmanned aerial vehicles (UAVs) capable of enacting military strikes such as rocket or missile launches while going virtually undetected by radar. The US government has used such technology (including the Predator drone) to destroy terrorist positions, including in remote territory that would otherwise be difficult and dangerous to access, but there have also been notable examples of misidentified targets and civilian deaths caused by drone strikes. Opponents of drones argue that the potential for mistakes or abuse of their capabilities is dangerous.

SOCIAL CONTEXT AND FUTURE PROSPECTS
In the twenty-first century, the presence of robots in factories all over the world is taken for granted. Meanwhile, robots are also increasingly entering daily life in the form of automated self-service kiosks and spill-detecting robots at supermarkets, electronic lifeguards that detect when swimmers in pools are struggling, and cars whose robotic speech-recognition software enables them to respond to verbal commands. A science-fiction future in which ubiquitous robotic assistants perform domestic tasks such as cooking and cleaning may not be far away, but many technological limitations must be overcome for that to become a reality. For example, it can be difficult for robots to process multipart spoken commands that have not been preprogrammed—a problem for researchers in the AI field of natural language processing. However, the voice-activated personal assistant software in smartphone and computer operating systems, such as Apple's Siri and Google's Google Assistant, shows how such technology is rapidly evolving.

Robots that provide nursing care or companionship to the infirm are not merely becoming important parts of the health-care industry but may also provide a solution to the problem increasingly faced by countries in the developed world—a growing aging population who need more caretakers than can be found among younger adults. Another area where robots can be particularly useful is in performing dangerous tasks that would otherwise put a human's life at risk. The use of robotics in the military remains a growing field—not only in the controversial use of combat drones, but also for tasks such as minesweeping. Robots are also more and more heavily used in space exploration. In the future, robots may be used in other dangerous fields as well. During the 2014 Ebola outbreak, roboticists discussed the possibility of using robots in future medical emergencies of the type for purposes such as disinfecting contaminated areas, while during the COVID-19 (coronavirus) pandemic in 2020 and 2021, the use of robots in environments such as hospitals and retail warehouses became more widespread.

There are also concerns about the growing use of robots to perform tasks previously performed by humans, however. As robotics technology improves and becomes less expensive, companies may well turn to cheap, efficient robots to do jobs that are typically performed by immigrant human labor, particularly in such areas as agriculture and manufacturing. Meanwhile, some observers are concerned that the rise of industrial and professional service robots is already eliminating too many jobs held by American workers. Many of the jobs lost in the 2008-9 recession within the struggling automotive industry, for example, are gone for good, because costly human workers were replaced by cheaper robotic arms. However, the issue is more complicated than that. In certain situations, the addition of robots to a factory's workforce can actually create more jobs for humans. Some companies, for example, have been able to increase production and hire additional workers with the help of robot palletizers that make stacking and loading their products much faster.

Safety concerns can sometimes hinder the acceptance of new robotic technologies, even when they have proven to be less likely than humans to make dangerous mistakes. Robotic sheep shearers in Australia, for example, have met with great resistance from farmers because of the small risk that the machines may nick a major artery as they work, causing the accidental death of a sheep. Similarly, while fully autonomous vehicles, including self-driving cars, are seen by many automotive and technology companies alike as a major area of innovation, crashes and other accidents by several prototypes in the 2010s drew significant concerns from regulators and the general public. It is critical in the field of robotics not only to develop the technology necessary to make a design a reality but also to understand the cultural and economic landscape that will determine whether a robot is a success or failure.

—M. Lee, BA, MA

Further Reading

Ackerman, Daniel. "Computer-Aided Creativity in Robot Design." *MIT News*, 30 Nov. 2020, news.mit.edu/2020/computer-aided-robot-design-1130. Accessed 28 Nov. 2021.

Floreano, Dario, and Claudio Mattuissi. *Bio-Inspired Artificial Intelligence: Theories, Methods, and Technologies*. MIT Press, 2008.

Hughes, Cameron, and Tracey Hughes. *Robot Programming: A Guide to Controlling Autonomous Robots*. Pearson Education, 2016.

Husband, T. M. "Robots, CAM and O.R." *Journal of the Operational Research Society*, vol. 34, no. 4, 1983, pp. 303-7.

Lynch, Kevin M., and Frank C. Park. *Modern Robotics: Mechanics, Planning, and Control*. Cambridge UP, 2017.

Popovic, Marko B. *Biomechanics and Robotics*. CRC Press, 2013.

Samani, Hooman, editor. *Cognitive Robotics*. CRC Press, 2016.

Siciliano, Bruno, et al. *Robotics: Modeling, Planning, and Control*. Springer-Verlag London, 2009.

Siciliano, Bruno, and Oussama Khatib, editors. *Springer Handbook of Robotics*. 2nd ed., Springer International Publishing, 2016.

Silva Sequeira, João, editor. *Robotics in Healthcare: Field Examples and Challenges*. Springer International Publishing, 2019.

Springer, Paul J. *Military Robots and Drones: A Reference Handbook*. ABC-CLIO, 2013.

Stroehle, Helga. "CAD Design and Robotics: A Great Combination." *PTC*, 22 Feb. 2016, www.ptc.com/en/blogs/cad/cad-design-and-robotics-a-great-combination. Accessed 28 Nov. 2021.

Thomas, Zoe. "Coronavirus: Will Covid-19 Speed Up the Use of Robots to Replace Human Workers?" *BBC*, 19 Apr. 2020, www.bbc.com/news/technology-52340651. Accessed 28 Nov. 2021.

ROLLER-COASTER DESIGN

ABSTRACT

Roller coasters are entertainment rides designed to put the rider through loops, turns, and falls, inducing sudden gravitational forces. The rapid ascents and descents coupled with sharp turns create momentary sensations of weightlessness. One known precursor of roller coasters are seventeenth-century Russian ice slides, which sent riders down a tall, ice-covered incline of roughly 50 degrees. Modern roller coasters can be traced to the late 1800s. As of 2021, California's Six Flags Magic Mountain held the world record for the most roller coasters—nineteen—in a single amusement park.

CONSERVATION OF ENERGY

The law of conservation of energy states that energy can neither be created nor destroyed but can only be converted from one form to another. Roller coasters exploit this law by converting the potential energy gained by the car as it ascends to the top of a hill into kinetic energy as it descends and goes through the turns and loops. The potential energy of the car at the top of the loop is given by $E = m \times g \times h$ where E is the total potential energy (joules), m is the total mass of the car (kg), g is the acceleration due to gravity (9.8 m/s2), and h is the height (m).

Simulation software enables designers to run virtual tests on each roller coaster design to evaluate the ride's ability to withstand the physical stresses to which it will be subjected. Photo via iStock/DougLemke. [Used under license.]

As the car expends potential energy, it is converted into kinetic energy, propelling it forward. In an ideal situation where there is no friction or air drag, the car would travel forever. However, because of friction and other resistive forces, the car decelerates and finally stops when it has expended all its potential energy.

CENTRIPETAL FORCE

Centripetal force is responsible for keeping the rider glued to the seat as the car executes turns and loops and even puts the rider upside down. Centripetal and centrifugal forces act on a body that is traveling on a curved path. Whereas centrifugal force is directed outwards, toward the center of curvature, centripetal force acts inward on the body.

G-FORCE AND LOOP DESIGN

G-forces are nongravitational forces and can be measured using an accelerometer. Humans have the ability to sustain a few times the force of gravity, but deleterious effects are a function of duration, amount, and location of the g-force. Many roller coasters accelerate briefly up to six g, depending on the shapes, angles, and inclines of loops, turns, and hills. Early roller-coaster loops were circles. To overcome gravity, the cars entered the circle hard and fast, which pushed riders' heads continually into their chests as the coaster changed direction. In the 1970s, coaster engineer Werner Stengel worked with National Aeronautics and Space Administration (NASA) scientists to determine how much force riders could safely tolerate. As a result of this and other

Photo via iStock/AleksandarGeorgiev. [Used under license.]

mathematical investigations, he began to use somewhat smoother clothoid loops, which are based on Euler spirals, named for Leonhard Euler. In 2010, using the same equations that describe how planets orbit the sun, mathematician Hanno Essén drew a new and unique series of potential roller-coaster loops. Riders would get the thrilling visual experience of a loop without any of the typical jolting and shaking, because the force that riders would feel pushing them into their seats would stay exactly the same all the way around the loop.

COMPUTER-AIDED ROLLER-COASTER DESIGN
In the first decades of the twenty-first century, roller-coaster designers increasingly used specialized computer software to aid in the design and testing of their coasters. Computer-aided design (CAD) software enabled designers to create three-dimensional (3D) models of the rides and modify the designs as needed in response to feedback. Simulation software enabled designers to run a host of virtual tests on each proposed design in order to evaluate the ride's ability to withstand the physical stresses to which it would be subjected. Such analyses likewise aided designers in ensuring that roller coasters in development would adhere to all relevant safety regulations.

—*Ashwin Mudigonda*

Further Reading
Alcom, S. *Theme Park Design: Behind the Scenes with an Engineer*. Theme Perks Press, 2010.
Koll, Hilary, Steve Mills, and Korey Kiepert. *Using Math to Design a Rollercoaster*. Gareth Stevens Publishing, 2006.
Mason, Paul. *Roller Coaster!: Motion and Acceleration*. Heinemann-Raintree, 2007.
Molitch-Hou, Michael. "Apollo Engineering Takes Amusement Park CAD for a Ride in the Cloud." *Engineering.com*, 28 Mar. 2017, www.engineering.com/story/apollo-engineering-takes-amusement-park-cad-for-a-ride-in-the-cloud. Accessed 28 Nov. 2021.
"Most Rollercoasters in One Theme Park." *Guinness World Records*, www.guinnessworldrecords.com/world-records/69225-most-roller-coasters-in-one-theme-park. Accessed 28 Nov. 2021.
Rutherford, Scott. *The American Rollercoaster*. MBI, 2000.
Weisenberger, Nick. "Coasters-101: What Software Do Roller Coaster Engineers Use?" *Coaster101*, 3 Nov. 2015, www.coaster101.com/2015/11/03/coasters-101-what-software-do-roller-coaster-engineers-use/. Accessed 28 Nov. 2021.

Douglas T. Ross

ABSTRACT
Douglas Taylor Ross (1929-2007) held several positions at the Massachusetts Institute of Technology (MIT), where he led the MIT Computer-Aided Design Project. He is widely credited with originating the term "CAD." Ross later founded the SofTech Corporation in 1969 and served as its president until 1975, when he became chair of SofTech's board of directors.

BACKGROUND
Douglas Taylor Ross was born in Canton, China, on December 21, 1929. His parents, Robert and Margaret, were psychiatrists who were serving as medical missionaries at the time of his birth. When he was six months of age, his family returned to the United States. The family eventually settled in Canandaigua, New York. As a young man in high

school, Ross was heavily involved in music and played piano, saxophone and clarinet. He was also adept at mathematics and sciences. His father died when Ross was eleven, and his mother continued to run the psychiatric hospital where they had been stationed.

When Ross completed high school, he enrolled in Oberlin College, which two of his siblings had also attended. He was attracted by Oberlin's schools of music, theology, mathematics, and science, as well as by the liberal culture of the college, which was historically one of the first US colleges to admit women and people of color. His major course of study at Oberlin was mathematics, and his strong mathematical ability gained him the special privilege of using the upper-class and graduate reading room in the mathematics library; he was the only Oberlin freshman to be accorded that privilege.

Ross married midway through his senior year at Oberlin. He and his wife, Patricia, spent their honeymoon touring various graduate schools, including that at Massachusetts Institute of Technology (MIT). He graduated from Oberlin College with a degree in mathematics in 1951.

MIT

Ross completed a master's degree at MIT in 1954 and a PhD in mathematics in 1956. During his early years at MIT, he was given a teaching assistantship of two units of mathematics when a visiting professor who would normally have taught the course became unavailable. During the summer of 1952, Ross worked a summer job operating a Marchant calculator in the Servomechanisms Laboratory. The Marchant calculator was a mechanical calculating device in which the hundreds of small gears used in its construction were worked in concert with each other to carry out relatively complex calculations. Early models employed a hand crank to operate the gears, and later models used an electric motor to replace the function of the hand crank. In the Servomechanisms Laboratory at MIT, they were being operated to carry out the calculations associated with military airborne fire control systems.

During that same summer, Ross designed what amounted to a computer programming language for which the "computer" was the group of people operating the Marchant calculators. The "language" consisted of a sheet of printed instructions stating what value to enter in a certain location on a Marchant calculator, where to read the calculated values, and where to enter them on a printed data recovery form. The first true computer Ross was involved with during that period in his career was MIT's Whirlwind computer, a computer with a paltry 1024 bytes of memory that was programmed in assembly language. It was with this machine that Ross taught himself how to write an actual computer program.

COMPUTER-AIDED DESIGN (CAD)

Ross continued to work in the Servomechanisms Laboratory for the next seventeen years. During those seventeen years he held several positions at MIT, serving as head of the Computer Applications Group at the Electronics Systems Laboratory and as a lecturer in the Electrical Engineering Department. With his colleagues in the Computer Applications Group, Ross created the Automatically Programmed Tool (APT) programming language, which would play an important role in the development of computer numerical control (CNC) technology.

Beginning in 1959, Ross also served as project engineer for the MIT Computer-Aided Design Project. In that project, Ross and his colleagues sought to "evolve a man-machine system which will permit the human designer and the computer to work together on creative design problems," as noted in Ross's 1960 technical memorandum *Computer-Aided Design: A Statement of Objectives*. In light of his early work and publications on computer-aided design, which he also referred to as computer-aids to design, Ross would later be widely credited with having coined the term "CAD."

LATER YEARS

In 1969, Ross founded the company SofTech, for which he served as president. He held that position until 1975, when he became chair of SofTech's board of directors. While with SofTech, Ross was responsible for developing the software engineering methodology Structured Analysis and Design Technique (SADT).

Ross received a number of prestigious awards throughout his career, including the Prize Paper Award of the Association for Computing Machinery in 1967, the Joseph Marie Jacquard Award of the Numerical Control Society in 1975, and the Society of Manufacturing Engineers' Distinguished Service Award in 1980. He died in Lexington, Massachusetts, on January 31, 2007.

—*Richard M. Renneboog, MSc*

Further Reading

Bi, Zhuming, and Xiaoqin Wang. *Computer Aided Design and Manufacturing*. Wiley-ASME Press, 2020.

"Douglas T. Ross." *Boston Globe*, 5 Feb. 2007, www.legacy.com/us/obituaries/bostonglobe/name/douglas-ross-obituary?id=25676072. Accessed 16 Dec. 2021.

Lee, J. A. N. "Douglas T. Ross." *Computer Pioneers*, 2013, history.computer.org/pioneers/ross.html. Accessed 16 Dec. 2021.

Llach, Daniel Cardoso. *Builders of the Vision: Software and the Imagination of Design*. Routledge, 2015.

Ross, Douglas T. *An Algorithmic Theory of Language*. MIT Press, 1962.

———. *Applications and Extensions of SADT (Structured Analysis and Design Technique)*. SofTech, 1984.

———. *Computer-Aided Design: A Statement of Objectives*. MIT Press, 1960.

———. "Oral History Interview with Douglas T. Ross." Interview with William Aspray. *Charles Babbage Institute*, 21 Feb. 1984, conservancy.umn.edu/handle/11299/107610. Accessed 16 Dec. 2021.

———, and Jorge E. Rodriguez. "Theoretical Foundation for the Computer-Aided Design System." *SIMULATION*, vol. 2, no. 3, 1964, pp. R-3-R-20.

S

SCANDINAVIAN DESIGN

ABSTRACT

Scandinavian design is a way of building and decorating a home or other building that uses light colors, natural elements, and a minimalist style with an emphasis on function. It is based on the style of construction and decor popular in the Scandinavian countries of Europe. The design style was first recognized outside of Scandinavia in the early twentieth century, when it was exhibited in the United States and other countries.

BACKGROUND

Scandinavia is a name used for a collection of neighboring northern European countries that are on or near the Scandinavian Peninsula. The peninsula reaches from the Baltic Sea in the south to the Arctic Circle in the north. It was home to the earliest people in Europe. The countries of Norway, Sweden, Denmark, Finland, Iceland, and sometimes Greenland are considered Scandinavian countries.

The area is harsher in climate than some areas of Europe, and its northern location means that there are long stretches of the year where it is dark and there is little natural light. In addition, the cost of dwellings in the area is higher than in many areas, which results in many people living in smaller homes. These factors, combined with a preference for little clutter and a natural look, led to the Scandinavian design aesthetic.

Scandinavian design originated at the beginning of the twentieth century. People moved away from the ornate, dark design that was typical of the late nineteenth century and began incorporating light colors, sleeker lines, and lighter woods into home decor. The Scandinavians had a longstanding preference for utilitarian decor that was driven partly by the harsh climate and the challenges of procuring resources in the area. Designers using this style began to be noticed. Some of the architects and designers who had a strong influence on the origins of Scandinavian design include Alvar Aalto, Eero Arnio, Arne Jacobsen, and Hans Wegner. Swedish entrepreneur Ingvar Kamprad, who founded the furniture company IKEA when he was seventeen years old, also helped popularize Scandinavian design by making affordable items in that style readily available.

The trend toward light-colored design and clean furniture lines began to grow in the days following World War II (1939-45). A number of postwar conferences were held in Scandinavian countries where the world took notice of the decor. The design style became associated with modernist designs, an association that was strengthened by the establishment of the Lunning Prize for Scandinavian design in 1951. Named after Frederik Lunning, a Danish-born New York importer, the prize was awarded annually for about twenty years to two promising designers who worked with the Scandinavian style. The cash prize given with the award helped promote Scandinavian design by supporting careers and providing recognition to new designers.

The Scandinavian style gained popularity in North America after it was featured in a traveling exhibition that spent three years touring the continent in the late 1950s. After a dip in popularity between the 1960s and 1980s, a renewed interest in minimalism, bright interiors, and sustainability revived attention on the design style. In the early part of the twenty-first century, furniture, household accessories, and other elements of Scandinavian design once again had a strong influence on home decor and design.

In addition to popularizing the Scandinavian design aesthetic, some manufacturers and retailers working within that field engaged in technological experimentation during the first decades of the twenty-first century, to great success. IKEA, for instance, made extensive use of computer technology in its design and manufacturing processes throughout that period, utilizing computer-aided design (CAD), computer-aided manufacturing (CAM), and three-dimensional (3D) printing technologies. By 2021, IKEA included digitally modeled 3D renderings of its products in catalogs rather than photographs of those products, a strategy that enabled the company to save money and resources when compiling catalogs.

OVERVIEW

Scandinavian design focuses on light, bright spaces with minimal clutter. The long, dark stretches of the year in the Scandinavian countries are made more

The Brooklyn Museum's 1954 "Design in Scandinavia" exhibition launched "Scandinavian Modern" furniture on the American market. Photo via Wikimedia Commons. [Public domain.]

bearable by having the walls and other surfaces inside reflect as much light as possible. Walls, ceilings, and furniture are often white, though other colors such as soft greens or pinks may also be used. However, the design aesthetic is not pale or stark. Instead, contrasting colors such as black and brown are often used in bold graphic patterns on pillows and other design pieces. Windows are often left uncovered to allow in as much natural light as possible, and there is special emphasis on the design of the light fixtures that are so important to brightening homes in areas without much natural light. Candles are also often featured in Scandinavian design as a way of increasing warmth and light in the inside environment.

Furniture is often made with simple lines and fashioned from light-colored woods that are left unpainted. Floors, too, are often made of wood and left bare except for throw rugs intended to add coziness to certain areas. Scandinavian-designed furniture also emphasizes function. Functional elements might include using coffee tables with storage and choosing throws that add patterns or color to the space while also providing warmth.

The use of wood is in keeping with the Scandinavian preference for natural materials and eco-friendly design. Scandinavian people generally enjoy outdoor activities and like to bring the outdoors into their homes through plants and other natural design elements. The area is also known for its interest in energy efficiency and being environmentally friendly, so cluttering the home with many pieces of furniture and belongings is not part of Scandinavian style. Instead, pieces are chosen to serve a purpose or multiple purposes. They are selected with an eye toward being in the home for many years.

The overall mission of Scandinavian design is making life better for the people who are spending time in the building. The emphasis on adding brightness to dark areas, using textures and patterns to add interest, and including functional pieces of furniture that require little upkeep are key design elements. All are intended to inspire the Danish ideal of *hygge* (pronounced "hoo-gah"), a cozy mind-state that results from living in an area that is clean and uncluttered but made cozy with lighting and soft furniture.

—*Janine Ungvarsky*

Further Reading

Blundell, Danielle. "The 10 Commandments of Scandinavian Design, According to Experts." *Apartment Therapy*, 29 Sept. 2018, www.apartmenttherapy.com/scandinavian-design-rules-262980. Accessed 28 Nov. 2021.

Briney, Amanda. "Countries of Scandinavia." *Thought Co.*, 10 Dec. 2019, www.thoughtco.com/countries-of-scandinavia-1434588. Accessed 28 Nov. 2021.

Fox, Danielle. "Scandinavian Design vs. Minimalist Design: What's the Difference?" *Elle Decor*, 21 Dec. 2017, www.elledecor.com/design-decorate/trends/a14479450/scandinavian-design-vs-minimalism/. Accessed 28 Nov. 2021.

Hobbs, Jordan. "Why IKEA Uses 3D Renders vs. Photography for Their Furniture Catalog." *CAD Crowd*, 20 Apr. 2021, www.cadcrowd.com/blog/why-ikea-uses-3d-renders-vs-photography-for-their-furniture-catalog/. Accessed 28 Nov. 2021.

"IKEA Design through the Years." *IKEA*, 2021, about.ikea.com/en/about-us/history-of-ikea/ikea-design-through-the-years. Accessed 28 Nov. 2021.

"Kamprad, King of Ikea." *Sweden*, 1 June 2021, sweden.se/life/people/kamprad-king-of-ikea. Accessed 28 Nov. 2021.

Livermore, Sienna. "Everything You Need to Know about Scandinavian Design." *House Beautiful*, 18 Sept. 2018, www.housebeautiful.com/design-inspiration/a23087463/scandinavian-design-style-trends/. Accessed 28 Nov. 2021.

Milliner-Waddell, Jenna. "6 Key Home Pieces to Nail the Scandinavian Design Trend." *Forbes*, 24 Jan. 2019, www.forbes.com/sites/forbes-finds/2019/01/24/key-pieces-to-nail-the-scandinavian-design-trend/#ef0035621f5e. Accessed 28 Nov. 2021.

O'Neill, Meaghan. "How Scandinavian Modern Design Took the World by Storm." *Architectural Digest*, 23 Oct.

2017, www.architecturaldigest.com/story/how-scandinavian-modern-design-took-the-world-by-storm. Accessed 28 Nov. 2021.

"The Philosophy of Scandinavian Design." *Smith Brothers*, smithbrothersconstruction.com/the-philosophy-of-scandinavian-design/. Accessed 28 Nov. 2021.

SKETCHPAD

ABSTRACT
Sketchpad was an intuitive computer graphics program created by Ivan E. Sutherland as part of his doctoral research at the Massachusetts Institute of Technology (MIT). He described the program in his 1963 thesis, Sketchpad, a Man-Machine Graphical Communication System. Sutherland's work proved to be foundational to the development of later computer-aided design (CAD) programs as well as to the concept of the graphical user interface (GUI).

OVERVIEW
In 1963, Ivan Sutherland presented the results of his doctoral research at the Massachusetts Institute of Technology (MIT), a thesis titled *Sketchpad, a Man-Machine Graphical Communication System* in which he described a groundbreaking computer program that would dramatically shape the future of both computer-aided design (CAD) and human-computer interaction. At the time Sketchpad was developed, computer programs were carried out by means of punched cards. Commands and data were communicated to a computer via a device that interpreted the series of punched holes on each card. The system was time-consuming and fraught with the potential for errors, in that a single misplaced hole in a single card, or a card that had been placed out of sequence, could prevent the program from executing. If that occurred, the user would be required to search through the stack of punched cards, which could number in the hundreds, to locate the error and repair the program.

As Sutherland noted, the punched card method was not conducive to graphics applications. Although a punched card program could be produced that would render a static drawing, any change to that drawing required a significant rewriting of the program, no matter how insignificant the change to be made. The aim of Sutherland's Sketchpad program was to allow the user to draw images and make changes to them by selecting points on a display screen. Due to the visual nature of that process, Sketchpad would later come to be considered to feature the first known example of a graphical user interface (GUI), an omnipresent feature of computer programs by the early twenty-first century.

IVAN SUTHERLAND AND SKETCHPAD
Ivan Edward Sutherland was born in Hastings, Nebraska, on May 16, 1938. His father was a civil engineer, and his mother was a teacher. Long intrigued by computer technology, Sutherland completed a bachelor's degree in electrical engineering at Carnegie Mellon University and a master's degree in the same field at the California Institute of Technology. He went on to pursue doctoral studies in electrical engineering at MIT, a major center of research in the burgeoning field of CAD. There, Sutherland developed his doctoral thesis project, which he initially named Robot Draftsman before settling on the name Sketchpad.

Sketchpad was developed on MIT's Lincoln TX-2 computer. The TX-2 included a 9-inch cathode-ray tube (CRT) display and a light pen that allowed the user to select items that appeared on the small display screen. Given the similarity in the way a light pen and a drawing pencil are used, Sutherland felt it should be possible to use the light pen to draw on the screen in much the same way one would draw with a pencil on a sheet of paper.

HOW SKETCHPAD WORKED

Like all computer programs, Sketchpad contained program code for input, output, and computation. Unlike other computer programs, Sketchpad was designed to accept input drawn directly on a display screen, interpret and compute that input, and output the result directly to the display screen. The input was provided using a light pen, which allowed the user to sketch directly on the screen. The user could draw line segments and arcs and then consolidate them into a shape or symbol that could be stored and reused at will. Any number of symbols could be defined in this way, and any change made to a symbol would be automatically reflected in all instances of that symbol. To modify a sketched item—for instance, to delete or move a line segment—the user could select that item using the light pen and then push the appropriate button on a push-button control device used with the computer.

Another important feature of Sketchpad was its ability to maintain topological information about a drawing, such as the connections of lines and other drawing components. This allowed the shape of a drawn structure to be altered while maintaining the integrity of the structure. For example, moving one corner of a rectangle would change the shape of the rectangle, but the result would still be a four-sided figure, as the connections to the other three corners were maintained. Similarly, moving a symbol to another location in the drawing dragged any connections to that symbol along with it.

Conditions within objects in a drawing could be changed by identifying the objects and selecting an assistant function. One example would be to select two nonparallel line segments and make them parallel to each other. With Sketchpad's computational abilities, any condition that could be computed could be added to Sketchpad's repertoire of functions. One could, as Sutherland noted in his thesis, compute the distribution of forces within a structure such as a truss bridge. In practice, composite conditions could be defined by combining a number of individual conditions.

LEGACY OF SKETCHPAD

Though capable of running on the computers of the 1960s, Sketchpad was an application well ahead of its time, in that it would take several years of development for computer technology to progress to the point at which Sketchpad's full potential could be realized. When technology eventually did reach that point, other programs and applications quickly surpassed Sketchpad. However, while the program was quickly superseded by more advanced CAD technologies, Sketchpad's legacy remained vast, rich, and far reaching. Sutherland's experiments with Sketchpad and GUIs enabled the development of point-and-click methods of human-computer interaction that would define the computer technology of the late twentieth and early twenty-first centuries, and the concepts he presented in his thesis would go on to serve as the foundation for essentially all later CAD and graphics programs. Sutherland himself earned widespread recognition for his groundbreaking research and in 1988 was honored with the A. M. Turing Award for his contributions to computer graphics.

—*Richard M. Renneboog, MSc*

Further Reading

Armstrong, Helen, editor. *Digital Design Theory. Readings from the Field*. Princeton Architectural Press, 2016.

"Ivan Sutherland." *A. M. Turing Award*, 2019, amturing.acm.org/award_winners/sutherland_3467412.cfm. Accessed 16 Dec. 2021.

Lee, Ji-Hyun, editor. *Computer-Aided Architectural Design*. Springer, 2019.

MacPherson, Cory. *Inventions in the Visual Arts: From Cave Paintings to CAD*. Cavendish Square, 2017.

Smith, Alvy Ray. *A Biography of the Pixel*. MIT Press, 2021.

Sutherland, Ivan Edward. *Sketchpad, a Man-Machine Graphical Communication System*. 1963. MIT, PhD dissertation.

Solar Panel Design

ABSTRACT
Solar panels are interconnected assemblies of photovoltaic cells that collect solar energy as part of a solar power system, either on Earth or in space. Typically, several solar panels will be used together in a photovoltaic array along with an inverter and batteries to store collected energy. Photovoltaic cells convert the energy of sunlight into electricity via the photovoltaic effect: the creation of electric current in a material when it is exposed to electromagnetic radiation.

HISTORY
The photovoltaic effect, a key principle of solar panel design, was observed by French physicist Alexandre-Edmond Becquerel in 1839. Prior to that time, many scientists and mathematicians built and researched parabolic burning mirrors, which are another way to focus solar energy. Diocles of Carystus showed that a parabola will focus the rays of the sun most efficiently. Archimedes of Syracuse may have built burning mirrors that set ships on fire. George LeClerc, Comte de Buffon, apparently tested the feasibility of such a mirror by using 168 adjustable mirrors in order to vary the focal length to ignite objects that were 150 feet away. Mathematics teacher Augustin Mouchot investigated solar energy in the nineteenth century and designed a steam engine that ran on sun rays. Some consider this invention to be the start of solar energy history.

The first working solar cells were built by the American inventor Charles Fritts in 1883, using selenium with a very thin layer of gold. The energy loss of Fritts's cells was enormous—less than 1 percent of the energy was successfully converted to electricity—but they demonstrated the viability of light as an energy source. Engineer Russell Ohl's semiconductor research led to a patent for what are considered the first modern solar cells, and Daryl Chapin, Calvin Fuller, and Gerald Pearson, working at Bell Labs in the 1950s, developed the silicon-based Bell solar battery. There were fewer than a single watt of solar cells worldwide capable of running electrical equipment at that time. Roughly fifty years later, solar panels generated a billion watts of electricity to power technology on Earth, satellites, and space probes headed to the far reaches of the galaxy.

In the twenty-first century, scientists and mathematicians continue to collaborate to improve solar panel technology. One such focus is on creating scalable systems that are increasingly efficient and economically competitive with various other energy technologies. Professionals in the field make use of a host of technologies and computer-based tools when designing solar panel technology and planning out solar arrays, including computer-aided design (CAD) programs such as AutoCAD and SolidWorks. A CAD software specifically dedicated to solar design, PVCAD Mega, made its debut in 2020.

PHYSICS AND MATHEMATICS OF SOLAR PANELS
In 1905, Albert Einstein published both a paper on the photoelectric effect and a paper on his theory of relativity. His mathematical description of photons (or "light quanta") and the way in which they produce the photoelectric effect earned him the Nobel Prize in Physics in 1921. In general, the photons or light particles in sunlight that are absorbed by semiconducting materials in the solar panel transfer energy to electrons—though some is lost in other forms, such as heat. Added energy causes the electrons to break free of atoms and move through the semiconductor. Solar cells are constructed so that the electrons can move in only one direction, producing electrical flow. A solar panel or array of connected solar panels produces direct current, like chemical batteries, which can be stored. An inverter can convert the direct current to alternating current for household use.

A CAD software specifically dedicated to solar design, PVCAD Mega, made its debut in 2020. Photo via iStock/baranozdemir. [Used under license.]

Mathematics is involved in many aspects of solar panel design, operation, and installation. For example, the perimeter of an array of multiple solar panels may change with rearrangement of the panels, but the area stays the same. Since area is one critical variable for power collection, this suggests different optimal arrangements for surfaces where solar panels might be arranged, like walls and roofs. Satellites often use folding arrays of solar panels that deploy after launch, and folding portable solar panel arrays have been designed for applications like camping and remote or automated research and monitoring stations. Space scientist Koryo Miura developed the Muria-Ori map folding technique, which involves mathematical ideas of flexible polygonal structures and tessellations. It has been incorporated into satellite solar panels that can be unfolded into a rectangular shape by pulling on only one corner.

ARRAYS

A solar panel array may be fixed, adjustable, or tracking. Each method has trade-offs in installation cost versus efficiency and energy over the lifetime of the installation, which can be analyzed mathematically in order to optimize an individual setup. Fixed arrays are solar panels that stay in one position. Optimal positioning of such arrays usually involves facing the equator (true south, not magnetic south, when in the northern hemisphere), with an angle of inclination roughly equal to their latitude. Using an angle of inclination slightly higher than the latitude has been shown in some studies to improve energy collection in the winter, which can help balance shorter days or increased heating energy needs. Setting the inclination slightly less than the latitude optimizes collection for the summer. Adjustable panels can have their tilt manually adjusted throughout the year. Tracking panels follow the path of the sun during the day, on either one or two axes: a single-axis tracker tracks the sun east to west only, while a double-axis tracker also adjusts for the seasonal declination movement of the sun.

Tracking panels may lead to a gain in power, but for some users, the cost trade-off might suggest adding additional fixed panels for some applications instead. Solar power companies and other entities provide maps showing the yearly average daily sunshine in kilowatt hours per square meter of solar panel. Combined with the expected energy consumption of a building, this data helps determine how many solar panels and batteries will be needed for an installation. Science and mathematics teachers often have students build solar panels and collect data to facilitate mathematical understanding and critical thinking, as well as make mathematics, science, and technology connections.

—Bill Kte'pi

Further Reading

Anderson, Edward E. *Fundamentals of Solar Energy Conversion*. Addison Wesley Longman, 1982.

Hull, Thomas. "In Search of a Practical Map Fold." *Math Horizons*, vol. 9, no. 3, 2002, pp. 22-24.

Kryza, Frank. *The Power of Light: The Epic Story of Man's Quest to Harness the Sun*. McGraw-Hill, 2003.

Misbrener, Kelsey. "PVComplete Launches Utility-Scale CAD Solar Design Software." *Solar Power World*, 26 Mar. 2020, www.solarpowerworldonline.com/2020/03/pvcomplete-launches-utility-scale-cad-solar-design-software/. Accessed 28 Nov. 2021.

"Solar Photovoltaic System Design Basics." *Office of Energy Efficiency and Renewable Energy*, www.energy.gov/eere/solar/solar-photovoltaic-system-design-basics. Accessed 28 Nov. 2021.

SolidWorks

ABSTRACT

SolidWorks is a computer-aided design (CAD) software produced by Dassault Systèmes. Used for a variety of CAD and computer-aided engineering (CAE) purposes, SolidWorks is a popular software solution in manufacturing, the automotive industry, and other fields.

UNDERSTANDING SOLIDWORKS

In 1993, engineering professional Jon Hirschtick founded the company SolidWorks Corporation with the goal of producing a new three-dimensional (3D) computer-aided design (CAD) software application that would be capable of running on computers using the Microsoft Windows operating system. The resulting software, SolidWorks 95, was released two years later. The SolidWorks Corporation's move into the CAD software market drew the attention of the French software company Dassault Systèmes, then known for the CAD software computer-aided three-dimensional interactive application (CATIA). Dassault Systèmes purchased the SolidWorks Corporation in 1997 and would continue to develop and market SolidWorks software throughout the first decades of the twenty-first century.

A continually evolving software, SolidWorks was updated annually in the decades following its initial release. SolidWorks 2022, released to the public late in 2021, offered a host of improvements to the software's existing tools and also incorporated fixes to software bugs reported by users. In keeping with its origin as a software designed for use with the Microsoft Windows operating system, SolidWorks continued to be officially supported for Windows use only, although the associated product SolidWorks eDrawings was supported for use with Apple's macOS.

SolidWorks, as its name would suggest, is software primarily designed for solid modeling. That is, the software is used to create digital models of solid objects. However, the software can also be used to create surface models, in which a design's external surfaces are modeled but not its interior, and wireframe models, in which the model exists as a 3D outline. SolidWorks is likewise capable of producing two-dimensional (2D) drawings.

CAD AND CAE
Due to its wide range of functions, SolidWorks is generally considered to be both a CAD software and a computer-aided engineering (CAE) software. CAD and CAE are complementary categories of software. CAD programs are used to produce technical drawings and models that specify the form and structural dimensions of a designed product. A drawing or model, however, is only a 2D- or 3D representation, with no functional characteristics or engineering factors incorporated. CAE software is a computational adjunct to CAD. The CAE software accepts data from the associated CAD program and from user input, and that data is used to compute performance factors and simulate the performance of the designed object. The results of these computations may be used by design engineers to refine the design of the object. CAE software is capable of carrying out various analyses on a design, such as the sensitivity of the design's performance to changes of dimension or other factors, and report results back to the CAD software. One of the greatest advantages of CAD/CAE software such as SolidWorks is the ability to simulate the performance of a design numerically and with animation of the 3D design. In animation, the designer can observe virtually the expected performance of the design according to the parameters of the design being animated.

LICENSING AND SOLUTIONS
SolidWorks is a proprietary software, and users must purchase a license to be able to use the software legally. SolidWorks licenses range from individual user licenses to corporate multiuser licenses. In addition to offering SolidWorks packages for commercial use, Dassault Systèmes offered several additional SolidWorks solutions as of 2021, including solutions designed for research and educational use. The company also offered SolidWorks for Students, a lower-cost package available in both cloud-based and desktop-based editions.

In addition to a host of design and engineering tools, Dassault Systèmes by 2021 offered users of both SolidWorks and the CAD software CATIA access to its 3DEXPERIENCE Marketplace, a means of connecting with vendors and service providers. The marketplace enabled companies to design parts or components in SolidWorks and subsequently hire computer-aided manufacturing (CAM) companies to produce physical versions of those products. In addition, the 3DEXPERIENCE Marketplace likewise offered both SolidWorks and CATIA users the option to search for and select existing 3D models of components that could then be integrated into their in-progress designs. SolidWorks users seeking to search the catalog of components directly from within the SolidWorks software could do so after installing the free 3DExperience Marketplace for SW add-in.

SOLIDWORKS CERTIFICATION
Alongside its software and digital marketplace, Dassault Systèmes operates a SolidWorks Certification Program, which as of 2021 encompassed professional certifications in relevant fields such as design, manufacturing, and education. Designers working in SolidWorks, for instance, could attain certification in disciplines such as mechanical design, model-based design, mold making, and electrical design, among others. Manufacturing offerings including certifications in CAM and in additive manufacturing. Teachers could pursue the SolidWorks Accredited Educator Certification, while students could attain academic versions of a number of the

program's certifications. To become certified, designers and other professionals were tasked with passing an online exam focused on the relevant skill or discipline. Dassault Systèmes presented its SolidWorks certifications as a means of demonstrating one's knowledge of the software and suitability for a career with a company that uses the software in its CAD/CAE/CAM operations.

—*Richard M. Renneboog, MSc*

Further Reading

King, Robert H. *Finite Element Analysis with SOLIDWORKS Simulation*. Cengage Learning, 2018.

Raoufi, Cyrus. *Applied Finite Element Analysis with SolidWorks Simulation*. 4th ed., CYRA Engineering Services, 2021.

Reyes, Alejandro. *Beginner's Guide to SolidWorks 2021: Level 1; Parts, Assemblies, Drawings, PhotoView 360, SimulationXpress and CSWA Preparation*. SDC Publications, 2020.

Shih, Randy, and Paul Schilling. *Parametric Modeling with SolidWorks 2021*. SDC Publications, 2021.

SolidWorks, 2021, www.solidworks.com/. Accessed 16 Dec. 2021.

Tran, Lani. *Mastering Surface Modeling with SolidWorks 2021: Basic through Advanced Techniques*. SDC Publications, 2020.

Spacecraft Engineering

ABSTRACT

Spacecraft engineering is an interdisciplinary engineering field concerned with the design, development, and operation of unmanned satellites, interplanetary probes, and crewed spacecraft. Unmanned satellite missions include commercial communications and remote sensing (including meteorological satellites), scientific research, military communications, navigation, and reconnaissance. Interplanetary probes are used for scientific and exploratory missions. Crewed spacecraft missions carried out by the National Aeronautics and Space Administration (NASA) are largely confined to long-duration assignments at the International Space Station (ISS) and short duration flights in support of the ISS. However, private aerospace companies such as SpaceX and Blue Origin worked to expand the private sector's involvement in spaceflight during the early twenty-first century, overseeing a number of additional crewed missions.

DEFINITION AND BASIC PRINCIPLES

Spacecraft engineering is the process of designing, constructing, and testing vehicles for deployment and operation in the full expanse of space above the earth's atmosphere, generally regarded as beginning at an altitude of 50 miles. Launch vehicles and rocket propulsion are considered part of the related but separate field of rocketry.

Spacecraft have to be robust enough to survive several harsh environments. The vibrational loads generated by the launch vehicle will damage or destroy weak or poorly designed structures. The electronic components must function reliably in a high-radiation environment. All parts of the spacecraft cycle from extreme heat to extreme cold each orbit as the spacecraft moves into and out of the earth's shadow. Outgassing in a vacuum can contaminate solar panels and camera optics. Motion through the plasma of the ionosphere creates potentially damaging static-electric charges.

Energy is expensive in space: It must either be gathered from sunlight from solar panels of limited area or generated from onboard fuel supplies, the exhaustion of which will end the mission. Batteries wear out through repeated charging and discharging and must be managed carefully to last as long as possible. Electrical components must operate with high efficiency and draw as little power as possible; inactive components have to be kept off or in a low-power standby state. Everything must be designed with the knowledge that repairs or replacements will be impossible at worst and difficult, dangerous, and expensive at best.

Batteries, fuel cells, pressure vessels, propulsion systems, and nuclear power modules are all inherently hazardous devices; a launch failure can be catastrophic. All launch ranges operate under rigidly enforced safety standards for the protection of the spacecraft, the launch vehicle, and the personnel working around them. Reliability, survivability, and safety have to be designed into the spacecraft from conception. Rigorous testing throughout the development and manufacturing process plays a major role in spacecraft engineering.

BACKGROUND AND HISTORY

Spacecraft engineering did not exist before the development of the A-4 (more popularly known as the V-2) rocket by the German army during World War II. Both the United States and the Soviet Union integrated technology gotten from captured German scientists, engineers, and rocket hardware into their domestic long-range ballistic-missile development efforts. The primary goal was the development of intercontinental-range ballistic missiles for the delivery of nuclear warheads in case of war. The A-4, however, flew very poorly without the ton of high explosives it was originally designed to carry. The ordnance payload was replaced with scientific instruments for exploration of atmospheric conditions at high altitude and astronomical observations unimpeded by atmospheric interference. The extreme conditions of rocket flight and the harsh environment of space posed new challenges to the instrument developers. Techniques that evolved to meet those challenges laid the foundation for the new field of spacecraft engineering.

In the early years, spacecraft were of necessity small and lightweight. The main challenges were miniaturizing components and operating on small amounts of electrical power. The newly invented

Used by spacecraft engineers throughout its existence, CAD software became an essential tool by the early twenty-first century, facilitating the design, modeling, and testing of crewed spaceships, satellites, probes, and other types of spacecraft. Photo via iStock/gorodenkoff. [Used under license.]

transistor and its packaging into integrated circuits were adopted by spacecraft engineers immediately in spite of their initially high cost. Power came from compact high-performance batteries supplemented by recently developed silicon solar cells to produce electricity from sunlight. The initiation of crewed spaceflight added the challenges of providing a livable environment for the crew and returning them safely to Earth. Spacecraft engineering had to confront the biological issues of providing air, water, and food while disposing of waste products. Long-duration manned missions raised quality-of-life issues such as comfort, privacy, personal hygiene, and physical fitness.

In the 1970s, interplanetary spacecraft ranged far from the sun and strained the capabilities of solar panels to provide sufficient electrical power. Spacecraft engineers harnessed the energy of radioactive decay to power deep-space missions and to keep the spacecraft warm so far from the Sun. Missions to Mercury and Venus, so near the sun, posed the opposite challenge of keeping the spacecraft from overheating. Command, control, and data acquisition from remote platforms with limited power available for broadcasting was likewise a major communications challenge for the spacecraft engineer.

Used by spacecraft engineers throughout its existence, computer-aided design (CAD) software became an essential tool within that field by the early twenty-first century, facilitating the design, modeling, and testing of crewed spaceships, satellites, probes, and other types of spacecraft. In addition to NASA and other nations' space agencies, dedicated users of CAD software for spacecraft-engineering purposes included designers and engineers employed by aerospace companies within the private sector. During the first several decades of the twenty-first century, a number of private aerospace companies established themselves as influential forces in the field, designing rockets as well as autonomous and crewed crafts for use in space missions. One major contributor to the private-spaceflight industry was SpaceX, which, in addition to launching its own space missions, established itself as a supplier of technology and components to NASA.

HOW IT WORKS

Spacecraft. Spacecraft are composed of a payload and a bus. The bus is designed as a major system composed of seven or more subsystems. The electrical power system (EPS) provides the power to operate the active components. The communications system (comms) maintains contact with ground control. The command and data handling system (C&DH) issues electronic commands to all onboard units and collects data from each unit for transmission to the ground. The thermal control system (TCS) regulates the temperatures of all onboard units to keep them within acceptable operating ranges. The attitude control system (ACS) controls the rotational dynamics of the spacecraft to achieve and maintain the required orientation in space. The propulsion system (PS) makes necessary changes in the trajectory of the spacecraft to keep it on course. The structure holds all of the spacecraft components and provides the mechanical support necessary during manufacture, transport, and launch. Crewed spacecraft include additional environmental control and life-support systems (ECLSS). Redundant (duplicate) components and subsystems are used as much as possible to maximize reliability.

Electrical power. The electrical power system is responsible for power generation, capture, or storage, plus delivery of conditioned electrical power to all parts of the spacecraft. Power may be generated by onboard reactors such as fuel cells, or captured from sunlight by solar panels. Power from sunlight is stored in rechargeable batteries for later use when the spacecraft is in eclipse, or for times when power demand temporarily exceeds the total available from solar panels alone. Power-conditioning circuits are necessary to provide electricity at the voltage, current, and stability required by individual components.

Communications. Communications, also known as "comms," consists of the antennas, transmitters, receivers, amplifiers, modulators, and demodulators necessary for communications with the ground. Comms may also include equipment for encrypting and decrypting the signal to prevent interception and to block attempts at illegally seizing control of the spacecraft with false messages. Communication must be maintained across distances that may stretch billions of miles in the case of interplanetary probes using signals of modest strength because of the limited amount of electrical power available. Static-free frequency modulation (FM) signals are preferred to minimize errors in transmission. High frequencies, on the order of billions of cycles per second, allow large amounts of data to be moved quickly. Spacecraft engineers are also experimenting with internet-type communications protocols, as well as laser communication systems that encode data onto a beam of light.

Command and data handling. The command and data handling system centers on the flight computer. The computer monitors the status of all components, turns them on and off in accordance with schedules transmitted up from the ground, and collects housekeeping data from all units and science data from any science packages onboard.

Altitude control system. High-gain antennas must be accurately pointed toward the earth to maintain communications with ground control. Remote-sensing instruments and science packages need to be pointed at their study targets. Crewed spacecraft must maintain proper attitude for safe re-entry. To achieve all of these, the altitude control system senses the orientation of the spacecraft relative to the fixed stars and reorients the spacecraft as necessary to fulfill the mission.

Spacecraft orientation is determined by reference to the sun, the earth, and the brightest stars. The sun and the bright stars can be located optically; the earth can be sensed even during eclipse by the infrared radiation emitted by its warm surface. Interplanetary probes can locate the earth by homing in on the radio signal coming from ground control.

Some spacecraft require three-axis stability where rotation about any axis must be rigorously suppressed. If the spacecraft begins to rotate in an undesired manner, onboard gyroscopes are spun up to absorb the additional rotational momentum and, by reaction, leave the spacecraft as a whole stationary. Many other spacecraft maintain stability by rotation about a fixed axis. Control of the altitude control system is the responsibility of the command and data handling system. When total rotational momentum of the spacecraft gets too large, the excess is eliminated by firing the attitude thrusters in the propulsion system.

Propulsion system. The propulsion system performs occasional maneuvers required to keep Earth-orbiting satellites on station or interplanetary probes on course. The propulsion system consists of rocket thrusters, propellant, pumps, valves, and pressure vessels. Attitude control thrusters control the rotational dynamics of the spacecraft. Course correction thrusters change the speed or direction of motion of the spacecraft. The propellant must be storable for long periods of time under the harsh conditions of space. Special pressurization techniques are necessary to move liquid propellants from tanks to thrusters in zero gravity. The spacecraft must carry enough propellant for the planned mission lifetime plus a reserve necessary for deorbit at end of life.

Structure. Spacecraft structures must satisfy the competing requirements of strength and low weight. Spacecraft structures must not bend or sag under the acceleration loads experienced during launch. Nuts and bolts must contain a locking feature to prevent them from loosening under vibrational loads. The mass of the structure plays a passive role in thermal control by conducting heat from warmer to colder parts of the spacecraft.

Thermal control system. The thermal control system uses active and passive methods of moving heat to maintain normal operating temperatures for critical components. Active methods include the use of heaters to warm cold objects and pump-driven fluids to move heat from hot to cold areas. Passive devices include reflective coatings and insulation.

Environmental control and life-support systems (ECLSS). Life-support systems manage air, water, food, and waste. Humans require a pressurized atmosphere that provides oxygen for respiration and humidity for comfort, while removing carbon dioxide. Too little oxygen leads to hypoxia, while too much leads to oxygen toxicity. Too much carbon dioxide leads to carbon dioxide poisoning. Too little humidity leads to extreme crew discomfort and possibly dangerous electrostatic discharges; too much humidity leads to condensation, which can interfere with electrical systems and nurture the growth of bacteria and fungi. Humans need about 7 pounds of water a day for proper hydration plus an additional 7 pounds for hygiene and housekeeping. Active adults require 2,500 to 5,000 calories a day to function without losing body mass. Corresponding amounts of waste are generated.

Captured waste products must either be recycled, returned to Earth, or dumped overboard. Short-duration flights can be open-loop, that is to say, all the required consumables can be onboard at launch and the waste products dumped overboard or disposed of after landing. The mass involved is prohibitive for long-duration flights. Open-loop systems can continue to be used if regular resupply flights are possible, as is done for the ISS. For crewed missions to Mars, by contrast, resupply would be difficult if not impossible, driving the ECLSS design toward full regenerative recycling, where carbon dioxide is taken up by plants that provide food and oxygen and wastewater is purified and reused. The ISS has an important role as a test bed for these emerging technologies.

APPLICATIONS AND PRODUCTS

Commercial spacecraft. To date, most commercial spacecraft have been communications satellites or remote-sensing satellites. Geosynchronous satellites appear stationary in the sky to an observer on Earth and make radio contact through fixed antennas possible. Television and radio programming sent up from the ground are amplified and rebroadcast to anyone with a line of sight to the spacecraft. Because the satellite never sets, the signal is uninterrupted. These satellites also provide radio and telephone communications for ships at sea and people living in remote locations. The market for these satellites supports a number of spacecraft manufacturers worldwide.

Remote-sensing satellites observe the surface of the earth across a broad range of the electromagnetic spectrum that stretches from radio waves, through the infrared and optical bands, and into the ultraviolet. The oldest and most mature application of remote sensing is in the field of weather forecasting. Infrared and optical photography from space is used in land-use planning, mapping, crop surveys, and pollution monitoring.

Passenger-carrying suborbital spacecraft were under development throughout the early twenty-first century. In July of 2021, the private company Virgin Galactic launched a crewed test flight the commercial craft VSS *Unity*. Later that month, Blue Origin launched the first crewed flight of the craft *New Shepard 4*. Though still experimental in nature, those missions demonstrated the viability of commercial suborbital flight.

Scientific spacecraft. The first US spacecraft, *Explorer I*, made the first major scientific discovery of the space age when it discovered belts of protons and electrons trapped by the earth's geomagnetic field. Discoveries by scientific spacecraft of all nations have profoundly changed mankind's knowledge of the earth and its place in the universe. Interplanetary probes have mapped almost every significant body in the solar system and discovered dozens of planetary moons undetectable from earthbound telescopes. The Hubble Space Telescope has photographed stars at birth, stars at death, and a black hole at the center of the Milky Way. Energy that does not penetrate the earth's atmosphere such as X-rays, gamma rays, and high-energy ultraviolet rays can be studied only from space platforms.

Military spacecraft. Military spacecraft include communications satellites, reconnaissance and surveillance satellites, missile-attack early-warning satellites, and navigation-support satellites such as the global positioning system (GPS) constellation. Military spacecraft are considered force-enhancement or force-support assets. They do not directly engage in hostilities.

CAREERS AND COURSEWORK

Undergraduate study in almost any field of engineering is sufficient entry-level training, but this should be followed up with graduate study at an institution with a strong spacecraft-design program—preferably one with faculty involved in an ongoing spacecraft project. Entry-level jobs are available with spacecraft manufacturers, government space agencies, intelligence agencies, and military departments. Entry into the field is also possible through appointment as a commissioned officer in the armed forces that have assigned space missions and responsibilities.

Upper- and mid-level-management jobs require administrative and budgeting skills that can be acquired on the job but are significantly enhanced by business or financial management courses. These courses can be completed as part of a secondary master's degree, through professional development training, or continuing education. Strong written and oral communication skills are essential.

Most spacecraft development work involves trade secrets and access to classified information. Individuals who cannot qualify for a security clearance, have a bad credit history or a criminal record, or who are not a citizen of the country in which they reside will not readily find employment in this field.

SOCIAL CONTEXT AND FUTURE PROSPECTS

Spacecraft and the services they provide are now part of everyday life. Airliners navigating across oceans and pedestrians navigating city streets rely on GPS devices to find their destinations, and embedded GPS chips in cell phones allow parents to track their children anywhere. Satellites bring television straight to the home and radio straight to the automobile. Public databases allow anyone connected to the internet to acquire a satellite photo of almost any spot on Earth. Accurate long-range weather forecasting exerts a daily influence on almost all business and personal planning. Spacecraft are an indispensable part of the global economic and social infrastructure. This infrastructure must be replaced as it ages and wears out, creating a continuing demand for the services of the spacecraft engineer.

Spacecraft have become so numerous in low-Earth orbit (LEO) that disposal of spacecraft at end of life is a major design challenge for the spacecraft engineer. On February 10, 2009, Iridium-33, a US communications satellite, collided with Cosmos-2251, a defunct Russian military communications satellite. The debris generated by the collision, as well as other debris, threatens other satellites at the same orbital altitude. Future collisions are certain to happen more often as the population of spacecraft increases and are best prevented by deliberately deorbiting nonoperational spacecraft so that they burn up in the atmosphere in reentry or by moving them up to orbits at seldom-used altitudes. Tougher regulation by United States and international agencies is highly probable.

In 2011, NASA shut down the Space Shuttle program, which provided crewed spaceflights to the ISS, with the anticipation that commercial firms would take over that function. Companies such as Boeing and SpaceX received funding from NASA for this purpose, and in 2018, SpaceX provided the first private spacecraft to reach the ISS. SpaceX went on to complete its first crewed mission to the ISS in May of 2020.

—*Billy R. Smith Jr., PhD*

Further Reading

Anderson, John D., Jr., and Mary L. Bowden. *Introduction to Flight*. 9th ed., McGraw-Hill, 2021.

Edwards, Bradley C., and Eric A. Westling. *The Space Elevator: A Revolutionary Earth-to-Space Transportation System*. B. C. Edwards, 2003.

Foust, Jeff. "Will Suborbital Space Tourism Take a Suborbital Trajectory?" *Space News*, 17 Aug. 2021, spacenews.com/will-suborbital-space-tourism-take-a-suborbital-trajectory/. Accessed 28 Nov. 2021.

Goldstein, Phil. "How Computer-Aided Design Is Used in Government." *FedTech*, 24 June 2020, fedtechmagazine.com/article/2020/06/how-computer-aided-design-used-government-perfcon. Accessed 28 Nov. 2021.

Mishkin, Andrew. *Sojourner: An Insider's View of the Mars Pathfinder Mission*. Berkeley Books, 2003.

Seedhouse, Erik. *Tourists in Space: A Practical Guide*. Praxis, 2008.

Sellers, Jerry Jon. *Understanding Space: An Introduction to Astronautics*. Edited by Douglas K. Kirkpatrick, 3rd ed., McGraw-Hill, 2005.

Swinerd, Graham. *How Spacecraft Fly: Spaceflight without Formulae*. Copernicus Books, 2008.

Wall, Mike. "The Private Spaceflight Decade: How Commercial Space Truly Soared in the 2010s." *Space.com*, 20 Dec. 2019, www.space.com/private-spaceflight-decade-2010s-retrospective.html. Accessed 28 Nov. 2021.

SPORTS ENGINEERING

ABSTRACT

Sports engineering is the study of how sports equipment affects performance and safety. Sports engineers use technologies such as three-dimensional (3D) imaging and computer modeling in combination with engineering analysis to optimize the overall performance of athletes and their equipment. The scope of sports engineering includes safety equipment such as helmets and pads, fields and buildings such as hockey arenas, and equipment required for sports such as skis and racquets. Sports engineering is a relatively new discipline, founded as a degree program in 1998 at the University of Sheffield in the United Kingdom. The International Sports Engineering Association (ISEA) was subsequently formed to promote the field of sports engineering and to provide a forum for sports engineers to discuss and collaborate.

DEFINITION AND BASIC PRINCIPLES

Sports engineering is the application of engineering principles to the study of sports equipment and sports venues. This field most closely resembles mechanical engineering. Mechanical engineering uses physics and mathematics to study and design physical processes and mechanical systems and also makes use of a variety of computer-based tools, including computer-aided design (CAD) and simulation software. Sports engineering uses the same techniques to study and design sport-specific equipment and venues. Since the 1990s, sports engineers have been involved in sports as varied as golf, hockey, speed skating, and tennis.

BACKGROUND AND HISTORY

Sports engineering is a relatively new field that was formed as a subdiscipline of mechanical engineering. The best-known sports engineering program is at the University of Sheffield in the United Kingdom. Founded in 1998, the program divides the discipline into the areas of aerodynamics, sports surfaces, impact, and friction. Although the specific field of sports engineering is new, the fundamentals that make up this subdiscipline are based on centuries of study.

The earliest recorded Olympic competition dates back to ancient Greece. As technology improves it has been applied to virtually all sports. Even clothing has advanced to provide sports specific advantages such as improved aerodynamics, breathable fabric, thinner insulating fabrics, and superior waterproofing. Sports engineers also work with the governing bodies of sports organizations to meet the regulations of those specific sports.

The fields of engineering evolved from physics and mathematics. The first societies were formed in the nineteenth century. As the specific field of mechanical engineering evolved, the principles of physics and mathematics were already being applied to sports equipment. Biomechanics and kinesiology developed as specialized fields in the subject of human movement; however, these fields did not specifically address sports equipment. The University of Sheffield provided a focused area of study in sports equipment and venues by founding the sports engineering program along with the Sports Engineering Research Group (SERG). The International Sports Engineering Association (ISEA) was then founded to provide a forum for engineers interested in this subject. There are now a handful of universities around the world that offer degrees in sports engineering and other mechanical engineering programs that offer classes in sports engineering.

HOW IT WORKS

Mechanical engineering applies mathematics and physics to the design and study of physical and mechanical processes. Sports engineering uses mechanical engineering knowledge to focus on the study and design of sports equipment and venues. Refinements in equipment lead to improved performance by athletes as well as improved safety for participants. Regulations of various sports have been modified in order to accommodate new forms of equipment while maintaining fairness between competitors and improving sports safety. It is useful to use the University of Sheffield's divisions of aerodynamics, sports surfaces, impact, and friction to understand the areas of study that make up sports engineering.

Aerodynamics. Aerodynamics uses mathematics and physics to describe and model the airflow around objects. For any sport that uses balls, it is helpful to understand the trajectories that may result under different circumstances to develop techniques for improved accuracy and speed. Aerodynamics also applies to any sports that involve speed. Skeleton, speed skating, bobsledding, sprinting, downhill skiing, and many other sports use specialized equipment and clothing to reduce the effects of air flow on performance.

To study the aerodynamics of sports equipment, there are a variety of techniques that can be employed. Wind-tunnel tests and laser scanners are used in the study of sports aerodynamics along with sophisticated mathematics techniques such as computational fluid dynamics (CFD). Forces such as lift and drag can be calculated using these methods. Variations in surface roughness of a ball or of clothing, spin on a ball, or other factors will change the way an object moves through space. The most familiar example of this is the variation in the behavior of a baseball depending on the pitch.

Sports surfaces. The interactions of athletic shoes or equipment and the sports surface play a large role in performance and can result in injuries. Surfaces may vary even within a sport, such in as tennis and soccer. Information about these interactions is used by shoe manufacturers and other manufacturers to design equipment that will reduce injuries and optimize performance. Traction-test devices are used to simulate conditions in some cases. A traction-test device is simply a shoe surface that is mounted on a plate that can be tested on various surfaces.

There are numerous variables involved in the interactions of surfaces. Each sport has different materials and different requirements for movements on the surface, and there are also inter-athlete differences. The mathematic models needed to study these interactions are so complex that SERG researchers have turned to neural-network modeling to generate information that can be used to design better equipment.

Impacts. One of the most-studied sports has been tennis. The variables of racquet design, swing technique, ball design, and area of the strings used will all change the trajectory and speed of the tennis ball in play. Numerous other sports can be studied in terms of impacts, including baseball, squash, hockey, field hockey, and cricket.

Three-dimensional (3D) ideography and high-speed photography can be used to study the effects of different variables in the impact stage and resulting trajectory of the ball. This information can then be used to refine the athlete's technique and to design more effective equipment.

Friction. Surface characteristics of balls, fields, and other sports equipment will affect sports performance. The interactions between the athlete's skin and grip must be considered in these circumstances in addition to environmental conditions such as moisture. The effects of sports surfaces on human skin are also studied to reduce injuries.

This area of sports engineering has overlap with biomechanics, since it involves the interaction of the skin and other tissues with the sports equipment or sports surface.

Special considerations. There are areas where these SERG divisions will overlap or where specialized knowledge is required. For speed skaters, the interaction of the skate blade and the ice surface creates a melting effect that must be understood in order to design faster skates. There are experts in this specific interaction that are working to improve skate-blade design. For changing conditions such as outdoor skiing or biking, there are different types of equipment that are designed for specific conditions. One example of this is the powder ski, which has different characteristics in terms of shape and design as compared with slalom or downhill skis. The varied requirements for each sport results in a wide array of specialization for sports engineers.

APPLICATIONS AND PRODUCTS

Engineering techniques have been used to improve sports equipment of all types even before there was a designation called "sports engineering." There are many examples of this in sporting history. The pole vault record increased to 6.14 meters as a result of improvements in materials and design during the twentieth century. This was a 53 percent increase from the first official competition. Sports engineering has resulted in improvements in areas as diverse as fly-fishing rods and Frisbees. Amateur, professional, and Olympic competitors have all benefited from improvements in equipment and venues.

Olympic sports. Sports engineering has increasingly been used to improve Olympic-athlete performance. Researchers at the University of Sheffield were credited with helping the British cycling team win four gold medals at the 2004 summer Olympic Games in Athens. Researchers then turned to studying skeleton and used complex modeling and digital shape sampling and processing to improve performances in the 2006 winter Olympic Games in Turin, Italy. Sports engineering can be particularly helpful in those sports where one-hundredth of a second might be the difference between a gold and silver medal.

Amateur sports. Sporting-equipment manufacturers use designers and engineers to produce better-performing shoes, skis, racquets, and other products intended for the general public.

Well-known sports manufacturers hire sports engineers to improve on existing products continually. These improvements have benefited the casual sportsman as well as more serious amateurs.

For example, lighter materials and the development of the oversize tennis racquet in the 1970s made it easier for beginners. Improved materials have increased racquet stiffness, which allows for a more efficient transfer of force to the ball, which leads to faster speeds.

In mountain biking, the addition of front and rear shock absorbers, lightweight frames, improved gearing, and step-in toe clips have made it easier for the less experienced riders to navigate difficult terrain. Similarly, skis and snowboards have evolved to provide increased ease of turning, which helps beginner and intermediate skiers and snowboarders.

Lightweight helmets are now worn by most bikers and skiers, which improves safety. Many of the ski helmets have improved features such as removable inserts for warmth and vents that can be opened or closed for cooling. Wearable water backpacks are now commonplace among many athletes and are more convenient than the standard water bottle.

As of 2021, virtually every sport has benefitted from sports engineering.

Professional sports. Improvements in sports equipment is driven by the demand for increased performance by Olympians and professional athletes. Advances in technology, such as the larger tennis racquet head and increased racquet stiffness, that have benefited amateur tennis players have also benefited professional tennis players. The larger head allows highly skilled professionals to achieve more topspin and higher speeds.

Advanced golf club and ball designs have been used by professional golfers. Differences in weighting and shaft construction influence performance. Golf balls are also evolving with the introduction of solid cores, which lead to longer drives. The dimpling on the golf balls is designed to give maximum flight. These dimples are modified in some newer balls to optimize flights. Equipment improvements have benefited professional sports of all types, and professional organizations continue to push for the technologic edge that will make them more competitive.

Sports venues. Sports engineers are also involved in designing and studying sports venues. An example of this is the development by SERG engineers of a trueness meter for greens evaluation. This is a device that helps greens keepers evaluate the smoothness of turf. This improves the ability of the greenkeeper to achieve optimum conditions for best performance.

Throughout the first decades of the twenty-first century, the National Hockey League (NHL) discussed the need for improved safety to reduce concussions in players. Discussions included possible changes to the glass surrounding the rinks. This type of design change to improve the safety of a sporting venue is an area in which sports engineers may get involved.

Sports safety. Sports-equipment engineering has had an impact on injury prevention at all levels. Helmets have become commonplace for sports such

A tennis racket made of an advanced material such as carbon fibre reinforced plastic can have a larger head than a traditional racket made of wood. Photo by CORE-Materials, via Wikimedia Commons.

as downhill skiing and bicycling, and in sports such as hockey, a helmet is required at both the amateur and professional levels. Baseball is another sport in which a helmet is required for certain positions. In some jurisdictions, bicycle helmets are required by law to be worn by riders under the age of eighteen. Many amateur participants will wear helmets to reduce the chance of injury even if they are not mandatory. There is evidence in the peer-reviewed medical literature that helmet use for sports such as bicycling and hockey does reduce injury. Full facial protection has also been shown to reduce injury in hockey players. In football, another high-contact sport, the first decades of the twenty-first century have seen an increased effort to find a helmet design that can protect players against not only the worst injuries but also the types of injuries that have become of increasing concern for the long-term health of players. The biggest issue facing designers is the prevalence of concussions, which research, sparked by several high-profile deaths and suicides of football players, has increasingly shown can cause long-term brain damage and related psychological trauma.

For venues, sports engineering can be used to modify existing venues or to design newer, safer venues. In the 2010 winter Olympic Games in Vancouver, the death of twenty-one-year-old Georgian athlete Nodar Kumaritashvili during a skeleton run sparked a public debate about the track safety. Some modifications were made shortly after the accident to improve safety, although debate continued about the role of inexperience versus track design as a cause for the accident.

Safety considerations include the durability of equipment and risk of sudden failure of equipment and impact the choice of materials that sports engineers consider when they design sports equipment. These considerations affect athletes at all levels, sporting organizations, governing bodies, and manufacturers.

Clothing. Clothing for high-speed sports has been improved to reduce the drag from air flow. High-tech clothing has been credited with improvements in sprinters, speed skaters, and downhill skiers. Shoes are another area of innovation, with improvements in material durability and performance characteristics. Weight, durability, cushioning, spikes, and flexibility are engineered to provide the best attributes for each sport.

CAREERS AND COURSEWORK

Sports engineering is a newer field compared with other engineering disciplines. There are some university programs that offer a sports engineering degree and others that have courses in sports engineering within their mechanical engineering degree program. Bachelor of engineering degrees will usually require three to five years to complete. A strong background in mathematics and physics is needed. Advanced degrees such as a master's degree or doctorate may be required for some career paths, such as teaching. Specific jobs may require some knowledge of biomechanics, kinesiology, or anatomy.

An interest in sports or a particular skill in sports can be helpful in the field of sports engineering. In some cases, athletes will go on to become sports engineers. For example, British aerospace engineer and Olympic skeleton competitor Kristan Bromley has done research on sled design to optimize performance.

For some applications, additional expertise or training in materials, architecture, physiology, kinesiology, or biomechanics may be needed. This type of specialization might come with an advanced degree or through work experience. The applications of sports engineering are wide ranging, so there are a number of paths an individual career might take.

SOCIAL CONTEXT AND FUTURE PROSPECTS

As sports engineers become more commonplace and sports engineering degree programs are created, this discipline is likely to be more widely recognized as a field separate from mechanical engineering. It is similar to the field of geomatics engineering, which was a branch of civil engineering and is now recognized as a separate field of engineering.

Since the middle of the twentieth century, new sports have evolved through material and design changes. The Frisbee and in-line skates were invented, and snowboarding was created. In Nordic skiing, a new technique called "skate skiing" became popular as a result of technique and equipment changes. This in turn changed the way many Nordic trails are prepared, such that the classic ski tracks are to one side and a larger flat area of packed snow is created for the skate skiers. Skatboarding and skateboard parks are another example of a sport and venue that have become popular as a result of improvements in equipment. These types of innovations will continue to occur in the future with modifications to existing sports and inventions of new sports.

The benefits to amateur and leisure sports will be enhanced comfort, performance, and safety as manufacturers continually improve their products. Entrepreneurs will create new products with the help of sports engineers, who will likely play an important role in the evolution of sports going forward.

—*Ellen E. Anderson Penno, MD, MS, FRCSC, Dip ABO*

Further Reading

Baine, Celeste. *High Tech Hot Shots: Careers in Sports Engineering*. National Society of Professional Engineers, 2004.

Cho, Adrian. "Engineering Peak Performance." *Science*, vol. 305, no. 5684, 2004, pp. 643-44.

Estivalet, Margaret, and Pierre Brisson, editors. *The Engineering of Sport 7*. Vol. 2. Springer, 2009.

Farish, Mike. "Bottoms Up." *Engineering*, vol. 248, no. 3, 2007, pp. 45-47.

Hamilton, Tracy Brown. *Dream Jobs in Sports Equipment Design*. Rosen Publishing Group, 2018.

James, David. "Design Engineering—Managing Technology: Slight Advantage." *Engineer*, 5 May 2008, p. 34.

Moore, Jack. "The Limits of Football Helmets." *The Atlantic*, 5 Feb. 2016, www.theatlantic.com/health/archive/2016/02/super-bowl-football-helmet-concussion/460092/. Accessed 28 Nov. 2021.

Moritz, Eckehard Fozzy, and Steve Haake, editors. *The Engineering of Sport 6: Developments for Disciplines*. Vol. 2. Springer, 2006.

"A Powerful Duo; HPC and Graphene Paving the Way for Cutting-Edge Sports Gear Design." *NIMBIX*, 21 Sept. 2021, www.nimbix.net/blog-graphene-hpc-sports-gear. Accessed 28 Nov. 2021.

Romeo, Jim. "Using 3D Printing to Improve Sports Equipment." *GrabCAD*, 6 July 2020, blog.grabcad.com/blog/2020/07/06/3d-printing-sports-equipment/. Accessed 28 Nov. 2021.

SUBMARINE ENGINEERING

ABSTRACT

Submarines are naval vessels capable of operating beneath the surface of the water. The early models were powered by simple diesel engines, but most modern submarines are nuclear powered. The world's navies operate most of the submarines, which are used as military vessels during wars. The submarine's ability to submerge beneath the waves allows it to hide from adversaries and avoid detection while carrying out its mission. Submarines are also used in civilian scientific capacities to study the deep portions of the ocean inaccessible by traditional diving methods.

DEFINITION AND BASIC PRINCIPLES

Submarine engineering is the field of designing, constructing, and improving submarines to work in their unique environment. Submarines are the only moving human-made objects designed to operate underwater, a hostile environment with many hazards and potential dangers to both vessel and crew.

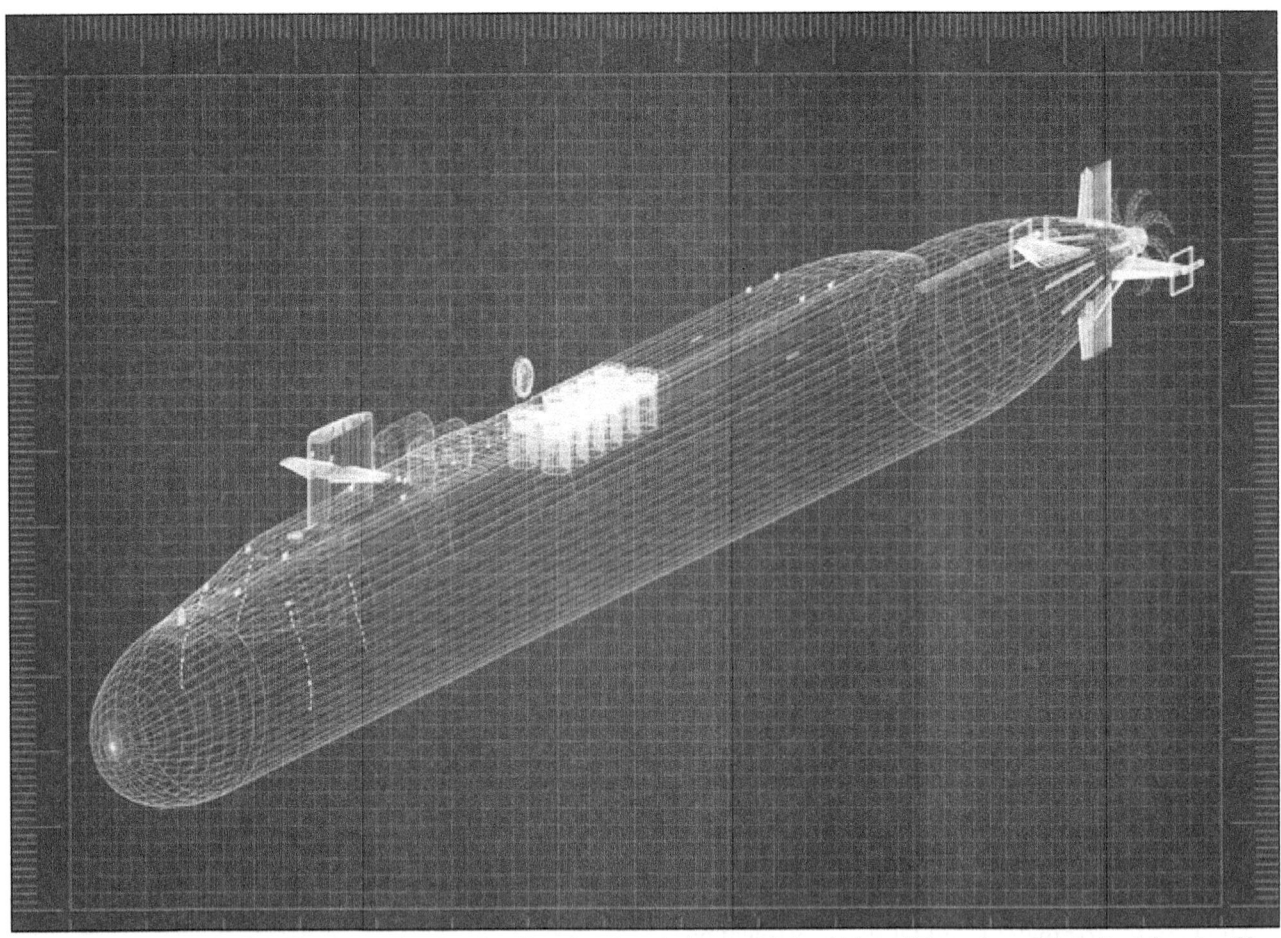

The Naval Undersea Warfare Center created a virtual replica of a submarine's control hub, which could be used to solicit feedback from possible future operators. Photo via iStock/Jelena83. [Used under license.]

In addition, most submarines are weapons of war and must deal with the threat of combat in addition to the perils of the sea. Early submarines were more accurately submersibles, craft that could submerge beneath the surface but that spent most of their time on the surface. Early submarines possessed only limited electric battery power to drive the engines while submerged and had to return to the surface after a relatively short period of time to recharge their batteries. Modern submarines, especially those with nuclear power, are true submarines, spending most of their time submerged and little time on the surface.

As tools of war, the weapons found on submarines have also changed over time to deal with different threats. Early submarines were armed with simple explosive charges on the end of a pole, but the invention of the torpedo in the late nineteenth century gave submarines a long-distance weapon that allowed them to take full advantage of their ability to hide underwater, sneak up on an enemy vessel, and destroy it. By the late twentieth century, submarines came equipped with modern offensive and defensive systems.

Submarines are also used in peaceful pursuits. Small research submarines are ideally suited to explore the depths of the ocean because they can go much deeper than divers equipped with portable sources of oxygen. Because of the intense water pressure found in deep waters, these research submarines must be built very strong. Despite the dangers of operating at depth, submarines have visited even the deepest portions of the ocean, thousands of feet beneath the surface.

BACKGROUND AND HISTORY

Although several inventors tried to construct submarines before the Industrial Revolution, none succeeded because they lacked an effective power source. These early submersibles, such as David Bushnell's *Turtle*, built in 1776, failed because they had to rely on human power. Later, when steam power became available, inventors such as Robert Fulton designed powered submarines, but the steam engines could not work underwater because they needed a source of oxygen for the fires in their boilers.

In 1897, the American inventor John Holland solved most of these problems. His submarines, albeit small, featured two power sources. The submarine had an electric motor that ran on large batteries for operating underwater and a diesel engine for cruising on the surface. The diesel engine also ran a dynamo to recharge the batteries so that the submarine could spend more time underwater. The US Navy, along with agencies from several other countries, purchased Holland's submarine design. By the twentieth century, submarines had matured into advanced weapons of war, and in both World War I and World War II, submarines sank thousands of enemy ships on both sides of the conflict.

The biggest weakness of the submarine was its periodic need to resurface to recharge its batteries. That problem was solved in 1954, when the US Navy commissioned the USS *Nautilus*, the first nuclear-powered vessel in the world. With an unlimited amount of power that did not need an oxygen supply, nuclear-powered submarines could stay submerged indefinitely, and because they did not need to take on diesel fuel, they could also operate at full power indefinitely, allowing them to range across the ocean with little fear of discovery. Innovations of the late twentieth and early twenty-first centuries included the use of computer-aided design (CAD) and simulation software, which aided designers in creating schematics and models of submarines and submarine components. Advances in computer graphics likewise aided submarine engineers in other ways: by 2009, for instance, the Naval Undersea Warfare Center had created a virtual replica of a submarine's control hub, which could be used to solicit feedback from those who would potentially operate the submarine.

HOW IT WORKS

Diving and maneuvering. Submarines, with their ability to operate beneath the surface, require special equipment to disappear below the surface (and come back up) and to maneuver while in the water. On the surface, the submarine operates like a traditional ship, relying on buoyancy to remain afloat and a rudder to maneuver. To submerge, however, submarines need to lose their buoyancy, which is accomplished using ballast tanks. When the submarine is on the surface, the ballast tanks are filled with air. When the air is compressed into tanks and the ballast tanks fill with water, the submarine becomes heavy enough to submerge. Once submerged, the submarine maneuvers using diving planes, small "wings" attached to the hull that direct the water flow past the submarine, to maneuver the submarine up or down. To surface, the submarine blows the stored air back into the ballast tanks, and the submarine rises. In the late 2010s, scientists began experimenting with electromagnetic propulsion systems. That kind of system could take up less space in the submarine and make it quieter.

Propulsion. Early submarines required two things that limited their range and ability to stay underwater: air and battery power. Large battery arrays allowed submarines to remain submerged but only for a limited time. Submarines had to use their diesel engines to recharge the batteries, but the diesel engines needed air, so the recharging had to occur on the surface. The advent of nuclear power in the 1950s, however, removed the major limitations on propulsion. Nuclear power plants did not need air to operate, and the nuclear submarine's steam turbine did not need batteries. Because of these features, some modern submarines are employed on missions during which they may not surface for six months or more. By the 1990s, new air-independent propulsion systems permitted the operation of diesel engines underwater without the expense of a nuclear power plant.

Sensors. Early submarines relied on human sight to sense obstacles and targets around them. This led to the creation of the conning tower, a structure built atop the submarine hull that allowed a lookout to view the area around the submarine while the bulk of the vessel remained just below the surface of the water. Once submerged, early submarines were blind and needed other means to find their way. After World War I, submarines used hydrophones, sensitive microphones mounted on the submarine hull, to listen for other ships and submarines around them. By the 1950s, sonar allowed submarines to actively detect other vessels.

Navigation. When early submarines submerged, they lost their ability to navigate because they lacked external reference points, such as the stars, by which to navigate. Submarines had to navigate into the general area of a target, then submerge to conduct their attack. When nuclear submarines began to spend more time submerged than surfaced, however, crews needed a more accurate means of establishing their location, especially after submarines were armed with nuclear missiles that required precise targeting. The solution was inertial navigation, whereby the submarine crew took extremely precise measurements from motion sensors mounted throughout the submarine and used the data relative to the amount of time and direction the submarine had traveled to calculate their location.

Stealth. Submarines can hide beneath the ocean, but that does not mean they are not detectable. Sonar allows aircraft, surface ships, and other submarines to detect the presence of submarines because of the noise they generate. To counter this, submarines strive to be extremely quiet, and all efforts are made to eliminate or suppress noise. Submarine propellers move very slowly to limit cavitation, the creation of air bubbles as the propeller blade moves through the water. A submarine's machinery is placed on racks fitted with rubber cushions so that the machinery vibration is not transmitted into the hull and then into the water. Many submarines are coated on the outside with anechoic tiles, material that absorbs sonar waves instead of bouncing them back.

Shape. Early submarines were shaped like surface craft. They were long and narrow and had a pointed bow to pierce the waves. Although this shape worked well on the surface, it was not suitable for underwater speed, as the hull shape created drag that was not hydrodynamic. When nuclear power permitted submarines to spend virtually all of their time submerged, hull forms began to reflect the change. Early nuclear submarines had hulls with a tubular cigar shape, but by the 1960s, US nuclear submarines had adopted a teardrop shape that emulated the shape of whales, with a bulbous bow and a stern that tapered to a point. This proved to be the most hydrodynamic shape, and all subsequent submarines have copied it.

Armament. The invention of the torpedo in the late nineteenth century made the submarine an effective ship-destroying weapon, but submarines had other weapon systems as well. Most submarines carried a deck gun in the 4- to 6-inch caliber range to deal with unarmed targets. When aircraft became a viable weapon, submarines began to carry light anti-aircraft guns, in the 20- to 40-millimeter caliber range, for self-defense. After nuclear power permitted submarines to stay underwater most of the time, these deck-mounted weapons became unnecessary. Instead, submarines added missiles to their armament. Submarines still used increasingly advanced torpedoes, but by the late twentieth century, they could fire either ballistic missiles armed with nuclear weapons or long-range cruise and antiship missiles.

APPLICATIONS AND PRODUCTS

Military use of submarines. The technological breakthroughs that led to the modern submarine make it the most lethal naval weapons system available to any nation that can afford it. As military craft, submarines fulfill three functions: defending shores, attacking enemy ships and submarines in the open ocean, and launching ballistic missiles.

Small diesel-electric submarines, usually equipped with air-independent propulsion systems, are used for coastal defense and short-range local operations, where their limited diving depth and relatively short operational range is not a limitation. As diesel-electric submarines are less expensive than nuclear-powered submarines, they are most common in the navies of smaller countries with less money to spend on defense.

Larger attack submarines, usually nuclear powered, are used to patrol the open ocean during wartime, searching for and sinking enemy surface ships and submarines. Submarines can sneak up close to possible targets and destroy them with either modern torpedoes or long-range cruise missiles. Because of their stealth features, attack submarines are also often used for intelligence-gathering missions against possible enemies.

The last military use of submarines is as missile carriers. These submarines, known as "ballistic missile submarines," carry a number of long-range ballistic missiles armed with nuclear warheads and act as a reliably safe deterrent to enemy nuclear attack. Land-based nuclear forces are vulnerable because they are visible and therefore vulnerable to enemy attack, but submarine-based missiles hiding and moving beneath the ocean are virtually untraceable. The first ballistic missile submarine, the USS *George Washington*, was commissioned into the US Navy in 1959. A number of countries other than the United States also operate ballistic missile submarines.

Civilian use of submarines. Not all submarine engineering is for military purposes. Technological advances allowed for expanded civilian use of submarines. A number of oceanographic and scientific institutes operate deep diving research submarines, known as "bathyscaphs" or deep submergence research vessels (DSRVs), to explore the depths of the ocean. They are also used for inspection and maintenance of underwater facilities, oil exploration, and salvaging. These scientific submarines are very different from military submarines. Although military submarines must be large in order to range across the oceans, research submarines are typically small, have a limited range, and must be conveyed to their research area by a supporting surface ship. Although military submarines have a relatively limited maximum diving depth, generally about 1,000 feet, research submarines are constructed with thick walls to survive depths significantly deeper. In 1960, a US-Swiss research submarine, the *Trieste*, reached the bottom of Challenge Deep, the deepest point in the world, at a depth of more than 36,000 feet.

The other primary civilian use of submarines is as entertainment and tourism. A number of resorts, especially in the Caribbean, use small submarines to take fee-paying tourists on a short and shallow ride into the ocean. The submarines are popular because they allow the rider to view the ocean and its wildlife in a comfortable, safe environment. The submarine also eliminates the need for bulky scuba gear and being trained in its use. Instead, tourists can simply climb aboard and see much of what a scuba diver would without the expense and inconvenience.

CAREERS AND COURSEWORK

Submarine engineering requires very specialized and advanced training, usually a doctorate, in addition to a number of years of experience in the form of training or apprenticeship. In addition to basic shipbuilding, engineers in the submarine field require advanced training in the particular attributes and challenges of constructing ships designed to go underwater. Materials engineering, especially involving high-tensile steels, is a prime example of a specialized skill required to construct a submarine. Engineering of nuclear power plants is a process separate from ship construction and requires an equal amount of specialized training in the design, use, and handling of nuclear fuels. Because of the myriad subsystems in every submarine, engineering related to submarine construction includes fields ranging from electrical/electronics engineering to environmental engineering and waste management. Coursework required for such a level of engineering involves advanced engineering in a range of subdisciplines, including chemistry, metallurgy, and computer-aided design.

SOCIAL CONTEXT AND FUTURE PROSPECTS

As a military weapon, submarines, especially nuclear ones, are stealthy, capable, and flexible in the missions they can accomplish. They can dominate large areas of ocean, and their ability to carry a variety of weapons systems makes them useful to navies that have them and attractive to navies that want them. As the backbone of a nation's nuclear deterrent force, missile-firing submarines, although expensive, are less vulnerable than land-based systems, guaranteeing their presence in the world's major navies for the foreseeable future.

Civilian submarines are also an area of growing interest. Although scientific submarines have mapped significant portions of the oceans, the majority of the ocean floor remains unexplored. As natural resources on the land become scarcer, humanity will rely more and more on the ocean to fill the need for materials, and the exploration of the ocean will take on even more significance. Civilian submarines also fill the need to educate the public about environmental protection. By providing a view of the ocean and demonstrating its importance to human survival, civilian submarines promote the cause of environmentalism and the preservation of natural resources. In the first decades of the twenty-first-century, civilian submarines grew in number, with ports in areas such as Hawaii and Australia that provide customers with underwater tours. There were also a number of submarines built for private ownership. These are smaller, with the ability to carry only a few passengers at a time, and are intended for recreational use.

—*Steven J. Ramold, PhD*

Further Reading

Burcher, Roy, and Louis Rydill. *Concepts in Submarine Design*. Cambridge UP, 1995.

Chakraborty, Soumya. "Introduction to Submarine Design." *Marine Insight*, 8 Jan. 2021, www.marineinsight.com/naval-architecture/introduction-to-submarine-design/. Accessed 28 Nov. 2021.

Friedman, Thomas. *US Submarines Through 1945: An Illustrated Design History*. Naval Institute Press, 1995.

Friedman, Thomas, and James L. Christley. *US Submarines Since 1945: An Illustrated Design History*. Naval Institute Press, 1994.

Jackson, Joab. "Navy Creates a Virtual World to Test Submarine Design." *CGN*, 24 Aug. 2009, gcn.com/articles/2009/08/24/data-visualization-sidebar-2-navy-sub.aspx. Accessed 28 Nov. 2021.

National Research Council, Committee on Future Needs in Deep Submergence Science. *Future Needs in Deep Submergence Science: Occupied and Unoccupied Vehicles in Basic Ocean Research*. National Academies Press, 2004.

Parrish, Thomas. *The Submarine: A History*. Penguin, 2004.

"Why Is CAD/CAM Crucial in the Design Process?" *BBC*, 4 Nov. 2019, www.bbc.co.uk/programmes/p07sxzpv. Accessed 28 Nov. 2021.

Technical Drawing

ABSTRACT

A technical drawing is a precise representation of a physical object or space drawn to a specific scale of proportions and specifying all dimensions of its subject. There are many different types of technical drawings relating to different fields of endeavor and ranging in complexity.

BASIC TECHNICAL DRAWING

Students in scientific and technical programs learn the most basic types of technical drawing. A student in a science course may be required to include a drawing of the apparatus used for a particular operation such as distillation. A student in a physics course or an electrical trades program may be required to produce a drawing showing the layout of a certain electrical circuit. A student in an art program may be required to produce a drawing of a particular building or the design of the stage for a certain play, and so on. All are types of technical drawings. However, students in courses related to technical trades are generally instructed in fundamental technical drawing, beginning with orthographic representation and isometric projection.

An orthographic representation of an object consists of three views: the front, top, and side. Each view depicts essentially how the object appears as though the viewer is looking directly at it along one of its three major axes (length, width, or depth) using just one eye. As a very simple example, the front, top, and side orthographic views of a cube are simple, two-dimensional (2D) squares. No other parts of the cube can be seen in an orthographic view. But as objects represented in orthographic views become more complex, so too do the orthographic views. The key feature of all such views in an orthographic representation is that only the features of the object that are visible are drawn. Technical drawings using orthographic views are completed by indicating the dimensions of the actual object.

The other fundamental representation used in basic technical drawing is isometric projection. An isometric projection can be thought of as an orthographic view of an object that has been rotated toward the viewer by 15 degrees and then dextrorotated (turned clockwise) by 15 degrees as well. The isometry in an isometric projection is due to the fact that the scale of the drawing along all three-dimensional (3D) axes (length, width, and depth) is the same. An isometric projection is produced by transferring the dimensions of an orthographic drawing point by point to an isometric grid. The isometric grid, typically ruled on isometric graphing paper, is scaled with lines at mutual angles of 120 degrees corresponding to the three axes of the object. Transferring the main dimensions of the object in the orthographic drawing to the isometric grid generates the isometric view of the object in three dimensions, much as it would appear in reality. As with an orthographic view, the more complex the object, the more complex is the isometric drawing.

Orthographic drawings and isometric projections are the foundation of all forms of technical drawing. A completed technical drawing, such as an engineering blueprint or a drawing of a newly designed proprietary device, becomes the legal documentation of its subject, as well as being the key to its reproduction as an actual physical entity.

TRADITIONAL TECHNICAL DRAWING

Traditional, or manual, technical drawing is carried out using a set of precision-made instruments. The first of these is the drafting table. The tops of such tables are made to different dimensions to facilitate their use in different working spaces. Each tabletop is made perfectly even and is often covered with a sheet of dense vinyl that can be replaced when necessary. The tabletops can be tilted to provide a comfortable working position for the draftsperson. Each tabletop is bordered by a precisely engineered and machined hardwood frame. The purpose of this border is to provide a precise match for the second essential drafting tool, the T-square.

A T-square is made to fit squarely to the edge of the drafting table, allowing the draftsperson to draw perfectly parallel horizontal lines. Other lines are generated using standard precision-made 30-60 and 45-90 triangle templates in conjunction with the T-square. Setting the base of the template against the crossbeam of the T-square guarantees that the lines drawn are at precise angles. All other dimension lines in the drawing are made using an appropriate template as a straightedge. Circles are generally drawn using a drafting compass or precision-made circle and ellipse templates. Constructing an ellipse using a drafting compass is a technique that demands definite skill.

The remaining essential tools of basic technical drawing are also the simplest: very sharp pencils and a gum eraser. Through all progressive developments of manual drafting, these are the only tools that have remained constant. All of the other tools of manual drafting have been replaced by the mechanical drafting table. A mechanical drafting table has a precision-engineered articulated arm that ends with two orthogonal straightedges attached to a hub that can be rotated to any desired angle, enabling the draftsperson to make any desired line in the drawing.

The technical drawing itself begins when the draftsperson positions the drawing paper on the drafting table and inscribes a fixed border around it, typically one centimeter from all four sides of the paper. This border defines the area of the drawing that will contain the legal content of the drawing. The legal content of the drawing, as an intellectual property, exists only within the area bounded by the border, regardless of the nature of the drawing. The drawing may be a map, an architectural blueprint, a design for an engineered device, a flow chart, a patent sketch, or something else.

SKETCHING

A sketch is a type of technical drawing that is carried out freehand, without the use of any of the standard drafting tools. It is not meant to be an accurate representation of the subject matter and can be thought of as analogous to the first draft of an essay. Sketching is primarily used to capture the essence of the thing being drawn so that it can be rendered accurately in a formal technical drawing. A sketch may also be used simply as a guide to record the locations and dimensions of certain features of an actual object for comparison to those features in an existing technical drawing.

Since sketching does not employ precise drafting tools, perhaps not even the pencils, sketches appear in a range of quality, depending on the conditions under which they were produced. One can, for example, imagine a technician attempting to sketch the appearance of a part located underneath a large machine while lying supine and trying to make the sketch on a piece of paper held in the palm of one hand. Accordingly, the technique of sketching is intended to minimize the negative effects of environmental conditions. In a formal drawing, straight lines are drawn in a single fluid motion while holding the tip of the pencil against a straight edge and turning the pencil as it moves to keep the line of uniform thickness. But in sketching, straight lines are drawn using short, straight-line segments that one hopes will produce a line that is more-or-less

Drafter at work. Photo via Wikimedia Commons. [Public domain.]

straight overall. Sketching is very much an acquired skill that calls for a great deal of practice.

COMPUTER-AIDED TECHNICAL DRAWING

Manual technical drawing continued to be the only accepted standard of technical drawing until well after computer graphic resolution became equal to that of manual drawing methods. It is still the preferred standard in many areas and applications that do not justify the cost or use of computer-aided drawing. That being said, however, nearly all graphics applications—whether incorporated into office software suites or existing as standalone applications—can be used to generate technical drawings. The benefits of such applications are their low cost and ease of use. Also beneficial is the ability to print out the drawing from any suitable printer on paper of the appropriate size. The applications typically have standard drafting line types and symbols that further enhance their capability as basic drafting implements.

High-end, and therefore high-cost, computer-aided drafting applications have far greater capabilities. Such applications are often referred to as either computer-aided design (CAD) or computer-aided design and drafting (CADD) tools. Software of that type is able to produce precise technical drawings on screen that can then be printed out as hard copies or be maintained as electronic files.

CAD, or CADD, programs allow real-time manipulation of a drawing as an animation through the use of rotation matrix functions. These computational methods demand significant computing power and allow the user to rotate the object being drawn through any angle in three dimensions. This enables designers to observe the function and performance of the object in a simulated environment before the investment is made to produce the object, a process that may itself be very costly due to the materials and production methods required to produce the actual object.

With the object finally designed, CAD/CADD programs have a singularly valuable feature in their ability to interface with other programs such as product lifecycle management (PLM), computer-aided manufacturing (CAM), or computer-aided engineering (CAE) programs. CAM programs, for example, control the operations of production machines such as milling machines, lathes, and 3D printers. By such digital transfer of data, the CAM programs can perform a dimensional analysis of the object from its drawing parameters, determine the order of operations its machinery should carry out to produce the shape of the object, and then direct that machinery in carrying out those operations. This ensures that each unit of the object in question is produced in precisely the same way and to the same dimensions given in the technical drawing. PLM programs are used throughout the lifecycle of a product, from its inception and design to the end of its useful life. CAD programs are of primary importance at the beginning of that lifetime, but less so thereafter.

A large number of CAD/CADD software options are available, spanning a range of costs from free to several thousand dollars annually. Proprietary CAD software applications typically have the highest costs but also the greatest capability with regard to interconnection and usability. Many of the free-for-use CAD programs are scaled-down versions of the high-end proprietary programs, designed for organizations and users that do not require the full functionality of the high-end program. Often, these programs can be upgraded to the high-end version after the user has had the opportunity to assess their needs against the capability of the particular CAD program. Some CAD programs are provided as open-source software, for which the end user is allowed to alter the source code of the program to suit particular needs that may not be adequately covered. Proprietary software, on the other hand, can only be legally altered by the proprietor of the software. Open-source applications generally also have the advantage of a large number of users and developers globally who will seek to find ways to improve the software and enhance its usability, as opposed to the proprietor organization having to maintain a large stable of in-house developers for the same purpose.

—*Richard M. Renneboog, MSc*

Further Reading

McHenry, David. *Drawing the Line: Technical Hand Drafting for Film and Television*. Routledge, 2018.

Ostrowsky, O. *Engineering Drawing with CAD Applications*. Routledge, 2019.

Plantenberg, Kirstie. *Engineering Graphics Essentials with AutoCAD 2022 Instruction*. SDC Publications, 2021.

Simmons, Colin H., Dennis E. Maguire, and Neil Phelps. *Manual of Engineering Drawing: British and International Standards*. Butterworth-Heinemann, 2020.

Singh, Lakhwinder Pal, and Harwinder Singh. *Engineering Drawing: Principles and Applications*. Cambridge UP, 2021.

Szkutnicka, Basia. *Flats: Technical Drawing for Fashion; A Complete Guide*. Lawrence King, 2017.

3D Printing

ABSTRACT

Three-dimensional (3D) printing, also known as additive manufacturing (AM), comprises several automated processes for building 3D objects from layers of plastic, paper, glass, or metal. 3D printing creates strong, light 3D objects quickly and efficiently.

ADDITIVE MANUFACTURING

Three-dimensional (3D) printing, also called "additive manufacturing" (AM), builds 3D objects by adding successive layers of material onto a platform. AM differs from traditional, or subtractive, manufacturing, also called "machining." In machining, material is removed from a starting sample until the desired structure remains. Most AM processes use less raw material and are therefore less wasteful than machining.

The first AM process was developed in the 1980s, using liquid resin hardened by ultraviolet (UV) light. By the 2000s, several different AM processes had been developed. Most of those processes use liquid, powder, or extrusion techniques. Combined with complex computer modeling and robotics, AM could launch a new era in manufacturing in which even complex mechanical objects could be created by AM.

SOFTWARE AND MODELING

3D printing begins with a computer-aided design (CAD) drawing or 3D scan of an object. Those draw-

3D printing, also called "additive manufacturing" (AM), builds 3D objects by adding successive layers of material onto a platform. Photo via iStock/vgajic. [Used under license.]

ings or scans are usually saved in a digital file format known as STL, originally short for "stereolithography" but since given other meanings, such as "surface tessellation language." STL files "tessellate" the object—that is, cover its surface in a repeated pattern of shapes. Though any shape can be used, STL files use a series of nonoverlapping triangles to model the curves and angles of a 3D object. Errors in the file may need repair. "Slices" of the STL file determine the number and thickness of the layers of material needed.

LIQUID 3D PRINTING

The earliest AM technique was stereolithography (SLA), patented in 1986 by Chuck Hull. SLA uses liquid resin or polymer hardened by UV light to create a 3D object. A basic SLA printer consists of an elevator platform suspended in a tank filled with light-sensitive liquid polymer. A UV laser hardens a thin layer of resin. The platform is lowered, and the laser hardens the next layer, fusing it to the first. This process is repeated until the object is complete. The object is then cleaned and cured by UV. This technique is also called "vat photopolymerization" because it takes place within a vat of liquid resin. Various types of SLA printing processes have been given alternate names, such as "photofabrication" and "photosolidification."

POWDER-BASED 3D PRINTING

In the 1980s, engineers at the University of Texas created an alternate process that uses powdered solids instead of liquid. Selective layer sintering (SLS), or powder bed fusion, heats powdered glass, metal, ceramic, or plastic in a powder bed until the material is "sintered." To sinter something is to cause its particles to fuse through heat or pressure without liquefying it. A laser is used to sinter thin layers of the powder selectively, with the unfused powder underneath giving structural support. The platform is lowered and the powder compacted as the laser passes over the object again.

EXTRUSION PRINTING

Material extrusion printing heats plastic or polymer filament and extrudes it through nozzles to deposit a layer of material on a platform. One example of this process is called "fused deposition modeling" (FDM). As the material cools, the platform is lowered, and another layer is added atop the last layer. Creating extruded models often requires the use of a structural support to prevent the object from collapsing. Extrusion printing is the most affordable and commonly available 3D printing process.

EMERGING AND ALTERNATIVE METHODS

Several other 3D printing methods are also emerging. In material jetting, an inkjet printer head deposits liquefied plastic or other light-sensitive material onto a surface, which is then hardened with UV light. Another inkjet printing technique is binder jetting, which uses an inkjet printer head to deposit drops of glue-like liquid into a powdered medium. The liquid then soaks into and solidifies the medium. In directed energy deposition (DED), metal wire or powder is deposited in thin layers over a support before being melted with a laser or other heat source. Sheet lamination fuses together thin sheets of paper, metal, or plastic with adhesive. The resulting object is then cut with a laser or other cutting tool to refine the shape. This method is less costly but also less accurate than others.

THE FUTURE OF 3D PRINTING

While AM techniques have been in use since the 1980s, engineers believe that the technology has not yet reached its full potential. Its primary use has been in rapid prototyping, in which a 3D printer is used to quickly create a 3D model that can be used to guide production. In many cases, 3D printing can create objects that are stronger, lighter, and more customizable than objects made through machining. Printed parts are already being used for planes, race cars, medical implants, and dental crowns, among other items. Because AM wastes far less material than subtractive manufacturing, it is of interest for conservation, waste management, and cost reduction. The technology could also democratize manufacturing, as small-scale 3D printers allow individuals and small businesses to create products that traditionally required industrial manufacturing facilities. However, intellectual property disputes could also occur more often as 3D printing becomes more widespread.

—*Micah L. Issitt*

Further Reading

Hutchinson, Lee. "Home 3D Printers Take Us on a Maddening Journey into Another Dimension." *Ars Technica*, 27 Aug. 2013, arstechnica.com/gadgets/2013/08/home-3d-printers-take-us-on-a-maddening-journey-into-another-dimension/. Accessed 28 Nov. 2021.

Matulka, Rebecca, and Matty Greene. "How 3D Printers Work." *Energy.gov*, 19 June 2014, www.energy.gov/articles/how-3d-printers-work. Accessed 28 Nov. 2021.

"The Printed World." *Economist*, 10 Feb. 2011, www.economist.com/briefing/2011/02/10/the-printed-world. Accessed 28 Nov. 2021.

UNISURF

ABSTRACT

UNISURF was an early computer-aided design (CAD) program created for use in designing surfaces. It was used primarily by European automakers Renault and Peugeot. It introduced and relied heavily on the design capabilities of the Bézier curve, developed by Pierre Bézier and Paul de Casteljau.

THE BÉZIER CURVE

Essentially all computer-aided design (CAD) and graphics programs of the early twenty-first century include a Bézier curve function, named for Pierre Bézier. A French design engineer working for the Renault automotive corporation, Bézier developed a matrix transformation process for producing a specialized curve-drawing function in CAD programs. This type of curve function quickly became known as the Bézier curve and was a powerful design tool, effectively the heart of the UNISURF CAD system Bézier designed around it. A Bézier curve may be generated in a CAD or graphics drawing by specifying a line with multiple points of attachment. The points at either end of the line are the anchor points of the line and remain in a fixed position. The remaining points that are situated between the end points may be moved to any location in the drawing, but the anchor points remain fixed in position. As the movable points are moved, the line between the anchor points bends and shifts to produce a curve.

Using the Bézier curve function, a designer can generate a precise curve of any desired arc or combination of arcs. The matrix mathematics that underlie the Bézier curve drawing function also allow the user to choose a desired number of movable points between the two anchor points. This allows the designer to generate smooth curves having sections with different radii, inflection points, maxima, and minima. Successive arcs can be generated that, when stacked together, produce representations of curved surfaces with features that cannot easily be produced in CAD drawings without the Bézier curve function.

Bézier curves are vitally important in automobile design and other three-dimensional (3D) surface applications and are used to design autobody panels, boat hulls, trains, aircraft, machine parts, and heating, ventilation, and air-conditioning (HVAC) systems. They are also used in architecture, computer-generated graphics, and many other fields of design that make use of curved surfaces. While the majority of users may seldom have a need to use Bézier curves to produce a CAD-type drawing, Bézier curves are an essential tool for advanced CAD users.

PIERRE BÉZIER AND PAUL DE CASTELJAU

Pierre Bézier was a design engineer for the French automaker Renault. His educational background was in electrical and mechanical engineering. However, he also possessed a longtime interest in mathematics and ultimately earned a PhD in mathematics from the Université de Paris later in life, based on his 1977 doctoral thesis *Essai de définition numérique des courbes et surfaces expérimentales* (Numerical Definition Test of Experimental Curves and Surfaces). In 1933, Bézier joined Renault, where he was able to apply his mathematical interest and engineering background to the design of the curved surfaces of car bodies and other Renault products. In the 1950s, numerical control (a form of computer-aided manufacturing [CAM]) was a very new technology that had not yet been accepted by car manufacturers. The concept that Renault should invest in numerical control research was soundly rejected when Bézier proposed the idea in the late 1950s. Despite the rejection, or perhaps because of it, Bézier undertook the research to apply numerical control methodology for the design of autobody tooling and die-cast models. He designed a drawing system for those purposes and named it UNISURF. Bézier would remain at Renault until his retirement in 1975. In addition to working in automotive manufacturing, he held a professorship at the Conservatoire National des Arts et Métiers for more than a decade and served for a time as an advisory editor for the journal *Computer-Aided Design*.

Bézier's UNISURF introduced the Bézier curve function into regular use within the field of CAD. However, Bézier himself was not the first figure to articulate the concept of the Bézier curve. That honor belonged to Paul de Casteljau, a mathematician working for rival French automaker Citroën. De Casteljau invented the algorithm, later called the "de Casteljau Algorithm," that calculates the Bézier curve based on the Bernstein Polynomial, which was discovered in 1912. De Casteljau defined the Bézier curve while working for Citroën in 1959, but it was Bézier at Renault who popularized its use in the UNISURF program he had developed. Bézier's research and development of UNISURF languished until 1966, when Renault and Peugeot, another French automaker, made an agreement to cooperate in research and development of numerical control. Peugeot engineers who were impressed by Bézier's UNISURF concept aided in furthering its development, and in 1968 the entire body of the Peugeot 204 was designed in UNISURF. The Peugeot 204 was the first car to be completely designed using UNISURF and one of the first automobiles ever to be designed using a CAD system.

UNISURF CAD/CAM

UNISURF reportedly remained in use among Renault employees through at least 1990. UNISURF was designed to reside on a mainframe computer and was not adapted for personal computers. Because it was proprietary and intended for use within Renault, detailed information about the program and its features was not typically made available to the public. However, Bézier described aspects of the system in his paper "Example of an Existing System in the Motor Industry: The Unisurf System," published in *Proceedings of the Royal Society A* in 1971, and later published the 1986 work *The Mathematical Basis of the UNIURF CAD System*, in which he detailed the complex mathematics underlying his creation. Bézier designed the UNISURF system for use with multiple technologies, including drawing machines and milling machines. Such functions extended the usefulness of UNISURF from CAD to CAD/CAM.

—Richard M. Renneboog, MSc

Further Reading

Bar-Cohen, Yoseph, editor. *Advances in Manufacturing and Processing of Materials and Structures*. CRC Press, 2019.

Barfield, Rose. "The Bézier Curve—How Car Design Influenced CAD." *Bricsys Blog*, blog.bricsys.com/the-bezier-curve-how-car-design-influenced-cad/. Accessed 16 Dec. 2021.

Bézier, Pierre. "Example of an Existing System in the Motor Industry: The Unisurf System." *Proceedings of the Royal Society A*, vol. 321, no. 1545, 1971, pp. 207-18.

Bézier, Pierre. *The Mathematical Basis of the UNISURF CAD System*. Butterworth-Heinemann, 1986.

Godse, Atul P., and Deepali A. Godse. *Computer Graphics*. Technical Publications, 2021.

Ko, Joy, and Kyle Steinfeld. *Geometric Computation: Foundations for Design*. Routledge, 2018.

Metwalli, Sayed M. *Machine Design with CAD and Optimization*. Wiley, 2021.

"Professor Bézier: A Short Biography." *Computer-Aided Design*, vol. 22, no. 9, 1990, p. 523. Sloman, Adam. *Peugeot 205: The Complete Story*. Crowood Press, 2015.

Urban Planning and Engineering

ABSTRACT

Urban planning and engineering is an interdisciplinary field focusing on the study of land within cities, towns, and metropolitan areas and the ways in which it is used. Urban planners conduct thorough assessments of specific areas of land, often with the support of statistical tools and mapping software such as geographic information systems (GIS). They analyze historical trends affecting the land's physical, economic, and social environments. Based on these findings, planners make recommendations about ways in which land can be used more effectively in the future. Planners advise lawmakers, government agencies, commercial developers, businesses, and residents. The rapid growth of urban areas worldwide fuels demand for professionals in the field.

DEFINITION AND BASIC PRINCIPLES

Urban planning and engineering is the design of cities and towns according to a plan. Such plans provide guidance on questions ranging from where to place new roads to how many supermarkets are needed in a neighborhood. Urban planning, also known as "urban studies" or "city planning" and often overlapping with regional planning, ensures that the land in a city or town will be used in a way that will benefit the largest number of people living and working there. It helps officials in local government and land developers avoid problems such as traffic, overcrowding, and urban sprawl.

Geography is a major factor affecting a city's urban planning efforts. The types of businesses that make up the local economy are another factor. Cities that rely on heavy industry such as oil refining, for example, have different urban planning needs than those for which technology or agriculture is more important. The topic of urban planning is often associated with newer high-growth cities where vacant land is being developed for the first time. Older urban areas also must depend on planning when urban renewal is needed.

Urban engineering is a specific field within urban planning and is more commonly known as "civil engineering" or "municipal engineering." It includes the design of transportation and its infrastructure.

BACKGROUND AND HISTORY

Urban planning and engineering in North America began with the development of the first large cities on the East Coast. These cities started as small settlements. As they grew, particularly in the seventeenth and eighteenth centuries, their roads and buildings were influenced by the design of European cities.

The use of a grid-based system for laying out streets and neighborhoods became popular in the 1800s, led by innovations in cities such as New York and Philadelphia. As railroads crossed the continent, many cities followed standard plans developed by the railroad companies. The Industrial Revolution led many cities to place the needs of manufacturing operations over those of citizens, creating pollution, overcrowding, and slums.

In the twentieth century, the US government passed several major laws to guide the development of cities and towns. The US Department of Housing and Urban Development (HUD), created in 1965, addressed common problems of urban growth on a national level. The rise of suburbs, influenced by the spread of automobiles and highway systems, created new challenges for city planners. As metropolitan areas have sought ways to fight urban sprawl and to redevelop land left underutilized by a general movement toward the suburbs, the demand has grown for urban planners in the twenty-first century.

HOW IT WORKS

Land-use study. When developing a new plan for a city or region, urban planners start by assessing the way in which the land is being used. Planners identify who is using the land and how. In urban areas, land use is often classified into business use (such as retail or manufacturing) and residential use (such as houses and parks). Even if land is vacant, it is likely to have been business or residential property at some point in the city's history. Once planners have defined who the land's users are, they create a detailed report and a map. The report and the map are known as the "land-use study." The report contains information on the types of businesses in the area, the population living there, and the ways in which both have changed over time. The map covers geographic features such as mountains and lakes, but its primary focus is on the features added by businesses and people using the land. It includes information about transportation infrastructure, utilities such as power and sewer lines, and the location and density of public resources such as fire stations, hospitals, and libraries.

Urban plan development. Once the land-use study is complete, urban planners evaluate the ways in which the land's present uses meet or fail to meet the needs of its businesses and inhabitants. Most urban planners are hired by officials from city and regional governments. These officials are likely to bring in urban planners to help solve problems such as traffic congestion or economic stagnation. Because of this, an urban plan often focuses on the ways in which land use could be improved. Urban

Urban planning and engineering is an interdisciplinary field focusing on the study of land within cities, towns, and metropolitan areas and the ways in which it is used. Photo via iStock/ AndreyPopov. [Used under license.]

planners apply their professional knowledge about the best ways in which an area of a city can be designed. Planners also spend time with business owners and residents to learn more about their specific needs. Planners consult with government officials on budget matters, as land-use changes are often financed by tax revenues. Finally, urban planners research zoning and building codes and environmental regulations. Planners must ensure that any recommended changes to land use are legal and will receive all necessary approvals.

Conflict management. Urban planners are most frequently hired to help resolve conflicts about land use. One of the most important roles played by many urban planners is that of mediator. Planners, as outside parties, gather information from all sides and incorporate this information into their recommended plans. This process can involve participating in community meetings and defending findings in front of businesses, residents, and government committees that may be critical of the planners' advice.

Technology. To create plans, urban planners rely on tools such as mapping software and geographic information systems (GIS). These systems help planners assess existing land use and forecast the impact of recommended changes. Computer-aided design (CAD) software such as AutoCAD can be useful for urban planners seeking to create digital plans and other drawings. Planners must also be skilled in the use of databases on population statistics and trends, laws and regulations, and geographic and environmental data.

APPLICATIONS AND PRODUCTS

Most professionals in the urban planning field have an area of specialty. Some of the most common areas are residential planning, transportation engineering and design, business and economic planning, historic preservation, environmental planning, and zoning and code enforcement.

Residential planning. Planners who focus on residential issues answer questions such as whether a community offers enough housing to meet its existing needs and how these needs will change in the next ten, twenty, or fifty years. They make recommendations that guide the building of single-family homes, townhouses, and apartment buildings within a community. Residential planners also study community income levels and develop plans for housing that will be affordable as well as comfortable. A subfield within residential planning is public housing. Many cities have moved away from public housing models in which residents were concentrated within single, large-scale communities, where problems such as crime and economic blight developed. Residential planners in this subfield are creating new approaches to public housing that improve the quality of life for all community members.

Transportation engineering and design. If a main road is choked with traffic, does the road need to be rebuilt or is a new highway needed? What is the best route for a new train line between the suburbs and downtown? Transportation engineers help cities find the best ways for people and commercial goods to get from one point to another. They evaluate whether existing structures are working and develop plans for the building of new roads, bridges, tunnels, rail lines, and public transit systems. Transportation engineers also measure the impact that the building of new structures will have on communities.

Business and economic planning. Planners who focus on business and economic issues work in one of the most diverse areas of urban planning. They address questions such as how a city that depended on heavy manufacturing can adapt when companies close their factories and whether a neighborhood should build a large shopping mall or several small groups of stores. Some planners specialize in guiding the long-term economic health of a community. Others specialize in the design, creation, and refurbishing of business and retail buildings. When economic planners succeed, communities can support a range of businesses that, in turn, create jobs. Some subfields of economic planning extend beyond the businesses themselves. For example, economic planners might recommend that a city build more schools to equip residents with new skills. The workforce created by these schools might attract industries to the area, which would boost economic growth in the long run.

Historic preservation. Historic preservation tries to determine issues such as whether decrepit older houses that make up the bulk of homes in a neighborhood should be protected or torn down and what elements give a city's downtown its unique character. This field has been on the rise since the 1960s and 1970s, when residents and businesses of many cities began to migrate from the urban core to newly built suburbs. Many urban planners in this field are involved with the creation of urban historic districts, neighborhoods that receive economic support from the city in exchange for preserving the architectural styles of their older buildings. Other specialists in historic preservation advise city governments on ways to reuse buildings that have historical value but have outlived their original purpose. Urban planners in this field help cities retain their distinct personalities while meeting the needs those who live and work in these cities.

Environmental planning. What is the most cost-effective way to clean up a river full of industrial pollutants? How can a city encourage more of its residents to take public transit or bike to work? Environmental planners help urban areas address questions such as these. Like the movement toward historic preservation, the importance of environmental protection has been on the rise since the 1960s and 1970s. Businesses and city governments must comply with increasingly strict laws about the cleanliness of air, water, and land. There is also greater public interest in protecting the environment, which has led to changes such as the increase in citywide recycling programs. Green buildings, or those that use materials with a minimal environmental impact and seek to conserve as much energy as possible, have become a priority for many cities and are becoming a larger part of their urban plans. Planners who specialize in this field help cities benefit as much as possible from new approaches to environmental protection.

Zoning and code enforcement. What kinds of businesses should be built around a new sports stadium? How far from a power plant should homes be built? Zoning and code enforcement is a specialty within urban planning that focuses on the laws and regulations that govern the ways land can be used. It includes both the writing of new codes and the process of ensuring that governments, businesses, and residents comply with them. Zoning specialists protect an urban plan's long-term vision by defining the ways in which specific projects must follow the plan.

CAREERS AND COURSEWORK

Although governmental agencies employ the largest number of urban planners and engineers, consulting firms in the private sector are increasingly hiring urban planners and engineers. Planners many increase their earning power and promotion opportunities by developing areas of specialty. Fields such as environmental sustainability and transportation engineering are areas of strong growth.

Many bachelor's and master's degree programs in urban planning exist at US colleges and universities; additional programs can be found in many major universities in other countries. Many students who enter the field at the graduate level hold bachelor's degrees in fields such as environmental science, geography, or political science. Coursework covers urban design, economic and environmental planning, community development, land use, and zoning and code enforcement. Related coursework might include architecture, public administration, economics, and law. A specialization in GIS would require a student to take classes in mathematics, statistics, and computer science. At the graduate level, most students take internships or part-time jobs in applied settings such as government agencies. In addition, urban planners may seek certification from the American Institute of Certified Planners to increase their skills and earning potential. In some jurisdictions, planners must be registered, a process that involves passing examinations and verifying professional experience.

SOCIAL CONTEXT AND FUTURE PROSPECTS

Demand for urban planners and engineers is on the rise. The Bureau of Labor Statistics forecast that jobs in the urban and regional planning sector would grow at a rate of 7 percent from 2020 to 2030. Planning jobs in the private sector that involve scientific and technical services are expected to see especially strong growth.

Many jobs in the private sector can be found with consulting firms that specialize in architecture and engineering services. An increase in demand for environmentally sustainable development is fueling the need for urban planners with up-to-date knowledge. This type of development includes everything from green buildings to the preservation of natural resources. The rise of new urbanism in the redevelopment of older communities and the building of new ones will continue to foster a need for urban planners familiar with its principles. As cities continue to grow and change, urban planners will be needed to manage the expansion of transportation and other infrastructure in a way that will avoid problems such as traffic congestion and pollution.

As reliance on GIS, CAD, and other technologies increases, urban planners and engineers will be expected to have strong backgrounds in statistics and computer science. Professionals who focus on these areas are likely to see the strongest possibilities for long-term career growth.

—*Julia A. Rosenthal, BA, MS*

Further Reading

Ascher, Kate. *The Works: Anatomy of a City*. 2005. Penguin Press, 2007.

Bayer, Michael, Nancy Frank, and Jason Valerius. *Becoming an Urban Planner: A Guide to Careers in Planning and Urban Design*. John Wiley & Sons, 2010.

Bokhari, Ali. "Urban Planning Education and Using CityCAD to Transform Our Cities." *Journal of Education*, 13 Dec. 2020, journals.sagepub.com/doi/abs/10.1177/0022057420979593. Accessed 28 Nov. 2021.

Chavan, Abhijeet, Christian Peralta, and Christopher Steins. *Planetizen's Contemporary Debates in Urban Planning*. Island Press, 2007.

Couch, Chris. *Urban Planning: An Introduction*. Palgrave Macmillan, 2016.

Duany, Andres, Elizabeth Plater-Zyberk, and Jeff Speck. *Suburban Nation: The Rise of Sprawl and the Decline of the American Dream*. 10th anniversary ed., North Point Press, 2010.

Jacobs, Jane. *The Death and Life of Great American Cities*. 1961. Random House, 2002.

Levy, John M. *Contemporary Urban Planning*. 11th ed., Routledge, 2016.

Maantay, Juliana, John Ziegler, and John Pickles. *GIS for the Urban Environment*. ESRI Press, 2006.

Song, Yang, and Yang Jin. "Urban Planning and Design Based on AutoCAD to Expand GIS Function." *Computer-Aided Design and Applications*, vol. 17, no. S2, 2020, pp. 11-21.

"Urban and Regional Planners." *US Bureau of Labor Statistics*, 8 Sept. 2021, www.bls.gov/ooh/life-physical-and-social-science/urban-and-regional-planners.htm. Accessed 28 Nov. 2021.

Yamagata, Yoshiki, and Ayoob Sharifi. *Resilience-Oriented Urban Planning: Theoretical and Empirical Insights*. Springer, 2018.

V

Vectors

ABSTRACT

Vectors express magnitude and direction and have applications in physics and many other areas. There are some quantities, like time and work, that have only a magnitude (also called "scalars"). If one says the time is 6 a.m., it is adequate. When discussing velocity or force, however, then magnitude is not enough. If a particle is said to have a velocity of 5 meters per second, this is not sufficient information because the direction of movement is unknown. Quantities that require both a magnitude and a sense of direction for their complete specifying are called "vectors." Pilots use vectors to compensate for wind to navigate airplanes, sport analysts use vectors to model dynamics, and physicists use vectors to model the world. "Vector" is also used to describe a category of computer graphic that is based on mathematically defined points and paths.

HISTORY AND DEVELOPMENT OF VECTORS

The term "vector" originates from *vectus*, a Latin word meaning "to carry." However, astronomy and physical applications motivated the concept of a vector as a magnitude and direction. Aristotle recognized force as a vector. Some historians question whether the parallel law for the vector addition of forces was also known to Aristotle, although they agree that Galileo Galilei stated it explicitly, and it appears in the 1687 work *Principia Mathematica* by Isaac Newton. Aside from the physical applications, vectors were useful in planar and spherical trigonometry and geometry. Vector properties and sums continue to be taught in high schools in the twenty-first century.

The rigorous development of vectors into the field of vector calculus in the nineteenth century resulted in a debate over methods and approaches. The algebra of vectors was created by Hermann Grassmann and William Hamilton. Grassmann expanded the concept of a vector to an arbitrary number of dimensions in his book *The Calculus of Extension*, while Hamilton applied vector methods to problems in mechanics and geometry using the concept of a "quaternion." Hamilton spent the rest of his life advocating for quaternions. James Maxwell published his *Treatise on Electricity and Magnetism* in which he emphasized the importance of quaternions as mathematical methods of thinking, while at the same time critiquing them and discouraging scientists from using them. Extending Grassmann's ideas, Josiah Gibbs laid the foundations of vector analysis and created a system that was more easily applied to physics than Hamilton's quaternions. Oliver Heaviside independently created a vector analysis and advocated for vector methods and vector calculus. Mathematicians such as Peter Tait, who preferred quaternions, rejected the methods of Gibbs and Heaviside. However, their methods were eventually accepted and they are taught as part of the field of linear algebra. The quaternionic method of Hamilton remains extremely useful in the twenty-first century. Vector calculus is fundamental in understanding fluid dynamics, solid mechanics, electromagnetism, and in many other applications.

During the nineteenth century, mathematicians and physicists also developed the three fundamental theorems of vector calculus, often referred to in the twenty-first century as the "divergence theorem," "Green's theorem," and "Stokes's theorem." Mathematicians with diverse motivations all contributed to the development of the divergence theorem. Michael Ostrogradsky studied the theory of heat, Simeon Poisson studied elastic bodies, Frederic Sarrus studied floating bodies, George Green studied electricity and magnetism, and Carl Friedrich Gauss studied magnetic attraction. The theorem is sometimes referred to as "Gauss's theorem." George Green, Augustin Cauchy, and Bernhard Riemann all contributed to Green's theorem, and Peter Tait and James Maxwell created vector versions of Stokes's theorem, which was originally explored by George Stokes, Lord Kelvin, and Hermann Hankel. Undergraduate college students often explore these theorems in a multivariable calculus class.

The concept of a space consisting of a collection of vectors, called a "vector space," became important in the twentieth century. The notion was axiomatized earlier by Jean-Gaston Darboux and defined by Giuseppe Peano, but their work was not appreciated at the time. However, the concept was rediscovered and became important in functional analysis because of the work by Stefan Banach, Hans Hahn, and Norbert Wiener, as well as in ring theory because of the work of Emmy Noether. Vector spaces and their algebraic properties are regularly taught as a part of undergraduate linear algebra.

MATHEMATICS

A vector is defined as a quantity with magnitude and direction. It is represented as a directed line seg-

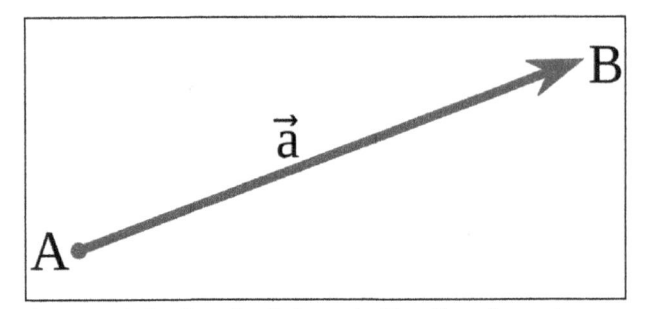

A vector pointing from A to B. Image by Oleg Alexandrov, via Wikimedia Commons.

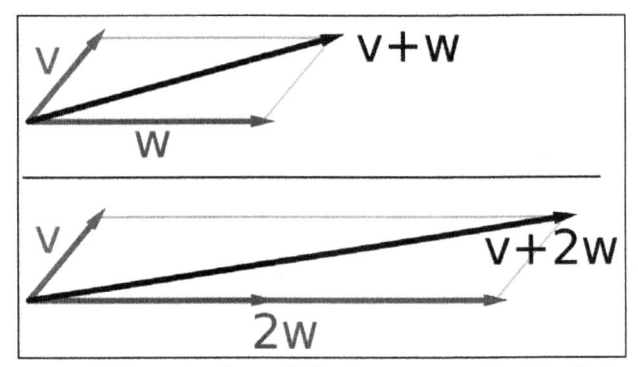

Vector addition and scalar multiplication: a vector v (blue) is added to another vector w (red, upper illustration). Below, w is stretched by a factor of 2, yielding the sum v + 2w. Image by IkamusumeFan, via Wikimedia Commons.

ment with the length proportional to the magnitude and the direction being that of the vector. If represented as an array, it is often represented as a row or column matrix. Vectors are usually represented as boldface capital letters, such as **A**, or with an arrow overhead. The Triangle Law states that while adding, "if two vectors can be represented as the two sides of a triangle taken in order then the resultant is represented as the closing side of the triangle taken in the opposite order."

Any vector can be split up into components, meaning to divide it into parts having directions along the coordinate axes. When added, these components return the original vector. This process is called "resolution into components." Clearly, this resolution cannot be unique as it depends on the choice of coordinate axes. However, for a given vector and specified coordinate axes, the resolution is unique. When two vectors are added or subtracted, these components along a specific axis simply "add up" (like 2 + 2 = 4 or 7 - 2 = 5), but the original vectors do not, which follow the rule of vector addition that can be obtained by the Parallelogram Law of Vector Addition. Vector addition is commutative and associative in nature.

Multiplication for vectors can be of a few types. For scalar multiplication (multiplication by a quantity that is not a vector), each component is multiplied by that scalar. Vector multiplication by a scalar is commutative, associative, and distributive in nature. For the multiplication of two vectors, one can obtain both a scalar (dot product) or a vector (cross product). For a cross product the resultant lies in a plane perpendicular to the plane containing the two original vectors. Dot product is both commutative and distributive. But cross product is neither commutative nor associative in nature because the result is a vector and depends on the direction.

APPLICATIONS

Obtaining components. Occasionally, one needs a part (or component) of a vector for a given purpose. For example, suppose a rower intends to cross over to a point on the other side of a river that has a great current. The rower would be interested to know if any part of that current could help in any way to move in the desired direction. To find the component of the current's vector along any specified direction, take the dot product of that vector with a unit vector (vector of unit magnitude) along the specified direction. This method is of particular importance in studying of particle dynamics and force equilibria.

Evaluating volume, surface, and line integrals. In many problems of physics, it is often necessary to shift from either closed surface integral (over a closed surface that surrounds a volume) to volume integral (over the whole enclosed volume), or from closed line integral (over a loop) to surface integrals (over a surface). To accomplish these shifts, it is often very useful to apply two fundamental theorems of vector calculus, namely Gauss's divergence theorem and Stokes's theorem, respectively.

Particle mechanics. In the study of particle mechanics, vectors are used extensively. Velocity, acceleration, force, momentum, and torque all being vectors, a proper study of mechanics invariably involves extensive applications of vectors.

Vector fields. A field is a region over which the effect or influence of a force or system is felt. In physics, it is very common to study electric and magnetic fields, which apply vectors and vectorial techniques in their description.

ALTERNATIVE DEFINITION OF VECTOR

The term "vector" is also used to describe a vector image, a type of computer graphic.

Vector images are based on points and the paths between them, which can be defined by mathematical equations. However, the mathematics of vector graphics are largely distinct from the mathematics of vector calculus.

Vector graphics are used in a variety of computer-graphics programs, including computer-aided design programs such as AutoCAD. Because the points, lines, curves, and other features of the images are defined mathematically, the resulting images remain true to scale even when enlarged or made smaller. Vector images are considered preferable for certain applications because they retain their original image quality even after their size has been modified.

—*Abhijit Sen*

Further Reading

Katz, Victor. "The History of Stokes' Theorem." *Mathematics Magazine*, vol. 52, no. 3, 1979, pp. 146-56.

"Mathematics of Vector Art." *Interactive Mathematics*, 23 Nov. 2019, www.intmath.com/vectors/math-vector-art.php. Accessed 28 Nov. 2021.

Matthews, Paul. *Vector Calculus*. Springer, 1998.

Stroud, K. A., and Dexter Booth. *Differential Equations*. Industrial Press, 2005.

Web Graphic Design

ABSTRACT

Web graphic design is the use of graphic design techniques in designing websites. Web graphic designers must balance the marketing aspects of a website with aesthetic design criteria. They also attempt to increase the likelihood that the website will be found in search results and therefore be an effective advertising tool.

DESIGNING FOR THE WEB

Web graphic design is a subfield of graphic design that focuses on designing for the web. It typically involves a blend of graphic design techniques and computer programming. Many websites are used as marketing materials for businesses and organizations. Consequently, web designers often incorporate business logos and other promotional materials. They also use search engine optimization (SEO) techniques to increase the likelihood that the web page will be found by search engines.

When creating graphics for use on the web, designers typically use any of a number of graphic-design programs, such as Adobe Photoshop and Corel's PaintShopPro. In some cases, however, web graphic designers may choose to utilize computer-aided design (CAD) or three-dimensional (3D) modeling software to create 3D graphics or icons for use online.

WEB DESIGN FUNCTIONALITY

Most websites, whether business, advocacy, news, or personal sites, serve as both marketing and informational tools. A website that represents a specific brand will incorporate iconic logos, logotypes, or combination marks to aid brand recognition. An iconic logo is a symbol or emblem that represents a person, business, or organization. A logotype is a company or brand name rendered in a unique or proprietary font and style. Combination marks combine icons with logotypes.

In addition to being informative, a website should be visually appealing and easy to understand. Skilled use of typography helps web designers achieve these goals. For example, while logotypes are designed to catch the eye, important information should be presented in a font that is aesthetically pleasing yet unobtrusive. A font that draws attention to itself will detract from the message of the text. Typography techniques such as this help web designers make websites easy to read and navigate.

In addition, web designers must be familiar with SEO, which relies on elements such as keywords and links to ensure that users can find a website using a search engine. SEO techniques are most effective when incorporated into the overall design of a website. As such, many web graphic designers also help users optimize their websites for better search results.

By the 2010s, web design had begun to focus on designing for the mobile web, creating websites and e-commerce sites that could be viewed and accessed using mobile devices. Many do-it-yourself (DIY) website builders started offering mobile web design templates and conversions.

DEVELOPMENT OF WEB DESIGN TECHNIQUES

Modern web design began in the 1990s, with the creation and adoption of hypertext markup language (HTML). This markup language specifies the

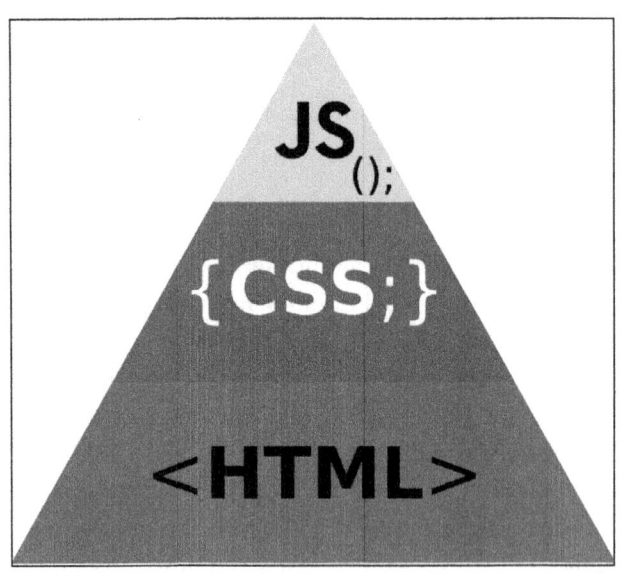

Web graphic design—the order of progressive enhancement. Image by CaptainT7, via Wikimedia Commons.

location and appearance of objects displayed on a web page. In the mid-1990s, web designers began using HTML tables. These consist of static cells that can be arranged on a page to specify the location of text or objects. By placing tables within tables, designers could create a richer experience for websites.

The programming language JavaScript was developed in 1995 to code website behavior. This made individual web pages interactive for the first time. With JavaScript, web designers could embed image galleries, add functions such as drop-down menus, and make websites respond visually when a user clicked on text or images. Flash, developed in 1996, allowed designers to add animated elements to websites. However, not all browsers supported Flash, so it was not as universally useful as JavaScript.

The next major step in web graphic design was the introduction of tableless web design. This approach to web design does not rely on HTML tables. Instead, it uses style sheets to format pages. The Cascading Style Sheets (CSS) language, first introduced in 1996, allows designers to separate the visual elements of the design from the content. CSS can determine the appearance and spacing, while individual elements are still described in HTML. Personal Home Page (PHP), another language used in web design, was developed in 1994 but gained in popularity during the late 1990s. It provides further options for making web pages interactive. When used with HTML, PHP allows websites to create new content based on user information and to collect information from visitors.

As of the third decade of the twenty-first century, most web design is still based on a combination of CSS and HTML. Programming in PHP and the database server software MySQL provide options for greater flexibility and interactivity. New versions of web design languages, such as HTML5, offer more ways of incorporating multimedia, better support for multilingual websites, and a wider array of aesthetic options for designers.

USER-GENERATED WEB DESIGN

The popular website WordPress is actually a content management system (CMS) built on PHP and MySQL. It debuted in 2003 as a blogging website, offering users templates and tools to design blogs. The site soon became popular as a basic web design system, allowing users with limited knowledge of HTML or other coding to build basic and functional, if aesthetically rudimentary, websites. Soon web designers began tailoring WordPress sites for customers. This has essentially served as a shortcut for the web design industry. As of 2021, WordPress remained among the most popular web design systems in the world, accounting for more than half of all CMS-based websites on the internet.

The debut of WordPress launched a new era in DIY web graphic design. Companies such as Squarespace, Wix, and Weebly soon began offering users the ability to design websites quickly and easily, without the need to understand programming languages. Most such sites provide users templates in the form of wireframes. Wireframes are structural layouts that specify the location of images, text, and interactive elements on a web page but are not themselves interactive. Users can then insert their own images and text and, depending on the underlying program, also rearrange the layout of the wireframe. Like most elements of online commerce and marketing, web graphic design is moving toward user-generated and user-influenced design in order to open up to broader audiences.

—*Micah L. Issitt*

Further Reading

Allanwood, Gavin, and Peter Beare. *User Experience Design: Creating Designs Users Really Love*. Fairchild, 2014.

Hagen, Rebecca, and Kim Golombisky. *White Space Is Not Your Enemy: A Beginner's Guide to Communicating Visually through Graphic, Web & Multimedia Design*. 3rd ed., A. K. Peters/CRC Press, 2016.

Mings, Josh. "3D CAD Smack! Graphic Design for Print and Web Using SolidWorks." *SolidSmack*, 25 June 2009, www.solidsmack.com/cad/solidworks-3d-web-rpint-graphic-design/. Accessed 28 Nov. 2021.

Schmitt, Christopher. *Designing Web & Mobile Graphics: Fundamental Concepts for Web and Interactive Projects*. New Riders, 2013.

Tupper, Shelby. "The Best Graphic Design Software for 2021." *PCMag*, 22 Oct. 2021, www.pcmag.com/picks/the-best-graphic-design-software. Accessed 28 Nov. 2021.

Williams, Brad, David Damstra, and Hal Stern. *Professional WordPress: Design and Development*. 3rd ed., Wiley, 2015.

"WordPress Market Share in 2021." *Envisage Digital*, 2021, www.envisagedigital.co.uk/wordpress-market-share/. Accessed 28 Nov. 2021.

Wireframes

ABSTRACT

A wireframe visually represents the basic elements of a proposed product, such as a physical item or a website, before a manufacturer or designer actually builds it. Creating a wireframe ensures that all stakeholders agree on the basic appearance and functionality of the product. It also allows them to map out how the end user will ultimately interact with the final product.

WIREFRAMES IN COMPUTER-AIDED DESIGN

Used in a multitude of industries, computer-aided design (CAD) software enables designers of products as varied as machine parts, dental appliances, furniture, automobiles, and spacecraft to create digital representations of their creations prior to beginning the fabrication of such products. Designs created via CAD software can include both two-dimensional (2D) diagrams and three-dimensional (3D) models. When building a 3D wireframe model, a designer uses lines and curves to represent the edges of the item being designed, creating a 3D outline of the complete object. A 3D wireframe model does not display a great level of detail, and exterior solid surfaces are not pictured. In creating such a model, a designer is able to create a useful view of the basic geometric structure of the object in development.

WIREFRAMES IN WEB DESIGN

In the field of web design, a wireframe is a visual, noninteractive representation of a proposed website. A web designer may use a wireframe to determine how best to lay out the elements of the site. If the site is being designed for a client, the designer may show the client a wireframe to get approval for the final product. To create the wireframe, a web designer will block out the basic elements of the proposed website first, most often drawing them on paper. This drawing is the wireframe. Though it may be no more than a set of squares, circles, columns, and lines that represent the individual elements of the pages, it allows the designer and the client to review the site concept together before it is built. Any changes in the website format can be easily made at this stage.

A wireframe also allows the designer to sort the content of the proposed website into an information hierarchy. The designer can then determine how best to arrange it on the page. When designing a website, particularly for a business or other organization, certain elements are standard. These elements may include a logo, a navigation bar, a header containing an index of the major elements of the website, and a footer containing contact information, privacy guidelines, and other legal information. A wireframe should incorporate any and all of elements that will be included in the final website. In most cases, the wireframe serves as a blueprint, with no distracting aesthetic features such as font, color, or images. The emphasis is on functionality—that is, how the proposed site will accommodate the end user. This type of wireframe is also called a "low-fidelity wireframe."

Once the client is on board with the concept, the designer may produce a more sophisticated, high-fidelity wireframe. This type of wireframe is usually created using dedicated software. It represents the final website in much more detail. It incorporates such design elements as images, color schemes, and typography. Sequences of images are used to represent how users will interact with the site. However, the wireframe itself is still noninteractive.

PROTOTYPING

While design processes vary among different industries, a common step that takes place between the creation of a wireframe and the creation of the final product is the development of a prototype. In the case of web design, a designer will sometimes produce an interactive prototype that simulates the user experience with the completed website. In fields that make extensive use of CAD software, the creation of a wireframe model will often be followed by the creation of a solid, rather than outline-based, digital model of the given object or structure. The creation of a physical prototype may follow, particularly in manufacturing sectors that utilize the strategy known as rapid prototyping. Prototypes are ideal for the testing of both physical products and virtual products such as websites. Any problems with the product or website in development can be addressed before the fabrication process begins or the designer begins coding for the final site.

IMPACT OF WIREFRAMES

Much as an architect creates a blueprint for a skyscraper or a director storyboards a film, a designer uses a wireframe to spot potential problems before building the final product. This saves both time and money and, ultimately, shields the end user from frustration—all critical factors in highly competitive fields such as manufacturing and web design.

—*Joseph Dewey*

Further Reading

"About Creating 3D Wireframe Models." *Autodesk*, 16 Dec. 2015, knowledge.autodesk.com/support/autocad/learn-explore/caas/CloudHelp/cloudhelp/2016/ENU/AutoCAD-Core/files/GUID-84E193D7-A18D-4EE2-B978-19E4AFBCAEEC-htm.html. Accessed 28 Nov. 2021.

Bi, Zhuming, and Xiaoqin Wang. *Computer Aided Design and Manufacturing*. Wiley-ASME Press, 2020.

Greenberg, Saul, et al. *Sketching User Experiences: The Workbook*. Morgan, 2012.

Hamm, Matthew J. *Wireframing Essentials: An Introduction to User Experience Design*. Packt, 2014.

Klimczak, Erik. *Design for Software: A Playbook for Developers*. Wiley, 2013.

Krug, Steve. *Don't Make Me Think, Revisited: A Common Sense Approach to Web Usability*. 3rd ed., New Riders, 2014.

Marsh, Joel. *UX for Beginners: A Crash Course in 100 Short Lessons*. O'Reilly, 2016.

Norman, Don. *The Design of Everyday Things*. Rev. and expanded ed., Basic, 2013.

"Wireframe Modeling." *PCMag*, www.pcmag.com/encyclopedia/term/wireframe-modeling. Accessed 28 Nov. 2021.

"Wireframe Modeling." *Spatial*, www.spatial.com/resources/glossary/wireframe-modeling. Accessed 28 Nov. 2021.

Timeline of Computer-aided Design and Manufacturing

The timeline below lists milestones in the history of computer-aided design and manufacturing, in addition to selected major developments in the fields of manufacturing and computer science.

Year	Event
1642	Mechanical calculator (Blaise Pascal): Eighteen-year-old Pascal invents the first mechanical calculator, which helps his father, a tax collector, count taxes.
1672	Leibniz's calculator (Gottfried Wilhelm Leibniz): Leibniz develops a calculator that can add, subtract, multiply, and divide, as well as the binary system of numbers used by computers today.
1767	Dividing engine (Jesse Ramsden): Ramsden develops a machine that automatically and accurately marks calibrated scales.
1785	Automated flour mill (Oliver Evans): Evans's flour mill lays the foundation for continuous production lines.
1822	Difference engine (Charles Babbage): Babbage's "engine" was a programmable mechanical device used to calculate the value of a polynomial-a precursor to modern computers.
1873	QWERTY keyboard (Christopher Latham Sholes): After patenting the first practical typewriter, Sholes develops the QWERTY keyboard, designed to slow the fastest typists, who otherwise jammed the keys. The basic QWERTY design remains the standard on most computer keyboards.
1884	Census tabulating machine (Herman Hollerith): Hollerith's machine uses punch cards to tabulate 1890 census data. He goes on to found the company that later becomes International Business Machines (IBM).
1892	Calculator (William Seward Burroughs): Burroughs builds the first practical key-operated calculator; it prints entries and results.
1894	Automatic loom (James Henry Northrop): Northrop builds the first automatic loom.
1926	Automatic power loom (Sakichi Toyoda): Toyoda's loom helps Japan catch up with the western Industrial Revolution.
1927	Analogue computer (Vannevar Bush): Bush builds the first analogue computer. He is also the first person to describe the idea of hypertext.
1928	New punch card: IBM introduces a new punch card that has rectangular holes and eight columns.
1937	Concepts of digital circuits and information theory (Claude Elwood Shannon): Shannon's most important contributions were electronic switching and using information theory to discover the basic requirements for data transmission.

Year	Event
1937	Model K computer (George Stibitz): The model K, an early electronic computer, employs Boolean logic.
1937-1938	Analogue computer (George Philbrick): Philbrick builds the Automatic Control Analyzer, which is an electronic analogue computer.
1939	Atanasoff-Berry Computer (John Vincent Atanasoff and Clifford Berry): The ABC, the world's first electronic digital computer, uses binary numbers and electronic switching, but it is not programmable.
1941	Z3 programmable computer (Konrad Zuse): Zuse and his colleagues complete the first general-purpose, programmable computer, the Z3, in December.
1944	Electromechanical computer (Howard Aiken and Grace Hopper): The Mark series of computers is built, designed by Aiken and Hopper. The US Navy uses it to calculate trajectories for projectiles.
1944	Colossus: Colossus, the world's first vacuum-tube programmable logic calculator, is built in Britain for the purpose of breaking Nazi codes.
1945	Automatic Computing Engine (Alan Mathison Turing): While the Automatic Computing Engine (ACE) was never fully built, it was one of the first stored-program computers.
1945	ENIAC computer (John William Mauchly and John Presper Eckert): The Electronic Numerical Integrator and Computer, ENIAC, is the first general-purpose, programmable, electronic computer. (The Z3, developed independently by Konrad Zuse from 1939 to 1941 in Nazi Germany, did not fully exploit electronic components.) Built to calculate artillery firing tables, ENIAC is used in calculations for the hydrogen bomb.
1947	Transistor (John Bardeen, Walter H. Brattain, and William Shockley): Hoping to build a solid-state amplifier, the team of Bardeen, Brattain, and Shockley discover the transistor, which replaces the vacuum tube in electronics.
1949	Magnetic core memory (Jay Wright Forrester): Core memory is used from the early 1950s to the early 1970s.
1950s	Fortran (John Warner Backus): Backus develops the computer language Fortran, which is an acronym for "formula translation." Fortran allows direct entry of commands into computers with Englishlike words and algebraic symbols.
1951	UNIVAC (John Mauchly and John Presper Eckert): Mauchly and Eckert invent the Universal Automatic Computer (UNIVAC). UNIVAC is competitor of IBM's products.
1952	Language compiler (Grace Murray Hopper): Hopper invents the compiler, an intermediate program that translates English-language instructions into computer language, followed in 1959 by Common Business Oriented Language (COBOL), the first computer programming language to translate commands used by programmers into the machine language the computer understands.
1954	Machine vision (Jerome H. Lemelson): Machine vision allows a computer to move and measure products and to inspect them for quality control.

Year	Event
1954	IBM 650: The IBM 650 computer becomes available. It is considered by IBM to be its first business computer, and it is the first computer installed at Columbia University in New York.
1955	Floppy disk and floppy disk drive (Alan Shugart): Working at the San Jose, California, offices of IBM, Shugart develops the disk drive, followed by floppy disks to provide a relatively fast way to store programs and data permanently.
1956	350 RAMAC: IBM produces the first computer disk storage system, the 350 RAMAC, which retrieves data from any of fifty spinning disks.
1957	PRONTO (Patrick J. Hanratty): While working for General Electric, Patrick J. Hanratty develops the numerical-control program PRONTO (Program for Numerical Tooling).
1958	Integrated circuit (Robert Norton Noyce and Jack St. Clair Kilby): The microchip, independently discovered by Noyce and Kilby, proves to be the breakthrough that allows the miniaturization of electronic circuits and paves the way for the digital revolution.
1958	TX-2: The digital computer TX-2 is completed at the Massachusetts Institute of Technology (MIT). Located within that institution's Lincoln Laboratory, the TX-2 will later run doctoral student Ivan Sutherland's groundbreaking computer-aided design program, Sketchpad.
1959	MIT CAD Project launches: The MIT Computer-Aided Design Project begins operations. The researcher leading the project, Douglas T. Ross, will later be credited with coining the term computer-aided design.
1959	Work on DAC-1 commences: Employees at General Motors begin work on the Design Augmented by Computer (DAC-1) system.
1960	*Computer-Aided Design: A Statement of Objectives* (Douglas T. Ross): On behalf of the MIT Computer-Aided Design Project, Douglas T. Ross publishes the technical memorandum *Computer-Aided Design: A Statement of Objectives*, in which he articulates the group's definition of computer-aided design.
1963	Sketchpad (Ivan Sutherland): MIT doctoral student Ivan Sutherland introduces the computer-aided design program Sketchpad in his 1963 doctoral thesis, *Sketchpad, a Man-Machine Graphical Communication System*. Its user interface will later be identified as the first example of a graphical user interface (GUI).
1964	BASIC programming language (John Kemeny and Thomas Kurtz): Kemeny and Kurtz develop the BASIC computer programming language. BASIC is an acronym for Beginner's All-purpose Symbolic Instruction Code.
1965	Minicomputer (Ken Olsen): Perhaps the first true minicomputer, the PDP-8 is released by Digital Equipment Corporation. Founder Olsen makes computers affordable for small businesses.
1965	CADAM: Originally known as Project Design, the computer application Computer-graphics Augmented Design and Manufacturing (CADAM) is developed at the Lockheed Corporation.
1968	*Computer-Aided Design*: The journal *Computer-Aided Design* publishes its first issue.

Year	Event
1968	Computer mouse (Douglas Engelbart): Engelbart presents the computer mouse, which he had been working on since 1964.
1968	UNISURF (Pierre Bézier): The computer-aided design and manufacturing system UNISURF, developed Pierre Bézier, comes into use at Renault.
1968	Peugeot 204: The body of the Peugeot 204 automobile is designed in UNISURF.
1969	ARPANET launches: The Advanced Research Projects Agency starts ARPANET, which is the precursor to the Internet. UCLA and Stanford University are the first institutions to become networked.
1970	UNIX (Dennis Ritchie and Kenneth Thompson): Bell Laboratories employees Ritchie and Thompson complete the UNIX operating system, which becomes popular among scientists.
1970	Network Control Protocol: The Network Working Group deploys the initial ARPANET host-to-host protocol, called the Network Control Protocol (NCP), establishing connections, break connections, switch connections, and control flow over the ARPANET.
1971	ADAM (Patrick J. Hanratty): While working at his own company Manufacturing Consulting Services, Patrick J. Hanratty creates the computer-aided design and manufacturing program ADAM (Automated Drafting and Machining).
1971	Microprocessor (Ted Hoff): The computer's central processing unit (CPU) is reduced to the size of a postage stamp.
1971	Touch screen (Sam Hurst): Hurst's touch screen can detect if it has been touched and where it was touched.
1972	Pong video game (Nolan K. Bushnell and Ted Dabney): Bushnell and Dabney register the name of their new computer company, Atari, and issue Pong shortly thereafter, marking the rise of the video game industry. Digital graphics and modeling software will later become common tools in that industry.
1975	Unigraphics: United Computing introduces the computer-aided design software Unigraphics, one of the forerunners of the software NX. The software will later be acquired by Electronic Data Systems.
1976	Apple computer (Steve Jobs): Jobs cofounds Apple Computer with Steve Wozniak.
1976	Microsoft Corporation (Bill Gates): Gates, along with Paul Allen, found Microsoft, a software company. Gates will remain head of Microsoft for twenty-five years.
1979	First commercially successful application: The VisiCalc spreadsheet for Apple II, designed by Daniel Bricklin and Bob Frankston, helps drive sales of the personal computer and becomes its first successful business application.
1979	USENET (Tom Truscott, Jim Ellis and Steve Belovin): Truscott, Ellis, and Belovin create USENET, a "poor man's ARPANET," to share information via e-mail and message boards between Duke University and the University of North Carolina, using dial-up telephone lines.

Year	Event
1981	First IBM personal computer: The first IBM PC, the IBM 5100, goes on the market with a $1,565 price tag.
1982	CATIA: Dassault Systèmes, an offshoot of Dassault Aviation, launches Version 1 of its flagship computer-aided design and manufacturing software, CATIA.
1982	AutoCAD: The software company Autodesk releases the first version of its flagship computer-aided design software, AutoCAD.
1982	I-DEAS: The Structural Dynamics Research Corporation introduces its Integrated Design and Engineering Analysis System (I-DEAS), one of the forerunners of the later software NX.
1984	CD-ROM: Philips and Sony introduce the CD-ROM (compact disc read-only memory), which has the capacity to store data of more than 450 floppy disks. The CD-ROM goes on to become a principal means of distributing computer software, including computer-aided design software.
1985	Windows operating system (Bill Gates): The first version of Windows is released.
1987	3D printer: 3D Systems releases the first commercial 3D printer.
1989	World Wide Web (Tim Berners-Lee and Robert Cailau): Berners-Lee finds a way to join the idea of hypertext and the young Internet, leading to the Web, coinvented with Cailau.
1995	SolidWorks: The SolidWorks Corporation releases SolidWorks 95, the debut version of its flagship software. The company will be acquired by Dassault Systèmes in 1997.
1995	Boeing 777: Commercial flights begin for the Boeing 777, the first commercial airliner designed and modeled entirely through digital means.
2011	Autodesk 360: Autodesk introduces its first cloud-based product offerings with Autodesk 360.
2012	3DEXPERIENCE: Dassault Systèmes introduces its 3DEXPERIENCE platform, a cloud-based platform that will come to be integrated with computer-aided design software such as CATIA and SolidWorks.
2018	3DEXPERIENCE Marketplace: Dassault Systèmes introduces the 3DEXPERIENCE Marketplace, a means of connecting companies using the 3DEXPERIENCE platform with manufacturers and design resources.

Source: Charles W. Rogers, Southwestern Oklahoma State University, Department of Physics; updated by the editors of Salem Press

Glossary

additive manufacturing: a form of manufacturing in which layers of a material are added and joined together to construct an object.

algorithm: a set of step-by-step instructions for performing computations.

animation variables (avars): defined variables that control the movement of an animated character or object.

applications: programs that perform specific functions that are not essential to the operation of the computer or mobile device; often called "apps."

application-specific GUI: a graphical user interface designed to be used for a specific application.

artificial intelligence (AI): the intelligence exhibited by machines or computers, in contrast to human, organic, or animal intelligence.

AutoCAD: the flagship computer-aided design software developed by Autodesk.

Automated Drafting and Machining (ADAM): a 1971 program created by American computer scientist Patrick J. Hanratty; one of the first commercially applied computer-aided design programs.

automation: a phenomenon in which computers or other machines, such as those used in manufacturing, carry out tasks without direct human guidance.

autonomous: able to operate independently, without external or conscious control.

Bézier curve: a parametric curve commonly used in CAD software, first articulated by French mathematician Paul de Casteljau and later popularized by French engineer Pierre Bézier.

Bézier, Pierre: a French engineer and the creator of UNISURF.

binder jetting: a form of additive manufacturing in which a liquid binding agent is used to fuse layers of powder together.

biomaterials: natural or synthetic materials that can be used to replace, repair, or modify organic tissues or systems.

bioprinting: the process of producing biomaterials such as living tissues through additive manufacturing.

bit: a single binary digit that can have a value of either 0 or 1.

building information modeling (BIM): the creation of a model of a building or facility that accounts for its function, physical attributes, cost, and other characteristics.

byte: a group of eight bits.

cathode ray tube (CRT): a vacuum tube used to create images in devices such as older television and computer monitors.

CATIA: a computer-aided design, manufacturing, and engineering software developed by Dassault Systèmes.

cellular manufacturing: the arrangement of production work stations and equipment in a sequence that supports a smooth flow of materials and components through the production process with minimal transport or delay.

central processing unit (CPU): electronic circuitry that provides instructions for how a computer handles, processes, and manages data from applications and programs.

character: a unit of information that represents a single letter, number, punctuation mark, blank space, or other symbol used in written language.

cloud services: computing services that are hosted on external servers and made available to users via the internet.

command line: an interface that accepts text-based commands to navigate and control the computer system.

command-line interpreter: an interface that interprets and carries out commands entered by the user.

computer numerical control (CNC): the process of using a computer program to provide instructions for the automated operation of machines, particularly those used in manufacturing.

computer: any device that can be programmed to perform mechanical or electrical computation, processing numbers. Since the middle of the twentieth century, the term is commonly used for equipment that can be programmed using a binary number system to perform a variety of work. For a computer to process letters, words, graphic images, or maps, human programmers have to encode nonnumerical data in a numeric form.

computer-aided design (CAD): the use of computer technology to create designs or virtual models of objects or structures.

computer-aided engineering (CAE): the use of computer technology to perform various analyses of computer-stored designs for factors such as structural integrity and performance.

computer-aided manufacturing (CAM): the use of computer technology to control the manufacturing process.

concurrent engineering: a method of product or process design that includes simultaneous input from every individual with a stake or role (including engineers, salespersons, support personnel, vendors, and customers) throughout the entire design process.

contract manufacturing: the process of hiring a manufacturing firm to produce one or more components, assemblies, or completed products.

data source: the origin of the information used in a computer model or simulation, such as a database or spreadsheet.

defect: the result of any deviation from product specifications that may lead to customer dissatisfaction.

Design Augmented by Computer (DAC-1): a forerunner of later graphics and computer-aided design programs developed in the 1960s by General Motors and IBM.

design for manufacturability (DFM): the tailoring of product designs to eliminate manufacturing difficulties and minimize costs.

device: equipment designed to perform a specific function when attached to a computer, such as a scanner, printer, or projector.

direct-access storage: a type of data storage in which the data has a dedicated address and location on the storage device, allowing it to be accessed directly rather than sequentially.

direct manipulation interface: a computer interaction format that allows users to directly manipulate graphical objects or physical shapes that are automatically translated into coding.

directed energy deposition: a form of additive manufacturing in which wire or powdered material is deposited onto an object and then melted using a laser, electron beam, or plasma arc.

electronic computer-aided design (ECAD): the use of computer technology to design electronic components and systems.

engineering: practical application of the knowledge of pure science, and sometimes of art as well, not only to construct buildings, bridges, infrastructure, and engines, but to plan and organize industrial and community processes. There are many branches of engineering, including electrical, industrial, mechanical, civil, aeronautical, geotechnical, transportation, water management, disaster preparedness and management, and telecommunications.

error: any deviation from a specified manufacturing process.

error-proofing: designing the process to prevent mistakes, to stop errors from occurring, to warn that an error has occurred, and to prevent assembly errors through design strategies.

four-dimensional building information modeling (4D BIM): the process of creating a 3D model that incorporates time-related information to guide the manufacturing process.

fuel cell: a source of electric current that operates in a manner similar to a battery, generating electricity as a by-product of a chemical reaction. The difference is that a fuel cell continues generating power as long as it is supplied with fuel. The hydrogen fuel cell, one of the most commonly known, generates electricity, heat, and water.

generative design: a form of computer-aided design in which the computer software automatically generates potential designs that meet a user-specified set of parameters.

geometry: literally "earth measurement," the branch of mathematics concerned with the properties and relationships of points, lines, and surfaces and the space contained by those entities.

globalization: the process of businesses or technologies spreading across the world, creating an interconnected, global marketplace operating outside constraints of time zone or national boundary.

graphical user interface (GUI): a computer interface in which the user controls the computer by interacting with menus, icons, and other graphical elements.

Hanratty, Patrick J.: an American computer scientist and the creator of Automated Drafting and Machining (ADAM).

hardware: the physical parts that make up a computer. These include the motherboard and processor, as well as input and output devices such as monitors, keyboards, and mice.

hydroponics: growing plants in a solution of water and selected nutrients, without need for soil.

information technology: the use of computers and related equipment for the purpose of processing and storing data.

input: data supplied to some program, subprogram, operating system, machine, system, or abstraction.

integration: in computer science, the process of combining individual system components, whether hardware or software, into a single, unified system.

intellectual property: intangible assets, including creative ideas and specialized knowledge that has commercial value; some can be protected by patents, trademarks, and copyrights.

interface metaphors: linking computer commands, actions, and processes with real-world actions, processes, or objects that have functional similarities.

internal-use software: software developed by a company for its own use to support general and administrative functions, such as payroll, accounting, or personnel management and maintenance.

International System of Units: also called SI units, the units of measurement used in most of the world for measurements. The seven basic SI units are the kilogram (for mass), the second (for time), the Kelvin (for temperature), the ampere (for electric current), the mole (for the amount of a substance), the candela (for luminous intensity), and the meter (for distance).

isometric drawing: a form of two-dimensional drawing in which the object being depicted is represented in such a way that it appears to be three dimensional and positioned at a specific angle.

just-in-time manufacturing (JIT): a manufacturing strategy in which products are manufactured as needed and little inventory is maintained.

kaizen: a manufacturing strategy based on continuous improvement.

laser: a light source that emanates from a well-defined wavelength; originally an acronym for light amplified by stimulated emission of radiation.

lean manufacturing: an approach to manufacturing that emphasizes flexibility, versatility, and the elimination of waste.

light pen: a device, used with early computer-aided design systems such as Sketchpad, that enabled users to select and manipulate graphics visible on a computer's display screen.

light-emitting diode (LED): a diode constructed to provide illumination from the movement of electrons through a semiconductor, which is housed in a bulb that concentrates the light in a desired direction.

machine code: system of instructions and data directly understandable by a computer's central processing unit.

machine learning algorithm: an algorithm that is capable of being trained and of learning based on the datasets to which it is exposed and the tasks it completes.

magnetic storage: a device that stores information by magnetizing certain types of material.

manufacturability: the features that make a product suitable for manufacture on a large-scale basis.

manufacturing process management (MPM): collection of technology and methods used to manufacture products.

material extrusion: a form of additive manufacturing in which heated filament is extruded through a nozzle and deposited in layers, usually around a removable support.

material jetting: a form of additive manufacturing in which drops of liquid photopolymer are deposited through a printer head and heated to form a dry, stable solid.

metals: a majority of known elements, generally shiny in appearance and good conductors of heat and electricity. In ionic compounds, metals usually provide the positive ion. Many metals react with acids and therefore act as a base.

micron: a unit of measurement equaling one millionth of a meter; typically used to measure the width of a core in an optical figure or the line width on a microchip.

milling: a form of subtractive manufacturing in which material is cut away using a machine equipped with rotary cutters.

modeling: the process of creating a two-dimensional (2D) or three-dimensional (3D) representation of the structure being designed.

nanotechnology: technology built on a very small scale.

network: two or more computers being linked in a way that allows them to transmit information back and forth.

nongraphical: not featuring graphical elements.

NX: a computer-aided design, engineering, and manufacturing software developed by Siemens.

object-oriented programming: a type of programming in which the source code is organized into objects, which are elements with a unique identity that have a defined set of attributes and behaviors.

object-oriented user interface: an interface that allows users to interact with onscreen objects as they would in real-world situations, rather than selecting objects that are changed through a separate control panel interface.

offshore manufacturing: the practice of moving manufacturing to overseas locations, usually for the purpose of lowering costs through cheaper labor, land, and materials.

open-source software: software for which users have permission to modify the source code.

operating system (OS): a specialized program that manages a computer's functions.

optical storage: storage of data by creating marks in a medium that can be read with the aid of a laser or other light source.

outsourcing: the practice of contracting with another firm to complete work that would normally be completed by the hiring firm.

parameter: a measurable element of a system that affects the relationships between variables in the system.

peripherals: devices connected to a computer but not part of the computer itself, such as scanners, external storage devices, and so forth.

platform: the underlying computer system on which an application is designed to run.

poka-yoke: a concept introduced at Toyota Motor Corporation in 1961 that uses process or design features to error-proof the manufacturing process by preventing the manufacture of a nonconforming or faulty product, promoting safer working conditions, and preventing machine damage.

postproduction: the period after a model has been designed and an image has been rendered, when an individual may manipulate the created image by adding effects or making other aesthetic changes.

powder bed fusion: a form of additive manufacturing in which a laser is used to heat layers of powdered material in a movable powder bed.

prime contractor: a company with overall responsibility for completing work contracted for by another firm. The prime contractor may use many subcontractors to complete the work required by the contract.

printed circuit board (PCB): a flat copper sheet shielded by fiberglass insulation in which numerous lines have been etched and holes have been punched, allowing various electronic components to be connected and to communicate with one another and with external components via the exposed copper traces.

process design: the development of procedures, flow, and quality practices needed to produce a product.

product lifecycle management (PLM): a strategic business approach that applies a consistent set of business solutions in support of the collaborative creation, management, dissemination, and use of product definition information across the extended enterprise from concept to end of life, thus integrating people, process, and information.

proprietary software: software owned by an individual or company that places certain restrictions on its use, study, modification, or distribution and typically withholds its source code.

prototype: an early version of product that is still under development, used to demonstrate what the finished product will look like and what features it will include.

quality assurance: the practice of improving processes and empowering employees to make decisions that enable avoidance of errors and defects.

random-access memory (RAM): memory that the computer can access very quickly, without regard to where in the storage media the relevant information is located.

rapid prototyping: the process of quickly creating physical prototypes that are then tested, evaluated, and potentially improved upon.

raster: a means of storing, displaying, and editing image data based on the use of individual pixels.

reconfigurable manufacturing system (RMS): a manufacturing system designed so that its structure, hardware, and software components can be rapidly changed to adjust production capacity in response to new market circumstances or to alter their functionality.

rendering: the process of transforming one or more models into a single image.

request for proposal (RFP): a formalized document created by hiring firms that details work to be completed and the terms under which it should be completed. Firms respond to RFPs with proposals on how they would accomplish the work specified, and at what price.

robotics: an interdisciplinary field concerned with the design, development, operation, and assessment of electromechanical devices used to perform tasks that would otherwise require human action.

Ross, Douglas T.: an American computer scientist credited with coining the term CAD.

sheet lamination: a manufacturing process in which thin layered sheets of material are adhered or fused together and extra material is then removed with cutting implements or lasers.

simulation: a computer model executed by a computer system.

Sketchpad: an early CAD software created by American computer scientist Ivan Sutherland as part of his 1963 doctoral thesis.

software as a service (SaaS): a cloud service in which users subscribe to software and access that software via the internet.

software patches: updates to software that correct bugs or make other improvements.

software: the sets of instructions that a computer follows in order to carry out tasks. Software may be stored on physical media, but the media is not the software.

solid modeling: the process of creating a 3D representation of a solid object.

solid-state storage: computer memory that stores information in the form of electronic circuits, without the use of disks or other read/write equipment.

SolidWorks: a computer-aided design, engineering, and manufacturing software developed by Dassault Systèmes.

source code: the set of instructions written in a programming language to create a program.

stereolithography: a form of additive manufacturing in which a layering technique is used to build physical objects.

subtractive manufacturing: a manufacturing process in which pieces of material are removed from a larger whole in order to form the desired product.

supercomputer: an extremely powerful computer that far outpaces conventional desktop computers.

supply chain: the entire network of suppliers, retailers, distributors, transporters, and warehousers that are involved in the sale, delivery, and production of a product.

surface modeling: the process of creating a 3D representation of an object in which all surfaces are modeled but the model itself is not solid.

Sutherland, Ivan: an American computer scientist and the creator of Sketchpad.

system: a set of interacting or interdependent component parts that form a complex whole.

third-party data center: a data center service provided by a separate company that is responsible for maintaining its infrastructure.

time to market: the length of time it takes to bring a product from the initial concept to the marketplace.

transistor: a computing component generally made of silicon that can amplify electronic signals or work as a switch to direct electronic signals within a computer system.

UNISURF: an early computer-aided design and manufacturing system developed by French engineer Pierre Bézier in the 1960s.

user-centered design: design based on a perceived understanding of user preferences, needs, tendencies, and capabilities.

variable: a symbol representing a quantity with no fixed value.

vat photopolymerization: a form of additive manufacturing in which a laser hardens layers of light-sensitive material in a vat.

vector: a means of storing, displaying, and editing image data based on the use of defined points and lines.

virtual reality: a form of technology that enables the user to view and interact with a simulated environment.

web application: an application that is downloaded either wholly or in part from the Internet each time it is used.

wireframe modeling: the process of creating a 3D representation of an object in which all edges are outlined, surfaces are not modeled, and the model itself is not solid.

Organizations

Additive Manufacturer Green Trade Association (AMGTA)
2500 SW 39th St.
Hollywood, FL 33312
954-308-0888
amgta.org

American Design Drafting Association (ADDA)
105 E Main St.
Newbern, TN 38059
731-627-0802
www.adda.org

American Institute of Aeronautics and Astronautics (AIAA)
12700 Sunrise Valley Dr.
Ste. 200
Reston, VA 20191-5807
800-639-2422
www.aiaa.org

American Institute of Architects (AIA)
1735 New York Ave, NW
Washington, DC 20006-5292
800-242-3837
www.aiaonline.com

American Institute of Architecture Students (AIAS)
1735 New York Ave NW
Third floor
Washington, DC 20006
202-808-0075
www.aias.org

American Institute of Building Design (AIDB)
7059 Blair Rd. NW
Ste. 400
Washington, DC 20012
800-366-2423
www.aibd.org

American Society of Mechanical Engineers (ASME)
2 Park Ave.
New York, NY 10016-5990
800-843-2763
www.asme.org

Association for Computer-Aided Design in Architecture (ACADIA)
communications@acadia.org
www.acadia.org

CAD/BIM Technology Center
US Army Corp of Engineers
441 G St. NW
Washington, DC 20314-1000
202-761-0011
wwwcadbimcenter.erdc.dren.mil

Industrial Designers Society of America (IDSA)
950 Herndon Pkwy
Ste. 250
Herndon, VA 20170
703-707-6000
www.idsa.org

Institute of Electrical & Electronics Engineers (IEEE)
445 and 501 Hoes Lane
Piscataway, NJ 08854-4141
732-981-0060
www.ieee.org

National BIM Standard-United States Project Committee (NBIMS-US)
(formerly Facility Information Council)
National Institute of Building Sciences (NIBS)
1090 Vermont Ave. NW
Ste. 700
Washington, DC 20005-4950
202-289-7800
wwwnationalbimstandard.org
www.nibs.org

National Tooling & Machining Association (NTMA)
1357 Rockside Rd.
Cleveland, OH 44134
800-248-6862
ntma.org

Society of Automobile Engineers (SAE) International
400 Commonwealth Dr.
Warrendale, PA 15096
724-776-4841
www.sae.org

Society of Computer Aided Drafting Designers
www.thescadd.org

Texas Society of Architects
500 Chicon St.
Austin, TX 87802
512-478-7386
www.texasarchitects.org

United States National CAD Standard (NCS)
National Institute of Building Sciences (NIBS)
1090 Vermont Ave. NW
Ste. 700
Washington, DC 20005-4950
202-289-7800
www.nationalcadstandard.org
www.nibs.org

World Design Organization (WDO)
455 St. Antoine St. West
Ste. SS10
Montreal, Quebec, Canada H2Z 1J1
514-448-4949
wdo.org

Bibliography

"3D Bioprinting of Living Tissues." *Wyss Institute*, 2021, wyss.harvard.edu/technology/3d-bioprinting/. Accessed 28 Nov. 2021.

"3-D Human CAD." *United States Ergonomics*, 2021, us-ergo.com/ergonomics-laboratory/measurement-technologies/human-cad-analysis/. Accessed 28 Nov. 2021.

"3D Modeling and CAD Design in Plastic Manufacturing." *Advanced Plastiform, Inc.*, 2021, advancedplastiform.com/process/3d-modeling-and-cad-drawings/. Accessed 28 Nov. 2021.

"3D Printing Technology for Improved Hearing." *Sonova*, www.sonova.com/en/story/innovation/3d-printing-technology-improved-hearing. Accessed 28 Nov. 2021.

"3D-4D Building Information Modeling." *US General Services Administration*, 4 Sept. 2020, www.gsa.gov/real-estate/design-construction/3d4d-building-information-modeling. Accessed 28 Nov. 2021.

"6 Contract Manufacturing Issues (and How to Avoid Them)." *Smart Machine Technologies*, 26 Sept. 2019, www.smartmachine.com/6-contract-manufacturing-issues-how-to-avoid-them/. Accessed 28 Nov. 2021.

"777 Commercial Transport." *Boeing*, www.boeing.com/history/products/777.page. Accessed 28 Nov. 2021.

Abbasov, Iftikhar B., editor. *Computer Modeling in the Aerospace Industry*. Wiley/Scrivener Publishing, 2020.

Abdi, M. Reza, and Ashraf Labib. "A Design Strategy for Reconfigurable Manufacturing Systems (RMSs) Using Analytical Hierarchical Process (AHP): A Case Study." *International Journal of Production Research*, vol. 41, no. 10, 2003, pp. 2273-99.

———. "Grouping and Selecting Products: The Design Key of Reconfigurable Manufacturing Systems (RMSs)." *International Journal of Production Research*, vol. 42, no. 3, 2004, pp. 521-46.

"About Additive Manufacturing." *Additive Manufacturing Research Group*, 2021, www.lboro.ac.uk/research/amrg/about/. Accessed 28 Nov. 2021.

"About Creating 3D Wireframe Models." *Autodesk*, 16 Dec. 2015, knowledge.autodesk.com/support/autocad/learn-explore/caas/CloudHelp/cloudhelp/2016/ENU/AutoCAD-Core/files/GUID-84E193D7-A18D-4EE2-B978-19E4AFBCAEEC-htm.html. Accessed 28 Nov. 2021.

"About Us." *Enabling the Future*, 2019, enablingthefuture.org/about/. Accessed 28 Nov. 2021.

Abrahamson, Eric, and David H. Freedman. *A Perfect Mess: The Hidden Benefits of Disorder*. Little, Brown, 2006.

Acheson, David. *The Wonder Book of Geometry*. Oxford UP, 2020.

Ackerman, Daniel. "Computer-Aided Creativity in Robot Design." *MIT News*, 30 Nov. 2020, news.mit.edu/2020/computer-aided-robot-design-1130. Accessed 28 Nov. 2021.

Adams, Nico, and Peter Murray-Rust. "Engineering Polymer Informatics: Towards the Computer-Aided Design of Polymers." *Macromolecular Rapid Communications*, vol. 29, no. 8, 2008, pp. 615-32.

Adhami, Reza, Peter M. Meenen III, and Dennis Hite. *Fundamental Concepts in Electrical and Computer Engineering with Practical Design Problems*. 2nd ed., Universal, 2005.

Agkathidis, Asterios. *Generative Design: Form-Finding Techniques in Architecture*. Laurence King, 2015.

Agrawal, Manindra, S. Barry Cooper, and Angsheng Li, editors. *Theory and Applications of Models of Computation: 9th Annual Conference, TAMC 2012, Beijing, China, May 16-21, 2012*. Springer, 2012.

Akhmedzyanov, D. A., A. E. Kishalov, and K. V. Markina. "Computer-Aided Design of Aircraft Gas Turbine Engines and Selection of Materials for Their Main Parts." *Vestnik*, vol. 14, no. 1, 2015, pp. 101-11.

Albert, Mark. "Always in the Learning Mode." *Modern Machine Shop*, 1 Mar. 2007, www.mmsonline.com/articles/always-in-the-learning-mode. Accessed 28 Nov. 2021.

Alcorn, S. *Theme Park Design: Behind the Scenes with an Engineer*. Theme Perks Press, 2010.

Allanwood, Gavin, and Peter Beare. *User Experience Design: Creating Designs Users Really Love*. Fairchild, 2014.

Allen, Theodore T. *Introduction to Engineering Statistics and Six Sigma: Statistical Quality Control and Design of Experiments and Systems*. 2nd ed., Springer-Verlag, 2010.

Allison, Eric, and Lauren Peters. *Historic Preservation and the Livable City*. Wiley, 2011.

Al-Maadeed, Mariam, Deepalekshmi Ponnamma, and Marcelo Carignano, editors. *Polymer Science and Innovative Applications: Materials, Techniques, and Future Developments*. Elsevier, 2020.

Alqahtan, Ammar Y., Elif Kongar, Kishore K. Pochampally, and Surendra M. Gupta, editors.

Responsible Manufacturing: Issues Pertaining to Sustainability. CRC Press, 2019.

"Alternative Fuels Data Center: Hybrid Electric Vehicles." *Energy Efficiency & Renewable Energy*, US Department of Energy, 28 Sept. 2016, www.afdc.energy.gov/vehicles/electric_basics_hev.html. Accessed 28 Nov. 2021.

Alton, Larry. "How CAD Software and 3D Printing Are Allowing Customized Products at Scale." *Inc.*, 1 Feb. 2020, www.inc.com/larry-alton/how-cad-software-3d-printing-are-allowing-customized-products-at-scale.html. Accessed 16 Dec. 2021.

"*Alvin* Upgrade." *WHOI*, 2021, www.whoi.edu/what-we-do/explore/underwater-vehicles/hov-alvin/history-of-alvin/alvin-upgrade/. Accessed 28 Nov. 2021.

Ambrose, Gavin, Paul Harris, and Sally Stone. *The Visual Dictionary of Architecture*. AVA, 2008.

Amin, M., and M. A. Karim. "A Time-Based Quantitative Approach for Selecting Lean Strategies for Manufacturing Organisations." *International Journal of Production Research*, vol. 51, no. 4, 2013, pp. 1146-67.

Anderl, Reiner, and Peter Binde. Simulations with NX/Simcenter 3D: Kinematics, FEA, CFD, EM and Data Management. 2nd ed., Hanser Publications, 2018.

Anderson, David M. *Design for Manufacturability*. 2nd ed., Routledge/Productivity Press, 2020.

Anderson, Edward E. *Fundamentals of Solar Energy Conversion*. Addison Wesley Longman, 1982.

Anderson, John D., Jr., and Mary L. Bowden. *Introduction to Flight*. 9th ed., McGraw-Hill, 2021.

Andrews, Wen. *CAD Tools for Interior Design*. Autodesk Press, 2008.

Anton, Howard. *Calculus: A New Horizon*. 6th ed., Wiley, 1999.

Aravind Raj, S., A. Sudheer, S. Vinodh, and G. Anand. "A Mathematical Model to Evaluate the Role of Agility Enablers and Criteria in a Manufacturing Environment." *International Journal of Production Research*, vol. 51, no. 19, pp. 5971-84.

Archer, L. Bruce. "Whatever Became of Design Methodology?" *Design Studies*, vol. 1, no. 1, 1979, pp. 17-20.

Armstrong, Helen, editor. *Digital Design Theory. Readings from the Field*. Princeton Architectural Press, 2016.

Arroyo, Sheri, and Rhea Stewart. *How Deep Sea Divers Use Math*. Chelsea House, 2009.

Arruñada, Benito, and Xosé H. Vázquez. "When Your Contract Manufacturer Becomes Your Competitor." *Harvard Business Review*, Sept. 2006, hbr.org/2006/09/when-your-contract-manufacturer-becomes-your-competitor. Accessed 28 Nov. 2021.

Arteaga, Robert F. *The Building of the Arch*. 10th ed., Jefferson National Parks Association, 2002.

Ascher, Kate. *The Works: Anatomy of a City*. 2005. Penguin Press, 2007.

Ashby, Darren. *Electrical Engineering 101: Everything You Should Have Learned in School—But Probably Didn't*. 3rd ed., Newnes, 2012.

Ashter, Syed Ali. *Introduction to Bioplastics Engineering*. Elsevier, 2016.

Askeland, Donald R., and Wendelin J. Wright. *The Science and Engineering of Materials*. 7th ed., Cengage Learning, 2015.

"Aspects of Energy Efficiency in Machine Tools." *Heidenhain*, 5 Oct. 2011, www.heidenhain.us/resources-and-news/aspects-of-energy-efficiency-in-machine-tools/. Accessed 28 Nov. 2021.

Asperl, Andreas. "How to Teach CAD." *Computer-Aided Design & Applications*, vol. 2, no. 1-4, 2005, pp. 459-68.

Astall, Chris. "Lean Manufacturing and IT: No Oxymoron." *Manufacturers' Monthly*, Apr. 2006, p. 20.

"Autodesk Research." *Autodesk*, 2021, www.autodesk.com/research/overview. Accessed 16 Dec. 2021.

Ayhan, Mustafa Batuhan, Ercan Öztemel, Mehmet Emin Aydin, and Yong Yue. "A Quantitative Approach for Measuring Process Innovation: A Case Study in a Manufacturing Company." *International Journal of Production Research*, vol. 51, no. 11, 2013, pp. 3463-75.

Azar, Dimitri T. *Clinical Optics, 2014-2015*. American Academy of Ophthalmology, 2014.

Baatz, E. "Rapid Growth Changes Rules for Purchasing." *Purchasing*, vol. 126, no. 10, 1999, pp. 33-35.

Babcock and Wilcox Company. *Steam: Its Generation and Use*. Kessinger, 2010.

Bacus, John. *Digital Sketching: Computer-Aided Conceptual Design*. Wiley, 2020.

Bagotsky, Vladimir S. *Fuel Cells: Problems and Solutions*. 2nd ed., John Wiley & Sons, 2012.

Baine, Celeste. *High Tech Hot Shots: Careers in Sports Engineering*. National Society of Professional Engineers, 2004.

Bajaj, Varun, and G. R. Sinha, editors. *Computer-Aided Design and Diagnosis Methods for Biomedical Applications*. CRC Press, 2021.

Baker, R. Jacob. *CMOS: Circuit Design, Layout, and Simulation*. 4th ed., Wiley-IEEE Press, 2019.

Bandyopadhyay, Amit, and Susmita Bose, editors. *Additive Manufacturing*. 2nd ed., CRC Press, 2020.

Baran, Stanley J., and Dennis K. Davis. *Mass Communication Theory: Foundations, Ferment, and Future.* 8th ed., Oxford UP, 2020.

Bar-Cohen, Yoseph, editor. *Advances in Manufacturing and Processing of Materials and Structures.* CRC Press, 2019.

Barfield, Rose. "The Bézier Curve—How Car Design Influenced CAD." Bricsys Blog, blog.bricsys.com/the-bezier-curve-how-car-design-influenced-cad/. Accessed 16 Dec. 2021.

Bar-Lev, Adi. "Big Waves: Creating Swells, Wakes and Everything In-Between." *Game Developer*, Feb. 2008, pp. 14-24.

"The Basics of Designing PCBs with CAD." *PCB Train*, 29 Sept. 2015, www.pcbtrain.co.uk/blog/the-basics-of-designing-pcbs-with-cad. Accessed 28 Nov. 2021.

Baukh, Oleksandra. "Pre-production Processes in Garment Manufacturing." *Techpacker*, 14 Oct. 2020, techpacker.com/blog/manufacturing/pre-production-processes-in-garment-manufacturing/. Accessed 28 Nov. 2021.

Bayer, Michael, Nancy Frank, and Jason Valerius. *Becoming an Urban Planner: A Guide to Careers in Planning and Urban Design.* John Wiley & Sons, 2010.

Beer, Jeroen de. *Potential for Industrial Energy-Efficiency Improvement in the Long Term.* Kluwer Academic, 2000.

Bell, Michael. *Incremental Software Architecture: A Method for Saving Failing IT Implementations.* John Wiley & Sons, 2016.

Ben Manmoud-Jouini, Sihem, Christophe Midler, and Philippe Silberzahn. "Contributions of Design Thinking to Project Management in an Innovation Context." *Project Management Journal*, vol. 47, no. 2, 2016, pp. 144-56.

Benford, Harry. *Naval Architecture for Non-Naval Architects.* Society of Naval Architects and Marine Engineers, 1991.

Benyoucef, Lyes, editor. *Reconfigurable Manufacturing Systems: From Design to Implementation.* Springer Nature Switzerland, 2020.

Bergin, Michael S. "A Brief History of BIM." *ArchDaily*, 7 Dec. 2012, www.archdaily.com/302490/a-brief-history-of-bim. Accessed 28 Nov. 2021.

Bernard, Francis. "How the Inventor of CATIA Became the Founder of Dassault Systèmes." *Isicad*, 3 Mar. 2021, isicad.net/articles.php?article_num=21729. Accessed 10 Jan. 2022.

———. *A Short History of CATIA & Dassault Systemes.* Bernard, 2003.

Bernier, Samuel N., Bertier Luyt, Tatiana Reinhard, and Carl Bass. *Design for 3D Printing: Scanning, Creating, Editing, Remixing, and Making in Three Dimensions.* Maker Media, 2014.

Bernstein, Larry. "What Is Computer-Aided Design (CAD) and Why It's Important." *Jobsite*, 11 Oct. 2021, www.procore.com/jobsite/what-is-computer-aided-design-cad-and-why-its-important. Accessed 16 Dec. 2021.

Bessieİre, Pierre, Emmanuel Mazer, Juan Manuel Ahuactzin, and Kamel Mekhnacha. *Bayesian Programming.* CRC Press, 2014.

Bethscheider-Kieser, Ulrich. *Green Designed: Future Cars.* Avedition, 2008.

Bézier, Pierre. "Example of an Existing System in the Motor Industry: The Unisurf System." *Proceedings of the Royal Society A*, vol. 321, no. 1545, 1971, pp. 207-18.

———. *The Mathematical Basis of the UNISURF CAD System.* Butterworth-Heinemann, 1986.

Bhattacharya, Amit, and James D. McGlothin, *Occupational Ergonomics: Theory and Applications.* 2nd ed., CRC Press, 2019.

Bi, Zhuming, and Xiaoqin Wang. *Computer Aided Design and Manufacturing.* Wiley-ASME Press, 2020.

"Biomechanics." *Engineering in Medicine and Biology Society*, 2018, www.embs.org/about-biomedical-engineering/our-areas-of-research/biomechanics/. Accessed 28 Nov. 2021.

Bird, Frederick, and Joseph Smucker. "The Social Responsibilities of International Business Firms in Developing Areas." *Journal of Business Ethics*, vol. 73, no. 1, 2007, pp. 1-9.

Bitonti, Francis. *3D Printing Design: Additive Manufacturing and the Materials Revolution.* Bloomsbury, 2019.

Blanchard, Dave. "When Not to Go Lean." *Industry Week*, 10 Apr. 2007, www.industryweek.com/operations/continuous-improvement/article/21935329/when-not-to-go-lean. Accessed 28 Nov. 2021.

Blank, David A., Arthur E. Bock, and David J. Richardson. *Introduction to Naval Engineering.* 2nd ed., Naval Institute Press, 2005.

Blockley, David. *Bridges: The Science and Art of the World's Most Inspiring Structures.* Oxford UP, 2010.

Blundell, Danielle. "The 10 Commandments of Scandinavian Design, According to Experts." *Apartment Therapy*, 29 Sept. 2018, www.apartmenttherapy.com/scandinavian-design-rules-262980. Accessed 28 Nov. 2021.

Bokhari, Ali. "Urban Planning Education and Using CityCAD to Transform Our Cities." *Journal of Education*, 13 Dec. 2020, journals.sagepub.com/doi/abs/10.1177/0022057420979593. Accessed 28 Nov. 2021.

Borowitz, Sidney. *Farewell Fossil Fuels: Reviewing America's Energy Policy*. Plenum Trade, 1999.

Borrmann, André, Markus König, Christian Koch, and Jakob Beetz, editors. *Building Information Modeling: Technology Foundations and Industry Practice*. Springer International Publishing, 2018.

Bosch-Mauchand, Magali, Farouk Belkadi, Matthieu Bricogne, and Benoît Eynard. "Knowledge-Based Assessment of Manufacturing Process Performance: Integration of Product Lifecycle Management and Value-Chain Simulation Approaches." *International Journal of Computer Integrated Manufacturing*, vol. 26, no. 5, 2013, pp. 453-73.

Boulos, Paul F., Kevin E. Lansey, and Bryan W. Karney. *Comprehensive Water Distribution Systems Analysis Handbook for Engineers and Planners*. 2nd ed., MWH Soft Press, 2006.

Boyce, Meherwan P. *Gas Turbine Engineering Handbook*. 4th ed., Butterworth-Heinemann, 2012.

Boyer, Carl B. *History of Analytic Geometry*. Dover, 2004.

Breeze, Paul. *Power Generation Technologies*. 3rd ed., Elsevier, 2019.

Brewer, Barry L., Bryan Ashenbaum, and Joseph R. Carter. "Understanding the Supply Chain Outsourcing Cascade: When Does Procurement Follow Manufacturing Out the Door?" *Journal of Supply Chain Management*, vol. 49, no. 3, 2013, pp. 90-110.

Briney, Amanda. "Countries of Scandinavia." *Thought Co.*, 10 Dec. 2019, www.thoughtco.com/countries-of-scandinavia-1434588. Accessed 28 Nov. 2021.

Brito, Allan. *FreeCAD for Architectural Drawing: Create Technical Drawings with a Free and Open-source CAD*. Brito, 2020.

Britt, Hugo. "How to Produce an Effective Contract Manufacturing Agreement." *Thomas*, 28 July 2020, www.thomasnet.com/insights/contract-manufacturing-agreement/. Accessed 28 Nov. 2021.

The Britannica Guide to the One Hundred Most Influential Scientists. Constable & Robinson, 2008.

Brockotter, Robin. "Key Design Considerations for 3D Printing." *HUBS*, www.hubs.com/knowledge-base/key-design-considerations-3d-printing/. Accessed 28 Nov. 2021.

Brown, Adrian. "Graphics File Formats." *National Archives*, Aug. 2008, www.nationalarchives.gov.uk/documents/information-management/graphic-file-formats.pdf. Accessed 28 Nov. 2021.

Brown, Charles B., Terry R. Collins, and Edward L. McCombs. "Transformation from Batch to Lean Manufacturing: The Performance Issues." *Engineering Management Journal*, vol. 18, no. 2, 2006, pp. 3-14.

Brown, Eric. "True Physics." *Game Developer*, vol. 17, no. 5, 2010, pp. 13-18.

Brown, Julian R. *Minds, Machines, and the Multiverse: The Quest for the Quantum Computer*. New York: Simon & Schuster, 2000.

Brown, William Christopher. "An Effective AutoCAD Curriculum for the High School Student." *CSUSB ScholarWorks*, 1999, scholarworks.lib.csusb.edu/etd-project/1791/. Accessed 16 Dec. 2021.

Buettner, Timothee, Atanas Tanev, Lars Pfotzer, Arne Roennau, and Ruediger Dillmann. "The Intelligent Computer Aided Satellite Designer iCASD—Creating Viable Configurations for Modular Satellites." *2018 NASA/ESA Conference on Adaptive Hardware and Systems (AHS)*, 2018, pp. 25-32.

Burcher, Roy, and Louis Rydill. *Concepts in Submarine Design*. Cambridge UP, 1995.

Butcher, Kenneth S., Linda D. Crown, and Elizabeth J. Gentry, editors. *The International System of Units (SI): Conversion Factors for General Use*. National Institute of Standards and Technology, 2006.

Cagan, Marty. *Inspired: How to Create Products Customers Love*. SVPG, 2008.

Callen, Jeffrey L., Mindy Morel, and Chris Fader. "The Profitability-Risk Tradeoff of Just-in-Time Manufacturing Technologies." *Managerial & Decision Economics*, vol. 24, no. 5, 2003, pp. 393-402.

Calvo, R., R. Domingo, R., and M. A. Sebastián. "Systemic Criterion of Sustainability in Agile Manufacturing." *International Journal of Production Research*, vol. 46, no. 12, 2008, pp. 3345-58.

Cancilla, Riccardo, and Monte Gargano, editors. *Global Environmental Policies: Impact, Management and Effects*. Nova Science Publishers, 2010.

Cardarelli, Francois. *Encyclopedia of Scientific Units, Weights and Measures: Their SI Equivalences and Origins*. Springer, 2003.

Carraher, Charles E., Jr. *Giant Molecules: Essential Materials for Everyday Living and Problem Solving*. 2nd ed., John Wiley & Sons, 2003.

———. *Introduction to Polymer Chemistry*. 4th ed., CRC Press, 2017.

"CATIA." *Dassault Systèmes*, 2021, www.3ds.com/products-services/catia/. Accessed 10 Jan. 2022.

"CATIA CAD/CAM/CAE System Version 3 Release 2 Overview." *IBM*, 2 Oct. 1990, www.ibm.com/common/ssi/cgi-bin/ssialias?appname=skmwww&htmlfid=897%2FENUS290-643&infotype=AN&mhq=service%20initial

izer&mhsrc=ibmsearch_a&subtype=CA. Accessed 10 Jan. 2022.

Cazares, A. "Reconfigurable Manufacturing Systems." *Production and Manufacturing Management*, World Technologies, 2012, pp. 101-6.

Chakraborty, Soumya. "Introduction to Submarine Design." *Marine Insight*, 8 Jan. 2021, www.marineinsight.com/naval-architecture/introduction-to-submarine-design/. Accessed 28 Nov. 2021.

Chang, Kuang-Hua. *Design Theory and Methods Using CAD/CAE*. Academic Press, 2014.

———. *e-Design: Computer-Aided Engineering Design*. Academic Press, 2016.

———. *Product Design Modeling Using CAD/CAE*. Academic Press, 2014.

Chau, Brian. "iMedicalApps: CAD Beats Casting for Prosthetic Limbs." *MedPageToday*, 29 Aug. 2017, www.medpagetoday.com/opinion/iltifathusain/67598. Accessed 28 Nov. 2021.

Chavan, Abhijeet, Christian Peralta, and Christopher Steins. *Planetizen's Contemporary Debates in Urban Planning*. Island Press, 2007.

"Chemical Manufacturing." *US Environmental Protection Agency*, 20 Feb. 2020, archive.epa.gov/sectors/web/html/chemical.html. Accessed 28 Nov. 2021.

Chen, C. C., T. M. Yeh, and C. C. Yang, "The Establishment of Project-Oriented and Cost-Based NPD Performance Evaluation." *Human Systems Management*, vol. 25, no. 3, 2006, pp. 185-96.

Childs, P. R. N. *Mechanical Design: Theory and Applications*. 3rd ed., Butterworth-Heinemann, 2021.

Ching, Francis D. K. *Architectural Graphics*. 6th ed., Wiley, 2015.

Cho, Adrian. "Engineering Peak Performance." *Science*, vol. 305, no. 5684, 2004, pp. 643-44.

Chorafas, Dimitris N. *Quality Control Applications*. Springer, 2012.

Chow, Ven Te. *Open-Channel Hydraulics*. 1959. Blackburn, 2008.

Chua, C. K., K. F. Leong, and C. S. Lim. *Rapid Prototyping: Principles and Applications*. World Scientific, 2010.

Chua, Chee Kai, Chee How Wong, and Wai Yee Yeong. *Standards, Quality Control, and Measurement Sciences in 3D Printing and Additive Manufacturing*. Academic Press, 2017.

Clarke, Dave, James Noble, and Tobias Wrigstad, editors. *Aliasing in Object-Oriented Programming: Types, Analysis and Verification*. Springer, 2013.

Clarke, Peter. "Why Contract Manufacturing Is Getting into Design." *eeNews*, 11 Apr. 2017, www.eenewseurope.com/news/why-contract-manufacturing-getting-design. Accessed 28 Nov. 2021.

Cleaverland, Peter. "Building a Better Manufacturing Future." *Product Design & Development*, vol. 61, no. 8, 2006, pp. 8-9.

Clemens, Kevin. *The Crooked Mile: Through Peak Oil, Hybrid Cars and Global Climate Change to Reach a Brighter Future*. Demontreville Press, 2009.

Cohen, Michael. *Classical Mechanics: A Critical Introduction*. University of Pennsylvania, 2013, live-sas-physics.pantheon.sas.upenn.edu/sites/default/files/Classical_Mechanics_a_Critical_Introduction_0_0.pdf. Accessed 28 Nov. 2021.

———. "The Long-Term Problem of Outsourcing." *IndustryWeek*, 18 Feb. 2021, www.industryweek.com/the-economy/competitiveness/article/21155621/the-longterm-problem-of-outsourcing. Accessed 28 Nov. 2021.

Collinson, R. P. G. *Introduction to Avionics Systems*. 3rd ed., Springer Netherlands, 2011.

"Commercial Aircraft: Global Market Trajectory & Analytics." *StrategyR*, 2021, www.strategyr.com/market-report-commercial-aircraft-forecasts-global-industry-analysts-inc.asp. Accessed 28 Nov. 2021.

"The Complete Engineering Guide: CNC Machining." *Hubs*, 2021, www.hubs.com/guides/cnc-machining/. Accessed 28 Nov. 2021.

"Computational Fluid Dynamics in Heat Exchanger Design and Analysis." *HRS Heat Exchangers*, www.hrs-heatexchangers.com/us/resource/computational-fluid-dynamics-in-heat-exchanger-design-and-analysis/. Accessed 28 Nov. 2021.

"Computational Modeling." *National Institute of Biomedical Imaging and Bioengineering*, May 2020, www.nibib.nih.gov/science-education/science-topics/computational-modeling. Accessed 28 Nov. 2021.

"Computer-Aided Design (CAD) and Computer-Aided Manufacturing (CAM)." *Inc.*, 6 Feb. 2020, www.inc.com/encyclopedia/computer-aided-design-cad-and-computer-aided-cam.html. Accessed 16 Dec. 2021.

"Computer Aided Design (CAD) vs. Manual Drafting." *Electrical Engineering* 123, electricalengineering123.com/computer-aided-design-cad-vs-manual-drafting/. Accessed 28 Nov. 2021.

"Computer Animator." *Art Career Project*, 15 July 2021, theartcareerproject.com/careers/computer-animation/. Accessed 28 Nov. 2021.

"Computer Graphics, Purpose and Function, Care and Use, Types of Drawings." *Aeronautics Guide*, Oct. 2019, www.aircraftsystemstech.com/2019/10/aircraft-drawings-computer-graphics.html. Accessed 28 Nov. 2021.

Congdon-Fuller, Ashleigh, Antonio Ramirez, and Douglas Smith. *Technical Drawing 101 with AutoCAD 2022: A Multidisciplinary Guide to Drafting Theory and Practice*. SDC Publications, 2021.

Constant, Edward W. *The Origin of the Turbojet Revolution*. Johns Hopkins UP, 1980.

Conway, Erik M. *High-Speed Dreams: NASA and the Technopolitics of Supersonic Transportation, 1945-1999*. 2005. Johns Hopkins UP, 2008.

Cook, Jacob. "The Five Steps to Starting PAT." *PharmTech*, 1 Mar. 2007, www.pharmtech.com/view/five-steps-starting-pat. Accessed 28 Nov. 2021.

Cooper, J. F. "Computer Aided Design of Modern Power Plant." *ETDEWEB*, www.osti.gov/etdeweb/biblio/6912842. Accessed 28 Nov. 2021.

Cormen, Thomas H. *Algorithms Unlocked*. MIT Press, 2013.

Costello, Vic, Susan Youngblood, and Norman E. Youngblood. *Multimedia Foundations: Core Concepts for Digital Design*. 2nd ed., Routledge, 2017.

Couch, Chris. *Urban Planning: An Introduction*. Palgrave Macmillan, 2016.

"Court Rules USDA Authorized to Certify Soil-less Hydroponic Operations as Organic." *Center for Food Safety*, 22 Mar. 2021, www.centerforfoodsafety.org/press-releases/6314/court-rules-usda-authorized-to-certify-soil-less-hydroponic-operations-as-organic. Accessed 28 Nov. 2021.

Courtnell, Jane. "What Is Business Process Management: For Industrial Companies." *Thomas Industrial Marketing and Manufacturing Blog*, 25 Nov. 2019, blog.thomasnet.com/what-is-business-process-management-for-industrial-companies?hs_amp=true. Accessed 28 Nov. 2021.

Cox, Cody R., and Jeffrey M. Ulmer. "Lean Manufacturing: An Analysis of Process Improvement Techniques." *Franklin Business and Law Journal*, vol. 2015, no. 2, 2015, pp. 70-77.

Crawford, Roy J., and Peter Martin. *Plastics Engineering*. 4th ed., Butterworth-Heinemann, 2020.

Crone, Mark. "Are Global Supply Chains Too Risky?" *Logistics Management*, vol. 46, no. 4, 2007, pp. 37-40.

Cummins, Fred. *Building the Agile Enterprise*. Elsevier, 2016.

Dailey, Franklyn E., Jr. *The Triumph of Instrument Flight: A Retrospective in the Century of US Aviation*. Dailey International, 2004.

Dale, Nell, and John Lewis. *Computer Science Illuminated*. 6th ed., Jones & Bartlett Learning, 2016.

Dalebout, Susan. *The Praeger Guide to Hearing and Hearing Loss: Assessment, Treatment, and Prevention*. Praeger, 2009.

Daniel, M. E., and C. W. Gwyn. "CAD Systems for IC Design." *IEEE Transactions on Computer-Aided Design of Integrated Circuits and Systems*, vol. 1, no. 1, 1982, pp. 2-12.

Darling, David. *The Universal Book of Mathematics: From Abracadabra to Zeno's Paradoxes*. Castle, 2007.

Darwin, David, and Charles Dolan. *Design of Concrete Structures*. 16th ed., McGraw-Hill, 2021.

Das, Sumitabha. *Your UNIX: The Ultimate Guide*. 3rd ed., McGraw-Hill, 2012.

"Data Measurement Chart." *University of Florida*, www.wu.ece.ufl.edu/links/dataRate/DataMeasurementChart.html. Accessed 28 Nov. 2021.

Davidson, Frank Paul, and Kathleen Lusk Brooke, editors. *Building the World: An Encyclopedia of the Great Engineering Projects in History*. 2 vols. Greenwood, 2006.

Davis, Daniel. "Generative Design Is Doomed to Fail." Daniel Davis, 20 Feb. 2020, www.danieldavis.com/generative-design-doomed-to-fail/. Accessed 16 Nov. 2021.

Davis, L. J. *Fleet Fire: Thomas Edison and the Pioneers of the Electric Revolution*. Arcade, 2003.

Davis, Mackenzie L., and Susan J. Masten. *Principles of Environmental Engineering and Science*. 4th ed., McGraw-Hill, 2020.

De Courtenay, Nadine, Olivier Darrigol, and Oliver Schlaudt, editors. *The Reform of the International System of Units (SI): Philosophical, Historical and Sociological Issues*. Routledge, 2019.

De Haan, Lex, and Toon Koppelaars. *Applied Mathematics for Database Professionals*. Springer, 2007.

Dean, Marti. "What Is CAM (Computer-Aided Manufacturing)?" *Autodesk*, 17 Mar. 2021, www.autodesk.com/products/fusion-360/blog/computer-aided-manufacturing-beginners/. Accessed 28 Nov. 2021.

DeBonis, David A., and Constance L. Donohue. *Survey of Audiology: Fundamentals for Audiologists and Health Professionals*. 3rd ed., Slack Incorporated, 2020.

DeKay, Mark, and G. Z. Brown. *Sun, Wind, and Light: Architectural Design Strategies*. 3rd ed., Wiley, 2014.

Deming, W. Edwards. *Out of the Crisis*. 1982. MIT Press, 2006.

Design Engineering Technical Committee. *AIAA Aerospace Design Engineers Guide*. 6th ed., American Institute of Aeronautics and Astronautics, 2012.

"Design for Manufacturability: Reducing Costs through Design." *Aved*, 22 Sept. 2021, aved.com/design-for-manufacturability-the-economics-of-design/. Accessed 28 Nov. 2021.

"Designing Small Fuel Cells for Homes." *3D CAD World*, 14 Apr. 2009, www.3dcadworld.com/designing-small-fuel-cells-for-homes/. Accessed 28 Nov. 2021.

Despommier, Dickson. *The Vertical Farm: Feeding the World in the Twenty-First Century*. St. Martin's Press, 2010.

Deutsch, Randy. *BIM and Integrated Design: Strategies for Architectural Practice*. Wiley, 2011.

Dhillon, Gupreet. "Dimensions of Power and IS Implementation." *Information and Management*, vol. 41, no. 5, 2004, pp. 635-44.

DiChristina, Mariette. "How Human Creativity Arose." *Scientific American*, 1 Mar. 2013, www.scientificamerican.com/article/how-human-creativity-arose. Accessed 28 Nov. 2021.

Dicks, Andrew L., and David A. J. Rand. *Fuel Cell Systems Explained*. John Wiley & Sons, 2018.

Dieny, Bernard, Ronald B. Goldfarb, and Kyung-Jin Lee. *Introduction to Magnetic Random-Access Memory*. IEEE Press/John Wiley & Sons, 2017.

"Different Types of Machining Operations and the Machining Process." *Thomas*, 2021, www.thomasnet.com/articles/custom-manufacturing-fabricating/machining-processes/. Accessed 28 Nov. 2021.

Dijksterhuis, Eva, and Gilbert Silvius. "The Design Thinking Approach to Projects." *Project Management Development—Practices and Perspectives*, vol. 5, no. 6, 2016, pp. 67-81.

Dillon, Andrew P., translator. *Zero Quality Control: Source Inspection and the Poka-Yoke System*. CRC Press, 2021.

"DMAIC vs. DMADV." *Purdue University*, 28 May 2021, www.purdue.edu/leansixsigmaonline/blog/dmaic-vs-dmadv/. Accessed 28 Nov. 2021.

Doheny, Mike, Venu Nagali, and Florian Weig. "Agile Operations for Volatile Times." *McKinsey and Company*, 1 May 2012, www.mckinsey.com/business-functions/operations/our-insights/agile-operations-for-volatile-times. Accessed 28 Nov. 2021.

Dorr, Barry L. *Ten Essential Skills for Electrical Engineers*. Wiley-IEEE Press, 2014.

"Douglas T. Ross." *Boston Globe*, 5 Feb. 2007, www.legacy.com/us/obituaries/bostonglobe/name/douglas-ross-obituary?id=25676072. Accessed 16 Dec. 2021.

Douglas, Kenneth. *Bioprinting: To Make Ourselves Anew*. Oxford UP, 2021.

Drexler, K. Eric. *Engines of Creation: The Coming Era of Nanotechnology*. Anchor Books, 1990.

Droege, Peter, editor. *Urban Energy Transition: From Fossil Fuels to Renewable Power*. Elsevier, 2008.

Duany, Andres, Elizabeth Plater-Zyberk, and Jeff Speck. *Suburban Nation: The Rise of Sprawl and the Decline of the American Dream*. 10th anniversary ed., North Point Press, 2010.

Duelm, Brian Lee. "Computer Aided Design in the Classroom." *LearnTechLib*, Dec. 1986, files.eric.ed.gov/fulltext/ED276885.pdf. Accessed 16 Dec. 2021.

Dul, Jan, and Bernard Weerdmeester. *Ergonomics for Beginners: A Quick Reference Guide*. 3rd ed., CRC Press, 2008.

Dye, Christopher, Joseph B. Staubach, Diane Emmerson, and C. Greg Jensen. "CAD-Based Parametric Cross-Section Designer for Gas Turbine Engine MDO Applications." *Computer-Aided Design and Applications*, vol. 4, no. 1-4, 2007, pp. 509-18.

Dym, Clive L., and Patrick Little. *Engineering Design: A Project-Based Introduction*. 4th ed., John Wiley and Sons, 2013.

Eastman Kodak Company. *Kodak's Ergonomic Design for People at Work*. 2nd ed., Wiley, 2003.

Ebewele, Robert O. *Polymer Science and Technology*. CRC Press, 2000.

Eckhouse, Brian, and Jennifer A. Dlouhy. "Electric Buses Are Poised to Get a US Infrastructure Boost." *Bloomberg*, 13 Aug. 2021, www.bloomberg.com/news/newsletters/2021-08-13/electric-buses-are-poised-to-get-a-u-s-infrastructure-boost. Accessed 28 Nov. 2021.

"Ecodesign." *Sustainability Guide*, 2018, sustainabilityguide.eu/ecodesign/. Accessed 28 Nov. 2021.

"Ecodesign." *Sustainable Minds*, 2021, www.sustainableminds.com/software/ecodesign-and-lca. Accessed 28 Nov. 2021.

Edwards, Bradley C., and Eric A. Westling. *The Space Elevator: A Revolutionary Earth-to-Space Transportation System*. B. C. Edwards, 2003.

Edwards, Paul N. *A Vast Machine: Computer Models, Climate Data, and the Politics of Global Warming*. MIT Press, 2010.

Eide, Arvid, Roland Jenison, Larry Northup, and Steven Mickelson. *Engineering Fundamentals and Problem Solving*. 7th ed., McGraw-Hill, 2018.

Eitel, Elisabeth. "3D Printing Goes Big-Time for Small Production Runs." *Machine Design*, 15 July 2014, www.machinedesign.com/3d-printing-cad/article/21831798/3d-printing-goes-bigtime-for-small-production-runs. Accessed 28 Nov. 2021.

Eiteljorg, Harrison II, Kate Fernie, Jeremy Huggett, Damian Robinson, Bernard Thomason, et al. "CAD: A Guide to Good Practice." *Archaeology Data Service/Digital*

Antiquity Guides to Good Practice, 2011, guides.archaeologydataservice.ac.uk/g2gp/Cad_Toc. Accessed 28 Nov. 2021.

Elangovan, Uthayan. Product Lifecycle Management (PLM): A Digital Journey Using Industrial Internet of Things (IIoT). CRC Press, 2020.

Elbert, Bruce R. *Introduction to Satellite Communication*. 3rd ed., Artech House, 2008.

"Electric Power Sector Consumption of Fossil Fuels at Lowest Level since 1994." *Today in Energy*, 29 May 2018, www.eia.gov/todayinenergy/detail.php?id=33543. Accessed 28 Nov. 2021.

Eli Whitney Museum and Workshop, www.eliwhitney.org/. Accessed 28 Nov. 2021.

Elias, Hans-Georg. *An Introduction to Plastics*. 2nd ed., Wiley-VCH, 2003.

Ellenberg, Jordan. *Shape: The Hidden Geometry of Information, Biology, Strategy, Democracy, and Everything Else*. Penguin Press, 2021.

El-Rabbany, Ahmed. *Introduction to GPS: The Global Positioning System*. 2nd ed., Artech House, 2006.

Engle, Emily. "What Is CAD (Computer-Aided Design)?" *Autodesk*, 27 Apr. 2021, www.autodesk.com/products/fusion-360/blog/what-is-cad-computer-aided-design/. Accessed 28 Nov. 2021.

"Environmental Sustainability." *Thwink.org*, 2014, www.thwink.org/sustain/glossary/EnvironmentalSustainability.htm. Accessed 28 Nov. 2021.

"EQUISat." *Brown Space Engineering*, 2020, brownspace.org/equisat/. Accessed 28 Nov. 2021.

Essex, David. "Manufacturing Process Management (MPM)." *SearchERP*, Feb. 2017, searcherp.techtarget.com/definition/manufacturing-process-management-MPM. Accessed 28 Nov. 2021.

Estivalet, Margaret, and Pierre Brisson, editors. *The Engineering of Sport 7*. Vol. 2. Springer, 2009.

Ethier, C. Ross, and Craig A. Simmons. *Introductory Biomechanics: From Cells to Organisms*. Cambridge UP, 2007.

Evans, Robert L. *Fueling Our Future: An Introduction to Sustainable Energy*. Cambridge UP, 2007.

Ewen, Dale, Neill Schurter, and P. Erik Gundersen. *Applied Physics*. 11th ed., Pearson, 2017.

Faeth, G. M. *Centennial of Powered Flight: A Retrospective of Aerospace Research*. American Institute of Aeronautics and Astronautics, 2003.

Falzon, Pierre. *Constructive Ergonomics*. CRC Press, 2019.

Fantoni, G., C. Taviani, and R. Santoro. "Design by Functional Synonyms and Antonyms: A Structured Creative Technique Based on Functional Analysis." *Proceedings of the Institution of Mechanical Engineers, Part B: Journal of Engineering Manufacture*, vol. 221, no. 4, 2007, pp. 673-83.

Farin, Gerald, Joseph Josef Hoschek, and Myung-Soo Kim. *Handbook of Computer-Aided Geometric Design*. Elsevier, 2002.

Farish, M. "Our Flexible Friends [factory automation]." *Engineering & Technology*, vol. 3, no. 8, 2008, pp. 62-67.

Farish, Mike. "Bottoms Up." *Engineering*, vol. 248, no. 3, 2007, pp. 45-47.

Fay, Cormac D. "Computer-Aided Design and Manufacturing (CAD/CAM) for Bioprinting." *Methods in Molecular Biology*, no. 2140, 2020, pp. 27-41.

Federal Aviation Administration. *Instrument Flying Handbook*. US Department of Transportation, 2012.

Fenichell, Stephen. *Plastic: The Making of a Synthetic Century*. HarperBusiness, 1997.

Ferguson, R. Stuart. *Practical Algorithms for 3D Computer Graphics*. 2nd ed., AK Peters/CRC Press, 2013.

Ferreira, Paulo, Victoria Reyes, and João Mestre. "A Web-Based Integration Procedure for the Development of Reconfigurable Robotic Work-Cells." *International Journal of Advanced Robotic Systems*, vol. 10, no. 7, 2013, journals.sagepub.com/doi/full/10.5772/54641. Accessed 28 Nov. 2021.

Ferreiro, Larrie D. *Ships and Science: The Birth of Naval Architecture in the Scientific Revolution, 1600-1800*. MIT Press, 2007.

Fielding, John P. *Introduction to Aircraft Design*. 2nd ed., Cambridge UP, 2017.

Filipovic, Nenad. *Computational Modeling in Bioengineering and Bioinformatics*. Academic Press, 2020.

Fink, Zachary L. *Encyclopedia of Electrical Engineering Research*. Nova Science, 2013.

Finnemore, E. John, and Joseph B. Franzini. *Fluid Mechanics with Engineering Applications*. 10th international ed., McGraw-Hill, 2009.

Fisanick, Christina, editor. *Eco-Architecture*. Greenhaven, 2008.

Fish, Tom. "The 10 Most Popular Hybrid Car Models in America." *Newsweek*, 14 May 2021, www.newsweek.com/most-popular-hybrid-car-models-america-1590402. Accessed 28 Nov. 2021.

Fitter, Hetal N., Akash B. Pandey, Divyang D. Patel, and Jitendra M. Mistry. "A Review on Approaches for Handling Bezier Curves in CAD for Manufacturing." *Procedia Engineering*, vol. 97, 2014, pp. 1155-66.

Floreano, Dario, and Claudio Mattuissi. *Bio-Inspired Artificial Intelligence: Theories, Methods, and Technologies*. MIT Press, 2008.

Forde, Morgan. "Survey: 59% of US Companies Would Have 2 Weeks of Stock after Halting Production." *Supply Chain Dive*, 27 Mar. 2020, www.supplychaindive.com/news/coronavirus-survey-us-companies-shipments-after-production-stops/575026/. Accessed 28 Nov. 2021.

Foust, Jeff. "Will Suborbital Space Tourism Take a Suborbital Trajectory?" *Space News*, 17 Aug. 2021, spacenews.com/will-suborbital-space-tourism-take-a-suborbital-trajectory/. Accessed 28 Nov. 2021.

Fox, Danielle. "Scandinavian Design vs. Minimalist Design: What's the Difference?" *Elle Decor*, 21 Dec. 2017, www.elledecor.com/design-decorate/trends/a14479450/scandinavian-design-vs-minimalism/. Accessed 28 Nov. 2021.

Fried, Joel R. *Polymer Science and Technology*. 3rd ed., Prentice Hall, 2014.

Friedl, Gunther, and Horst J. Kayser, editors. *Valuing Corporate Innovation: Strategies, Tools and Best Practice from the Energy and Technology Sector*. Springer, 2018.

Friedman, Daniel P., and Mitchell Wand. *Essentials of Programming Languages*. 3rd ed., MIT Press, 2008.

Friedman, Thomas. *US Submarines Through 1945: An Illustrated Design History*. Naval Institute Press, 1995.

Friedman, Thomas, and James L. Christley. *US Submarines Since 1945: An Illustrated Design History*. Naval Institute Press, 1994.

Fu, Chung C., and Shuqing Wang. *Computational Analysis and Design of Bridge Structures*. CRC Press, 2015.

Gaboury, Jacob. *Image Objects: An Archaeology of Computer Graphics*. MIT Press, 2021.

Gaget, Lucie. "How to Learn CAD in Schools: Top 15 of the Best Educational Software." *Sculpteo*, 26 Dec. 2017, www.sculpteo.com/blog/2017/12/26/how-to-learn-cad-in-schools-top-15-of-the-best-educational-software/. Accessed 16 Dec. 2021.

Gaha, Raoudha, Bernard Yannou, and Benamara Abdelmajid. "A New Eco-Design Approach on CAD Systems." *International Journal of Precision Engineering and Manufacturing*, vol. 15, no. 7, 2014, pp. 1443-51.

Gambetta, Gabriel. *Computer Graphics from Scratch*. No Starch Press, 2021.

Gamble, Clive. *Archaeology: The Basics*. 3rd ed., Routledge, 2015.

Garbovskiy, Yuriy A., and Anatoliy V. Glushchenko. *A Practical Guide to Experimental Geometrical Optics*. Cambridge UP, 2017.

"Gardening without Soil." *U of California at Berkeley Wellness Letter*, vol. 28, no. 4, 2012, p. 4.

Gardiner, Robert, editor. *The Earliest Ships: The Evolution of Boats into Ships*. Conway Maritime, 2004.

Garino, Brian W., and Jeffrey D. Lanphear. "Spacecraft Design, Structure, and Operations." *AU-18 Space Primer*. Air U, 2009, www.airuniversity.af.edu/Portals/10/AUPress/Books/AU-18.PDF. Accessed 28 Nov. 2021.

Garrison, Ervan G. *A History of Engineering and Technology: Artful Methods*. 2nd ed., CRC Press, 1999.

Garstki, Kevin. *Digital Innovations in European Archaeology*. Cambridge UP, 2020.

Gaudin, Sharon. "WPI Researcher Develops Self-Healing Concrete That Could Multiply Structures' Lifespans, Slash Damaging CO_2 Emissions." *WPI*, 8 June 2021, www.wpi.edu/news/wpi-researcher-develops-self-healing-concrete-could-multiply-structures-lifespans-slash. Accessed 28 Nov. 2021.

Gelfand, Stanley A. *Essentials of Audiology*. 4th ed., Thieme Medical, 2016.

Generative Design Primer, 2021, generativedesign.org. Accessed 16 Nov. 2021.

Geng, Hwaiyu. *Manufacturing Engineering Handbook*. 2nd ed., McGraw-Hill Professional, 2015.

Giacomelli, Gene A., et al. "CEA in Antarctica: Growing Vegetables on 'the Ice.'" *Resource: Engineering & Technology for a Sustainable World*, vol. 13, no. 1, 2006, pp. 3-5.

Giampaolo, Tony. *Gas Turbine Handbook*: Principles and Practices. 5th ed., River Publishers, 2013.

Giancoli, Douglas C. *Physics for Scientists and Engineers with Modern Physics*. 4th ed., Pearson, 2008.

Glawion, Alex. "Building the Best PC for 3D Animation [2021 Guide]." *CGDirector*, 5 Oct. 2021, www.cgdirector.com/best-computer-for-animation/. Accessed 28 Nov. 2021.

"Global Electronic Design Automation Software Market by Application, by End User, by Regional Outlook, Industry Analysis Report and Forecast, 2021-2027." *Research and Markets*, June 2021, www.researchandmarkets.com/reports/5354457/global-electronic-design-automation-software. Accessed 16 Dec. 2021.

Göbel, Ernst O., and Uwe Siegner. *The New International System of Units (SI): Quantum Metrology and Quantum Standards*. Wiley VCH, 2019.

Godse, Atul P., and Deepali A. Godse. Computer Graphics. Technical Publications, 2021.

Gohde, Justin, and Marius Kintel. *Programming with OpenSCAD. A Beginners Guide to Coding 3D-Printable Objects*. No Starch Press, 2021.

Golann, Bret. "Achieving Growth and Responsiveness: Process Management and Market Orientation in Small

Firms." *Journal of Small Business Management*, vol. 44, no. 3, 2006, pp. 369-85.

Goldberger, Paul. *Why Architecture Matters*. Yale UP, 2009.

Goldstein, Phil. "How Computer-Aided Design Is Used in Government." *FedTech*, 24 June 2020, fedtechmagazine.com/article/2020/06/how-computer-aided-design-used-government-perfcon. Accessed 28 Nov. 2021.

———. "What Is Building Information Modeling Technology in Government?" *FedTech*, 16 June 2020, fedtechmagazine.com/article/2020/06/what-building-information-modeling-technology-government-perfcon. Accessed 28 Nov. 2021.

Gonzalez-Salazar, Miguel Angel, et al. "Review of the Operational Flexibility and Emissions of Gas- and Coal-Fired Power Plants in a Future with Growing Renewables." *Renewable and Sustainable Energy Reviews*, vol. 82, 2018, pp. 1497-1513.

Goodship, Vanessa. *Injection Moulding: A Practical Guide*. 3rd ed., De Gruyter, 2020.

Grand View Research. "Hydroponics Market Size, Share & Trends Analysis Report by Type (Aggregate Systems, Liquid Systems), by Crops (Tomatoes, Lettuce, Peppers, Cucumbers, Herbs), by Region, and Segment Forecasts, 2021-2028." *Research and Markets*, Oct. 2021, www.researchandmarkets.com/reports/5457654/hydroponics-market-size-share-and-trends. Accessed 28 Nov. 2021.

Grant, August E., and Jennifer Meadows. *Communication Technology Update and Fundamentals*. 16th ed., Routledge, 2018.

"Graphene Transistor Could Mean Computers That Are 1,000 Times Faster." *Science Daily*, 13 June 2017, www.sciencedaily.com/releases/2017/06/170613145144.htm. Accessed 28 Nov. 2021.

"Graphical User Interface (GUI)." *Techopedia*, 28 May 2021, www.techopedia.com/definition/5435/graphical-user-interface-gui. Accessed 28 Nov. 2021.

Green, Mark M., and Harold A. Wittcoff. *Organic Chemistry Principles and Industrial Practice*. Wiley-VCH, 2006.

Green, Robert. *Expert CAD Management*. Sybex, 2007.

Greenberg, Saul, et al. *Sketching User Experiences: The Workbook*. Morgan, 2012.

Grossman, Elizabeth. "If Your Veggies Weren't Grown in Soil, Can They Be Organic?" *Civil Eats*, 28 July 2016, civileats.com/2016/07/28/if-your-veggies-were-grown-hydroponic-can-they-be-organic/. Accessed 28 Nov. 2021.

Grover, William H. "The Rise (and Risks) of Resin-Based 3D Printers." *Grover Lab*, 13 June 2021, groverlab.org/hnbfpr/2021-06-13-3d-printer-risks.html. Accessed 28 Nov. 2021.

Gudmundsson, Snorri. *General Aviation Aircraft Design: Applied Methods and Procedures*. 2nd ed., Butterworth-Heinemann, 2021.

Guelich, Scott, Shishir Gundavaram, and Gunther Birznieks. *CGI Programming with Perl*. 2nd ed., O'Reilly, 2000.

"Guide to Stereolithography (SLA) 3D Printing." *Formlabs*, 2021, formlabs.com/blog/ultimate-guide-to-stereolithography-sla-3d-printing/. Accessed 28 Nov. 2021.

Gülen, S. Can. *Gas Turbines for Electric Power Generation*. Cambridge UP, 2019.

Gupta, Kapil, and J. Paulo Davim, editors. *High-Speed Machining*. Academic Press, 2020.

Hagen, Rebecca, and Kim Golombisky. *White Space Is Not Your Enemy: A Beginner's Guide to Communicating Visually through Graphic, Web & Multimedia Design*. 3rd ed., A. K. Peters/CRC Press, 2016.

Hai, Yao, Bao Jinsong, Hu Xiaofeng, and Jin Ye. "Dynamics Simulation Research on Load Vehicle of Deep Submergence Rescue Vehicle (LV-DSRV)." *International Journal for Engineering Modelling*, vol. 22, no. 1, 2009, pp. 71-79.

Haindl, Michal, and Matej Sedlácek. "Virtual Reconstruction of Cultural Heritage Artifacts." *2016 International Workshop on Computational Intelligence for Multimedia Understanding (IWCIM)*, 2016, pp. 1-5.

Hall, Susan J. *Basic Biomechanics*. 9th ed., McGraw-Hill, 2021.

Halpern, Daniel Noah. *Becoming a Video Game Designer*. Simon & Schuster, 2020.

Hamill, Joseph, Kathleen M. Knutzen, and Timothy R. Derrick. *Biomechanical Basis of Human Movement*. 5th ed., Wolters Kluwer, 2021.

Hamilton, Tracy Brown. *Dream Jobs in Sports Equipment Design*. Rosen Publishing Group, 2018.

Hamm, Matthew J. *Wireframing Essentials: An Introduction to User Experience Design*. Packt, 2014.

Hansen, Robert, et al. "Development and Operation of a Hydroponic Lettuce Research Laboratory." *Resource: Engineering & Technology for a Sustainable World*, vol. 17, no. 4, 2010, pp. 4-7.

Harbour, Jonathan S. *Beginning Game Programming*. 4th ed., Cengage Learning, 2015.

"Hard Drive." *Computer Hope*, 2 Aug. 2020, www.computerhope.com/jargon/h/harddriv.htm. Accessed 28 Nov. 2021.

Hardin, Brad, and Dave McCool. *BIM and Construction Management: Proven Tools, Methods, and Workflows*. 2nd ed., Wiley, 2015.

Harris, A. "Reaping the Rewards of Agile Thinking." *Manufacturing Engineer*, vol. 83, no. 6, 2004, pp. 24-27.

Hasan, Anwarul, editor. *Tissue Engineering for Artificial Organs*. 2 vols. Wiley, 2017.

Hawkins, Amanda, and Sam Aquillano. *Bespoke Bodies: The Design & Craft of Prosthetics*. Design Museum Press, 2020.

Hayashi, Alden M. "Building Better Teams." *MIT Sloan Management Review*, 15 Jan. 2004, sloanreview.mit.edu/article/knowledge-management-building-better-teams/. Accessed 28 Nov. 2021.

Hayenga, Heather N., and Helim Aranda-Espinoza. *Biomaterials Mechanics*. CRC Press, 2017.

Hays, Kevin. "What CAD Software Does SpaceX Use?" *Departing Earth*, departingearth.com/what-cad-software-does-spacex-use/. Accessed 28 Nov. 2021.

Heilbron, J. L. *Geometry Civilized: History, Culture, and Technique*. Oxford UP, 2000.

Helfrick, Albert D. *Principles of Avionics*. 9th ed., Avionics Communication, 2015.

Heller, Steven. "The Evolution of Design." *The Atlantic*, 9 Apr. 2015, www.theatlantic.com/entertainment/archive/2015/04/a-more-inclusive-history-of-design/390069. Accessed 28 Nov. 2021.

Helliwell, T. M., and V. V. Sahakian. *Modern Classical Mechanics*. Cambridge UP, 2021.

Hench, Larry L., and Julian R. Jones, editors. *Biomaterials, Artificial Organs, and Tissue Engineering*. CRC Press, 2005.

Hendry, Linda C. "Applying World Class Manufacturing to Make-to-Order Companies: Problems and Solutions." *International Journal of Operations & Production Management*, vol. 18, no. 11, 1998, pp. 1086-1100.

Henry, Gary N., Wiley J. Larson, and Ronald W. Humble. *Space Propulsion Analysis and Design*. McGraw-Hill 1995.

Herstatt, Cornelius, and Daniel Ehls, editors. *Open-Source Innovation: The Phenomenon, Participant's Behavior, Business Implications*. Routledge, 2015.

Herz-Fischler, Roger. *A Mathematical History of the Golden Number*. Dover, 1998.

Hesmondhalgh, David. *The Cultural Industries*. 4th ed., SAGE Publications, 2018.

Hesselgreaves, J. E., Richard Law, and David Reay. *Compact Heat Exchangers: Selection, Design and Operation*. 2nd ed., Butterworth-Heinemann, 2016.

Hey, Tony, and Gyuri Pápay. *The Computing Universe: A Journey through a Revolution*. Cambridge UP, 2015.

Higham, Nicholas J., editor. *The Princeton Companion to Applied Mathematics*. Princeton UP, 2015.

Highfield, Roger. "Fast Forward to Cartoon Reality." *Telegraph*, 13 June 2006, www.telegraph.co.uk/technology/3346141/Fast-forward-to-cartoon-reality.html. Accessed 28 Nov. 2021.

"Highway History." *Federal Highway Administration*, 27 Apr. 2021, www.fhwa.dot.gov/interstate/faq.cfm. Accessed 28 Nov. 2021.

Hill, Philip Graham, and Carl R. Peterson. *Mechanics and Thermodynamics of Propulsion*. 2nd ed., Addison-Wesley, 2010.

Himbert, M. E. "A Brief History of Measurement." *European Physical Journal Special Topics*, vol. 172, 2009, pp. 25-35.

Hirz, Mario, Patrick Rossbacher, and Jana Gulanová. "Future Trends in CAD—From the Perspective of Automotive Industry." *Computer-Aided Design and Applications*, vol. 14, no. 6, 217, pp. 734-41.

"History." *Dassault Systèmes*, 2021, www.3ds.com/about-3ds/what-we-are/history. Accessed 10 Jan. 2022.

"The History and Design of Milling Machines." *Plethora*, 8 Aug. 2017, www.plethora.com/insights/the-history-and-design-of-milling-machines. Accessed 28 Nov. 2021.

"History of CNC Machining." *Bantam Tools*, 12 Apr. 2019, medium.com/cnc-life/history-of-cnc-machining-part-1-2a4b290d994d. Accessed 28 Nov. 2021.

"The History of Design, Model Making and CAD." *Creative Mechanisms*, 14 Dec. 2015, www.creativemechanisms.com/blog/the-history-of-design-model-making-and-cad. Accessed 16 Dec. 2021.

"History of the Space Shuttle." *NASA*, history.nasa.gov/shuttlehistory.html. Accessed 28 Nov. 2021.

"History of Universal Design." *Centre for Excellence in Universal Design*, 2020, universaldesign.ie/what-is-universal-design/history-of-ud/. Accessed 28 Nov. 2021.

Hobbs, Jordan. "Why IKEA Uses 3D Renders vs. Photography for Their Furniture Catalog." *CAD Crowd*, 20 Apr. 2021, www.cadcrowd.com/blog/why-ikea-uses-3d-renders-vs-photography-for-their-furniture-catalog/. Accessed 28 Nov. 2021.

Hoel, Michael, and Snorre Kverndokk. "Depletion of Fossil Fuels and the Impact of Global Warming." *Resource and Energy Economics*, vol. 18, no. 2, 1996, pp. 115-36.

Holme, Audun. *Geometry: Our Cultural Heritage*. 2nd ed., Springer, 2010.

Hoogers, Gregor, editor. *Fuel Cell Technology Handbook*. CRC Press, 2003.

Horstmann, Cay. *Big Java: Early Objects*. 7th ed., John Wiley & Sons, 2018.

Horvath, Joan. *Mastering 3D Printing: Modeling, Printing, and Prototyping with Reprap- Style 3D Printers*. Apress, 2014.

Hoskins, Stephen. *3D Printing for Artists, Designers and Makers*. Bloomsbury, 2013.

Hoss, Marcelo, and Carla Schwengber ten Caten. "Lean Schools of Thought." *International Journal of Production Research*, vol. 51, no. 11, 2013, pp. 3270-82.

"How 3D Modeling Software Meet the Requirements of the Automotive Industry." *ZWSoft*, 28 May 2021, www.zwsoft.com/news/zwschool/how-3d-modeling-software-meet-the-requirements-of-the-automotive-industry. Accessed 28 Nov. 2021.

"How 3D Printed Hearing Aids Silently Took Over the World." *3D Sourced*, www.3dsourced.com/editors-picks/custom-hearing-aids-3d-printed/. Accessed 28 Nov. 2021.

"How Computers Work: The CPU and Memory." *University of Rhode Island*, homepage.cs.uri.edu/faculty/wolfe/book/Readings/Reading04.htm. Accessed 28 Nov. 2021.

"How Proswith AutoCAD Training Design Prosthetics." *Digital School*, www.digitalschool.ca/pros-autocad-training-design-prosthetics/. Accessed 28 Nov. 2021.

Howison, Sam. *Practical Applied Mathematics: Modelling, Analysis, Approximation*. Cambridge UP, 2005.

Hughes, Cameron, and Tracey Hughes. *Robot Programming: A Guide to Controlling Autonomous Robots*. Pearson Education, 2016.

Hull, Thomas. "In Search of a Practical Map Fold." *Math Horizons*, vol. 9, no. 3, 2002, pp. 22-24.

Husain, Iqbal. *Electric and Hybrid Vehicles: Design Fundamentals*. 3rd ed., CRC Press, 2021.

Husband, T. M. "Robots, CAM and O.R." *Journal of the Operational Research Society*, vol. 34, no. 4, 1983, pp. 303-7.

Husby, Paul. "Becoming Lean." *Material Handling Management*, vol. 62, no. 8, 2007, pp. 42-45.

Hutchinson, Lee. "Home 3D Printers Take Us on a Maddening Journey into Another Dimension." *Ars Technica*, 27 Aug. 2013, arstechnica.com/gadgets/2013/08/home-3d-printers-take-us-on-a-maddening-journey-into-another-dimension/. Accessed 28 Nov. 2021.

Huth, Mark W. *Understanding Construction Drawings*. 7th ed. Cengage Learning, 2019.

Hwang, H. C., and B. K. Choi. "Workflow-Based Dynamic Scheduling of Job Shop Operations." *International Journal of Computer Integrated Manufacturing*, vol. 20, no. 6, 2007, pp. 557-66.

Ida, Nathan. *Engineering Electromagnetics*. 3rd ed., Springer, 2015.

"IKEA Design through the Years." *IKEA*, 2021, about.ikea.com/en/about-us/history-of-ikea/ikea-design-through-the-years. Accessed 28 Nov. 2021.

Ingrassia, Michael. *Maya for Games*. Focal Press, 2009.

"Introduction to Image Files Tutorial." *Boston University Information Services and Technology*, www.bu.edu/tech/support/research/training-consulting/online-tutorials/imagefiles/image101-1/. Accessed 28 Nov. 2021.

"Introduction to Memory." *CCM Benchmark Group*, 22 Jan. 2021, ccm.net/contents/396-computer-introduction-to-memory. Accessed 28 Nov. 2021.

"IonQ Chooses Onshape's Cloud CAD Platform for Quantum Computer Design." *Duke*, 23 Jan. 2019, otc.duke.edu/news/ionq-chooses-onshapes-cloud-cad-platform-for-quantum-computer-design/. Accessed 28 Nov. 2021.

Irwin, J. David, and R. Mark Nelms. *Basic Engineering Circuit Analysis*. 12th ed., Wiley, 2021.

"Is It Too Late to Prevent Climate Change?" *NASA*, 2019, climate.nasa.gov/faq/16/is-it-too-late-to-prevent-climate-change/. Accessed 28 Nov. 2021.

Isakov, Edmund. *International System of Units (SI): How the World Measures Everything, and the People Who Made It Possible*. Industrial Press, 2013.

"Ivan Sutherland." *A. M. Turing Award*, 2019, amturing.acm.org/award_winners/sutherland_3467412.cfm. Accessed 16 Dec. 2021.

"Ivan Sutherland Creates the First Graphical User Interface." *Historyofinformation.com*, historyofinformation.com/detail.php?id=805. Accessed 28 Nov. 2021.

Jackson, Chad. "What Is Mechanical Computer Aided Engineering (MCAE)?" *Lifecycle Insights*, 2021, www.lifecycleinsights.com/tech-guide/mcae/. Accessed 16 Dec. 2021.

Jackson, Joab. "Navy Creates a Virtual World to Test Submarine Design." *CGN*, 24 Aug. 2009, gcn.com/articles/2009/08/24/data-visualization-sidebar-2-navy-sub.aspx. Accessed 28 Nov. 2021.

Jacobs, Jane. *The Death and Life of Great American Cities*. 1961. Random House, 2002.

James, David. "Design Engineering—Managing Technology: Slight Advantage." *Engineer*, 5 May 2008, p. 34.

James, Hubert M. *Theory of Servomechanisms*. McGraw, 1947.

Jayaswal, Bijay K., and Peter C. Patton. *Design for Trustworthy Software: Tools, Techniques, and Methodology of Developing Robust Software*. Prentice Hall, 2007.

Jensen, Cecil H., and Ed Espin. *Interpreting Engineering Drawings*. 7th Canadian ed., Nelson Education, 2015.

Jepson, Phil. "The CNC Milling Process Explained." *EGL Vaughan*, 4 Aug. 2020, eglvaughan.co.uk/cnc-milling-process-explained/. Accessed 28 Nov. 2021.

Jiang, Wenbo, and Yuan Zhang. "Application of 3D Visualization in Landscape Design Teaching." *International Journal of Emerging Technologies in Learning (JET)*, vol. 14, no. 6, 2019, pp. 53-62.

Jimenez, Jorge, et al. "Destroy All Jaggies." *Game Developer*, vol. 18, no. 6, 2011, pp. 13-20.

"John H. Hall." *National Park Service*, www.nps.gov/hafe/learn/historyculture/john-h-hall.htm. Accessed 28 Nov. 2021.

Johnson, Jeff. *Designing with the Mind in Mind*. 2nd ed., Morgan Kaufmann, 2014.

Johnson, Khari. "Researchers Seek to Advance Predictive AI for Engineers with CAD Model Data Set." *VentureBeat*, 21 July 2020, venturebeat.com/2020/07/21/researchers-seek-to-advance-predictive-ai-for-engineers-with-cad-model-data-set/. Accessed 16 Dec. 2021.

Jones, J. Benton, Jr. *Hydroponics: A Practical Guide for the Soilless Grower*. 2nd ed., CRC Press, 2005.

Joyappa, P. "Lean and Green Manufacturing." *Flexible Packaging*, vol. 14, 2012, pp. 42-45.

Julien, Pierre Y. "Our Hydraulic Engineering Profession." *Journal of Hydraulic Engineering*, vol. 143, no. 5, 2017.

Juuti, Petri S., Tapio S. Katko, and Heikki Vuorinen. *Environmental History of Water: Global Views on Community Water Supply and Sanitation*. IWA, 2007.

"Kamprad, King of Ikea." *Sweden*, 1 June 2021, sweden.se/life/people/kamprad-king-of-ikea. Accessed 28 Nov. 2021.

Karwowsi, Waldemar, Marcelo Soares, and Neville A. Stanton, editors. *Handbook of Human Factors and Ergonomics in Consumer Product Design*. 2 vols. CRC Press, 2020.

Katz, Victor. "The History of Stokes' Theorem." *Mathematics Magazine*, vol. 52, no. 3, 1979, pp. 146-56.

Kaye, Naomi. "Best Open-Source CAD Software of 2021." *ALL3DP*, 16 July 2021, all3dp.com/2/best-open-source-cad-software/. Accessed 16 Dec. 2021.

Keane, Phillip. "Shipbuilding Sets Sail with CAD." *Engineers Rule*, 30 Aug. 2018, www.engineersrule.com/shipbuilding-sets-sail-cad/. Accessed 28 Nov. 2021.

Kehlhofer, Rolf, et al. *Combined-Cycle Gas and Steam Turbine Power Plants*. 3rd ed., PennWell, 2009.

Keivanpour, Samira. *Approaches, Opportunities, and Challenges for Eco-Design 4.0: A Concise Guide for Practitioners and Students*. Springer Nature Switzerland, 2022.

Kelly, Robert L., and David Hurst Thomas. *Archaeology*. 7th ed., Cengage Learning, 2017.

Kemp, John F., and Peter Young. *Ship Construction Sketches and Notes*. 2nd ed., Butterworth, 1997.

Kendall, Bonnie. *Opportunities in Dental Care Careers*. Rev. ed., McGraw-Hill, 2006.

Kenney, W. F. *Energy Conservation in the Process Industries*. Academic Press, 1984.

Kensek, Karen M., and Douglas E. Noble. *Building Information Modeling: BIM in Current and Future Practice*. Wiley, 2014.

Khan, Omera. *Product Design and the Supply Chain: Competing through Design*. Kogan Page, 2019.

Kilkelly, Michael. "Which Architectural Software Should You Be Using?" *ArchDaily*, 4 May 2015, www.archdaily.com/626972/which-architectural-software-should-you-be-using. Accessed 28 Nov. 2021.

Kim, Chang-Hun, et al. *Real-Time Visual Effects for Game Programming*. Springer, 2015.

Kim, Chulhan, and Tae-Eog Lee. "Modelling and Simulation of Automated Manufacturing Systems for Evaluation of Complex Schedules." *International Journal of Production Research*, vol. 51, no. 12, 2013, pp. 3734-47.

Kim, Minkyun, Nallan C. Suresh, and Canan Kocabasoglu-Hillmer. "An Impact of Manufacturing Flexibility and Technological Dimensions of Manufacturing Strategy on Improving Supply Chain Responsiveness: Business Environment Perspective." *International Journal of Production Research*, vol. 51, no. 18, 2013, pp. 5597-5611.

"The Kinematic Equations." *Physics Classroom*, www.physicsclassroom.com/class/1DKin/Lesson-6/Kinematic-Equations. Accessed 28 Nov. 2021.

King, Robert H. *Finite Element Analysis with SOLIDWORKS Simulation*. Cengage Learning, 2018.

Kishita, Yusuke, Mitsutaka Matsumoto, Masato Inoue, and Shinichi Fukushige, editors. *EcoDesign and Sustainability*

I: Products, Services, and Business Models. Springer Nature Singapore, 2021.

Klimczak, Erik. *Design for Software: A Playbook for Developers*. Wiley, 2013.

Knapp, Chris. "Forward History: Practice Beyond BIM." *ArchitectureAU*, 5 Apr. 2013, architectureau.com/articles/forward-history-practice-beyond-bim/. Accessed 28 Nov. 2021.

Ko, Joy, and Kyle Steinfeld. *Geometric Computation: Foundations for Design*. Routledge, 2018.

Ko, Kuo-Cheng, and Pius J. Egbelu. "Reconfiguration of a Job Shop to Respond to Product Mix Changes Based on a Virtual Production System Concept." *International Journal of Production Research*, vol. 42, no. 22, 2004, pp. 4641-72.

Kojic, Miloš, et al. *Computer Modeling in Bioengineering: Theoretical Background, Examples and Software*. Wiley, 2008.

Kolko, Jon. "Design Thinking Comes of Age." *Harvard Business Review*, Sept. 2015, hbr.org/2015/09/design-thinking-comes-of-age. Accessed 28 Nov. 2021.

Koll, Hilary, Steve Mills, and Korey Kiepert. *Using Math to Design a Rollercoaster*. Gareth Stevens Publishing, 2006.

Kotas, T. J. *The Exergy Method of Thermal Plant Analysis*. Krieger Publications, 1995.

Kramer, Steven, and David K. Brown. *Audiology: Science to Practice*. 3rd ed., Plural, 2018.

Krar, Steve, Arthur Gill, and Peter Smid. *Technology of Machine Tools*. 8th ed., McGraw-Hill, 2020.

Krug, Steve. *Don't Make Me Think, Revisited: A Common Sense Approach to Web Usability*. 3rd ed., New Riders, 2014.

Krull, Fred N. "The Origin of Computer Graphics within General Motors." IEEE Annals of the History of Computing, vol. 16, no. 3, 1994, pp. 40-56.

Kryza, Frank. *The Power of Light: The Epic Story of Man's Quest to Harness the Sun*. McGraw-Hill, 2003.

Kuhn, Karl F. *In Quest of the Universe*. 6th ed., Jones and Bartlett, 2010.

Kumar, Kaushik, Chikesh Ranjan, and J. Paulo Davim. *CNC Programming for Machining*. Springer Nature Switzerland, 2020.

Kumar, Kaushik, Divya Zindani, and J. Paulo Davim. *Design Thinking to Digital Thinking*. Springer Nature Switzerland, 2020.

Kumar, Sudheer. "Recent Development of Biobased Epoxy Resins: A Review." *Polymer-Plastics Technology and Engineering*, vol. 57, no. 3, 2017, pp. 133-55.

Kurzweil, Ray. *The Age of Spiritual Machines: When Computers Exceed Human Intelligence*. Penguin, 2000.

Kutz, Myer. *Environmentally Conscious Manufacturing*. Wiley, 2007.

Kyratsis, Panagiotis, Konstantinos G. Kakoulis, and Angelos P. Markopoulos, editors. *Advances in CAD/CAM/CAE Technologies*. MDPI, 2020.

La Roche, Pablo. *Carbon-Neutral Architectural Design*. 2nd ed., CRC Press, 2017.

Labi, Samuel. *Introduction to Civil Engineering Systems: A Systems Perspective to the Development of Civil Engineering Facilities*. Wiley, 2014.

Lanza, Robert, Robert Langer, Joseph Vacanti, and Anthony Atala, editors. *Principles of Tissue Engineering*. 5th ed., Academic Press, 2020.

Larrañaga, Michael D., Richard J. Lewis, and Robert A. Lewis. *Hawley's Condensed Chemical Dictionary*. 16th ed., John Wiley & Sons, 2016.

Larson, Eric D., Marc H. Ross, and Robert H. Williams. "Beyond the Era of Materials." *Scientific American*, vol. 254, no. 6, 1986, p. 34.

Lass, Norman J., and Charles M. Woodford. *Hearing Science Fundamentals*. Mosby, 2007.

Lavagno, Luciano, Igor L. Markov, Grant Martin, and Louis K. Scheffer, editors. *Electronic Design Automation for IC Implementation, Circuit Design, and Process Technology*. 2nd ed., CRC Press, 2016.

Law, Averill M. *Simulation Modeling and Analysis*. 5th ed., McGraw, 2015.

Leach, Richard, and Stuart T. Smith, editors. *Basics of Precision Engineering*. CRC Press, 2018.

"Lean Manufacturing and the Environment." *EPA*, 17 Mar. 2021, www.epa.gov/sustainability/lean-manufacturing-and-environment. Accessed 28 Nov. 2021.

Lee, J. A. N. "Douglas T. Ross." *Computer Pioneers*, 2013, history.computer.org/pioneers/ross.html. Accessed 16 Dec. 2021.

Lee, Ji-Hyun, editor. *Computer-Aided Architectural Design*. Springer, 2019.

Lee, Kent D. *Foundations of Programming Languages*. Springer, 2014.

Lee, S. M., R. Harrison, and A. A. West. "A Component-Based Control System for Agile Manufacturing." *Proceedings of the Institution of Mechanical Engineers—Part B—Engineering Manufacture*, vol. 219, no. 1, 2005, pp. 123-35.

Leifer, Larry J., Christoph Meinel, and Hasso Plattner. *Design Thinking: Understand—Improve—Apply*. Springer, 2011.

Leonard, Kathleen M. "Brief History of Environmental Engineering: 'The World's Second Oldest Profession.'"

ASCE Conference Proceedings, vol. 265, no. 47, 2001, pp. 389-93.

Leseure, Michel. "Trust in Manufacturing Engineering Project Systems: An Evolutionary Perspective." *Journal of Manufacturing Technology Management*, vol. 26, no. 7, 2015, pp. 1013-30.

Levy, John M. *Contemporary Urban Planning*. 11th ed., Routledge, 2016.

Lewrick, Michael, Patrick Link, and Larry Leifer. *The Design Thinking Toolbox*. Wiley, 2020.

Leyzerovich, Alexander S. *Steam Turbines for Modern Fossil-Fuel Power Plants*. River Publishers, 2020.

Liang, Xinyuan, Xiang Zhang, Lei Zhang, et al. "Computer-Aided Polymer Design: Integrating Group Contribution and Molecular Dynamics." *Industrial & Engineering Chemistry Research*, vol. 58, no. 34, 2019, pp. 15542-52.

Liarokapis, Fotis, Athanasios Voulodimos, Nikolaos Doulamis, and Anastasios Doulamis, editors. *Visual Computing for Cultural Heritage*. Springer Nature Switzerland, 2020.

Liedtka, Jeanne. "Why Design Thinking Works." *Harvard Business Review*, Sept. 2018, hbr.org/2018/09/why-design-thinking-works. Accessed 28 Nov. 2021.

Lienig, Jens, and Juergen Scheible. *Fundamentals of Layout Design for Electronic Circuits*. Springer, 2020.

Liepmann, H. W., and A. Roshko. *Elements of Gas Dynamics*. Dover, 2001.

Lim, Kieran. *Hybrid Cars, Fuel-Cell Buses and Sustainable Energy Use*. Royal Australian Chemical Institute, 2004.

Lindell, James E. *Handbook of Hydraulics*. 8th ed., McGraw Hill Professional, 2017.

Lipson, Hod, and Melba Kurman. *Fabricated: The New World of 3D Printing*. Wiley, 2013.

Livermore, Sienna. "Everything You Need to Know about Scandinavian Design." *House Beautiful*, 18 Sept. 2018, www.housebeautiful.com/design-inspiration/a23087463/scandinavian-design-style-trends/. Accessed 28 Nov. 2021.

Llach, Daniel Cardoso. *Builders of the Vision: Software and the Imagination of Design*. Routledge, 2015.

Lloyd, Marion. "Gardens of Hope on the Rooftops of Rio." *Chronicle of Higher Education*, vol. 52, no. 8, 2005, p. A56.

Lobos, Alex, and Callie W. Babbitt. "Integrating Emotional Attachment and Sustainability in Electronic Product Design." *Challenges*, vol. 4, no. 1, 2013, pp. 19-33.

Long, Simon. *An Introduction to C & GUI Programming*. Raspberry Pi Press, 2019.

Lou, Shuqin, and Chunling Yang. *Digital Electronic Circuits: Principles and Practices*. De Gruyter, 2019.

Lusardi, Michelle M., and Caroline C. Nielsen, editors. *Orthotics and Prosthetics in Rehabilitation*. 3rd ed., Elsevier, 2013.

Lynch, Kevin M., and Frank C. Park. *Modern Robotics: Mechanics, Planning, and Control*. Cambridge UP, 2017.

Maantay, Juliana, John Ziegler, and John Pickles. *GIS for the Urban Environment*. ESRI Press, 2006.

MacCormick, John. *Nine Algorithms That Changed the Future: The Ingenious Ideas That Drive Today's Computers*. Princeton UP, 2012.

MacPherson, Cory. *Inventions in the Visual Arts: From Cave Paintings to CAD*. Cavendish Square, 2017.

Madhav, Sanjay. *Game Programming Algorithms and Techniques: A Platform-Agnostic Approach*. Addison-Wesley, 2014.

Mahdoum, Ali. *CAD of Circuits and Integrated Systems*. Wiley-ISTE, 2020.

Maiti, Chinmay Kumar. *Computer Aided Design of Micro- and Nanoelectronic Devices*. World Scientific, 2017.

Malhotra, Vasdev, Tilak Raj, and Ashok Arora. "Evaluation of Barriers Affecting Reconfigurable Manufacturing Systems with Graph Theory and Matrix Approach." *Materials and Manufacturing Processes*, vol. 27, no. 1, 2012, pp. 88-94.

Manivannan, Subramaniam. "Lean Error-Proofing for Productivity Improvement." *Forging*, 27 Apr. 2007, www.forgingmagazine.com/issues-and-ideas/article/21922032/lean-errorproofing-for-productivity-improvement. Accessed 28 Nov. 2021.

"Manufacturing Industry Statistics." *National Institute of Standards and Technology*, 2 Nov. 2021, www.nist.gov/el/applied-economics-office/manufacturing/manufacturing-industry-statistics. Accessed 28 Nov. 2021.

"Manufacturing: NAICS 31-33." *US Bureau of Labor Statistics*, 28 Nov. 2021, www.bls.gov/iag/tgs/iag31-33.htm. Accessed 28 Nov. 2021.

Marchant, Ben. "Game Programming in C and C++." *Cprogramming.com*, www.cprogramming.com/game-programming.html. Accessed 28 Nov. 2021.

Margolin, Victor. *World History of Design: Two-Volume Set*. Bloomsbury, 2015.

Margolis, James M., editor. *Plastics Engineering Handbook*. McGraw-Hill, 2006.

Marks, Myles H. *Basic Integrated Circuits*. Tab Books, 1986.

Marras, William S., and Waldemar Karwowski, editors. *Interventions, Controls, and Applications in Occupational Ergonomics*. 2nd ed., CRC Press, 2019.

Marschner, Steve, and Peter Shirley. *Fundamentals of Computer Graphics*. 4th ed., CRC Press, 2016.

Marsh, Joel. *UX for Beginners: A Crash Course in 100 Short Lessons*. O'Reilly, 2016.

Martin, Richard. "The Race for the Ultra-Efficient Jet Engine of the Future." *MIT Technology Review*, 23 Mar. 2016, www.technologyreview.com/s/601008/the-race-for-the-ultra-efficient-jet-engine-of-the-future/. Accessed 28 Nov. 2021.

Martins, Ricardo, Nuno Lourenço, and Nuno Horta. *Analog Integrated Circuit Design Automation: Placement, Routing and Parasitic Extraction Techniques*. Springer, 2017.

Mason, Paul. *Roller Coaster!: Motion and Acceleration*. Heinemann-Raintree, 2007.

Mataigne, Fen. *Medicine by Design: The Practice and Promise of Biomedical Engineering*. Johns Hopkins UP, 2006.

"Mathematics of Vector Art." *Interactive Mathematics*, 23 Nov. 2019, www.intmath.com/vectors/math-vector-art.php. Accessed 28 Nov. 2021.

Matheson, Rob. "MIT Engineers Build Advanced Microprocessor Out of Carbon Nanotubes." *MIT News*, 28 Aug. 2019, news.mit.edu/2019/carbon-nanotubes-microprocessor-0828. Accessed 28 Nov. 2021.

Mattelart, Armand. *Networking the World: 1794-2000*. Translated by Liz Carey-Libbrecht and James A. Cohen. U of Minnesota P, 2000.

Matthews, Paul. *Vector Calculus*. Springer, 1998.

Mattingly, Jack. *Elements of Gas Turbine Propulsion*. 1996. American Institute of Aeronautics and Astronautics, 2005.

Matulka, Rebecca, and Matty Greene. "How 3D Printers Work." *Energy.gov*, 19 June 2014, www.energy.gov/articles/how-3d-printers-work. Accessed 28 Nov. 2021.

May, Bella J., and Margery A. Lockard. *Prosthetics and Orthotics in Clinical Practice: A Case Study Approach*. Davis, 2011.

McClellan, Marilyn. *Organ and Tissue Transplants: Medical Miracles and Challenges*. Enslow, 2003.

McClenahen, J. S. "Factory of the Future." *Industry Week*, vol. 256, no. 2, 2007, pp. 21-22.

———. "JIT Tops Management Practices." *Industry Week/IW*, vol. 255, no. 12, 2006, p. 13.

McElroy, Kathryn. *Prototyping for Designers*. O'Reilly Media, 2017.

McGeorge, H. D. *Marine Auxiliary Machinery*. 7th ed., Butterworth, 1995.

McHaney, Roger. *Computer Simulation: A Practical Perspective*. Academic Press, 1991.

McHenry, David. *Drawing the Line: Technical Hand Drafting for Film and Television*. Routledge, 2018.

McLachlin, Ron. "Internal Plant Environment and Just-in-Time Manufacturing." *International Journal of Manufacturing Technology & Management*, vol. 6, no. 1/2, 2004, pp. 112-24.

McLoughlin, Ian. *Computer Systems: An Embedded Approach*. McGraw-Hill, 2018.

McMorrough, Julia. *The Architecture Reference & Specification Book*. Rev. ed., Rockport, 2018.

McNichol, Tom. *AC/DC: The Savage Tale of the First Standards War*. Jossey-Bass, 2006.

Mealing, Stuart, editor. *Computers and Art*. 2nd ed., Intellect, 2008.

Medina, Lourdes A., Gul E. Okudan Kremer, and Richard A. Wysk. "Supporting Medical Device Development: A Standard Product Design Process Model." *Journal of Engineering Design*, vol. 24, no. 2, 2013, pp. 83-119.

Mehta, B. R., and Y. Jaganmohan Reddy. *Industrial Process Automation Systems: Design and Implementation*. Butterworth-Heinemann, 2014.

Memon, Afaque Rafique, Enpeng Wang, Junlei Hu, Jan Egger, and Xiaojun Chen. "A Review on Computer-Aided Design and Manufacturing of Patient-Specific Maxillofacial Implants." *Expert Review of Medical Devices*, vol. 17, no. 4, 2020, pp. 345-56.

Meschede, Dieter. *Optics, Light and Lasers: The Practical Approach to Modern Aspects of Photonics and Laser Physics*. 2nd ed., Wiley, 2007.

Metta, Haritha, and Fazleena Badurdeen. "Integrating Sustainable Product and Supply Chain Design: Modeling Issues and Challenges." *IEEE Transactions on Engineering Management*, vol. 60, no. 2, 2013, pp. 438-46.

Metwalli, Sayed M. *Machine Design with CAD and Optimization*. Wiley, 2021.

Milliner-Waddell, Jenna. "6 Key Home Pieces to Nail the Scandinavian Design Trend." *Forbes*, 24 Jan. 2019, www.forbes.com/sites/forbes-finds/2019/01/24/key-pieces-to-nail-the-scandinavian-design-trend/#ef0035621f5e. Accessed 28 Nov. 2021.

Milton, Alex, and Paul Rodgers. *Product Design*. Laurence King, 2011.

Mings, Josh. "3D CAD Smack! Graphic Design for Print and Web Using SolidWorks." *SolidSmack*, 25 June 2009, www.solidsmack.com/cad/solidworks-3d-web-rpint-graphic-design/. Accessed 28 Nov. 2021.

Minoli, Daniel. *Innovations in Satellite Communications and Satellite Technology*. John Wiley & Sons, 2015.

Mironov, Vladimir, Thomas Boland, Thomas Trusk, Gabor Forgacs, and Roger R. Markwald. "Organ Printing: Computer-Aided Jet-Based 3D Tissue Engineering." *Trends in Biotechnology*, vol. 21, no. 4, 2003, pp. 157-61.

Misbrener, Kelsey. "PVComplete Launches Utility-Scale CAD Solar Design Software." *Solar Power World*, 26 Mar. 2020, www.solarpowerworldonline.com/2020/03/pvcomplete-launches-utility-scale-cad-solar-design-software/. Accessed 28 Nov. 2021.

Mishkin, Andrew. *Sojourner: An Insider's View of the Mars Pathfinder Mission*. Berkeley Books, 2003.

Mityushev, Vladimir, Wojciech Nawalaniec, and Natalia Rylko. *Introduction to Mathematical Modeling and Computer Simulations*. CRC Press, 2018.

Mitzner, Kraig, Bob Doe, Alexander Akulin, et al. *Complete PCB Design Using OrCAD Capture and PCB Editor*. 2nd ed., Academic Press, 2019.

Moaveni, Saeed. *Engineering Fundamentals: An Introduction to Engineering*. 6th ed., Cengage Learning, 2020.

Molitch-Hou, Michael. "Apollo Engineering Takes Amusement Park CAD for a Ride in the Cloud." *Engineering.com*, 28 Mar. 2017, www.engineering.com/story/apollo-engineering-takes-amusement-park-cad-for-a-ride-in-the-cloud. Accessed 28 Nov. 2021.

Mondal, S. C., J. J. Maiti, and P. K. Ray. "Modelling Robustness in Serial Multi-Stage Manufacturing Processes." *International Journal of Production Research*, vol. 51, no. 21, 2013, pp. 6359-77.

"Monte Carlo Simulation." *IBM*, 24 Aug. 2020, www.ibm.com/cloud/learn/monte-carlo-simulation. Accessed 28 Nov. 2021.

Moore, Brian C. J. *Cochlear Hearing Loss: Physiological, Psychological and Technical Issues*. 2nd ed., Wiley, 2007.

Moore, David S., William I. Notz, and Michael Fligner. *The Basic Practice of Statistics*. 9th ed., Macmillan, 2021.

Moore, Jack. "The Limits of Football Helmets." *The Atlantic*, 5 Feb. 2016, www.theatlantic.com/health/archive/2016/02/super-bowl-football-helmet-concussion/460092/. Accessed 28 Nov. 2021.

Morawetz, Herbert. *Polymers: The Origins and Growth of a Science*. Dover, 2002.

Moritz, Eckehard Fozzy, and Steve Haake, editors. *The Engineering of Sport 6: Developments for Disciplines*. Vol. 2. Springer, 2006.

Morris, Richard. *The Fundamentals of Product Design*. 2nd ed., Fairchild Books, 2016.

Morrison, Foster. *The Art of Modeling Dynamic Systems: Forecasting for Chaos, Randomness, and Determinism*. 1991. Dover, 2008.

Morse, Philip, and George Kimball. *Methods of Operations Research*. Kormendi Press, 2008.

Mosher, D. C., Craig Shipp, Lorena Moscardelli, Jason Chaytor, Chris Baxtor, Homa Lee, and Roger Urgeles, editors. *Submarine Mass Movements and Their Consequences*. Springer, 2009.

"Most Rollercoasters in One Theme Park." *Guinness World Records*, www.guinnessworldrecords.com/world-records/69225-most-roller-coasters-in-one-theme-park. Accessed 28 Nov. 2021.

Mota, Carlos, Sandra Camarero-Espinosa, Matthew B. Baker, Paul Wieringa, and Lorenzo Moroni. "Bioprinting: From Tissue and Organ Development to *in Vitro* Models." *Chemical Reviews*, vol. 120, no. 19, 2020, pp. 10547-607.

Motoyama, Yasuyuki. *Global Companies, Local Innovations: Why the Engineering Aspects of Innovation Making Require Co-Location*. Routledge, 2016.

"Moving from CATIA V5 to 3DEXPERIENCE CATIA." *Dassault Systèmes*, 2021, www.3ds.com/3dexperience/cloud/moving-catia-v5-3dexperience-catia. Accessed 10 Jan. 2022.

Mughal, Ghulam Rasool. "Impact of Semiconductors in Electronics Industry." *PAF-KIET Journal of Engineering and Sciences*, vol. 1, no. 2, 2007, pp. 91-98.

Murray, Tim. *Milestones in Archaeology: A Chronological Encyclopedia*. ABC-CLIO, 2007.

National Research Council, Committee on Future Needs in Deep Submergence Science. *Future Needs in Deep Submergence Science: Occupied and Unoccupied Vehicles in Basic Ocean Research*. National Academies Press, 2004.

National Research Council. *Decreasing Energy Intensity in Manufacturing: Assessing the Strategies and Future Directions of the Industrial Technologies Program*. National Academies Press, 2004.

Neapolitan, Richard E. *Foundations of Algorithms*. 5th ed., Jones, 2015.

"Next Generation Air Transportation System (NextGen)." *Federal Aviation Administration*, 7 Sept. 2021, www.faa.gov/nextgen/. Accessed 28 Nov. 2021.

Noorani, Rafiq. *3D Printing: Technology, Applications, and Selection*. CRC Press, 2017.

Norman, Don. *The Design of Everyday Things*. Rev. and expanded ed., Basic, 2013.

Norton, Bill. *STOL Progenitors: The Technology Path to a Large STOL Aircraft and the C-17A*. American Institute of Aeronautics and Astronautics, 2002.

NSF ERC for Reconfigurable Manufacturing Systems, 2021, erc.engin.umich.edu/. Accessed 28 Nov. 2021.

"NX." Siemens, 2021, www.plm.automation.siemens.com/global/en/products/nx/. Accessed 16 Nov. 2021.

O'Hayre, Ryan, Suk-Won Cha, Whitney Colella, and Fritz B. Prinz. *Fuel Cell Fundamentals*. 3rd ed. John Wiley & Sons, 2016.

O'Leary, Timothy, Linda O'Leary, and Daniel O'Leary. *Computing Essentials 2021*. McGraw-Hill, 2020.

O'Neill, Meaghan. "How Scandinavian Modern Design Took the World by Storm." *Architectural Digest*, 23 Oct. 2017, www.architecturaldigest.com/story/how-scandinavian-modern-design-took-the-world-by-storm. Accessed 28 Nov. 2021.

Ocak, Z. "Streamlining Waste." *Industrial Engineer: IE*, vol. 43, no. 5, 2011, pp. 38-40.

Ogewell, Verdi. "Dassault Launches Long-Awaited Migration Bridge for CATIA V5 to 3DEXPERIENCE." *Engineering.com*, 20 Nov. 2018, www.engineering.com/story/dassault-launches-long-awaited-migration-bridge-for-catia-v5-to-3dexperience. Accessed 10 Jan. 2022.

"Oral Conditions." *Healthy People 2030*, health.gov/healthypeople/objectives-and-data/browse-objectives/oral-conditions. Accessed 28 Nov. 2021.

"Organ Donation Statistics." *Health Resources & Services Administration*, Oct. 2021, www.organdonor.gov/learn/organ-donation-statistics. Accessed 28 Nov. 2021.

Osakue, Edward E. *Introductory Engineering Graphics*. Momentum Press, 2018.

Ostrowsky, O. *Engineering Drawing with CAD Applications*. Routledge, 2019.

Ott, Ellis R., Edward G. Schilling, and Dean V. Neubauer. *Process Quality Control: Troubleshooting and Interpretation of Data*. 4th ed., American Society for Quality, 2005.

Ott, Katherine, et al., editors. *Artificial Parts, Practical Lives: Modern Histories of Prosthetics*. New York UP, 2002.

Otte, Lea. "Computer-Aided-Design in Electronics Engineering." *Celus*, 25 June 2020, www.celus.io/en/blog/cad. Accessed 28 Nov. 2021.

"Our Story." *Pixar*, 2021, www.pixar.com/our-story-pixar. Accessed 28 Nov. 2021.

Özkaya, Nihat, David Goldsheyder, and Margareta Nordin. *Fundamentals of Biomechanics: Equilibrium, Motion, and Deformation*. 4th ed., Springer International Publishing, 2018.

Pahl, Gerhard, Wolfgang Beitz, Jörg Feldhusen, and Karl-Heinrich Grote. *Engineering Design: A Systematic Approach*. 3rd ed., Springer, 2007.

Painter, Paul C., and Michael M. Coleman. *Essentials of Polymer Science and Engineering*. DEStech Publications, 2009.

Palmeri, Christopher. "Mattel Takes the Blame for Toy Recalls." *Business Week*, 21 Sept. 2007, www.bloomberg.com/news/articles/2007-09-21/mattel-takes-the-blame-for-toy-recallsbusinessweek-business-news-stock-market-and-financial-advice. Accessed 28 Nov. 2021.

Papanikolaou, Apostolos, editor. *A Holistic Approach to Ship Design: Volume 1; Optimisation of Ship Design and Operation for Life Cycle*. Springer Nature Switzerland, 2019.

Parent, Rick. *Computer Animation: Algorithms and Techniques*. 3rd ed., Elsevier, 2012.

Parker, Matt. *Things to Make and Do in the Fourth Dimension: A Mathematician's Journey through Narcissistic Numbers, Optimal Dating Algorithms, at Least Two Kinds of Infinity, and More*. Farrar, 2014.

Parras, Toni. "Opening Our Eyes to the Deep: Molly Curran." *WHOI*, 12 Mar. 2020, www.whoi.edu/news-insights/content/opening-our-eyes-to-the-deep-molly-curran/. Accessed 28 Nov. 2021.

Parrish, Thomas. *The Submarine: A History*. Penguin, 2004.

Parry, G. C., and C. E. Turner. "Application of Lean Visual Process Management Tools." *Production Planning & Control*, vol. 17, no. 1, 2006, pp. 77-86.

"Part I. Historical Context." *Space Transportation System*. Historic American Engineering Record, Nov. 2012.

Pavey, Lisa. "Never a Dull Moment." *Tesla*, 22 Nov. 2006, www.tesla.com/blog/never-dull-moment. Accessed 28 Nov. 2021.

Pavlidis, Vasilis F., Ioannis Savidis, and Eby Friedman. *Three-Dimensional Integrated Circuit Design*. 2nd ed., Morgan Kaufman, 2017.

Pedrotti, Frank L., Leno M. Pedrotti, and Leno S. Pedrotti. *Introduction to Optics*. 3rd ed., Cambridge UP, 2017.

Peebles, Curtis. *Road to Mach 10: Lessons Learned from the X-43A Flight Research Program*. American Institute of Aeronautics and Astronautics, 2008.

Peng, William W. *Fundamentals of Turbomachinery*. Wiley, 2008.

Penn, C. "Inquiring Minds Want to Know." *Private Label Buyer*, no. 21, 2007, pp. 36-37.

Peterson, Donald R., and Joseph D. Bronzino, editors. *Biomechanics: Principles and Practices*. CRC Press, 2017.

Pham, D., and A. Thomas, A. "Fighting Fit Factories: Making Industry Lean, Agile and Sustainable." *Manufacturing Engineer*, vol. 84, no. 2, 2005, pp. 24-29.

"The Philosophy of Scandinavian Design." *Smith Brothers*, smithbrothersconstruction.com/the-philosophy-of-scandinavian-design/. Accessed 28 Nov. 2021.

Picard, Alyssa. *Making the American Mouth: Dentists and Public Health in the Twentieth Century*. Rutgers UP, 2009.

Pinto, José Luís Quesado, João Carlos O. Matas, Carina Pimental, et al. *Just in Time Factory: Implementation through Lean Manufacturing Tools*. Springer International Publishing, 2018.

Pipinato, Alessio, editor. *Innovative Bridge Design Handbook: Construction, Rehabilitation, and Maintenance*. 2nd ed., Elsevier, 2021.

Pitkin, Mark R. *Biomechanics of Lower Limb Prosthetics*. Springer, 2010.

Plantenberg, Kirstie. *Engineering Graphics Essentials with AutoCAD 2022 Instruction*. SDC Publications, 2021.

Platt, Charles. *Make: Electronics*. 2nd ed., Maker Media, 2015.

Plonus, Martin. *Electronics and Communications for Scientists and Engineers*. 2nd ed., Butterworth-Heinemann, 2020.

Poggenpohl, Sharon, and Keiichi Sato. *Design Integration: Research and Collaboration*. Intellect, 2009.

Pohl, Jens G. *Building Science: Concepts and Applications*. Wiley, 2011.

Polito, Tony, and Kevin Watson. "Just-in-Time under Fire: The Five Major Constraints upon JIT Practices." *Journal of American Academy of Business, Cambridge*, vol. 9, no. 1, 2006, pp. 8-13.

Popovic, Marko B. *Biomechanics and Robotics*. CRC Press, 2013.

Porterfield, Jason. *Creating with Milling Machines*. Rosen, 2017.

"A Powerful Duo; HPC and Graphene Paving the Way for Cutting-Edge Sports Gear Design." *NIMBIX*, 21 Sept. 2021, www.nimbix.net/blog-graphene-hpc-sports-gear. Accessed 28 Nov. 2021.

Prendergast, Patrick, editor. *Biomechanical Engineering: From Biosystems to Implant Technology*. Elsevier, 2007.

Pringle, Heather. "The Origins of Creativity." *Scientific American*, Oct. 2016, www.scientificamerican.com/article/the-origins-of-creativity/. Accessed 28 Nov. 2021.

"The Printed World." *Economist*, 10 Feb. 2011, www.economist.com/briefing/2011/02/10/the-printed-world. Accessed 28 Nov. 2021.

"Product Lifecycle Management (PLM) Software." Siemens, 2021, www.plm.automation.siemens.com/global/en/our-story/glossary/product-lifecycle-management-plm-software/12506. Accessed 16 Dec. 2021.

Productivity Press Development Team. *Kanban for the Shopfloor*. CRC Press, 2019.

"Professor Bézier: A Short Biography." Computer-Aided Design, vol. 22, no. 9, 1990, p. 523.

Prust, Z. A., and Peggy B. Deal. *Graphic Communications: Digital Design and Print Essentials*. 6th ed., Goodheart-Willcox, 2019.

Psomas, Evangelos L., Christos V. Fotopoulos, and Dimitrios P. Kafetzopoulos. "Core Process Management Practices, Quality Tools and Quality Improvement in ISO 9001 Certified Manufacturing Companies." *Business Process Management Journal*, vol. 17, no. 3, 2011, pp. 437-60.

Pyzdek, Thomas, and Paul Keller. *The Six Sigma Handbook*. 5th ed., McGraw-Hill Education, 2018.

Qin, Zheng, Huidi Zhang, Xin Qing, et al. Fundamentals of Software Culture. Springer, 2018.

"Quality Assurance & Quality Control." *ASQ*, asq.org/quality-resources/quality-assurance-vs-control. Accessed 28 Nov. 2021.

Rafiquzzaman, M. *Fundamentals of Digital Logic and Microcontrollers*. 6th ed., John Wiley & Sons, 2014.

Ramey, Jay. "Electric Semi-Trucks Are on Their Way, at Last." *Autoweek*, 22 Apr. 2021, www.autoweek.com/news/green-cars/a36201258/electric-semi-trucks-arrive/. Accessed 28 Nov. 2021.

Ranganayakulu, C., and K. N. Seetharamu. *Compact Heat Exchangers: Analysis Design and Optimization Using FEM and CFD Approach*. Wiley-ASME Press, 2018.

Rangwala, A. S. *Turbo-Machinery Dynamics: Design and Operation*. McGraw-Hill, 2005.

Raoufi, Cyrus. Applied Finite Element Analysis with SolidWorks Simulation. 4th ed., CYRA Engineering Services, 2021.

Rathnam, K. A First Course in Engineering Drawing. Springer, 2018.

Ratti, Carlo, and Matthew Claudel. *Open Source Architecture*. Thames & Hudson, 2015.

Rauf, S. Bobby. *Electrical Engineering Fundamentals*. CRC Press, 2020.

Reddy, Thomas B., editor. *Linden's Handbook of Batteries*. 4th ed., McGraw-Hill, 2011.

"The Redefinition of the SI Units." *NPL*, www.npl.co.uk/si-units/the-redefinition-of-the-si-units. Accessed 28 Nov. 2021.

Reimer, Jeremy. "A History of the GUI." *Ars Technica*, 5 May 2005, arstechnica.com/features/2005/05/gui/. Accessed 28 Nov. 2021.

Rempel, Gerhard. "The Industrial Revolution." *University of Delaware*, www1.udel.edu/fllt/faculty/aml/201files/IndRev.html. Accessed 28 Nov. 2021.

Renfrew, Colin, and Paul G. Bahn, editors. *Archaeology: The Key Concepts*. Routledge, 2005.

Retna, Kala S. "Thinking about 'Design Thinking': A Study of Teacher Experiences." *Asia Pacific Journal of Education*, vol. 36, suppl. 1, 2016, pp. 5-19.

Reyes, Alejandro. *Beginner's Guide to SolidWorks 2021: Level 1; Parts, Assemblies, Drawings, PhotoView 360, SimulationXpress and CSWA Preparation*. SDC Publications, 2020.

Robbins, Charles. *Applied Mechanical Physics Using Computer Aided Design*. World Class CAD, 2007.

Rogers, Jerry R., and Augustine J. Fredrich, editors. *Environmental and Water Resources History*. American Society of Civil Engineers, 2003.

Rolls Royce. *The Jet Engine*. 5th ed., Wiley, 2015.

Romeo, Jim. "Using 3D Printing to Improve Sports Equipment." *GrabCAD*, 6 July 2020, blog.grabcad.com/blog/2020/07/06/3d-printing-sports-equipment/. Accessed 28 Nov. 2021.

Ronquillo, Romina. "Understanding CNC Milling." *Thomas*, 2021, www.thomasnet.com/articles/custom-manufacturing-fabricating/understanding-cnc-milling/. Accessed 28 Nov. 2021.

Root, Michael. *The TAB Battery Book: An In-Depth Guide to Construction, Design, and Use*. McGraw-Hill, 2011.

Rosato, Dominick V., Donald V. Rosato, and Matthew V. Rosato. *Plastic Product Material and Process Selection Handbook*. Elsevier, 2004.

Ross, Douglas T. *An Algorithmic Theory of Language*. MIT Press, 1962.

———. *Applications and Extensions of SADT (Structured Analysis and Design Technique)*. SofTech, 1984.

———. *Computer-Aided Design: A Statement of Objectives*. MIT Press, 1960.

———. "Oral History Interview with Douglas T. Ross." Interview with William Aspray. *Charles Babbage Institute*, 21 Feb. 1984, conservancy.umn.edu/handle/11299/107610. Accessed 16 Dec. 2021.

Ross, Douglas T., and Jorge E. Rodriguez. "Theoretical Foundation for the Computer-Aided Design System." *SIMULATION*, vol. 2, no. 3, 1964, pp. R-3-R-20.

Ross, Marc H., and Daniel Steinmeyer. "Energy for Industry." *Scientific American*, vol. 263, no. 3, 1990, p. 89.

Rossomando, Edward F., and Mathew Moura. "The Role of Science and Technology in Shaping the Dental Curriculum." *Journal of Dental Education*, vol. 72, no. 1, 2008, pp. 19-25.

Rowe, Jeff. "3D Model-Based Design: Setting the Definitions Straight." *MCADCafe*, 27 Sept. 2010, www10.mcadcafe.com/nbc/articles/2/867959/3D-Model-Based-Design-Setting-Definitions-Straight. Accessed 16 Dec. 2021.

Rowe, Peter G. *Design Thinking*. MIT Press, 1987.

Rowen, Alan L., et al. *Introduction to Practical Marine Engineering*. Society of Naval Architects and Marine Engineers, 2005.

Rubin, Jean E. *Mathematical Logic: Applications and Theory*. Saunders College Publishing, 1990.

Rutherford, Scott. *The American Rollercoaster*. MBI, 2000.

Sacks, Rafael, Chuck Eastman, Ghang Lee, and Paul Teicholz. *BIM Handbook: A Guide to Building Information Modeling for Owners, Designers, Engineers, Contractors, and Facility Managers*. 3rd ed., Wiley, 2018.

Samani, Hooman, editor. *Cognitive Robotics*. CRC Press, 2016.

Sandals, Jonathan. "Top Programming Languages of 2021." *Coding Dojo*, 7 Feb. 2020, www.codingdojo.com/blog/top-7-programming-languages. Accessed 28 Nov. 2021.

Saran, Cliff. "How 3D Printing Is Growing One Step at a Time." *ComputerWeekly.com*, 26 Aug. 2021, www.computerweekly.com/news/252505878/How-3D-printing-is-growing-one-step-at-a-time. Accessed 16 Dec. 2021.

Sarkar, Jayanta. *Computer Aided Design: A Conceptual Approach*. CRC Press, 2017.

"Save Energy Now LEADER." *US Department of Energy*, Feb. 2011, www1.eere.energy.gov/manufacturing/tech_assistance/pdfs/leaderpledgefaq.pdf. Accessed 28 Nov. 2021.

Schaberg, Christopher. "The Jet Engine Is a Futuristic Technology Stuck in the Past." *The Atlantic*, 11 Feb. 2018, www.theatlantic.com/technology/archive/2018/02/engine-failure/552959/. Accessed 28 Nov. 2021.

Schapire, Robert E., and Yoav Freund. *Boosting: Foundations and Algorithms*. MIT Press, 2012.

Scherer, Michael. "3D Printing Same-Day Permanent Crowns with a Desktop Printer and Helping Out a Patient at the Same Time!" *LearnDentistry*, learndentistry.com/3d-printing-same-day-permanent-crowns-with-a-desktop-printer/. Accessed 28 Nov. 2021.

Schmitt, Christopher. *Designing Web & Mobile Graphics: Fundamental Concepts for Web and Interactive Projects*. New Riders, 2013.

Schobeiri, Meinhard T. *Gas Turbine Design, Components and System Design Integration*. 2nd ed., Springer Nature Switzerland, 2019.

Schwartz, Ephraim. "Evaluating Anti-Terror Technology." *InfoWorld*, 20 Feb. 2006, www.infoworld.com/article/2656261/evaluating-anti-terror-technology.html. Accessed 28 Nov. 2021.

Scott, Michael L. *Programming Language Pragmatics*. 4th ed., Morgan Kaufmann, 2016.

Seal, Anthony M. *Practical Process Control*. Butterworth, 1998.

Seames, Warren S. *Computer Numerical Control Concepts and Programming*. 4th ed., Delmar, 2002.

Sedivy, Josef, and Stepan Hubalovsky. "Mathematical Foundations and Principles in Practice of Computer Aided Design Simulation." *International Journal of Mathematics and Computers in Simulation*, vol. 6, no. 1, 2012, pp. 230-37.

Seedhouse, Erik. *Tourists in Space: A Practical Guide*. Praxis, 2008.

Segura, Diana. "13 Best CAD Programs for Kids." *3DPrinterChat.com*, 8 Feb. 2020, 3dprinterchat.com/13-best-cad-programs-for-kids/. Accessed 16 Dec. 2021.

Seibert, B. "Design Agility Achieved with PDM/PLM." *Apparel Magazine*, May 2005, pp. 22-26.

Seidl, Martina, et al. *UML@Classroom: An Introduction to Object-Oriented Modeling*. Springer, 2015.

Seliger, Günther, Marwan K. Khrasheh, and I. S. Jawahir, editors. *Advances in Sustainable Manufacturing*. Springer-Verlag, 2011.

Sellers, Jerry Jon. *Understanding Space: An Introduction to Astronautics*. Edited by Douglas K. Kirkpatrick, 3rd ed., McGraw-Hill, 2005.

Sen, P. C. *Principles of Electric Machines and Power Electronics*. 3rd ed., Wiley, 2014.

Sexton, Timothy J. *A Concise Introduction to Engineering Graphics Including Worksheet Series B*. 6th ed., SDC Publications, 2019.

Seymour, Raymond B., editor. *Pioneers in Polymer Science: Chemists and Chemistry*. Kluwer Academic Publishers, 1989.

Sharifzadeh, Mahdi, editor. *Design and Operation of Solid Oxide Fuel Cells*. Academic Press, 2020.

Sharp, Lesley A. *Bodies, Commodities, and Biotechnologies: Death, Mourning, and Scientific Desire in the Realm of Human Organ Transfer*. Columbia UP, 2008.

Shearer, Allan W. "Abduction to Argument: A Framework of Design Thinking." *Landscape Journal*, vol. 34, no. 2, 2015, pp. 127-38.

Shepherd, D. *Aerospace Propulsion*. Elsevier, 1972.

Sherman, Don. "How a Car Is Made: Every Step from Invention to Launch." *Car and Driver*, 18 Nov. 2015, www.caranddriver.com/news/a15350381/how-a-car-is-made-every-step-from-invention-to-launch/. Accessed 28 Nov. 2021.

Shih, Randy, and Paul Schilling. *Parametric Modeling with SolidWorks 2021*. SDC Publications, 2021.

———. *Parametric Modeling with Siemens NX*. Spring 2020 ed., SDC Publications, 2020.

Shih, Willy C. "Computer Simulations Are Better—and More Affordable—Than Ever." *Harvard Business Review*, 2 Oct. 2020, hbr.org/2020/10/computer-simulations-are-better-and-more-affordable-than-ever. Accessed 28 Nov. 2021.

"Ship Design Computer Laboratory." *University of New Orleans*, 2020, www.uno.edu/academics/coe/name/facilities/ship-design-computer-laboratory. Accessed 28 Nov. 2021.

Shukla, Arun. "Proactive People Management One Key to Lean Success." *Plant Engineering*, 1 July 2006, www.plantengineering.com/articles/proactive-people-management-one-key-to-lean-success/. Accessed 28 Nov. 2021.

Shurkin, Joel N. *Broken Genius: The Rise and Fall of William Shockley, Creator of the Electronic Age*. Macmillan, 2006.

Shurr, Donald G., and John W. Michael. *Prosthetics and Orthotics*. 2nd ed., Prentice Hall, 2002.

"SI Redefinition." *NIST*, www.nist.gov/si-redefinition. Accessed 28 Nov. 2021.

Siciliano, Antonio. *Optics: Problems and Solutions*. World Scientific, 2006.

Siciliano, Bruno, and Oussama Khatib, editors. *Springer Handbook of Robotics*. 2nd ed., Springer International Publishing, 2016.

Siciliano, Bruno, et al. *Robotics: Modeling, Planning, and Control*. Springer-Verlag London, 2009.

Siddiqi, Muzaffer A. *Dynamic RAM: Technology Advancements*. CRC Press, 2013.

Silva Sequeira, João, editor. *Robotics in Healthcare: Field Examples and Challenges*. Springer International Publishing, 2019.

Simmons, Colin H., Dennis E. Maguire, and Neil Phelps. *Manual of Engineering Drawing: British and International Standards*. Butterworth-Heinemann, 2020.

Simpson, Timothy W., Zahed Siddique, and Jianxin Jiao, editors. *Product Platform and Product Family Design*. Springer, 2007.

Singh, Lakhwinder Pal, and Harwinder Singh. *Engineering Drawing: Principles and Applications*. Cambridge UP, 2021.

Singmin, Andrew. *Beginning Digital Electronics through Projects*. Butterworth-Heinemann, 2001.

Sito, Tom. *Moving Innovation: A History of Computer Animation*. MIT Press, 2013.

"SK Hynix Launches World's First DDR5 DRAM." *HPC Wire*, 7 Oct. 2020, www.hpcwire.com/off-the-wire/

sk-hynix-launches-worlds-first-ddr5-dram/. Accessed 28 Nov. 2021.

Skinner, Wickham. "The Focused Factory." *Harvard Business Review*, May 1974, hbr.org/1974/05/the-focused-factory. Accessed 28 Nov. 2021.

Slack, Nigel. *Operations and Process Management: Principles and Practice for Strategic Impact*. 5th ed., Pearson, 2018.

Sloman, Adam. *Peugeot 205: The Complete Story*. Crowood Press, 2015.

Sly, David. "Manufacturing Process Management." *Technology Trends in PLM*, 17 June 2004, www.proplanner.com/media/cms/MPM_Whitepaper_Tech_Trend_PDF_CDF4B29897EE8.pdf. Accessed 28 Nov. 2021.

Smith, Alvy Ray. *A Biography of the Pixel*. MIT Press, 2021.

Smith, Carlos A. *Automated Continuous Process Control*. Wiley, 2002.

Smith, Marquard, and Joanne Morra, editors. *The Prosthetic Impulse: From a Posthuman Present to a Biocultural Future*. MIT, 2006.

Soares, Claire. *Gas Turbines: A Handbook of Air, Land and Sea Applications*. 2nd ed., Butterworth-Heinemann, 2015.

Soares, Marcelo M., and Francisco Rebelo. *Ergonomics in Design: Methods & Techniques*. CRC Press, 2017.

"Solar Photovoltaic System Design Basics." *Office of Energy Efficiency and Renewable Energy*, www.energy.gov/eere/solar/solar-photovoltaic-system-design-basics. Accessed 28 Nov. 2021.

SolidWorks, 2021, www.solidworks.com/. Accessed 16 Dec. 2021.

Song, Yang, and Yang Jin. "Urban Planning and Design Based on AutoCAD to Expand GIS Function." *Computer-Aided Design and Applications*, vol. 17, no. S2, 2020, pp. 11-21.

"Space Systems Computer-Aided Design Technology." *NASA*, ntrs.nasa.gov/citations/19840046682. Accessed 28 Nov. 2021.

SpaceX, 2021, www.spacex.com/. Accessed 28 Nov. 2021.

Spellman, Frank R., and Nancy E. Whiting. *Environmental Science and Technology: Concepts and Applications*. 2nd ed., Government Institutes, 2006.

Spitzer, Cary R., editor. *Avionics: Development and Implementation*. CRC Press, 2007.

Springer, Paul J. *Military Robots and Drones: A Reference Handbook*. ABC-CLIO, 2013.

Stanton, Neville A., Paul M. Salmon, Laura A. Rafferty, et al. *Human Factors Methods: A Practical Guide for Engineering and Design*. 2nd ed., CRC Press, 2013.

Stark, John. Product Lifecycle Management (Volume 2): The Devil is in the Details. 3rd ed., Springer, 2016.

Steiner, Christopher. *Automate This: How Algorithms Came to Rule Our World*. Penguin, 2012.

"The STEP Standard." *STEP Tools, Inc.*, 2021, www.steptools.com/stds/step/. Accessed 28 Nov. 2021.

Stokes, Vijay K. *Introduction to Plastics Engineering*. Wiley-ASME Press, 2020.

Stone, Sarah. "Textile Engineering Student Helping to Develop Tesla Seat Covers." *NC State University*, 11 Oct. 2021, textiles.ncsu.edu/news/2021/10/textile-engineering-student-helping-to-develop-tesla-seat-covers/. Accessed 28 Nov. 2021.

"Storage vs. Memory." *PCMag*, www.pcmag.com/encyclopedia/term/storage-vs-memory. Accessed 28 Nov. 2021.

Streib, James T., and Takako Soma. *Guide to Java: A Concise Introduction to Programming*. Springer, 2014.

Stroehle, Helga. "CAD Design and Robotics: A Great Combination." *PTC*, 22 Feb. 2016, www.ptc.com/en/blogs/cad/cad-design-and-robotics-a-great-combination. Accessed 28 Nov. 2021.

Strong, A. Brent. *Plastics: Materials and Processing*. 3rd ed., Pearson Prentice Hall, 2006.

Stroud, K. A., and Dexter Booth. *Differential Equations*. Industrial Press, 2005.

Sun, Haiyin. *Basic Optical Engineering for Engineers and Scientists*. SPIE, 2019.

Sutherland, Ivan Edward. *Sketchpad, a Man-Machine Graphical Communication System*. 1963. MIT, PhD dissertation.

Sutton, George P., and Oscar Biblarz. *Rocket Propulsion Elements*. 9th ed., Wiley, 2016.

Swinerd, Graham. *How Spacecraft Fly: Spaceflight without Formulae*. Copernicus Books, 2008.

Syddell, M. "Going Lean Can Mean Plump Profits." *Manufacturers' Monthly*, Mar. 2005, pp. 19-20.

Szkutnicka, Basia. *Flats: Technical Drawing for Fashion; A Complete Guide*. Lawrence King, 2017.

Tamimi, Faleh, and Hiroshi Hirayama, editors. *Digital Restorative Dentistry: A Guide to Materials, Equipment, and Clinical Procedures*. Springer, 2019.

Tang, C. Y., et al. "Product Form Design Using Customer Perception Evaluation by a Combined Superellipse Fitting and ANN Approach." *Advanced Engineering Informatics*, vol. 27, no. 3, 2013, pp. 386-94.

Tartakovskii, Alexander, editor. *Quantum Dots: Optics, Electron Transport and Future Applications*. Cambridge UP, 2012.

Tavernor, Robert. *Smoot's Ear: The Measure of Humanity*. Yale UP, 2007.

Taylor, Andrew, Margaret Taylor, and Andrew McSweeney. "Towards Greater Understanding of Success and Survival of Lean Systems." *International Journal of Production Research*, vol. 51, no. 22, 2013, pp. 6607-30.

Taylor, Frederick Winslow. *The Principles of Scientific Management*. Harper & Brothers, 1913.

Taylor, Peter J., and Frederick H. Buttel. "How Do We Know We Have Global Environmental Problems? Science and the Globalization of Environmental Discourse." *Geoforum* vol. 23, no. 3, 1992, pp. 405-16.

Thakur-Weigold, Bublu, Stephan Wagner, and Tee Bin Ong. "The Challenging Business of Nuts and Bolts." *ISE Magazine*, Nov. 2016, pp. 44-48.

Thomas, Katie Lloyd, Timo Amhoff, and Nick Beech. *Industries of Architecture*. Routledge, 2016.

Thomas, Zoe. "Coronavirus: Will Covid-19 Speed Up the Use of Robots to Replace Human Workers?" *BBC*, 19 Apr. 2020, www.bbc.com/news/technology-52340651. Accessed 28 Nov. 2021.

Thompson, Avery. "Scientists Have Made Transistors Smaller Than We Thought Possible." *Popular Mechanics*, 12. Oct. 2016, www.popularmechanics.com/technology/a23353/1nm-transistor-gate/. Accessed 28 Nov. 2021.

Tickoo, Sham. Siemens NX 2020 for Designers. 13th ed., CADCIM Technologies, 2020.

Tidwell, Jenifer, Charles Brewer, and Aynne Valencia. *Designing Interfaces: Patterns for Effective Interaction Design*. 3rd ed., O'Reilly Media, 2020.

"Timeline of Computer History." *Computer History Museum*, www.computerhistory.org/timeline/computers/. Accessed 28 Nov. 2021.

Tipler, Paul A., and Gene Mosca. *Physics for Scientists and Engineers*. 6th ed., extended version, Macmillan Learning, 2020.

Toller, Jonathan. "The History of Agile Manufacturing." *Kloeckner Metals*, 26 May 2020, www.kloecknermetals.com/blog/agile-manufacturing/. Accessed 28 Nov. 2021.

Tonias, Demetrios E., and Jim J. Zhao. *Bridge Engineering: Design, Rehabilitation, and Maintenance of Modern Highway Bridges*. 4th ed., McGraw-Hill, 2017.

Tooley, Mike. *Aircraft Digital Electronic and Computer Systems: Principles, Operation and Maintenance*. 2nd ed., Routledge, 2013.

Tooley, Mike, and David Wyatt. *Aircraft Communications and Navigation Systems*. 2nd ed., Routledge, 2017.

"Toyota Production System." *Toyota*, 2021, global.toyota/en/company/vision-and-philosophy/production-system/. Accessed 28 Nov. 2021.

Tran, Lani. Mastering Surface Modeling with SolidWorks 2021: Basic through Advanced Techniques. SDC Publications, 2020.

Tremblay, Thom. Fusion 360: Generative Design. LinkedIn Learning, 2019.

Tripathi, Anuj, and Jose Savio Melo, editors. *Advances in Biomaterials for Biomedical Applications*. Springer Nature Singapore, 2017.

Troughton, Michael J. *Handbook of Plastics Joining: A Practical Guide*. 2nd ed., William Andrew, 2008.

Tupper, Shelby. "The Best Graphic Design Software for 2021." *PCMag*, 22 Oct. 2021, www.pcmag.com/picks/the-best-graphic-design-software. Accessed 28 Nov. 2021.

Tyler, Dustin. "Graphic Design vs Video Game Design: Which Career Match Your Skills?" *GameDesigning*, 25 June 2021, www.gamedesigning.org/learn/graphic-design-vs-game-design/. Accessed 28 Nov. 2021.

Tyulin, Andrey, and Alexander Chursin. *The New Economy of the Product Life Cycle: Innovation and Design in the Digital Era*. Springer, 2020.

Udroin, Azvan, and Paul Bere, editors. *Product Lifecycle Management: Terminology and Applications*. IntechOpen, 2018.

Udroiu, Razvan, editor. *Computer-Aided Technologies: Applications in Engineering and Medicine*. IntechOpen, 2016.

Ulrich, Karl, Steven Eppinger, and Maria C. Yang. *Product Design and Development*. 7th ed., McGraw-Hill, 2020.

Um, Dugan. *Solid Modeling and Applications: Rapid Prototyping, CAD and CAE Theory*. Springer, 2016.

Unsworth, John F. *Design and Construction of Modern Steel Railway Bridges*. 2nd ed., CRC Press, 2018.

"Urban and Regional Planners." *US Bureau of Labor Statistics*, 8 Sept. 2021, www.bls.gov/ooh/life-physical-and-social-science/urban-and-regional-planners.htm. Accessed 28 Nov. 2021.

"Use of Energy Explained." *US Energy Information Administration*, 2 Aug. 2021, www.eia.gov/energyexplained/use-of-energy/industry.php. Accessed 28 Nov. 2021.

"User Interface Design Basics." *Usability.gov*, www.usability.gov/what-and-why/user-interface-design.html. Accessed 28 Nov. 2021.

V., Carlotta. "What Is the Current State of Microscale 3D Printing?" *3DNatives*, 16 Apr. 2020, www.3dnatives.com/en/what-is-the-current-state-of-microscale-3d-printing/. Accessed 28 Nov. 2021.

Valencia, Raymond P., editor. *Applied Physics in the Twenty-First Century*. Nova Science, 2010.

Valiant, Leslie. *Probably Approximately Correct: Nature's Algorithms for Learning and Prospering in a Complex World*. Basic, 2013.

Van der Zwaag, Sybrand, editor. *Self-Healing Materials: An Alternative Approach to Twenty Centuries of Materials Science*. Springer, 2007.

Van Dokkum, Klaas. *Ship Knowledge: Ship Design, Construction and Operation*. 10th ed., Dokmar Maritime Publishers, 2020.

Van Roy, Peter, and Seif Haridi. *Concepts, Techniques, and Models of Computer Programming*. MIT Press, 2004.

Van Vliet, Hans Willem, and Kees van Luttervelt. "Development and Application of a Mixed Product/Process-Based DFM Methodology." *International Journal of Computer Integrated Manufacturing*, vol. 17, no. 3, 2007, pp. 224-34.

Wall, Mike. "The Private Spaceflight Decade: How Commercial Space Truly Soared in the 2010s." *Space.com*, 20 Dec. 2019, www.space.com/ private-spaceflight-decade-2010s-retrospective.html. Accessed 28 Nov. 2021.

Walsh, Bryan. "Indoor Vertical Farming Grows Up." *Axios*, 26 May 2021, www.axios.com/vertical-farming-e6137f78-6a73-46e6-9277-5f8d22b6a2fc.html. Accessed 28 Nov. 2021.

Walski, Thomas M. *Advanced Water Distribution Modeling and Management*. Methods, 2003.

Wang, Guoqing, and Wenhao Zhao. *The Principles of Integrated Technology in Avionics Systems*. Academic Press, 2020.

Wang, John, editor. *Optimizing, Innovating, and Capitalizing on Information Systems for Operations*. Business Science Reference, 2013.

Wang, Yongtian, Xueming Li, and Yuxin Peng, editors. *Image and Graphics Technologies and Applications*. Springer Singapore, 2020.

Washington, Allyn J. *Basic Technical Mathematics with Calculus*. 10th ed., Pearson, 2014.

Watson, Catie. "What Are the Four Basic Functions of a Computer?" *Techwalla*, 21 Sept. 2018, www.techwalla.com/articles/what-are-the-four-basic-functions-of-a-computer. Accessed 28 Nov. 2021.

Weingardt, Richard G. *Engineering Legends: Great American Civil Engineers; 32 Profiles of Inspiration and Achievement*. American Society of Civil Engineers, 2005.

Weisberg, David E. "Chapter 13: IBM, Lockheed and Dassault Systèmes." *The Engineering Design Revolution: The People, Companies and Computer Systems That Changed Forever the Practice of Engineering*. Weisberg, 2008, www.cadhistory.net/13%20IBM,%20Lockheed%20and%20Dassault.pdf. Accessed 10 Jan. 2022.

Weisenberger, Nick. "Coasters-101: What Software Do Roller Coaster Engineers Use?" *Coaster101*, 3 Nov. 2015, www.coaster101.com/2015/11/03/coasters-101-what-software-do-roller-coaster-engineers-use/. Accessed 28 Nov. 2021.

West, Nick. "Practical Fluid Dynamics: Part 1." *Game Developer*, Mar. 2007, pp. 43-47.

"What Can You 3D Print with Plastics?" *3D Systems*, 2021, www.3dsystems.com/what-can-you-3d-print-with-plastics. Accessed 28 Nov. 2021.

"What Do We Mean by Design?" *Design Council*, www.designcouncil.org.uk/news-opinion/what-do-we-mean-design. Accessed 28 Nov. 2021.

"What Goes into Meeting the Workstation Requirements for CAD Systems." *Infratech*, 13 Jan. 2019, www.infratechcivil.com/pages/Workstation-requirements-for-CAD-systems-for-autocad-revit. Accessed 28 Nov. 2021.

"What Is 3Dponics?" *3Dponics*, 2021, www.3dponics.com/what-is-3dponics/. Accessed 28 Nov. 2021.

"What Is CAD/CAM Dentistry?" *Colgate*, 2021, www.colgate.com/en-us/oral-health/dental-visits/cad-cam-dentistry-what-is-it. Accessed 28 Nov. 2021.

"What Is Design?" *University of Illinois at Chicago College of Architecture, Design, and the Arts*, design.uic.edu/what-is-design. Accessed 28 Nov. 2021.

"What Is Design for Manufacturing (DFM)?" *TWI*, 2021, www.twi-global.com/technical-knowledge/faqs/faq-what-is-design-for-manufacture-dfm. Accessed 28 Nov. 2021.

"What Is the Difference between CAD, CAE, and CAM?" *Michigan State University*, 2 Apr. 2021, online.egr.msu.edu/articles/cad-vs-cae-vs-cam-what-is-the-difference/. Accessed 28 Nov. 2021.

"What Is Electrical CAD (ECAD)?" *Arena*, www.arenasolutions.com/resources/glossary/electrical-cad/. Accessed 28 Nov. 2021.

"What Is the Engineering Design Process?" *TWI*, www.twi-global.com/technical-knowledge/faqs/engineering-design-process. Accessed 28 Nov. 2021.

"What Is Global Climate Change?" *NASA*, 2019, climatekids.nasa.gov/climate-change-meaning/. Accessed 28 Nov. 2021.

"What Is PLM (Product Lifecycle Management)?" Oracle, 2021, oracle.com/scm/product-lifecycle-management/what-is-plm/. Accessed 16 Dec. 2021.

"What Is a Projectile?" *Physics Classroom*, www.physicsclassroom.com/class/vectors/Lesson-2/What-is-a-Projectile. Accessed 28 Nov. 2021.

"What Is Rapid Prototyping?-Definition, Methods and Advantages." *TWI*, www.twi-global.com/technical-knowledge/faqs/faq-manufacturing-what-is-rapid-prototyping. Accessed 28 Nov. 2021.

"What Is Simulation Modeling (and How Does It Work)?" *Spatial*, 25 Mar. 2020, blog.spatial.com/simulation-in-cad. Accessed 28 Nov. 2021.

Wheeler, Donald J., and David S. Chambers. *Understanding Statistical Process Control*. 3rd ed., Statistical Process Controls Press, 2010.

White, Annie. "12 Best-Selling Electric Vehicles of 2021 (So Far)." *Car and Driver*, 29 Oct. 2021, www.caranddriver.com/features/g36278968/best-selling-evs-of-2021/. Accessed 28 Nov. 2021.

"Why Is CAD/CAM Crucial in the Design Process?" *BBC*, 4 Nov. 2019, www.bbc.co.uk/programmes/p07sxzpv. Accessed 28 Nov. 2021.

Williams, Brad, David Damstra, and Hal Stern. *Professional WordPress: Design and Development*. 3rd ed., Wiley, 2015.

Winchester, Simon. *The Perfectionists: How Precision Engineers Created the Modern World*. HarperCollins, 2018.

Winder, Catherine, and Zahra Dowlatabadi. *Producing Animation*. Focal, 2011.

———. *Science in the Age of Computer Simulation*. U of Chicago P, 2010.

Winsberg, Eric. "Computer Simulations in Science." *Stanford Encyclopedia of Philosophy*, 26 Sept. 2019, plato.stanford.edu/entries/simulations-science/. Accessed 28 Nov. 2021.

"Wireframe Modeling." *PCMag*, www.pcmag.com/encyclopedia/term/wireframe-modeling. Accessed 28 Nov. 2021.

"Wireframe Modeling." *Spatial*, www.spatial.com/resources/glossary/wireframe-modeling. Accessed 28 Nov. 2021.

Wolfe, William J. *Optics Made Clear: The Nature of Light and How We Use It*. SPIE, 2007.

Wong, Kenneth. "Fly into a Wind Tunnel with Autodesk Project Falcon." *Digital Engineering 247*, 14 Dec. 2011, www.digitalengineering247.com/article/fly-into-a-wind-tunnel-with-autodesk-project-falcon/. Accessed 28 Nov. 2021.

Wood, David. *Interface Design: An Introduction to Visual Communication in UI Design*. Fairchild Books, 2014.

"WordPress Market Share in 2021." *Envisage Digital*, 2021, www.envisagedigital.co.uk/wordpress-market-share/. Accessed 28 Nov. 2021.

"World Population to Reach 9.9 Billion by 2050." *IISD*, 6 Aug. 2020, sdg.iisd.org/news/world-population-to-reach-9-9-billion-by-2050/. Accessed 28 Nov. 2021.

Wynbrandt, James. *The Excruciating History of Dentistry: Toothsome Tales and Oral Oddities from Babylon to Braces*. St. Martin's Press, 1998.

Wypych, George. *Handbook of Polymers*. 3rd ed., ChemTec, 2022.

Wysocki, Robert K. *Effective Project Management: Traditional, Agile, Extreme*. 7th ed., John Wiley & Sons, 2014.

Yamagata, Yoshiki, and Ayoob Sharifi. *Resilience-Oriented Urban Planning: Theoretical and Empirical Insights*. Springer, 2018.

Yamamoto, Jazon. *The Black Art of Multiplatform Game Programming*. Cengage Learning, 2015.

Yanev, Bojidar. *Bridge Management*. Wiley, 2007.

Yasinski, Emma. "On the Road to 3-D Printed Organs." *Scientist*, 26 Feb. 2020, www.the-scientist.com/news-opinion/on-the-road-to-3-d-printed-organs-67187. Accessed 28 Nov. 2021.

Yasmin, Nighat. *Introduction to AutoCAD 2022 for Civil Engineering Applications*. SDC Publications, 2021.

Yock, Paul G., Stefanos Zenios, Josh Makower, et al., editors. *Biodesign: The Process of Innovating Medical Technologies*. 2nd ed., Cambridge UP, 2015.

Yu, Rongrong, Ning Gu, and Michael J. Ostwald. *Computational Design: Technology, Cognition and Environments*. CRC Press, 2021.

Zabihian, Farshid. *Power Plant Engineering*. CRC Press, 2021.

Zhao, Pengfei, et al., editors. *Advanced Graphic Communications and Media Technologies*. Springer Singapore, 2017.

Ziden, Azidah Abu, Fatariah Zakaria, and Ahmad Nizam Othman. "Effectiveness of AutoCAD 3D Software as a Learning Support Tool." *International Journal of Emerging Technologies in Learning (JET)*, vol. 7, no. 2, 2012, pp. 57-60.

Ziliak, Stephen T., and Deidre N. McClosky. *The Cult of Statistical Significance: How the Standard Error Costs Us Jobs, Justice, and Lives*. U of Michigan P, 2008.

Zubaly, Robert B. *Applied Naval Architecture*. Cornell Maritime, 1996.

Subject Index

3D CAD models, 54
3D polymers, 194, 346
3D printing technology, 52, 86, 349

Accreditation Board for Engineering and Technology (ABET), 93, 192
actuarial science, 18, 20
additive manufacturing (AM), 52, 85, 228, 323, 334, 417, 438
advanced project management, 381
aerial reconnaissance techniques, 32
aeroderivative turbine, 224
aerodynamic lift, 1, 3, 368
aeroelasticity, 7
aeronautic design, 8
aeronautics, 1, 3
aerospace design, 8-9, 11-12, 99, 282
aerospace engineering, 1, 7-8
aerospace engineers, 7, 9
afterburner, 284
agile manufacturing, 386-387
air traffic control (ATC), 61-62, 67
air-pollution control, 188, 191, 193
algorithm, 13-15, 18-19, 115, 124, 228-230, 238-239, 243, 381, 392, 398-399, 442
alternating current (AC), 169, 178-179, 208, 414
Alexander, Christopher, 38
American Academy of Orthotists and Prosthetists, 373
American Board for Certification in Orthotics and Prosthetics, 371, 373
American Board of Audiology and the American Speech-Language-Hearing Association (AHSA), 53
American Dental Association (ADA), 148
American Institute of Architects Committee on the Environment (AIA/COTE), 39
analytical hierarchical process, 390, 393-394
Aphotic Zone, 142
Apollo program, 211, 401
apparel manufacturing, 302-304
application programming interface (API), 220
application-specific integrated circuit (ASIC), 170
applied mathematics, 15, 17-21, 349
applied physics, 22-27
archaeologists, 27-33, 149, 178
archaeology, 27-29, 32-33
Architect Registration Examination, 40

architectural engineering, 34, 36, 38-40, 105
architecture, 30, 38-43, 70, 76, 78, 82, 113, 155, 229, 263, 280, 327, 331, 388, 447
architecture software, 41-43
artificial intelligence (AI), 101-102, 127, 219, 221, 396
Artificial Intelligence robot (AIBO), 400
artificial organs, 44, 46-48, 69, 72, 84, 86-87
astronautical design, 8
astronomy, 123, 322, 338, 340-341, 449
asynchronous SRAM (ASRAM), 383
Atanasoff, J.V., 121
Atlantis (space shuttle), 2, 12
attitude control system (ACS), 420
audiology program, 53
audiovisual representation, 37
Australian Center for Plant Functional Genomics, 87
AutoCAD, 54-56, 78-79, 94, 101, 111, 168, 193, 234, 259, 280, 337, 374, 414, 438, 445, 447
Autodesk, 8, 54-56, 75, 78, 90, 103, 110, 112, 191, 212, 220
autoimmune diseases, 143
Automated Drafting and Machining (ADAM), 107
automated process, 56-61, 106, 438
autonomous underwater vehicles, 140
aviation, 3, 5-9, 61, 63, 66, 125, 214, 222, 225
avionics, 6-7, 61-67, 98

barodynamics, 73-74, 77
basic input/output system (BIOS), 385
bathyscaphs, 433
battery technology, 162
Becquerel, Alexandre-Edmond, 414
Bézier, Pierre, 125, 441
Bézier curve, 441-442
bioartificial devices, 86
bioartificial liver, 86
bioartificial organ, 85
biochemical oxygen demand (BOD), 191
biodegradable polymers, 355
biodegradable scaffolds, 86
bioengineering, 44, 48, 83-84, 86-87, 264, 355, 370
biological oxidation, 190
biological treatment processes, 190, 192
biological wastewater treatment, 190
biomaterials, 43-44, 48, 77
biomechanical engineering, 69-70, 72

Subject Index

biomechanical engineers, 72
biomechanics, 46, 69-70, 73, 370, 372, 426, 428
bioprinting, 85-86, 88
bioreactor, 86
biotechnology, 48, 73, 352, 355
Boolean algebra, 181
Bourne, William, 140
Brayton thermodynamic cycle, 282, 365
building description system (BDS), 78
building information modeling (BIM), 41, 113

C++ language, 118-120
CAD education, 99
CAD research and theory, 101-102
calendering, 349
cardiopulmonary resuscitation (CPR), 401
CD-ROM, 122
cell and tissue engineering, 83-87
cell biology, 87
cell phone technology, 173, 202
cellular manufacturing, 295, 309, 391, 394
Centers for Disease Control and Prevention (CDC), 200
central processing unit (CPU), 169, 242, 267, 384, 397
centrifugal force, 3
centripetal force, 404
chain-reaction polymerization, 351
chemical CAE, 105
chemical energy, 211, 213
chemical engineering, 105, 192, 214, 277, 354-355
chemotherapy, 51
civil engineering, 75, 88-94, 106, 188, 254, 258, 429
civil engineers, 90
Clarke, Arthur C., 95-96
classical archaeology, 27
Clean Air Act of 1970, 189, 191
Clean Water Act of 1977, 192
close-ended prototyping, 375
CMYK model, 238
CNC lathing, 59, 125
cochlear implants, 51-52
code enforcement, 446
cognitive ergonomics, 201
Cold War, 9
Columbia (space shuttle), 12, 49
combustion, 24, 161-162, 164-167, 172, 186, 205-210, 213-215, 221-222, 247, 250-251, 284-285, 331, 364-368
combustor, 224, 283, 367
commercial spacecraft, 422
Common Business-Oriented Language (COBOL), 119
Communications Satellite Act of 1962, 95

communications satellite technology, 94, 97-98
Communications Workers of America (CWA), 98
compact disk (CD), 172, 182
competent cells, 48
Comprehensive Environmental Response, Compensation, and Liability Act of 1980, 192
computational mathematics, 18
computer animation, 114-116, 240
computer graphics, 243, 412, 431
computer modeling, 106, 424, 438
computer numerical control (CNC), 103, 112-113, 125, 187, 332, 387-388, 406
computer programmers, 169, 174, 219
computer programming language, 170, 398, 406
computer programming, 58, 170, 215, 381, 398, 406, 453
computer simulation, 70, 123, 128-129
computer-aided design (CAD) and drafting, 437
computer-aided design (CAD) programs, 451
Computer-Aided Design Project, 405-406
Computer-Aided Design: A Statement of Objectives, 406-407
computer-aided drawing, 437
computer-aided engineering (CAE), 82, 103, 152-153, 280, 328, 332, 337, 349, 363, 387, 416-417, 437
computer-aided manufacturing (CAM), 21, 44, 63, 72, 81, 85, 96, 106, 110, 112, 130, 144, 187, 301, 332, 337, 349, 363, 374, 387, 397, 410, 417, 437, 442
computer-aided polymer design (CAPD), 351-352
computer-aided process planning (CAPP), 360
computer-aided production engineering (CAPE), 360
computer-assisted engineering, 103
computer-generated imagery (CGI), 234, 240, 242, 278
computer-simulation programs, 163
concurrent engineering, 153, 309
content management system (CMS), 454
contract manufacturing, 131-133
control processing unit (CPU), 176
COVID-19 pandemic, 7, 290
cross-linking bonds, 196
crude oil, 205, 207, 209, 330, 332
cultural resource management (CRM), 31
customer information exchange, 135

Darwin, Charles, 29
Dassault Systèmes, 81-83, 90, 168, 191, 416-418
database management, 219
deaerator, 248
de Casteljau, Paul, 441-442
deep submergence vehicle (DSV), 142
Defense Advanced Research Projects Agency (DARPA), 214
dental care, 143, 146, 148

dentistry, 143-149
deoxyribonucleic acid, 352
Design Augmented by Computer (DAC-1), 54, 139
design calculations, 246
design for manufacturability (DFM), 135, 152, 308
design processes, 157, 226, 456
design thinking, 155-156
digital design, 52, 77, 112, 179-180, 323
digital images, 238, 370
digitized diagrams, 139
direct current (DC), 169, 175, 208, 414
direct manipulation interface (DMI), 237
direct-access storage, 383
disk operating system (DOS), 55, 118, 236
dynamic random-access memory (DRAM), 383

Ebola outbreak, 402
ecodesign, 159-161
Edison, Thomas, 169, 171, 173
Einstein, Albert, 230, 338-339, 414
electric vehicles, 162, 164, 166-167, 173, 253
electrical energy, 11, 211, 213, 251, 253
electrical engineering, 105, 168, 170-171, 173-174, 412
electrical engineers, 168-169, 171, 173-174
electrical power system (EPS), 420
electrical resistivity, 23
electrical theory, 168, 173
electrochemistry, 167, 214
electromagnetism, 111, 449
electromotive force (EMF), 208
electronic circuit diagrams, 177
Electronic Data Systems (EDS), 333
electronic design automation (EDA), 177
electronic engineering, 178, 181
Electronic Numerical Integrator and Computer (ENIAC), 117, 272
electronic technology, 178, 182
electrostatic precipitators, 191
empirical engineering, 88, 188
endodontics, 147
Energy Research and Development Administration, 250
energy-conversion methods, 167
engineering design, 183-185
engineering design process, 183-185
engineering management, 93
Engineering Research Center for Reconfigurable Machining Systems, 392
enterprise resource planning (ERP), 358, 387
environmental archaeologists, 32

environmental control and life-support systems (ECLSS), 420
environmental engineering, 88, 90, 93, 167, 188-193, 254-255, 258-259, 434
environmental engineers, 189-191, 193
environmental protection, 446
Environmental Protection Agency (EPA), 250, 305, 307, 315
environmental sciences, 199
environmental sustainability, 446
epidemiology, 19, 147
epoxy, 193, 196-198, 343
Ergonomics Research Society, 199
ergonomics, 199-203
Ericsson cycle, 222
Euclidean geometry, 230-231
European Organisation for the Exploitation of Meteorological Satellites, 96
evolutionary prototyping, 376
extended data out DRAM, 383
external hard drive, 122
extracellular matrix, 85
extracorporeal membrane oxygenation (ECMO), 46

fast page mode DRAM, 383
fatal accidents, 5
Fauchard, Pierre, 143
Federal Aviation Administration (FAA), 66-67
Federal Highway Act, 92
feedwater heater, 248
fiber-reinforced polymer (FRP), 343-344, 347, 349
field-programmable gate array (FPGA), 170
flexible manufacturing system (FMS), 136
flight instrumentation, 61-62, 65-66
flocculation, 190-191
fluid mechanics, 90, 190, 256, 258
Ford, Henry, 57, 188, 286, 306, 391
FORTRAN, 118-119, 140
fossil fuel power plants, 210
fossil fuels, 159, 161, 167, 205-207
Frederick Winslow Taylor, 312-313
fuel cells, 161-162, 164-167, 211-215, 226, 252, 419-420
fuel economy, 215, 224, 229, 253
functional design, 180, 215-216
fused deposition modeling (FDM), 440
Future Farmers of America, 263

game programming, 56, 114-115, 171, 219-221, 234-235, 242-243, 278, 280
garbage archaeology (garbology), 32

501

gas turbine technology, 222-224, 226
gearbox, 252, 284-285, 367
General Conference on Weights and Measures, 275, 323
General Motors (GM), 54, 59, 107, 111, 139-140, 162, 234, 252, 333
generative design, 104, 227-230
geocaching, 65
geographic information systems (GIS), 90, 191, 443, 445
geological processes, 205
geometric optics, 339
geometry, 15, 106, 183, 185, 230-235, 283, 293, 322, 366, 389, 449
geotechnical engineering, 90-91
g-forces, 404
global climate change, 159, 167
global economy, 109-110, 203, 319
Global Industry Analysts, 7
global positioning system (GPS), 7, 62, 233, 423
global warming, 21, 159, 193, 206, 264
globalization, 385, 391
Golann Brett, 357
Graphical Language for Interactive Design (GLIDE), 78
graphical user interface (GUI), 107, 121, 236, 412
graphics processing unit (GPU), 242
graphics programs, 29, 55, 177, 278, 413, 441, 451
graphics technology, 241, 243
Grassmann, Hermann, 449
Gray code, 60
green buildings, 447
greenhouse gas emissions, 210
gross domestic product (GDP), 302
group technology, 286, 393
gyroscopes, 6, 61-63, 65, 421

Hall, John H. 312
Hamilton, William, 449
Hanratty, Patrick J. 111
Harvard Business Review, 129, 133, 157, 288, 292
hazardous-waste management, 188-189, 193
Health Insurance Portability and Accountability Act (HIPAA), 147
health-care providers, 143
hearing aids, 47-49, 51-53
hearing loss, 48-53
heat exchanger, 207, 245-249, 301, 330
heating, ventilation, and air-conditioning (HVAC) systems, 38
hemodynamics, 46-47
heteropolymer, 351
homopolymer, 351

Human Factors and Ergonomics Society, 203
human intervention, 26, 95, 274, 395, 399
human-computer interaction (HCI), 102, 236, 412-413
hybrid electric vehicle (HEV), 253
hybrid paradigm, 399
hybrid power systems, 213
hydraulic engineering, 254-259
hydraulic engineers, 255-256, 258
hydrocarbon fuels, 205, 212, 214
hydrodynamics, 70, 327
hydrology, 90, 93, 188, 190, 193
hydroponics, 259-264
hydrostatics, 256
hypertext markup language (HTML), 119, 376, 453

IC design engineering, 168
image compression, 239
immune system, 83-84
immunoprotective artificial membranes, 48
in vitro engineering, 84, 86
in vivo engineering, 84-85
incremental prototyping, 376
Indian National Satellite System (INSAT), 96
Industrial Revolution, 17, 22, 57, 125, 187, 205, 274, 312-313, 316, 322, 379, 431, 443
industrial robots, 57, 59, 397, 400
IndustryWeek, 287
inertial navigation systems (INS), 62
information technology (IT), 100, 201, 358-359, 388
Initial Graphics Exchange Specification (IGES), 389
Institute for Defense Analysis (IDA), 360
Institute of Ergonomics and Human Factors, 203
integrated circuit (IC), 60, 154, 168-170, 175, 178, 180-181, 196, 241, 267, 269, 332, 383, 396-397, 420
Integrated Design and Engineering Analysis System (I-DEAS), 333
intelligent Computer Aided Satellite Designer (iCASD), 96
Interactive Design and Evaluation of Advanced Spacecraft (IDEAS), 95
internal combustion engines, 161-162, 166, 186, 205, 208, 250, 364
International Business Machines (IBM), 54, 81, 119, 131, 140, 383
International Ergonomics Association (IEA), 199, 203
International Society for Occupational Ergonomics and Safety, 203
International Space Station (ISS), 26, 39, 418
International Sports Engineering Association (ISEA), 424-425
International Standards Organization (ISO), 380, 389

International System of Units (Le Système International d'Unités, or SI), 272-274, 276-277, 318, 323
iRobot Corporation, 400
isentropic compression, 282
isometric drawing, 278-280, 435
isometry, 280, 435

Java Virtual Machine, 119
Jefferson, Thomas, 28, 312
jet engine technology, 285
jet engine, 2, 6, 24, 221-224, 226, 241, 281-285, 364-368
Journal of Small Business Management, 357, 361
just-in-time manufacturing (JIT), 134, 136, 286-292, 295-296, 306, 309, 315

Kaizen, 296, 309
Kanban, 136-137, 288-289, 296-297, 309, 311
Kennedy Space Center, 12
kinematics, 111, 256, 293-294
kinesiology, 425, 428
knowledge-based engineering, 102

labor tracking, 134
Leadership in Energy and Environmental Design, 37
lean manufacturing, 134, 136, 287, 295-297, 308-310, 312, 315, 358, 380
light-emitting diode (LED), 173
Linux operating system, 177, 219, 242, 336
liquefied natural gas (LNG) ship, 330

magnetic resonance imaging (MRI), 19, 25, 147, 173
magnetic susceptibility, 23, 105
Manhattan Project, 123, 128
manufacturing process management (MPM), 356, 359
manufacturing processes, 102, 132, 151-152, 154, 288-289, 291, 303, 307-308, 358, 360, 387, 410
manufacturing resource planning (MRPII), 135
manufacturing strategies, 134, 297
manufacturing systems design, 312, 315
marine engineering, 327, 331, 429, 433-434
marine engineers, 327, 330-331, 431
market intelligence, 357
mass transfer efficiency, 46
Massachusetts Institute of Technology (MIT), 54, 62, 98, 107, 110, 405-406, 412
mastectomy, 372
material requirements planning, 360, 387
maxillofacial surgery, 146
mechanical CAE, 105

mechanical engineering, 69-73, 89, 170, 174, 203, 214, 235, 249, 253, 255, 277, 322, 397, 424-425, 428-429, 441
mechanobiology, 69
medical imaging, 18-19, 25, 72
medical science, 71, 86, 371
metal oxide semiconductor field effect transistor (MOSFET) technology, 170, 267-268, 270-272
metalworking, 186-187, 343
meteorology, 22, 123, 340-341
metrology, 234, 277, 319, 322, 378, 380
microelectromechanical gas turbines, 281
microscale 3D printing, 323-325
microscopes, 337-338, 340
Microsoft.NET, 120
microwave radio, 96
Molniya orbits, 96
molten carbonate fuel cell (MCFC), 164
monocoque concept, 5
municipal engineering, 443

nanotechnology, 22, 230, 301
National Aeronautics and Space Administration (NASA), 26, 39, 66, 214, 263, 285, 368, 404, 418
National Airspace System (NAS), 66
National Alliance for Communications Technology Education and Learning (NACTEL), 98
National Council of Examiners for Engineering and Surveying, 40
National Deep Submergence Facility (NDSF), 142
National Institute for Occupational Safety and Health (NIOSH), 200
National Institute of Dental and Craniofacial Research (NIDCR), 147
National Institute of Standards and Technology (NIST), 277, 302, 307, 323
National Institutes of Health (NIH), 147
National Renewable Energy Laboratory, 214
natural gas, 165, 205, 207, 209-210, 223, 251, 255, 301, 327, 330, 332
naval architecture, 327, 331
network management, 219
Newton, Isaac 1, 17, 22, 70, 256, 338, 449
New World, 195, 345
next-generation (NextGen) air transportation system, 66
Nixon, Richard, 12
nondirectional radio beacon (NDB), 63
nonmechanical memory devices, 121
nonrenewable resources, 159, 205

North American Industry Classification System (NAICS), 303
nuclear power plants, 249, 434
Nuclear Regulatory Commission, 249
nutrient film technique (NFT), 261

object-oriented programming (OOP), 219
Occupational Safety and Health Administration (OSHA), 147, 305-306
occupational therapists, 203
oceanography, 22
operating system, 55, 81, 118-120, 140, 177, 220, 236, 242, 336, 383, 389, 402, 416
optical instruments, 337, 340
oral and maxillofacial pathology, 147
oral and maxillofacial radiology, 147
oral hygiene, 143, 146-148
oral surgery, 146
original equipment manufacturer (OEM), 130
orthodontics, 146
orthosis, 370
orthotics, 370, 373
osseointegration, 373
otorhinolaryngologists, 53
outsourcing, 130-131, 133, 303, 305, 310
oxidation-reduction process, 207

pacemakers, 26, 47, 174, 369, 372-373
paleogenetics, 352
passive thermal control, 11
pedodontics, 146
periodontics, 146
phase-change material (PCM), 11
photochemistry, 352
photovoltaic effect, 414
physical optics, 337
Pixar, 114-116
plastics engineering, 343, 345-346, 349-350
poka-yoke, 152-153, 296, 309-310
polyethylene terephthalate, 47
polymer science, 352, 354-355
polymerization reactions, 347, 354
polymerization, 193-197, 324, 345-348, 351-354, 439
polymorphism, 216
polysaccharides, 352
polysilicon, 268
polyvinyl chloride (PVC), 354
pontoon bridge, 76
population dynamics, 21
positron emission tomography (PET), 147

postprocessors, 105
power consumption, 175, 180, 332
POWER-GEN Asia conference, 209
prehistoric archaeology, 27
principle of uniformitarianism, 29
Principles of Scientific Management, 313
printed circuit board (PCB), 175, 177, 179-180, 241, 268
process analytical technology (PAT), 307
product data management (PDM), 356
product design, 56, 69, 82, 131, 133, 135, 153, 183, 185, 197, 201, 309, 356, 361-362, 393
product development, 48, 159, 290, 357, 389-390
product lifecycle management (PLM), 309, 361-364
programmable logic controller (PLC), 57
programmable read-only memory (PROM), 121
propulsion, 5, 285, 327, 329, 364-369, 418-421, 431-433
propulsion system, 364-369, 419-421, 431-433
propulsion technologies, 368
prosthesis, 369-371, 373
prosthetic devices, 369-373
prosthetic limbs, 183, 371
prosthetics, 370-374
prosthetist, 369-371, 373
prosthodontics, 146
proton exchange membrane fuel cell (PSTN), 164, 211-212
prototype development, 105, 374
prototyping, 46, 105, 111, 114, 132, 152, 185, 219, 309, 374-376, 440, 456
pseudocode, 219
public switched telephone network (PSTN), 97
pultrusion, 193, 344, 347-348
Pythagorean theorem, 232-233

quality control (QC), 20, 114, 134-135, 137, 267, 297, 310, 377, 379-381
quality-control process, 380
quality-control programs, 380-381
quality-control technique, 319, 379
quantum optics, 341

radio frequency identification (RFID), 136
radio signals, 62, 94-95
ramjet engines, 285
random-access memory (RAM), 121, 242, 383-384
rapid prototyping, 105, 111, 114, 152, 309, 374, 440, 456
read-only memory (ROM), 121, 383
reconfigurable agile manufacturing, 386-387
reconfigurable manufacturing system, 386, 390-393, 395
regenerative medicine, 84

renewable energy sources, 37, 210
resin technologies, 197-198
resins, 144, 193, 195-198, 334, 345, 347-348, 352
RGB color model, 238-23
robopets, 400
robotic submarine vehicles, 140
roboticists, 402
robotics applications, 396-397
robotics, 101, 127, 177, 264, 293, 396-399, 401-403, 438
roller coasters, 403-405
roller-coaster designers, 405
Ross, Douglas Taylor, 54, 405-407
rotational molding, 348
rudimentary application, 60

Safe Drinking Water Act of 1974, 189
sanitary engineering, 188-189, 255
Satellite-Based Alarm and Surveillance System (SASS), 234
Save Energy Now, 302
Scandinavian design, 409-411
search engine optimization (SEO), 453
Selective Compliant Assembly Robot Arm, 400
selective layer sintering (SLS), 440
semi-automatic ground environment (SAGE), 110
semiconductor technology, 175-176
servomechanism, 57-60
Siemens NX, 333-334
simulation data management (SDM), 106
simulation programs, 102, 142, 163, 246, 328, 367
Six Sigma, 308, 310-311, 380, 382
sketching, 155, 436
Sketchpad, 54, 77, 107, 110, 236, 412-413
Sketchpad, a Man-Machine Graphical Communication System, 412
Society of Cable Telecommunications Engineers (SCTE), 98
SofTech, 405, 407
software-as-a-service (SaaS) model, 82
software development, 54, 219, 374-375
software engineering, 105, 219, 407
soil mechanics, 89-91, 93, 188, 190, 193
solar panel design, 414-415
solar panels, 414-416, 418, 420
solid oxide fuel cell (SOFC), 164, 211
solid rocket booster (SRB), 12
solid-waste management, 188, 192-193
SolidWorks, 82, 96, 100-101, 168, 414, 416-418
sound waves, 49-50, 52, 71, 373
Space Race, 9, 95
Space Shuttle program, 9, 12, 424

Space Task Group, 12
Space Transportation System, 12, 424
spacecraft engineers, 419-420
SpaceX, 9, 365, 369, 418, 424
sports engineering, 424-426, 428-429
Sports Engineering Research Group, 425
sports engineers, 424, 427-429
Sputnik 1, 9, 94-95
Standard for Exchange of Product Model Data (STEP), 109
static RAM (sRAM), 383-384
stationary power plants, 213-214
statistical process control (SPC), 20, 234, 319, 378
steam generator, 245, 248
stereolithography, 108, 195, 439
strategic management, 308
stratigraphy, 30
stroboscope, 60
Structural Dynamics Research Corporation, 333
submarine engineering, 433
submarines, 65, 331, 429-434
subsonic flow, 6
supersonic waves, 6
supply chain management (SCM) system, 388
suspension bridges, 75
Sutherland, Ivan Edward, 54, 77, 107, 110, 412-413
synchronous DRAM, 383
synchronous SRAM, 383

tankers, 330, 332
targeted muscle reinnervation (TMR), 372
technical drawing, 54, 103, 177, 187, 226, 322, 335, 417, 435-437
technology development, 48, 314, 357
telemetry, tracking, and commanding (TT&C) subsystem, 11
telescopes, 26, 337-340, 423
television broadcast technology, 98
Tesla, Nikola, 179
theory of evolution, 29
thermal conductivity, 23, 246
thermal control system (TCS), 420, 422
thermal energy, 221, 245, 321
thermal stability, 196
thermodynamic temperature, 273, 316, 320
thermodynamics, 7, 90, 249, 254, 285, 331, 368
thermoforming process, 348
thermoplastic materials, 344, 348
thermoplastics, 343-344, 346, 348-349, 353
thermoset, 194, 198, 344-348

505

thermosetting resin, 194, 198, 347-348
three-dimensional (3D) printing, 41, 44, 46, 52, 72, 86, 105, 109, 193, 195, 215-216, 228-229, 260, 288, 323-325, 334, 349, 374, 410, 438-440
throwaway prototyping, 375-376
tolerance range, 187
torpedo, 330, 430, 432-433
total quality management (TQM), 287, 377
Toxic Substances Control Act of 1976, 189
Toxics Use Reduction Act, 305
Toyota Production System (TPS), 286, 292, 298, 315, 380
transportation engineering, 445-446
transportation equipment manufacturing, 302-304
truss bridge, 76, 413
turbochargers, 225, 248-249, 285
turbofan, 222, 224, 281, 284-285, 366-367
turbojet, 222, 281, 284, 366
turbomachine aerodynamics, 285
turbomachines, 281, 283, 285
turboprop engine, 283-284
turboshaft engines, 285

ultraviolet (UV) light, 324, 337, 422-423, 438
UNISURF, 126, 441-442
universal milling machine, 125
UNIX operating system, 81, 242
unmanned aerial vehicle (UAE), 1, 6, 65, 214, 402
urban planners, 443-447
urban planning, 56, 150, 443, 445-446
US Bureau of Labor Statistics (BLS), 307, 447
US Census Bureau, 302
US customary system, 275, 277, 316
US Department of Agriculture (USDA), 264
US Department of Defense (DoD), 285
US Department of Energy (DoE), 165, 250, 254, 302
US Department of Health and Human Services (HHS), 147
US Department of Housing and Urban Development (HUD), 443
US Department of Labor (DoL), 305

US Food and Drug Administration (FDA), 52, 71
US Navy, 331, 431, 433
USS *Nautilus*, 431
US Nuclear Detonation Detection System, 65
utilitarian agriculture, 259

vacuum tube technology, 175, 180
vacuum tubes, 49, 121, 169, 175-176, 180-181, 267, 383
vat photopolymerization, 324, 439
vector image, 43, 113, 238-239, 451
vectors, 20, 293-294, 449-451
vendor managed inventory (VMI), 290
Venturi principle, 24
Veterans Sustainable Agriculture Training, 263
videoconferencing applications, 97

Walt Disney Studios, 114
waste management, 32, 188-189, 192-193, 434, 440
wastewater biosolids, 190
wastewater treatment, 94, 188, 190, 192-193
water resources engineering, 92
water-pollution control, 188, 193
waterproofing, 195, 345, 425
wavelet theory, 19
web graphic design, 454-455
Whitney, Eli, 312, 316, 379
wireframe, 54-55, 111, 113, 234-235, 241, 417, 454, 455-456
wireframe models, 54-55, 113
Wireless World, 95
Woods Hole Oceanographic Institution (WHOI), 142
World War I, 2, 5-6, 9, 24, 57, 62, 128-129, 155, 195, 199, 261, 281, 346, 352, 365, 379, 409, 419, 431-432
World War II, 2, 5-6, 9, 24, 57, 62, 128-129, 155, 195, 199, 261, 281, 346, 352, 365, 379, 409, 419, 431
World Wide Web, 33, 119, 398
Wright brothers, 1, 6

X-rays, 25, 144, 146-147, 173, 180, 423

The Principles of... Series

Principles of Science
Principles of Anatomy
Principles of Astronomy
Principles of Behavioral Science
Principles of Biology
Principles of Biotechnology
Principles of Botany
Principles of Chemistry
Principles of Climatology
Principles of Computer Science
Principles of Computer-Aided Design
Principles of Ecology
Principles of Energy
Principles of Fire Science
Principles of Geology
Principles of Information Technology
Principles of Marine Science
Principles of Mathematics
Principles of Microbiology
Principles of Modern Agriculture
Principles of Pharmacology
Principles of Physical Science
Principles of Physics
Principles of Programming & Coding
Principles of Robotics & Artificial Intelligence
Principles of Scientific Research
Principles of Sports Medicine & Kinesiology
Principles of Sustainability
Principles of Zoology

The Principles of... Series

Principles of Health
Principles of Health: Allergies & Immune Disorders
Principles of Health: Anxiety & Stress
Principles of Health: Depression
Principles of Health: Diabetes
Principles of Health: Nursing
Principles of Health: Obesity
Principles of Health: Pain Management
Principles of Health: Prescription Drug Abuse

Principles of Business
Principles of Business: Accounting
Principles of Business: Economics
Principles of Business: Entrepreneurship
Principles of Business: Finance
Principles of Business: Globalization
Principles of Business: Leadership
Principles of Business: Management
Principles of Business: Marketing

Principles of Sociology
Principles of Sociology: Group Relationships & Behavior
Principles of Sociology: Personal Relationships & Behavior
Principles of Sociology: Societal Issues & Behavior

SALEM PRESS · https://salempress.com · (800) 221-1592